Ius Comparatum – Global Studies in Comparative Law

Volume 22

D1824674

Series Editors

Katharina Boele-Woelki, Bucerius Law School, Germany
Diego P. Fernández Arroyo, Institut d'Études Politiques de Paris, Sciences Po, France

Founding Series Editors

Jürgen Basedow, Max Planck Institute for Comparative and International Private Law, Germany
George Bermann, Columbia University School of Law, USA

Editorial Board

Bénédicte Fauvarque-Cosson, Université Panthéon-Assas, Paris 2, France
Joost Blom, University of British Columbia, Canada
Giuseppe Franco Ferrari, Università Bocconi, Milan, Italy
Toshiyuki Kono, Kyushu University, Fukuoka, Japan
Marek Safjan, Court of Justice of the European Union, Luxembourg
Jorge Sanchez Cordero, Mexican Center of Uniform Law, Mexico
Ulrich Sieber, Max Planck Institute for Foreign and International Criminal Law, Germany

More information about this series at http://www.springer.com/series/11943

Académie Internationale de Droit Comparé
International Academy of Comparative Law

Souichirou Kozuka
Editor

Implementing the Cape Town Convention and the Domestic Laws on Secured Transactions

 Springer

Editor
Souichirou Kozuka
Faculty of Law
Gakushuin University
Toshima-ku, Tokyo, Japan

ISSN 2214-6881 ISSN 2214-689X (electronic)
Ius Comparatum – Global Studies in Comparative Law
ISBN 978-3-319-83527-3 ISBN 978-3-319-46470-1 (eBook)
DOI 10.1007/978-3-319-46470-1

© Springer International Publishing AG 2017
Softcover reprint of the hardcover 1st edition 2017
This work is subject to copyright. All rights are reserved by the Publisher, whether the whole or part of the material is concerned, specifically the rights of translation, reprinting, reuse of illustrations, recitation, broadcasting, reproduction on microfilms or in any other physical way, and transmission or information storage and retrieval, electronic adaptation, computer software, or by similar or dissimilar methodology now known or hereafter developed.
The use of general descriptive names, registered names, trademarks, service marks, etc. in this publication does not imply, even in the absence of a specific statement, that such names are exempt from the relevant protective laws and regulations and therefore free for general use.
The publisher, the authors and the editors are safe to assume that the advice and information in this book are believed to be true and accurate at the date of publication. Neither the publisher nor the authors or the editors give a warranty, express or implied, with respect to the material contained herein or for any errors or omissions that may have been made.

Printed on acid-free paper

This Springer imprint is published by Springer Nature
The registered company is Springer International Publishing AG
The registered company address is: Gewerbestrasse 11, 6330 Cham, Switzerland

Foreword

The 2001 Cape Town Convention on International Interests in Mobile Equipment, with its associated Protocols relating to aircraft objects, railway rolling stock and space assets, is undoubtedly one of the most important private commercial law conventions of recent times. The Convention has now received 72 ratifications and the Aircraft Protocol (the only one currently in force) 65 ratifications, an astonishing achievement in under 15 years. Now a new Protocol, devoted to agricultural, mining and construction equipment, is on the horizon, and the first meeting of a UNIDROIT Committee of governmental experts is to be held in the first half of 2017.

There has been a growing amount of literature devoted to the analysis of the Convention and its economic impact, including numerous doctoral theses, but relatively little has been written on the mode and adequacy of its implementation in the legislation of Contracting States. The appearance of this volume, which is based on the general report and national reports presented at the XIXth International Congress of Comparative Law held at Vienna in July 2014, is therefore most timely. An opening chapter by Professor Jeffrey Wool, who himself played a leading role in the development of these instruments, notes the importance of ensuring that they are properly implemented and given priority over domestic law, a point which he has previously developed in a series of articles. Skilfully introduced and edited by Professor Souichirou Kozuka, who was also heavily involved in the Cape Town project, *Implementing the Cape Town Convention and the Domestic Laws of Secured Transactions* contains an incisive general report by Professor Kozuka outlining the key features of the Convention and Protocols. This is followed by contributions from leading scholars, government lawyers and legal practitioners in private practice, which examine the existing national laws governing security and title-retention interests in nine Contracting and nine non-Contracting States, the impact of the Convention on the existing laws of Contracting States and the techniques adopted to implement the Convention and Aircraft Protocol.

This volume provides both a rich comparative law feast and an examination of the Cape Town instruments from a variety of national law viewpoints which serve to emphasise the remarkable degree to which they have proved responsive to the needs of widely differing legal systems. *Implementing the Cape Town Convention and the Domestic Laws of Secured Transactions* is essential reading for all those with a serious interest in Cape Town, and I warmly recommend it.

Oxford   Roy Goode
28 July 2016

Contents

Part I
Introduction

About This Book: Why National Implementation of the Cape Town Convention Matters

Souichirou Kozuka

1.1 The Cape Town Convention as a Successful Uniform Law Instrument

1.1.1 History of the Cape Town Convention

The Cape Town Convention is a uniform law instrument initiated by the International Institute for the Unification of Private Law (UNIDROIT). It is one of the most recent instruments, but has become one of the most successful.

The drafting of the Cape Town Convention dates back to 1992. Following the adoption of two UNIDROIT Conventions on leasing and factoring,[1] it was one of the projects of UNIDROIT on unification of finance law.[2] The original idea was to draft a general convention on security interests in mobile equipment, broadly covering every kind of high-value mobile assets. However, this approach was abandoned in 1997, and the "umbrella" structure of the Base Convention and three Protocols was adopted instead.[3] The Base Convention (Convention on International Interests

---

[1] The UNIDROIT Convention on International Financial Leasing, 1988; the UNIDROIT Convention on International Factoring, 1988.

[2] Herbert Kronke (2011), Financial Leasing and its Unification by UNIDROIT – General Report, [2011-1/2] *Uniform Law Review* p.23; also published in: K.B. Brown and D.V. Snyder (eds.), *General Reports of the XVIIIth Congress of the International Academy of Comparative Law* (Springer, 2012).

[3] It was the proposal made by the aircraft manufacturing industry and airlines industry on the initiative of Lorne S Clark, then General Counsel of the International Air Transport Association (IATA). See Lorne S. Clark, The 2001 Cape Town Convention on International Interests in Mobile Equipment and Aircraft Equipment Protocol: Internationalizing Asset-Based Financing Principles for the Acquisition of Aircraft and Engines, *Journal of Air law and Commerce*, vol. 69, p.3, at p.5 (2004); Roy Goode, From Acorn to Oak Tree: the Development of the Cape Town Convention and Protocols, [2012] *Uniform Law Review* p.599, at p.603.

S. Kozuka (✉)
Faculty of Law, Gakushuin University, Toshima-ku, Tokyo, Japan
e-mail: souichirou.kozuka@gakushuin.ac.jp

in Mobile Equipment) and the first Protocol on Aircraft (Protocol to the Convention on International Interests in Mobile Equipment on Matters Specific to Aircraft Equipment) were adopted at the Diplomatic Conference in Cape Town in 2001. Since then, the Convention has been known by the popular name after the name of the city. The second Protocol relating to the Railway Rolling Stock (Luxembourg Protocol to the Convention on International Interests in Mobile Equipment on Matters Specific to Railway Rolling Stock) was adopted in 2007 at the Diplomatic Conference hosted by the Grand Duchy of Luxembourg and features Luxembourg as part of its name. The third Protocol (Protocol to the Convention on International Interests in Mobile Equipment on Matters Specific to Space Assets), which applies the rules of the Cape Town Convention with necessary adaptations to the space business, was adopted in Berlin in 2012 and is known as the Space Protocol.

Since 2014, a fourth Protocol on mining, agricultural and construction equipment (MAC Protocol) has been discussed by the MAC Study Group.[4] With the preliminary draft text having been finalised, the Governing Council of UNIDROIT found it "sufficiently developed to warrant the convening of a Committee of Governmental Experts in early 2017".[5] It has also been argued that a Protocol on ship might be worth considering.[6]

Because of the umbrella structure, the following terms are employed throughout this book. The term "Cape Town Convention" is used to refer to the Convention and its Protocols as a whole. When referring specifically to the Convention itself and not Protocols, the term "the Base Convention" is used. The use of these terms is justified by the requirement that the Convention and Protocol should be read and interpreted together as a single instrument (Art. 6 of the Base Convention). The three Protocols are, respectively, mentioned by the common names "Aircraft Protocol", "Luxembourg Rail Protocol" and "Space Protocol".

1.1.2 Current Status

The Cape Town Convention has proven to be an enormous success. The Base Convention and the Aircraft Protocol entered into force in 2006, only 5 years after their adoption. As of December 2015, the Convention has 70 Contracting States, and the Aircraft Protocol has 63 States Parties (besides the European Union as the Regional Economic Integration Organisation being a Party to both instruments).[7] Only a few other uniform law instruments have paralleled such achievements of the

---

[4] Henry Deep Gabriel, The MAC Protocol: we aren't there yet – how far do we have to go?, *The Cape Town Convention Journal* Vol.4, p.67 (2015); Charles W. Mooney Jr, The MAC Protocol: some comments and a challenge, *The Cape Town Convention Journal* Vol.4, p.76 (2015).

[5] UNIDROIT 2016 – C.D. (95) Misc.2, para.7.

[6] Ole Böger, The Cape Town Convention and Proprietary Security over Ships, [2014] *Uniform Law Review* p.24.

[7] The text, States Parties, list of declarations and other information are available on the UNIDROIT website and Aviation Working Group website.

Cape Town Convention. Not only has it had a significant impact on the practice of aircraft financing,[8] but also their intellectual influence on the designing of secured transactions law has been significant.[9]

Remarkably, the Cape Town Convention does not merely provide a set of uniform rules to be applied by the courts of the States Parties. Some mechanisms to ensure its implementation and enforcement exist, which make the Cape Town Convention an operating institution by itself. One of such mechanisms is the International Registry established under each Protocol for the asset covered by the Protocol. The International Registry for Aircraft Equipment has been in operation since 2006 and has been widely used in practice. As of 2014, the number of aircraft objects against which the international interests are registered reached 340,000, and the number of registrations recorded 613,900.[10] Another mechanism relevant to the Aircraft Protocol is the reference in the Aircraft Sector Understanding (ASU) of the Organisation for Economic Co-operation and Development (OECD), most recently revised in September 2015. The ASU provides for the agreement among the export credit agencies on the conditions that they can offer and approves a beneficial treatment of the debtor (acquirer of an aircraft) in a State Party to the Cape Town Convention, as long as certain conditions are satisfied and the Convention is found to be implemented effectively in the relevant State. Thus, a State has an incentive for effective implementation of the Cape Town Convention if it wishes to enable its airline to enjoy the beneficial treatment under the ASU.

Furthermore, effectiveness of the implementation of the Cape Town Convention is monitored by the Aviation Working Group (AWG). The AWG is a private body originally formed to provide the drafters with expertise in aircraft financing. It has now become an organisation to promote ratification of the Convention and to monitor the implementation within the States Parties.

Two other Protocols are on their way to catch up with the Aircraft Protocol. The Luxembourg Rail Protocol has one Contracting State, namely, Luxembourg, and has been approved by the European Union as the Regional Economic Integration Organisation. It has also been signed by five States, most recently by the UK in February 2016, a fact which may indicate its significance. An industry group named the Rail Working Group (RWG) has been making efforts to promote ratification. The Space Protocol has four Signatories but no Party yet. Still, it is recognised as the first private law instrument in space law and has attracted much attention from the experts in space law.[11]

---

[8] Dirk Schmalenbach, Recent Developments in Aircraft Finance with Special Regard to the Cape Town Convention, *Zeitschrift für Luft- und Weltraumrecht*, 64. Jg, S.270 (2015).

[9] See, as an example of a general theory developed from the experiences of the Cape Town Convention, Jeffrey Wool, Treaty Design, Implementation, and Compliance Benchmarking Economic Benefit – a Framework as Applied to the Cape Town Convention, [2012] *Uniform Law Review* p.633.

[10] Ludwig Weber, Public and private features of the Cape Town Convention, *The Cape Town Convention Journal*, Vol.4, p.53 (2015).

[11] See, for example, Francis Lyall and Paul B. Larsen, *Space Law: A Treatise*, pp.446 et seq. (Ashgate, 2009); Mark Sundahl, Financing space ventures, in: Frans von der Dunk and Fabio Tronchetti (eds.), *Handbook of Space Law* (Edward Elgar, 2015), pp.874 et seq.

1.2   The Aim of This Book

1.2.1   The Significance of Implementation of the Cape Town Convention

This book is a study on the domestic implementation of the Cape Town Convention. The subject has both practical and theoretical significance. The practical significance of examining the national implementation is obvious when the effective implementation of the Convention is focused. Even before deciding to become a Party to the Convention, a State needs to know in what respects the Cape Town Convention differs from the domestic law and what steps are required, if it is to ratify and implement the Convention. Furthermore, there are several options in the provisions of the Cape Town Convention, many of them enabling the State to opt in by making a declaration, but a few providing for the possibility to opt out. A State may wish to examine carefully the differences between the rules of the Cape Town Convention and domestic law to decide which option to choose.

The theoretical significance of looking into the national implementation derives from the nature of the Cape Town Convention as an international treaty for the unification of private law. The international instruments to unify private laws, by their very nature, stand on the interface of the international law and private law. Examining the domestic implementation will reveal the actual functions of the uniform private law: whether, and how, it affects the national laws of the States. As a uniform law instrument, the primary function of the Cape Town Convention is to provide for a set of rules to replace divergent existing laws. However, it does not stop there.

The traditional idea about the unification of law is that it is beneficial to overcome the divergences among laws of various countries. The technique used for this aim has been to codify a set of compromised rules acceptable to all the countries.[12] Contrary to such a traditional idea, the Cape Town Convention is designed by a problem-solving approach and aims to introduces rules based on the new concept that are considered more suitable to the modern type of transactions and more efficient in generating the economic benefits than the existing rules. In this context, implementation forms part of the mechanism of generating economic benefits and has greater importance than in the case of a traditional uniform law. Thus, the goal of this book is to identify the uniqueness of the Cape Town Convention and, more

---

[12] There can be a few reasons why States accept the compromised rules produced in this way (Souichirou Kozuka, The Economic Implications of Uniformity in Law, in: Jürgen Basedow and Toshiyuki Kono (eds.), *An Economic Analysis of Private International Law* (Tübingen: Mohr Siebeck, 2006); reprinted with slight modifications in: [2007-4] *Uniform Law Review* p.683). In the simplest case, the divergence itself causes significant costs in transactions across the borders, while it makes little difference among the various rules. In other words, everyone benefits from agreeing to a single rule, but which rule it is does not matter. Another scenario is that the uniform rule is, though not considered as the best one, accepted as better than some other rule, which would be applicable if the uniform rule were not agreed on.

generally, to find out the functions of uniform law in the modern world, through the examination of the national implementation of the Convention.

1.2.2   The Approach of Analysis

To achieve the goal, this book has collected reports from various countries. Some of them are States Parties to the Cape Town Convention. For these States, the reports literally cover the issue of implementation of the Convention. They describe, as technical aspects of implementation, what laws have been enacted or amended, which laws were abolished and then whether there remains any uncertainty. They also discuss the substantive issues, namely, how the domestic law before ratification differed from the Cape Town Convention and what arguments were made when changing such substantive rules.

For those States that are not Parties yet, the reports discuss how their laws differ from the Cape Town Convention and then evaluate whether such existing laws are satisfactory. In some contributions, there are implications about whether the State will benefit from becoming a Party to the Convention and what, if any, the hurdles are against doing so.

Recently it has been emphasised that, once adopted, the Convention needs to be interpreted by the autonomous interpretation, free from the legal concepts, terminology or interpretive techniques of the domestic law.[13] From that perspective, the analysis of the existing domestic law, in particular the domestic law that a State Party used to have, might seem irrelevant. However, this author believes that the comparison of the Convention and the existing domestic law is useful to highlight the changes the Convention has made, or is going to make, to the domestic law. As mentioned above, such an analysis will also reveal the unique features of the Cape Town Convention as the uniform law instrument.

1.2.3   How This Book Has Developed

The book developed from a session at the XIXth International Congress of Comparative Law held at the University of Vienna on 22 July 2014. As general reporter of the session, this author received twelve national reports and presented the general reports based on them.[14] The national reports were prepared in response

---

[13] Jeffrey Wool and Andrej Jonovic, The relationship between transnational commercial law treaties and national law – A framework as applied to the Cape Town Convention, *The Cape Town Convention Journal* Issue 2, p.65 at p.69 (2013).

[14] The general report, slightly rewritten after the Congress, is published in Martin Schauer and Bea Verschraegen (eds.), *General Reports of the XIXth Congress of the International Academy of Comparative Law/Rapports Généraux du XIXème Congrès de L'Académie Internationale de Droit*

to the Questionnaire that the author sent to the reporters in advance, which is reproduced in the Annex of this book. After the Congress was over, the national reporters were asked to revise their reports to fit in this book's format. This author, on the other hand, sought for contributions from other countries as well as from some practitioners, to make the book as comprehensive as possible. The latter contributions do not necessarily cover all the questions in the questionnaire, but focus on what the contributor thought unique to, or important under, the legal system of their countries.

1.3 The Structure of This Book

This book consists of three parts. In the first part on the general perspectives on the subject, Chap. 1 by Jeffrey Wool, one of the core drafters of the Cape Town Convention, elaborates on the design of the Convention and the meaning of national implementation in the context. It is followed by Chap. 2 by Souichirou Kozuka, which is the general report giving the overall analysis of the subject. This chapter briefly reviews the main features of the Cape Town Convention and then discusses the three main values that the Cape Town Convention brings to the domestic law.

The second part collects contributions on various nations' implementation. Among the eighteen contributions, nine are from Contracting States, while another nine came from non-Contracting States. Subpart A consists of the former contributions, namely, Chap. 3 (Canada) by Frédérique Sabourin, Chap. 4 (England and Wales) by George Leloudas, Chap. 5 (Indonesia) by Prita Amalia, Chap. 6 (Malaysia) by Mary George, Chap. 7 (the Netherlands) by Sjef van Erp, Chap. 8 (Russia) by Nataliya Doronina, Chap. 9 (South Africa) by Phetole Sekhula, Chap. 10 (Spain) by Teresa Rodríguez de las Heras Ballell and Chap. 11 (USA) by Charles W. Mooney, Jr. Subpart B includes the latter chapters, namely, Chap. 12 (Finland) by Teemu Juutilainen; Chap. 13 (France) by Philippe Delebecque; Chap. 14 (Germany) by Benjamin von Bodungen; Chap. 15 (Greece) by Elina N. Moustaira; Chap. 16 (Italy) by Anna Veneziano; Chap. 17 (Japan) by Haruna Fujisawa; Chap. 18 (Poland) by Maria Dragun-Gertner, Zuzanna Pepłowska-Dąbrowska and Jacek Krzemiński; Chap. 19 (Portugal) by Maria Helena Brito; and Chap. 20 (Switzerland) by Bénédict Foëx.

The third part is made up of three chapters, commenting on each of the three Protocols by a practitioner knowledgeable about the subject: Chap. 21 (Aircraft Protocol) by Patrick Honnebier, Chap. 22 (Luxembourg Rail Protocol) by Howard Rosen and Chap. 23 (Space Protocol) by Daniel A. Porras. Although the Base Convention and the three Protocols are constructed by a consistent design, it should not be overlooked that the three Protocols differ from each other, corresponding to

---

Comparé (Springer, forthcoming). Some of the original national reports are available on the Repository of the Cape Town Academic Project's website, because they have had to be made much shorter for the purpose of this book.

the different nature of the relevant transactions. The three chapters in this part give the readers insights into these Protocol-specific issues.

At the end of the book, the questionnaire used to invite national reporters to develop their analysis is included as Appendix. When chapters on individual jurisdictions mention the questionnaire or a specific question in it, the reader is referred to this Appendix.

References

1. Böger, Ole. 2014. The Cape Town Convention and proprietary security over ships, [2014]. *Uniform Law Review* 19: 24.
2. Clark, Lorne S. 2004. The 2001 Cape Town Convention on international interests in mobile equipment and aircraft equipment protocol: Internationalizing asset-based financing principles for the acquisition of aircraft and engines. *Journal of Air law and Commerce* 69: p.3, at p.5.
3. Gabriel, Henry Deep. 2015. The MAC protocol: We aren't there yet – How far do we have to go? *The Cape Town Convention Journal* 4: 67.
4. Goode, Roy. 2012. From acorn to oak tree: The development of the Cape Town Convention and protocols, [2012]. *Uniform Law Review* p.599, at p.603.
5. Kozuka, Souichirou. 2006. The economic implications of uniformity in law. In *An economic analysis of private international law* (Mohr Siebeck) ed. Jürgen Basedow and Toshiyuki Kono (reprinted with slight modifications in: [2007–4] *Uniform Law Review* p.683).
6. Kozuka, Souichirou. 2016. Security interests in transport vehicles – The Cape Town Convention and its implementation in national law. In *General Reports of the XIXth Congress of the International Academy of Comparative Law/Rapports Généraux du XIXème Congrès de L'Académie Internationale de Droit Comparé* (Springer) ed. Martin Schauer and Bea Verschraegen.
7. Kronke, Herbert. 2011. Financial leasing and its unification by Unidroit – General report, [2011-1/2] *Uniform Law Review* p.23 (also published in: K.B. Brown and D.V. Snyder (eds.), *General reports of the XVIIIth congress of the International Academy of Comparative Law* (Springer, 2012)).
8. Lyall, Francis, and Paul B. Larsen. 2009. *Space law: A treatise*. Farnham: Ashgate.
9. Mooney Jr, Charles W. 2015. The MAC protocol: Some comments and a challenge. *The Cape Town Convention Journal* 4: 76.
10. Schmalenbach, Dirk. 2015. Recent developments in Aircraft finance with special regard to the Cape Town Convention. *Zeitschrift für Luft- und Weltraumrecht* 64: Jg, S.270.
11. Sundahl, Mark. 2015. Financing space ventures. In *Handbook of space law,* ed. Edward Elgar, Frans von der Dunk and Fabio Tronchetti.
12. Weber, Ludwig. 2015. Public and private features of the Cape Town Convention. *The Cape Town Convention Journal* 4: 53.
13. Wool, Jeffrey. 2012. Treaty design, implementation, and compliance benchmarking economic benefit – A framework as applied to the Cape Town Convention, [2012]. *Uniform Law Review* 17: 633.
14. Wool, Jeffrey, and Andrej Jonovic. 2013. The relationship between transnational commercial law treaties and national law – A framework as applied to the Cape Town Convention. *The Cape Town Convention Journal* 2, p.65 at p.69.

Chapter 1
Implementation of the Cape Town Convention into and Its Relationship with National Law

Jeffrey Wool

The Cape Town Convention and its Aircraft Protocol (read together, the 'convention') is a groundbreaking substantive law instrument designed to facilitate a transaction type. It does so by setting out risk-reducing rules, which, if effectively implemented into national law and complied with by national authorities, produces substantial economic benefit.

Early in the developmental process, there were proposals for a short conflict-of-law-type instrument, which would help determine which state's substantive law applies to the transaction. The aviation industry already had such an instrument: the Geneva Convention of 1948. Beyond that, at a conception level, although such an instrument would simplify conflicts analysis (thus lightly reducing information-related transaction costs), it would not have delivered the best practice, risk-reducing legal predictability that creditors and debtors maximize economic benefit.

To deliver that level of predictability and risk-reduction, the convention needed to deal with substantive legal issues that had previously been considered beyond the scope of what was politically feasible in earlier commercial law harmonization attempts. More specifically, at the core of the transactions the convention governs are legal subjects that were long considered inherently domestic: fundamental concepts of *property law* and *insolvency*. To complicate matters further, the international nature of the transactions necessitated a registry which could be used instantly and universally, all at a time when modern electronic systems were still in their infancy. These items were boldly addressed, leading to the success of the instrument. The use of an innovative declaration structure, permitting states to opt into

J. Wool (✉)
School of Law, University of Washington, Seattle, WA, USA

Aviation Working Group, 65 Fleet Street, London EC4Y 1HS, UK

Harris Manchester College, University of Oxford, Oxford, UK
e-mail: jeffrey.wool@awg.aero

© Springer International Publishing AG 2017
S. Kozuka (ed.), *Implementing the Cape Town Convention and the Domestic Laws on Secured Transactions*, Ius Comparatum - Global Studies in Comparative Law 22, DOI 10.1007/978-3-319-46470-1_1

and out of some of the further reaching provisions, greatly assisted in the politics needed to address these topics.

The approach of dealing with core notions of property and insolvency law, together with the wide scope of sub-topics addressed (creation, registration, priority, enforcement, and dispute resolution), however, entailed intimate interaction between the convention and national law. While a contracting state's international obligations, supported by the (Vienna Treaty on Treaties) rule that national law may not excuse non-compliance with such obligations, are helpful and signal the applicability and reliability of the convention's rules, transacting parties need to know that *such rules have the effect of national law in a contracting state with priority over other national law in the case of conflict*. Both *de jure* and *de facto*. This '***primacy criterion***' has driven, and will continue to drive, the analysis and utility of the convention over the years.

The threshold question, now addressed at length in the literature, is whether the convention's rules have been 'implemented' into, and, thus, have the force of national law. In another words, will the convention's provisions apply to transactions within its scope. The exact process of implementation (noting that the term used for this legal process and its effect differs by legal system) varies from state to state. At the most basic level, the starting point is whether the state has a monist legal system—which views the international and domestic legal spheres as one—or a dualist legal system—which views international law as a separate plane from domestic law with international law governing the relations between states rather than relations between individuals. In dualistic states, the convention has limited or no direct effect on the legal relationships between transacting parties; rather, those relationships will be governed by a domestic law passed to give the convention the force of law within that state. In reality, most legal systems have aspects of monism and dualism, and, accordingly, these concepts should be viewed as setting out a continuum. For example, many states with monist legal systems must pass publicity-ensuring basic legislation and may need to amend conflicting laws. Without exception, they also need to provide practical rules dealing with changes to aviation regulations (on de-registration of aircraft, a core concept in the instrument).

The second feature of the primacy criterion, while receiving less attention, is much more important: does the convention prevail in the case of conflict with other national law. The answer to that question implicates, depending on the subject legal system, fundamental questions of treaty implementation, interpretation, and legislative and regulatory technique. The assumption that the convention has primacy— that is, that the international obligation aligns with the effect under national law—may be false. That depends on whether such primacy has been established and remains effective based on one of four legal principles. Does the convention prevail in the case of conflict with other national law: (1) as a higher legal norm (based on the role of treaties in the constitutional or hierarchical system), (2) based on express legislation to that effect, (3) based on the principle of *lex specialis*, or (4) based on the principle of *lex posteriori*. A summary of the position on this critical question can be found on www.awg.aero (summary of national implementation).

This book—arising out of Prof. Kozuka's presentation to the 19th International Congress of Comparative Law—offers an important comparative look at the convention from the vantage point of major jurisdictions around the world. A close reading of these chapters gives much detailed information about, highlights and shows the importance of, and suggests points requiring further assessment and work on, the main implementation themes, including the primacy criterion, outlined above. It also sets the stage for, and provides elements relating to, the analysis of treaty compliance: will the convention's rule actually and accurately be applied, assuming threshold implementation in countries around the world.

Finally, this book serves an important educational function with links to implementation features. This educational function is especially needed now. As states consider ratifying the rail and space protocols and work on developing other protocols continues, these issues of implementation will remain central to their success. All states, whether monist or dualist and regardless of the applicable primacy technique, must work to educate their judges and administrative officials on the convention and protocols. When applying new international norms to areas of law that were previously domestic, there is a risk (as Prof Brian Havel and others have said) of 're-nationalization.' This process is often unintentional; legislators, judges, and officials are more familiar with their domestic law than with an international instrument like the convention, and, thus, have a natural tendency to implement, interpret, and apply treaties in a way that makes them accord with their prior national law. That would fail to reflect the international character of the convention, an objective expressly set out in the text.

Jeffrey Wool is professor of global business law, University of Washington and an associate faculty member, University of Oxford. He is secretary general, Aviation Working Group, and head of aerospace law and policy, Freshfields Bruckhaus Deringer. Professor Wool is also the executive director of the Cape Town Convention Academic Project, the general editor of the *Cape Town Convention Journal*, and the chair of the Advisory Board to the International Registry (Aircraft Protocol).

Part II
General Report

Chapter 2
The Cape Town Convention and Its Implementation in Domestic Law: Between Tradition and Innovation

Souichirou Kozuka

2.1 The Features of the Cape Town Convention

The Cape Town Convention is a uniform law treaty on the security interests in mobile equipment. It provides a set of rules that the courts in the States Parties shall apply. In the absence of the Convention, the court must first look up its choice of law rules to determine which law should govern the security interests at issue. The governing law may be the law of the place where the asset is located (*lex rei siate* or *lex situs*). Or, in particular in the case of security interests in aircraft, it may be the law of the country for whose registry the aircraft is registered (*lex registri*). In any case, the rules on the creation and perfection of the security interests differ from country to country. The uncertainty arising from these complexities is itself a legal risk to parties to the secured transactions. In some cases, the rules chosen as the governing law could lead to a problematic outcome.[1]

Under the Cape Town Convention, if the security interest satisfies the condition for the creation of a valid international interest, the provisions of the Convention apply in place of the applicable domestic law. Furthermore, the rules under the Convention are designed to facilitate asset based financing. The asset based financing has been a primary method used for the acquisition of transport vehicles such as aircrafts and railway rolling stock. Therefore, the Cape Town Convention is expected

---

[1] This was so in the *Blue Sky* case. See William J Glaister, Robert Murphy, Marisa Chan, Ellie Dunne & Julian Acratopulo, *Lex situs* after *Blue Sky*: is the Cape Town Convention the solution?, *The Cape Town Convention Journal* Issue1, p.3 (2012); Dirk Schmalenbach, Recent Developments in Aircraft Finance with Special Regard to the Cape Town Convention, *Zeitschrift für Luft- und Weltraumrecht*, 64. Jg, S.270 (2015).

S. Kozuka (✉)
Faculty of Law, Gakushuin University, Toshima-ku, Tokyo, Japan
e-mail: souichirou.kozuka@gakushuin.ac.jp

© Springer International Publishing AG 2017
S. Kozuka (ed.), *Implementing the Cape Town Convention and the Domestic Laws on Secured Transactions*, Ius Comparatum - Global Studies in Comparative Law 22, DOI 10.1007/978-3-319-46470-1_2

to contribute to the growth of the relevant industries using these transport vehicles covered by the Protocols.

The remainder of this Sect. 2.1 offers a concise overview of the Cape Town Convention. In the following sections, it is discussed how the rules of the Cape Town Convention differ from the domestic laws of various countries, and what are the values that the Cape Town Convention as a uniform law treaty brings about to this subject. First, the value in providing for a uniform set of rules when the laws of countries are different is identified (Sect. 2.2). Secondly, the economic benefits to be achieved by applying the Cape Town Convention is discussed (Sect. 2.3). Thirdly, the virtues of the establishment of global institutions, including the International Registry, which is by its nature impossible for a single country, are considered (Sect. 2.4). The final section includes conclusions, offering perspectives for the general theory on the role of private law unification (Sect. 2.5).

As noted in "About This Book," the term "Cape Town Convention" is used to refer to the Convention and its Protocols as a whole. When referring specifically to the Convention itself and not to Protocols, the term "the Base Convention" is used. The three Protocols are respectively mentioned by the common names "Aircraft Protocol", "Luxembourg Rail Protocol" and "Space Protocol."

2.1.1 The International Registry and Priority of International Interests

When the Cape Town Convention is applicable, the creditor can constitute an "international interest" according to the rules of the Convention. An international interest under the Cape Town Convention includes a security interest granted by the chargor under a security agreement, an interest vested in a person who is the conditional seller under a title reservation agreement, and an interest vested in a person who is the lessor under a leasing agreement.[2] These types of interests are non-possessory security interests, which do not require the creditors (holders of the security interest) to take possession of the secured object.

2.1.1.1 Creation and Registration of an International Interest

The creditor may constitute a valid international interest by concluding an agreement that satisfies certain formalities with the debtor. The required formalities are that the agreement: (a) is in writing; (b) relates to an object of which the debtor has the power to dispose; (c) enables the object to be identified in conformity with the

---

[2] Art.2 (2) of the Base Convention.

Protocol; and (d) in the case of a security agreement, enables the secured obligations to be determined.[3]

To register international interests and publicise them, the International Registry is set up under the Cape Town Convention. For each type of objects covered by each Protocol, different Registries may be established.[4] There is required to be a Supervisory Authority for the International Registry.[5] The Supervisory Authority appoints the Registrar that operates the International Registry and supervises it.[6]

2.1.1.2   Priorities Between Interests in the Object

The registration of an international interest with the International Registry determines the priorities among the competing interests by the timing of registration. The first to register is granted the first priority. Whether or not the first registrant had actual knowledge of the existence of a subsequently registered international interest or unregistered interest does not matter.[7]

The establishment of the International Registry does not, by itself, abolish the domestic registry that has existed. However, an interest registered only with the domestic registry and not with the International Registry is treated as an unregistered interest and cannot claim its priority vis-à-vis a registered international interest, unless it is a pre-existing right or interest protected its priority under the transitional provision.[8] Even after the Cape Town Convention enters into force with a Contracting State, the State may designate the office for the domestic registration as the entry point for the International Registry.[9] There are a few States that have made a declaration to designate such entry points with regard to the Aircraft Protocol.

As an exception to the rule that the first to register is granted the first priority, a Contracting State may declare that a non-consensual right or interest of a certain category enjoys priority without any registration.[10] Besides that, a Contracting State may declare that other categories of non-consensual rights or interests may be registered with the International Registry, in which case the priority between such a

---

[3] Article 7 of the Base Convention.

[4] Article 16 of the Base Convention.

[5] Article 17 (1) of the Base Convention.

[6] Article 17 (2) (b), (f) of the Base Convention. More details of the appointment of the Registrar is provided in the Protocols. For the Aircraft Protocol, the Registrar's term of appointment is 5 years (Article XVII (5) of the Aircraft Protocol). The Luxembourg Rail Protocol does not specify the exact term, but provides that the first Registrar shall be appointed for a period of not less than 5 and more than 10 years and that the following terms shall not exceed ten years (Article XII (11) of the Luxembourg Rail Protocol). The Space Protocol has no equivalent provision.

[7] Art.29 of the Base Convention.

[8] Article 60(1) of the Base Convention.

[9] Article XIX of the Aircraft Protocol; Article XIII of the Luxembourg Rail Protocol; Article XXXI of the Space Protocol.

[10] Article 39(1) of the Base Convention.

non-consensual right or interest and a registered international interest is to be determined according to the timing of registration.[11]

2.1.2 Assuring the Enforcement of International Interests

2.1.2.1 Possibility of Private Enforcement

To the eyes of the creditor, the effective enforcement of the security interest as remedies for the default by the debtor is one of the key elements to evaluate the law on secured transactions. In this regard, the Cape Town Convention requires the States Parties to choose whether the remedies provided in the Convention are available out of court or only with leave of the court (art.54 (2) of the Convention). This is a mandatory declaration that must be made when a State becomes a Party to the Cape Town Convention. Even if the Contracting State declares that the remedies are available without going through the court procedure and, therefore, the private enforcement of its international interest may lawfully be exercised in that State, the creditor may apply for a court order granting the remedies anyway.[12]

Whether or not the private enforcement is possible, the creditor must exercise its right "in a commercially reasonable manner."[13] It is obvious that the intention of the requirement is to protect the debtor's interest. Still, the same provision deems the exercise of an international interest in conformity with a provision of the agreement to be exercised in a commercially reasonable manner, except where such a provision is manifestly unreasonable. Therefore, the provision in the agreement for creating an international interest is basically decisive.

2.1.2.2 The Remedies Available Under the Cape Town Convention

The creditor under the Cape Town Convention is entitled to a variety of remedies in case of default of the debtor. A chargee is entitled to: (a) take possession or control of any object charged to it; (b) sell or grant a lease of any such object; or (c) collect or receive any income or profits arising from the management or use of any such object.[14] Thus, besides selling the object and applying the collected, the creditor can grant a lease of the object to a third party and apply the income collected. It is also

---

[11] Article 40 of the Base Convention. Further on non-consensual right or interest, John Prichard & David Lloyd, Analysis of Non-Consensual Rights and Interests under Article 39 of the Cape Town Convention, *The Cape Town Convention Journal*, Issue 2, p.3 (2013).

[12] Article 8(2) and Article 10 (b) of the Base Convention.

[13] Article IX (3) of the Aircraft Protocol; Article VII (3) of the Luxembourg Rail Protocol; Article XVII (1) of the Space Protocol. The same phrase is used in Article 8(3) of the Base Convention, but the latter provision is excluded in the abovementioned provisions in the Protocols, to adapt to the wider variety of remedies available under the Protocols.

[14] Article 8(1) of the Base Convention.

possible to satisfy the secured obligation by vesting the ownership of the object in the chargee, upon agreement of the chargee and other interested parties or by the court order.[15] Further, if the international interest is a title reserved by the conditional seller or a lessor's right (as opposed to a security interest under a security agreement), there is no need for the creditor to pay the balance to the debtor even when the amount of the balance is larger than the amount of the secured obligation.[16] It is important to note that the distinction of a security interest and an interest of a conditional seller or lessor shall be made according to the applicable law.[17]

The Aircraft Protocol adds an aircraft-specific remedy to the list of available remedies, namely to (a) procure the de-registration of the aircraft and (b) procure the export and physical transfer of the aircraft object from the territory in which it is situated.[18] To facilitate these types of remedy, the Aircraft Protocol introduces the system of irrevocable de-registering and export request authorisation (IDERA). It is an option that a Contracting State may opt in by making a declaration. Because it is usually the debtor as current user of the aircraft that must apply for de-registration of the aircraft and permission to export it to another state, the creditor wishing to exercise these two remedies could face difficulties if the debtor does not voluntarily cooperate. An IDERA is a letter of attorney authorising the creditor or its designee to make these applications on behalf of the debtor. Holding an IDERA in advance, the creditor can take necessary steps by itself, once the event of default occurs. Because the IDERA is not revocable, the creditor may trust in the authority that it has. If a Contracting State opts in this provision, an IDERA made pursuant to the Annex of the Aircraft Protocol shall be recorded by the registry authority (the office maintaining the aircraft register in accordance with the Chicago Convention).[19] The registry authority and other authorities of the Contracting States must affirm the validity of the recorded IDERA and enable the creditor to exercise the remedies.[20]

The Luxembourg Rail Protocol also provides, as the additional type of remedy, that the creditor may procure the export and physical transfer of railway rolling stock from the territory in which it is situated.[21] However, it has no provision on an IDERA equivalent to that in the Aircraft Protocol. The difference may due to the fact that there is no universal system of registering railway rolling stock, as opposed to the aircraft register based on the Chicago Convention.

The Space Protocol provides for no additional type of remedies. However, because of the technical difficulty of repossessing a space asset in the orbit, two special mechanisms are introduced. For one, when a space asset is in orbit, physical

---

[15] Article 9(1) and (2) of the Base Convention.

[16] Compare art.10 with art.8 (6) of the Convention. Sir Roy Goode, *Convention on International Interests in Mobile Equipment and Protocol Thereto on Matters Specific to Aircraft Equipment: Official Commentary*, Third Edition, para.4.101 (Unidroit, 2013).

[17] Article 2(4) of the Base Convention.

[18] Article IX (1) of the Aircraft Protocol.

[19] Article XIII (2) of the Aircraft Protocol.

[20] Article XIII (4) of the Aircraft Protocol.

[21] Article VII (1) of the Luxembourg Rail Protocol.

repossession is possible only through transfer of control from the earth, which may be exercised by changing the command code to an alternative one escrowed in advance. To make sure that such an arrangement is permissible, the Space Protocol provides that the creditor and debtor may agree for the placement of command codes and related data and materials with another person.[22] For another, the creditor may wish to collect the secured debt by applying the payments that the user of the space asset makes to the debtor, since the economic value of the space asset is, after all, realised in such revenue stream, which is assigned to the creditor as additional collateral.[23] To enable it, the Space Protocol introduces "rights assignment", by which a debtor agrees with the creditor to grant an interest in or over the whole or part of existing or future debtor's rights.[24] The rights assignment can be recorded with the International Registry, but only at the same time as the registration of an international interest.[25] This is because the assignment of receivables as such is not the subject of the Cape Town Convention.[26]

2.1.2.3   "Relief Pending Final Determination"

Besides the remedies available to the creditor in any case, a few "speedy reliefs" are obtainable from the court unless a Contracting State excludes their application by making a declaration. At first sight it might look like interim reliefs to preserve the claimant's position. However, the "relief pending final determination" under the Cape Town Convention differs from the ordinary structure of interim reliefs in that it requires the evidence of default, while not requiring the danger of harm to the creditor, and that the availability of reliefs depends on the agreement by the debtor.[27] It may better be viewed as a *sui generis* remedy to give satisfaction to the creditor in advance of the final determination on the merits.[28]

Such reliefs available under the Base Convention are: (a) preservation of the object and its value; (b) possession, control or custody of the object; (c)

---

[22] Article XIX of the Space Protocol. See Chap. 23.

[23] MJ Stanford, The availability of a new form of financing for commercial space activities: the extension of the Cape Town Convention to space assets, *The Cape Town Convention Journal*, Issue1, p.109, at p.121 (2012).

[24] Article I (2)(h) of the Space Protocol.

[25] Article XII (1) of the Space Protocol.

[26] Sir Roy Goode, *Convention on International Interests in Mobile Equipment and Protocol Thereto on Matters Specific to Space Assets: Official Commentary*, para.5.49 (Unidroit 2013).

[27] Gilles Cuniberti, Advance relief under the Cape Town Convention, *The Cape Town Convention Journal*, Issue 1, p.79 (2012).

[28] Anna Veneziano, Advance relief under the Cape Town Convention and its Aircraft Protocol: A comment on Gilles Cuniberti's interpretative proposal, *The Cape Town Convention Journal*, Issue 2, p.185 (2013). Because the remedies under the Cape Town Convention is the exercise of an international interest (property right or *in rem* right) and not the enforcement of a claim (right to obligations or *in personam* right), it is not convincing to regard the reliefs under this provision as a measure to preserve the creditor's position.

immobilization of the object; and (d) lease or management of the object and the income therefrom.[29] The Protocols, subject to a separate declaration to opt in by a Contracting State, add (e) sale and application of the proceeds therefrom.[30] Each Protocol also requires that the State opting in under the Protocol specify the number of working days needed for the court to grant a "speedy" relief.

2.1.2.4   Events of Default

Under the recent practice of financing, default does not simply mean the failure to pay the due monetary claim. Various covenants accompany the financing agreement and a breach of those covenants constitutes an event of default, which entitles the creditor to demand remedies. The Cape Town Convention reflects such a practice by affirming the validity of an agreement in writing between the creditor and debtor on the events that constitute "default".[31]

2.1.3   Status of International Interests in Insolvency Proceedings

2.1.3.1   Basic Rule: Applicable Law – Functionalism

The Cape Town Convention requires that a registered international interest remains effective even after the insolvency proceedings commence against the debtor.[32] However, the Base Convention leaves the issue of the international interest's status under the insolvency proceedings to the applicable law. Therefore, whether the exercise of an international interest is stayed or whether the obligation under the agreement may be modified, is determined by the applicable law of insolvency.

2.1.3.2   The Alternatives on the Enforceability of International Interests After Commencement of Insolvency Proceedings

It is, however, critical in structuring the asset based financing, in particular with regard to credit rating of equipment trust certificates, whether or not the right of the creditor is affected by the commencement of insolvency proceedings. For this reason, the Protocols provide detailed rules on the issue, applicable if a Contracting State opts in by a declaration. Basically, a registered international interest can be

---

[29] Article 13 of the Base Convention.

[30] Article X of the Aircraft Protocol; Article VIII of the Luxembourg Rail Protocol; Article XX of the Space Protocol.

[31] Article 11(1) of the Base Convention.

[32] Article 30(1) of the Base Convention.

enforced even after an insolvency proceedings are commenced against the debtor, without being stayed either automatically or by an order of the court.[33] Thus, the registered international interest under the Cape Town Convention is "bankruptcy remote."

Furthermore, all three Protocols provide a provision that differ in the extent of the power that the creditor with a registered international interest can exercise in insolvency proceedings, and require the State that opts in the provision to choose one of these alternatives. Alternative A under all three Protocols ensure that the creditor is entitled to private enforcement of its international interest: the insolvency administrator or debtor, unless it cures all defaults (other than the opening of insolvency proceedings, which may itself be an event of default) and agrees to perform all future obligations under the agreement within the waiting period, must give possession of the object encumbered with an international interest to the creditor.[34] The length of the waiting period is specified by the State in its declaration.[35] Alternative A is apparently inspired by sections 1110 and 1168 of the Bankruptcy Code of the United States, which is known to have supported the development of equipment trust certificates market.

Even under Alternative B of all the Protocols, it remains the case that the insolvency administrator or debtor must choose either to cure all defaults and agree to perform all future obligations or to give the creditor the opportunity to take possession of the object in accordance with the applicable law. However, pursuant to the applicable law, the court may require that the creditor take additional steps or provide an additional guarantee. This means that the "bankruptcy remote" structure is somewhat qualified if Alternative B is applicable.[36] Under Alternative C, contained only in the Luxembourg Rail Protocol, private enforcement can be suspended by the court order on condition that all the sums accruing to the creditor continue to be paid and that the insolvency administrator or debtor performs all other obligations. The insolvency administrator or debtor must first choose, within the cure period, either to cure all defaults and agree to perform all future obligations or to give the creditor the opportunity to take possession of the object. Then it may, before the cure period ends, apply for a court order suspending the repossession by the creditor.[37] Limiting the private enforcement in such a manner reflects the nature of enforcement over

---

[33] Article XI of the Aircraft Protocol; Article IX of the Luxembourg Rail Protocol; Article XXI of the Space Protocol.

[34] Alternative A, Article XI (2) and (7) of the Aircraft Protocol; Alternative A, Article IX (3) and (7) of the Luxembourg Rail Protocol; Alternative A, Article XXI (2) and (8) of the Space Protocol. The Space Protocol entitles the creditor also to private enforcement over the debtor's rights covered by a rights assignment (Article XXI (3) of the Space Protocol).

[35] Alternative A, Article XI (3) of the Aircraft Protocol; Alternative A, Article IX (4) of the Luxembourg Rail Protocol; Alternative A, Article XXI (4) of the Space Protocol.

[36] Alternative B, Article XI (2) and (3) of the Aircraft Protocol; Alternative B, Article IX (3) and (4) of the Luxembourg Rail Protocol; Alternative B, Article XXI (2) and (3) of the Space Protocol.

[37] Alternative C, Article IX (3) and (4) of the Luxembourg Rail Protocol. See Chap. 22 for the background.

railway rolling stock: because it may be delivered only by driving on the rail, the support by the court will anyway be required.[38]

2.1.4   The Emphasis of the Policy Intent

The unique features of the Cape Town Convention discussed above resulted from the approach to drafting which is much different from traditional uniform law instruments. The Cape Town Convention does not aim at merely unifying the laws of various jurisdictions by choosing one of the existing domestic laws or creating a "middle ground" rule among them. Rather, the drafters had the clear goal of establishing a legal framework conducive to asset based financing that will bring about the economic benefit from larger availability of financing to the State Party.[39] It was recognised that three principles were needed to achieve this goal, namely: (1) transparency in the priority among secured interests, (2) the prompt enforcement of secured interests in case of default by the debtor, including the admissibility of private enforcement, and (3) the enforcement of the secured interests without being qualified or modified under the insolvency proceedings.[40]

This approach reflects the evaluations by the market for enhanced equipment trust certificates (EETCs). EETCs are securities to finance acquisition of equipment from the capital market. Since the latter half of the nineteenth Century, railway companies in the United States have developed a scheme of equipment trust of railway rolling stock that enabled the issuance of equipment trust certificates (ETCs) to the capital market. Originally it was bailment with purchase option of rolling stock held by the trustee, but later the conditional sale agreement appeared, followed by the leasing agreement.[41] After the Second World War, the scheme started to be used for aircraft financing. Now, a scheme of "enhanced" equipment trust certificates, distinguishing several tranches and introducing cross subordination, is commonly used.[42]

As bankruptcy procedure was gradually formed in the United States since the end of the nineteenth Century, the status of equipment trust in the procedure began

---

[38] Howard Rosen, Martin Fleetwood & Benjamin von Bodungen, The Luxembourg Rail Protocol – Extending Cape Town Benefits to the Rail Industry, [2012] *Uniform Law Review* p.609, at p.613.

[39] Jeffrey Wool, The case for a commercial orientation to the proposed Unidroit Convention as applied to aircraft equipment, [1999] *Uniform Law Review* p.289.

[40] Anthony Saunders, Anand Srinivasan, Ingo Walter & Jeffrey Wool, The Economic Implications of International Secured Transactions Law Reform: A Case Study, *The University of Pennsylvania Journal of International Economic Law*, vol. 20, p.309, at p. 324 (1999).

[41] Michael Downey Rice, Railroad Equipment Financing, *Transportation Law Journal*, Vol.18, p.85 (1989); For the detailed history of the development of ETCs of railway rolling stock, see Francis Rawle, Car Trust Securities, *Annual Report of the American Bar Association*, p.277 (1885).

[42] Ronald Scheinberg, Enhanced Equipment Trust Certificates in the Downturn: An Assessment for Banks, *Banking Law Journal*, Vol.121, p.108 (2004).

to be questioned. The concerns from the market resulted in the amendment of 1935 to the Bankruptcy Act of 1898, adding a paragraph to the provision on bankruptcy of railway operators that allowed the owner of conditionally sold or leased railway rolling stock to take possession of the collateral even after the commencement of the reorganisation procedure.[43] The provision is currently codified in section 1168 of the 1978 Bankruptcy Code of the United States,[44] and a similar provision exists with regard to aircraft and ships as section 1110.[45] The latter provision has been considered as "one of the linchpins of EETCs, and indeed all U.S. aircraft, financings."[46] If one compares the texts of section 1110 and Article XI of the Aircraft Protocol, it is easy to see that Alternative A of the latter provision intended to replicate the former, expecting the economic benefit realised by sections 1110 and 1168 to become available to borrowers outside the United States.

Because the policy intent was so strong, it was feared that a compromise on the text would mitigate the expected economic benefit. For this reason, when the negotiations on the text encountered difficulties, it was preferred to incorporate options. As a result, the Cape Town Convention has options (possibilities to opt in and opt out) in various provisions. The strategy was to accommodate conflicting views on the policies at the stage of negotiations, and to postpone the decisions on which policy to choose until the time when states ratify the Cape Town Convention and decide whether or not to make declarations on opt-in's and opt-out's.[47] Under this mechanism, the economic benefit to be achieved will vary, depending on the set of rules opted by the ratifying states. To give guidance on the combination of options acceptable to the market, the Aviation Working Group (AWG) and the Rail Working Group (RWG) have prepared "a matrix of recommended declarations".[48] For the Aircraft Protocol, almost identical set of declarations is treated as "qualifying declarations" in the Aircraft Sector Understanding (ASU) of the OECD (Organisation for Economic Cooperation and Developments). It is one of the conditions for the discount in premium rate to be applicable (see Sect. 2.4.2.2).

---

[43] See Gregory Ripple, Note, special Protection in the air[line Industry]: The Historical Development of Section 1110 of the Bankruptcy Code, *Notre Dame Law Review*, Vol.78, p.281, at pp.287–288 (2002); On the background of the amendments, Max Lowenthal, The Railroad Reorganization Act, *Harvard Law Review*, Vol.47, p.18 (1933).

[44] 11 USC §1168.

[45] 11 USC §1110.

[46] Scheinberg, supra note 55, p.114.

[47] Ikumi Sato & Yoshinobu Zasu, Beyond Conflict of Interest: Lessons from the Cape Town Convention, *Asian Journal of Law and Economics*, Vol.1, Issue 1, p.1 (2010).

[48] http://www.awg.aero/assets/docs/matrixofrecommendeddeclarations.pdf

2.1.5 The Application of the Cape Town Convention

2.1.5.1 Sphere of Application

As a uniform law treaty, the Cape Town Convention binds the courts of States Parties to apply the provisions of the Base Convention and the Protocol that the State ratifies. In such courts, the Cape Town Convention applies when the debtor is situated in a Contracting State at the time of the conclusion of the agreement creating or providing for the international interest. The location of the creditor is not relevant.[49] If the State of the court is a Party to the Aircraft Protocol, the court must apply the Base Convention as modified by the Aircraft Protocol also when the airframe or helicopter is registered in an aircraft register of a Contracting State which is the State of registry.[50] The other two Protocols do not have an equivalent to the last provision.

2.1.5.2 Internal Transactions

If a Contracting State makes a declaration to opt in, several provisions of the Cape Town Convention are not applicable to "internal transactions."[51] Still, some of the remedial provisions and all of the provisions on registration and priorities remain applicable. A transaction that could otherwise be a transaction covered by the Convention becomes an internal transaction (i) when the centre of the main interests of all parties to the transaction is situated, and the relevant object is located, in the same Contracting State at the time of the conclusion of the contract, and (ii) where the interest created by the transaction has been registered in a national registry in the same Contracting State, and (iii) the same Contracting State has made a declaration to opt in to Article 50 of the Base Convention.[52]

For a transport vehicle as mobile equipment, the location of the object under the condition (i) is not easy to determine. Each Protocol offers guidance in this respect. Under the Aircraft Protocol, the location of object is determined by the State of registry of the aircraft (for an airframe and engine installed on an aircraft) or the State of registry of the helicopter (for a helicopter).[53] The Space Protocol provides that a space asset on orbit is deemed to be in the Contracting State which registers the space asset, or on the registry of which the space asset is carried, as a space object under the relevant space law instruments.[54] The railway rolling stock might appear to be easier in determining a physical location of the object, but the

---

[49] Article 3 of the Base Convention.

[50] Article IV (1) of the Aircraft Protocol.

[51] Article 50 of the Base Convention.

[52] Article 1(n) of the Base Convention.

[53] Article IV (2) of the Aircraft Protocol.

[54] Article I (3) of the Space Protocol.

Luxembourg Rail Protocol adds an additional case of an internal transaction. It is when the rolling stock is only capable of being operated on a single railway system within the Contracting State concerned, because of track gauge or other elements of the design of such railway rolling stock.[55]

2.1.5.3   Special Rules for the Equipment Used for a Public Service

The Aircraft Protocol does not apply to aircraft objects, if the airframe, aircraft engine or helicopter is used in military, customs or police services.[56] In this sense, it excludes the aircraft objects from the sphere of applications in its entirety. The Luxembourg Rail Protocol and Space Protocol, on the other hand, do not exclude objects used for public services, as these types of equipment are more often used for what might be considered as public services or for both public and commercial purposes at the same time (as with dual use space assets). As a result, a problem arose in these two Protocols on how to reconcile the public interests and financier's demands.[57]

The Luxembourg Rail Protocol introduced an opt-in provision that allows a Contracting State to declare that the "rules of its law in force at that time which preclude, suspend or govern the exercise within its territory of any of the remedies … in relation to railway rolling stock habitually used for the purpose of providing a service of public importance ('public service railway rolling stock')."[58] The condition for precluding, suspending or otherwise governing the exercise of remedies is that the money is paid to the creditor every month in the amount specified under the domestic law in force or the amount of market lease rental, whichever is larger.[59] The system appears similar to the German Law in respect of Measures for the Maintenance of the Operation of Railways Providing Public Transportation of 1934. It is an exchange for the prevention of repossession by the creditor vis-à-vis the assured payment of compensation.[60] One of the primary drafters of the Luxembourg Rail Protocol warns that opting in to this provision could limit the ability to finance from the market severely and that a Contracting State is advised to make careful consideration before opting in.[61]

---

[55] Article XXIX (2) of the Luxembourg Rail Protocol.

[56] Article I (2) (b), (e) & (l) of the Aircraft Protocol.

[57] Howard Rosen, Public Service and the Cape Town Convention, *The Cape Town Convention Journal*, Issue 2, p.131 (2013).

[58] Article XXV (1) of the Luxembourg Rail Protocol.

[59] Article XXV (3) of the Luxembourg Rail Protocol.

[60] Rosen, supra note 70, at p.141 (2013). On the German Law in respect of Measures for the Maintenance of the Operation of Railways Providing Public Transportation (Gesetz über Maßnahmen zur Aufrechterhaltung des Betriebs von Bahnunternehmen des öffentlichen Verkehrs), see Benjamin von Bodungen && Konrad Schott, The Public Service Exemption under the Luxembourg Rail Protocol: a German Perspective, [2007] *Uniform Law Review* p.573.

[61] Howard Rosen, The Luxembourg Rail Protocol: a Major Advance for the Railway Industry, [2007] *Uniform Law Review* p.427, at pp.439–440.

Under the Space Protocol, the provision limiting the exercise of remedies when the space asset is used for providing a public service is not an option by declaration. When the space asset is used for providing a public service in a Contracting State, that Contracting State may register a public service notice with the International Registry.[62] Once such a public service notice is registered, the creditor with an international interest registered after the public service notice (or had knowledge of the agreement to provide a public service) may not render the space asset unavailable for the provision of the public service during a certain period of time by exercising the remedies.[63] The idea is obviously to ensure some time to coordinate on how best to continue the use of the space asset and maintain the public service after the debtor becomes insolvent.[64] As in the case of public service exemption under the Luxembourg Rail Protocol, this mechanism could compromise the appetite of the capital market severe. Because the register of a public service notice is made on the basis of an agreement between the debtor, public service provider and the Contracting State, the creditor might require the debtor not to agree on the public service notice as a covenant of the loan or lease agreement.[65]

2.2   Unification in the Traditional Sense: Choosing from the Varieties

The Cape Town Convention is a uniform law instrument, with the aim of converging the domestic law rules that vary from one jurisdiction to another. However, such unification is achieved only on some issues. On several other issues, the Cape Town Convention leaves options that are open to State Parties to choose through declaration.

Limiting the uniform rules to some important issues is not exceptional. In fact, it has been quite common for a traditional uniform law treaty to explicitly state in its title that only "certain rules" are regulated.[66] In such a case, the applicable domestic law determines the issues that fall beyond the scope of the treaty. The Cape Town Convention is not different, though it requires the solution "in conformity with the general principles on which it [the Convention] is based" to be considered, before resorting to the applicable law.[67]

---

[62] Article XXVII (1) of the Space Protocol.

[63] Article XXVII (3) & (9) of the Space Protocol.

[64] See the duty to "co-operate in good faith with a view to finding a commercially reasonable solution permitting the continuation of the public service" in Article XXVII (7) (a) of the Space Protocol.

[65] Goode, *Official Commentary on Space Protocol*, supra note 39, para.5.105.

[66] Examples are the International Convention for the Unification of Certain Rules of Law Relating to the Bills of Lading, 1924 (the so-called Hague Rules) and the Convention for the Unification of Certain Rules Relating to International Carriage by Air (the Warsaw Convention), 1929.

[67] Article 5(2) of the Base Convention.

The following sections describe the issues on which laws of various states differ and for which the Cape Town Convention provides for a uniform solution. Here the Cape Town Convention serves as the uniform law treaty in the traditional sense.

2.2.1 Non-possessory Security Interests in Transport Vehicles

2.2.1.1 Creation of Non-possessory Interests and Their Registries

An international interest under the Cape Town Convention will in practice be a non-possessory security interest in a movable asset.[68] Jurisdictions are divided over whether movables can generally be the subject of such non-possessory security interest. As far as aircraft is concerned, however, it seems universal that such an interest can be constituted in an aircraft and registered in the relevant registry in all the reported jurisdictions.

In some jurisdictions, movable assets in general can be mortgaged and no special law is needed with regards to aircraft. Such is the case in Canada (the Personal Property Security Act (PPSA) in common law provinces and *Code Civil* in Québec) and Poland (Registered Pledge Act). In Poland, a registered pledge is distinguished from a regular pledge in that the possession need not be transferred to the pledgee and that registration with the registry operated by the district courts suffices. Spain also has a registry for non-possessory pledge and mortgage in movables, and the mortgages in aircrafts are also registered in this registry (*Ley sobre Hipoteca Mobiliaria y prenda sin desplazamiento de posesión* of 16 December 1954). In the United States, the general filing system for security interests under the Uniform Commercial Code (UCC) does not govern aircrafts and railway rolling stock, as these assets have their specialised recording system. For space assets, though, an interest equivalent to an international interest under the Cape Town Convention is subject to the UCC filing.

Many other jurisdictions have special rules on aircraft mortgages with a registry for that purpose being established. England (Mortgaging of Aircraft Order 1972), Finland (Aviation Act (1194/2009)), Greece (Law 1340/1983), Italy (*Codice della navigazione*), Portugal (*Decreto* No.20.062, 25 October 1930) and Switzerland (*Loi fédérale sur le registre des aéronefs, du 7 octobre 1959*: LRA) are the jurisdictions of this group. Malaysia (Civil aviation regulations 1996) and the United States (recording of transaction documents with the Federal Aviation Authority (FAA)) are the States Parties to the Convention and Aircraft Protocol, but they also maintain their domestic registries for registering mortgages on aircraft.

A few jurisdictions have a similar registry for railway rolling stock. The United States requires the secured transactions over rolling stock to be filed with the Surface

---

[68] Though not likely to be relevant in practice, the Cape Town Convention also covers pledges, under which the creditor possesses the secured object. Goode, supra note 29, para 2.37.

Transportation Board (STB). In Finland, mortgages in railway rolling stock may be created under the Vehicle Mortgage Act (810/1972).

For space assets, no state appears to have a special registry for registration of security interests. As noted above, in some jurisdictions such as Canada, Poland and the United States, an interest in a space asset may be registered in the general registry for security interests. In the absence of specific registry, a pledge may also be created through taking possession of a space asset. As space assets are controlled from the ground through the TTC (telemetry, tracking and command) center, if the domestic law recognises the indirect possession through the operator of such TTC center, it is possible that a pledge is validly constituted.[69]

2.2.1.2   The Solution Provided by the Cape Town Convention

While the domestic laws on security interests have a wide variety, the Cape Town Convention provides a simple solution. Independently from any domestic law, it introduces a set of rules on the creation and registration of security interests as *sui generis* rights and establishes a registry specific to each type of equipment for which a Protocol exists.[70] Then it determines priorities according to the registration with the International Registry, which rule overrides the domestic law. In this respect, the Cape Town Convention is a uniform law. For aircraft, the Cape Town Convention and the International Registry established by the Aircraft Protocol override (but do not replace) the domestic law on registration and the national registry, which exists in most jurisdictions. As regards space assets and, in many jurisdictions railway rolling stock as well, the International Registry is a novel scheme enabling the asset based registration of security interests in such mobile equipment.

An important implication from the priority rules of the Cape Town Convention is that a registered international interest prevails over a creditor that has a priority under the domestic law. This is of particular importance in those countries where railway rolling stock cannot be separately financed once the whole railway facility is mortgaged. For example, in Switzerland the *gage* over the whole railway facility enterprise has existed under the law of 1917 (*la Loi fédérale concernant la constitution de gages sur les entreprises de chemins de fer et de navigation et la liquidation forcée de ces entreprises, du 25 septembre 1917*).[71] Japan also has the Railway Mortgage Act, according to which the whole set of assets of the railway company constitutes an estate and can be mortgaged, in which case the mortgage can be registered in a special registry.[72] Also in some states of Germany, there are statutes that treat all the properties of railway operator as one unit (*Bahneinheit*) for the purpose

---

[69] See discussions in Chaps. 10 and 20.

[70] Article 16(2) of the Base Convention.

[71] See Chap. 20.

[72] See Chap. 17.

of mortgaging.[73] Under these laws, the mortgagee of the whole facility, if registered, may claim priority over the financier of railway rolling stock. Under the Cape Town Convention, the outcome would be different, as a mortgage over the whole facility cannot be registered with the International Registry. Recognising this point, the Swiss government recently excluded the rolling stock from the subject of gage on the railway business in preparation for the entry into force of Rail Protocol.[74] In some other jurisdictions, such as England and Malaysia, a floating charge can be created over a fund of assets and be registered in a companies register.[75] Again, such a floating charge is not covered by the Cape Town Convention, because the International Registry is asset-based and registration with it is only available to uniquely identifiable assets. As a result, a registered international interest will have a priority.

A similar observation may be made with regards to international interests in space assets. The space operator seldom creates a floating charge on its assets, but several cases of leveraged buy outs (LBO) targeted satellite operators in the first few years of the twenty-first Century. A leveraged buy out has some common elements with a floating charge, as its finance is based on the value of the whole corporation. Now that the rush of LBOs in the space sector seems to have become an anecdote in the past, assuring the right of a creditor of asset based financing by the Space Protocol might have merits in space financing.[76]

2.2.2   Title-Based Security (Quasi-security)

Other than the security interest (movable mortgage), the Cape Town Convention governs the retention of title and lease. In jurisdictions where the *numerus clausus* rule is adopted for secured transactions, these transactions are not secured transactions. Still, the creditor's interest can be secured through the title (ownership) to the object and is enforceable by termination of the contract accompanying recovery of the title (ownership). These transactions are known as "title-based security," "*quasi-sûretés*" or "quasi-security interests."

A major issue with respect to the title-based security is whether or not they are subjected to the same or parallel rules as the mortgage or *hypothèque*. In some jurisdictions, it is considered that a transaction-type with the same function must be regulated in the same manner. This may be called "functional approach." In others, emphasis is given more on the differences in the form, in which case a title-based security is not subjected to the same rules as a mortgage or *hypothèque*.

---

[73] Benjamin von Bodungen, *Mobiliarsicherungsrechte an Luftfahrzeugen und Eisenbahnrollmaterial im nationalen und internationalen Rechtsverkehr*, S.173 ff (Lit Verlag, 2009).

[74] Recueil officiel du droit fédéral 2009 pp. 5622 et 5628.

[75] See Chaps. 4 and 6.

[76] Souichirou Kozuka & Fuki Taniguchi, An Economic Assessment of the Space Protocol to the Cape Town Convention, [2012] *Uniform Law Review* p.927.

A jurisdiction known for its functionalist approach is the United States, where Article 9 of the Uniform Commercial Code (UCC) covers secured transactions broadly. However, as far as the lease is concerned, UCC Article 9 only applies to leases for security purposes, and the lease not for security purposes (true lease) is governed by Article 2A. The PPSA of common law provinces in Canada has a larger scope of application and applies not only to transactions creating security interests but to non-financial lease of more than 1 year. The *Code Civil* of Québec distinguishes property law and contractual "quasi-sûretes", but generally parallel rules apply to both, including the registration.

In contrast, the traditional formalism is maintained in such jurisdictions as England, Germany, Greece and Poland. In England, the finance lease, conditional sales agreement, hire-purchase agreement and retention of title clause, collectively known as title-retention agreements, are not subject to registration, unless the court recharacterises the transaction as a secured transaction because the document does not truly reflect what the parties have agreed. Nor are they governed by the same rules with regard to their enforcement. Further, the operating lease is entirely out of the scope of mortgage registration. Similarly, in Greece the distinction between the mortgage (simple and preferred mortgages) as property right (real right) on the one hand and leases and title-reservation agreements as contractual right on the other hand is emphasised. This is so notwithstanding that there is a special statute on aircraft leasing (Law 1665/1986). Poland shares the same distinction as the basic approach, though there is a special rule that a conditional sale becomes opposable vis-à-vis the buyer's creditor through production of confirmation in writing with the authenticated date.

Even in jurisdictions where the law appears to treat the title-based transaction according to its form, academic theories are familiar with the functional approach.[77] Furthermore, for the purposes of registration, the functional approach is sometimes adopted as a statutory rule. This is the case in Portugal, where the title reservation agreement and financial leasing are registered if the object of the transaction is a movable subject to registration, and in Spain, where any agreement with the same economic goal as a hire purchase agreement is registered in the Registry of Movables. Still, in these jurisdictions the functional approach is confined to registration and the court usually treats the title-based security as fully fledged property right. The opposite is true in Japan, where the Supreme Court employs a functionalist view and treats the owner under a title-based security agreement as a secured creditor in the corporate reorganisation procedure.[78]

On this issue, the Cape Town Convention unifies the divergent rules only to the minimum. The unification is achieved to the extent that the title reserved by a conditional seller and the interest of a person who is the lessor under a leasing agreement can be registered in the International Registry. It has gone even further than the UCC of the United States in that a lessor's interest under any kind of leasing agreement is registrable. However, with regard to the exercise of remedies, the Cape

---

[77] See Chaps. 10, 16 and 19.

[78] See Chap. 17.

Town Convention distinguishes the security interest and the title reserved by the conditional seller and the lessor's interest. In this connection, characterization is made according to the applicable law.[79] Thus, the meaning of "charge" or "lease" will be different in those jurisdictions adopting the functional approach and those not. This means that the divergence in domestic law is not entirely overcome.

2.2.3   The Enforcement of Security and Private Autonomy

2.2.3.1   The Variety of Remedies

When the debtor defaults, the creditor must be entitled to remedies. However, the variety of available remedies is not the same in every jurisdiction. In some jurisdictions, a broad range of remedies are available. England is such a jurisdiction, where the four main methods of enforcement for the holder of a security interest (as opposed to a title-based security) are the repossession of the asset, sale of the asset, foreclosure (satisfaction by the secured object through court order) and appointment of receiver.[80] In Canada, under both the PPSA in common law provinces and the *Code civil* of Québec the secured creditor may take possession of the object and lease it to apply the revenues from it, satisfy its claim by the secured object, have the object sold or sell the object by the creditor himself.[81] The remedies available under the UCC Article 9 of the United States are also broad in variety, including taking of proceeds and applying it to the secured obligation, taking possession of the collateral, rendering the equipment unusable, selling, leasing, licensing or otherwise disposing of collateral in its present condition, applying the cash proceeds from such disposition, as well as accepting the collateral in full or partial satisfaction of the secured obligation.[82]

A few jurisdictions accommodate parties' agreement on the variety of remedies. Finland affirms the parties' freedom of agreement and holds an agreement (typically as a clause in the financing agreement in practice) on the types of remedy available to the creditor as valid. Also in France, the reform of 2006 brought much flexibility to the secured transactions law so as to affirm the validity of agreement on satisfaction by secured object and to authorise the court to order transfer of the secured object as the remedy. The Swiss law also upholds the validity of an agreement on the manner of enforcement, though private enforcement is considered not allowed with regard to the exercise of a mortgage in aircraft, due to the Convention on the International Recognition of Rights in Aircraft, 1948 (Geneva Convention).[83] In Canada, the common law provinces affirm the parties' agreement on remedies,

---

[79] Article 2(4) of the Base Convention.

[80] See Chap. 4.

[81] See Chap. 3.

[82] See Chap. 11.

[83] See Chap. 20.

while the *Code civil* of Québec limits the available remedies to those listed in the *Code*.[84]

2.2.3.2 Private Enforcement and *Pactum Commissorium*

Besides the variety of remedies, a controversial issue is whether the creditor may exercise the remedy without resorting to the court. In the United States, UCC Article 9 allows a secured party to take possession of collateral following a default without the judicial process unless it breaches the peace in doing so. Under the Greek law, the mortgagee of a preferred mortgage in aircraft may take possession of the aircraft without any court procedure, on condition that the mortgage is in the form of a notarial deed, which is regarded as one of the enforceable titles in Greece. In Canada, the *Code civil* of Québec, as opposed to PPSA of common law provinces, requires the procedure before the court unless the debtor voluntarily delivers the secured object.[85]

In other jurisdictions, the secured creditor can only avail itself of the judicial enforcement (judicial sale). This is so, for example, with the pledgee of a registered pledge in Poland.[86] On a particular issue of whether an agreement to grant the secured object in satisfaction of the claim (*pactum commissorium*) is valid, jurisdictions are divided. Italy, Portugal and the Netherlands deny the validity of such an agreement.[87] In fact, it is one of the reasons why the Netherlands chose not to accede to the Cape Town Convention with the effect over the European part of the Kingdom. In contrast, France affirms the validity of *pacte commissoire* after the reform of 2006.[88] A halfway solution is found in Germany, where it is implied by the Aircraft Mortgage Act that the mortgagor and mortgagee of an aircraft may enter into an agreement of this kind after the mortgage becomes enforceable.[89] The academic literature in Spain holds the same view, namely an agreement of vesting an object in satisfaction of the claim (*pacto comisorio*) is valid if made after the claim becomes due.[90] Finally, under the *Code civil* of Québec, taking the creditor's secured object in satisfaction requires the court's permission when the debtor has discharged half or more of the secured debt. Thus, the timing of entering into the agreement is not the only element for consideration.[91]

---

[84] See Chap. 3.

[85] See Chaps. 3, 11 and 15. Canada made a declaration under Article 54 (2) of the Base Convention that the court order is not required for the exercise of remedies when acceding to the Cape Town Convention. As a result, Québec's *Code civil* providing for a contrary rule had to be amended.

[86] See Chap. 18.

[87] See Chaps. 7, 16 and 19.

[88] See Chap. 13.

[89] See Chap. 14.

[90] See Chap. 10.

[91] See Chap. 3.

2.2.3.3   The Enforcement of Title-Based Securities

The remedies available to the holder of a title-based security are even more divergent. It is no surprise, as jurisdictions vary in whether the functional approach shall
be adopted to treat a title-based security as equivalent to a mortgage. On the one
hand, there are jurisdictions in which the form of title is emphasised and the creditor
is given a status of the owner, with a larger power than a mortgagee. England is typically such a formalist jurisdiction, where the owner under a title-retention agreement (such as seller reserving the title or lessor under a lease) may reclaim the full
ownership upon the occurrence of the repudiatory breach of the agreement. The
remedy is available with or without the court procedure and the owner is under no
obligation to account for the balance of the value of the object and the secured
claim.[92] The right of the conditional sellers and lessors in Italy is the same.[93]

On the other side of the continuum stands the jurisdiction that is "functionalist."
The UCC Article 9 of the United States adopts this approach, treating the conditional seller as a chargee and applies the same rules.[94] Similarly in Poland, the law
requires the payment for the balance between the value of the object and the remaining amount of claims when the creditor of a security or title-based security repos-
sesses the object.[95] Such a duty to pay for the balance can be waived by the agreement
in case of a lease and conditional sale, but not in case of a registered pledge. Then,
the hybrid solution is taken by France, where the owner repossessing the object is
required to pay the balance in the case of a reservation of title, but not under a
finance lease.[96]

2.2.3.4   The Protection of the Debtor's Interests

While the creditor achieves its economic interest by exercising the remedies, the
interest of the debtor also needs due consideration. The extent to which the debtor's
interest is protected, however, differs from one jurisdiction to another. The UCC
Article 9 of the United States provides that every aspect of a disposition of collateral
must be commercially reasonable.[97] Seemingly in contrast, under the English law,
the mortgagee enjoys the "unfettered discretion" as to the timing of enforcement.
However, English law also assumes that the mortgagee must act fairly towards the
mortgagor, and that the mortgagee having determined to proceed to the sale of the

---

[92] See Chap. 4.

[93] See Chap. 16.

[94] See Chap. 11. However, even in the United States, the right of a lessor is governed by Article 2A
of the UCC, not Article 9. See Sect. 2.2.2.

[95] See Chap. 18.

[96] See Chap. 13.

[97] See Chap. 11.

asset owes the duty to take reasonable care about achieving a proper price.[98] As a result, both jurisdictions may not be different in reality.

Sometimes the legislator is more specific in preserving the interest of the debtor. In Italy, the *Codice della navigazione* provides that the court may order the continued use of the aircraft against provision of security and apply the proceeds from such continued use. It is different from the rules on the general mortgage under the *Codice civile*. With the high value that aircraft usually has, it is reasonable to enable avoiding the forced sale in this way.[99]

2.2.3.5   Events of Default

Traditionally, in particular in jurisdictions influenced by the German legal doctrine, the concept of "default" has been considered as including three types, namely non-performance, impossibility of performance and delay in performance. In those jurisdictions, the parties' freedom to stipulate the meaning of "default" in an agreement is doubted. In the Netherlands, the "open-ended concept of default" under the Cape Town Convention is considered to be significantly different from its Civil Code.[100] In Poland, while a conditional sale and a lease agreement may be flexibly drafted, a registered pledge is strict with regard to the concept of default, since only the monetary claim can be secured by it.[101]

However, other jurisdictions are more generous in upholding the validity of agreements on what constitutes default. Such jurisdictions include Canada (both common law provinces and Québec), England, Finland, Switzerland and the United States.[102] The English court seems to be the most flexible and maintains the view that the parties to the agreement are the best judge of the commercial fairness.

2.2.3.6   The Solution Provided by the Cape Town Convention

On many of these issues relating to the enforcement, the Cape Town Convention adopts a strong solution. It authorises parties to entertain a wide range of freedom of agreement, both with regard to the remedies available and the meaning of default. In this sense, the Cape Town Convention introduces a uniform set of rules to replace the existing domestic law, just like traditional uniform law treaties. The uniqueness may be found, though, in that the adopted solution is apparently not the middle ground of the various laws in different jurisdictions. It is closer to one end of the continuum, clear preference being given to private autonomy.

---

[98] See Chap. 4.

[99] See Chap. 16.

[100] See Chap. 7.

[101] See Chap. 18.

[102] See Chaps. 3, 4, 11, 12 and 20.

Still, the Cape Town Convention has not entirely unified the rules. An important issue of the admissibility of private enforcement is not determined by the Convention's rule, but is left to the choice of Contracting States to be made through declarations under Article 54(2). Under that provision, a Contracting State must declare whether or not the remedies are available without leave of the court. Until now, only a few States, including Brazil, China, Mexico and Spain, chose to require leave of the court and, therefore, the rules are highly uniform. Still, it is a result of choices of Contracting States and not the uniformity through the provisions of the Convention.

Further, as a result of not deeming a title-based security as equal to a security interest, the rules on the remedies available to a chargee of a security interest and those available to a conditional seller and lessor are different under the Cape Town Convention. In this respect also, the unification achieved by the Cape Town Convention has remained modest.

2.2.4 Summary: The Insignificance of the Legal Family

As overviewed in this chapter, the laws of security and title-based security are more than diverse among jurisdictions. It is worth noting that the diversity does not correspond to the difference between the common law and Civil law. On the one hand there are issues such as the functional approach, over which the English and American law differ significantly. While both English and American law admit the private enforcement to a large extent, South Africa, which is a mixed jurisdiction of common law and Roman Dutch law, viewed it as infringing on the Constitutional principle.[103] On the other hand, unlike the secured transactions law in general, the law on aircraft finance has historically responded to the practice in the specific sector, as shown in the fact that most jurisdictions have a special register for mortgages in aircraft. Further, recent reforms on secured transactions law, as the 2006 law of France or 1996 law of Poland, have diminished the differences between the common law and Civil law.

As regards the remaining divergences, the Cape Town Convention has achieved unification, but rather modestly. It has ensured the registrability of title-based securities as well as lease (even non-financial leases), which in many jurisdictions are not regarded as security interests. It also has validated the agreement on the meaning of "default" and on a variety of remedies available to the creditor in case of default of the debtor. However, the Cape Town Convention has not gone beyond there and has reserved the room for a choice by Contracting States on such issues as the admissibility of private enforcement. Furthermore, some important issues are left to the court, as with characterisation of the transaction or interpretation of the requirement of "commercially reasonable" manner in the enforcement.

---

[103] See Chap. 9.

2.3 Creating a New Scheme: Improving the Law on Secured Transactions

As noted earlier (Sect. 2.1.4), the Cape Town Convention adopted a novel approach to drafting. Different from the traditional approach of finding a "compromise" without a bias on any of the divergent domestic laws, or of playing "give and take" game in which each camp makes a concession on some issues, the drafters focused on the conditions facilitative to asset based financing and incorporated them in the Convention.

This approach is useful, among others, on issues where existing laws are outdated or too complicated. It is also critical when the prevailing view on the issue is in fact detrimental to the practice of asset based financing. These issues are discussed in the following sections.

2.3.1 Modernisation of Filing System for Security Interests

2.3.1.1 The Design of Aircraft Registry

As already noted, most jurisdictions have a registry to record security interests in aircraft under the existing domestic law. It does not mean, however, that those existing domestic registries are similarly designed. Rather, there is a large variety in the manner how they are designed.

First, the registry can be indexed by the asset (aircraft) or by the debtor. Where the domestic registry for rights in aircraft exists, it is usually indexed by the aircraft. Such asset-based registries are found in Finland (register maintained by the Finnish Transport Safety Agency (TraFi)), Germany, Greece (records maintained by the Civil Aviation Authority), Italy, Japan and Switzerland.[104] In the United States, while the filing system under UCC Article 9 is debtor-based, security interests in aircraft are recorded with the aircraft-based file with the FAA, and the same is true with the recordation of secured transactions over railway rolling stock with STB.[105]

Where the relevant registry is not specific to aircraft, there are both possibilities. The Registry of Pledges in Poland, for example, is an asset-based registry. So is Spain's Registry of Movables.[106] On the other hand, the Canadian Registers under the PPSA (in common law provinces) and the *Code civil* (of Québec) are debtor-based. In France, the registry for *hypothèque* in aircraft is asset-based, but there is another registry for financial lease (*credit-bail*) based on the *Code monétaire et financier*. The latter registry is debtor-based.[107]

---

[104] See Chaps. 12, 14, 15, 16, 17 and 20.

[105] See Chap. 11.

[106] See Chap. 18.

[107] See Chap. 3.

Some jurisdictions have a system for registering a floating charge. By its nature, a floating charge can only be registered in the debtor-based registry. In England, most charges, fixed or floating, must now be registered with the debtor-based Register of Company Charges, if the debtor is a company or a limited liability partnership. Failure to do so will make the charge void against a liquidator, an administrator or creditor of the company.[108] In Malaysia, a charge used to be registered in the debtor-based registration under subsection 108 (3) of the Companies Act 1965 (Act 125) prior to its accession to the Cape Town Convention.[109] Under these systems, the transaction parties have to consult two registries, an asset-based registry for aircraft mortgages and a debtor-based registry for floating charges. In both Malaysia and the United Kingdom, the Cape Town Convention has now simplified the system.[110]

Secondly, some jurisdictions has a notice filing registry, while others not. A notice filing registry accepts filing without reviewing it. As a result, there is no guarantee that the filed security interest truly exists or is validly constituted. The United States (the UCC filing), Canada (both PPSA registries in common law provinces and the registry under the *Code civil* of Québec) and South Africa maintain notice filing registries.[111]

Other jurisdictions have title-registry, under which the application is reviewed by the registrar. The application for registration is accepted only after the registrar is convinced that a valid security interest has been created. The registry for registered pledges in Poland and the Registry of Movables in Spain are of this type.[112] Aircraft specific registries of several jurisdictions, such as Italy or Switzerland, are not notice filing system, but entail review by the registrar.[113]

Still another variant is the document recordation system of the FAA and STB in the United States. It is different from simply filing a notice of financing agreement in that the transaction document itself is recorded. However, the system differs from the aircraft specific registries in many other jurisdictions in that the FAA or STB does not review the recorded document to check whether the security interest is validly constituted.[114]

---

[108] See Chap. 4.

[109] See Chap. 6.

[110] In Malaysia, the International Interests in Mobile Equipment (Aircraft) Act 2006 (Act 659), which implements the Convention and Aircraft Protocol in Malaysia, explicitly excludes the application of the debtor-based registration of a charge under subsection 108 (3) of the Companies Act 1965 (Act 125).

[111] See Chaps. 3, 9 and 11.

[112] See Chap. 10.

[113] See Chaps. 16 and 20.

[114] See Chap. 11.

2.3.1.2   Procedure and Practice of Filing

The procedure for filing with the domestic registry is determined in the law or regulation of that jurisdiction. However, sometimes the practice finds strict compliance inconvenient. In such a case, the practice starts deviating from the prescribed procedure.

For example, in Finland, the basic rule for filing with the registry for mortgage in aircraft requires that the secured amount is fixed. However, the practice has demanded more flexible arrangements and developed the use of a bearer bond. The bearer bond does not reflect an actual debt, but is used only to satisfy the formality. There are even forms for a bearer bond made available on the website of the TraFi. Under such a practice, a mortgage becomes opposable vis-à-vis third parties (or "perfected") not by registering the mortgage but by acquiring a possession of a "bearer bond that contains the register authority's entry concerning the mortgage." There was a proposal to make a reform to the current practice in 1992, but without any outcome.[115]

In Switzerland, the practice has derogated from the law in the opposite direction. The aircraft mortgage registry in Switzerland has a constitutive effect, which means that a mortgage is validly created upon registration. Under the registry system in Switzerland, the priority is determined not by who registers first, but how the registration is made: even if the mortgage of the first rank is deleted as a result of discharge of the secured debt, the second ranked mortgage does not go up, unless otherwise agreed. The vacated first rank is to be used by a new creditor appearing later, thus prevailing over the second ranked mortgagee who registered earlier. In practice, however, the parties may agree on promoting the second ranked mortgage to the first.[116] In contrast to Finland, where the status of the registered mortgagee is transferred by using a bearer bond, the practice in Switzerland makes it possible to erase the upper rank status that will maintain the priority according to the law.

2.3.1.3   Multiple Layers of Special Laws

Another source of complications to the practice is the parallel existence of more than one registration system. It is typically observed in Italy, where the charge under the 1993 Banking Law ("Art.46 Bank Charge"), only available to a bank extending finance, is registered with *Tribunale* independently from the ordinary aircraft chattel mortgage. The priority between two Art.46 Bank Charges is determined by the first-to-file rule, whereas the priority between an Art.46 Bank Charge and another right, including an aircraft chattel mortgage, depends on the ascertained date of the latter right and the date of registration of the Art.46 Bank Charge. Furthermore, Italy

---

[115] See Chap. 12.
[116] See Chap. 20.

maintains the registry for retention of title. A creditor trading with an Italian debtor will suffer from the inconvenience of having to look up all these registries.[117]

To a lesser extent, the Greek law has some complications as well. There are two types of mortgages under the law of Greece: simple mortgage and preferred mortgage. Both are registered in the same Registry, and the priority is determined by the date of registration. However, the remedies available to the mortgagee are different.[118] This might imply that the mortgagee of the lower priority needs to check which type of mortgage is registered with priority to it.

2.3.1.4   The Solution Provided by the Cape Town Convention

Under the Cape Town Convention, there is only the International Registry to consult. It is an asset-based registry of notice-filing system, operated all electronically and accessible on 24 h/7 days basis. Under the Cape Town Convention, the priority between registered international interests is determined solely by the first-to-file rule, and a registered international interest enjoys priority over any right or interest not registered with the International Registry, except the non-consensual rights or interests specified in the declaration of a Contracting State. It is no longer necessary to look up the registry of floating charges, because a floating charge, not registrable with an asset-based International Registry by definition, will never have priority over a registered international interest.

What the Cape Town Convention introduces here is the modernisation of outdated or complicated domestic system. As a single and simple system with a clear rule on priority, it will improve the practice of aircraft financing. Unlike the modest unification discussed above (see Sect. 2.2.4), the modernisation effect of the Cape Town Convention is significant, as no compromise has been made with the simplicity of first-to-file principle.

Still, even after a State becomes a Party to the Cape Town Convention, the domestic registry need not be abandoned. It may be used as the entry point, as in the case of the FAA recordation in the United States.[119] Registration with the domestic registry may also be considered useful to benefit from the remedies under the domestic law, in particular, to obtain proceeds from the object, which fall outside the limited definition in the Convention except under the Space Protocol.

---

[117] See Chap. 16.

[118] See Chap. 15.

[119] It is possible that the domestic registry remains valid with regard to internal transactions. For this, however, it will be necessary for the Contracting State to make a declaration under Article 50 of the Base Convention. In Malaysia, the Regulations based on the Civil Aviation Act 1969 have not been abolished when it became a Party to the Base Convention and Aircraft Protocol. As Malaysia has not made a declaration to opt in to the exclusion of internal transactions, the usefulness of the retained domestic registry for internal transactions is doubted. See Chap. 6.

2.3.2 Rights in Aircraft Engines and Components

One of the largest gaps between the current law and practice of aircraft financing lies with financing and leasing of aircraft engines. No jurisdiction covered by this volume maintains a registry for recording interests in aircraft engines. In many jurisdictions, an engine loses a status as an independent object by way of the rules on accession.[120] These rules are outdated in a day when an aircraft engine costs tens of millions of dollars and the practice of leasing has become so common.

There is a similar issue concerning transponders and other payloads on space assets. "Hosted payloads" are frequently employed in space financing when the government does not want to procure the whole satellite but wish to own only a payload on a satellite, the remaining part of which is used for commercial purposes.[121] The difference from the case of aircraft engines is that a payload cannot practically be removed from the satellite bus once the satellite is placed on orbit, while engines can be installed on or removed from an airframe easily. As a result, financing of the "remainder" of the satellite (in an extreme case, a satellite bus only) usually does not take place, but the whole of the satellite including the hosted payload is the subject of financing. No domestic law appears to have an explicit rule to govern such a situation.

The Cape Town Convention addresses these demands of the most recent practice. In particular, the Aircraft Protocols has created a system for registering rights in aircraft engines. Aircraft engines are separate type of "aircraft objects",[122] and international interests created in them can be registered with the International Registry. The rules on accession under the domestic law do not apply when an aircraft engine is installed on an airframe.[123] The Space Protocol, in a similar manner, provides that a payload and "a part of a spacecraft or payload such as a transponder" may be treated as an independent space asset on condition that a separate registration may be effected for these pursuant to the regulation.[124] As with an aircraft engine, installation of and removal from a space asset (payload) from another space asset (satellite), if it ever occurs, does not affect the ownership or other rights or interests by way of accession.[125]

---

[120] See Chap. 21.

[121] Maria Buzdugan, Satellite Financing through Hosted Payloads: Benefits and Challenges, *Air and Space Law*, Vol.36, p.139 (2011).

[122] Article I (2) (c) of the Aircraft Protocol.

[123] Article XIV (3) of the Aircraft Protocol.

[124] Article I (ii) (k) of the Space Protocol.

[125] Article III (b) of the Space Protocol.

2.3.3 Enforcement of Security Interests in Insolvency Proceedings

2.3.3.1 Status of Mortgage After the Commencement of the Insolvency Proceedings

Among the insolvency proceedings, many jurisdictions distinguish the liquidation-type and the reorganisation-type. The goal of the liquidation-type procedure is to maximise the amount of debtor's asset (estate) that can be distributed to creditors. Under this type of procedure, a secured claim usually retains the priority that it enjoys in the absence of the commencement of the insolvency proceedings. On the other hand, the reorganisation-type procedure has the prevailing goal of restructuring the debtor's business to maintain its going concern value, which is considered as larger than the liquidation value. While the goal will be in the benefit of the whole group of creditors, the individual interest of a secured creditor could be compromised.

Generally speaking, the insolvency law of the reorganisation-type provides that the exercise of the security interest must be suspended ("stayed"), either automatically or by the court order after the commencement of the procedure and that the restructuring plan could request a secured claim to be modified in the amount of interests and/or principal, though its priority vis-à-vis non-secured claims is generally or necessarily respected. The plan will be voted by the creditors, usually in classes of secured and non-secured creditors. For example, in Finland, while the mortgagee enjoys the "separatist" position in the liquidation-type bankruptcy procedure, its exercise of right is stayed by the commencement of reorganisation procedure. Italy also distinguishes the general insolvency proceedings for liquidation and extraordinary receivership for reorganisation. While the mortgagee is, in principle, not preempted under the general insolvency proceedings, once the extraordinary receivership is opened, the mortgagee's exercise is restrained. The Japanese law is similar in that both of the two reorganisation-type laws, the Civil Rehabilitation Act and Corporate Reorganisation Act, authorise the court to issue an order for stay of exercise of security interests and subject the secured claims to the rehabilitation or reorganisation plan. These two laws further provide that, if the secured object is indispensable to the continuation of the insolvent debtor's business, the debtor (under the Civil Rehabilitation Act) or trustee (under both Acts) may file a petition with the court, seeking that the security interests be extinguished by paying the amount equivalent to the present value of the secured object.[126]

A more creditor-friendly approach is adopted in England. Like other jurisdictions, the liquidation and administration are distinguished and the enforcement of interests over assets is subject to consent of the administrator under the administration. However, even under the administration, due consideration will be given to the

---

[126] See Chaps. 12, 16 and 17.

interest of the secured creditor in balancing with the interests of other creditors. As a result, it is anticipated that a leave to enforce should normally be granted.[127]

In contrast, Portugal's new Insolvency and Recovery Code of 2004 (CIRE) has integrated the procedures of bankruptcy (liquidation) and restructure (recovery). Under the integrated "insolvency" procedure, the emphasis is placed more on reorganisation of the insolvent debtor and the exercise of rights is restrained.[128]

Among the various jurisdictions, the United States is unique. Chapter 11 of the Bankruptcy Code of 1978 provides for a reorganisation-type procedure. The exercise of any security interest is automatically stayed upon the commencement of the procedure[129] and the reorganisation plan could impair the right of secured creditors.[130] However, the Bankruptcy Code has incorporated special rules to protect the equipment security interests. Section 1110 of the Bankruptcy Code for aircraft (and vessels) and section 1168 for railway rolling stock, in a close resemblance to Alternative A under the three Protocols of the Cape Town Convention, provides that a secured party with a security interest in, or a lessor or conditional vendor of, equipment can enforce its rights or remedies notwithstanding the commencement of the bankruptcy procedure, unless the trustee agrees to perform all obligations of the debtor and cures any default within 60 days (see Sect. 2.1.4). The uniqueness of the United States law lies in the idea to give special status only to the security interest of equipment finance (asset-based finance), as distinguished from the general security interest.

2.3.3.2   Title Based Security (Quasi Security) Under Insolvency Proceedings

Existing laws are divided as regards the status of title-based securities in insolvency proceedings. The differences in rules may, in part, derive from the different attitude toward the functional approach (see Sect. 2.2.2). If the jurisdiction adopts the functional approach and treats a title-based security as a security interest, the rules on a security interest in insolvency proceedings will apply to a title-based security. Thus, in the United States, both section 1110 and section 1168 of the Bankruptcy Code treat a "secured party," a conditional vendor and a lessor in the equal manner. The Japanese cases similarly treat a title-based security as if it were a security interest without formally recharacterising it. Contrary to the United States, the Japanese rules of insolvency law, as mentioned above, is restrictive of the exercise of a

---

[127] See Chap. 4. It notes that the "creditor-friendly approach" of English insolvency law was well recognised by rating agencies in enabling the British Airways to place Enhanced Equipment Trust Certificates (EETC) in the US market even before becoming a Party to the Cape Town Convention.

[128] See Chap. 19.

[129] 11 USC §362.

[130] See 11 USC §1123 (a)(3).

security interest, not distinguishing a security interest in general and an interest to secure asset-based financing (equipment financing).[131]

In jurisdictions that do not adopt the functional approach, the law does not recharacterise a title-based security as a security interest. Among these jurisdictions, the rules further diverge. On the one side, some jurisdictions treat a conditional seller or a lessor as an owner of the object and do not require it to file its "claim" in the insolvency proceedings. This is the case in France and Switzerland.[132] On the other side are jurisdictions that focus on the agreement of conditional sale or lease. In these jurisdictions, such agreements are subject to the insolvency administrator's option to either maintain the agreement or terminate it. This is the case in Germany and Italy.[133]

In a few jurisdictions, a title-based security could be even more disadvantaged than a security interest. Under CIRE of Portugal, a title reservation agreement is opposable in the insolvency proceedings on condition that the agreement is in writing before the delivery of the asset. However, this rule does not apply to a lease agreement.[134] In Greece, there are court decisions from some years ago that denied the effect of a title reservation agreement in the insolvency proceedings. However, the opposite view seems to be becoming prevalent recently.[135]

2.3.3.3   The Solution Provided by the Cape Town Convention

The Cape Town Convention's rule on the insolvency proceedings is nuanced. The Base Convention leaves the matter to the applicable law, while the Protocols provide two (the Luxembourg Rail Protocol provides three) alternatives for a Contracting State to opt in by declaration. It is apparent that the Cape Town Convention does not aim to unify rules on this issue. A chosen alternative must be applied in its entirety, without allowing a Contracting State to cherry-pick, though the declaration of a Contracting State may apply different alternatives to different types of insolvency proceedings.[136] Then, as one of the alternatives to opt in, Alternative A of each Protocol closely traces sections 1110 and 1168 of the Bankruptcy Code of the United States. The latter is a unique legislation, very different from the laws in majority of the jurisdictions, but has been well reputed for facilitating the growth of EETC market.

The rules on the insolvency proceedings under the Cape Town Convention do not distinguish a security interest and a conditional seller's title and a lessor's right. However, it should be noted that the remedies that a creditor can exercise, whether

---

[131] See Chap. 17.

[132] See Chaps. 13 and 20.

[133] See Chaps. 14 and 16.

[134] See Chap. 19.

[135] See Chap. 15.

[136] Article XXX (3) of the Aircraft Protocol; Article XXVII (3) of the Luxembourg Rail Protocol; Article XLI of the Space Protocol.

with little qualification under Alternative A or subject to conditions under other Alternatives (or applicable law, when none of the Alternatives is opted in), are determined by the rules on the enforcement in general and, therefore, are different depending on whether the international interest is a security interest or a title of a conditional seller or a lessor.

Because of the expectation that opting in to Alternative A will replicate the reputation that the American law has entertained, most of the States Parties of the Aircraft Protocol have opted in to Alternative A. In Canada, the federal laws on insolvency (Bankruptcy and Insolvency Act (*Loi sur la faillite et l'insolvabilité*),[137] Companies' Creditors Arrangement Act (*Loi sur les arrangements avec les créanciers des compagnies*),[138] and Winding-up and Restructuring Act (*Loi sur les liquidation et les restructurations*)[139]) were amended in order to implement Alternative A fully, since the latter federal laws were not compatible with Alternative A in that, for example, the secured creditor must notify its intention to exercise its right in advance and could be subject to a suspension.[140] In contrast, Malaysia made no reference to the exclusion of existing insolvency statutes in the implementing law (International Interests in Mobile Equipment (Aircraft) Act of 2006), despite the fact that there could have been modifications to the rules in insolvency law by opting in to Alternative A. Still, the compliance with the Convention and Aircraft Protocol will be ensured by the general clause in the same Act providing that the Base Convention and Aircraft Protocol prevails in case of conflict with any domestic law.[141]

Among the States Parties, the United States did not make any declaration under Article XI of the Aircraft Protocol. As a result, according to Article 30(2) of the Convention, the applicable law determines the status of the international interest. It is easy to see that the United States will suffer no disadvantage if section 1110 of the Bankruptcy Code applies.

Finally, in Europe, the European Community (now the European Union) claimed competence on the Protocol insolvency provisions under the Treaty on the Functioning of the European Union. Therefore, the European Community as a Regional Economic Integration Organisation acceded to the Base Convention and the Aircraft Protocol, and approved the Luxembourg Rail Protocol, to the extent these matters are concerned.[142] In doing so, the European Community made no declaration as to the alternatives on insolvency proceedings under the two Protocols. Still, a member state of the European Union can amend its insolvency law to make it in line with the Alternative A, and the insolvency law as so amended will apply as

---

[137] R.S.C., 1985, c. B-3.

[138] R.S.C., 1985, c. C-36.

[139] R.S.C., 1985, c. W-11.

[140] See Chap. 3.

[141] See Chap. 6.

[142] See Article 48 of the Base Convention; Article XXVII of the Aircraft Protocol; Article XXII of the Luxembourg Rail Protocol.

the applicable law in the absence of choice of any Alternative.[143] In this way, just as the United States applying section 1110 of the Bankruptcy Code, a European state can enjoy the same benefits as expected from opting in to Alternative A.

2.3.4 Summary: Law Market for the Asset Based Financing

On the issues discussed in this section, the Cape Town Convention does not simply "unify" the laws of various jurisdictions, but improves them. For the registries and the registration practice, it modernises the existing law of states, which are often outdated, complicated or maintained only by the practice unintended by the original lawmaker. On the status of international interests in insolvency proceedings, it offers (in the form of an alternative) a set of rules responsive to the market's demands. In other words, the benefits of the Cape Town Convention derive not merely from eliminating the differences, but from replacing its rules for the existing, less efficient law.[144]

In the background of such a focus on modernisation is the emergence of the competition of legislation, sometimes referred to as the "law market." The competition of legislation has been a well known phenomenon in American corporate law. In the United States, a large number of public companies are incorporated in Delaware, while their business activities are conducted elsewhere. It was once argued that Delaware's victory in attracting incorporation was due to its law's indulging corporate directors by applying lax rules on directors' liability ("race to the bottom"),[145] but the more recent view attributes it to the development by the equity court and legislature of efficient rules that the market finds reasonable ("race to the top").[146] According to the last view, the genius of the American corporate law lies in the competition of law-making among the states.

The law market on the global level is not based on the freedom of choosing the law of incorporation as in the traditional competition for charter in the United States. Rather, it is a competition between the countries motivated by the firms' pursuit for a cheaper finance.[147] A study by a group of economists assessing the relationship between the legal system and economic growth of the countries in the world may be

---

[143] Cf. Article 4 of the Appendix 2 to the ASU.

[144] For distinction between eliminating the differences and introducing a better law, see Souichirou Kozuka, The Economic Implications of Uniformity in Law, in: Jürgen Basedow & Toshiyuki Kono (eds.), *An Economic Analysis of Private International Law*, p.73 (Mohr Siebeck, 2006), reprinted in: [2007] *Uniform Law Review* p.683.

[145] William L. Cary, Federalism and Corporate Law: Reflections Upon Delaware, *Yale Law Journal*, Vol.83, p.663 (1974).

[146] Roberta Romano, *The Genius of American Corporate Law* (The AEI Press, 1993).

[147] Henry Hansmann and Reinier Kraakman, The End of History for Corporate Law, *Georgetown Law Journal* Vol.89, p.439, at p.454 (2001).

relevant here.[148] While the technical details of the study has been extremely controversial,[149] the idea that the legal environment favourable to the suppliers of finance, whether investors or creditors, leads to larger economic welfare has come to be widely accepted.

It was no surprise in this context that an economic impact assessment was conducted in the course of drafting the Cape Town Convention to find how beneficial the instrument could be to the debtor and, ultimately, society as a whole. In the sector of aircraft financing, where asset based financing has become the mainstream method of financing, the enhanced status of the secured creditor will bring about a larger legal certainty and foreseeability, which will be reflected in the more favourable conditions for finance that the debtor can avail of. The empirical study assessed the impact by referring to the reform of section 1110 of the United States Bankruptcy Code as an event study and concluded that the estimated economic benefit will be a decrease in interest spread by 150 basis points, which will generate "pass through" benefits to passengers and users of airline services, reduction in transaction costs and profits from enhanced fleet efficiency.[150] It seems that the study played an important role in convincing many States to adopt the Cape Town Convention, and then to ratify it.

The result of empirical study indicates that strengthening the rights of a secured creditor will be beneficial to the aviation industry and, therefore, should be the goal to pursue in the competition of legislation. Such an implication, however, appears contrary to the path that the bankruptcy laws of many jurisdictions are taking. The general trend is to limit the creditors' rights and promote early reorganisation of the debtor to avoid the quick deterioration of the value of the debtor's business.[151] One possible view is that the policy of the Cape Town Convention can be justified only "in a restricted and highly specialized economic sector."[152] Alternatively, a distinction might be found useful between the creditors in general and the financier of asset-based financing. A further exploration in the economic theory in this respect is called for.

---

[148] Rafael La Porta, Florencio Lopez-de-Silanes, Andrei Shleifer & Robert Vishny, Legal Determinants of External Finance, *Journal of Finance*, Vol.52, p.1131 (1997); Rafael La Porta, Florencio Lopez-de-Silanes, Andrei Shleifer & Robert Vishny, Law and Finance, *Journal of Political Economy*, Vol.106, p.40 (1998); Rafael La Porta, Florencio Lopez-de-Silanes, Andrei Shleifer & Robert Vishny, Investor Protection and Corporate Valuation, *Journal of Finance*, Vol.42, p.1147 (2002).

[149] See for example, Holger Spamann, The "Antidirector Rights Index" Revisited, *Review of Financial Studies*, Vol.23, p.467 (2010).

[150] Saunders, Srinivasan, Walter & Wool, supra note 53.

[151] See Chaps. 13 and 19.

[152] See Chap. 16.

2.4 Ensuring the Outcome: Mechanisms to Achieve the Intended Goal

Besides adopting unified rules to replace the divergent domestic laws and introducing rules to improve the legal environment for aircraft financing, the Cape Town Convention has established a global institution operative in the real world. It is yet another feature of the Cape Town Convention that was absent in traditional uniform law instruments. In most cases, a uniform law treaty was merely a set of rules, and its implementation was entirely left to the States Parties. The only exception may be the International Convention on the Establishment of an International Fund for Compensation for Oil Pollution Damage, which actually creates a pool of contributed money and makes available compensation to the victims of oil pollution from the Fund.[153] The Convention on Compensation for Damage to Third Parties, Resulting from Acts of Unlawful Interference Involving Aircraft of 2009, adopted under the auspices of ICAO (International Civil Aviation Organization) provides for the establishment of the ICAO Fund to compensate the victims of aircraft accident due to an unlawful interference, but it has so far been unsuccessful in attracting many Parties.

The most visible part of the global scheme established by the Cape Town Convention is the International Registry. Further, there are several mechanisms to make the Convention operative in practice. On the side of the State Parties, the full compliance with the Convention has been strictly required. The following sections visit these issues in turn.

2.4.1 The Global Scheme Realised by the International Registry

The Cape Town Convention provides that an International Registry is established under each Protocol to register international interests in the equipment covered by the Protocol. The International Registry for aircraft equipment has been in operation since 2006, operated by Aviareto Ltd. as registrar. The International Registry for railway rolling stock is to be operated by Regulis SA in Luxembourg as registrar. For the Space Protocol, the Preparatory Commission is still working on the preparation to establish the International Registry.

With the International Registry for aircraft equipment, 613,900 registrations are recorded against 340,000 objects as of 2014.[154] Not only has it received such a large number of registrations, but also the quality of the services it offers has met a high

---

[153] See Souichirou Kozuka, The Bifurcated World of Uniform Law: uniform law of "islands" and of "the ocean", in: Eppur si mouve: The age of Uniform Law (2016).

[154] Ludwig Weber, Public and private features of the Cape Town Convention, *The Cape Town Convention Journal*, Vol.4, p.53 (2015).

standard. The records are stored by the technology adaptable to the future innovations. While keeping the accessibility open to the public, the security over the identity of the users is controlled by using Public Key Infrastructure (PKI). The integrity of the data is securely protected against tampering by the original software.[155]

The International Registry has also been responsive to the demands of the users. From 2013 it has entered "the Generation II" by developing the functions not foreseen in the Base Convention and Aircraft Protocol.[156] The Generation II of the International Registry started when multiple object registration became acceptable in 2013. When the parties create international interests in several aircraft objects under the same agreement, such as international interests in airframe and two engines of the same aircraft or those in a fleet of aircrafts, the creditor can now register all the international interests by one application instead of registering the international interests one by one. In the next year, the Closing Room was created to enable coordination among the parties to a series of transactions regarding the same aircraft object.[157] As if it were an electronic folder of documents, the data to be registered are entered into a closing room with a sequential order for registration, and "locked" when negotiations are completed. Then the consents are sought from all the parties, followed by the payment of registration fee to the International Registry. After everything is set, all the registrations in the electronic folder are submitted and recorded.[158]

The International Registry has taken advantage of its global scale to achieve both the high quality of service and responsiveness to the industry's demands. Without sufficient funding from a large number of registrations, it could not have been possible. It is argued that the United States took this point seriously when deciding to ratify the Aircraft Protocol.[159] By making the volume of transactions recorded within the United States registrable under the Cape Town Convention, the International Registry became viable, which in turn has helped asset-based financing to develop globally.

---

[155] Rob Cowan and Donal Gallagher, The International Registry for Aircraft Equipment – The First Seven Years, What We Have Learned, *Uniform Commercial Code Law Journal*, Vol.45, p.225 (2014).

[156] William B. Piels & Tan Siew Huay, Generation II Of The International Registry Website – The Closing Room: A Transactional Approach to Registries, *The Cape Town Convention Journal*, Issue 2, p.165 (2013); Cowan and Gallagher, supra note 168, p.243.

[157] By borrowing the example in Cowan and Gallagher, supra note 168, if an aircraft is sold, financed by a senior lender and a junior lender, and leased to an airline, there will be five parties (seller, buyer (lessor), bank 1, bank 2, airline (lessee)) and five registrations to be made (sale, loan 1, loan 2, lease and assignment of lease).

[158] Piels and Tan, supra note 169, p.175; Cowan and Gallagher, supra note 168, p.243.

[159] See Chap. 11.

2.4.2   Mechanisms to Keep the Cape Town Convention Relevant

2.4.2.1   The Regulations for the International Registry

The practical rules on how the International Registry operates are not prescribed in the Base Convention or Protocols in detail, but are provided in the regulations. The regulations are published by the Supervisory Authority.[160] The Supervisory Authority is the Council of the ICAO for the Aircraft Protocol,[161] a body established by the representatives appointed by State Parties, Unidroit and the Intergovernmental Organisation for International Carriage by Rail (OTIF) for the Luxembourg Rail Protocol.[162] For the Space Protocol, the negotiation with the International Telecommunications Union (ITU) has been continuing pursuant to the resolution at the Diplomatic Conference of 2012.[163]

As the creation of the Closing Room has shown, the regulations can go beyond what is explicitly foreseen by the Base Convention and the Protocol, if it is needed by the users of the system. In order to remain responsive to the users' demands, the Supervisory Authority may establish a commission of experts.[164] ICAO has benefited from the expertise of the Commission of Experts of the Supervisory Authority of the International Registry (CESAIR). The International Registry for aircraft objects, on their side, established the International Registry Advisory Board (IRAB) to advise it on the needs of users. These experts have made the regulations to be user-oriented and kept the scheme workable.

2.4.2.2   Aircraft Sector Understanding of OECD and Qualifying Declarations

The Cape Town Convention relates to the creation and enforcement of international interests. How they are used for financing transactions is, although critical as economic motivations, not addressed in the Convention itself. The reference to the Cape Town Convention in the Sector Understanding on Export Credits for Civil Aircraft (ASU) of OECD fills this gap. Though ASU, which is Annex III of the Arrangement on Officially Supported Export Credits,[165] is applicable only to

---

[160] Article 17 (2) (d) of the Base Convention. See also Article XVIII of the Aircraft Protocol and Article XXIX of the Space Protocol.

[161] Article XVII (1) of the Aircraft Protocol and the Resolution No.2 of the Diplomatic Conference.

[162] Article XII (1) of the Luxembourg Rail Protocol. OTIF serves as its secretariat (Article XII (6) of the Luxembourg Rail Protocol).

[163] Article XXVIII (1) of the Space Protocol; Resolution No.1.

[164] Article XVII (4) of the Aircraft Protocol; Article XII (5) of the Luxembourg Rail Protocol; Article XXVIII (3) of the Space Protocol.

[165] The most updated version is of 1 February 2016, TAD/PG(2016)1 (hereinafter "ASU 2016").

financing by export credit agencies, it is in practice critical, as most aircraft financing involves export credit agencies.

The ASU is an agreement among major aircraft manufacturing states to provide "a framework for the predictable, consistent and transparent use of officially supported export credits for the sale or lease of aircraft".[166] In particular, the ASU places limits on the premium rates on the credit that export credit agencies extend in its Appendix II. In this context, if the operator of the aircraft is situated in a State on the list of State Parties to the Cape Town Convention that qualifies certain conditions ("Cape Town List"), reduction of up to 10% from the minimum premium rate is permitted.[167] This mechanism, known as the "Cape Town Discount," visualises the economic benefit of the Cape Town Convention that the empirical research predicted.

To be on the Cape Town List, a State must (besides being a Contracting Party to the Cape Town Convention) have made the "qualifying declarations" and have implemented the Cape Town Convention "in its laws and regulations, as required, in such a way that the Cape Town Convention commitments are appropriately translated into national law."[168] The "qualifying declarations" are a combination of required opt-ins and prohibited opt-outs. The required opt-ins are to (a) choose Alternative A with regard to the exercise of international interests in insolvency proceedings (under Article XI of the Aircraft Protocol) with the waiting period being no more than 60 calendar days, (b) authorise de-registration and export as additional remedies for a creditor (under Article XIII of the Aircraft Protocol), (c) assure the freedom to agree on the choice of law (under Article VIII of the Aircraft Protocol), and either (d) authorise remedies without court procedure (under Article 54 (2) of the Base Convention) or (e) ensure the grant of relief pending determination (under Article 13 of the Base Convention) within a limited period of time.[169] The prohibited opt-outs are to exclude (a) the availability of relief pending final determination and the jurisdictions for them (under Article 43 of the Base Convention) unless the State authorises the remedies without court procedure, (b) the priority of the Cape Town Convention over the Convention for the Unification of Certain Rules Relating to the Precautionary Attachment of Aircraft (1933 Rome Convention) (under Article XXIV of the Aircraft Protocol), or (c) authorising the grant of a lease of the aircraft object as a remedy (option provided for in Article 54(1) of the Base Convention).

It is noteworthy that the modest unification by incorporating many options in the text is complemented by the requirement of "qualifying declarations." Among the

---

[166] ASU 2016, Article 1.a).

[167] Articles 37 and 38 of the Appendix II to the ASU 2016.

[168] Article 39 of the Appendix II to the ASU 2016.

[169] Annex 1 of the Appendix II to the ASU 2016. For (e), the time period shall be not more than ten calendar days for (i) preservation of the aircraft objects and their value, (ii) possession, control or custody of the aircraft objects, and (iii) immobilisation of the aircraft objects, and not more 30 calendar days for (iv) lease or management of the aircraft objects and the income thereof and (v) sale and application of proceeds from the aircraft equipment.

States Parties that wish to realise the economic benefit from the Cape Town Convention, the rules will be unified to a large extent after all. The fact that the unification takes place not by drafting of the text but from the choices made by the State Parties is consistent with the idea of regulatory competition in the law market.

2.4.2.3 Ensuring the Prevailing Effect of the Cape Town Convention

If the economic benefit from the rules conducive to asset-based financing is not only theoretical but is realised through the Cape Town Discount under the ASU, it is important to ensure that the rules in the Cape Town Convention are implemented with strict compliance in the States Parties. Some States Parties have assured, when ratifying the Convention, that any conflicting rules in the domestic law will be excluded. For example, the implementation law of Indonesia provides that the Cape Town Convention directly applies and that the Convention prevails over the domestic law in case there is a conflict. The same legislative technique is adopted also by other States, such as Malaysia and the Russian Federation.[170]

Still, there could be the problem of actual compliance, namely the application of the Cape Town Convention's rules by government officials or interpretation of the Convention by the court. The AWG as a group of industry experts monitors such actual compliance through a network of national contacts groups.[171] The finding of non-compliance may result in the removal of the State from the Cape Town List.[172]

While all these will be valid mechanisms to ensure compliance, the Cape Town Convention stopped short of including the dispute resolution mechanism between the creditor and the non-complying State. One commentator argues that a dispute resolution mechanism modelled after the investor-State dispute resolution will be useful in enhancing the trust in the Convention, given the commonality in nature of the Cape Town Convention with investment treaty.[173] The question here is whether the incentives due to the pressure of the "law market" is sufficient to ensure compliance, or the Cape Town Convention needs to create a global regime accompanying a judicial mechanism for the strict compliance.

---

[170] See Chaps. 5, 6 and 8.

[171] http://www.awg.aero/projects/capetownconvention/

[172] Article 44 of the Appendix II to the ASU 2016.

[173] Charles W. Mooney, Jr., The Cape Town Convention's Improbable-but-Possible Progeny Part Two: Bilateral Investment Treaty-Like Enforcement Mechanism, *Virginia Journal of International Law*, Vol.55, p.451 (2015).

2.5   Conclusion: The Cape Town Convention as Innovative Uniform Law

The Cape Town Convention is one of the uniform law treaties. It is one of the most successful instruments of this kind, judging from the number of States Parties. A closer examination of the Convention, based on the comparison with domestic laws of major jurisdictions on the subject, reveals that it goes beyond a simple unification.

First, the Cape Town Convention unifies the rules on secured transactions, in particular its formation, registration and enforcement upon default by the debtor, over mobile equipment. Its scope is broad enough to cover not only the security proper or "real rights" such as mortgage, *hypothèque* or pledge, but also title-based transactions that have equivalent functions. However, the unification by the Cape Town Convention is rather modest. On some important issues, options are open to States, which could end up with a large variety in rules under the Convention. Some other issues are left to the applicable law or the court.

Secondly, the Cape Town Convention does not simply unify the laws. It modernises the domestic laws that are outdated or complicated. It also introduces rules to adapt to the new developments of practice (as in the case of engine finance) or rules facilitative to asset based financing (as with rules on insolvency proceedings).

The shift of focus from simple unification to modernisation should not be seen as an isolated anecdote. The United Nations Commission on International Trade Law (UNCITRAL), an international body within the United Nations to promote unification of commercial law, has recently added to its mission the modernisation of law.[174] Recent law reforms in the area of financial and insolvency law, such as those advanced under the auspices of the World Bank, European Bank for Reconstruction and Development (EBRD) or Organization of American States (OAS), usually target at modernising the local law.[175] The Cape Town Convention must be seen as forming a part of such law reform movements.

The law reform inevitably requires a convincing argument that the adopted rules will be more efficient than the existing law. In the case of the Cape Town Convention, an economic assessment was made to quantify the enhanced efficiency that it will bring about. While the theoretical study on the assessment of laws by economics has been known since the last few decades, such use of empirical study in the legislative process is not common at all. In many jurisdictions, "the economic effect" in the abstract term is one of the elements to be considered when enacting or reforming a law, but there are few, if any, cases where an empirical assessment is actually

---

[174] Gerard McCormack, *Secured Credit and the Harmonisation of Law: The UNCITRAL Experience*, p.17 (Edward Elgar, 2011).

[175] European Bank for Reconstruction and Development, Model Law on Secured Transactions, 1994; Organization for American States, Model Inter-American Law on Secured Transactions, 2002.

conducted. The actual use of economic empirical study is another innovating feature of the Cape Town Convention.

Finally, the third aspect of the Cape Town Convention is that it has established a global scheme that operates in reality. For one thing, international interests are registered with the International Registry, which is an entity established by the Protocol, independent from domestic registries. For another, the ASU is applicable to finance transactions making use of an international interest, and the benefit from the Cape Town Convention becomes visible by the Cape Town Discount under it. The traditional uniform law treaties seldom establish such global schemes. This is another innovation that the Cape Town Convention realised. And it has been successful with it, supported by both the industry and regulators, including the international orgnisations.

Thus, the Cape Town Convention is a uniform law treaty, not only a successful one but an innovative one. To see exactly how innovative it is, one needs to analyse the functions that a uniform law instrument can have, and then examine in what respects the Convention changes the existing laws, and how.

Acknowledgements The author acknowledges the informative and insightful analysis of each chapter's contributors. The remaining errors are all attributable to the author. This work is a product supported by the Grant-in-aid of the Japan Society for Promotion of Research (JSPS grant no.15H01917).

References

1. Buzdugan, Maria. 2011. Satellite financing through hosted payloads: Benefits and challenges. *Air and Space Law* 36: 139.
2. Cary, William L. 1974. Federalism and corporate Law: Reflections upon Delaware. *Yale Law Journal* 83: 663.
3. Cowan, Rob, and Donal Gallagher. 2014. The international registry for aircraft equipment – the first seven years, what We have learned. *Uniform Commercial Code Law Journal* 45: 225.
4. Cuniberti, Gilles. 2012. Advance relief under the Cape Town convention. *The Cape Town Convention Journal* 2012(1): 79–94.
5. Rice, Michael Downey. 1989. Railroad equipment financing. *Transportation Law Journal* 18: 85.
6. Glaister, William J., Robert Murphy, Marisa Chan, Ellie Dunne, and Julian Acratopulo. 2012. *Lex situs* after *blue Sky*: Is the Cape Town convention the solution? *The Cape Town Convention Journal* 2012(1): 3–23.
7. Goode, Roy. 2013. *Convention on international interests in mobile equipment and protocol thereto on matters specific to aircraft equipment: Official commentary*, 3rd ed, para.4.101. Rome: UNIDROIT.
8. Goode, Roy. 2013. *Convention on international interests in mobile equipment and protocol thereto on matters specific to space assets: Official commentary*, para.5.49. Rome: UNIDROIT.
9. Hansmann, Henry, and Reinier Kraakman. 2001. The end of history for corporate law. *Georgetown Law Journal* 89: 439, at p.454.
10. Kozuka, Souichirou. 2006. The economic implications of uniformity in law. In *An economic analysis of private international law*, ed, Jürgen Basedow and Toshiyuki Kono, 73 (Mohr Siebeck) (reprinted in: [2007] *Uniform Law Review*, 683).

11. Kozuka, Souichirou. 2016. The bifurcated world of uniform law: Uniform law of "islands" and of "the ocean". In *Eppur si muove: The age of uniform law – Festschrift for Michael Joachim Bonell to celebrate his 70th birthday*, ed. UNIDROIT, Rome: UNIDROIT.
12. Kozuka, Souichirou, and Fuki Taniguchi. 2012. An economic assessment of the space protocol to the Cape Town convention, [2012]. *Uniform Law Review* 16(4): 927–941.
13. La Porta, Rafael, Florencio Lopez-de-Silanes, Andrei Shleifer, and Robert Vishny. 1997. Legal determinants of external finance. *Journal of Finance* 52: 1131.
14. La Porta, Rafael, Florencio Lopez-de-Silanes, Andrei Shleifer, and Robert Vishny. 1998. Law and finance. *Journal of Political Economy* 106: 40.
15. La Porta, Rafael, Florencio Lopez-de-Silanes, Andrei Shleifer, and Robert Vishny. 2002. Investor protection and corporate valuation. *Journal of Finance* 42: 1147.
16. Lowenthal, Max. 1933. The railroad reorganization act. *Harvard Law Review* 47: 18.
17. McCormack, Gerard. 2011. *Secured credit and the harmonisation of law: The UNCITRAL experience*. Cheltenham/Northampton: Edward Elgar.
18. Mooney, Jr, and W. Charles. 2015. The Cape Town convention's improbable-but-possible progeny part two: Bilateral investment treaty-like enforcement mechanism. *Virginia Journal of International Law* 55: 451.
19. Piels, William B., and Tan Siew Huay. 2013. Generation II of the international registry website – the closing room: A transactional approach to registries. *The Cape Town Convention Journal*, (2): 165.
20. Prichard, John, and David Lloyd. 2013. Analysis of non-consensual rights and interests under article 39 of the Cape Town convention. *The Cape Town Convention Journal* 2: 3.
21. Rawle, Francis. 1885. Car trust securities. *Annual Report of the American Bar Association*, 277.
22. Ripple, Gregory. 2002. Note, special protection in the air[line industry]: The historical development of section 1110 of the bankruptcy code. *Notre Dame Law Review* 78: 281.
23. Romano, Roberta. 1993. *The genius of American corporate law*. Washington, DC: The AEI Press.
24. Rosen, Howard. 2007. The Luxembourg rail protocol: A major advance for the railway industry, [2007]. *Uniform Law Review* 12: 427.
25. Rosen, Howard. 2013. Public service and the Cape Town convention. *The Cape Town Convention Journal* 2: 131.
26. Rosen, Howard, Martin Fleetwood, and Benjamin von Bodungen. 2012. The Luxembourg rail protocol – extending Cape Town benefits to the rail industry, [2012]. *Uniform Law Review* 17: 609.
27. Sato, Ikumi and Yoshinobu Zasu. 2010. Beyond conflict of interest: Lessons from the Cape Town convention. *Asian Journal of Law and Economics* 1(1): 1.
28. Saunders, Anthony, Anand Srinivasan, Ingo Walter, and Jeffrey Wool. 1999. The economic implications of international secured transactions law reform: A case study. *The University of Pennsylvania Journal of International Economic Law* 20: 309.
29. Scheinberg, Ronald. 2004. Enhanced equipment trust certificates in the downturn: An assessment for banks. *Banking Law Journal* 121: 108.
30. Schmalenbach, Dirk. 2015. Recent developments in Aircraft Finance with special regard to the Cape Town convention. *Zeitschrift für Luft- und Weltraumrecht*, 64. Jg, S.270.
31. Spamann, Holger. 2010. The "antidirector rights index" revisited. *Review of Financial Studies* 23: 467.
32. Stanford, M.J. 2012. The availability of a new form of financing for commercial space activities: the extension of the Cape Town convention to space assets. *The Cape Town Convention Journal* 2012(1): 109.
33. Veneziano, Anna. 2013. Advance relief under the Cape Town convention and its aircraft protocol: A comment on Gilles Cuniberti's interpretative proposal. *The Cape Town Convention Journal, Issue* (2): 185

34. Von Bodungen, Benjamin, and Konrad Schott. 2007. The public service exemption under the Luxembourg Rail protocol: A German perspective, [2007] *Uniform Law Review,* 12(3): 573.
35. Von Bodungen, Benjamin. 2009. *Mobiliarsicherungsrechte an Luftfahrzeugen und Eisenbahnrollmaterial im nationalen und internationalen Rechtsverkehr* (Lit Verlag).
36. Weber, Ludwig. 2015. Public and private features of the Cape Town convention. *The Cape Town Convention Journal* 4: 53.
37. Wool, Jeffrey. 1999. The case for a commercial orientation to the proposed Unidroit convention as applied to aircraft equipment, [1999]. *Uniform Law Review* 4: 289–302.

Souichirou Kozuka (PhD, Tokyo) is Professor of Law at Gakushuin University, Tokyo. He specialises in commercial law, corporate law and maritime, air and space law. His recent publications in English include: "An Economic Assessment of the space Assets Protocol to the Cape Town Convention" (co-authored with Fuki Taniguchi) [2011–2014] *Uniform law Review* pp. 927–941; "Law in a changing economy: law of trade credit and security interests in context", in: *The Changing Role of Law in Japan* (Dimitri Vanoverbeke et al. (eds.) pp. 81–94 (Edward Elgar, 2014); "Policy and Politics in Contract Law Reform in Japan" (co-authored with Luke Nottage), in: *The Method and Culture of Comparative Law* (Maurice Adams & Dirk Heirbaut (eds.)), pp.235–253 (2014); "Licensing and regulation of Japan's offshore resources", in: Tina Hunter (ed.), *Regulation of the Upstream Petroleum Sector: A Comparative Study of Licensing and Concession Systems* (2015, Edward Elgar). He is chair of the Space Law Committee of the International Bar Association (IBA) for 2016 and 2017, correspondent of UNIDROIT (the International Institute for the Unification of Private Law) and Associate Member of the International Academy of Comparative Law (IACL).

Part III
National Reports

Chapter 3
Les sûretés sur des aéronefs en droit canadien, la *Convention relative aux garanties internationales portant sur des matériels d'équipement mobiles* et son *Protocole aéronautique*

Frédérique Sabourin

Abstract On April 1, 2013, the Convention and the Protocol entered into force in Canada in Alberta, British Columbia, Manitoba, Nova Scotia, Nunavut, Ontario, Quebec, Saskatchewan, Newfoundland and Labrador and the Northwest Territories. On October 1, 2014, these instruments have become applicable to Prince Edward Island and Yukon. They are applicabled across Canada since July 1st, 2016, following a new declaration of Canada, this time concerning New Brunswick.

In many ways, the fact that Canada has become party to the Convention and the Protocol did not alter the provincial, territorial or federal law that already existed. In other respects, the entry into force of these instruments in Canada has required legislative changes. The Convention and Protocol have thus been implemented federally and in all provinces and territories, because of the constitutional division of powers and the need to implement international treaties to which Canada is a party.

At the moment of Canada's ratification, Alternative A of Article XI of the Protocol was declared applicable. The federal implementation act that was adopted has been modified before its entry into force to give the force of law in particular to this article and to repeal the amendments made to various federal statutes to that effect, that would have become redundant. Therefore Canada qualifies for favorable financial conditions under Appendix II of the Sector Understanding on Export Credits for Civil Aircraft (ASU).

F. Sabourin (✉)
Ministère de la Justice du Québec, Québec, QC, Canada
e-mail: frederique.sabourin@justice.gouv.qc.ca

© Springer International Publishing AG 2017
S. Kozuka (ed.), *Implementing the Cape Town Convention and the Domestic Laws on Secured Transactions*, Ius Comparatum - Global Studies in Comparative Law 22, DOI 10.1007/978-3-319-46470-1_3

Canada has not made the declaration that would have allowed him to exclude the application of the Convention for internal operations. The Convention and the Protocol has thus enabled the creation of a single registry for securities in aircraft objects covered by the Convention and the Protocol, which was not the case before.Résumé

Le 1er avril 2013, la Convention et le Protocole sont entrés en vigueur au Canada en Alberta, en Colombie-Britannique, au Manitoba, en Nouvelle-Écosse, au Nunavut, en Ontario, au Québec, en Saskatchewan, à Terre-Neuve-et-Labrador et aux Territoires du Nord-Ouest. Le 1er octobre 2014, ces instruments sont devenus applicables à l'île-du-Prince-Edouard et au Yukon. Ils s'appliquent dans tout le Canada depuis le 1er juillet 2016, à la suite d'une nouvelle déclaration du Canada concernant cette fois le Nouveau-Brunswick.

À plusieurs égards, le fait pour le Canada de devenir partie à la Convention et au Protocole n'a pas modifié le droit fédéral, provincial ou territorial existant. À d'autres égards, l'entrée en vigueur de ces instruments au Canada a nécessité des modifications législatives. La Convention et le Protocole ont donc fait l'objet de lois de mise en oeuvre au fédéral et dans toutes les provinces et territoires, à cause de la répartition constitutionnelle des pouvoirs et de la nécessité de mettre en oeuvre les traités internationaux auxquels le Canada est partie.

Au moment de sa ratification, le Canada a déclaré applicable la Variante A de l'article XI du Protocole. La loi fédérale de mise en oeuvre qui avait antérieurement été adoptée a été modifiée avant son entrée en vigueur pour donner force de loi notamment à cet article et pour abroger les modifications introduites dans différentes lois fédérales à cet effet et qui auraient alors fait double emploi. Le Canada bénéficie donc de conditions financières favorables en application de l'Appendice II de l'Accord sectoriel sur les Crédits à l'Exportation d'Aéronefs Civils (ASU).

Le Canada n'a pas fait la déclaration qui lui aurait permis d'exclure de l'application de la Convention les opérations internes. La Convention et le Protocole ont donc permis la création d'un registre unique pour les garanties sur les biens aéronautiques couverts par la Convention et le Protocole, ce qui n'était pas le cas jusqu'alors.

3.1 Contexte et introduction

3.1.1 Contexte

Le texte qui suit répond aux questions posées par le Dr. Souichirou Kozuka, professeur de droit à l'université Gakushuin, à Tokyo, au Japon, et rapporteur général pour la session III.D du XIXe Congrès de l'Académie internationale de droit comparé qui s'est déroulée à Vienne du 20 au 27 juillet 2014. Il se limite à répondre aux questions adressées aux États parties à la *Convention relative aux garanties internationales portant sur des matériels d'équipement mobiles* (« Convention ») et au *Protocole portant sur les questions spécifiques aux matériels d'équipement* aéronautiques à la *Convention relative aux garanties internationales portant sur des matériels d'équipement mobiles* (« Protocole »), lesquels sont applicables sur l'ensemble du territoire canadien. Il ne se prononce pas sur les incidences du *Protocole portant sur les questions spécifiques aux biens spatiaux à la Convention relative aux garanties internationales portant sur des matériels d'équipement mobiles* (Berlin, 2012), ni sur celles du *Protocole de Luxembourg portant sur les questions spécifiques au matériel roulant ferroviaire à la Convention relative aux garanties internationales portant sur des matériels d'équipement mobiles* (Luxembourg, 2007) auxquels le Canada n'est pas partie.

3.1.2   Introduction

Le 1er avril 2013, la Convention et le Protocole sont entrés en vigueur au Canada. Le gouvernement du Canada a alors déclaré, en vertu de l'article 52 de la Convention et de l'article XXIX du Protocole, qu'ils s'appliquent aux provinces et territoires suivants : l'Alberta, la Colombie-Britannique, le Manitoba, la Nouvelle-Écosse, le Nunavut, l'Ontario, le Québec, la Saskatchewan, Terre-Neuve-et-Labrador et les Territoires du Nord-Ouest. Le 1er octobre 2014, à la suite d'une nouvelle déclaration du Canada, ces instruments sont devenus applicables à la province de l'Île-du-Prince-Édouard et au territoire du Yukon. Ils s'appliquent également au Nouveau-Brunswick depuis le 1er juillet 2016.

Au Canada, la *Loi constitutionnelle de 1867* (L.C. 1867) distribue les pouvoirs législatifs entre le fédéral et les provinces et territoires. L'aéronautique n'est prévue dans aucune des catégories établies.[1] La conclusion et la mise en oeuvre des traités non plus[2] mais la banqueroute et la faillite sont attribuées de façon exclusive au gouvernement fédéral.[3] Suivant la jurisprudence,[4] l'aéronautique relève du pouvoir du fédéral de faire des lois pour la paix, l'ordre et le bon gouvernement du Canada.[5]

---

[1] Peter Hogg, *Constitutional Law in Canada*, volume 1, Toronto, éd. Thomson Carswell, éd. sur feuilles mobiles, p. 22–23 et s.

[2] Ibid., p. 11–11. Hormis l'article 132 de la *Loi constitutionnelle de 1867* (L.C. 1867) qui traite des traités conclus avant l'accession du Canada à la souveraineté, et qui confie la mise en oeuvre de ces traités au fédéral. Cet article est depuis devenu désuet. *A.G. Canada c. A.G. Ontario (Conventions du travail)*, [1937] A.C. 326. Henri Brun, Guy Tremblay, Eugénie Brouillet, *Droit constitutionnel*, Cowansville, éd. Yvon Blais, 2008, 5e éd., pp. 564–565; Stéphane Beaulac, « Interlégalité et réception du droit international en droit interne canadien et québécois », dans *JurisClasseur Québec*, coll. « Droit public », Droit constitutionnel, fasc. 23, Montréal, LexisNexis Canada, 2011, feuilles mobiles, par. 16.

[3] Art. 91 (21) L.C. 1867.

[4] *Re Regulation and Control of Aeronautics in Canada*, [1932] A.C. 54; *Johannesson* v. *Municipality of West St. Paul*, [1952] 1 S.C.R. 292; *Construction Montcalm Inc.* c. *Commission du salaire minimum*, [1979] 1 R.C.S. 754, p. 770–771; *Air Canada* c. *Ontario (Régie des alcools)*, [1997] 2 R.C.S. 581, par. 72; *Québec* v. *Canadian Owners and Pilots Association*, 2010 2 SCR 536.

[5] Art. 91 paragraphe introductif L.C. 1867.

Cependant, les provinces ont la compétence pour légiférer sur la propriété et les droits civils.[6] Par conséquent, les sûretés sur des biens aéronautiques sont de compétence partagée. De plus, suivant la jurisprudence,[7] les traités doivent être mis en oeuvre par voie législative pour s'appliquer au Canada et cette mise en œuvre relève de la compétence du fédéral ou des provinces suivant la répartition de la L.C. 1867 et la matière visée par le traité. Cette répartition des compétences est peut être l'une des raisons pour lesquelles le Canada est partie à la *Convention relative à l'aviation civile internationale de 1944* (Convention de Chicago) mais pas à la *Convention relative à la reconnaissance internationale des droits sur aéronefs de 1948* (Convention de Genève).

À plusieurs égards, la Convention et le Protocole ne diffèrent pas du droit fédéral, provincial ou territorial par ailleurs applicable au Canada.[8] En effet, le Canada s'est

---

[6] Art. 92 (13) L.C. 1867.

[7] *A.G. Canada* c. *A.G. Ontario (Conventions du travail)*, précité note 2.

[8] (Alberta), *Personal Property Security Act*, RSA 2000, c. P-7; (Colombie-Britannique), *Personal Property Security Act*, RSBC 1996, c. 359; (Île-du-Prince-Édouard), *Personal Property Security Act*, RSPEI 1998, c P-3.1; (Manitoba), *Personal Property Security Act*, CCSM, c. P35; (Nouveau-Brunswick), *Personal Property Security Act*, SNB 1993, c. P-7.1; (Nouvelle-Écosse), *Personal Property Security Act*, SNS 1995–96, c. 13; (Nunavut), *Personal Property Security Act*, SNWT (Nu) 1994, c. 8 (2001); (Ontario), *Personal Property Security Act*, RSO1990, c. P.10; (Saskatchewan), *Personal Property Security Act*, SS 1993, c. P-6.2; (Terre-Neuve et Labrador), *Personal Property Security Act*, SNL 1998, c. P-7.1; (Territoires-du-Nord-Ouest), *Personal Property Security Act*, SNWT 1994, c. 8; (Yukon), *Personal Property Security Act*, RSY 2002, c. 169; désignés collectivement « PPSA ». Les PPSA sont inspirés de l'article 9 du *Uniform Commercial Code américain*. Ils sont issus d'une loi modèle proposée par la Conférence canadienne sur les sûretés mobilières. Les lois des provinces de l'Atlantique, de l'Ontario et des provinces de l'Ouest diffèrent quelque peu entre elles mais ces différences tendent à s'amenuiser au fil des amendements plus récents qui ont été apportés. Ronald C.C. Cuming, Catherine Walsh, Roderick J. Woods, *Personal Property Security Law*, coll. Essentials of Canadian Law, Toronto, éd. Irwin Law Inc., 2e éd., 2012, p. 65 à 70. Au Québec, le Code civil présente des similarités et des divergences avec les PPSA. Ibid., pp. 89–114. Michel Deschamps, « Les lois sur les sûretés mobilières canadiennes et le Code civil du Québec, Similitudes et différences », exposé présenté le 30 mai 2000 à la Conférence canadienne sur les sûretés mobilières et en août de la même année à la réunion annuelle de la Conférence pour l'harmonisation des lois au Canada, « Sûretés mobilières canadiennes et le Code civil du Québec similitudes et différences » à Victoria, en Colombie-Britannique à http://www.ulcc.ca/fr/2000-victoria-bc-fr-fr-1/342-documents-de-la-section-civile-2000/179-suretes-mobilieres-canadiennes-et-le-code-civil-du-quebec-similitudes-et-differences-2000 et « The perfection and priority rules of the Cape Town Convention and the Aircraft Protocol, A comparative law analysis », (2013) *Cape Town Convention Journal* 51–64.

beaucoup impliqué dans la négociation de ces instruments internationaux qui sont largement inspirés du droit canadien.[9]

À d'autres égards, l'entrée en vigueur de ces instruments au Canada a nécessité que des modifications législatives soient apportées. Ces changements se justifiaient plus aisément du fait du caractère hautement spécialisé du domaine et des connaissances techniques présumées des parties concernées.

---

[9] « Canadian representatives were instrumental in persuading Unidroit to take on the Convention project, and Canadian representatives were actively involved in the development of the regulations for the international registries contemplated by the convention and its Protocols. » Ronald C.C. Cuming et al., *op. cit.*, note 8, p. 81–82. Il s'agit notamment de Mes T. Bradbrook Smith (Stikeman Elliott), Ronald Cuming (University of Saskatchewan), Donald Gray (Blake, Cassels & Graydon), Michel Deschamps (McCarthy Tétrault), Suzanne Potvin-Plamondon (ministère de la Justice du Québec), David J. Shapiro (Air Canada) pour n'en mentionner que quelques uns. Voir Roy Goode, « From Acorn to Oak Tree : The Development of the Cape Town Convention and Protocols », (2012) *Rev. dr. unif.* 599; Ronald C.C. Cuming, « Le Registre international pour les garanties internationales portant sur des biens aéronautiques : présentation de sa structure », (2006) *Rev. dr. unif.* 18; Ronald C.C. Cuming, « Considerations in the design of an International Registry for interests in mobile equipment », (1999) *Rev. dr. unif.* 275; Ronald C.C. Cuming, « La réglementation internationale de certains aspects des sûretés grevant le matériel susceptible d'être déplacé d'un État dans un autre », (1990) *Rev. dr. unif.* 62; Donald Gray and Jean Surette « History and Details of Canada's Ratification, Seminar on the Cape Town Convention held in Toronto, April 29th and 30th, 2013 » à http://www.capetowntreatyforum.com/toronto/2013/presentation_files.cfm; Ronald Cuming, « The Convention on International Interests in Mobile Equipment, When it applies and with what consequences, a paper presented to the Canadian Cape Town Convention Seminar Toronto Ontario, April 29–30, 2013 », à la même adresse.

« [...] Canada has been a global pioneer in the design and operation of electronic secured transactions systems. » Ronald C.C. Cuming et al., *op.cit.*, note 8, p. 85.

« The implementation of the Convention in PPSA jurisdictions will result in the introduction of very little that is novel to or asymmetrical with personal property security law. The underlying concept of the Convention and the central role of a registry in his priority structure are very familiar to Canadian legal practitioners. Indeed, the structure and many of the provisions of the Convention are patterned on Canadian secured financing regimes ». Ronald C.C. Cuming et al., *op.cit.*, note 8, p. 727.

La Convention et le Protocole ont donc fait l'objet de lois de mise en oeuvre au fédéral[10] et dans toutes les provinces[11] et territoires,[12] y compris au Nouveau-Brunswick.[13] En outre, un Règlement d'application de la Convention et du Protocole a été adopté par le Québec.[14] Par ailleurs, il faut souligner, que les provinces et les territoires canadiens sont régis par la *common law* à l'exception du Québec, seule province de droit civil.

---

[10] *Loi de mise en œuvre de la Convention relative aux garanties internationales portant sur des matériels d'équipement mobiles et du Protocole portant sur les questions spécifiques aux matériels d'équipement aéronautiques à la Convention relative aux garanties internationales portant sur des matériels d'équipement mobiles*, L.C. 2005, ch. 3. Cette loi a été modifiée à quelques reprises à la suite de son adoption en 2005. De plus, en 2008 et en 2009 des modifications ont été apportées à diverses lois fédérales pour éliminer les incompatibilités entre d'une part, le droit canadien et, d'autre part, la Convention et le Protocole. Voir Auriol Marasco, « Turning the Cape Town Convention into a reality : The status of Cape Town in Canada » dans Association du Barreau canadien, *Altitudes*, janvier 2012, à http://www.cba.org/abc/nouvelles-sections/2012/PrintHTML. aspx?Docld=47396#article4 et *infra* notes 48 et 60.

[11] *International Interests in Mobile Aircraft Equipment Act*, SA 2006, c I-6.5 (Alberta); *International Interests in Mobile Equipment (Aircraft Equipment) Act*, SBC 2011, c 12 (Colombie-Britannique); *International Interests in Mobile Equipment (Aircraft Equipment) Act*, RSPEI 1988, c I-5.1 (Île-du-Prince-Édouard); *International Interests in Mobile Aircraft Equipment Act*, SNS 2004, c 5 (Nouvelle-Écosse); *Loi sur les garanties internationales portant sur des matériels d'équipement mobiles (matériels d'équipement aéronautiques)*, CPLM c 163 (Manitoba); *Loi de 2002 sur les garanties internationales portant sur des matériels d'équipement mobiles (équipements aéronautiques)*, LO 2002, c 18, ann B (Ontario); *Loi assurant la mise en oeuvre de la Convention relative aux garanties internationales portant sur des matériels d'équipement mobiles et du Protocole portant sur les questions spécifiques aux matériels d'équipement aéronautiques à la Convention relative aux garanties internationales portant sur des matériels d'équipement mobiles*, RLRQ, c. M-35.1.2.1 (Québec); *Loi sur les garanties internationales portant sur des matériels d'équipement aéronautiques mobiles*, LS 2013, c I-10.201 (Saskatchewan); *International Interests in Mobile Aircraft Equipment Act*, SNL 2006, c I-15.1 (Terre-Neuve et Labrador).

En outre, le *Règlement d'application de la Convention relative aux garanties internationales portant sur des matériels d'équipement mobiles et du Protocole portant sur les questions spécifiques aux matériels d'équipement aéronautiques à la Convention relative aux garanties internationales portant sur des matériels d'équipement mobiles*, RLRQ, c. M-35.1.2.1, r. 1, a été adopté par le Québec.

[12] *Loi sur les garanties internationales portant sur des matériels d'équipement mobiles*, LY 2013, c 6 (Yukon); *Loi sur les garanties internationales portant sur des matériels d'équipement mobiles*, S. Nu. 2011, c. 5 (Nunavut); *Loi sur les garanties internationales portant sur des matériels d'équipement aéronautiques mobiles*, LTN O 2009, c 4 (Territoires-du-Nord-Ouest).

[13] *Loi sur les garanties internationales portant sur des matériels d'équipement mobiles*, 2014, ch. 34, modifiée par 2014, ch. 72 (Nouveau-Brunswick). Bien que le Nouveau-Brunswick ait adopté une loi de mise en œuvre dès 2014, le Canada n'a déposé une nouvelle déclaration le concernant, conformément à l'article 52(1) de la Convention et à l'article XXIX(1) du Protocole, que le 23 décembre 2015. Cette déclaration n'a pu, conformément à l'article 57(2) de la Convention et à l'article XXXIII (2) du Protocole prendre effet avant le premier jour du mois suivant l'expiration d'une période de six mois à compter de la date de réception de la notification par le Dépositaire.

[14] *Règlement d'application de la Convention relative aux garanties internationales portant sur des matériels d'équipement mobiles et du Protocole portant sur les questions spécifiques aux matériels d'équipement aéronautiques à la Convention relative aux garanties internationales portant sur des matériels d'équipement mobiles*, précité note 11.

3.2 Biens, garanties, opposabilité aux tiers et inscription aux registres

3.2.1 Biens garantis (question 1 b))

Avant l'entrée en vigueur de la Convention et du Protocole au Canada, les biens aéronautiques (cellules d'aéronef, moteurs d'avion et hélicoptères) pouvaient généralement déjà être hypothéqués, soumis à des sûretés ou faire l'objet d'autres formes de garantie en vertu des lois canadiennes sur les sûretés mobilières («*PPSA*»)[15] et du Code civil du Québec («C.c.Q.»).[16] Il n'y avait pas de loi spéciale ou de système d'inscription particulier pour les sûretés garantissant ces biens, qui les auraient opposés aux biens mobiliers en général.

3.2.2 Garanties (question 1 d))

Suivant Mᶜ Michel Deschamps, « l'aspect le plus novateur des règles [...] de la Convention du Cap est de soumettre au même régime le droit d'un créancier garanti et le droit de propriété d'un vendeur conditionnel ou d'un bailleur ».[17]

En effet, selon le deuxième alinéa de l'article 2 de la Convention, une garantie conférée par le constituant en vertu d'un contrat constitutif de sûreté, détenue par une personne qui est le vendeur conditionnel en vertu d'un contrat réservant un droit de propriété ou détenue par une personne qui est le bailleur en vertu d'un contrat de bail, peut être considérée comme une garantie internationale portant sur des matériels d'équipement mobiles.

Or, en droit québécois, une sûreté réelle[18] est un droit garantissant une obligation créé sur un bien appartenant à celui qui constitue le droit (le « constituant »);

---

[15] Voir les définitions de « collateral » et de « personal property » dans les PPSA précités note 8, et Ronald Cuming, « The Convention on International Interests in Mobile Equipment, When it applies and with what consequences, a paper presented to the Canadian Cape Town Convention Seminar Toronto Ontario, April 29–30, 2013 », *loc.cit.*, note 9.

[16] Au Québec, en vertu de l'article 2683 C.c.Q., à moins qu'elle n'exploite une entreprise et que l'hypothèque ne grève les biens de l'entreprise, une personne physique ne peut consentir une hypothèque mobilière sans dépossession que dans les conditions et sur les véhicules routiers et autres biens meubles déterminés par règlement. Or, l'article 15.01, 6° du *Règlement sur le registre des droits personnels et réels mobiliers*, RLRQ, chapitre CCQ, r. 8, réfère spécifiquement aux aéronefs. Il s'en suit qu'une personne physique peut donc consentir une hypothèque mobilière sans dépossession sur un aéronef.

[17] Michel Deschamps, « Les règles de priorité de la Convention et du Protocole du Cap », 2002–1, *Rev. Dr. Unif.*, p. 45.

[18] Une sûreté peut également être « personnelle ». Voir Denise Pratte, *Priorités et hypothèques*, Sherbrooke, éd. Revue de droit de l'Université de Sherbrooke, p. 5.

un tel droit prend le nom d'hypothèque. Le Code civil, entré en vigueur en 1994, a opéré un regroupement de toutes les formes de sûretés réelles qui existaient alors (cession de biens en stock, nantissement, etc.) et la constitution d'un registre unique, le Registre des droits personnels et réels mobiliers (« RDPRM »). Le régime des sûretés réelles du C.c.Q. s'applique seulement à l'hypothèque. L'hypothèque ne peut grever un bien n'appartenant pas au constituant (art. 2670 C.c.Q.).[19]

D'autre part, un particulier doit en général exploiter une entreprise pour consentir une hypothèque sans dépossession et l'hypothèque ne peut alors affecter que les biens de son entreprise. Plusieurs quasi-sûretés échappent cependant à cette règle (réserve de propriété, bail autre qu'un crédit-bail, fiducie pour fins de garantie[20]).

Les opérations juridiques où le droit de propriété sert de garantie sans appartenir au constituant (e.g. une réserve de propriété) ne sont pas des hypothèques; par commodité, ces opérations peuvent être qualifiées de « quasi-sûretés ». Les quasi-sûretés sont des institutions juridiques distinctes de l'hypothèque et ont leurs propres règles. Cependant, l'exercice des recours découlant d'une quasi-sûreté est souvent assujetti aux mêmes formalités qu'en matière d'hypothèque.[21]

De plus, plusieurs quasi-sûretés du droit québécois sont assujetties à des exigences de publicité (c.a.d. d'inscription) semblables à celles applicables à l'hypothèque sans dépossession: la réserve de propriété, le crédit-bail, la vente avec faculté de rachat et la fiducie à des fins de garantie.[22] La cession d'une universalité de créances[23] et le bail de plus d'un an sont aussi soumis au Québec à des mesures de publicité similaires, et ce, même si ces opérations ne sont pas réalisées à des fins de garantie.

---

[19] Il est possible d'hypothéquer le bien d'autrui ou à venir quoique l'hypothèque ne prenne effet qu'à compter de son acquisition par le constituant.

[20] Selon l'article 1263 C.c.Q., la fiducie établie par contrat à titre onéreux peut avoir pour objet de garantir l'exécution d'une obligation.

[21] Tel est le cas de la réserve de propriété et de la fiducie pour fins de garantie. Par contre, les recours résultant d'un crédit-bail et d'un bail ordinaire ne sont assujettis à aucun préavis particulier et à aucune autorisation judiciaire. Michel Deschamps, *loc.cit.*, note 8.

[22] Une opération autre que celles-ci et où le droit de propriété est utilisé à des fins de garantie n'est toutefois pas soumise à aucune mesure de publicité; ainsi, une entente de consignation n'aurait pas à être inscrite et serait opposable aux tiers, dans la mesure où cette entente ne serait pas considérée comme une réserve de propriété déguisée. Michel Deschamps, *loc.cit.*, note 8.

[23] Il n'en est toutefois pas ainsi dans le cas de la cession d'une créance particulière. Michel Deschamps, *loc.cit.*, supra 8.

Pour leur part, les *PPSA* s'appliquent à toute transaction qui crée une sûreté sur un bien meuble. Le constituant doit avoir des droits dans les biens grevés, mais il n'est pas nécessaire qu'il en soit propriétaire. Les *PPSA* s'appliquent aussi à certaines opérations qui n'ont pas pour but de garantir l'exécution d'une obligation telle que la vente d'une créance et au bail non financier de plus d'un an. Les *PPSA* considèrent comme étant une sûreté tout droit dans un bien qui garantit l'exécution d'une obligation, quel qu'en soit sa forme et sans égard à la personne qui est propriétaire du bien. Ainsi, une personne peut être considérée comme titulaire d'une sûreté sur un bien dont elle a la propriété, lorsque le droit de propriété est utilisé à titre de garantie; à titre d'exemple, une réserve de propriété dans un contrat de vente est une sûreté aux termes des *PPSA*, malgré le fait que le titre de propriété soit détenu par le créancier (art. 2).[24]

Aux termes de la Convention et du Protocole, et contrairement au droit québécois,[25] le bail ordinaire est considéré comme une garantie même s'il n'a pas été consenti principalement à des fins de financement. Contrairement aux *PPSA*[26] et au droit québécois,[27] les baux ordinaires ne sont pas assujettis à la condition d'avoir une durée de 12 mois ou plus pour être soumis aux règles d'opposabilité aux tiers de la Convention et du Protocole.

---

[24] « The PPSA concept of security [...] include [...] conditional sales and financial leases ». Ronald C.C. Cuming et al., *op.cit.*, note 8, p. 12. « [It] also captures certain deemed security interest; namely the title of an assignee under an assignment of accounts or chattel paper and, except for the Ontario Act, the title of a consignor under a commercial consignment. The Atlantic Acts also extend the deemed security concept to the title of a buyer under a sale of goods outside the ordinary course of business where the seller remains in possession after the sale. [...] Bringing them within the Act removes the need for characterization except at the level of enforcement on default [...] ». *Ibid.*, p. 13.

[25] Art. 3 de la Convention; art. 1851 à 1891 C.c.Q.

[26] Art. 2 PPSA Ontario, à titre d'exemple. Les PPSA soumettent toutefois un bail ordinaire de 12 mois ou plus à presque toutes les règles régissant les sûretés.

[27] Les règles du crédit-bail (art. 1842 à 1850 C.c.Q.) ne s'appliquent pas forcément à une convention de louage qui dans les faits sert d'instrument de financement. Pierre-Gabriel Jobin, *Le louage*, 2e éd., éd. Yvon Blais, 1996. p. 56. Le droit québécois applique toutefois au bail ordinaire de 12 mois ou plus la même règle d'opposabilité aux tiers qu'en matière d'hypothèque. Michel Deschamps, *loc.cit.*, note 8.

3.2.3   Opposabilité aux tiers (question 1 a))

La Convention donne la priorité au créancier qui a inscrit sa garantie[28] le premier, que le créancier ait eu ou non connaissance réelle de l'existence d'une autre garantie non inscrite[29] tout comme c'est le cas généralement pour les sûretés sans dépossession[30] tant suivant les *PPSA*[31] que suivant le C.c.Q.[32]

---

[28] La Convention ne fait aucune distinction entre une garantie avec ou sans dépossession. Suivant l'article 2702 C.c.Q., l'hypothèque mobilière avec dépossession est constituée par la remise matérielle du bien ou du titre au créancier ou, si le bien est déjà entre ses mains, par le maintien de la détention matérielle, du consentement du constituant, afin de garantir sa créance. La possession du bien par le créancier ou pour son compte par un tiers rend opposable aux tiers une sûreté avec dépossession, aussi bien en vertu des PPSA qu'en vertu du Code civil. Les catégories de biens pouvant faire l'objet d'un gage sont cependant moins nombreuses en droit québécois; par exemple, le droit québécois ignore la notion de « chattel paper » et il est douteux que la remise d'un tel document serait suffisante pour déposséder le constituant. Michel Deschamps, *loc.cit.*, note 8.

[29] Article 29 Convention.

[30] Tant les PPSA que le Code civil permettent généralement de rendre opposable aux tiers toute sûreté mobilière au moyen d'une inscription au registre des sûretés mobilières. En règle générale, tant les PPSA que le Code civil déterminent la priorité du titulaire d'une sûreté en fonction de la date d'opposabilité aux tiers de la sûreté.

Les exceptions à cette règle sont moins nombreuses sous le Code civil que sous les PPSA. Ainsi, sous les PPSA, une personne qui obtient de bonne foi un gage sur des valeurs mobilières aura priorité sur le titulaire d'une sûreté sans dépossession antérieurement consentie à un tiers sur les mêmes valeurs mobilières et ce, bien que cette dernière sûreté ait été inscrite antérieurement. Dans une situation semblable, le Code civil accorde plutôt priorité au titulaire de la sûreté sans dépossession.

La sûreté en garantie du prix d'acquisition (purchase-money security interest ou PMSI) constitue également en vertu des PPSA une exception à la règle voulant que la priorité d'une sûreté soit établie selon la date où elle devient opposable aux tiers. Dans les PPSA, la protection accordée par un PMSI bénéficie aussi bien au vendeur à crédit du bien qu'à un prêteur qui finance l'acquisition du bien. Dans le droit québécois, une protection équivalente n'existe que pour le vendeur à crédit ou le crédit-bailleur; le prêteur qui obtient une sûreté sur un bien dont il a financé l'acquisition prendra rang après le titulaire d'une hypothèque inscrite antérieurement sur l'ensemble des biens du débiteur. Michel Deschamps, *loc.cit.*, supra note 8.

[31] Voir Ronald Cuming, « The Convention on International Interests in Mobile Equipment, When it applies and with what consequences, a paper presented to the Canadian Cape Town Convention Seminar Toronto Ontario, April 29–30, 2013 », *loc.cit.*, note 9. « Under the Act, priority among security interests that have been perfected by registration generally is determined by the order of registration without regard to actual knowledge, and the holder of a registered or otherwise perfected security interest generally has priority against subsequent claimants. ». Ronald C.C. Cuming et al., *op.cit.*, note 8, p. 11. « For reasons of commercial necessity or practice, the Act recognizes significant exceptions to temporal ranking in favour of: (1) secured parties who finance the debtor's acquisition of the collateral; (2) secured parties who obtain physical possession of money or collateral represented by a negotiable or quasi-negotiable instrument or document and (3) secured parties who obtain control of collateral that qualifies as investment property». *Ibid.*, p. 19–20; « […] actual knowledge combined with other factors – for example, […] abuse of a non-arm's length relationship, or […] misleading or fraudulent conduct – may deny a person the right to rely on an otherwise applicable PPSA priority rule». *Ibid.*, p. 53. Voir également *ibid.*, p. 55–59.

[32] Art. 2941 à 2945 et 2963 C.c.Q.; Ronald C.C. Cuming et al., *op.cit.*, note 8, p. 96–97.

3.2.4 Inscription aux registres (question 1 c))

Tout comme le Registre international constitué en vertu de la Convention (article 17) prévoit l'inscription de certaines données de base relatives aux droits susceptibles d'inscription et non pas le dépôt des documents constitutifs de ces droits,[33] tant le RDPRM, constitué en vertu du C.c.Q.,[34] que les Registres constitués en vertu des *PPSA* («PPR»), sont des registres de « notice filing ».[35] Ils ne donnent à une personne qui les consulte que certains renseignements généraux.[36]

Contrairement au Registre international en vertu de la Convention du Cap qui est un système basé sur l'inscription contre un bien, pas contre le nom du débiteur (voir art. 18 (1) de la Convention), le RDPRM du Québec est basé sur l'inscription nominative en ce qui concerne tout autre bien qu'un véhicule routier défini à l'article 15 du *Règlement sur le registre des droits personnels et réels mobiliers*.[37] Les aéronefs étant mentionnés à l'art. 15.01, 6°, il s'ensuit que ceux-ci étaient déjà sujets à une inscription. Cependant, contrairement aux véhicules routiers faisant aussi l'objet d'une fiche descriptive permettant la recherche par numéro d'identification, les inscriptions au sujet des aéronefs ne se retrouvent que sur la base d'un nom.[38] Les PPR, sauf en Ontario, prévoient des inscriptions par un numéro de série ou une description des biens, en plus du nom du débiteur.

De plus, le Registre international comme les PPR dispensent de fournir le montant maximum garanti par la sûreté contrairement à l'article 2689 C.c.Q.[39]

Tant suivant les *PPSA* que le Code civil, mais contrairement à la Convention et au Protocole, il est possible de constituer une garantie sur une universalité de biens.[40]

---

[33] Michel Deschamps, *loc.cit.*, note 17, p. 21.

[34] Denys-Claude Lamontagne et Pierre Duchaine, *La publicité des droits*, 5e édition, Cowansville, éd. Yvon Blais, 2012, p. 434, par. 723.

[35] « All that has to be registered is a simple notice (called a financial statement) containing the basic information necessary to alert a searcher to the potential existence of a security interest – the names and addresses of the parties, a description of the collateral, and the duration of the registration. There is no need to file the underlying security documentation, or tender it for scrutiny by registry staff ». Ronald C.C. Cuming et al., *op.cit.*, note 8, p. 9.

[36] Le RDPRM est toutefois plus complet que ses homologues canadiens puisqu'il faut inscrire tous les droits que le requérant souhaite rendre opposables aux tiers (art. 2981 et 2986 C.c.Q.); il n'est donc pas utile de consulter les documents contrairement à ce qui est le cas avec les autres registres canadiens.

[37] Précité note 16.

[38] La recherche au RDPRM pour une fiche nominative se fait à l'aide du nom du constituant, et non pas celui du titulaire, auquel peut s'ajouter un code postal lorsqu'il s'agit d'un constituant « personne morale ». S'il s'agit d'une personne physique, le nom est requis ainsi que la date de naissance. L'adresse ne constitue pas une clé de recherche au RDPRM. La recherche permettrait ainsi de découvrir les charges pesant sur un avion mais peut-être aussi sur d'autres biens du constituant.

[39] La somme peut être un estimé si elle est incertaine. Ronald C.C. Cuming et al., *op.cit.*, note 8, p. 92; M. Deschamps, *loc.cit.*, note 17, p. 22, note 21.

[40] Au Québec, suivant les articles 2684 et 2684.1 C.c.Q., seule la personne ou le fiduciaire qui exploite une entreprise peut consentir une hypothèque sur une universalité de biens, meubles ou

Ainsi si un transporteur aérien accordait une sûreté en désignant les biens grevés comme étant « tous les avions et les moteurs lui appartenant présentement ou pouvant dans l'avenir lui appartenir », la sûreté serait formellement valable en vertu de ces régimes mais pas au regard de la Convention et du Protocole. Il en serait de même si les obligations garanties par la sûreté étaient décrites comme étant « toutes les obligations présentes et futures du constituant envers le débiteur », sans autre forme d'identification.[41]

Enfin, suivant la Convention,[42] les PPR et le RDPRM, le Conservateur ou l'officier de la publicité des droits ne vérifie pas l'exactitude du contenu des informations qui lui sont soumises. Il n'encourt donc pas de responsabilité à cet égard.

Le Canada n'a pas fait la déclaration prévue à l'article 50(1) de la Convention qui lui aurait permis d'exclure de l'application de la Convention les opérations internes, définies à l'article 1 n) de la Convention et à l'article IV du Protocole. La Convention et le Protocole ont donc permis la création d'un registre unique aux garanties sur les biens aéronautiques couverts par la Convention, ce qui n'était pas le cas jusqu'alors.

3.3   Défaut, recours et autorisation judiciaire

3.3.1   Défaut (question 2 b))

Tant selon la Convention et le Protocole, qu'en vertu des *PPSA* ou du Code civil, les parties sont libres de définir les cas de défauts (art. 11 (1) de la Convention).

Cependant, les mesures par lesquelles les créanciers exercent leurs recours sont, tant selon les *PPSA* que selon le Code civil, assujetties à des règles procédurales standardisées et obligatoires.[43]

---

immeubles, présents ou à venir, corporels ou incorporels. Par exception, la personne physique qui n'exploite pas une entreprise peut, si ces valeurs ou titres sont de la nature de ceux qu'elle peut grever d'une hypothèque sans dépossession, consentir une hypothèque sur une universalité de valeurs mobilières ou de titres intermédiés, présents ou à venir, visés par la *Loi sur le transfert de valeurs mobilières et l'obtention de titres intermédiés* (chapitre T-11.002). Elle peut aussi, si les biens sont de la nature de ceux qu'elle peut grever d'une hypothèque sans dépossession, consentir une hypothèque sur toute autre universalité de biens, présents ou à venir, déterminée par règlement. Article 15.02 du *Règlement sur le registre des droits personnels et réels mobiliers*, précité note 16.

[41] Michel Deschamps, *loc. cit.*, note 17, notes 22 et 23, voir l'article 10 PPSA (Nouveau-Brunswick) ainsi que les articles 2697 et 2950 C.c.Q.

[42] Art. 28(2) de la Convention.

[43] Ronald C.C. Cuming et al., *op.cit.*, note 8, p. 7.

3.3.2   Recours et autorisation judiciaire (questions 2 a) et c))

Tant suivant la Convention, le Code civil[44] que les *PPSA*, le créancier garanti bénéficie d'un large éventail de recours au cas de défaut de son débiteur: il peut prendre
possession du bien grevé pour l'administrer (donner à bail le bien, en percevoir tout
revenu ou bénéfice), le prendre en paiement de sa créance, le faire vendre ou le
vendre lui-même. Cependant, les recours du créancier sont limités à ces hypothèses
en droit québécois, alors que dans les provinces de common law et sous la Convention
et le Protocole, les parties sont libres d'en imaginer d'autres tant que la méthode
employée est commercialement raisonnable (art. 8 de la Convention).

Le Code civil requiert une autorisation judiciaire pour que le créancier puisse
prendre possession des biens si le débiteur ne les lui remet pas volontairement.[45]

Le gouvernement du Canada a déclaré, en vertu de l'article 54 de la Convention,
qu'une mesure ouverte à un créancier en vertu d'une disposition de la Convention
dont la mise en œuvre n'est pas subordonnée à une demande à un tribunal peut être
prise sans l'autorisation du tribunal. Le droit québécois a ainsi dû être modifié pour
correspondre à cette déclaration du Canada.[46]

Ainsi, alors que le Code civil[47] exige l'autorisation du tribunal pour que le créancier puisse exercer la prise en paiement si le débiteur ne délaisse pas volontairement
le bien et qu'il avait déjà acquitté, au moment de l'inscription du préavis du créancier, la moitié, ou plus, de l'obligation garantie par hypothèque, la Convention vient
en contrepartie permettre que soit rendu au débiteur l'excédent du montant garanti
par la sûreté et des frais raisonnables engagés au titre de l'une quelconque de ces
mesures, après paiement des autres créanciers.

---

[44] Art. 2748 C.c.Q. Il s'agit de recours « hypothécaires ». Le créancier peut en outre exercer ses
recours « personnels ».

[45] Art. 2765 C.c.Q. : « Le délaissement est forcé lorsque le tribunal l'ordonne, après avoir constaté
l'existence de la créance, le défaut du débiteur, le refus de délaisser volontairement et l'absence
d'une cause valable d'opposition.

Le jugement fixe le délai dans lequel le délaissement doit s'opérer, en détermine la manière et
désigne la personne en faveur de qui il a lieu. »

De plus, bien que les PPSA et le Code civil posent comme principe que le créancier doit donner
au débiteur un préavis de son intention de faire vendre les biens grevés, les PPSA comportent de
nombreuses exceptions à ce principe, alors que le Code civil, même s'il permet au tribunal
d'abréger le délai du préavis, n'en dispense complètement le créancier que dans des circonstances
très limitées. Ainsi, le titulaire d'une sûreté sur des biens périssables ou se dépréciant rapidement
et qui voudrait les vendre n'est pas dispensé d'en donner avis au débiteur et il devra obtenir
l'autorisation du tribunal pour procéder à la vente avant l'expiration du délai de préavis.

[46] Voir *supra* note 14.

[47] Art. 2778 C.c.Q.

3.4   Faillite et l'insolvabilité ((questions 3 a) et b)

Le gouvernement du Canada a déclaré, en vertu de l'article XXX du Protocole, qu'il applique la Variante A de l'article XI du Protocole dans son intégralité à tous les types de procédures d'insolvabilité et tous les événements liés à l'insolvabilité et que le délai d'attente aux fins du paragraphe 3 de l'article XI de cette Variante est de soixante (60) jours civils.

L'article 20 de la *Loi n° 2 portant exécution de certaines dispositions du budget déposé au Parlement le 29 mars 2012 et mettant en oeuvre d'autres mesures*[48] est venu modifier la *Loi sur les garanties internationales portant sur des matériels d'équipement mobiles* de manière à donner force de loi au Canada à la Variante A de l'article XI du Protocole, comme le recommande l'Accord sectoriel sur les aéronefs (ASU) élaboré sous la direction de l'Organisation de coopération et de développement économiques (OCDE). En conséquence, les dispositions se rapportant expressément au Protocole introduites en 2005 dans la *Loi sur la faillite et l'insolvabilité*[49] (LFI), la *Loi sur les arrangements avec les créanciers des compagnies*[50] (LACC) et la *Loi sur les liquidations et les restructurations*[51] (LLR) n'ont plus été requises et ont été abrogées de manière à assurer une plus grande clarté et à éliminer le double emploi. Ces lois fédérales s'appliquent sur l'ensemble du territoire canadien.

Ainsi, la garantie inscrite est opposable dans les procédures d'insolvabilité dont le débiteur fait l'objet (art. 30 (1) de la Convention).

La Variante A ne correspond que partiellement au droit canadien applicable lorsque la Convention et le Protocole ne s'appliquent pas. En effet, les créanciers garantis doivent donner un préavis d'au moins dix jours de leur intention d'exercer leurs recours sur certaines catégories de biens de leur débiteur (art. 243, 244 LFI[52]). Le débiteur insolvable qui exploite une entreprise peut au cours de ce délai se mettre sous la protection de la LFI ou de la LACC. Les créanciers garantis visés par la proposition ou l'arrangement se voient alors imposer une suspension de leurs recours et cette suspension peut se prolonger (art. 69.1 et 69.2 LFI ou 10.02 LACC).

---

[48] Projet de loi C-45, *Loi no 2 portant exécution de certaines dispositions du budget déposé au Parlement le 29 mars 2012 et mettant en oeuvre d'autres mesures*: http://www.parl.gc.ca/ HousePublications/Publication.aspx?Language=F&Mode=1&DocId=5765988&File=470.   Au moment de son adoption en 2005, la Loi de mise en oeuvre fédérale ne donnait pas force de loi à l'article XI du Protocole. Des modifications à différentes lois fédérales avaient par la suite été adoptées afin de prévoir comme en droit américain un régime similaire à la Variante A du Protocole sans la déclarer applicable. En 2012, lorsque la loi de mise en oeuvre a été à nouveau modifiée notamment pour donner force de loi à l'article XI du Protocole, les dispositions introduites dans ces différentes lois ont été abrogées.

[49] *Loi sur la faillite et l'insolvabilité*, L.R.C. (1985), ch. B-3.

[50] *Loi sur les arrangements avec les créanciers des compagnies*, L.R.C. (1985), ch. C-36.

[51] *Loi sur les liquidations et les restructurations*, L.R.C. (1985), ch. W-11.

[52] Au Québec, le préavis de l'article 2757 C.c.Q. remplit ce rôle. Jacques Deslauriers, *La faillite et l'insolvabilité au Québec*, Montréal, éd. Wilson et Lafleur, 2e éd., 2011, p. 541, par. 1797. Le débiteur qui ne se prévaut pas de la protection de ces lois dans le délai de dix (10) jours, n'est plus protégé contre les recours de ses créanciers.

La suspension résultant d'une proposition prend fin si les créanciers garantis visés votent contre la proposition (art. 69. 1 (5) LFI). Le syndic peut toutefois obtenir la suspension de la réalisation des garanties pendant une période maximale de six mois, pour lui permettre de décider s'il abandonne sa saisie sur les biens affectés à la garantie, s'il en force la réalisation ou s'il rachète la garantie (art. 69.3 et 128 et s. LFI). Les tribunaux accordent très généralement cette suspension des recours.[53]

3.5 Droits non-consensuels et incompatibilité

3.5.1 *Droits non-consensuels*

Les *PPSA* ne s'appliquent pas aux droits non-consensuels mais dans certaines provinces et territoires de common law,[54] le créancier d'un jugement se voit conférer un statut qui est assimilé à une sûreté laquelle est traitée comme les autres en vertu des *PPSA*. Également, les contributions impayées d'un employeur à un régime de pension en faveur de ses employés, la créance d'un réparateur et celle d'un aéroport ou autre autorité de navigation font également l'objet de droits non-consensuels pouvant avoir priorité sur les sûretés consensuelles en droit canadien.[55]

Au Québec, les droits non-consensuels sont codifiés. Il s'agit des créances prioritaires et des hypothèques légales.

Suivant l'article 2650 C.c.Q., est prioritaire la créance à laquelle la loi attache, en faveur d'un créancier, le droit d'être préféré aux autres créanciers, même hypothécaires, suivant la cause de sa créance. Les créances prioritaires qui sont pertinentes au contexte de la Convention et du Protocole, sont les suivantes et, lorsqu'elles se rencontrent, elles sont, malgré toute convention contraire, colloquées dans cet ordre[56]:

    1° Les frais de justice et toutes les dépenses faites dans l'intérêt commun;
    2° La créance du vendeur impayé pour le prix du meuble vendu à une personne physique
       qui n'exploite pas une entreprise;
    3° Les créances de ceux qui ont un droit de rétention sur un meuble, pourvu que ce droit
       subsiste;
    4° Les créances de l'État pour les sommes dues en vertu des lois fiscales;
    [...]

---

[53] Jacques Deslauriers, *op.cit.*, note 52, p. 130–131; 529–565.

[54] Ronald C.C. Cuming et al., *op.cit.*, note 8, p. 69. *Civil Enforcement Act*, RSA 2000, c. C- 15 (Alberta), *The Executions Act*, CCSM c E160 (Manitoba, 2004 c.4), *Enforcement of Money Judgments Act*, SNB 2013, c 23, (Nouveau-Brunswick); *Exemptions Act*, RSNWT (Nu) 1988, c E-9 (Nunavut, SNu 2006, c 3); *The Enforcement of Money Judgments Act*, SS 2010 c. E-9.22 (Saskatchewan, S 2012, c. 23); *Judgment Enforcement Act*, SNL 1996, c J-1.1 (Terre-Neuve et Labrador), voir http://www.ulcc.ca/images/stories/Uniform_Acts_EN/Table%205%20E%202012. pdf, p. 519.

[55] Donald Gray and Jean Surette, *loc.cit.*, note 9.

[56] Art. 2651 C.c.Q.

Suivant l'article 2724 C.c.Q., les seules créances qui peuvent donner lieu à une hypothèque légale, et qui sont pertinentes au contexte de la Convention et du Protocole, sont les suivantes:

1° Les créances de l'État pour les sommes dues en vertu des lois fiscales, ainsi que certaines autres créances de l'État ou de personnes morales de droit public, spécialement prévues dans les lois particulières;
[…]
4° Les créances qui résultent d'un jugement.

Ces hypothèques ne sont acquises que par leur inscription sur le RDPRM si elles grèvent des meubles.[57]

Un règlement[58] d'application de la Convention et du Protocole a été adopté par le Québec qui prévoit:

En vertu de l'article 39 (1) *a* et (2) de la Convention, un droit ou une garantie non conventionnel portant sur un bien qui, en vertu du droit québécois en vigueur à la date de la présente déclaration ou après cette date, prime une garantie équivalente à celle du titulaire d'une garantie internationale inscrite, primera de la même façon une garantie internationale inscrite, que ce soit ou non en cas de procédure d'insolvabilité.

Plus particulièrement:

1° une créance prioritaire prendra rang avant une garantie internationale inscrite au Registre international constitué en vertu de la Convention et du Protocole, que ce soit ou non dans le cadre d'une procédure d'insolvabilité;

2° une hypothèque légale inscrite au registre des droits personnels et réels mobiliers prendra rang avant une garantie internationale subséquemment inscrite au Registre international constitué en vertu de la Convention et du Protocole, que ce soit ou non dans le cadre d'une procédure d'insolvabilité.

En vertu de l'article 39 (1) *b* de la Convention, aucune disposition de la Convention ne porte atteinte au droit du gouvernement du Canada, d'une province ou d'un territoire, d'une entité gouvernementale, d'une organisation intergouvernementale ou d'un autre fournisseur privé de services publics, de saisir ou de retenir un bien en vertu du droit québécois pour le paiement des redevances dues à ce gouvernement, entité, organisation ou fournisseur qui sont directement liées aux services fournis concernant ce bien ou à un autre bien.

En vertu de l'article 39 (4) de la Convention, un droit ou une garantie visé par la déclaration faite en vertu de l'article 39 (1) *a* prime une garantie internationale inscrite avant la date de la ratification par le Canada.

Le Canada a fait une déclaration correspondante conformément aux articles 39 et 40 de la Convention. Ainsi, il a notamment déclaré en vertu de l'alinéa a) du paragraphe 1 de l'article 39 de la Convention, qu'un droit ou une garantie non conventionnel, établi en vertu du droit canadien, existant au moment de la présente déclaration, ou après cette date, et primant une garantie portant sur un bien équivalente à celle du titulaire d'une garantie internationale inscrite, prime de la même

---

[57] Art. 2725 C.c.Q.
[58] Précité note 14.

façon une garantie internationale inscrite, que ce soit ou non en cas de procédure d'insolvabilité.

Il a également déclaré en vertu de l'alinéa a) du paragraphe 1 de l'article 39 de la Convention, qu'une hypothèque légale en vertu du droit de la province de Québec, existant au moment de la présente déclaration, ou après cette date, inscrite au registre des droits personnels et réels mobiliers de cette province prime une garantie internationale subséquemment inscrite au Registre international constitué en vertu de la Convention et du Protocole, que ce soit ou non en cas de procédure d'insolvabilité.

Enfin, il a déclaré en vertu de l'alinéa a) du paragraphe 1 de l'article 39 de la Convention, qu'une créance prioritaire en vertu du droit de la province de Québec, existant au moment de la présente déclaration, ou après cette date, à laquelle la loi attache en faveur du créancier d'être préféré aux autres créanciers, prime une garantie internationale subséquemment inscrite au Registre international constitué en vertu de la Convention et du Protocole, que ce soit ou non en cas de procédure d'insolvabilité.

3.5.2 Incompatibilité

Il est d'usage dans les lois de mise en oeuvre adoptées au fédéral ou dans les provinces de common law, d'annexer les instruments internationaux auxquels il est donné force de loi. Il est également d'usage d'y prévoir que les dispositions des instruments internationaux, auxquels il est donné force de loi, l'emportent sur toute règle de droit incompatible. Au Québec, alors que la technique de la loi annexe est également utilisée, on semble se reposer sur les règles d'interprétation pour parvenir à ce même résultat, c'est-à-dire que les instruments internationaux priment sur les autres lois.[59]

---

[59] La loi de mise en oeuvre est plus précise que l'autre loi (*lex specialis derogat legi generali*), et plus récente que cette autre loi (*lex posterior derogat legi priori*), l'autre loi dont il s'agit étant généralement le Code civil. Il existe également une présomption en droit canadien suivant laquelle le législateur est censé avoir légiféré conformément aux obligations internationales contractées. Voir Arrangement sur les crédits à l'exportation bénéficiant d'un soutien public, Annexe 2: Questionnaire sur la Convention du Cap, note 4 p. 88 à http://search.oecd.org/officialdocuments/displaydocumentpdf/?cote=tad/pg(2013)11&doclanguage=fr et Frédérique Sabourin, « Une perspective québécoise sur la Convention pour le règlement des différends relatifs aux investissements entre États et ressortissant d'autres États », dans Sylvette Guillemard, dir., *Mélanges en l'honneur du professeur Alain Prujiner*, Cowansville, éd. Yvon Blais, 2011, p. 337; Frédérique Sabourin, « Les conventions multilatérales de droit international privé conclues par le Canada et leur mise en oeuvre en droit québécois » dans Nathalie Vézina, dir., *Le droit uniforme : limites et possibilités*, Cowansville, éd. Yvon Blais, 2009; Frédérique Sabourin, « Le cycle de vie d'un instrument international », *XIXe Conférence des juristes de l'État*, Cowansville, éd. Yvon Blais, 2011.

La Loi de mise en oeuvre fédérale[60] a précisé que les dispositions de la *Loi réglementant certaines drogues et autres substances,*[61] des parties II.1 et XII.2 et des articles 487 à 490.01 et 490.1 à 490.9 du *Code criminel,*[62] de la *Loi sur les licences d'exportation et d'importation,*[63] de la *Loi sur les mesures économiques spéciales*[64] et de la *Loi sur les Nations Unies,*[65] ainsi que de leurs règlements d'application, l'emportent sur toute disposition incompatible de la présente loi ou des règlements ainsi que sur toute disposition incompatible de la Convention ou du Protocole aéronautique à laquelle l'article 4 donne force de loi.

Enfin, le Canada a déclaré également en vertu de l'article 60 de la Convention, que celle-ci s'applique à un droit ou une garantie préexistant régi par les articles 426 à 436 de la *Loi sur les banques*[66] aux fins de déterminer sa priorité, y compris la protection d'une priorité existante, cinq ans après la date d'entrée en vigueur au Canada du Protocole aéronautique. Jusqu'alors, ce droit ou cette garantie sera régi par lesdits articles. Apparemment, cette loi n'est pas utilisée au Canada pour le financement d'aéronefs et autres biens visés par la Convention.[67]

Sauf cette exception, la priorité d'un droit ou d'une garantie préexistant continuera d'être régie par le droit antérieur, sans limite dans le temps. Les *PPSA* et le Code civil continueront en outre de s'appliquer : (1) chaque fois que la Convention et le Protocole renvoient au droit national; (2) aux biens aéronautiques qui ne sont pas couverts par la Convention et le Protocole; (3) ainsi qu'aux aspects du droit des sûretés auxquels la Convention et le Protocole n'apportent pas de réponses ou auxquels ils apportent une réponse incomplète.[68] Les différents registres provinciaux et territoriaux continueront donc de servir.

---

[60] Précitée note 10.

[61] *Loi réglementant certaines drogues et autres substances*, L.R.C. (1985), C-38.8.

[62] *Code criminel*, L.R.C. (1985), C-46.

[63] *Loi sur les licences d'exportation et d'importation*, L.R.C. (1985), E-19.

[64] *Loi sur les mesures économiques spéciales*, L.R.C. (1985), S-14.5.

[65] *Loi sur les Nations Unies*, L.R.C. (1985), U-2.

[66] *Loi sur les banques*, L.C. 1991, c. 46.

[67] Donald Gray et Jean Surette, *loc.cit.*, note 9.

[68] Articles 2 et 5 de la Convention, notamment. Ronald Cuming, «The Convention on International Interests in Mobile Equipment, When it applies and with what consequences, a paper presented to the Canadian Cape Town Convention Seminar Toronto Ontario, April 29–30, 2013 », *loc.cit.*, note 9; M. Deschamps, « The perfection and priority rules of the Cape Town Convention and the Aircraft Protocol, A comparative law analysis », *loc.cit.*, note 8.

3.6   Conclusion (question 4)

Il est d'usage au Canada d'évaluer les impacts économiques d'une mesure législative proposée.[69] L'industrie de l'aérospatiale est importante au Canada. Le Canada compte plus de 400 entreprises aérospatiales employant près de 80 000 spécialistes qualifiés; elles ont enregistré des ventes totales de 22,1 milliards de dollars en 2006. L'industrie exporte 80 pourcent de sa production.[70]

L'idée de base de la Convention et du Protocole est que leur ratification bénéficiera à toutes les parties impliquées dans une transaction internationale, le débiteur en ayant accès à de meilleures conditions de financement et le créancier à de meilleures méthodes de réalisation de sa sûreté, et par conséquent à l'économie en général.[71]

Comme le rapportait le groupe de travail issu de la Conférence pour l'harmonisation des lois au Canada chargé d'étudier la façon de mettre en oeuvre la Convention et le Protocole au Canada[72]:

[...] la Convention/le Protocole [...] reflète les caractéristiques exposées en ce qui a trait à la nouvelle Architecture financière, [...] dans la mesure où ce document est favorable au financement garanti par un actif et du fait que ses caractéristiques principales couvrent la constitution d'une garantie internationale, un système d'inscription, une règle sur la priorité des garanties et des mesures promptes en cas d'inexécution, y compris celles qui n'appellent pas l'intervention d'un tribunal. On se souviendra que, sur le plan mondial, les aéronefs représentent 4 % du matériel d'équipement mobile.

[16] L'adoption et l'application des règles de la Convention/du Protocole sont destinées à faciliter l'acquisition rentable et l'utilisation de matériel aéronautique, qu'il s'agisse d'aéronefs neufs ou de pièces. Ceci devrait permettre aux exploitants d'acquérir du matériel d'équipement moderne et non polluant et de concentrer plus aisément leurs efforts sur la sécurité.

[70] [...] de tels gains économiques pourraient donner au Canada des gains intéressants au niveau de la concurrence économique.

L'Appendice II de l'Accord sectoriel sur les Crédits à l'Exportation d'Aéronefs Civils (ASU) soutient cette idée en prévoyant un abattement sur la prime minimale dans le cas où un État remplit les conditions énoncées à l'article 35 et 38 de cet Appendice lesquelles sont notamment d'être une partie contractante à la Convention

---

[69] Question 4(a).

[70] http://www.ic.gc.ca/eic/site/ad-ad.nsf/fra/ad03909.html.

[71] Question 4(b).

[72] Conférence pour l'harmonisation des lois au Canada, *Rapport sur la mise en oeuvre de la Convention sur les garanties sur les équipements mobiles*, Toronto, Ontario, 22 août 2001, http://www.ulcc.ca/fr/2001-toronto-on-fr-fr-1/324-documents-de-la-section-civile-2001/2076-garanties-internationales-equipements-mobiles-rapport-2001.

et au Protocole et d'avoir fait certaines déclarations et s'être abstenu d'en faire d'autres.[73]

Au 20 octobre 2014, le Canada faisait partie de la liste des 21 pays approuvés par les Participants à l'ASU des États pour lesquels un tel abattement est autorisé.[74] Cela permettra à l'industrie de réduire ses coûts de financement de façon significative.[75] On estime donc généralement que la Convention et le Protocole profiteront au Canada.[76]

Soulignons en terminant qu'Unidroit, en sa qualité de dépositaire, a apporté des modifications notamment à la version française des textes authentiques de la Convention et de l'Annexe du Protocole. Ces modifications entraînent la nécessité de lois modificatrices au Canada, Manitoba, Nouveau-Brunswick, Nunavut, Ontario, Saskatchewan, Territoires du Nord-Ouest et au Yukon, à défaut qu'elles puissent se faire en vertu d'un pouvoir correctif administratif.[77]

Frédérique Sabourin Avocate, ministère de la Justice du Québec. Les opinions exprimées dans cet article n'engagent que l'auteure. Celle-ci tient par ailleurs à exprimer toute sa gratitude envers sa directrice, Me Renée Madore, Direction des orientations et politiques, pour son soutien administratif, envers Me Michel Deschamps, avocat associé du cabinet McCarthy Tétrault, le professeur Ronald Cuming du College of Law de l'Université de la Saskatchewan, ainsi qu'envers M. François Dumas et Mes Lise Cadoret et Caroline Lavoie, de la Direction des registres et de la certification, pour leurs judicieux commentaires.

---

[73] http://search.oecd.org/officialdocuments/displaydocumentpdf/?cote=tad/pg(2013)11&doclanguage=fr

[74] http://www.oecd.org/fr/tad/xcred/ctc.htm. Question 4 c).

[75] Drew Hasselback, « Air Canada's top lawyer makes the investment grade, *Financial Post*, 12/06/13, http://business.financialpost.com/2013/06/12/air-canadas-top-lawyer-makes-the-investment-grade/.

[76] Donald Gray et Jean Surette, *loc.cit.*, note 9.

[77] Au Québec, le Service de refonte des lois et des règlements du ministère de la Justice a procédé aux modifications requises en vertu de l'article 3 de la Loi sur le Recueil des lois et des règlements du Québec, RLRQ, c. R-2.2.0.0.2: voir N.I. 2016-05-15.

Chapter 4
The Law of England and Wales on Secured Transactions as Compared with the Cape Town Convention

George Leloudas

4.1 Introduction

English law occupies a dominant position in aircraft financing. Understandably, it is the preferred choice of law in transactions which involve aircraft in the UK. Yet, its influence is far-reaching, since it is one of the most desirable choices of law in financial transactions which involve non-UK registered aircraft that may have little or no link to England.

The reasons for such extraterritorial application have been summarised in a report prepared by the Law Society of England and Wales that aims to promote English commercial law and the jurisdiction of English courts in international commercial transactions.[1] The report was not prepared with aircraft finance in mind, but its observations are of immediate relevance to our paper. In a nutshell, it argues that "at the specialised Commercial Court, a staggering 80 % of cases involve a foreign claimant or defendant".[2] This preference is arguably the result of "...English commercial law provid[ing] predictability of outcome, legal certainty and fairness. It is clear and is built upon well-founded principles, such as the ability to require exact performance and the absence of any general duty of good faith".[3] These characteristics would not have been sufficient to attract the attention of commercial people worldwide had it not been for the ability of English law to adapt to the evolving

---

[1] The Law Society of England and Wales, "England and Wales: the jurisdiction of choice. Dispute Resolution" (2007).

[2] *Ibid.*, p. 5 per the RT Hon Jack Straw MP, Secretary of State for Justice and Lord Chancellor (as he then was).

[3] *Ibid.*

G. Leloudas (✉)
College of Law and Criminology, Swansea University,
Singleton Park, Swansea SA2 8PP, UK
e-mail: G.Leloudas@swansea.ac.uk

© Springer International Publishing AG 2017
S. Kozuka (ed.), *Implementing the Cape Town Convention and the Domestic Laws on Secured Transactions*, Ius Comparatum - Global Studies in Comparative Law 22, DOI 10.1007/978-3-319-46470-1_4

needs of international commerce. The report attributes this ability to the flexibility of judge-made law and the doctrine of precedence as distinguished from what the report describes as the rigidity of statute-based laws.[4] Yet, this distinction does not tell the entire story, since the prevalence of the common law is eroded by the influence of EU law (until Brexit is concluded at least) and the on-going harmonisation of private international law.

It is arguable that the flexibility of English law is predominantly the result of the judiciary's ability to interpret statutes or create common law in a manner that is relevant for the on-going evolution of commerce. The example of the Marine Insurance Act 1906, which still serves the marine insurance industry despite its minor amendments since its entry into force more than 100 years ago, is a testament to the pragmatism of English commercial judges.[5]

In that respect, the question whether to ratify the Cape Town Convention posed the following conundrum to the drafters of English law: does this new instrument of international law serve the needs of the aviation industry in such a holistic manner that is worth replacing English law on aircraft finance? The advocates of the pre-Cape Town system were arguing that English law is a tested and internationally popular choice. Any change will mess with a perfectly good system and will undermine the influence of London as a finance and dispute-resolution centre. The advocates of change were arguing that English law on aircraft finance is not as user-friendly and transparent as the Cape Town Convention. It is a scattered amalgam of common law and statutory provisions that have served the industry well so far. Yet, it does not provide the same degree of certainty with the Cape Town Convention, especially vis-à-vis the registration and the ascertainment of priorities of interests.

After a long consultation period the British Government decided to ratify the Cape Town Convention as it "would benefit the UK economy by creating a harmonised legal framework to register interests against helicopters, aircraft frames and aircraft engines".[6] The International Interests in Aircraft Equipment (Cape Town Convention) Regulations 2015 implement the Cape Town Convention into English law.[7] The Regulations at large follow the text of the Cape Town Convention with minor textual amendments in regs. 16 and 31.

It is the aim of this report to look into the relevant provisions of English law through the prism of the Cape Town Convention. It is the belief of this author that the Cape Town Convention will remedy a good number of the drawbacks of English law. Using the international popularity of English law on aircraft finance as a reason to halt the implementation of the Cape Town Convention in English law was

---

[4] *Ibid.*, p. 8.

[5] The Consumer Insurance (Disclosure and Representations) Act 2012 and the Insurance Act 2015 are the most important amendments of the Marine Insurance Act 1906 since its enactment.

[6] Department for Business Innovation and Skills, *Convention on International Interests in Mobile Equipment and Protocol thereto on Matters Specific to Aircraft Equipment. Government Response to the Call for Evidence* (2013), at [3.19].

[7] SI 2015/912.

misleading for two reasons: (i) it overlooked its structural deficiencies by essentially arguing that there is no room for improvement; and (ii) it undermined the commercial needs of the UK aviation industry, especially of aircraft operators.

A note of caution to the readers: this report does not purport to "reinvent the wheel" which explains the large number of notes. Inevitably, its originality has been compromised for the sake of providing an accurate and all-embracing account of English law by reference to a wide range of materials while respecting the limits imposed by the editor.

4.2   Registration System

4.2.1   The Root of the Problem and the Effect of the Cape Town Convention

One of the main distinctions in the English law of personal property (as distinguished from real property) is between security interests and title-retention agreements or, as alternatively known, "quasi-security" interests.[8] Both terms will be used interchangeably.

English law divides the former category to interests which are created consensually and interests which are created by operation of law. Consensually-created security interests comprise of the following four which are subject to the *numerus clausus* principle: pledges, contractual liens, (legal or equitable) mortgages and (equitable, fixed or floating) charges. Interests created by operation of law are not subject to the *numerus clausus* principle. In the words of Professor McKendrick "[n]o useful purpose would be served by trying to catalogue all these (legal) securities, but they may be divided into five principal categories: the [possessory, equitable, maritime or statutory] lien, the equitable right of set-off, the equitable right to trace and, finally, a group of what may be conveniently termed procedural securities".[9]

Title-retention agreements comprise of finance leases, conditional sales agreements, hire-purchase agreements and retention of title clauses. What they have in common is that they "do not involve the taking of security but…have a similar economic function, in that a party that provides credit retains property rights over assets that in practice are being purchased by the debtor with the credit provided".[10]

The similarity of function between security interests and title-retention agreements is not a good enough reason for English law to treat them in the same manner with respect to registration. In sharp contrast to Article 9 of the Uniform Commercial

---

[8] A comprehensive analysis of this area of English law is outside the scope of this report.

[9] E McKendrick, *Goode on Commercial Law* (4th edn, 2010), p. 660.

[10] H Beale, M Bridge, L Gullifer, E Lomnicka, *The Law of Security and Title-Based Financing* (2nd edn, 2012), at [1.01].

Code (UCC) and a number of common law jurisdictions,[11] English law retains its focus on the form of the agreement rather than its function. As a result, it only provides for the registration of security interests. Title-retention agreements are not subject to registration.[12] This discrepancy has been the subject of academic criticism,[13] yet as at the time of writing no such requirement is imposed.

The Law Commission of England and Wales initially was supportive of registering title-retention agreements. The main argument in favour of the registration was that "it may be difficult for other creditors or buyers dealing with a company to find out which goods on a company's premises belong to it, and which still belong to the supplier under a conditional sale, hire-purchase agreement or finance lease".[14] The Commission even suggested that operating leases of over 1 year, which do not have a security purpose, should be registered in order to enhance the transparency of transactions over assets.[15] Yet, the Commission in its final recommendations backed down from their initial proposal following the lukewarm reception of the suggestion by financiers and practitioners who expressed concerns about the complexity of introducing such a scheme.

The irony of this (non) development is that English law is left with an uncertain system. The requirement to register (or not) the relevant interest depends on the characterisation of the agreement in question. Most structures will be taken at face value. Yet, English courts tend to take a good look into sophisticated structures of sale and lease/buy-back agreements or retention of title clauses of goods (e.g. proceeds of sale clauses or product clauses). Their main concern is to check whether the structure in question contains the incidents of security, the most important of which are: (i) the debtor's right to redeem the asset in question when the obligation is discharged (equity of redemption); (ii) accounting any profit achieved by the creditor upon realising the asset in question to the debtor; and (iii) not discharging the liability of the debtor for any shortfall upon the realisation of the asset in question.[16] When they are convinced that this is the case, English courts will re-characterise them as security interests which are subject to registration. By re-characterising them, courts in essence devoid them of any meaning, since the deadline for registration of the re-characterised security interests (21 days from the day of its creation) most probably would have passed.[17]

---

[11] For references see E McKendrick, *Goode on Commercial Law* (4th edn, 2010), p. 660, note 45.

[12] With the exception of two voluntary schemes of registration which are irrelevant for the purposes of this report.

[13] See E McKendrick, *Goode on Commercial Law* (4th edn, 2010), pp. 717–718.

[14] The Law Commission of England and Wales, *Company Security Interests. A Consultative Report* (2004), at [1.10].

[15] *Ibid.*, at [2.96].

[16] For English case law and analysis on the issue of characterisation see H Beale, M Bridge, L Gullifer, E Lomnicka, *The Law of Security and Title-Based Financing* (2nd edn, 2012), at [4.13]ff and M Bridge, L Gullifer, G McMeel, S Worthington, *The Law of Personal Property* (2013), at [7–102] ff.

[17] See below under "Registration or Registrations?".

In that respect, English law has a circular structure: it retains the formal division between security interests and "quasi-security" interests and it treats them differently with respect to registration. Yet, at the same time it looks into the substance of the agreement to decide its proper characterisation and consequently whether it shall be registered or not.

As such, English law falls into the category of States which treat conditional sellers and lessors of aircraft as full owners (subject to the qualifications referred to in the previous paragraph). For the purposes of Art. 2(2) of the Convention, English law differentiates among interests granted by the chargor under a security agreement [Art. 2(2)(a)],[18] interests vested in a person who is a conditional seller under a title reservation agreement [Art. 2(2)(b)][19] and interests vested in a person who is the lessor under the leasing agreement [Art. 2(2)(c)].[20]

In the first category, English law classifies mortgages or charges over an aircraft to secure a loan. In the second category, English law classifies hire-purchase agreements, conditional sales agreements and finance leases. In broad terms, in all three structures, the owner/seller/lessor retains title over the aircraft. What differentiates the first two structures is that in hire-purchases the hirer has the option to purchase the aircraft upon payment of the price,[21] whereas in conditional sales the buyer is bound to purchase it upon payment of the price.[22] Finance leases usually entail the leasing out of the aircraft for the entirety of its life to the lessee. The lessor retains nominal ownership with the lessee being the de facto owner and enjoying "substantially all the risks and rewards associated with the ownership of the asset".[23] Finance leases can take many forms with varied provisions on the rights of the lessee to create property rights on the leased aircraft or the fate of any residual value of

---

[18] Reg. 6(1) The International Interests in Aircraft Equipment (Cape Town Convention) Regulations 2015.

[19] Ibid.

[20] Ibid.

[21] See H Beale, M Bridge, L Gullifer, E Lomnicka, *The Law of Security and Title-Based Financing* (2nd edn, 2012), at [7.28] for analysis and case law on what a true option to purchase is.

[22] The characterisation of a structure as a hire-purchase or a conditional sale is also important for the application of s. 25(1) of the Sale of Goods Act 1979. A buyer under a conditional sale agreement will be a "buyer in possession" under the Act, whereas a hirer will not have this status until it exercises its option to purchase the aircraft. This distinction has implications for their respective rights vis-à-vis third parties: a buyer has the power to pass good title on the aircraft to a third party, whereas the hirer does not enjoy the same power unless it exercises the option to purchase. The said right of the buyer under a conditional sale agreement has been curtailed by statutory intervention, namely the Consumer Credit Act 1974, which essentially puts him in the position of a hirer with respect to passing title to a third party. Yet, the Act applies to transactions involving consumers and as such its importance in the context of the present report is limited.

[23] SSAP21 Accounting for Leases and Hire Purchase Contracts (1984). For that reason the aircraft is recorded on the balance sheet of the lessee, see D Mcclean (ed), *Shawcross and Beaumont on Air law* (2015), at IV[40].

the aircraft.[24] For the purposes of our discussion, their legal classification depends on the availability of the option to purchase the aircraft: (i) if the lease contains no such option/obligation, it will qualify as a contract of hire; (ii) if it contains an option to purchase the aircraft, it will qualify as a hire-purchase; and (iii) if it contains an obligation to purchase the aircraft, it will qualify as a conditional sale.[25]

In the third category, English law includes operational leases of aircraft. These do not have a security or a "quasi-security" function, since they transfer possessory rights (as distinguished from proprietary rights) over the aircraft for a portion of its life.[26] The implications of this feature of operating leases were recently explained by Hamblen J.:

> …[the lessor] retains a very real interest in the Aircraft themselves, including their proper maintenance, the extent of their use, their condition, and their rental and resale value. Possession of the Aircraft will revert to it at a time when the bulk of their economic life is still to run…[The lessor] therefore retains many of the risks and rewards of ownership.[27]

In that respect, the rental is calculated on the basis of "the prevailing supply and demand for aircraft of this type" rather than on "recouping the cost of the Aircraft together with interest and profit" as is the case with finance leases.[28]

Under English law it is only the interests that fall into the first category of Art. 2(2) of the Cape Town Convention that require registration. Conditional sales, hire-purchases, finance leases and operating leases of aircraft are not subject to any compulsory or voluntary registration regime, unless they are judicially re-characterised as security instruments. The implementation of the Cape Town Convention into English law by virtue of The International Interests in Aircraft Equipment (Cape Town Convention) Regulations 2015 increases its transparency, since all said interests are subject to registration in the International Registry.[29] Furthermore, it provides for the "back-door" realisation of the initial proposals of the Law Commission on the registration of "quasi-security" interests and operating leases, albeit in the limited context of aircraft finance.

---

[24] See H Beale, M Bridge, L Gullifer, E Lomnicka, *The Law of Security and Title-Based Financing* (2nd edn, 2012), at [7.43]ff and E McKendrick, *Goode on Commercial Law* (4th edn, 2010), p.767 ff.

[25] H Beale, M Bridge, L Gullifer, E Lomnicka, *The Law of Security and Title-Based Financing* (2nd edn, 2012), at [7.45].

[26] See D Hanley, *Aircraft Operating Leasing: A Legal and Practical Analysis in the Context of Public and Private International Air Law* (2012), Ch. 2 and *Celestial Aviation Trading 71 Limited v Paramount Airways Private Ltd* [2010] EWHC 185 (Comm), [2011] 1 All ER (Comm) 259, [2011] 1 Lloyd's Rep. 9.

[27] *Celestial Aviation Trading 71 Limited v Paramount Airways Private Ltd* [2010] EWHC 185 (Comm), [2011] 1 All ER (Comm) 259, [2011] 1 Lloyd's Rep. 9, at [54].

[28] *Ibid.*

[29] Regs. 6(1), 10 and Schedule 3 of The International Interests in Aircraft Equipment (Cape Town Convention) Regulations 2015, Art. 16(a) of the Cape Town Convention.

4.2.2 Registration or Registrations?

Professor McKendrick gave a critical snapshot of the registration system under English law:

[t]he present position with respect to registration/filing as a method of perfection is profoundly unsatisfactory on account of the multiplicity of registers, the varying, and sometimes uncertain effects of registration, and the lack of rational policy underlying the sanctions for non-registration. Several of the registers attract their own priority rules; and certain types of security interest are registrable in more than one register.[30]

Holders of security interests over aircraft are no strangers to the problems described by Professor McKendrick. Their source is the dual-registration requirement under both the Register of Aircraft Mortgages and the Register of Company Charges, the former being a specialist register of assets and the latter a register of debtors.

The UK Register of Aircraft Mortgages was created by the Mortgaging of Aircraft Order 1972.[31] It came into force on 1st October 1972 and since then the UK Civil Aviation Authority (CAA) administers it. The Order provides that only UK-registered aircraft together with their spare parts can be made security for a loan or other valuable consideration that is eligible for registration.[32] However, this broad statement is misleading, since the Order restricts the security interests over aircraft that are eligible for registration: it limits the ambit of the Register to (legal and equitable) mortgages over aircraft together with their spare parts, as well as to fixed charges over the same, while explicitly excluding floating charges over them.[33] In effect, this means that a mortgage covering spare engines or other spare parts alone is not eligible for registration. Having said that, it is arguable that "where the charge is over both a registered aircraft and a stock of spares of it, the charge is within the scheme even though the provisions that relate to the spares create a floating charge over them".[34] Opinion suggesting the contrary exists.[35]

The effects of registration of a mortgage at the Register of Aircraft Mortgages have been succinctly described as follows:

---

[30] E McKendrick, *Goode on Commercial Law* (4th edn, 2010), pp. 692–693 with notes omitted.

[31] See Arts 1 and 4 of the Mortgaging of Aircraft Order 1972, SI 1972/1268.

[32] Art. 3. Registration of a mortgage under the Order is not compulsory. Yet, the draconian effect of non-registration on its priority makes registration *de facto* compulsory. A mortgage over a non-UK registered aircraft "remains possible in law", yet it will not be subject to the Order that will inevitably impair its priority in D Mcclean (ed), *Shawcross and Beaumont on Air law* (2015), at IV[46].

[33] Art. 2(2) and 4(1). The term "charge" in the Order is used to "include charge 'within mortgage'" in H Beale, M Bridge, L Gullifer, E Lomnicka, *The Law of Security and Title-Based Financing* (2nd edn, 2012), at [14–51].

[34] H Beale, M Bridge, L Gullifer, E Lomnicka, *The Law of Security and Title-Based Financing* (2nd edn, 2012), at [14–51].

[35] J Edmunds, "Mortgages of Aircraft" in I Davies (ed), *Security Interests in Mobile Equipment* (2002), p. 145, 148.

first, the registered aircraft mortgage will take priority over all other mortgages and charges save for prior registered mortgages (or priority notices current in respect of them)…;second, all persons are deemed to have express notice of all facts appearing on the register although the registration of a mortgage does not contribute evidence of its validity; third, registered mortgages are not affected by or subject to the terms of the Bill of Sales Act 1878 and 1882; last, the CAA will indemnify any person suffering loss by reason of any error or omission on the register or of any inaccuracy in the copy of an entry in the register.…[36]

In that respect, the following considerations are relevant to our report:

1. entering the mortgage in the Register of Aircraft Mortgages gives notice of the interest and preserves its priority[37];
2. the said entry is not an element of its constitution, since the Order expressly provides that "the registration of a mortgage shall not be evidence of its validity".[38] This further means that any buyer of the aircraft "will not be able to take free of an equitable mortgage or charge over it as the bona fide purchaser of a legal estate for value and without notice"; [39]
3. the registrar does not guarantee that the registered information reflects the true state of the titles. Furthermore, the Order provides that any person who "makes any statement which he knows to be false in a material particular, or recklessly makes any statement which is false in a material particular" is guilty of a criminal offence.[40] However, the registrar is responsible for its own errors. The Order provides that the registrar will indemnify anyone who suffers loss as a result of an "error or omission in the Register or of any inaccuracy in a copy of an entry in the Register",[41] unless she/he has contributed to the loss fraudulently or "has derived title from a person so committing fraud".[42]

With respect to priorities, the Order creates the following rules:

1. A registered mortgage enjoys priority over any unregistered mortgage or charge on the same aircraft[43];
2. Priority between two (or more) registered mortgages on the same aircraft is determined on a first come, first served basis: it will depend on "the times at which they were respectively entered in the Register"[44];

---

[36] *Ibid.*, p. 152.

[37] Art. 14(1).

[38] Art. 13.

[39] H Beale, M Bridge, L Gullifer, E Lomnicka, *The Law of Security and Title-Based Financing* (2nd edn, 2012), at [14–59].

[40] Art. 17.

[41] Art. 18(1).

[42] Art. 18(2)(a).

[43] Art. 14(1).

[44] Art. 14(2).

3. Priority notices are registrable in the Register,[45] with the Order providing for a period of 14 days for them to be converted into proper mortgages and to be registered.[46] This registered mortgage will take priority retrospectively from the date of registration of the priority notice[47];
4. A mortgage that is registered in the knowledge that there is an earlier unregistered mortgage enjoys priority over the earlier one as per the rules above.[48]
5. The Order creates an exception to the aforementioned priority rules: possessory liens for unpaid work undertaken on the aircraft, as well as rights of detention of the aircraft deriving from an Act of Parliament,[49] enjoy priority over any registered mortgages or charges that are created or registered either before or after them.[50] It is noted that possessory liens and rights of detention are not registrable under this scheme.

Registration of the mortgage at the Register of Aircraft Mortgages is not the end of the story. So long as the mortgage or the charge is created by a company or a limited liability partnership, registration of the interest at the Register of Companies Charges under the Companies Act 2006 is also required. The Register of Company Charges, unlike the Register of Aircraft Mortgages, is a debtor-based registration scheme. The scheme went through a major amendment in 2013 (with effect from 6 April 2013) and as a result references to both the new (post-2013 scheme) and the old regime (pre-2013 scheme) are made where appropriate.[51] Under both regimes a charge on an aircraft created by a company registered in England, Wales or Northern Ireland (under the pre-2013 scheme) or created by a company registered in the UK (under the post-2013 scheme) requires registration, otherwise it is void against a liquidator, an administrator or a debtor of the company.[52] The term charge as used in both the pre-2013 and the post-2013 schemes of the Companies Act 2006 is wide enough to encompass mortgages and charges that are registrable in the Register of Aircraft Mortgages. The pre-2013 scheme contains a list of charges that shall be registered, which it expressly refers to charges on aircraft, while including floating

---

[45] Art. 5(1).

[46] Art. 14(2)(ii).

[47] Art. 14(2)(ii).

[48] Art. 14(4).

[49] Such as the fleet liens the CAA enjoys for unpaid route charges under s. 83 of the Transport Act 2000 and certain airports enjoy for unpaid charges under s. 88 of the Civil Aviation Act 1982. See also *Global Knafaim Leasing Ltd v Civil Aviation Authority* [2010] EWHC 1348 (Admin), [2011] 1 Lloyd's Rep. 324.

[50] Art. 14(5).

[51] The Companies Act 2006 (Amendment of Part 25) Regulations 2013, SI 2013/600, repealed ss. 860 to 892 of the Companies Act 2006 and replaced them with ss. 859A to 859Q. Relevant interests created on or after 1 April 2013 are governed by the new regime, with interests created before that day governed by the old regime.

[52] s. 859H(3) of the post-2013 registration scheme and s. 874 of the pre-2013 registration scheme.

charges that are expressly excluded from the Register of Aircraft Mortgages.[53] The post-2013 scheme does not contain a list. Instead, it provides that all charges,[54] as defined by the Act,[55] created by a company in the UK shall be registered, subject to three exceptions.[56]

Under the pre-2013 scheme it was the duty of the company/debtor to register the charge within 21 days beginning with the day after the date of creation of the charge.[57] Any failure to do so, opened up the company and its officers, who were in default, to criminal liability.[58] Most importantly for the purposes of this report, the failure to register the charge rendered it void vis-à-vis the liquidator or the administrator of the company, as well as a creditor of the company.[59] As such, "if a charge has not been registered in time…and the company becomes insolvent, the liquidator may take the property that would been subject to the charge for the benefit of the creditors generally".[60]

Under the post-2013 scheme the company/debtor is under no duty to register the charge, as the threat of criminal liability has been eliminated. However, failure to register the charge within 21 days of the date of its creation renders it void vis-à-vis the liquidator, the administrator or the creditor of the company, as per the pre-2013 regime. Essentially, non-registration of the charge converts its holder to an unsecured creditor.[61]

Under both schemes, failure to register the mortgage with the Register of Company Charges has a detrimental effect on its registration in the Register of Aircraft Mortgages. Registering a mortgage over an aircraft in the Register of

---

[53] For the list of charges see s. 860(7) Companies Act 2006 which includes the following: (a) a charge on land or any interest in land, other than a charge for any rent or other periodical sum issuing out of land; (b)a charge created or evidenced by an instrument which, if executed by an individual, would require registration as a bill of sale; (c)a charge for the purposes of securing any issue of debentures; (d)a charge on uncalled share capital of the company;(e)a charge on calls made but not paid; (f)a charge on book debts of the company; (g)a floating charge on the company's property or undertaking; **(h)a charge on a ship or aircraft, or any share in a ship** [emphasis added]; (i)a charge on goodwill or on any intellectual property.

[54] s. 859A (1) Companies Act 2006.

[55] s. 859A (7) Companies Act 2006 provides that a "charge includes a mortgage; a standard security; assignation in security, and any other right in security constituted under the law of Scotland, including any heritable security, but not including a pledge".

[56] The exceptions in s. 859A(6) are the following: a charge in favour of a landlord on a cash deposit given as a security in connection with the lease of land; a charge created by a member of Lloyd's [within the meaning of the Lloyd's Act 1982(3)] to secure its obligations in connection with its underwriting business at Lloyd's; and a charge excluded from the application of this section by or under any other Act.

[57] s. 870 Companies Act 2006.

[58] s. 860 (4) – (6) Companies Act 2006.

[59] s. 874 Companies Act 2006.

[60] H Beale, M Bridge, L Gullifer, E Lomnicka, *The Law of Security and Title-Based Financing* (2nd edn, 2012), at [10–32].

[61] M Bridge, L Gullifer, G McMeel, S Worthington, *The Law of Personal Property* (2013), at [14–090].

Aircraft Mortgages but not in the Register of Company Charges will render the mortgage void vis-à-vis any creditor, liquidator or administrator of the company. This omission will detrimentally affect its priority:

> if a first mortgage was duly registered at Companies House but the second one is not...the second mortgage will be void against the first creditor. If a first one was not duly registered at Companies House but only on the aircraft mortgage register, it will be void against the second mortgage provided that the second one was duly registered at Companies House. When neither has been registered in time, it seems likely that priority will depend on the date of registration on the aircraft mortgage register.[62]

At the same time, registration of the mortgage in both registers gives priority over floating charges even when they contain a negative pledge clause that is known to the subsequent mortgagee (floating charges are not registrable in the aircraft register, but they are to be registered in the companies register).[63] Considering that floating charges (or mortgages) over spare parts alone are not registrable in the Register of Aircraft Mortgages, any mortgage over this aircraft and its spare parts (which are registrable) would take priority over the floating charge.[64]

The ratification of the Cape Town Convention increases the transparency of English law because it creates a focal point for registrations and the ascertainment of priorities: (i) both security and "quasi-security" interests over aircraft and engines (alone) are registrable; and (ii) the existence of a single register simplifies the priority rules increasing the confidence of financiers and buyers in the quality of the transaction in question. There have been arguments in England that the pre-Cape Town system of registration of mortgages over aircraft works well and as such there is no need to change it.[65] It is true that overall the system works, but this is mostly the result of the sophistication and experience of the parties and their lawyers. However, it is submitted that its structure and organisation is complicated and not all-embracing with ample space for the Cape Town Convention to improve it.

---

[62] H Beale, M Bridge, L Gullifer, E Lomnicka, *The Law of Security and Title-Based Financing* (2nd edn, 2012), at [14–57]. The provisions of the Companies Act on the Register of Companies Charges, unlike the Mortgaging of Aircraft Order 1972, do not contain an express provision on constructive notice. In a case where the interest is registered in the Register of Companies Charges but not in the Register of Aircraft Mortgages the answer to the question whether a bona fide buyer of the aircraft is bound by the interest depends on the effect of registration: does the registration provide constructive notice to all the world or only to those who were reasonably expected to search the Register of Companies Charges. The prevailing view is the latter which means that the answer will depend on whether it is expected from the buyer in question to search the Register of Companies Charges. For a thorough analysis of constructive notice in the context of the Register of Companies Charges see H Beale, M Bridge, L Gullifer, E Lomnicka, *The Law of Security and Title-Based Financing* (2nd edn, 2012), at [12.04]ff. For the position under the Register of Aircraft Mortgages see above note 33.

[63] *Ibid.*, at [14.58].

[64] *Ibid.*

[65] See Department for Business, Innovation and Skills, *"Call for evidence: full list of responses. Convention on International Interests in Mobile Equipment and Protocol thereto on Matters Specific to Aircraft Equipment"* (2010), especially the response of Machins Solicitors.

Having said that, the UK Register of Aircraft Mortgages will remain open following the implementation of the Cape Town Convention into English law. Firstly, there is no compulsory requirement to register an international interest and parties might still opt for the domestic solution.[66] Secondly, Reg. 23 of the International Interests in Aircraft Equipment (Cape Town Convention) Regulations 2015 provides that "[a]ny additional remedies available in accordance with the applicable law…may be exercised to the extent that they are not inconsistent with provisions… under these Regulations or the Cape Town Convention". In that respect, retaining the UK Register is essential "if creditors wish to have access to remedies which are available under domestic UK law for domestic interests (which may or may not also be international interests under the Cape Town Convention), domestic law requirements in connection with those interests (including perfection and/or registration requirements) need to continue to be satisfied".[67] Furthermore, the International Interests in Aircraft Equipment (Cape Town Convention) Regulations 2015 provide that s. 859A of the Companies Act 2006 on the Register of Companies Charges "is not to apply to a charge which is an international interest", releasing *prima facie* the parties from the said additional domestic registration. However, a note of caution has already been raised: "if the security agreement creates a charge which would usually have been registrable under section 859A in any case, that charge should continue to be registered with Companies House in the usual way irrespective of whether or not it is also an international interest. This is important for two reasons: (a) failure to register a registrable charge with Companies House means not only that the charge is void as against an insolvency officer as a matter of domestic English law but it also means that the underlying debt secured by that charge becomes immediately repayable and (b) dual registration enables the chargee to have access to both Cape Town Convention remedies and any applicable domestic UK law remedies".[68]

4.3 Enforcement of Interests

One of the main reasons behind the popularity of English law is its commercial pragmatism in enforcing both security and "quasi-security" interests over aircraft. As a general comment, English law provides for few formalities, supports "self-help" remedies and in principle respects the contractual arrangements of the parties.

---

[66] Department for Business, Innovation and Skills, *"The International Interests in Aircraft Equipment (Cape Town Convention) Regulations 2015. Draft Guidance"* (2015), at [25].

[67] White & Case, "UK Ratification of the Cape Town Convention" (2015) available at http://www.whitecase.com/publications/article/uk-ratification-cape-town-convention (last accessed 23 March 2016).

[68] *Ibid.*

4.3.1   Security Interests

With respect to security interests proper, English law provides for four main methods of enforcement, namely (re)possession of the asset, sale of the asset, foreclosure and appointment of a receiver. Due to space constraints, our focus will be on the enforcement of mortgages by repossession, sale and foreclosure.

Unlike Art. 3 of the Cape Town Convention, English law does not impose on the mortgagee an overarching duty "to exercise its remedies in a commercially reasonable manner or, indeed, to exercise them at all".[69] In an often quoted extract Sir Donald Nicholls VC provided a succinct analysis of what is expected from a mortgagee:

> a mortgagee can sit back and do nothing. He is not obliged to take steps to realise his security. But if he does take steps to exercise his rights over his security, common law and equity alike have set bounds to the extent to which he can look after himself and ignore the mortgagor's interests. In the exercise of his rights over his security the mortgagee must act fairly towards the mortgagor. His interest in the property has priority over the interest of the mortgagor, and he is entitled to proceed on that footing. He can protect his own interest, but he is not entitled to conduct himself in a way which unfairly prejudices the mortgagor.[70]

Strictly speaking, a legal mortgagee, being the owner of the legal estate, has the right "to possession at any time, irrespective of default on the mortgagor's part, unless the parties have agreed otherwise".[71] Parties will invariably contract out, expressly or by implication, of this broad right and provide in their agreement for the right of the mortgagee to (re)possess the asset upon the default of the mortgagor. This broad right does not extend to equitable mortgages where an express provision is required for the equitable mortgagee to repossess the aircraft upon the mortgagor's default without a court's order or without appointing a receiver.[72] Judicial opinion supporting the right of the equitable mortgagee to (re)possess the asset in the absence of an express contractual provision exists, but it is submitted that it is a minority. In its absence (re)possession can take place by appointing a receiver.[73] Under a legal mortgage (with or without an express provision) or an equitable mortgage (with an express provision) (re)possession can take place without a court's order, provided that the aircraft "can be seized without entry on to the premises of

---

[69] S Saidova, "The Cape Town Convention: repossession and sale of charged aircraft objects in a commercially reasonable manner" [2013] LMCLQ 180, 193.

[70] *Palk v Mortgage Services Funding plc* [1993] 2 All ER 481,486 per Sir Donald Nicholls VC endorsing the opinion of Lord Templeman in *China and South Sea Bank Ltd v Tan* [1989] 3 All ER 839, 842.

[71] *Western Bank Ltd v Kurt Schindler* [1976] 2 All ER 393, 396 per Buckley LJ endorsing *Four-Maids Limited v Dudley Marshall (Properties) Limited* [1957] 2 All ER 35, [1957] Ch 317.

[72] M Bridge, L Gullifer, G McMeel, S Worthington, *The Law of Personal Property* (2013), at [18–007].

[73] H Beale, M Bridge, L Gullifer, E Lomnicka, *The Law of Security and Title-Based Financing* (2nd edn, 2012), at [18.33] with references to relevant case law.

the debtor".[74] Otherwise, the consent of the debtor or a court's order is required. If the cooperation of the debtor is not forthcoming, resort to the courts is also necessary.

Upon (re)possessing the asset what are the duties of the mortgagee? Lightman J applied the principles advanced by Sir Donald Nicholls VC and gave a concise response: "If the mortgagee takes possession, he becomes the manager of the charged property…He thereby assumes a duty to take reasonable care of the property secured…; and this requires him to be active in protecting and exploiting the security, maximising the return, but without taking undue risks…".[75]

Taking reasonable care of the asset is the beginning of the story with the inevitable question then arising: how do English courts interpret the duty of the mortgagee in possession to "protect and exploit the security, maximise the return"? Professor Beale et al reviewed numerous authorities and provided an accurate description of the current state of the law:

> a duty to use any income arising from the possession of the assets to reduce the amount due from the mortgagor, and any profit made must be strictly accounted for, although the mortgagee can set off against the income from the assets any expenses in taking and keeping possession…[it] is also under a duty to preserve and take reasonable care of the property [and] it will be liable for failure to obtain a reasonable income if this is due to wilful default, but…it is not liable to account for profits made by reason of possession of the mortgaged assets if the profits are not income generated by the assets themselves.[notes omitted][76]

As long as the mortgagee comes into possession of the asset in question, common law gives her/him the power to sell the asset in question upon the mortgagor's default without obtaining a court order.[77] The prevailing view is that an equitable mortgagee does not have the power to sell the asset without the court's intervention.[78]

It is submitted that s. 101(1) of the Law of Property Act 1935, which is applicable to mortgages made by deed,[79] gives both a legal and an equitable mortgagee the power "to sell…the mortgaged property…by public auction or by private contract" without the court's intervention. S. 103 of the Law of Property Act 1935 curtails this broad power by providing that it should be exercised (i) 3 months upon serving a notice requiring payment of the outstanding money on the mortgagor(s); or (ii) when interest under the mortgage has not been paid for over 2 months; or (iii) when the mortgagor has breached a condition of the mortgage deed that is not related to the payment of the mortgage money or interest. It is common practice for the parties

---

[74] E McKendrick, *Goode on Commercial Law* (4th edn, 2010), p. 680.

[75] *Silven Properties Ltd v Royal Bank of Scotland plc* [2003] EWCA Civ 1409, [2004] 4 All ER 484, at [13] per Lightman J.

[76] H Beale, M Bridge, L Gullifer, E Lomnicka, *The Law of Security and Title-Based Financing* (2nd edn, 2012), at [18.39].

[77] *Ibid.*, at [18.42] with references to case law.

[78] E McKendrick, *Goode on Commercial Law* (4th edn, 2010), p. 681.

[79] The prevailing opinion is that ss. 101 ff apply to personal property courtesy of s. 205(1)(xx).

to exclude the application of s. 103 in their agreement, as per the contractual freedom granted by s. 101(4) of the Law of Property Act 1935.

In any case, the parties are free to include express provisions in their agreement on the power of the mortgagee to sell the asset that will modify the common law, as well as the statutory powers.

Like the right to (re)possess, the mortgagee's right of sale is subject to the general principles pronounced by Sir Donald Nicholls VC in *Palk v Mortgage Services Funding plc*. Lightman J applied these principles in the context of the right of sale:

> In default of provision to the contrary in the mortgage, the power is conferred upon the mortgagee by way of bargain by the mortgagor for his own benefit and he has an unfettered discretion to sell when he likes to achieve repayment of the debt which he is owed... A mortgagee is at all times free to consult his own interests alone whether and when to exercise his power of sale...The mortgagee's decision is not constrained by reason of the fact that the exercise or non-exercise of the power will occasion loss or damage to the mortgagor...It does not matter that the time may be unpropitious and that by waiting a higher price could be obtained: he is not bound to postpone in the hope of obtaining a better price....[80]

Assuming the mortgagee decides to go ahead with the sale of the asset, she/he has the duty to take reasonable care to achieve a proper price;[81] proper price is equated with the "the true market value of the mortgaged property" at the day the decision was made.[82] English courts are in general reluctant to set overarching rules on the "informed judgment" of the mortgagee preferring a case by case approach.[83] Having said that, courts have set a few principles over the years with the burden of proof resting on the mortgagor to prove a breach, which in practice is a not such an easy task:

> [t]he duty includes drawing the sale to the attention of available buyers, and drawing the attention of potential buyers to all the features of the asset that affected its value...However, the duty will depend on the facts of the case, and a mortgagee will not be liable unless he is plainly 'on the wrong side of the line'. The mere fact that a higher price might have been obtained does not mean that there is a breach, if the price is a 'proper price'. There is also no duty to improve, as oppose to preserve, the assets prior to marketing them. [notes omitted][84]

Inevitably, English law would treat any sale of the asset to the mortgagee himself as void on policy grounds.[85] Yet, sale of the asset by the mortgagee to a connected

---

[80] *Silven Properties Ltd v Royal Bank of Scotland plc* [2003] EWCA Civ 1409, [2004] 4 All ER 484, at [14] per Lightman J.

[81] *Downsview Nominees Ltd v First City Corporation* [1993] 3 All ER 626, 637 per Lord Templeman endorsing *Cuckmere Brick Co Ltd v Mutual Finance Ltd* [1971] 2 All ER 633 and being endorsed by *Yorkshire Bank Plc v Hall* [1999] 1 WLR 1713 and *Den Norske Bank ASA v Acemex Management Co Ltd* [2003] EWCA Civ 1559.

[82] *Cuckmere Brick Co Ltd v Mutual Finance Ltd* [1971] 2 All ER 633, 646 per Salmon LJ.

[83] *Michael and others v Miller and others* [2004] EWCA Civ 282, at [132] per Parker LJ.

[84] H Beale, M Bridge, L Gullifer, E Lomnicka, *The Law of Security and Title-Based Financing* (2nd edn, 2012), at [18.50].

[85] *Farrar v Farrars Ltd* [1888] 40 Ch D 395.

party, i.e. a party in which the mortgagee has an interest, such as shares, is permitted, but is subject to stricter rules. The burden of proof is reversed and it is for the mortgagee to show that "he acted fairly to the borrower and used his best endeavours to obtain the best price reasonably obtainable for the mortgaged property".[86] English courts look carefully into any conflicts of interests that is resolved in favour of the connected party. Caesar's wife must be above suspicion: "the facts must show that the desire to obtain the best price was given absolute preference over any desire than an associate should obtain a good bargain…The inevitable conflict of interest which arises on a sale to a close associate may be not only consciously but also unconsciously resolved in favour of the associate…".[87] It is submitted that seeking the court's approval prior to undertaking such sale is the best way forward.

What is the effect of selling the asset on priorities?

> Sale by a first mortgagee extinguishes the debtor's equity of redemption and overrides the second mortgage, which then attaches to any surplus proceeds of sale remaining after the first mortgage has taken what is due to him. Sale by a second mortgagee takes effect subject to the first mortgagee unless that is discharged from the proceeds of sale…If the proceeds of sale of the mortgaged property produce a surplus remaining after the first mortgage has taken what is due to him, the mortgagee is accountable for it to next ranking incumbrances, if there is one, or, if not, then to the debtor. Where the sale leaves a deficiency this remains governed by the express covenant for payment, which the mortgagee is entitled to enforce.[88]

Foreclosure is essentially the "termination of the…right to redeem by court order…The mortgagee may then treat the property as absolutely his, and is therefore entitled to keep all the proceeds of any sale, even where there is a surplus over and above the amount of the debt and the costs of disposal".[89] Courts regard this remedy with caution considering its drastic impact on the mortgagor; as such they will initially issue an interim order giving the mortgagor time to pay the outstanding amount and redeem the asset. Failing that, they will issue a final order foreclosing the asset in question. At any time before the order turning final the court has the power to order the sale of the asset. Foreclosure is rarely used any more since (i) the court controls the process which inevitably causes delays; and (ii) the mortgagee loses the right to go after the mortgagor for recovering any deficit between the value of the foreclosed asset and the secured liability. In that respect, Art. 9 of the Cape Town Convention provides for a less draconian and more balanced procedure to be followed.[90]

---

[86] *Tse Kwong Lam v Wong Chit Sen* [1983] 3 All ER 54, 59 per Lord Templeman.

[87] *Australia and New Zealand Banking v Bangadilly* (1978) 139 CLR 195, 201 per Jacobs.

[88] E McKendrick, *Goode on Commercial Law* (4th edn, 2010), p. 682.

[89] M Bridge, L Gullifer, G McMeel, S Worthington, *The Law of Personal Property* (2013), at [18–22].

[90] English law is also prepared to implement Art. IX of the Aircraft Protocol. Both the remedy of de-registration of the aircraft under a power of attorney and its export outside the jurisdiction were remedies already available under English law and according to one commentator exercised without problems, see P. Farrell, "England and Wales" in B. Crans and R. Nath (eds), *Aircraft repossession and enforcement. Practical Issues* (2009), p. 285, 324 ff.

Overall, Art. 8(1) and (2) of the Cape Town Convention will not come as a surprise to an English lawyer, since the "self-help" remedies in Art. 8(1), as well as the court's assistance envisaged in Art. 8(2) are all options available to a mortgagee in this jurisdiction.[91] At the same time, English courts have produced an elaborate and evolving line of case law over the years exploring the practicalities of enforcing the mortgagee's remedies following a default of the mortgagor. How to distribute the proceeds of sale and any surplus remaining has also been analysed extensively by English courts which in principle echo Arts 8(5) and (6) of the Cape Town Convention (with the exception of foreclosure in Art. 9).[92] What constitutes "a commercially reasonable manner" under the Cape Town Convention will almost certainly be tested before English courts.[93] It is submitted that this new requirement is not a cause of concern: one commentator has already argued that the duties of the mortgagee vis-à-vis the exercise of the remedies under English law "appear... to be similar to the one intended under the Convention".[94]

4.3.2   "Quasi-security" Interests

The owner of the asset under a title-retention agreement enjoys the following remedies subject to contractual arrangements: "he may retake the goods, resell them and normally claim any loss he has suffered as damages from the buyer...As [he] does not have a true 'security' interest, there is no question of the buyer having an equity of redemption and hence the seller can keep all the proceeds of sale of the goods"[notes omitted].[95] As per our discussion under Sect. 4.3.1 these remedies can be exercised on a "self-help" basis or upon the court's approval.

In all three title-retention agreements, the owner of the asset is required to demonstrate that the buyer/hirer/lessee has lost its right to possession. At common law, this would take place upon a repudiatory breach of the agreement which is accepted by the owner, essentially treating the agreement as at an end. English courts have found the following instances of repudiatory breaches in the context of title-retention devices: "...prolonged non-payment of rentals..., renouncing the agreement..., and

---

[91] Reg. 19 of the International Interests in Aircraft Equipment (Cape Town Convention) Regulations 2015.

[92] Reg. 19(6) and (7) of the International Interests in Aircraft Equipment (Cape Town Convention) Regulations 2015.

[93] Reg. 24 of the International Interests in Aircraft Equipment (Cape Town Convention) Regulations 2015.

[94] S Saidova, "The Cape Town Convention: repossession and sale of charged aircraft objects in a commercially reasonable manner" [2013] LMCLQ 180, 194. The author provides an illuminating analysis on the implications of the requirement of "commercial reasonableness" both domestically and at an international level.

[95] H Beale, M Bridge, L Gullifer, E Lomnicka, *The Law of Security and Title-Based Financing* (2nd edn, 2012), at [19.09] on conditional sales. The authors make similar statements at [19.23] on hire purchase and at [19.30] on finance lease.

non-punctual payment of an instalment where punctual payment is of the essence…
"[notes omitted].[96] Furthermore, in hire-purchases and finance leases, which are
essentially contracts of bailments, "any act that is inconsistent with the lessor/bail-
or's rights as such (for example a sale, pledge, or even just offering the goods for
sale) automatically terminates the bailment and vests the immediate right to possession in the lessor/bailor" [notes omitted].[97]

To avoid difficult questions whether the breach in question justifies termination
of the agreement or whether the owner has affirmed it, the parties make provision in
their agreements for a list of repudiatory breaches/events of default that give the
right to the owner to terminate the contract and exercise the remedies (see under
Sect. 4.3.3). Using the term repudiatory breach in the agreement to describe such
events is a misnomer, since the list usually includes events that strictly speaking
cannot be qualified as repudiatory breaches, such as the insolvency/bankruptcy of
the seller/hirer/lessee or the non-payment of one rental.[98]

It is important to note again that, unlike the holders of security interests, the
owner of the asset under a title-retention agreement is not required to account to the
buyer/hirer/lessee for any surplus from the sale of the asset. However, this common
law right is subject to the parties' contractual arrangements. The parties usually
insert clauses in their title-retention agreements permitting the owners to retain the
instalments paid by the buyer/hirer/lessor prior to their termination. Although it is
not settled beyond doubt, English courts have upheld the validity of such clauses
(especially in cases of hire-purchases and finance leases) and are in general reluctant to grant such relief to the buyer, since they do not want to interfere with the
contractual arrangement of the parties.[99] What they are prepared to do is to give the
buyer more time to fulfil his/her obligations under the agreement.

In that respect, Article 10 of the Cape Town Convention will not come as a surprise to an English lawyer.[100] Both remedies provided therein are available under
English law either on a "self-help" basis or following the court's approval.

4.3.3   Events of Default

Art. 11(1) of the Cape Town Convention which permits the parties to define the
events of default in their agreement is a provision that fits well into English law.[101]
English courts are in principle reluctant to interfere with the provisions agreed

---

[96] *Ibid.*, at [19.32] note 220.

[97] *Ibid.*, at [19.31].

[98] *Ibid.*, at [7.29] on conditional sale; at [7.38] on hire-purchases; and at [7.50] on finance leases.

[99] *Ibid.*, at [19.16] on conditional sales; at [19.28] on hire-purchases; and at [19.38] on finance
leases.

[100] Reg. 21 of the International Interests in Aircraft Equipment (Cape Town Convention) Regulations
2015.

[101] Reg. 18 of the International Interests in Aircraft Equipment (Cape Town Convention) Regulations
2015.

between commercial parties on the basis of freedom of contract, subject to issues of "illegality, incapacity, mistake, duress, misrepresentation, frustration and restraint of trade".[102]

What is the reason behind the non-interventionism of English courts to bargains struck in commercial contracts? The following often-quoted opinion of Chadwick LJ in *Watford Electronics v Sanderson CFL Ltd* sheds light on their rationale:

> Where experienced businessmen representing substantial companies of equal bargaining power negotiate an agreement, they may be taken to have had regard to the matters known to them. They should, in my view be taken to be the best judge of the commercial fairness of the agreement which they have made; including the fairness of each of the terms in that agreement. They should be taken to be the best judge on the question whether the terms of the agreement are reasonable. The court should not assume that either is likely to commit his company to an agreement which he thinks is unfair, or which he thinks includes unreasonable terms. Unless satisfied that one party has, in effect, taken unfair advantage of the other—or that a term is so unreasonable that it cannot properly have been understood or considered—the court should not interfere.[103]

Considering this extract, it is not surprising (or at least it is less surprising) that the parties are given considerable leeway in identifying the events that will permit the non-breaching party to terminate the contract[104]: "this right of termination may be exercisable upon a breach of contract by the other party (whether or not the breach would amount to a repudiation of the contract), or upon the occurrence or non-occurrence of a specified event other than breach, or simply at the will of the party upon whom the right is conferred."[105]

---

[102] Halsbury's Laws of England, *Contract* (5th edn, 2012), Vol 22, at [213] it is also stated that "the courts have sometimes intervened by way of the classification of terms, and by their interpretation of the parties' agreement, or the implication of terms...In addition, [they have employed equity rules, such as] promissory estoppel, specific performance, injunction, undue influence and the notion of unconscionable bargains".

[103] [2001] EWCA Civ 317, [2001] 1 All ER (Comm) 696, at [55].

[104] *Lombard North Central plc v Butterworth* [1987] 1 All ER 267 with references in p 272 to cases that go back to 1876.

[105] H Beale (ed), *Chitty on Contracts* (31st edn, 2013), at [22–048]. As to what constitutes a repudiatory breach, Professor Peel recently provided a brief analysis that fits well into our discussion: "As a matter of general law, a contract may be terminated in the following circumstances: (i) where the defendant is guilty of renunciation; (ii) where the defendant is guilty of a substantial failure to perform; and (iii) where the defendant is guilty of a breach of condition. A little elaboration is called for in relation to each of these circumstances and it is helpful to start with the last of them. The designation of a term as a condition must be understood in the context of the tripartite classification of the terms of a contract into conditions, warranties and innominate (or intermediate) terms. A condition is a term of the contract which, if breached, entitles the innocent party to terminate the contract. A warranty is a term of the contract which, if breached, entitles the party only to damages and not to terminate the contract. An innominate (or intermediate) term, as the name suggests, is neither a condition nor a warranty. Whether, if breached, it entitles the innocent party to terminate the contract depends upon the seriousness of the breach. It is in relation to innominate terms, therefore, that the right to terminate accrues on the basis of a substantial failure to perform. By contrast, there is no requirement that a breach of condition should also amount to a substantial failure to perform; all that is required for the right to terminate is that the term should amount to a condition and that it should have been breached. A term of a contract may be a condition as a result

Professor Peel recently provided an instructive analysis of the benefits and the pitfalls of using such clauses:

> ...it can avoid the uncertainty inherent in termination for a repudiatory breach, though whether it does so depends on the extent to which the relevant event can be identified with certainty. If satisfied, the contract may be terminated notwithstanding that the breach is only a minor one and does not amount to a substantial failure to perform. If the other party has some bargaining power, the potential harshness of a termination clause may be mitigated by stipulating for an opportunity to cure the breach so that termination is available only if the time allowed for a cure has expired, or the attempted cure fails to remedy the initial breach. The courts have also insisted on strict compliance with the requirements that must be met before an express power to terminate may be invoked and with any procedure which must be followed to effect termination. [notes omitted][106]

Having said that, the use of an event of default clause raises the following issues under English law:

1. does the use of such clause exclude the common law right to terminate the contract for a repudiatory breach? The answer is no, unless the clause, expressly or impliedly, excludes such right[107];
2. can the parties take the flexibility of English law to the extreme and include a blanket default clause which provides that the "breach of any of its obligations under the contract" entitles the non-breaching party to terminate the contract for any breach no matter how minor it is? The answer is no. In a blanket default clause the right to terminate will only accrue in the case of a repudiatory breach

---

of legislation, or judicial precedent, or by express or implied agreement of the parties...As for substantial failure to perform, it is often captured by a number of differently formulated tests: did the breach go to the root of the contract; did it substantially deprive the innocent party of what he bargained for; did it frustrate his purpose in making the contract? In simple terms, the question to be asked is whether the breach was sufficiently serious to justify termination of the contract. It is the breach and its effects which are relevant; not the nature of the term broken. Whether the breach reaches the necessary threshold is often a question of 'very great difficulty'. The defendant is guilty of renunciation where he has demonstrated by his words or conduct his intention not to perform the contract, either at all, or in some respect which goes to the root of the contract. It is clear that renunciation and substantial failure to perform can overlap, since the conduct upon which a plea of renunciation may be based is a failure to perform obligations which have already fallen for performance. But renunciation may also be relied upon to terminate on the basis of an entirely anticipatory breach, ie before the time for performance...[A]ll three bases of termination under the general law will be referred to...as termination for a 'repudiatory breach'" in E Peel, "The termination paradox" [2013] LMCLQ 519, 520–521. How English law on repudiatory breach is going to fit into Art. 11(2) of the Cape Town Convention which speaks of "substantial deprivation" will be a matter for consideration. The "substantial failure to perform" seems to be its equivalent from an English law perspective, with the two notions being conceptually close. Yet, the question remains whether renunciation and breach of condition will be good enough reasons to trigger default in the absence of express contractual provisions; with the breach of condition arguably qualifying as such.

[106] E Peel, "The termination paradox" [2013] LMCLQ 519, 522.

[107] H. Beale (ed), *Chitty on Contracts* (31st edn, 2013), at [22–048] with analysis on the implications of having both running in parallel.

of a contractual obligation,[108] unless clear wording to the contrary is used in the contract.[109] The main reason behind this decision is that such an interpretation "flouts business commonsense. A reasonable commercial person would understand [it]... as meaning that if either party shall in any respect fail or neglect to observe or perform any provision of the Agreement in a way that amounts to a repudiatory breach, or if an insolvency event arises, then the innocent party may terminate by giving notice."[110]; and

3. the notion of business common sense is regularly used by English courts as a tool of interpreting commercial contracts: "if detailed semantic and syntactical analysis of words in a commercial contract is going to lead to a conclusion that flouts business common sense, it must yield to business common sense".[111] Yet, this statement must be approached with caution, because English courts are reluctant to use the notion of business common sense as giving them the green light to rewrite commercial contracts[112]: The decision in *Co-operative Wholesale Society Ltd v National Westminster Bank plc* [1995] 1 EGLR 97 where the Court of Appeal upheld a clause that produced an "improbable commercial result... [because] it flowed from the unambiguous language of the clause" is always a tale of caution for the unwary.[113] However, if the wording of the clause is ambiguous, English court will not hesitate to opt for the interpretation that makes commercial sense. Recently, Lord Clarke, with whom all the Lords agreed, explained what the search for commercial sense entails:

> ...the ultimate aim of interpreting a provision in a contract, especially a commercial contract, is to determine what the parties meant by the language used, which involves ascertaining what a reasonable person would have understood the parties to have meant...[T]he relevant reasonable person is one who has all the background knowledge which would reasonably have been available to the parties in the situation in which they were at the time of the contract.[114]

---

[108] *Rice (T/A the Garden Guardian) v Great Yarmouth Borough Council* 2000 WL 823961 endorsed by *Dominion Corporate Trustees Ltd v Debenham Properties Ltd* [2010] EWHC 1193 (Ch) and H. Beale (ed), *Chitty on Contracts* (31st edn, 2013), at [22–048].

[109] *Looney v Trafigura Beheer BV* [2011] EWHC 125 (Ch), [2011] All E.R. (D) 17 (Feb) with comments in H Beale (ed), *Chitty on Contracts* (31st edn, 2013), at [22–048].

[110] *Dominion Corporate Trustees Ltd v Debenham Properties Ltd* [2010] EWHC 1193 (Ch) at [32] per Kitchin J.

[111] *Antaios Cia Naviera SA v Salen Rederierna AB (The Antaios)* [1985] AC 191, 201 per Lord Diplock.

[112] In *Co-operative Wholesale Society Ltd v National Westminster Bank plc* [1995] 1 EGLR 97 Hofmann LJ (as he then was) delivered a strong statement to that effect at p. 99: "[t]his robust declaration does not, however, mean that one can rewrite the language which the parties have used in order to make the contract conform to business common sense. But language is a very flexible instrument and, if it is capable of more than one construction, one chooses that which seems most likely to give effect to the commercial purpose of the agreement".

[113] *Rainy Sky SA v Kookmin Bank* [2011] UKSC 50, [2012] 1 All ER 1137, at [23] per Lord Clarke.

[114] *Ibid.*, at [14].

In that respect, the extensive contractual freedom granted to the parties by Art. 11 of the Cape Town Convention will not suffer from its ratification from the British Government. Instead, I believe that the strong preference of English courts in providing a pragmatic, commercially-oriented interpretation of ambiguous clauses, including events of default clauses, will only strengthen the aims of Art. 11. At the same time, the dominant role that the notion of business common sense plays in the interpretation of commercial contracts is an assurance that English courts will easily embrace the concept of "commercial reasonableness" in Art. 8 of the Cape Town Convention.[115]

Having said that, the Consumer Rights Act 2015 and the Unfair Contract Terms Act 1977 (as amended) have in principle the potential to restrict the contractual freedom of parties to define events of default clauses. However, their influence over the issues regulated in the Cape Town Convention and are the subject of this report is limited; considering also the purposes of this report a very short analysis will be provided herein.

The Consumer Rights Act 2015 came into force on 1 October 2015 and replaces, among others, the Unfair Terms in Consumer Contracts Regulations 1999 which implemented into English law the EC Directive on Unfair Terms,[116] and for the first time introduced into English law a test of fairness. The Act applies to contracts between "a trader and a consumer for the trader to supply goods, digital content or services".[117] The term consumer is defined as "an individual acting for purposes that are wholly or mainly outside that individual's trade, business, craft or profession". [118] The Act gives the power to the court to set aside a term "if, contrary to the requirement of good faith, it causes a significant imbalance in the parties' rights and obligations under the contract to the detriment of the consumer".[119] The restrictive definition of consumer does not leave much room for the application of the Act to the definition of events of default in the commercial context of our discussion.

The Unfair Contract Terms Act 1977 (as amended by the Consumer Rights Act 2015) subjects exclusions and limitation of liability clauses in business-to-business contracts[120] (and consumer-to-consumer contracts) to a reasonableness test, namely that the term is "a fair and reasonable one to be included having regard to the circumstances which were, or ought reasonably to have been, known to or in the contemplation of the parties when the contract was made".[121] The Act covers clauses

---

[115] Reg 24 of the International Interests in Aircraft Equipment (Cape Town Convention) Regulations 2015.

[116] Council Directive 93/13/EEC of 5 April 1993 on unfair terms in consumer contracts, OJ L 095, 21/04/1993.p. 29.

[117] s 1(1).

[118] s. 2(3).

[119] s. 62(4).

[120] ss. 1(3) and 14.

[121] s. 11(1). The Act also provides in its Schedule 2 guidelines for the application of the reasonableness test.

that exclude liability for negligence,[122] and/or liability arising in contract[123] and treats them in one of the following two ways: either they are outright unenforceable without checking their reasonableness (e.g. clauses excluding negligence for death or injury) or they are unenforceable subject to satisfying the reasonableness test (e.g. clauses excluding negligence for loss or damage other than death or injury).

Broad this scope as it is, the Act has three major restrictions with respect to our discussion:

1. It is applicable to clauses excluding or limiting liability not to the entirety of the agreement. Strictly speaking events of default clauses in commercial contracts do not qualify as such and they remain outside the scope of the Act. Yet, English courts tend to look into the substance rather than the form of the clause in question taking a broad approach as to what constitutes an exclusion clause courtesy of s. 13(1) which essentially expand the meaning of exclusion clause, e.g. covering clauses excluding the right to set-off, or reversing the burden the proof etc.[124] As such, the drafting of the events of default clause is of paramount importance to avoid having its terms evaluated under the Act;

2. In a business to business context English courts are still reluctant to fiddle with the parties' arrangements: "I am less enthusiastic about [the] intrusion [of the Act] into contracts between commercial parties of equal bargaining strength, who should generally be considered capable of being able to make contracts of their choosing and expect to be bound by their terms".[125] Still, when the question whether a clause in a commercial contract is reasonable arises, English courts are cautious to avoid disturbing the parties' arrangements:

   it should be much easier to establish that the clause is reasonable, especially if the clause is question is contained in a standard form which is generally accepted in the industry. This accords with the approach adopted in *Photo Production v Securicor* [1980] AC 827 [1980] 1 All ER 556, of non-interventionism and leaving it to the parties to allocate the risks and responsibility for insurance cover[126];

3. The Act does not apply to international supply contracts which are defined as "either...a contract of sale of goods or...one under or in pursuance of which the possession or ownership of goods passes; and it is made by parties whose places of business...are in the territories of different States".[127] The Act further provides

---

[122] s. 2.

[123] ss. 3, 6, 7.

[124] s. 13(1) provides that the Act prevents "(a)making the liability or its enforcement subject to restrictive or onerous conditions; (b)excluding or restricting any right or remedy in respect of the liability, or subjecting a person to any prejudice in consequence of his pursuing any such right or remedy; (c)excluding or restricting rules of evidence or procedure". For case law on application of s. 13(1) see H Beale (ed), *Chitty on Contracts* (31st edn, 2013), at [14–062].

[125] *Granville Oil & Chemicals Ltd v Davis Turner & Co Ltd* [2003] EWCA Civ 570, [2003] 1 All ER (Comm) 819, [2003] 2 Lloyd's Rep 356 at [31] per Tuckey LJ.

[126] J. Poole, *Contract Law* (11th edn, 2012), p.288.

[127] s. 26(1), (3).

that for a contract to fit into this description one of the following three conditions must be satisfied: "(a)the goods in question are, at the time of the conclusion of the contract, in the course of carriage, or will be carried, from the territory of one State to the territory of another; or (b)the acts constituting the offer and acceptance have been done in the territories of different States; or (c)the contract provides for the goods to be delivered to the territory of a State other than that within whose territory those acts were done.".[128]

This section was examined by the Court of Appeal in *Trident Turboprop (Dublin) Limited v First Flight Couriers Limited.*[129] The claimant, which was an Irish company, entered into two aircraft operating leases with the defendant who was an Indian company. The aircraft were intended to be used in India in the defendant's courier business. The leases provided for delivery of the aircraft to the defendant in the UK, but one of them was actually delivered in Sweden and the other one in the UK. The leases contained an exclusion of the claimant's liability for misrepresentation. The defendant stopped paying rent on the aircraft on the basis that they were unreliable and he argued that he had terminated the lease as a result of the claimant's misrepresentation regarding the quality of the aircraft; with the clause excluding the liability of the lessor being unenforceable under the Unfair Contract Terms Act 1977. The claimant sought summary judgment requesting the court to decide, among other things, whether the Act is inapplicable to the exclusion clause in question as a result of s. 26. The Court rightly held that s. 26(3) was satisfied since the operating leases "provided for possession of the aircraft to pass under them and were made by parties whose places of business were in the territories of different states".[130] With ss. 26(4)(b) and s. 26(4)(c) inapplicable, because the negotiations took place in England and the aircraft were to be delivered in England, the focus turned into s. 26(4)(a). The Court avoided a technical reading of the section and looked into the intentions of the parties: "if a person who carries on business abroad hires equipment from a supplier in this country in circumstances where both know that the intention is for it to be used abroad, the lease is one pursuant to which the goods will be carried from the territory of one state to the territory of another within the meaning of section 26(4)(a) and can sensibly be described as an international supply contract".[131] Yet, the question remained whether the phrase "goods carried" in the section is broad enough to encompass aircraft which are flown in a foreign land under their own power. The Court gave a positive reply: "I am unable to accept that Parliament intended to draw a distinction for this purpose between vehicles capable of moving under their own power and other goods. In my view the aircraft in this case were to be 'carried' from the United Kingdom to India within the meaning of subsection 4(a), despite the fact that it was the intention of [the defendant] to

---

[128] s. 26(4).

[129] [2009] EWCA Civ 290.

[130] *Ibid.*, at [25] per Moore-Bick LJ.

[131] *Ibid.*, at [28].

fly them under their own power".[132] Considering the popularity of such leasing arrangements, it becomes obvious that this finding limits the number of aircraft leases that would be subject to the Act.

4.4 Treatment of Security Interests Under Insolvency Procedures

One of the fundamental principles of English corporate insolvency law is that insolvency "does not affect the rights and remedies of those who own property in the possession of the company or who hold a security interest over all or any of its assets".[133] This statement is subject to qualifications on the basis of the insolvency procedure followed and the nature of the rights to be enforced.

A commentator recently noted that "the proceedings now most commonly encountered in the context of airline insolvencies are administration, liquidation and receivership".[134] Detailed treatment of insolvency procedures on property rights shall be sought elsewhere. The aim of this section is to provide a bird's eye view of the general principles of English law on the rights and duties of holders of security and "quasi-security" interests in administration and liquidation.

We analysed in Sect. 4.2.2 that failure to register the security interest with the Register of Company Charges (under both the pre- and post-2013 schemes) makes it void against a liquidator, an administrator, and a creditor of the company. In practice the failure has the following effects: "the liquidator may take the property that would have been subject to the charge for the benefits of the creditors generally. If the company is put into administration, the administrator, acting on behalf of the company, may deal with the property as if there were no charge over it.".[135]

On the assumption that the security interest is properly registered, the rights of its holder will very much depend on which insolvency procedure is followed. In administration, the enforcement of their interests over assets in the company's possession are subject to the consent of the administrator or the permission of the court;[136] the same applies in the case of title-retention agreements.[137] Enforcing the

---

[132] *Ibid.*, at [32]

[133] E McKendrick, *Goode on Commercial Law* (4th edn, 2010), p. 907.

[134] P. Farrell, "England and Wales" in B. Crans and R. Nath (eds), *Aircraft repossession and enforcement. Practical Issues* (2009), p. 285, 310.

[135] H Beale, M Bridge, L Gullifer, E Lomnicka, *The Law of Security and Title-Based Financing* (2nd edn, 2012), at [10–32].

[136] Insolvency Act 1986, Schedule B1, s. 43(2). The Act defines security interests to include "any mortgage, charge, lien or other security" in s. 248.

[137] Insolvency Act 1986, Schedule B1, s. 43(3). The Act speaks of hire-purchase agreements, but for the purposes of administration they are defined broadly to include conditional sale agreements, a chattel leasing agreements and retention of title agreements in Schedule B1, s 101. In *Bristol Airport plc v Powdrill* [1990] Ch. 744 the Court of Appeal extended the application of this principle to the right of certain airport authorities to detain and sell aircraft for unpaid airport charges under s. 88 of the Civil Aviation Act 1982.

interest without prior approval would make the holder liable to pay damages.[138]
What would a court look in an application to allow enforcement? Professor Bridge
et al provide a useful synopsis:

> [t]he legitimate interests of the secured or hire purchase creditors have to be balanced
> against those of the other creditors of the company, with greater weight normally being
> given to the former. If the applicant would otherwise suffer a significant loss, leave to
> enforce should normally be granted. Relevant considerations also include the financial posi-
> tion of the company in administration, the length of the administration, and the conduct of
> the applicant.[139]

In the question of how likely it is for the court or the administrator to grant such
a relief one commentator recently gave an illuminating response:

> the Lessor should bear in mind that administration is primarily a rescue procedure; accord-
> ingly it is unlikely to obtain the agreement of the administrator or the court to its overstep-
> ping the moratorium by seeking to enforce its Security Interest or contractual rights where
> to do so would be inconsistent with the objectives of the administration. A Lessor's power
> to detain, repossess and/or sell aircraft operated by a lessor in administration are, therefore,
> severely circumscribed.[140]

Restrictive as this arrangement is, it supports the statutory aims of the administration which have been explained by Sir Nicolas Browne-Wilkinson VC:

> ...It is of the essence of administration...that the business will continue to be carried on by
> the administrator. Such continuation of the business by the administrator requires that there
> should be available to him the right to use the property of the company, free from interfer-
> ence by creditors and others during the, usually short, period during which such administra-
> tion continues.[141]

Having said that, the administrator is not permitted to act without any judicial
control: she/he can exercise the right to sell assets which are subject to "security" or
"quasi-security" interests (with the exception of floating charges) only upon the
court's approval;[142] such approval to be given "where the court thinks that disposal
of the property would be likely to promote the purpose of administration in respect
of the company".[143] Furthermore, the proceeds of any sale shall be directed towards
the interests-holders: the Insolvency Act 1986 expressly provides that any proceeds
from the disposal of the property shall be "applied towards discharging the sums
secured under the security [or payable under the "quasi-security" interest]".[144] In

---

[138] M Bridge, L Gullifer, G McMeel, S Worthington, *The Law of Personal Property* (2013), at
[38–036] with references to case law.

[139] *Ibid.*, at [38–037] with references to case law.

[140] P. Farrell, "England and Wales" in B. Crans and R. Nath (eds), *Aircraft repossession and
enforcement. Practical Issues* (2009), p. 285, 310.

[141] *Bristol Airport plc v Powdrill* [1990] Ch. 744, 758.

[142] Insolvency Act 1986, Schedule B1, ss.70–72.

[143] Insolvency Act 1986, Schedule B1, ss. 71(2)(b) for security interests and 72(2)(b) for "quasi-
security" interests.

[144] Insolvency Act 1986, Schedule B1, ss. 71(3)(a) for security interests and 72(3)(a) for "quasi-
security" interests.

case the asset is not sold in its market value, the Act provides that the administrator shall top up the proceeds of the sale with "any additional money required… so as to produce the amount determined by the court as the net amount which would be realised on a sale of the goods at market value".[145]

Liquidation (either voluntary or compulsory) does not have a rescue role and its main aim is to realise and distribute the assets of the company to its creditors. It is not surprising then that the Insolvency Act 1986 provides that the liquidator "shall take into his custody or under his control all the property and things in action to which the company is or appears to be entitled".[146] His/her main aim is "to secure that the assets of the company are got in, realised and distributed to the company's creditors and, if there is a surplus, to the persons entitled to it".[147] In that respect, assets which are subject to a security or a title-retention agreement do not belong to the company and as such they remain outside the distributable property. This further means that their owners can enforce their interests on a "self-help" basis, subject to any contractual restrictions/the equity of redemption/payment of the price.[148] As such "liquidation is of little concern to secured creditors except to the extent to which they are owed an amount in excess of the value of security. A fully secured creditor is able largely to ignore the liquidation process and to go his own way, enforcing his security very much as if the debtor were still solvent."[notes omitted].[149]

Does it work in practice? In the words of a practitioner, it does: "a…liquidator appointed to the Lessee has extremely limited powers to interfere with the exercise of the rights of the Lessors and other third parties. Any terminating provisions contained in the Lease, whether effective automatically or on the giving of notice to the Lessee, will normally be unrestricted, As such, the Lessor will be able to avail itself of any rights or detention, repossession or sale flowing from termination."[150]

A recent market development gave a strong endorsement on English corporate insolvency law. British Airways managed to raise capital in the US via the issuance of Enhanced Equipment Trust Certificates (EETC), becoming one of the very few non-US airlines being able to do so. If one considers that at the time of the deal the UK was not a party to the Cape Town Convention, this development becomes even more impressive. It goes without saying that the credit rating of British Airways played a major role in the decision to provide funding. Yet, this does not tell the full story. In the words of a commentator the certainty of English law contributed in a

---

[145] Insolvency Act 1986, Schedule B1, ss. 71(3)(b) for security interests and 72(3)(b) for "quasi-security" interests.

[146] s. 144(1).

[147] s. 143(1).

[148] The now repealed Art. 15 of the Mortgaging of Aircraft Order 1972 provided that "[a] registered mortgage of an aircraft shall not be affected by any act of bankruptcy committed by the mortgagor after the date on which the mortgage is registered…". The same result is now achieved by s. 285(4) of the Insolvency Act 1986.

[149] E McKendrick, *Goode on Commercial Law* (4th edn, 2010), pp. 908–909.

[150] P. Farrell, "England and Wales" in B. Crans and R. Nath (eds), *Aircraft repossession and enforcement. Practical Issues* (2009), p. 285, 311.

significant manner to the decision: "In the BA transaction, the rating agencies investigated the underlying English insolvency and administration regime in detail. They concluded that whilst the regime was not as certain as the s 1110 or Alternative A—lacking a definitive 60-day end point—the general creditor-friendly approach was sufficiently well established through case law precedent to afford the required level of comfort to allow a favourable rating. In particular, they concluded that an administrator appointed to manage the affairs of BA in a corporate administration should not be able to simply ignore the proprietary ownership rights in the aircraft, and should be required either to allow timely repossession of the aircraft, or to continue leasing—and paying rental for—the aircraft".[151]

The British Government was initially reluctant to implement Alternative A on the basis that it would "restrict the ability of an airline in financial difficulties from effecting a turnaround of its business using the rescue provisions of the UK's insolvency regime".[152] Yet, following consultation, it opted for Alternative A of Article XI of the Aircraft Protocol (with a period of 60 days).[153] To facilitate UK carriers taking advantage of the discounts offered by export credit agencies, it also made the declaration of Art XXIII of the Aircraft Protocol.[154]

4.5 General Considerations

During the consultation process on the ratification of the Cape Town Convention, the Government, reflecting the view of the majority of respondents, advanced the following reasons for recommending its ratification: (1) A single international regime will reduce the uncertainty of cross-border financing and leasing transactions; (2) The Cape Town Convention may increase the appeal of airlines to cheaper finance provided by Export Credit Agencies and with the use of EETCs; (3) It permits the separate registration of interests against engines (which is not an option under English law) that may reduce the cost of financing them; and (4) The continuous operation of the International Registry will reduce bureaucracy, simplify closings and increase certainty with respect to priorities: "a financier would only be checking one register rather than multiple national registers".[155] Overall, the British

---

[151] J Cameron and R Walton, "Take Off: British Airways' issuance of EETC" (2013) JIBFL 576, 577.

[152] Department for Business Innovation and Skills, *"Ratification of the Convention on International Interests in Mobile Equipment and Protocol thereto on Matters Specific to Aircraft Equipment. Consultation on Options for Implementation"* (2014), at [76].

[153] Reg. 37 of the International Interests in Aircraft Equipment (Cape Town Convention) Regulations 2015.

[154] Reg. 22 of the International Interests in Aircraft Equipment (Cape Town Convention) Regulations 2015.

[155] Department for Business Innovation and Skills, *"Convention on International Interests in Mobile Equipment and Protocol thereto on Matters Specific to Aircraft Equipment. Government Response to the Call for Evidence"* (2013), at [3.17].

government believed that "ratification of the treaty would benefit the UK economy by creating a harmonised legal framework to register interests against helicopters, aircraft frames and aircraft engines".[156]

There is no doubt that English law provided a creditor-friendly legal framework even before the implementation of the Cape Town Convention that treasured contractual freedom and facilitated the enforcement of both security and "quasi-security" interests. It is expected that the implementation of the Cape Town Convention will not bring a sea change to the existing legal framework. It remedies some of the admittedly few deficiencies of English law, with first among them, the limited transparency that is caused by the non-registration of title-retention agreements, the non-registration of engines alone, as well as by the multiplicity of registers. There will certainly be a period of adjustment when both lawyers and the judiciary will attempt to interpret terms like "commercial reasonableness" in the context of the Cape Town Convention's philosophy and in light of case law from other party jurisdictions. Judging from the past experience of English courts in other fields of private international air law, it is expected that this adjustment will not take time and the transition will take place smoothly.

References

1. Beale, H., M. Bridge, L. Gullifer, and E. Lomnicka. 2012. *The law of security and title-based financing*, 2nd ed. Oxford: Oxford University Press.
2. Beale, H. (ed), 2013. *Chitty on contracts*, 31st ed. Sweet & Maxwell.
3. Bridge, M., L. Gullifer, G. McMeel, and S. Worthington. 2013. *The law of personal property*. London: Sweet & Maxwell.
4. Cameron, J., and R. Walton. 2013. Take off: British airways' issuance of EETC. *JIBFL* 576, 577.
5. Department for Business Innovation and Skills. 2013. *Convention on international interests in mobile equipment and protocol thereto on matters specific to aircraft equipment. Government response to the call for evidence.*
6. Department for Business Innovation and Skills. 2014. *Ratification of the convention on international interests in mobile equipment and protocol thereto on matters specific to aircraft equipment. Consultation on options for implementation.*
7. Department for Business, Innovation and Skills. 2015. *The international interests in aircraft equipment (Cape Town Convention) regulations 2015. Draft guidance.*
8. Edmunds, J. 2002. Mortgages of aircraft. In *Security interests in mobile equipment*, ed. I. Davies, 145, 152–153. Aldershot: Ashgate.
9. Farrell, P. 2009. England and Wales. In *Aircraft repossession and enforcement. Practical issues*, eds. B. Crans and R. Nath, 285. Alphen aan den Rijn: Wolters Kluwer
10. Halsbury's Laws of England. 2012. *Contract*, 5th edn, Vol 22.
11. Hanley, D. 2012. *Aircraft operating leasing: A legal and practical analysis in the context of public and private international air law*. Alphen aan den Rijn: Kluwer Law International.
12. The Law Commission of England and Wales. 2004. *Company security interests. A consultative report.*

---

[156] *Ibid.*, at [3.19].

13. The Law Society of England and Wales. 2007. *England and Wales: The jurisdiction of choice*. Dispute Resolution.
14. Mcclean, D. (ed.). 2015. *Shawcross and Beaumont on Air law*. London: Butterworth.
15. McKendrick, E. 2010. *Goode on commercial law*, 4th edn. London: Penguin.
16. Peel, E. 2013. The termination paradox, LMCLQ 519.
17. Poole, J. 2012. *Contract law*, 11th edn. Oxford: Oxford University Press
18. Saidova, S. 2013. The Cape Town Convention: repossession and sale of charged aircraft objects in a commercially reasonable manner. LMCLQ 180.
19. White & Case. 2015. UK Ratification of the Cape Town Convention. Available at http://www.whitecase.com/publications/article/uk-ratification-cape-town-convention.

Cases

Antaios Cia Naviera SA v Salen Rederierna AB (The Antaios) [1985] AC 191.
Australia and New Zealand Banking v Bangadilly (1978) 139 CLR 195.
Bristol Airport plc v Powdrill [1990] Ch. 744.
Celestial Aviation Trading 71 Limited v Paramount Airways Private Ltd [2010] EWHC 185 (Comm), [2011] 1 All ER (Comm) 259, [2011] 1 Lloyd's Rep. 9.
China and South Sea Bank Ltd v Tan [1989] 3 All ER 839.
Co-operative Wholesale Society Ltd v National Westminster Bank plc [1995] 1 EGLR 97.
Cuckmere Brick Co Ltd v Mutual Finance Ltd [1971] 2 All ER 633.
Den Norske Bank ASA v Acemex Management Co Ltd [2003] EWCA Civ 1559.
Dominion Corporate Trustees Ltd v Debenham Properties Ltd [2010] EWHC 1193 (Ch).
Downsview Nominees Ltd v First City Corporation [1993] 3 All ER 626.
Farrar v Farrars Ltd [1888] 40 Ch D 395.
Four-Maids Limited v Dudley Marshall (Properties) Limited [1957] 2 All ER 35, [1957] Ch 317.
Global Knafaim Leasing Ltd v Civil Aviation Authority [2010] EWHC 1348 (Admin), [2011] 1 Lloyd's Rep. 324.
Granville Oil & Chemicals Ltd v Davis Turner & Co Ltd [2003] EWCA Civ 570, [2003] 1 All ER (Comm) 819, [2003] 2 Lloyd's Rep 356.
Lombard North Central plc v Butterworth [1987] 1 All ER 267.
Looney v Trafigura Beheer BV [2011] EWHC 125 (Ch), [2011] All E.R. (D) 17 (Feb).
Michael and others v Miller and others [2004] EWCA Civ 282.
Palk v Mortgage Services Funding plc [1993] 2 All ER 481.
Rainy Sky SA v Kookmin Bank [2011] UKSC 50, [2012] 1 All ER 1137.
Rice (T/A the Garden Guardian) v Great Yarmouth Borough Council 2000 WL 823961.
Silven Properties Ltd v Royal Bank of Scotland plc [2003] EWCA Civ 1409, [2004] 4 All ER 484.
Trident Turboprop (Dublin) Limited v First Flight Couriers Limited [2009] EWCA Civ 290.
Tse Kwong Lam v Wong Chit Sen [1983] 3 All ER 54.
Western Bank Ltd v Kurt Schindler [1976] 2 All ER 393.
Yorkshire Bank Plc v Hall [1999] 1 WLR 1713.

George Leloudas is an Associate Professor at the Institute of International Shipping and Trade Law (IISTL) of Swansea University that he joined in 2011. He is a graduate of the National and Kapodistrian University of Athens. He holds LLM degrees in Commercial Law from the University of Bristol (England, 2002) and in Air and Space Law from the Institute of Air and Space Law of McGill University (Montreal, Canada, 2003). He also completed his PhD degree in air law with emphasis on liability and insurance at Trinity Hall, Cambridge University in 2009.

Chapter 5
Indonesia's Report: The Implementation of The *Cape Town Convention 2001*

Prita Amalia

5.1 Introduction

The Cape Town Convention 2001,[1] which was ratified by Indonesia through the Presidential Decree Number 8/2007, is one of international conventions which fulfils the international convention threshold as regulated under *Vienna Convention on the law of treaties 1969.*[2] Ratification is one of the requirements under the Cape Town Convention 2001 in order for a State to become its Party.[3] According to Art. 26 of the Vienna Convention 1969,[4] Indonesia is bound to perform international obligation contained in the Cape Town Convention 2001 by ratifying it and must perform its international obligation in good faith.

There are several regulations concerning Indonesia's ratification of the Cape Town Convention 2001, namely ordinance of the Presidential Decree Number 8/2007 in order to know what kind of declaration Indonesia has submitted; Aviation Law Number 1/2009 which explains about Indonesia's implementation of the Cape Town Convention 2001 under Art.71–82; and some technical regulations.

---

[1] The Cape Town Convention 2001 in this article means the Cape Town Convention 2001 regarding Security Interest on Mobile Equipment and the Aircraft Protocol that Indonesia ratified by a single instrument, Presidential Decree No.8/2007.

[2] Vienna Convention 1969.

[3] Article 47 (2) Cape Town Convention 2001 *"This Convention shall be subject to ratification, acceptance or approval by states which have signed it".*

[4] Article 26 Vienna Convention 1969 *"Every Treaty in force is binding upon the parties and must be performed by them in good faith".*

P. Amalia (✉)
Faculty of Law, Universitas Padjadjaran, Bandung, Indonesia
e-mail: pritaamalia@unpad.ac.id; prita_amalia@yahoo.com

© Springer International Publishing AG 2017
S. Kozuka (ed.), *Implementing the Cape Town Convention and the Domestic Laws on Secured Transactions,* Ius Comparatum - Global Studies in Comparative Law 22, DOI 10.1007/978-3-319-46470-1_5

5.2   Ratification of the Cape Town Convention 2001

Indonesia ratified the Cape Town Convention 2001 through the Presidential Decree Number 8/2007 based on Indonesian Treaty Law No 24/2000, pursuant to Article 47 of the Cape Town Convention 2001.

Even though Indonesia was not a negotiating state at the diplomatic conference of the Cape Town Convention 2001 which was held by UNIDROIT and ICAO, Indonesia followed the development of the negotiation which occurred in Cape Town and acknowledged that the purpose of this Convention is to form a set of international law applicable in order to procure an aircraft that can promote the development of international carriage by air. As such, Indonesia felt the need to be bound by this Convention based on this consideration.[5]

In ratifying the Cape Town Convention 2001, Indonesia based its ratification on several laws which are Art. 4 and Art. 11 of Constitutional Law 1945, Aviation Law Number 15/1992 as replaced by Aviation Law Number 1/2009, Indonesian Treaty Law 24/2000, and the Formation of Legislation Law No. 12/2011.

Indonesia submitted its declarations according to Art. 39, 40, and 60 of the Cape Town Convention 2001, which provide that every Contracting State has the option to opt in or opt out under the Convention, by making mandatory declaration and other declarations.[6]

Indonesia declared that it was bound by the Cape Town Convention 2001 and adopted the opt-in provision under Art. 39 (1)(a) which states that Indonesia submitted declaration that the following categories of non-consensual right or interest have priority under its laws over an interest in an aircraft object equivalent to that of the holder of a registered international interest and shall have priority over a registered international interest, whether in or outside insolvency proceedings[7]:

(a) Liens in favour of airline employees for unpaid wages arising after the time of a declared default under a contract to finance or lease an aircraft object;
(b) Liens or other rights of an authority of Indonesia relating to taxes or other unpaid charges arising from or related to the use of that aircraft object, and arising after the time of a declared default under a contract to finance or lease that aircraft object;
(c) Liens or other rights in favour of repairers of an aircraft object in their possession to the extent of service or services performed on and value added to that aircraft object.

---

[5] Consideration of the Presidential Decree No. 8/2007.

[6] Goode, Roy, *Official Commentary on The Convention on International Interest in Mobile Equipment and the Protocol thereto on Matters specific to Aircraft Equipment*, UNIDROIT, p.29.

[7] Annex of the Presidential Decree No. 8/2007.

Indonesia also declared that it adopted and is bound by Art. 39 (1)(b),[8] which states that Indonesia declares that nothing in the Convention shall affect its right or that of any entity thereof, or any intergovernmental organization to which Indonesia is a member, or other private provider of public services in Indonesia, to arrest or detain an aircraft object under its law for payment of amount owed to the government of Indonesia, any such entity, organization or provider directly relating to the service or services provided by it in respect of that or another aircraft object.[9]

Indonesia adopted and is bound by Art. 40 as well.[10] It stated that Indonesia declares the following categories of non-consensual right or interest shall be registrabled under the Convention as regards any category of aircraft object as if the right or interest were an international interest and shall be regulated accordingly:

(a) Liens in favour of airline employee for unpaid wages arising prior to the time of declared default under a contract to finance or lease an aircraft object;
(b) Liens or other right of an authority of Indonesia relating to taxes or other unpaid charges arising from or related to the use of an aircraft object, and arising prior to the time of a declared default under a contract to finance or lease that aircraft object; and
(c) Rights of a person obtaining a court order permitting attachment of an aircraft object in partial or full satisfaction of a legal judgment.

Apart from Art. 39 and 40 which Indonesia has adopted and is bound by, Indonesia also made a mandatory declaration under Art. 53 and 54. Regarding Art. 53[11] declaration, Indonesia stated that all courts with the competent jurisidction under the law of Indonesia are the relevant courts for the purpose of Art. 1 and Chapter 12 of the Convention. Under Art. 54[12] Indonesia declared that any and all remedies available to the creditor under the Convention which are not express under

---

[8] Article 39 (1) (b) *"that nothing in this Convention shall affect the right of a State or State entity, intergovernmental organization or other private provider of public services to arrest or detain an object under the laws of that State for payment of amounts owed to such entity, organization or provider directly relating to those services in respect of that object or another object".*

[9] Annex of the Presidential Decree No. 8/2007.

[10] Article 40 *"A Contracting State may at any time in a declaration deposited with the Depositary of the Protocol list the categories of non-consensual right or interest which shall be registrable under this Convention as regards any category of object as if the right or interest were an international interest and shall be regulated accordingly. Such a declaration may be modified from time to time."*

[11] Article 53 *"A Contracting State may, at the time of ratification, acceptance, approval of, or accession to the Protocol, declare the relevant "court" or "courts" for the purposes of Article 1 and Chapter XII of this Convention."* This declaration give an authority to Contracting States to submit declaration regarding jurisdiction of the court based on Convention. But this not include privat court or administrative court. Roy, *Official Commentary.....*P.159.

[12] Article 54 *"A Contracting State shall, at the time of ratification, acceptance, approval of, or accession to the Protocol, declare whether or not any remedy available to the creditor under any provision of this Convention which is not there expressed to require application to the court may be exercised only with leave of the court".*

the relevant provision thereof to require application to the court may be exercise without a court action and without a leave of the court.[13]

Additionally, Indonesia also made a declaration under the Aircraft Protocol in which some of the article are adopted by and binding on Indonesia, such as Art. XXX (1) relating to Art. VIII concerning choice of law, Art. XXI concerning insolvency aid, Art. XIII concerning the authority to request the removal of the registration and export,[14] Art. XXX (2) relating to Art. X concerning changes in provisions concerning recovery before the final decision, and Art. XXX (3) relating to Art. XI concerning the recovery in the insolvency proceeding, which imposes alternative 'A'.

5.3   Indonesia's Air Law Based on Aviation Law No. 1/2009

Aviation Law No. 1/2009 is a new regulation concerning aviation which replaces the previous regulation Aviation Law No. 15/1992. The Aviation Law No. 1/2009 aims to perfect and to complete the previous law in order to confirm with the development of science and technology, the change in paradigm and strategic environment.

Cape Town Convention 2001 is one of international treaties in aviation, and one of many reasons for its ratification was to perfect Indonesian's Aviation Law in order to empower national aviation industry. It is in accordance with the explanation chapter of Aviation Law No. 1/2009.

In the effort to empower national aviation industry, this Law shall also contain provisions regarding international interests on aircraft objects regulating aircraft objects that may bear international interests arising from a security agreement, a title reservation agreement, and/or a leasing agreement. These regulations refer to the Convention on International Interest in Mobile Equipment and the protocol to the Convention on Interest in Mobile Equipment on Matters Specific to Aircraft Equipment, airplane engines, as a consequence of ratifying the convention and protocol normally called the Cape Town Convention.[15]

Based on this explanation, it could be understood that Indonesia's Government will enact international obligation after ratify international treaty as an effort to implement the treaty in good faith according to the Vienna Convention 1969. Although the purpose to ratify the Cape Town Convention 2001 is to perfect the Aviation law, the Aviation law does not clearly state that Art.71–82 are the implementing legislation of the Cape Town Convention 2001. As such, it is important to

---

[13] Annex of Presidential Decree No.8/2007.

[14] Kamran Radjab Lossen, Yurisdiksi Negara atas Pendaftaran Nasionalitas Pesawat Udara Leasing Transnasional dalam mendukung Industri Penerbangan Indonesia, Dissertation, Universitas Padjadjaran, Bandung, 2008, p. 262–267.

[15] Explanation chapter of Aviation Law No.1/2009.

discuss the international interest provisions under the Aviation law contained in the Section XI.

According to Art. 71 of Aviation Law, an aircraft object may be borne with international interests arising from a security agreement, title reservation agreement, and/or leasing agreement. The aircraft object includes airframe, its engine, and helicopter. Art. 71 also adopted provision of the Cape Town Convention 2001 are the definition of the aircraft object which could be borne with international interest as regulated under Art. 2(3) of the Cape Town Convention, the definition of international interest under Art. 2(1) of the Cape Town Convention, the agreement as the basis of international interest under Art. 2(2) of the Cape Town Convention.

Airframe which may be borne with international interests is airframe which is not used as the state aircraft that if an engine is assembled onto the body, it should be certified by the authorized official for at least 8 persons including its crew or goods which exceeds 2.750 kg with all of the equipments, components and tools which are installed, included or related (other than aircraft engines), and all data manuals and records relating to it.

Aircraft engine which may be borne with international interest is aircraft engine (apart from military, customs, or police purposes) powered by jet propulsion or turbine or piston technology. As for aircraft engine powered by jet propulsion, the Aviation Law requires thrust in 1750 lbs or equivalent, for engine powered by turbine or piston it requires 550 hp usually used to take off or anything equivalent, and all of moduls, gears, components, and other equipment which are installed, included or related (other than aircraft engines), and all data manuals and records relating to it.

Helicopter which may be borne with international interests is certain helicopter (apart from military, customs, or police purposes) which are certified by the authorized aviation institution to transport at least 5 persons including its crew or goods more than 450 kg and gears, components, and other equipment which are installed, included or related (rotor included), and all data manuals and records relating to it.

International interest is an interest acquired by creditor due to security agreements, title reservation agreement, and/or leasing agreement which comply to Cape Town Convention.

Art. 72 of Aviation law gives the parties right to choose their own choice of law. Chargor vs chargee or lessor vs lessee could choose the governing law for the agreement, be it title reservation agreement or leasing agreement, in accordance with private international law. Principle of private international law could be invoked by the parties in order to choose the law that would govern the contractual rights and obligations under the agreement or in the absence of a link between the choice of law chosen by one of the parties to the agreement or the implementation of the obligations under the agreement. Besides the freedom of choice of law principle, Art. 72 also gives the parties the freedom of choice of forum.

Art. 72 is an implementing provision on choice of law under Art. VIII of the Protocol which Indonesia adopted and is bound by. Hence, it could be concluded that Art. 72 is an implementing legislation based on the Cape Town Convention 2001.

Art. 73 provides that in the case the agreement as meant in Article 71 is a subject under the Indonesian laws, the agreement must be drawn in an authentic deed containing, at the least: identities of all the parties; identification of the aircraft object; and the rights and obligations of the parties. Art. 73 is not regulated under the Cape Town Convention 2001, however this provision is intended for an agreement which cause an international interest and use Indonesian law according to the requirements set out by Art. 73.

Art. 74 concerns the Power of Attorney. This provision regulate that the debtor may issue power of attorney in regard to application of *irrevocable de-registration and export request authorization* to creditor to apply deregistration and export of the Indonesia's aircraft or helicopter. The power of attorney to application of deregistration should be claimed and listed by the Minister of Transportation and could not be annulled without creditor's consent. Creditor is the one and only person to apply for deregistration of the nationality of the aircraft[16] or helicopter based on rules.

Provisions referred to in Article 74 called IDERA is one of remedies set forth in the Cape Town Convention 2001, Chapter 3 on Default Remedies (recovery measures). The explanation of this article states clearly that the power to apply for deregistration and export can not be withdrawn, the corresponding provisions of the Cape Town Convention in 2001 (Explanation of Article 74 of Aviation Law 2009). Regarding IDERA also the further provisions laid down in the Protocol Article XIII adopted by and binding on Indonesia through declarations (opt-in) made at the time of ratification.

The authorization to apply for deregistration and export of the aircraft that can not be withdrawn is one of the remedies that may be filed by the creditor in case of default in the implementation of the agreement. This is provided for in Article 75 of the Aviation Law 2009, which is the basis of the power to apply deregistration and export that can not be withdrawn. Furthermore, this article provides that the petition be submitted to the Minister of Transportation, to apply deregistration and export of aircraft and helicopters. The Minister of Transportation shall remove the registration marks and nationality of aircraft and helicopters in less than 5 working days from the receipt of the application. Removal of the nationality of the aircraft is set also in Article 29. The Indonesia's Aviation Law regulates that for an aircraft that has a nationality and registration marks of aircraft removal of nationality and registration may be requested when default is committed by the aircraft's tenant without a court decision (Article 29 of The Aviation Law 2009).

The provision concerning the removal of registration under Article 29, stating that removal can be done without a court decision is in line with the provisions of Article 54 (2) of the Convention on the remedies, which Indonesia has declared to be bound by the declaration at the time of ratification, that Indonesia declared that all remedies available to the creditor under the Convention can be implemented without the need for court action and without notifying the court.

The provisions of Article 74 and Article 75 regulate the available remedies in the event of default for creditors. Regarding the obligations in the implementation of

16 Article 17 Chicago Convention 1944.

the remedies in accordance with these provisions, Article 76 stipulates that the ministry in charge of the affairs of aviation and other government agencies should assist and expedite the implementation of the remedies made by the creditor under a security agreement, title reservation agreement, and/or leasing agreement. Explanation of this article clarifies that what is meant by "other government agencies" are, among other agencies, those that have the duty and responsibility in customs, taxation, foreign affairs and defense. Remedies and creditor rights referred to in this article is the creditor's rights and remedies that arise from the agreement by the parties in accordance with the given constraints of Article 77 of Aviation Law 2009. These articles are the implementation of the default remedies of the Cape Town Convention in 2001.

The appointment of the Ministry of Transportation as a representative in the implementation of the remedies of the Cape Town Convention 2001 should constitute one of the mandates of the Aviation Law 2009 to give mandate to several related government institutions. The Provision concerning the remedies is one of the cross-cutting provisions that are already in case the implementation of this article should be equivalent provisions of the Presidential Decree.[17]

International interest is one of the most important things under the Cape Town Convention 2001. An international interest has priority or precedence rights over the rights that are not registered or subsequently registered rights as stipulated in Article 29 of the Convention called Priority Rules. Aviation Law 2009 has formulated what is meant by the international interest in the law and in line with the Convention as well as giving priority rights or the rights of precedence as stipulated in Article 78. This section further regulates that the right of priority of the international interest is a right granted after the international interest is registered in the office of the international registration.

International registration office referred to in this act is the International Registry established for the purposes of the Cape Town Convention 2001 and will be the only office for the registration of international interests for the aircraft object (Explanation of Article 78 of Aviation Law 2009). The International Registry is an electronic registration system under the coordination of the ICAO, which is the only registry for the international interest. Currently, the international registration office in question has been established and can be visited via the website (https://www.internationalregistry.aero). However, this article does not set out more about the implementation of the registration of international interest as provided in detail in Chapter 4 of the Convention on the International Registration System (See Articles 16 and 17 of the Cape Town Convention 2001, which regulates the international registration system).

International interest, priority rules, the international registration and default remedies are four main things in the Cape Town Convention 2001. In order to determine the effectiveness of the implementation of this Convention, it shall be assessed with the implementing regulations for the four important issues whether it is sufficient or not. The fact that there is no regulation of the international registration in

---

[17] The Formation of Regulation Law of Indonesia No. 12 in 2011.

detail in this legislation makes it less effective in implementing the obligations under the Convention, as Art. 78 clearly provides that the limitation of international interest which has priority is an interest which has been registered through the office of the international registration.

Furthermore, Art. 79 set the decision of the district court, namely that when the debtor did default then the creditor can ask for the decision of the court chosen by the parties or the district court of Indonesia which has a relative competence in the absence of a choice of forum in the agreement to acquire an interim measure based on agreements on aircraft object that may be borne with international interest without any prior claim to carry out the principal case demands in Indonesia and without the parties to follow the mediation ordered by the court. Regarding the decision of the court, the Aviation Law has assigned ten (10) calendar days in respect of the remedies specified in Article 13(1)(a), (b) and (c) of the Convention and thirty (30) calendar days in respect of the remedies specified in Article 13(d) and (e) of the Convention in accordance with the declaration submitted Indonesia under the Protocol Article XXX (2) in respect of Article X. This period is also the time period that must be complied with by the court, curator, bankruptcy administrators, and/or debtor to hand over control of aircraft object to the creditor as provided for in Article 80 of Aviation Law.

In addition to the priority rules, international interest which has been registered by Indonesia also specify some bills or certain rights precedence or has priority over the international interest that has been registered in the aircraft object. It is stipulated in Article 81 of Aviation Law and the implementation of the declaration made by Indonesia to Art. 39 and 40 of the Convention. Such provisions allow the Contracting States to determine what rights have priority over an international interest.

Article 82 of Aviation Law is the last article in the section governing the international interest. This article provides that the provisions of the International Convention on Security Interest on mobile equipment and the Aircraft Protocol, to which Indonesia is a party, shall have the force of law in Indonesia and is a specific legal provision. According to its explanation, specific legal provision is in the case of inconsistency or discrepancy between the provisions of the Convention, protocols and declarations with Indonesian Law, the provisions of the Convention, the Protocol and the declaration should be applied.

The last provision in the chapter of international interest under Aviation Law, according to the authors' opinion, this article gives a description of the Indonesia's view towards international treaty that had always been a subject of debate. By putting the provisions of the convention, it can be said that Indonesia adheres to monism with the primacy of international law that international law enjoys precedence when there is a conflict between international law and national law proposed by Mochtar Kusumaatmadja. This article also states that although the convention is a non-self-executing treaty, there are some provisions that could be self-executing. Of the provisions of international interest on movable equipment or property, Indonesia will prioritize the provisions contained in the Cape Town Convention 2001.

The Cape Town Convention 2001 covers not only the legal scope of the Aviation law, but also bankruptcy. Aviation Law 2009 indirectly regulates bankruptcy to the extent international interest is related. The presence of the bankruptcy provisions in the Aviation Law 2009 could cause an overlap or conflict of law between the Cape Town Convention 2001 and Law No. 37 Year 2004 on Bankruptcy. The provisions contained in the tangent to the bankruptcy declaration made in Indonesia at the time of ratification, especially declarations under Article XXX (3) in respect of Article XI of the Protocol on measures to be taken in the event of bankruptcy.

The possibility of this conflict of law would be anticipated with the provision of Art. 82 of Aviation Law 2009. In case its implementation is contrary to the Bankruptcy Law, the provisions of the Cape Town Convention in 2001 are to be used. However, the intention of the legislator to include the term '*lex specialis*' according to the author is incorrect, because it does not indicate the terms of the provisions of this specialist provision apart from generalist. Except where the provisions mentioned in the explanation of which is the provision of *lex specialis* and *lex generalis*.[18]

5.4 Conclusions

After Indonesia ratified the Cape Town Convention 2001 and the Aircraft Protocol through Presidential Decree No. 8 in 2007, Indonesia, according to its domestic law, has also made some adjustments to the Aviation Law 2009 and some other technical implementing regulations. However, because the Cape Town Convention 2001 is not only related to aviation law, especially related to the procurement of aircraft as well as with other legal fields such as Civil Law and Security Law, it seems that there are still laws that should be reviewed in order to implement the Cape Town Convention 2001 in Indonesia more effectively. Knowledge and information about how the State parties implement the Cape Town Convention 2001 will be a comparative study useful for Indonesia in implementing this convention.

Prita Amalia is a Lecturer at the Faculty of Law, Universitas Padjadjaran, Indonesia. She obtained her Master of Laws degree on 2012 from the Faculty of Law, Universitas Padjadjaran, with her thesis concerning the 2001 Cape Town Convention. She conducted numerous researches and publications in International Trade Law, International Economic Law, International Commercial Arbitration Law, Aircraft Financing and Air and Space Law. She has been appointed as faculty advisor for Universitas Padjadjaran's Willem C. Vis Team since 2009 until now.

---

[18] Hikmahanto Juwana, "Kewajiban Negara Mentransformasikan ketentuan Perjanjian Internasional kedalam Peraturan perundang-undangan: Studi Kasus Pasca Keikutsertaan dalam Cape Town Convention 2001", *Jurnal Hukum Bisnis*, Vol 28 No. 4 Tahun 2009, P. 56.

Chapter 6
Implementation of the Cape Town Convention in Malaysia

Mary George and See Eng Teong

Foreword This Report has five sections. Section 6.1 outlines the aviation industry in Malaysia. Section 6.2 deals with an analysis of the role of equity, common law and statutory rules in aircraft secured transactions law in Malaysia. Section 6.3 sets out the Malaysian Declarations to the Convention and Protocol. Section 6.4 deals with the local legislation that implement the Cape Town Convention and Aircraft Protocol. Section 6.5 provides answers to the Questionnaire. I would like to thank Dato' Azharuddin Abdul Rahman, the Director-General of the Department of Civil Aviation, Ministry of Transport, Malaysia for the interview on the implementation aspects of the Cape Town Convention in Malaysia and its interactions with other domestic legislation. Having ratified the Convention and implemented domestic law in this regard, the Director-General of the Department of Civil Aviation, Ministry of Transport is of the view that so far no conflicts have arisen between the two systems.

I also thank Dr See Eng Teong for his input into Part IV.

All views expressed here are from an academic perspective.

M. George (✉) • S.E. Teong
Faculty of Law, University of Malaya, 50603 Kuala Lumpur, Malaysia
e-mail: maryg@um.edu.my; set2law@gmail.com

© Springer International Publishing AG 2017
S. Kozuka (ed.), *Implementing the Cape Town Convention and the Domestic Laws on Secured Transactions*, Ius Comparatum - Global Studies in Comparative Law 22, DOI 10.1007/978-3-319-46470-1_6

6.1   An Overview of the Aviation Industry in Malaysia

6.1.1   Introduction

This overview provides a brief insight into the background and current developments in the aviation industry in Malaysia. In the 2014 National Budget, the Government has endorsed that a new National Aviation Policy will be adopted soon.[1]

6.1.2   Background

Scheduled air passenger and mail services in Malaya commenced in 1937, when Wearne's Air Service (WAS) began operating services between Singapore, Kuala Lumpur and Penang. The first flight, using an 8-seater de Havilland D.H.89A Dragon Rapide took place on 28 June 1937.[2] This inaugural flight departed Singapore from the then brand-new Kallang Airport which had opened earlier in the same month on 12 June.[3] Next to arrive on the scene was *Malayan Airways Limited (MAL)* incorporated in Singapore on 12 October 1937, an initiative of the Ocean Steamship Company of Liverpool, in partnership with the Straits Steamship Company[4] and Imperial Airways. The airline's inaugural flight on the "Raja Udang,"[5] with only five passengers was a charter from Kallang Airport in Singapore to Sungei Besi Airport in Kuala Lumpur, on 2 April 1947, using an Airspeed Consul twin-engined aircraft. Weekly scheduled flights then followed from Singapore to Kuala Lumpur, Ipoh and Penang from 1 May 1947 with the same aircraft type.[6] Its services expanded in the 1940s and 1950s. In 1960, the airline launched its first long-haul international flight, to Hong Kong and thereafter several new routes were added. The airlines has had a series of name change, for example, in 1963, the airline's name was changed, from "Malayan Airways" to "Malaysian Airlines" and then when Singapore joined the Federation of Malaya to Malaysia-Singapore

[1] Business News, Budget 2014: Logistics sector to be improved, aviation hub role e yed, http://www.thestar.com.my/Business/Business-News/2013/10/25/Logistics-sector-to-be-improved-Govt-eyes-aviation-hub-role/?style=biz, 28 November 2014.

[2] Mail takes flight. Singapore Philatelic Museum http://clients.theadventus.com/spm_revamp/web/htdocs/exhibition/past_exhibition/mail_takes_flight.html accessed 22 March 2014.

[3] Flight into fantasy, ALPAS Singapore http://www.alpas.org/list.php?c=aviationscene accessed 22 March 2014.

[4] Straits Steamship Company. http://infopedia.nl.sg/articles/SIP_1056_2008-01-05.html accessed 22 March 2014.

[5] Flight into Fantasy. ALPAS Singapore http://www.alpas.org/list.php?c=aviationscene accessed 22 March 2014.

[6] Singapore Airlines – Our History http://www.singaporeair.com/en_UK/about-us/sia-history/ accessed 22 March 2014.

Airlines. It also took over Borneo Airways. In 1966, following Singapore's separation from the Federation, the airline's name was changed again to Malaysia Airlines System and Singapore Airlines (SIA).[7] By 1987, it was called Malaysia Airlines, from its original name of Malaysian Airways in 1947.[8] The technical Regulatory Authority[9] is the Department of Civil Aviation (DCA),[10] Ministry of Transport Malaysia. Air Services are generally divided into Scheduled and Non-scheduled Services. The DCA processes applications to obtain an Air Service License (ASL) and Air Operators Certificate (AOC) to provide scheduled air services. As of 2012, Malaysia has bilateral Air Services Agreement with 100 countries.[11] As a country that sits on the International Civil Aviation Organization – ICAO, Malaysia has ratified several International Conventions as follows:

No	Convention	Year
1	Convention for the Unification of Certain Rules Relating to International Carriage by Air	1929
2	Convention on International Civil Aviation (Chicago Convention)	1944
3	Convention on the Privileges and Immunities of Specialized Agencies	1947
4	Convention on Offences and Certain Other Acts Committed on Board Aircraft	1963
5	Convention for the Suppression of Unlawful Seizure of Aircraft (Hague Convention 1970)	1970
6	Convention for the Suppression of Unlawful Acts against the Safety of Civil Aviation (Montreal Convention 1971)	1971
7	Convention on International Interests in Mobile Equipment (Cape Town Convention 2001)	2001

The Acts and Regulations in force in Malaysia that regulate all matters relating to aviation and the usage of mobile equipment (aircraft) are as follows:

- Civil Aviation Act 1969 [Act 3]
- Carriage By Air Act 1974 [Act 148]
- Aviation Offences Act 1984 [Act 307]
- Airport and Aviation Services Act (Operating Company) 1991 [Act 467]
- International Interest Act in Mobile Equipment (Aircraft) 2006 [Act 659]
- Civil Aviation Regulations 1996

In Malaysia, aviation operators consist of two distinct groups of companies, namely:

---

[7] Malaysia Airlines – Our Story. http://www.malaysiaairlines.com/my/en/corporate-info/our-story.html accessed 22 March 2014.

[8] http://www.malaysiaairlines.com accessed 22 March 2014.

[9] Aviation Department, Ministry of Transport http://www.mot.gov.my/en/Services/Pages/Aviation.aspx accessed 22 March 2014.

[10] Department of Civil Aviation http://www.mot.gov.my/en/Sectoral/Pages/Aviation.aspx accessed 22 March 2014.

[11] Air Services Agreement. Ministry of Transport http://www.mot.gov.my/en/Sectoral/Pages/Aviation.aspx accessed 22 March 2014.

(a) The companies that are responsible to develop, manage and operate the airport terminals such as Malaysia Airports Holdings Berhad, a government-linked entity (MAHB)[12] which after corporate re-structuring in November 2014 is called Malaysia Airports Berhad (MAB) and Senai Airport Terminal Services (SATS), a privately-owned company.[13]

(b) The companies which operate the air services are; Firefly,[14] MAS Wings,[15] AirAsia,[16] Air Asia X,[17] Berjaya Air,[18] Transmile, and Malindo.[19]

Malaysia Airports operates 40 airports in Malaysia including the Kuala Lumpur International Airport (KLIA) hub airport while the Senai Airport Terminal Services Sdn. Bhd. operates the Johor Baru airport. The KLIA airport included the Low Cost Carrier Terminal (LCCT) which is now replaced by the KLIA2[20]with a capacity of 45 million ppa. Following the KLIA, the next largest airports in passengers handled are Penang, Kota Kinabalu and Kuching each handling over one mppa over a similar period.[21]

Comparison between KLIA, LCCT, and KLIA2

	KLIA	LCCT	KLIA2
Capacity (passengers per year)	25 million	15 million	45 million
Terminal size (sqm)	479,404	64,067	257,000
Retail space (sqm)	19,425	8898	32,000 (estimated)
Car park (lots)	6208 (covered lots) 5509 (uncovered lots)	3000 (uncovered lots)	6000
Cost (RM billion)	About 10.0	0.3 (terminal cost only)	3.6–3.9 (latest estimate)
Runway access	Runway 1 and 2 at KLIA	Runway 1 and 2 at KLIA	4 km runway with a 2.2 km separation from Runway 2
Passenger comfort (capacity/floor space)	52 pax per sqm	234 pax per sqm	124 pax per sqm

[12] http://www.malaysiaairports.com.my/ accessed 22 March 2014.

[13] http://www.senaiairport.com/ accessed 22 March 2014.

[14] http://www.fireflyz.com.my/ accessed 22 March 2014.

[15] http://www.maswings.com.my/ accessed 22 March 2014.

[16] http://www.**airasia**.com/ accessed 22 March 2014.

[17] http://www.**airasia**.com/ accessed 22 March 2014.

[18] https://www.berjaya-air.com/about-us/our-history/ accessed 22 March 2014.

[19] http://www.malindoair.com/en/AboutUs accessed 22 March 2014.

[20] KLIA2 Malaysia's Next Generation Hub http://www.klia2.info/about-klia2 accessed 22 March 2014.

[21] Source: Malaysia Airports Holdings Berhad and Senai Airport Terminal Services Sdn. Bhd.

Malaysia Airlines once operated 118 domestic routes within Malaysia and 114 international routes across the continents. Its glorious past routes have come under scrutiny and reconsideration in Business Turn Around Plans for reasons of profitability. Air Asia has been expanding in route coverage and fleet size.[22]

6.2 An Analysis of the Role of Equity, Common Law and Statutory Rules in Aircraft Secured Transactions Law in Malaysia

6.2.1 Federal Constitution 1957

Malaysia comprises the States of Peninsular Malaysia and East Malaysia which in turn comprises the States of Sabah and Sarawak. Treaty ratification is the prerogative of the Federal Government under Article 76(1) of the Federal Constitution and not state governments.

Malaysia was a former British colony and upon independence on 31 August 1957, had a rich legacy of the rules of English equity supplanting the legal rules, both statutory and judge-made law where the latter is referred to as "common law" and in cases of conflict between the common law and equitable rules, equitable rules prevail. This body of equitable rules has over the years been enriched by the local courts in Malaysia too.

The Cape Town Convention and the Aircraft Protocol have not generated any reported litigation that have gone before the local courts in Malaysia. Both treaties have been implemented domestically and it is to these legislative aspects that we now turn to see the implications of the treaties before and after ratification by Malaysia in the law of secured transactions for aircraft in Malaysia.

---

[22] Malaysia Airlines Annual Report 2012 http://ir.chartnexus.com/mas/doc/ar/ar2012.pdf accessed 22 March 2014; Malaysia Airlines - Our Story http://www.malaysiaairlines.com/my/en/corporate-info/our-story.html accessed 22 March 2014; Singapore Philatelic Museum SPM "Mail Takes Flight" http://clients.theadventus.com/spm_revamp/web/htdocs/exhibition/past_exhibition/mail_takes_flight.html accessed 22 March 2014; Straits Steamship Company http://infopedia.nl.sg/articles/SIP_1056_2008-01-05.html Airline Pilots Association of Singapore ALPAS "Flight into Fantasy" http://www.alpas.org/list.php?c=aviationscene accessed 22 March 2014; Ministry of Transport, Malaysia Aviation Division http://www.mot.gov.my/en/Sectoral/Pages/Aviation.aspx accessed 22 March 2014; Malaysia Airports Holdings Berhad and Senai Airport Terminal Services Sendirian Berhad 2013 Unpublished Paper;

KLIA2 Malaysia's Next Generation Hub http://www.klia2.info/about-klia2 accessed 22 March 2014; Malaysia Airlines – Business Turnaround Plan 2011 http://www.malaysiaairlines.com/content/dam/mas/master/en/pdf/corporate-info/Business%20Turnaround%20Plan%20(BTP%201).pdf accessed 22 March 2014; Malaysia Airlines Fleet http://www.malaysiaairlines.com/au/en/mh-experience/our-fleet/boeing-737-800.html accessed 22 March 2014; Air Asia Annual Report 2012 http://www.airasia.com/iwov-resources/my/common/pdf/AirAsia/IR/annual-report-2012.pdf; Cape Town Convention 2001 http://www.unidroit.org/english/conventions/mobile-equipment/aircraftprotocol.pdf.

6.2.2   Civil Law Act 1956

Long before the adoption of the Cape Town Convention and the Aircraft Protocol, the Civil Law Act 1956 (Act 67) has played and continues to play a very important role in the Malaysian legal system as it states the importance of the role of English rules of equity in addition to or in the absence of legal rules. This piece of legislation applies to the administration of all civil laws in Malaysia as enumerated in the Act unless otherwise provided. It was first enacted as Ordinance No. 5 of 1956 and revised in 1972 as Act 67 with effect from 1 April 1972. It applies to Peninsular Malaysia with effect from 7 April 1956 and to the States of Sabah and Sarawak with effect from 1 April 1972, through subsidiary legislation *P.U.(A)* 424/1971. Sections 2, 3 and 5 of the Act in particular have some implications for the law of secured transactions in aircraft financing and mortgage before the adoption of the Convention and Protocol. This is because of the continuous weave of local and English statutory rules, common law rules and English equitable rules in the administration of civil law in this country. Of utmost importance to air carriers, is the law spelt out in section 5, discussed below. In brief, section 5 states very clearly that the law of the UK as decided in that subject-matter applies. Therefore, the adoption of the treaties above and the ensuing domestic legislation implementing the treaties, expressly exclude the application of section 5 which has been the hitherto governing section for aircraft carriers. This is one possible literal interpretation. It could always be argued that if the treaties created an unfair regime that caused injustice to either the chargor or chargee, then it is an unfair rule and should be struck down by the forum court as stipulated in the charge contract.

Besides, equitable maxims such as "equity prevails over the law" and "where the equities are equal the first in time prevails" are applicable in Malaysia. Therefore, it is important to outline the role equity plays in Malaysia to ensure justice is done at the end of the day.

Section 2 of the Civil Law Act interprets the term "Court" unless the context otherwise requires to mean any court in Malaysia of competent jurisdiction, and includes any Judge thereof whether sitting in court or in chambers and "written law" in relation to any part of Malaysia means written law as defined in the law relating to interpretation in that part of Malaysia.

PART II of the Act deals with general provisions. In particular section 3 on the **Application of U.K. common law, rules of equity and certain statutes** deserve special attention. This means that English common law, equitable rules and even in certain circumstances statutory rules, such as may be necessary in the states of Sarawak or Sabah, become applicable, as set out in section 3(3).

At the outset, this has far-reaching implications for the subject-matter of the treaties under consideration here. What this means is that the law of secured transactions in aircraft financing and mortgage was before the adoption of the treaties capable of being subject to section 3 as briefly described by its title above.

Section 3(1) provides that where other provisions have been made or shall be made hereafter by any written law in force in Malaysia, the Court in Malaysia shall *(a)* in Peninsular Malaysia or any part thereof, apply the common law of England and the rules of equity as administered in England on 7 April 1956; *(b)* in Sabah, apply the common law of England and the rules of equity, together with statutes of general application, as administered or in force in England on 1 December 1951; *(c)* in Sarawak, apply the common law of England and the rules of equity, together with statutes of general application, as administered or in force in England on 12 December 1949, subject however to subparagraph (3)(ii). This is subject to a Proviso which states that –

> Provided always that the said common law, rules of equity and statutes of general application shall be applied so far only as the circumstances of the States of Malaysia and their respective inhabitants permit and subject to such qualifications as local circumstances render necessary.

Section 3(2) is very important in that it states where there is a conflict between common law and the rules of equity with regard to the same subject-matter, the rules of equity shall prevail.

In the application of English law in commercial matters, section 5(1) governs all transactions unless special domestic law provides otherwise, as has happened in the context of the treaties. The scope of section 5(1) is that where questions or issues which arise or which have to be decided in the States of Peninsular Malaysia other than Malacca and Penang with respect to the law of partnerships, corporations, banks and banking, principals and agents, carriers by air, land and sea, marine insurance, average, life and fire insurance, and with respect to mercantile law generally, the law to be administered shall be the same as would be administered in England in the like case at the date of the coming into force of this Act, if such question or issue had arisen or had to be decided in England, unless in any case other provision is or shall be made by any written law. This means that the applicable law in the States of Peninsular Malaysia when this Act came into force was the law in the UK in 1956. While Courts and counsel in Malaysia are free to move from this ossification, the law in Section 5 of the Civil Law Act still remains unchanged. Further, section 5(2) provides that where these issues mentioned above have to be decided in Malacca, Penang, Sabah and Sarawak, the law to be administered shall be the same as would be administered in England in the like case at the corresponding period, if such question or issue had arisen or had to be decided in England, unless in any case other provision is or shall be made by any written law.

6.2.3 Civil Aviation Act 1969 and Civil Aviation Regulations 1996

The Civil Aviation Act 1969 (Act 3) gives effect to the 1944 Chicago Convention on Civil Aviation 1944, its Annexes and regulates civil aviation in Malaysia. Section 3 empowers the Minister to adopt the Civil Aviation Regulations 1996 which have been amended as recently as 2004. The Preamble to the Civil Aviation Regulations

1996 acknowledges this. These Ministerial regulations are called Federal Subsidiary Legislation, *P.U.(A)* 139/96. Two important areas of this subsidiary legislation for the present analysis of the Convention and its Protocol relate to aircraft detention, sale and lien and mortgage. Section 22 of the Civil Aviation Act provides that aircraft may be detained to secure compliance with this Act or any such regulations. If the rules on aircraft sale and lien and mortgage are not abrogated in the Civil Aviation Act, then two possible interpretations arise. First, that they are compatible with the treaty regimes that Malaysia has adopted and so these provisions continue to govern our internal transactions and second, in the event that they are inconsistent with Malaysia's international obligations under the treaty regimes, then the treaty obligations would prevail under the 1969 Vienna Convention on the Law of Treaties, as Malaysia is also a party to the latter.

6.2.3.1 Analysis of the Regulations on Aircraft Liens and Sale

Under the Civil Aviation Act 1969, Regulation 140 interprets several terms where "airport charges" mean any charges payable to a licensed company and a "charge" is *(a)* a charge for a service or a facility provided by the Director-General; or *(b)* a fee for other charge in respect of any matter specified in these Regulations. Importantly, the term "outstanding amount" includes reference to a statutory lien: it "means, in relation to an aircraft in respect of which an aircraft lien is in effect, in relation to a particular time, *(a)* the amount of any charge payable in respect of the aircraft that is unpaid at that time; *(b)* the amount of any penalty that is unpaid at that time, and *(c)* the amount of any debt payable under Regulation 156 in respect of the aircraft that is unpaid at that time, to the extent that any such amount has not been remitted, waived or written off."

The power to detain any aircraft is vested in the Director-General of Civil Aviation. Under Regulation 141 where an owner or operator of an aircraft has defaulted in the payment of any charge incurred by virtue of these Regulations, the Director-General "shall not" detain or continue to detain an aircraft under these Regulations by reason of any alleged default in the payment of any charge where the owner or operator of the aircraft or any other person claiming an interest therein disputes that charge or that it was incurred in respect of that aircraft. This Regulation requires the payment of a sufficient security to be given to the Director-General, pending the determination of the alleged dispute. Regulation 142 refers to the Director-General's duties upon detaining an aircraft. One such mandatory duty is to enter such detention in the Aircraft Register; and take all reasonable steps to give notice of detention to the concerned person who in his opinion, has a security interest in the aircraft; or to any owner, operator, lessee, hirer, charterer or pilot-in-command of the aircraft.

Regulation 143 also mandates the Director-General on the nature of the particulars to be entered in the Aircraft Register under Regulation 141, such as:

(a) the description and amount of the charge due and from whom it is due;

(b) the date on which and the time at which the aircraft was detained; and
(c) the date on which and the time at which the entry is made.

Regulation 144 deals with a statutory aircraft lien which emphasises the possessory nature of the holding and it is vested in the Director-General. It ranks lower than a legal mortgage. An aircraft lien shall be vested in the Director-General and he may keep possession of the aircraft until all outstanding amounts referred to above are paid.

Regulation 145 provides for consequences following a de-registration of Malaysian aircraft for default of payment of a secured amount where an aircraft lien has been entered. If a Malaysian aircraft is involved in default of payment, this regulation provides that "where an outstanding amount is secured by an aircraft lien is unpaid at the end of six months after the day on which it became an outstanding amount or the day on which the aircraft lien was registered, whichever is the later, the Director-General may, having regard to all the circumstances, including the steps, if any, taken by any person to pay the whole or part of outstanding amounts secured by the aircraft lien, cancel the certificate of registration of the aircraft in the Aircraft Register." Subsection (2) further provides: "If the certificate is cancelled, the aircraft shall not be registered until the aircraft lien ceases to have effect." For the aircraft lien to cease having effect, payment must be made or it will be subject to a sale.

Regulation 146 requires aircraft liens to be settled within a month of the aircraft lien registration. This Regulation empowers the Director-General to sell an aircraft, with the leave of the High Court, where the outstanding amount secured by an aircraft lien is unpaid at the end of 1 month after the date on which the aircraft lien was registered. The High Court is in turn instructed that such leave for the sale of the impugned aircraft should only be granted against proof that a sum is due to the Director-General for any charge; a default in payment has occurred and that the Director-General is in compliance with Regulation 147(1). The Director-General has to observe Regulation 147 on Notice of Application for *locus standi* purposes of bringing the matter to the notice of interested parties and for announcement in the newspapers. What this requires of the Director-General to do before applying to the High Court for leave to sell an aircraft, is to take the necessary steps required under this regulation "for bringing the proposed application to the notice of any interested person and for affording them an opportunity of becoming a party to the proceedings". The Director-General has to, at least 21 days before applying to the High Court, publish this matter in one or more national newspapers circulating in Malaysia.

Where it is impracticable to publish as aforementioned, then a notice must be served on interested parties, namely, *(a)* the registered owner of the aircraft; *(b)* the operator of the aircraft; *(c)* any charterer or hirer of the aircraft; *(d)* any registered mortgagee of the aircraft; and *(e)* any other person with a priority interest in the aircraft. Such notice shall include details on the nationality and registration marks of the aircraft; its type; statement of the default sum and requirement to make payment within a period of sixty days from the date when the detention began, or within twenty-one days of the date of service of the notice, whichever shall be the later, after which the application will be made to the High Court for sale of the aircraft; and invite such person to inform the Director-General within fourteen days of the service of the notice if he wishes to become a party to the proceedings.

It mandatory to cause this notice to be served by any one of the following processes, for example, by delivery to the person to whom it is to be sent; or by leaving it at his usual or last known place of business or abode. Other forms include "sending by post in a prepaid registered letter addressed to him at his usual or last known place of business or abode; or if the person to whom it is to be sent is a company or body corporate, by delivering it to the registered address or principal office address of the company or body corporate or by sending it by post in a prepaid registered letter."

Regulation 148 outlines the Notice of sale where the High Court has given the Director-General leave to sell the aircraft subject to any additional notice that the Court deems just. Then a notice to sell the aircraft shall be published in one or more national newspapers circulating in Malaysia and the aircraft is to be sold for the best price that can be reasonably obtained. Regulation 149 deals with the Proceeds of sale which are to be applied in the following order: *(a)* payment of any customs duty for bringing the aircraft into Malaysia; *(b)* payment of the Director-General's expenses incurred in detaining, keeping and selling the aircraft, including its expenses in connection with the application to the High Court and its insurance required under Regulation 156; *(c)* payment of any charge in respect of any aircraft which the High Court has found to be due; *(d)* payment of any airport charge due from the operator to the owner or manager of the aerodrome under Regulation 141. If there is a surplus, such shall be paid to those whose interest have been divested by the aircraft sale.

Regulation 150 regulates Equipment, store and aircraft documents. The power of the Director- General to detain and sell an aircraft also extends under this Regulation to **aircraft equipment** and any equipment and stores carried in the aircraft, irrespective of whether it is the property of the operator.

Regulation 151 gives the Director-General power to recover charges or any part by civil action.

Regulation 152 provides for cessation of aircraft lien where

(a) there is no outstanding amount secured by the aircraft lien;
(b) the aircraft is sold under this Part; or
(c) the Director-General directs in writing that the aircraft lien ceases to have effect, …

An entry to this effect shall be made by the Director-General in the Aircraft Register.

Regulation 153 mentions the duty of the Director-General to state on a Certificate the amount unpaid either as charge or as penalty in respect of an aircraft and its accompanying details where a prescribed person requests such information in writing.

Where such a certificate has been issued by the Director-General, any aircraft lien does not secure *(a)* any such charge or debt in respect of the aircraft that was payable and unpaid as at that time but was not specified in the certificate; or *(b)* any penalty relating to any such charge.

Prescribed persons refer to:

(a) the registered holder of the certificate or registration of the aircraft;
(b) a person with security interest in the aircraft;
(c) the owner, or the agent of the owner, of the aircraft; and
(d) an authorised person by writing referred to in paragraph *(a)*, *(b)* or *(c)*.

Regulation 154 criminalises anyone who dismantles or detaches an aircraft or its parts or equipment under lien without the prior permission of the Director-General. But if this is done pursuant to these Regulations, such act is not criminal in nature.

Regulation 155 provides for protection against an action against the Director-General for any loss of or damage to an aircraft during its detention or arrest or for any economic loss suffered by a person as a result of an arrest, unless wilfully or negligently caused by the Director-General.

Regulation 156 deals with compulsory payment of insurance of an aircraft where it is detained by or in the custody or possession of the Director-General. Such insurance shall be for the benefit of the prescribed person. Where a premium amount is paid by the Director-General, "an equivalent becomes a debt payable to the Director-General by the person by whom amounts secured by the aircraft lien in respect of the aircraft are payable." Prescribed persons refer to *(a)* the Director-General; *(b)* a person who has a security interest in the aircraft; and *(c)* the owner of the aircraft.

6.2.3.2 Analysis of the Regulations on Aircraft Mortgage

Regulation 157 states that a mortgage of an aircraft includes both a mortgage and a charge but does not include a floating charge. This would exclude naturally the crystallisation of the floating charge as a fixed charge. This Regulation interprets, unless the context otherwise requires, the "mortgage of an aircraft" as including a mortgage or charge which extends to any store or space parts for the aircraft but does not otherwise include a mortgage created as a floating charge.

Regulation 158 provides for the requirements to register, a Malaysian aircraft mortgage in the Aircraft Register. Once the mortgagee intends to apply for aircraft mortgage registration, it shall be submitted to the Director-General in the specified form and shall be accompanied by a certified true copy of the mortgage. The mortgagee can also include the terms "priority notice". Sub-regulation (3) provides: "A notice of intention to make an application to enter a contemplated mortgage of an aircraft in the Aircraft Register (hereinafter referred to as "a priority notice") may also be entered in the Aircraft Register." Sub-regulation 4 provides that the application to enter a priority notice in the aircraft register shall be made to the Director-General by or on behalf of the prospective mortgagee in the form specified by the Director-General. The following sub-regulations 5–9 are important to note as they deal with applications of mortgage notices and priority interests and their interrelationship in ranking. Sub-regulation 5 states that separate applications have to be made where there are two or more aircrafts that are the subject of one mortgage or where one aircraft is subject to two mortgages in such a case, "separate applications shall be made in respect of each aircraft or of each mortgage, as the case may be."

Sub-regulation 6 states that where a mortgage is not in *Bahasa Malaysia* or in English, the application for mortgage registration must be accompanied by the original document accompanied by a certified true translation thereof. Sub-regulation (7) states that upon receipt of an application to enter a mortgage or priority notice in the Aircraft Register, the Director-General shall enter the mortgage or the priority notice by placing the application form there and by noting on it the date and time of the entry. Sub regulation (8) provides: "Applications duly made shall be entered in the Aircraft Register in order of their receipt by the Director-General." Finally, sub-regulation (9) states: "The Director-General shall notify the applicant of the date and time of the entry of the mortgage or the priority notice … and of the register number of the entry and shall send a copy of the notification to the mortgagor and the owner."

Regulation 159 covers amendments of entries made in the aircraft register: such as in the name, status or address of mortgagee or mortgagor or description of the mortgaged property. Once the appropriate fee is paid, the Director-General shall enter the notification in the Aircraft Register and shall notify the mortgagee, the mortgagor and the owner that he has done so. Regulation 160 underscores the discharge of an aircraft mortgage when the debt owing by mortgagor to mortgagee has been settled. The Director-General shall then enter the form in the Aircraft Register and mark the relevant entry as "Discharged" and notify the mortgagee, mortgagor and the owner that he has done so. The power to rectify an entry in the aircraft register is found in Regulation 161 by order of the High Court being served on the Director-General. Regulation 162 provides that the removal of an aircraft from the aircraft register shall not affect the rights of any mortgagee under any registered mortgage, unless of course this happens before the notice of discharge of the mortgage takes place.

Regulation 163 provides for the discontinued application of the Bills of Sale Act 1950 and application of the registration provisions of the Companies Act 1965. This Regulation provides:

(1) The provisions of the Bills of Sale Act 1950 *[Act 268]* insofar as they relate to bills of sale and other documents given by way of security for the payment of money shall not apply to any mortgage of an aircraft registered in the Aircraft Register.
(2) Section 108 of the Companies Act 1965 *[Act 125]* , shall continue to have effect on a mortgage of an aircraft or any share in an aircraft created by a company incorporated pursuant to that Act.

It is noteworthy that domestic legislation implementing the treaties has subsequently declared inapplicable the provisions of section 108 of the Companies Act 1965 also. The net effect, today, then is that both these laws are inapplicable to aircraft mortgages.

Section 2C of the Civil Aviation Act 1969 provides that the powers, duties and functions of the Director-General may be delegated in writing conferred on him under the Act.

6.2.4 Compatibility with the Treaty Regimes: Cape Town Convention and Aircraft Protocol

The civil aviation regulations discussed above fall within the terms of an "internal transaction" as set out in <u>Article 1(n)</u> of the Convention and under the Aircraft Protocol. "Internal transaction" means a transaction of a type listed in Article 2(2) (a) to (c) <u>where the centre of the main interests of all parties to such transaction is situated, and the relevant object located (as specified in the Protocol), in the same Contracting State at the time of the conclusion of the contract and where the interest created by the transaction has been registered in a national registry in that Contracting State</u> which has made a declaration under Article 50(1)."

In the preceding discussion on the Civil Aviation Regulations, the place of transaction is Malaysia and the interest in the aircraft object was registered in the national registry. Hence, the civil aviation regulations are compatible with the Convention. But Malaysia has not made an opt-out declaration under Article 50 of the Convention which regulates internal transactions. Under this article the Contracting State may declare that the Cape Town Convention shall not apply to internal transactions. Paragraph 2 of Article 50 provides that certain other provisions continue to apply to internal transactions. These are the provisions of Articles 8(4) dealing with remedies of chargees, 9(1) dealing with vesting of property in satisfaction/redemption, 16 on validity of registration in the international register, Chapter V- other matters relating to registration as set out in Articles 18 to 26, Article 29 on priority of competing interests, and any provisions of this Convention relating to registered interests. The Relevant Contracting State here is the "State in which center of the main interests of all parties to a transaction is located, where the aircraft object is located, and where interest arising under that transaction has been registered in a national registry, as set out in Article 1(n) of the Convention." The Civil Aviation Regulations do not cross-refer to these Articles, namely: 8(4), 9(1), 16, Chapter V, Article 29 and any other provision relating to registered interests. Therefore, the present status of Article 50 is that Malaysia has not made a statement on internal transactions even though it seems on the basis of the foregoing analyses that Malaysia deems the preceding civil aviation regulations as internal transactions within the meaning of Article 50(1) of the Convention.

The priority of competing interests in Malaysia might therefore be along the following lines before the adoption of the Convention and Protocol:

(a) Legal or equitable mortgage that is registered in the national registry followed by a statutory lien that is likewise registered.
(b) Equitable liens and leases that are recognised at equity.
(c) Floating charges could have a place in aircraft mortgage unless expressly ruled out but fixed charges as in debenture holder rights must prevail as in company law under Section 108 of the Companies Act.

(d) Article 4(3) of the Civil Law Act 1956 on legal and equitable assignments of various rights would still be preserved.
(e) The Bill of Sales Act 1950 would not apply.

Last but not the least, equitable maxims such as "where the equities are equal, the first in time prevails" might continue to apply to internal transactions.

6.3   Declarations by Malaysia to the Cape Town Convention

Seven years ago, Malaysia ratified the 2001 Cape Town Convention on International Interests in Mobile Equipment and the Protocol to the Cape Town Convention on International Interests in Mobile Equipment on Matters specific to Aircraft Equipment on 1 March 2006 and deposited several Declarations under the Cape Town Convention and its Protocol.

The Protocol especially for aircraft (which can carry at least eight people or 2750 kg of cargo and engines (with thrust 1750 lb force [7800 N] or 550 horse power [410 kW] and helicopters carrying five or more passengers) took effect on 1 March 2006. Airlines operate as the owners or leaseholders of an aviation asset. The Registry is based in Dublin, Ireland.

Chapter X deals with the "Rights or interests subject to declarations by Contracting States". It covers Articles 39 and 40. With regard to Article 39(1)(a), "Malaysia declares that the following categories of non-consensual right or interest have priority under its laws over an interest in an aircraft object equivalent to that of the holder of a registered international interest and shall have priority over a registered international interest, whether in or outside insolvency proceedings.

1. liens in favour of airline employees for unpaid wages arising since the time of a declared default by that airline under a contract to finance or lease an aircraft object.
2. liens or other rights of an authority of Malaysia relating to taxes or other unpaid charges arising from or related to the use of that aircraft object and owed by the owner or operator of that aircraft object, and arising since the time of a default by that owner or operator under a contract to finance or lease that aircraft object; and
3. liens in favour of repairers of an aircraft object in their possession to the extent of service or services performed on and value added to that aircraft object."

On general opt-in declarations under Article 39(1)(b)

"Malaysia declares that nothing in the Convention shall affect its right or that of any entity thereof, or any intergovernmental organization in which Malaysia is a member, or other private provider of public services in Malaysia, to arrest or detain an aircraft object under its laws for payment of amounts owed to the Government of Malaysia, any such entity, organization or provider directly relating to the service or services provided by it in respect of that or another aircraft object."

Article 40 deals with registrable non-consensual rights or interests. On opt-in declarations under Article 40, "Malaysia declares that the following categories of non-consensual right or interest shall be registrable under the Convention as regards any category of aircraft object as if the right or interest were an international interest and shall be regulated accordingly.

1. Liens in favour of airline employees for unpaid wages arising prior to the time of a declared default by that airline under a contract to finance or lease an aircraft object.
2. Liens or other rights of an authority of Malaysia relating to taxes or other unpaid charges arising from or related to the use of an aircraft object and owed by the owner or operator of that aircraft object, and arising prior to the time of a declared default by that owner or operator under a contract to finance or lease that aircraft object; and
3. Rights of a person obtaining a court order permitting attachment of an aircraft object in partial or full satisfaction of a legal judgment.

Article 53 falls under Chapter XIV on Final Provisions covering Articles 47–62. Article 53 deals with Determination of courts. "Malaysia declares that all courts with competent jurisdiction under the laws of Malaysia are the relevant courts for the purposes of Article 1 and Chapter XII of the Convention."

Article 54 deals with Declarations regarding remedies. On the mandatory declaration under Article 54(2), "Malaysia declares that any and all remedies available to the creditor under the Convention which are not expressed under the relevant provision thereof to require application to the court may be exercised without court action and without leave of the court."

6.3.1 Declarations Deposited by Malaysia Under the Protocol to the Cape Town on International Interests in Mobile Equipment on Matters Specific to Aircraft Equipment

Opt-in declaration under Article XXX(1) in respect of Article VIII
"Malaysia declares that it shall apply Article VIII."
Opt-in declaration under Article XXX(1) in respect of Article XII
"Malaysia declares that it shall apply Article XII."
Opt-in declaration under Article XXX(1) in respect of Article XIII.
"Malaysia declares that it shall apply Article XIII."
Opt-in declarations deposited under Article XXX(2) in respect of Article X providing for the application of the entirety of Article X:
"Malaysia declares that it shall apply Article X of the Protocol in its entirety and that the number of working days to be used for the purposes of the time limit laid down in Article X(2) of the Protocol shall be no more than:

Ten (10) working days in respect of the remedies specified in Articles 13(1)(a) and
(b) and (c) of the Convention (respectively, preservation of aircraft objects and
their value; possession, control or custody of aircraft objects; and, immobilization of aircraft objects); and

Thirty working days in respect of the remedies specified in Articles 13(1)(d) and
(e)) of the Convention (respectively, lease, or management of aircraft objects and
the income thereof, and, sale and application of proceeds from aircraft objects)."

General opt-in declarations under Article XXX(3) in respect of Article XI providing for the application of Alternative A in its entirety to all types of insolvency
proceedings:

"Malaysia declares that it shall apply Article XI, Alternative A, of the Protocol in its
entirety to all types of insolvency proceedings, and that the waiting period for the
purposes of Article XI(3) of that Alternative shall be sixty (60) working days."

6.3.2   Notification to UNIDROIT

The Government of Malaysia has also entered the following in its notification to
UNIDROIT:

"[This declaration was notified to UNIDROIT by the Government of Malaysia, as a
subsequent declaration pursuant to Article XXXIII(1) of the Protocol, on 18
December 2006, and in accordance with Article XXXIII(2) of the Protocol it
took effect on 1 July 2007. A previous declaration by the Government of Malaysia
under Article XXX(3) of the Protocol was withdrawn by the Government of
Malaysia pursuant to Article XXXIV(1) of the Protocol, with the withdrawal
taking effect from 1 July 2007. The text of that previous declaration was as follows: "Malaysia declares that it shall apply Article XI, Alternative A, of the
Protocol in its entirety to all types of insolvency proceedings, and that the waiting period for the purposes of Article XI(3) of that Alternative shall be sixty (60)
working days."

6.4   The International Interests in Mobile Equipment (Aircraft) Act 2006 (Act 659)

6.4.1   The Cape Town Convention and Aircraft Protocol

This Convention and Protocol provide for two important bases of jurisdiction,
namely, the law of the contracting state where the aircraft is registered and the
where the debtor is situated. The two jurisdictions may or may not coincide. Owners
of aircraft and engines can now register their interests under the local domestic laws.

It is to be noted that aircraft can now be bought on hire-purchase. Before the dawn of the Convention, the owners registered their aircraft in any country but the International Civil Aviation Organisation (ICAO) now allows only for one registration because of cross-border leasing arrangements. When the aircraft are not airworthy problems can arise. However, registration under the Cape Town Convention protects the owner. Since the airlines suffered two major air disasters in 2015, the airlines is declared "technically bankrupt" with a re-structuring to follow.[23]

In Malaysia, MAS and other aircraft are registered in Ireland. All Malaysian registered civil aircraft have a prefix 9M. MAS has entered into dry and wet leasing arrangements too. The Cape Town Convention enables the tracking of the aircraft under various leasing and sub-leasing agreements for the regulation of the industry. In their airline manufacture and operating industries, several states are involved. For example, there is the state of design, the state of production, the state of registration and the state of the operator. The Cape Town Convention focuses on the registration of financial interests.

6.4.2   Act 659

This Act is published by the Commissioner for Law Revision, Malaysia under the Authority of the Revision of Laws Act 1968, 2012. The date of the Royal Assent is 30 August 2006 and the date of publication in the Gazette is 31 August 2006 and subsidiary legislation is made under *P.U. (B)* 281/2006. The Act incorporates the Convention and Protocol through two Schedules, First Schedule and Second Schedule. Experts point out that the Malaysian approach was not to rewrite the national aviation laws but to attach the Protocol and Convention and incorporate priority over inconsistent laws (Paul NG, Global Head of Aviation, Stephenson Harwood Outline who has entered a disclaimer that he is not Malaysian qualified but his work is based on the recollection of those persons who attended the event.) Malaysia's ratification brought the convention into force.

6.4.2.1   Structure of Act 659

This Act has seven sections and two schedules.

The Preamble to the Act states that it is "An Act to implement the Convention on the International Interests in Mobile Equipment, and the Protocol to that Convention on International Interests in Mobile Equipment on Matters Specific to Aircraft Equipment and to provide for matters connected therewith. The Preamble acknowledges that the Convention on International Interests in Mobile Equipment and the Protocol to the Convention on International Interests in Mobile Equipment on

---

[23] BBC News, Malaysia Airlines "technically bankrupt" http://www.bbc.com/news/business-32955818, accessed on 23 October 2015.

Matters Specific to Aircraft Equipment were opened for signature at Cape Town on 16 November 2001. Malaysia deposited her instruments of accession on 2 November 2005 and in accordance with Article 49 of the Convention and Article XXVIII of the Protocol, the said Convention and Protocol entered into force for Malaysia on 1 March 2006.

Act 659 is cited as the International Interests in Mobile Equipment (Aircraft) Act 2006.

Section 2(1) provides that the Convention on International Interests in Mobile Equipment as set out in the First Schedule and the Protocol set out in the Second Schedule, shall have the force of law in Malaysia and shall be construed in accordance with the provisions of this Act. Section 2(2) provides that notwithstanding Article 2 of the Convention on International Interests in Mobile Equipment, this Act shall apply to aircraft objects only.

Section 3 offers several Interpretations to the Act. Act 659 also includes any subsidiary legislation made under it unless the context otherwise requires,, according to section 3. "Cape Town Convention" means the Convention on International Interests in Mobile Equipment. "Aircraft objects" are defined in section 3(3) as "any frame, aircraft engine and helicopter as defined under Article 1(2) of the Aircraft Protocol. The national agency responsible for the convention is the Department of Civil Aviation, Ministry of Transport and "Minister" refers to the Minister charged with the responsibility for civil aviation. "Aircraft Protocol" means the Protocol to the Convention on International Interests in Mobile Equipment on Matters Specific to Aircraft Equipment.

Following on from Article 53 of the Cape Town Convention, "Relevant courts" under the Act refer to all courts with competent jurisdiction under the laws of Malaysia for purposes stated in Article 1 and Chapter XII of the Cape Town Convention, under section 4.

Section 5 empowers the Minister to make such regulations which are effective or necessary to (1) better implement the Act's provisions; (2) generally regulate and carry out the Cape Town Convention and the Aircraft Protocol; and (3) make any amendments to such Convention or Protocol.

The mandatory non-application of other local legislation (Acts) are stated in section 6. Under section 6(1), it is clearly stated that subsection 108(3) of the Companies Act 1965 (Act 125) shall not apply to a charge on any aircraft objects falling within the scope of the Cape Town Convention and the Aircraft Protocol. This is a significant departure as section 108 of the Companies Act requires a charge to be lodged with the Companies Commission of Malaysia: Writing in the context of immoveable property under the National Land Code, Lorraine Cheah and Grace CG Yeoh of Shearn Delamore & Co, pointed out: "If the provisions of section 108 of the Companies Act are not complied with, the undertaking purportedly secured by the charge shall be void against the liquidator and any creditor of the company."[24]

---

[24] Lorraine Cheah and Grace C G Yeoh, "Getting the Deal Through – Restructuring and Insolvency: Malaysia" (2009), http://www.shearndelamore.com/assets/templates/images/pdf/paper_publications/Restructuring_and_Insolvency_2009.pdf accessed on 22 March 2014.

The position with regard to movable property such as aircraft in Malaysia is summarized by Lee Tat Boon of Skrine, Malaysia as: "Any mortgage of a Malaysian aircraft may be entered in the aircraft register which is maintained by the Director-General of Civil Aviation Malaysia. Such application must be made to the Director-General by or on behalf of the mortgagee in the prescribed form and accompanied by a copy of the mortgage certified true copy by the applicant. "Mortgage of an aircraft" is defined under the Civil Aviation regulations 1996 to include a mortgage or charge which extends to any store or space parts for the aircraft but does not otherwise include a mortgage created as a floating charge.... The mortgagee's security in the aircraft under the mortgage may be enforced through a sale of the mortgaged aircraft under the provisions of either the Civil Aviation regulations 1996 or the Rules of the High Court 1980."[25]

Under the Cape Town Agreement, Article 1(a), an "agreement" refers to a security agreement, a title reservation agreement or a leasing agreement. Subsection 108 (3) of the Companies Act provides for the registration of charges including (i) a charge on a ship or aircraft or any share in a ship or aircraft.

This is followed by clause 2 which states that subsection 4(3) (on a right to sue under an assignment) of the Civil Law Act 1956 [Act 67] shall not apply to any assignment falling within the scope of the Cape Town Convention and the Aircraft Protocol. Under Article 1(b) of the Cape Town Convention, an "assignment" means a contract which, whether by way of security or otherwise, confers on the assignee associated rights with or without a transfer of the related international interest and Article 1.c defines "associated rights" as all rights to payment or other performance by a debtor under an agreement which are secured by or associated with the object. In Malaysia, an assignor is a person who transfers his interest or property to another called the assignee and the transaction is called an assignment. An assignment may also involve the transfer of obligations. The significance of subsection 4 (3) and a right to sue under an assignment has been considered elsewhere.[26]

The prevailing laws clause of the Act in section 7(1) states that subject to section 6, the provisions of Act 659 are additions and not derogations, to the prevailing written laws on the financing and leasing of aircraft object, creation of international interests in aircraft object and their registration. Subsection 7(2) also provides for resolution of conflict of laws where there is a conflict between Act 659 and other written laws. It states that Act 659 shall prevail in such cases where the matter is

---

[25] Lee Tat Boon, "Security over Collateral" http://www.lexmundi.com/Document.asp?DocID=1027 accessed on 22 March 2014 on the forms of security that may be created in Malaysia include a charge, pledge, lien, legal assignment, set-off, hypothecation, guarantee and indemnity.

[26] Roger Tan, "Rights of Assignors and Assignees to sue under an Absolute Assignment and Assignment by way of Charge Used as a Security for Loan" (2003), http://www.malaysianbar.org.my/index2.php?option=com_content&do_pdf=1&id=97, accessed on 26 December 2013. Upon receipt of the notice, the debtor must make all payments of the debt to the assignee and not the assignor and if he pays the assignor without the consent of the assignee, he may have to pay the assignee all over again. (Malayawata Steel Berhad v Government of Malaysia & Anor [1980] 2 MLJ 103, even though it involved an equitable assignment. See also Malaysian International Merchant Bankers Bhd v Malaysian Airlines Sytem Bhd [1982] 2 MLJ 59.)

governed by the Cape Town Convention and the Aircraft Protocol. The fate of the other inconsistent or conflicting laws is that to the extent of the conflict or inconsistency they are deemed to be superseded.

This is then followed by the First Schedule under subsection 2 (1) which sets out the provisions of the Convention on International Interests in Mobile Equipment and a Second Schedule under subsection 2 (1) setting out the provisions of the Protocol to the Convention on International Interests in Mobile Equipment on Matters specific to Aircraft Equipment.

Upon ratification of the Convention and Protocol, the priority of competing claims for internal transactions would now be as follows:

1. Legal or equitable mortgage that is registered in the national registry followed by a statutory lien that is likewise registered.
2. Perhaps, equitable liens and leases that are recognised at equity.
3. Floating charges do not have a place in aircraft mortgage. Fixed charges as in debenture holder rights also do not prevail due to the express ouster clause of Section 108 of the Companies Act by the local legislation: International Interests in Mobile Equipment (Aircraft) Act 2006, Act 659. Similarly, neither the Bill of Sales Act 1950 nor Article 4 (3) of the Civil Law Act 1956 apply to any assignment falling within the scope of the Convention and Protocol. The exclusion of Article 4 (3) of the Civil Law Act 1956 signifies that legal and equitable assignments of various rights will not be preserved.
4. Last but not the least, equitable maxims such as "where the equities are equal, the first in time prevails" might continue to apply to internal transactions.

6.5 Questionnaire for Session III D. at the Vienna Congress 2014 of AIDC

by Dr See Eng Teong,

[Questions for a national reporter in a Party Jurisdiction]
Note: VS- Dr See Eng Teong; MG- Mary George

1. Registration system

    (a) VS: In the absence of the Cape Town Convention registration system, the governing principle would probably have been the first to *create* a charge or mortgage and the priority would be *prima facie* based on registration of the charge/mortgage, if permissible under either the Companies Act or other relevant legislation, subject to any prior charge that would have been recognized in equity.

    (b) VS: Not sure about railway rolling stocks and space assets but a charge created over an aircraft would be registrable under s 108(3) of the Companies Act 1965. A mortgage created over an aircraft might also be registrable under Regulation 158 of the Civil Aviation Regulations 1996.

(c) VS: There are two separate issues here. In respect of the issue of registration against an asset, neither the Companies Act 1965 nor the Civil Aviation Regulations seem to expressly state whether registration is against a debtor or an asset though it appears that the two laws are more person-oriented as opposed to asset-oriented. In respect of the issue of accuracy of the information provided, Regulation 158(2) of the Civil Aviation Regulations does require attachment of a certified true copy of the mortgage.

(d) VS: Don't quite understand this question.

2. Enforcement of a security interest

(a) VS: It appears that an agreement on private enforcement of an international interest, similar to that provided for in the Cape Town Convention, was valid and enforceable.

(b) VS: Such a clause would be valid even in absence of Cape Town Convention. Based on principle of freedom of contract the parties to an agreement were free, subject to legal or statutory prohibitions otherwise which were and are rare, to define their terms of dealing in the agreement.

(c) VS: [Q1] Subject to any statutory intervention in respect of these three types of vehicles prior to the enforcement of the Cape Town Convention (which was probably none), a security agreement might spell out the exact remedies that would be available to the creditor/parties in the event of a default. [Q2] Subject to statutory intervention in respect of these three types of vehicles prior to enforcement of Cape Town Convention (which was probably none), a security agreement could spell out the order of application of the proceeds from the realization of the secured assets and the usual order was to satisfy the statutory authorities (if any), secured creditors, unsecured creditors (if any), and any balance would be returned to the debtor.

3. Treatment of Security Interests under the Insolvency Procedure[27]

(a) VS: Dr Mary George reported that Malaysia declared Alternative A. If it does, were the rules provided by the chosen alternative different from the treatment of a security interest under the domestic insolvency law of your jurisdiction in the absence of the Convention? If no alternative is chosen, what was the reason for doing so?

(b) VS: Alternative A of Article XI of the Aircraft Protocol appears to be different from the insolvency process.

(c) VS: Based on Alternative A of Article XI of the Aircraft Protocol, the rule would be different in the absence of the Cape Town Conv.

---

[27] All three Protocols provide alternatives that differ in the extent of the power that the creditor can exercise in case of insolvency of the debtor. However, even under an alternative less favourable to the creditor (Alternative B), the insolvency administrator or debtor in possession shall either cure all defaults and agree to perform all future obligations or give the creditor the opportunity to take possession of the secured object. Alternative C of Art.IX of the Rail Protocol seems to be the only exception, which enables the insolvency administrator or the debtor to apply to the court for an order suspending its obligation.

4. General Consideration[28]

(a) VS: It may or may not be usual to conduct an economic analysis prior to designing a law, whether on secured transactions or other private laws more generally. No idea whether any economic analysis was conducted prior to becoming a Party to the Cape Town Convention.[29]

(b) VS: Not sure but doubtful. The terms and conditions of financial institutions are more or less settled and they hardly negotiate on their terms, subject to State intervention or where the borrower is a large company or wields strong non-business influence. In most situations the determining factor tends to be the creditworthiness of the borrower.

(c) MG: The Federal Constitution of Malaysia has a dualist-transformation approach to the implementation of international treaty law and hence subscribes to the idea that international law rules must be incorporated into domestic law once a State is Party to a convention for the implementation of rights and obligations as the case may be, except where reservations or declarations are made thereto. There is no specific mention that the way to gain the economic benefits of the Cape Town Convention is through domestic implementation of its provisions. However, it could be inferred that based on the above, that the benefits of a Convention are obtained only when found in domestic law.

References

1. Lee Tat Boon, "Security over Collateral" http://www.lexmundi.com/Document. asp?DocID=1027.
2. Cheah, Lorraine and Grace C.G. Yeoh. 2003. Getting the deal through – Restructuring and insolvency: Malaysia, http://www.shearndelamore.com/assets/templates/images/pdf/paper_ publications/Restructuring_and_Insolvency_2009.pdf.
3. Wool, Jeffrey. Treaty design, implementation, and compliance benchmarking economic benefit – A framework as applied to the Cape Town Convention [2012–4]. *Uniform Law Review*, 633.
4. Roger Tan, "Rights of Assignors and Assignees to sue under an Absolute Assignment and Assignment by way of Charge Used as a Security for Loan" (2003), http://www.malaysianbar. org.my/index2.php?option=com_content&do_pdf=1&id=97.

---

[28] Anthony Saunders, Anand Srinivasan, Ingo Walter & Jeffrey Wool, The Economic Implications of Secured Transactions Law Reform: A Case Study, University of Pennsylvania Journal of International Economic Law, Vol. 20, p.309, at 324

[29] Jeffrey Wool, Treaty Design, Implementation, and Compliance Benchmarking Economic Benefit – a framework as applied to the Cape Town Convention, [2012-4] *Uniform Law Review*, 633.

Mary George is an Associate Professor at the University of Malaya, Faculty of Law and she also serves as the Head of the Law and Policy Unit of The Institute of Ocean and Earth Sciences, at the University. Having received her early legal education from the University of Bangalore (India), the Institute of Social Studies (The Hague), London School of Economics (England), she pursued her doctoral studies at the Faculty of Law, University of Sydney. Specialising in international air and space law, law of the sea and trust law, she teaches and supervises postgraduate and undergraduate students. She has presented many papers at numerous international and national conferences and published many articles and books. She received the Fulbright Award in 2009 and pursued ocean law research at the Georgetown University Law School. She is also involved in international and national consultancies such as the UN-IPBES Deliverable 4 (c) and the IMO-NORAD programme to assist the East Asian Seas in the Control of Marine Pollution. Till very recently she was also a member of the Malaysian National Law Reform Committee. She is currently a member of and serves the Asian Society of International Law.

Dr See Eng Teong read law at King's College London and practised law for a few years before pursuing his postgraduate study. He was awarded a *Monbukagakusho* scholarship to study at Nagoya University where he obtained his PhD on competition law and policy research. He has work experience in the academics and legal practice. He was once a law lecturer at a university, and General Counsel of an airline. He is called to the Honourable Society of Lincoln's Inn. His areas of academic interest include aviation law and policy, competition law and policy, and world trade law.

Chapter 7
The Cape Town Convention on International Interests in Mobile Equipment and Its Implementation in the Netherlands and on the Dutch Caribbean Islands

Sjef van Erp

7.1 Introduction

Already in 2004 I expressed the idea that the Cape Town Convention on International Interests in Mobile Equipment ("Cape Town Convention") with its first-in-time and object- based computerised notice filing system could be a workable model for a registration system of security interests in Europe and even be a model for a European mortgage registration system regarding immovable property.[1] This was at a moment when it was not clear yet whether this convention would be as global in its success as the drafters had hoped for. In the meantime that hope has become true and it was therefore an excellent choice of the International Academy of Comparative Law to devote one of its sessions to this topic during its XIXth International Congress of Comparative Law in Vienna.

---

[1] For the text of the Cape Town Convention see: www.unidroit.org/en/instruments/security-interests/cape-town-convention. Cf. S. van Erp, The Cape Town Convention: a Model for a European System of Security Interests Registration?, European Review of Private Law 2004, p. 91ff. See also my earlier contribution on registration principles: S. van Erp, A comparative analysis of mortgage law: Searching for principles, in: M.E. Sanchez Jordán and A. Gambaro, Land Law in Comparative Perspective (The Hague: Kluwer Law International, 2002), p. 69ff.

S. van Erp (✉)
Faculty of Law, Maastricht University, Maastricht, The Netherlands
e-mail: s.vanerp@maastrichtuniversity.nl

© Springer International Publishing AG 2017
S. Kozuka (ed.), *Implementing the Cape Town Convention and the Domestic Laws on Secured Transactions*, Ius Comparatum - Global Studies in Comparative Law 22, DOI 10.1007/978-3-319-46470-1_7

7.2   The Kingdom of the Netherlands, the European Union and the Cape Town Convention

The position of the Netherlands with regard to the Cape Town Convention is rather complicated. This is due to the internal (constitutional) structure of the country itself, the recent changes in that structure, and its position as a Member State of the European Union (EU). Let me first discuss the constitutional structure of the country, then the resulting (non-)applicability of European Union law, followed by the consequences for the (non-)applicability of the Cape Town Convention.

Until October 10, 2010 the Kingdom of the Netherlands consisted of three "countries": in Europe the Netherlands and overseas the Netherlands Antilles and Aruba. On that date this structure was modified, such that, next to the Netherlands, the islands of Aruba, Curaçao and Sint Maarten are now autonomous countries (with internal self-government) within the broader framework of the Kingdom of the Netherlands. The islands of Bonaire, Sint Eustatius/Statia and Saba (the so-called "BES islands") became public bodies (municipalities) of the Netherlands, constituting the Caribbean part of the Netherlands, next to a European part of the Netherlands.[2] Until that date all of the Caribbean islands were not a part of the European Union. They were "Overseas Countries and Territories" (they had "OCT status") in the sense of article 198 of the Treaty on the Functioning of the European Union (TFEU).[3] After the new structure of the Kingdom of the Netherlands became effective that status remained, also with regard to the islands of Bonaire, Sint Eustatius and Saba. This could change in case the Dutch government might decide to apply for any of the Caribbean islands to obtain the status of Outermost Region

---

[2] A visual explanation might clarify the situation. See http://isleofholland.com/images/2013/01/Kingdom-of-the-Netherlands.jpg.

[3] Article 198 TFEU reads:

The Member States agree to associate with the Union the non-European countries and territories which have special relations with Denmark, France, the Netherlands and the United Kingdom. These countries and territories (hereinafter called the 'countries and territories') are listed in Annex II.

The purpose of association shall be to promote the economic and social development of the countries and territories and to establish close economic relations between them and the Union as a whole.

In accordance with the principles set out in the preamble to this Treaty, association shall serve primarily to further the interests and prosperity of the inhabitants of these countries and territories in order to lead them to the economic, social and cultural development to which they aspire.

For more information on the OCT status see: http://ec.europa.eu/europeaid/where/octs_and_greenland/index_en.htm. Cf. also Council Decision of 27 November 2001 on the association of the overseas countries and territories with the European Community ('Overseas Association Decision') (2001/822/EC), OJ 30.11.2001, L 314/1.

("OR status") according to article 349 TFEU, in which case EU law would apply.[4] This could happen in a few years when the new status of the islands is evaluated.

Effective September 1, 2010 the Kingdom of the Netherlands acceded to the Cape Town Convention on May 17, 2010. The accession was explicitly limited to Aruba and the Netherlands Antilles.[5] According to a "Nota Verbale" of the Dutch government to UNIDROIT, the new structure of the Kingdom did not affect the applicability of treaties, even with regard to what is now the Caribbean part of the Netherlands (Bonaire, Sint Eustatius and Saba), although with regard to these islands, according to the nota verbale, "the Government of the Netherlands will now be responsible for implementing these agreements." This means that the Dutch government is responsible for the implementation of the Convention in the Caribbean part of the Netherlands, but that it is not bound by the Convention with regard to the European part of the Netherlands, except in as far as it is bound as an EU Member State because of the accession by the European Union on April 28, 2009, effective from August 1, 2009. For the implementation on Aruba, Curaçao and Sint Maarten their respective governments are responsible. It should also be noted that Dutch civil law is not applicable on these islands, which have their own Civil Code, although it should immediately be added that their civil law closely follows Dutch law.

The European part of the Netherlands, being a Member-State of the European Union, is bound by European Union law. Because the European Union has competence in the area of private international law and was therefore involved in the

---

[4] Article 349 TFEU reads:

Taking account of the structural social and economic situation of Guadeloupe, French Guiana, Martinique, Réunion, Saint-Barthélemy, Saint-Martin, the Azores, Madeira and the Canary Islands, which is compounded by their remoteness, insularity, small size, difficult topography and climate, economic dependence on a few products, the permanence and combination of which severely restrain their development, the Council, on a proposal from the Commission and after consulting the European Parliament, shall adopt specific measures aimed, in particular, at laying down the conditions of application of the Treaties to those regions, including common policies. Where the specific measures in question are adopted by the Council in accordance with a special legislative procedure, it shall also act on a proposal from the Commission and after consulting the European Parliament.

The measures referred to in the first paragraph concern in particular areas such as customs and trade policies, fiscal policy, free zones, agriculture and fisheries policies, conditions for supply of raw materials and essential consumer goods, State aids and conditions of access to structural funds and to horizontal Union programmes.

The Council shall adopt the measures referred to in the first paragraph taking into account the special characteristics and constraints of the outermost regions without undermining the integrity and the coherence of the Union legal order, including the internal market and common policies.

For more information see: http://ec.europa.eu/regional_policy/activity/outermost/index_en.cfm.

[5] See the parliamentary history of the so-called "tacit" acceptance by the Dutch Parliament: Parliamentary document no. 32 227 (R 1904), A and nr. 1, *Verdrag inzake internationale zakelijke rechten op mobiel materieel en Protocol bij het Verdrag inzake internationale zakelijke rechten op mobiel materieel betreffende voor luchtvaartmaterieel specifieke aangelegenheden; Kaapstad, 16 November 2001*, Letter by the Minister of Foreign Affairs and Informative Note.

negotiations resulting in the Cape Town Convention, the European Union had to accede to the Convention to facilitate accession by its Member States.[6] The accession was, however, limited to those legal aspects where it had explicit competence. The European Union acceded in its capacity as "Regional Economic Integration Organisation" under article 48 of the Convention and article XXVII of the Aircraft Protocol. To make clear that it had the explicit competence to act, the Council Decision by which it was approved that the European Union would accede to the Cape Town Convention made explicit reference to the Brussels I Regulation, the Insolvency Regulation, and the Rome I Regulation.[7] All three regulations deal with topics which were also dealt with in the Convention: recognition and enforcement of judgments, insolvency and choice of law. The European Union also made several so-called "declarations" or decided explicitly not to make a "declaration": statements to opt-in or opt-out of certain arrangements under the Convention regime. A declaration the European Union made concerns article XXI of the Aircraft Protocol. This article reads: "For the purposes of Article 43 of the Convention and subject to Article 42 of the Convention, a court of a Contracting State also has jurisdiction where the object is a helicopter, or an airframe pertaining to an aircraft, for which that State is the State of registry." Article 43 of the Convention is about jurisdiction and article 42 about choice of forum. The declaration made is the following: "In accordance with Article XXX(5) of the Aircraft Protocol, Article XXI thereof will not apply within the Community and Council Regulation (EC) No 44/2001 of 22 December 2000 on jurisdiction and the recognition and enforcement of judgments in civil and commercial matters will apply to this matter for the Member States bound by the said Regulation or by any other agreement designed to extend its effects." The background of this declaration is that the Brussels I Regulation should not be set aside by a special rule of jurisdiction based on the *lex situs* of the registry in cases where the object is a helicopter or an airframe.[8] This example concerns an opt-out declaration to protect the coherence of European law. An example of an

---

[6] Cf. Council Decision of 6 April 2009 on the accession of the European Community to the Convention on international interests in mobile equipment and its Protocol on matters specific to aircraft equipment, adopted jointly in Cape Town on 16 November 2001 (2009/370/EC), OJ 15.5.2009, L 121/3 and B. Crans, The implications of the EU accession to the Cape Town Convention, Air and Space Law 2010, p. 1 ff. Reference can be made particularly to recitals 6 and 7 of the Council Decision:

> (6) The Community has exclusive competence over some of the matters governed by the Cape Town Convention and the Aircraft Protocol, while the Member States have competence over other matters governed by these two instruments.
> (7) The Community should therefore accede to the Cape Town Convention and the Aircraft Protocol.

[7] See Council Regulation (EC) No 44/2001 of 22 December 2000 on jurisdiction and the recognition and enforcement of judgments in civil and commercial matters (Brussels I Regulation), OJ 16.01.2001, L 12/1; Council Regulation (EC) No 1346/2000 of 29 May 2000 on insolvency proceedings (Insolvency Regulation), OJ 30.06.2000, L 160/1; Regulation (EC) No 593/2008 of the European Parliament and of the Council of 17 June 2008 on the law applicable to contractual obligations (Rome I Regulation), OJ 4.7.2008, L 177/6.

[8] Council decision, COM(2008) 508 final, p. 5.

explicit choice not to opt-in by declaration, again to protect the coherence of European law, concerns article XI of the Aircraft Protocol. This article contains provisions of substantive law concerning remedies on insolvency and is aimed at the protection of secured creditors, e.g. by obliging the insolvency administrator or the debtor to give the creditor possession of an aircraft object. This article "applies only where a Contracting State that is the primary insolvency jurisdiction has made a declaration pursuant to Article XXX(3)". The EU Insolvency Regulation in its article 5, however, contains a substantive provision of private international law, stating that the rights *in rem* of third parties shall not be affected by the opening of insolvency proceedings. No reference is made here to the law of the state in which the proceedings are opened or to the *lex rei sitae* for deciding whether or not the object is part of the insolvent's estate.[9] The EU, therefore, decided not to opt in to this article of the Aircraft Protocol, although, remarkably enough, J. Wool (Secretary and General Counsel of the Aviation Working Group) at a UNIDROIT seminar on the European Community and the Cape Town Convention argued that article XI of the Aircraft Protocol is "the most important (...) by far" of "declarations that will maximise the economic advantages" of acceding to the Cape Town Convention.[10] It seems as if the European Union saw more economic advantage in regional than global integration or, at least, valued the internal coherence of European law more than global uniformity.

The position of the Netherlands is therefore as follows. The European part of the Netherlands is bound by the EU accession to the Cape Town Convention, but the Caribbean islands are not.[11] For these islands accession by the Kingdom of the Netherlands was required, which indeed happened. This means that in both the European and the Caribbean part of the Netherlands the conflict of laws provisions of the Convention regime apply, although for the European part of the Netherlands European private international law has been given precedence over this regime by explicit decisions either not to opt-in or to opt-out of Cape Town Convention provisions. The accession by the EU does not have an impact on the substantive insolvency law of the Member States. With regard to that legal area they remain

---

[9] Council decision, COM(2008) 508 final, p. 4.

[10] Seminar – The European Economic Community and the Cape Town Convention (Rome, 26 November 2009), Summary Report prepared by the UNIDROIT Secretariat, p. 3, to be found on the website of the Aviation Working Group: www.awg.aero. See also a paper by J. Wool and a. Littlejohns, Cape Town Treaty in the European context: The case for Alternative A, Article XI of the Aircraft Protocol, also to be found on the website of the Aviation Working Group. They argue (footnote 1): "It is understood that, based on issues of the respective competence of the EU and its Member States, it may be necessary, desirable, or otherwise agreed that countries should effect the decision to adopt Alternative A via amendments to national law".

[11] Council decision on accession, Annex I, under II(4): "This Declaration is not applicable in the case of the territories of the Member States in which the Treaty establishing the European Community does not apply and is without prejudice to such acts or positions as may be adopted under the Aircraft Protocol by the Member States concerned on behalf and in the interests of those territories."

competent.[12] That same conclusion was drawn by the Kingdom of the Netherlands regarding the insolvency law of the Caribbean islands – and consequently the European part of the Netherlands – when accession for these islands was proposed to the Dutch Parliament. The Kingdom of the Netherlands, as the European Union, explicitly decided not to opt-in to the insolvency regime of article XI of the Aircraft Protocol.[13] It is still unclear – and most likely will not become clear in the near future – where the exact border line can be found separating what falls under the exclusive competence of the European Union from what remains within the realm of the Member States.[14]

As mentioned earlier, in order to make the Cape Town Convention applicable on the Caribbean islands the Kingdom of the Netherlands had to accede to the Convention and Aircraft Protocol. It did this only for those islands and deliberately not for its European territory. The Caribbean islands are, therefore, bound by the full Convention regime, taking into account the various opt-in/opt-out choices made. As the Kingdom of the Netherlands decided only to accede to the Convention for, at present, Aruba, Curaçao and Sint Maarten as "countries" within the Kingdom and by *nota verbale* declared that the accession for the Caribbean part of the Netherlands (Bonaire, Sint Eustatius and Saba) remains to be effective, the European part of the Netherlands still is not bound by the substantive provisions of the Convention and the Aircraft Protocol.[15] The Dutch government, acting as the

---

[12] Council decision on accession, Annex I, Under II(6): "The Member States keep their competence concerning the rules of substantive law as regards insolvency."

[13] Parliamentary document no. 32 227 (R 1904), A and nr. 1, p. 6 and p. 19.

[14] Council Decision on accession, Annex I, under II(7): "The exercise of competence which the Member States have transferred to the Community pursuant to the Treaty establishing the European Community is, by its nature, liable to continuous development. In the framework of that Treaty, the competent institutions may take decisions which determine the extent of the competence of the Community. The latter therefore reserves the right to amend this Declaration accordingly, without this constituting a prerequisite for the exercise of its competence with regard to matters governed by the Aircraft Protocol." See also the Netherlands Minister of Foreign Affairs in his reaction to critical remarks by the Council of State on his draft proposal for tacit acceptance of the Cape Town Convention, asking for an (explicit) list of provisions from the Cape Town Convention which are binding upon the Netherlands and which are not (Parliamentary history, document no. 32 227 (R 1904), B and no. 2, p. 2): "*Een lijst van bepalingen die onder de exclusieve bevoegdheid van de EG vallen, is niet beschikbaar om de reden dat de uitoefening van bevoegdheden die de lidstaten uit hoofde van het EG-Verdrag aan de Gemeenschap hebben overgedragen uit de aard der zaak voortdurend aan ontwikkeling onderhevig is. Door in Hoofdstuk III, onder 1, te verwijzen naar de relevante Verordeningen zijn de onderdelen van het Verdrag en het Protocol aangegeven waar de EG in casu de exclusieve bevoegdheid heeft.*" (To summarise: No list of provisions from the Cape Town Convention which fall under the exclusive competence of the European Community can be offered in light of the continuous development of the competencies which the Member States have transferred to the Community. Only references to specific European regulations can be given.). Cf. also Crans, The implications of the EU accession to the Cape Town Convention, p. 5, who adds on that same page that the "practical consequences of the Community's accession appear to be limited".

[15] Before the 2010 changes in the internal structure of the Kingdom, as described above, the islands of Bonaire, Sint Eustatius and Saba belonged to the "Netherlands Antilles", being a "country" within the Kingdom of the Netherlands next to the Netherlands and Aruba.

government of the Caribbean part of the Netherlands, is bound by the full Convention, whereas the Dutch government acting as the government of the European part of the Netherlands is only bound by the limited EU accession.

In the following paragraphs I will briefly discuss why this for a small country as the Netherlands so incredibly complicated decision not to ratify the Cape Town Convention for the European part of the Netherlands, but to ratify it only for the Caribbean islands was taken.

7.3 No Accession for the European Part of the Netherlands

The arguments not to ratify the Cape Town Convention for the European part of the Netherlands (i.e.: the Netherlands which is a Member State of the European Union), presented by the Minister of Foreign Affairs, are briefly worded and almost scant. It is obvious from the critical remarks by the Council of State in its advice regarding the draft letter by the Minister of Foreign Affairs asking for tacit (i.e. without any oral or written discussion in Parliament) acceptance of the Convention and Aircraft Protocol that the Council of State would have valued more elaborate arguments. The Council of State explicitly asked the Dutch government to reconsider its decision not to ask for permission to accede for the whole Kingdom.[16] In his reply the Minister of Foreign Affairs makes clear that his decision remains unchanged not to join the Convention for the European part of the Netherlands.

In his letter to Parliament the Minister of Foreign Affairs puts forward several arguments against accession of the European part of the Netherlands. His arguments are based on an analysis of the Convention and the Protocol from the viewpoint of underlying policies. Each policy is first described, then it is concluded that for the European part of the Netherlands this policy is either irrelevant or not acceptable, followed by the (implicit) conclusion that the situation is different for the Caribbean islands.[17]

---

[16] Parliamentary history, document no. 32 227 (R 1904), B and nr. 2, p. 2. Particularly B.P. Honnebier has argued in favour of accession, both for the Netherlands and for the Dutch Caribbean islands. See, to mention only a few of his articles: B.P. Honnebier, The Cape Town Convention and International Registry for Mortgages and other Secured Interests in Aircraft/La Convention du Cap et le Registre International pour hypothèques et autres garanties constituées sur les aéronefs/Die Kapstadt-Konvention und das internationale Register über Pfandrechte und andere Sicherungsrechte an Luftfahrzeugausrüstungen/La Convenzione del Capo e il Registro Internazionale per ipoteche e altre garanzie su aeromobili/La Convención de Ciudad del Cabo y el Registro Internacional de Hipotecas y otras Garantías Reales en la Aviación, Notarius International 2006, p. 21ff.; B.P. Honnebier, Clarifying the alleged issues concerning the financing of aircraft engines. Some comments to the alleged pitfalls arising under Dutch, German and international law as proposed in the ZLW 1/2007 (pp. 33–44), Zeitschrift für Luft- und Weltraumrecht 2007, p. 383 ff.; P.B. Honnebier, The European air transport sector requires an international solid regime facilitating aircraft financing: The Cape Town Convention, Tijdschrift Vervoer & Recht 2007, p. 151ff.

[17] As the arguments are presented in an extremely brief manner, much is left implicit and open. This makes a critical analysis of the arguments against and in favour of accession rather difficult, because somewhat speculative.

The following policy aspects were put forward to justify non-accession for the European part of the Kingdom:

(a) The Convention aims to strengthen the position of aircraft manufacturers and financiers, particularly in developing countries.[18]
(b) Under the Convention regime financiers are given an unreasonably strong position vis-à-vis buyers of aircraft. The Convention promotes freedom of contract, which allows the financier to make agreements which are disadvantageous for the debtor. Reference is made to the open-ended concept of "default", which would give considerable freedom to act on the part of the creditor, and the consequences of default which differ from Dutch civil law.[19] The Minister mentions, e.g., that under the Convention regime the financier can agree with the debtor that he becomes the owner of the object, albeit under the obligation to deduct the value of the object from the existing debt. Such a clause could easily violate article 3:251 of the Netherlands Civil Code.[20]
(c) The Netherlands does not have an aircraft industry, it does not have an offshore aviation financing industry, nor are there are any problems in the Netherlands concerning the giving of security when it comes to financing of aircraft materials.
(d) Royal Dutch Airlines, at least for the time being, was not interested. The Netherlands Railways and the Netherlands Association of Banks even considered accession to the Cape Town Convention as undesirable ("*onwenselijk*").[21]
(e) Only EU Member States which have a direct interest in application of the Cape Town Convention had at that time become a party: Ireland and Luxemburg.

To summarise: Accession would, according to the Dutch government, not create any new economic benefits and Dutch civil law provides a better balance of interest between creditors and debtors. The Netherlands therefore did not have a direct interest in accession.

---

[18] Implicitly the Minister is stating that, because the Netherlands is not a developing country, no accession is needed.

[19] It is interesting to note that these arguments would also apply *mutatis mutandis* to the Caribbean islands, where, albeit with some changes, the new Netherlands Civil Code has been taken over.

[20] See also A.F. Salomons, Should we ratify the Convention on International Interests in Mobile Equipment and the Air Equipment Protocol? Some remarks from a Dutch point of view, European Review of Private Law, 2004, p. 67ff.

[21] No further explanation is given as to why it would be undesirable.

7.4   Accession for the Dutch Caribbean Islands

With regard to the Dutch Caribbean islands the viewpoint of the Dutch government is quite different. The following arguments were mentioned in favour of accession, stressing that it is useful and necessary to make a choice opposite to the decision made for the Netherlands:

(a) Accession could broaden and thus promote the financial and economic development of these islands through the creation of an offshore aviation financing industry.

(b) The Caribbean islands already had legislation which promotes investment. Mentioned are the economic zone for commercial activities, the special purpose vehicle for financing and investment activities (*"Vrijgestelde Vennootschap voor financierings- en beleggingsactiviteiten"* or A.V.V., a limited company, profiting from a special tax regime) and a special tax for registration of ships (*"tonnagebelasting"*). This legislation might be a ground for the aviation industry to establish itself on these islands, if financiers are offered investment protection under the Convention.

(c) Financial service providers (both institutions and individual financial advisers: civil law notaries, advocates, tax advisers, trust offices) could, in addition to already existing financial products, offer an extra financial product.

(d) Accession would have no direct impact on the applicable legislative framework. The Convention made a choice for a broad and pragmatic legal system which could be directly applicable in all countries, so also – although the conclusion is drawn implicitly! – on the Caribbean islands.

(e) The Convention assumes that countries have their own national system of property law. The legal qualification, the conditions for establishment and consequences of existing property rights are left to the national legislator (the Civil Codes of Aruba and the Netherlands Antilles). The existing national property security rights can be the basis for an international security right, as laid down in the Convention. As long as parties do not reach a written agreement on publication of that security right in the international registry no third party effect will follow and national law will remain applicable. In other words: the Convention would not lead to fundamental changes in the existing property law.[22]

(f) Only if the parties were to agree on establishment of an international security right and this right would be registered in the international registry, would the respective Codes of Civil Procedure be affected. If not, the law on civil procedure would not change and would not affect third parties. Again the (implicit) argument seems to be that the existing legal order would not directly be affected.

---

[22] Cf. B.P. Honnebier, The Dutch real rights can be the basis of International Interests under the Convention of Cape Town, just like their equivalent American security interests, European Review of Private Law, 2004, p. 46ff.

(g) There would be no effect regarding the seizure of aircraft: the existing laws and applicable treaties would remain applicable.

(h) The Regulation on Insolvency of Aruba and the Netherlands Antilles would also not be effected, given that the islands would not use article XXX(3) and XI of the Aircraft Protocol, in which a special insolvency regime is laid down.

To summarise: Accession would only benefit the economy and not create unacceptable burdens by changes in the national legal system. The opposite of the conclusion for the (European part of) the Netherlands!

7.5 Concluding Remarks

It seems that many of the arguments in favour of accession by the Caribbean islands could just as well have been put forward to defend accession by the European part of the Netherlands, whereas some of the negative arguments could just as well be applied to the Caribbean islands. If an aviation industry is absent in the Netherlands (as it is on the Caribbean islands) why then not accede to become more attractive for this branch of economic activity? If the concept of "default" is too ambivalent for application in the European part of the Netherlands, then why does not this also apply to the Caribbean islands? The islands have a legal system that closely follows the legal system of the European part of the Kingdom. Given that the Civil Codes of Aruba and the Netherlands Antilles are almost copies of the Netherlands Civil Code, how can the argument then be justified that the Convention creates a legal framework particularly for developing countries and consequently is not needed for the European part of the Netherlands, but is needed for the Dutch Caribbean islands? And, finally, if the Netherlands Association of Banks considers the Convention to be even undesirable, it is difficult to understand why financial service providers on the Caribbean islands are so in favour of the Convention. It is, furthermore, interesting to note that concerns which sometimes can be heard regarding – more generally – tax havens were obviously not seen as relevant with regard to the Dutch Caribbean islands. Although these islands in many respects are tax havens, such concerns were not even mentioned, let alone dealt with. Why was not the need discussed to prevent money laundering and set up an adequately functioning supervisory aviation authority to prevent that aircraft are leased or bought with illicit gains?

The legal status of the Convention in the Kingdom of the Netherlands is complex, to put it mildly. The European part of the Netherlands is now bound by the conflict of laws rules of the Convention as a consequence of the ratification by the European Union. The Caribbean part of the Kingdom, although it does not belong to the European Union, nevertheless is also bound by the Convention's conflict of laws rules, but stemming from the accession by the Kingdom of the Netherlands to the Cape Town Convention for the whole Dutch Caribbean region. As a result the substantive part of the Convention does not apply to the European part of the Netherlands, but its rules are applicable on the Caribbean islands: (1) the now autonomous countries within the Kingdom: Aruba, Curaçao and Sint Maarten and (2) the Caribbean part of the Netherlands: Bonaire, Sint Eustatius and Saba. The practical consequences are that an aircraft registration request coming from the Caribbean part of the Netherlands, although registered in the Netherlands (and therefore with the Dutch prefix: PH), will fall under the Convention regime, whereas aircraft with a PH prefix registered in the European part of the Netherlands only falls under the Convention in as far as the private international law provisions are concerned.[23] It is submitted that more coordination between the various parts of the Kingdom should have taken place to avoid this labyrinthine situation.[24]

Elsewhere I already expressed the view that the Convention creates a very workable regime even in a Civil Law setting, although it may be more inspired by the Common Law (particularly Article 9 of the US Commercial Code) than the Civil Law tradition.[25] As such the Convention is a good example to show the impact of globalisation on national law and how such impact can be beneficial. Uniform rules create more certainty, particularly in the area of mobile equipment, which by its very nature may cross borders. The number of countries which are now a party to the Convention is clear evidence to show the correctness of this statement. The Dutch Caribbean islands, no doubt because of their size, their location and the nature of the commercial activities in which they are involved, seem to have understood this better than the Netherlands.

Acknowledgements I would like to thank my student assistant Ralph Diederen for excellent research assistance, while also doing research for his Bachelor thesis on the Cape Town Convention, Duan Angela, a student at the University of Aruba, who, at the time of writing this report, was preparing his final thesis on the Convention and who provided me with information on the law of Aruba, and Anna Berlee, who, when I was writing this report, was PhD researcher at Maastricht University preparing a thesis on the principle of transparency in European property law and who made several useful comments on the draft. This chapter was previously published in: *Netherlands Reports to the Nineteenth International Congress of Comparative Law* (Intersentia, 2015) and is reproduced with permission.

---

[23] For the tax consequences see B.P. Honnebier and A.P. Berkhout, The new legal and fiscal regimes that facilitate the financing and easing of aircraft in the Netherlands and Dutch Caribbean, Tax Planning International Review 2012, p. 1ff.

[24] See, as to how complicated the situation is perceived in practice, the remarks by the International Registry of Mobile Assets in Ireland (https://www.internationalregistry.aero/ir-web/faq, Question 5: "What countries have raftified?"): "The Kingdom of the Netherlands comprises of several territorial units, the structure of which has changed recently. Further research may be required by you. Pursuant to Article 52, paragraph 1, of the Convention and Article XXIX of the Protocol, the Kingdom of the Netherlands declares that the Convention and the Protocol are to apply to the following territorial units, the Netherlands Antilles and Aruba. Please consult UNIDROIT website (www.unidroit.org) and your legal advisors or both if you query relates to any of the following territories: the Kingdom of the Netherlands, the Netherlands Antilles, Aruba, Caribbean part of the Netherlands (the islands of Bonaire, Sint Eustatius and Saba), European part of the Netherlands, Curacao and Sint Maarten."

[25] S. van Erp, The Cape Town Convention: a Model for a European System of Security Interests Registration?, European Review of Private Law 2004, p. 91 ff., already referred to above.

References

1. Seminar – The European Economic Community and the Cape Town Convention (Rome, 26 November 2009), Summary Report prepared by the UNIDROIT Secretariat, to be found on the website of the Aviation Working Group: www.awg.aero.
2. Crans, B. 2010. The implications of the EU accession to the Cape Town Convention. *Air and Space Law* 1 ff.
3. van Erp, S. 2004. The Cape Town Convention: A model for a European system of security interests registration? *European Review of Private Law*, 91ff.
4. van Erp, S. 2002. A comparative analysis of mortgage law: Searching for principles. In *Land law in comparative perspective*, ed. M.E. Sanchez Jordán and A. Gambaro, 69ff. The Hague: Kluwer Law International.
5. Honnebier, B.P. 2004. The Dutch real rights can be the basis of international interests under the Convention of Cape Town, just like their equivalent American security interests. *European Review of Private Law*, 46ff.
6. Honnebier, B.P. 2006. The Cape Town Convention and international registry for mortgages and other secured interests in aircraft/La Convention du Cap et le Registre International pour hypothèques et autres garanties constituées sur les aéronefs/Die Kapstadt-Konvention und das internationale Register über Pfandrechte und andere Sicherungsrechte an Luftfahrzeugausrüstungen/La Convenzione del Capo e il Registro Internazionale per ipoteche e altre garanzie su aeromobili/La Convención de Ciudad del Cabo y el Registro Internacional de Hipotecas y otras Garantías Reales en la Aviación. *Notarius International*, 21ff.
7. Honnebier, B.P. 2007. Clarifying the alleged issues concerning the financing of aircraft engines. Some comments to the alleged pitfalls arising under Dutch, German and international law as proposed in the ZLW 1/2007, 33–44. *Zeitschrift für Luft- und Weltraumrecht*, 383ff.
8. Honnebier, P.B. 2007. The European air transport sector requires an international solid regime facilitating aircraft financing: The Cape Town Convention. *Tijdschrift Vervoer & Recht*, p. 151ff.
9. Honnebier, B.P. and A.P. Berkhout. 2012. The new legal and fiscal regimes that facilitate the financing and easing of aircraft in the Netherlands and Dutch Caribbean. *Tax Planning International Review*, p. 1ff.
10. Salomons, A.F. 2004. Should we ratify the convention on international interests in mobile equipment and the air equipment protocol? Some remarks from a Dutch point of view. *European Review of Private Law*, 67ff.
11. Wool, J. and A. Littlejohns. Cape Town Treaty in the European context: The case for Alternative A, Article XI of the Aircraft Protocol, also to be found on the website of the Aviation Working Group: www.awg.aero.

Sjef van Erp holds a law degree from Tilburg University (1977) and also studied at the Faculté Internationale pour l'Enseignement du Droit Comparé and the The Hague Academy of International Law. After working as a research assistant and adviser at the Netherlands Royal Society of Notaries, he started working as an assistant professor at the Faculty of Law of Tilburg University. As a visiting scholar, he did comparative legal research at the Max-Planck-Institut für ausländisches und internationales Privatrecht (Germany), Wolfson College Cambridge (UK) and Berkeley (US). In 1990, he completed his doctorate thesis and continued his work at Tilburg University as an associate professor. He continued his research abroad and was visiting professor at Université Laval (Quebec, Canada) and Cornell University (US), and Socrates visiting professor at Trento University (Italy). In 1997, Sjef van Erp was appointed Professor of Civil Law and European Private Law at Maastricht University. From October 2004 until October 2006 he was Marie Curie Fellow and visiting professor at the Institute for Law and Politics at Bremen University (Germany). In 2009 he was elected fellow at the South African Research Chair in Property law at the University of Stellenbosch and in 2011 he was elected titular member of the International

Academy of Comparative Law and Member of the American Law Institute. He is Deputy Justice at the Court of Appeals of 's-Hertogenbosch (the Netherlands), past President of the Netherlands Comparative Law Association, Vice-President of the World Society of Mixed Jurisdiction Jurists, member of the Executive Committee of the International Association of Legal Science, co-founder and Advisory Editor (until 2014: Editor-in-Chief) of the European Journal of Comparative Law and Governance (continuation of the Electronic Journal of Comparative Law), co-founder and Editor-in-Chief of the European Property law Journal (published by DeGruyter in Berlin), Editor-in-Chief of the Ius Commune casebook "Property Law", member of the Advisory Board of the Edinburgh Law Review, coordinating programme leader "property law" of the Ius Coummune research school, co-founding Council Member and Member of the Executive Committee of the European Law Institute, foreign expert member of the Collegio dei docenti del Dottorato in Studi giuridici comparati ed europei of Trento University (Italy), he is a member of the Board of Directors of the American Association of Law, Property and Society and a member of the Board of Directors of the International Institute for Justice Excellence. Other professional activities include: lecturing comparative and European property law at the China-EU School of Law in Beijing, the University of Stellenbosch (South Africa), the Universities of Bremen and Oldenburg (Germany) and the Russian School for Private Law (connected with the Institute for State and Law) in Moscow. He was also involved as expert advisor in several law reform projects.

Chapter 8
Russian Legislation and the Cape Town Convention

Natalia Doronina

8.1 The Regulation of Security Interests in Russia

Chapter 23 of the Civil Code of Russian Federation (CC RF) includes the rules on the security of the performance of obligations. The §1 "The general provisions" in this chapter enumerates different instruments which may be used to secure the performance of obligations (penalty, pledge, withholding of property of the debtor, surety, bank guaranty, deposit of money and other means provided by a statute or a contract). There is also art. 824 in CC RF which provides the rules on the contract of financing with assignment of monetary claim. *The contract of financing* with assignment of monetary claim reflects the main features of the institute of the International investment law created by the Cape Town Convention.

The conventional rules on registration can have effect only if there is a system of registration of the rights reflecting the interests of the persons financing the acquisition of the equipment in national system of law (the rights in things). In Russian Federation According to Article 130 of the Civil Code of Russian Federation transport vehicles are immovable things. "Immovable things also include the following, if subject to state registration: *airships and ocean-going vessels, inland waterway vessels, outer space objects*." (part 2 of Art.130). The right of ownership and other *rights in things (property rights)* to immovable things, limitation of these rights; the origin, transfer and termination of these rights are subject to state registration in the single state register by the institutions of justice (Art.131 CC of RF). The mortgage is subject to such registration. Thus the equipment such as airships and ocean-going vessels, inland waterway vessels, outer space objects are subject to the registration. That means that the rules of the Convention are applicable to those kinds of

N. Doronina (✉)
Department of Economic and Legal Studies, Institute of Legislation and Comparative Law, Moscow, Russia
e-mail: nata@izak.ru

© Springer International Publishing AG 2017

157

S. Kozuka (ed.), *Implementing the Cape Town Convention and the Domestic Laws on Secured Transactions*, Ius Comparatum - Global Studies in Comparative Law 22, DOI 10.1007/978-3-319-46470-1_8

equipment that are mentioned above. As far as railway and space assets Protocols are concerned, the work on their content is going on in doctrine and in banking legislation. The regime of these objects as movables will be subject to their registration and the rights in the equipment of that kind can be guaranteed as any other form of financing (investments).

The applicability of Cape Town Convention in Russian practice is explained mostly by the effectiveness of the UNIDROIT Convention on leasing of 1988. Russia is a state party to that Convention. The Federal Law of 29-th of October of 1998 N. 164-FZ "On the financial lease or leasing" was formulated on the basis of the general rule of Civil Code, in which §6 of Chapter 34 "Lease" includes the rules on finance lease (leasing). "Under the Contract of finance lease (the contract of leasing) the lessor is obligated to obtain in ownership property indicated by the lessee and to provide the lessee this property for payment in temporary possession and use for entrepreneurial purposes" (art.665 of CC RF). The Law formulated the main purpose - to develop the forms of investments as a means of production. . That means the development of investment legislation in Russian Federation in direction of modernization of civil law relationship. The modern regulation of civil law relationship can ameliorate investment climate and make wider the sphere of applicability of other investment Conventions that like Cape Town Convention promote financing of modern economy.

8.2   The Current Status of Convention

Russian Federation accessed the Cape Town Convention ("Convention on international interests in mobile equipment") in 2010 (Federal Law of 23.12.2010 N.361-FZ // Sobr. Zakonod. RF. 2011, N.36, Item 5124). The Convention is in force in Russia from the 1st of September of 2011. It was enforced together with the Protocol to the Convention on international interests in mobile equipment on matters specific to aircraft equipment on the 1st of September of 2011 (Federal Law of 23.12.2010 N.361-FZ // Sobr. Zakonod. RF. 2011, N.36, Item 5124) with a declaration made in accordance with Article XXXI under Article 60 of the Convention. The Declaration provides that Russian Federation will apply articles VIII and XIII of the Protocol. The Federal Law of the 5-th of June of 2012 N.60-FZ "On the Declaration of Russian Federation concerning Protocol to the Convention on international interests in mobile equipment on matters specific to aircraft equipment" provides that according to Part of Article XXXIII of the Protocol Russian Federation as a State Party of the Protocol shall apply articles VIII and XIII of the Protocol (Sobr. Zakonod. RF. 2012, N.24, Item 3077).

To summarize the main acts of implementation of the Cape Town Convention and the Protocol on matters specific to aircraft equipment into Russian legislation one can say that the national law is to play the main role in regulation of financing transport equipment and aircraft equipment particularly. But the application of

Russian legislation is subordinated to the Rules of Convention, especially the rule on the obligatory international registration.

The registration of civil aircrafts is a function of a state body – Federal Agency on transportation by air - "Rosaviazia" (Rosaviation). It registers the rights in the aircrafts also. According to the Federal Law of 14th of March 2009 No.31-FZ "On State Registration of the rights in aircrafts" Rosaviazia determines the order of registration including the procedure of interconnection between the registration body and the applicant. The Administrative Regulation on services in form of registration of rights in aircraft is enacted by the Order of the Transport Ministry of the 6th of May 2013 No.170. It is necessary to pay attention to the fact that at preset Rosaviazia has no function to deregistrate in case of sale of aircraft or transfer of the right in aircraft. The procedure of deregistration is necessary to be introduced in Russian legislation in order to secure the creditors' interest as it is provided by the Cape Town Convention.[1]

The sphere of application of the Cape Town Convention and the sphere of application of Russian legislation on security interests do not coincide. The first is applicable in international business relations. Security interests have a wider sphere of application. The latter includes security interests in the business relations between national persons that is the relations which are developing within the state and are governed by the Russian legislation exclusively. Thus the absence of contradiction between national and international regulation was one of the arguments in favor of ratification of the Cape Town Convention. At the same time the rules coordinating different regimes of security interests were enforced in Russian Legislation by Federal Law on accession to the Cape Town Convention and the Protocol on the matters specific to Aircraft Equipment of 23 December of 2010 No.361-FZ.

1. According to Federal Law on accession to Cape Town Convention and Protocol on the matters specific to Aircraft Equipment of 23 December of 2010 No.361-FZ the following requirements of creditors will have priority when satisfied within the territory of Russian Federation in cases of insolvency: on current payments; on payments with the aim to prevent technological and ecological catastrophe caused by the insolvency of the debtor; the requirements of a person to the debtor responsible for damage of health and requirement of compensation of moral damage; salaries and payments according to labor contracts with hired personnel.

   The mentioned requirements will have priority before the requirements as a result of an – international interest registered in International Registry. Article 39 of Convention provides for the possibility of rights that have priority without registration in case of Contracting State deposit corresponding declaration with the depository.

2. According to Federal Law on accession to the Cape Town Convention and the Protocol on the matters specific to Aircraft Equipment of 23 December of 2010 No.361-FZ the disputes connected with the application of Convention and

---

[1] Юрьев Ю.С., Евстигнеева И.С. Особые способы защиты лизигодаелей по Кейптаурской Конвении о международных гараниях в отношении подвижного оборудования 2001г. // Закон.2014, №4, с.158

Protocol shall be solved by the state courts (arbitration courts) that are specialized in economic disputes. This provision corresponds to Art. 53 for the purposes of Art.1 and Chapter XII "Jurisdiction" of the Convention.

3. According to Federal Law on accession to the Cape Town Convention and the Protocol on the matters specific to Aircraft Equipment of 23 December of 2010 No.361-FZ the remedies available to creditors under any provision of the Convention, which are not expressly defined as a mode of protection of the secured interest that require application to the court, may be exercised without leave of the court (art 1 Part 4 of the Law). This provision of the Law corresponds to Part 2 of Art.54 of the Convention.

4. According to Federal Law on accession to Cape Town Convention and Protocol on the matters specific to Aircraft Equipment of 23 December of 2010 No.361-FZ The Russian Federation, following the Part 3 of Art. XXX of the Protocol, will apply the entirety of Alternative A of Art.XI of Protocol and time period will be 60 days.

According to Art. XI of the Protocol on matters specific to Aircraft equipment Alternative A applies only where the Contracting Party is the primary insolvency jurisdiction. So as it is provided in the abovementioned Law of Russian Federation the insolvency related event may result in the transfer of the possession of the aircraft object to the creditor by the order of insolvency administrator with the waiting period not later than 60 days.

8.3   Filing System for Security Interest

There is no system of registration in Russian Federation, which is equivalent to International Registry under Cape Town Convention. As it was said above there is the single state register of immovables and rights in things founded by the institutions of justice (Art.131 CC of RF). This register is fixing the right of ownership and other *rights in things (property rights)* to immovable things, limitation of these rights; the origin, transfer and termination of these rights. The mortgage is subject to such registration. The Federal Law of 21of July 1997N.122-FZ "On State Registry of Immovables and Transactions With Them" (In the reduction of Federal Law of 21 of July 2014N.224 –FZ) is the basis for rules on the registration and transfer of rights to immovable under the contract of purchase and sale (Art.551,558, and 560 of the CC of RF), under other contracts (for example, contract of gift – art. 573–574, contract of rent –art.584), including the contract of lease (Articles 651 and 658 of the Civil Code).

The Cape Town Convention provides for special protection equivalent to the protection of investments. According to the Russian legislation the investor providing investments in the form of, for example, leasing or factoring contracts is not protected as investor but as an ordinary creditor. The right or claim belonging to a creditor on the basis of obligation may be transferred by it to another to another person by a transaction (assignment of claim) (Art. 382 of the Civil Code).

Assignment of claim is considered as a changing persons in obligation. (См.: Гражданское право. Под редакцией Е.А. Суханова. М. 2002. С.37). The Procedure for Transfer of the rights to another person depends on the kind of the property being transferred. Assignment of a property that is to be registered (immovables or _airships and ocean-going vessels, inland waterway vessels, outer space objects_) is to be registered also. The contract of assignment does create a new obligation which continues to be connected with the main contract, for example, contract of sale. (См.: Брагинский М.И., Витрянский В.В. Договорное право. Часть c.373–374). This position of a doctrine makes the assignment according to Russian legislation different from the assignment according to Cape Town Convention. But this view does not prevent from applying the Cape Town Convention with the special regime of protection for assignor.

The assignment as a way to change the party to the contract (the dominant view in Russian doctrine) can infringe upon creditor's rights in case of insolvency of a debtor and in relations with the other creditors. The first rank creditor may be responsible for the validity of the obligation but not for the execution of the obligation. The debtor may become responsible for the period of payment but not for the execution of obligation in the case of his insolvency. So registration within the Cape Town Convention is a good guarantee of the rights of a party to the international contract in case of transfer of aircraft equipment.

Natalia Doronina   (Doctor of Law) is the Deputy chief of the Department of economic and legal studies of State and municipal activity of the Institute of Legislation and Comparative Law at the Government of Russian Federation, Doctor of Law, Professor, The Honored Jurist of Russian Federation. Prior to holding the current position, she had been researcher, senior researcher, leading researcher, Chief of Department of Private International Law of the Institute of Legislation and Comparative Studies of Law within the Government of Russian Federation during 1976–2009. She was Professor at the Chair of Civil Law of Moscow International University, The Program and the Course of Lectures on Investment Law, during 1996–1997; Professor at the Chair of Civil Law of the Academy of Labor and Social Relations, the Course of Lectures on Civil Law of foreign countries, The Program and the Course of Lectures on Investment Law in Russian Federation during 1997–2001; Professor at the Chair of Civil Law of the Russian State Academy of Taxes during 2001–2009; Deputy Director of the Institute of Legislation and Comparative Studies of Law within the Government of Russian Federation during 2010–2013; Deputy Director of the Center for Economic and Legal Studies of the Institute of Legislation and Comparative Studies of Law within the Government of Russian Federation during 2013–2014. Her publications include:

– Organizational and Legal Forms of Foreign Investments in Developing Countries, Dissertation & Thesis for academic degree of Doctor of Law, Moscow State Institute of Foreign Relations. 1979
– _Regulation of Foreign Investments in Russia and Abroad_ (with Natalya G. Semilutina as co-author). Moscow. Finstatinform. 1993.
– Regulation of Foreign Investments (the Evolution of Sources of Law and the Perspectives of the Development of Russian Legislation). Moscow 1995. Manuscript deposited in INION RAN N50171 of 16.03.1995
– Regulation of Foreign Investments (Legal Problems and Resolutions). Dissertation & Thesis for academic degree of Doctor of Law. Moscow 1996;
– _State and Investment Regulation. Moscow_. Gorodets. 2003. (with co-author);

– *The Commentary on the Law on Investment Funds*. Moscow. The Publishing House "Justicinform". 2003. (with co-author);
– "The Property Law", "The Law of Legal Persons" in *Private International Law*. (pp. 602). Editor: professor N I. Marysheva. Moscow. Jurist. 2004
– "Concession Agreements" in *Certain Kinds of Obligations in Private International Law*. Editor: V.P. Zvekov. Moscow. 2008.
– "The Property Law", "The Law of Legal Persons" in *Private International Law*. Editor: professor N I. Marysheva. Moscow. Walters Kluver 2010
– Private International Law and Investments. Cj-author Semilutina N. Moscow 2012

Chapter 9
The Cape Town Convention and Its Implementation in South African Air Law

Phetole Sekhula

9.1 Background

The Convention on International Interests in Mobile Equipment (**"the Convention"**) and the Protocol to the Convention on International Interests in Mobile Equipment on Matters Specific to Aircraft equipment (**"Aircraft Protocol"**)[1] were ratified by the Government of South Africa in 2003 and subsequently incorporated into domestic law by the promulgation of the Convention on International Interests in Mobile Equipment Act 4 of 2007 (**"the CIIME Act"**). The South African Government also made the required Declarations when ratifying the Convention (**"the SA Declarations"**).[2]

The effect of the incorporation of the Convention and the Aircraft Protocol, collectively referred to as the Convention, was to modify the practical administration of security interests in aircraft in the Republic, and put to the questions the legal effect of the enforcement of such international security interests under domestic judicial processes. Yet there is legal uncertainty in South Africa in regard to the effective incorporation and implementation of the Convention and Aircraft Protocol in domestic law. This is primarily due not only to the substantive requirements of the provisions of the Convention, but also uncertainty attendant to the adherence or

---

[1] Convention on International Interests in Mobile Equipment, 2001, Protocol to the Convention on International Interests in Mobile Equipment on Matters Specific to Aircraft Equipment, 2001, and also Protocol to the Convention on International Interests in Mobile Equipment on Matters Specific to Space Assets, 2012 and Luxembourg Protocol to the Convention on International Interests in Mobile Equipment on Matters Specific to Railway Rolling Stock, 2007, http://www.unidroit.org/english/conventions/mobileequipment/main.html

[2] Annex to the Instrument of Ratification in respect of the Cape Town Convention, http://www.unidroit.org/english/conventions/mobileequipment/main.html

P. Sekhula (✉)
South African Council for Space Affairs (SACSA), Pretoria, South Africa
e-mail: advppsekhula@gmail.com

© Springer International Publishing AG 2017   163
S. Kozuka (ed.), *Implementing the Cape Town Convention and the Domestic Laws on Secured Transactions*, Ius Comparatum - Global Studies in Comparative Law 22, DOI 10.1007/978-3-319-46470-1_9

non-fulfillment of constitutional prerequisites for effective incorporation of international agreements into domestic law. As a result of this legal uncertainty, South Africa has not enjoyed the benefits flowing from being a Contracting Party to the Convention.[3]

The benefits accruing to the airline industry in a fully compliant Party jurisdiction include, *inter alia*, less cumbersome contractual requirements and reduced financing or leasing costs. The confidence that financiers or lessors of aircraft have in the special protections afforded to creditors in terms of the Convention facilitates and reduces anxieties when concluding commercial transactions in the aircraft business in compliant jurisdictions. However, the associated formal requirements for acquiring the benefits of the Convention is compliance with the prerequisites contained in the Aircraft Sector Understanding, a "gentleman's agreement", amongst participant States that include Australia, Brazil, Canada, the EU, Japan, US, etc., which sets out the minimum premium rates charged for new and used aircraft, spare engines, spare parts, maintenance, service contracts as well as the conditions for reduction of premium rates.

In order to qualify for the reduction of premium rates, the buyer or lessor of the aircraft object must be situated in a State which, at the time of the conclusion of the disbursement, appears on the list of States which qualify for reductions (**"the Cape Town List"**). To be on the Cape Town List, a State must be a Contracting Party, made the specified declarations (**"the qualifying declarations"**), and incorporated the Convention in its domestic laws and regulations, including the qualifying declarations, in a satisfactory manner. While South Africa has satisfied the first two requirements, albeit with some reservations on the constitutionality of Declaration made in terms of Article 54(2), the validity of the qualifying declarations under domestic law is uncertain. Thus far, this has proved an Achilles heel to the local airline industry since South Africa is not on the Cape Town List.

South Africa has not ratified the Railway Protocol nor the Space Assets Protocol. In the main, the uncertainties surrounding the effectiveness of the Aircraft Protocol, coupled with the negative sentiments held by a very small satellite community aligned to the international satellite consortia, has negatively affected the impetus towards a positive consideration of the Space Asset Protocol. It has not been established, at the time of writing, what the relevant executive authority's position is as regards the railway Protocol. Hence, the tentative position is unless and until the uncertainties surrounding the Aircraft Protocol are adequately addressed, there is little chance of, at least as the Space Assets Protocol is concerned, any further ratification of these associated instruments.

---

[3] **See, e.g**, Airline Association of Southern Africa, Discussion Document on the Incorporation of the Convention on International Interests in Mobile Equipment, 22 August 2012, on file with author.

9.2   Principles Underlying the Convention System

The Cape Town Convention aims at establishing a legal framework that will facilitate financing and leasing of high value mobile equipment.[4] The Convention and Aircraft Protocol are premised on three Principles needed to establish such a framework. These are:

1. priority among secured interests ("international interests") evidenced by a transparent registration system,
2. prompt enforcement of secured interests in case of default by the debtor, including private enforcement, and
3. enforcement of the secured interests without being qualified or modified under the insolvency procedure.[5]

These principles have largely been adopted by the Convention and its Protocols. Since South Africa is a Contracting Party we are invited to analyse whether, and to what extent, these principles were consistent with the national law before becoming a Party to the Cape Town Convention.

9.2.1   Priority Among Secured Interests

South Africa became a signatory to the Convention on the International Recognition of Rights in Aircraft, and incorporated same in domestic law through the promulgation of Convention on the International Recognition of Rights in Aircraft Act 59 of 1993 (**"RAA"**).[6] Section 4 of the RAA provides for the creditor to register a security interest on an aircraft or share in aircraft, including spare parts and engines, where a loan or debt is acquired. A deed of mortgage is thereby created as evidence of such a security interest. The Director of Civil Aviation is authorized, upon production of such an instrument and payment of the prescribed fee, to record the mortgage in a register created for such purpose.

The Director records the mortgage in the order in which the deeds creating them are provided to him. They are endorsed with the date and time of that record. Where a mortgage is to be executed outside the Republic, a registered owner of an aircraft or share must apply to the Director for a certificate of mortgage. The certificate contains a statement of any registered mortgages or certificates of mortgage affecting

---

[4] Roy Goode, *Convention on International Interests in Mobile Equipment and Protocol Thereto on Matters Specific to Aircraft Equipment: Official Commentary*, para. 2.1. (Revised edition 2008, Rome).

[5] Anthony Saunders, Anand Srinivasan, Ingo Walter & Jeffrey Wool, The Economic Implications of Secured Transactions Law Reform: A Case Study, *University of Pennsylvania Journal of International Economic Law*, Vol. 20, p.309, at 324.

[6] *See, e.g.* Chris Christodoulou, International Comparative Legal Guide, Aviation Law 2015: 3st Edition,, Global Legal Group, www.iclg.co.uk, accessed 28 June 2015.

the aircraft or share in respect of which the certificate is given. Section 6 of RAA provides that priority of mortgages in respect of the same aircraft shall be determined in accordance to the date and time at which each mortgage is recorded not when it was executed. Thus, registration presumably affects the priority among creditors on a **"first in line"** basis.

9.2.2   Prompt Enforcement of Secured Interests in Case of Default by the Debtor, Including Private Enforcement

Common law remedies in case of default include the right of a creditor to take possession of an aircraft for debts owed by the debtor. However, since the advent of a constitutional dispensation in 1994, such a step needs to court authorization. While it may be permissible under very narrow circumstances for self-help remedies to be legal, *i.e.* debtor's rights to prevent prejudice by approaching the courts and no other unduly onerous conditions, the acceptable way is to access the court by way of an urgent application, which may include interim injunctions and ancillary relief.

9.2.3   Enforcement of the Secured Interests Without Being Qualified or Modified Under the Insolvency Procedure[7]

Under South African insolvency law, a secured creditor holds security covering his claim by a special mortgage, landlord's legal hypothec, pledge or right of retention. During insolvency proceedings, an insolvency administrator liquidates the estate of the insolvent party and applies the balance of the proceeds for the payment of all proven, claims secured by the property in question, in order of preference. A disposition made *in fraudem creditorium* is impeachable.[8] However, the Companies Act of 2008 provides a moratorium on actions against an entity that is in "business rescue" proceedings for companies in financial distress. The rights of creditors are severely limited under this Act.

---

[7] Anthony Saunders, Anand Srinivasan, Ingo Walter & Jeffrey Wool, The Economic Implications of Secured Transactions Law Reform: A Case Study, *University of Pennsylvania Journal of International Economic Law*, Vol. 20, p.309, at 324.

[8] So is disposition without value, voidable preferences, and undue preferences.

9.3   Domestic Implementation of the Convention System

9.3.1   Registration System

The Cape Town Convention provides for the manner of constituting an international interest in high value mobile equipment. In terms of Article 29, a registered interest enjoys priority over unregistered interests and any other subsequently registered interest. The Convention provides priority to the secured creditor who filed first, whether or not the creditor had actual knowledge of the existence of a prior security interest created before.

Prior to the adoption of the Convention and subsequent incorporation into domestic law, South Africa followed the registration system provided for in the RAA, which contains a principle different from the Convention's priority principle. Section 4 provides for the creditor to register a security interest on an aircraft or share in aircraft, including spare parts and engines, where a loan or debt is acquired. A deed of mortgage is thereby created as evidence of such a security interest. The Director of Civil Aviation is authorized, upon production of such an instrument and payment of the prescribed fee, to record the mortgage in a register created for such purpose.

The Director records the mortgage in the order in which the deeds creating them are provided to him. They are endorsed with the date and time of that record. Where a mortgage is to be executed outside the Republic, a registered owner of an aircraft or share must apply to the Director for a certificate of mortgage. The certificate contains a statement of any registered mortgages or certificates of mortgage affecting the aircraft or share in respect of which the certificate is given. Section 6 provides that priority of mortgages in respect of the same aircraft shall be determined in accordance to the date and time at which each mortgage is recorded and not when it was executed.

In terms of Section 3 of the RAA, it is impermissible to mortgage by bond registered in a deeds registry an aircraft or a share in an aircraft. The aircraft or share in an aircraft may be mortgaged as security for a loan or other debt by means of an instrument in prescribed form lodged with the Director of Aviation. Section 4 provides for a register where such mortgages must be registered.

A registered owner of an aircraft or share in an aircraft must apply to the Director for a certificate of mortgage where a mortgage is executed outside the Republic. A registered owner means a person who owns an aircraft or share in an aircraft, and whose name is registered as such in the register. The certificate contains a statement of any registered mortgages or certificates of mortgage affecting the aircraft or share in respect of which the certificate is given and is personal to the owner. The domestic registration system is thus similar to the International Registry under the Cape Town Convention which is a system based on registration against an asset, not against a debtor.

Both registrations are a "notice filing" system, which gives a notice to third parties that a security interest exist that deserves further enquiries.[9] Under both the Act and the Convention, the Director, like the Registrar assumes the accuracy of the provided information without any examination of it and records it accordingly.

A mortgagee under a registered mortgage is entitled to recover the amount due under the mortgage in any court of competent jurisdiction. The court may order that the mortgaged aircraft or share be sold in execution of the judgement (Section 7). Thus, a mortgage registered under the Act would qualify as an international interest and can be so registered in the international registry. If it is not registered in the International registry, but only contained in the local registry maintained by the Director of Civil Aviation, it would not enjoy priority consideration under the Convention system.

9.3.2 Enforcement of a Security Interest

Article 8 of the Convention provides for remedies that a creditor is entitled to in the event of default of a debtor under the security agreement relating to specific mobile equipment, subject to the provision that the debtor has agreed to such under the security agreement in question and further subject to any declaration contemplated in Article 54 of the Convention. Article 54 relates to the manner in which a creditor may exercise any of the enumerated remedies with or without Court's intervention and depends on the declarations made therein (**"Self Help Remedy"**).

The remedies include taking possession and control of the object concerned, selling or granting a lease, or collecting any income or profits arising out of the use of the object. Any of these remedies must be exercised in "*a commercially reasonable manner*". A remedy is deemed to be exercised in a commercially reasonable manner if it is exercised in conformity with a provision of the agreement, unless such a provision is manifestly unreasonable.[10] There are also procedural prerequisites that must be complied with before a creditor can exercise a remedy such as giving notice to the debtor and other interested parties.

South Africa elected to exclude the intervention of the Courts for the exercise of the remedies under the Convention, unless where expressly required. This election is, ***prima facie***, in conflict with constitutional provisions relating to right of access to courts. Any law that restricts a person's access to court is invalid to the extent of the inconsistence, albeit there may be permitted reasonable justifications for the inconsistency.[11] The effect of the SA Government allowing for exercise of the remedies without leave of Court deprives the debtor of his right to defending its rights or seeking recourse against the creditor's conduct. This type of proscription is

---

[9] Goode, Official Commentary, supra note 5, para. 4.132.

[10] Article IX (3) of the Protocol.

[11] *see*, Section 34, Constitution of the Republic of South Africa, 1994 read with Section 36 ("the limitations clause").

unconstitutional and therefore unlawful. However, the prerequisites to enforcement where a security agreement is in issue, may militate against the adverse consequences of Article 8 read with Article 54 and the Republic's declaration. Judicial decisions on the validity of self-help remedies is that such drastic actions is only permissible where the debtor has consented at the time of such an exercise or on the basis of a court order.[12]

Default means an occurrence of an event agreed to as default by a debtor and creditor which has an effect of depriving the creditor of its entitlements under the agreement. This accords well with the South African common law of freedom to contract: as long as the agreement reflects a mutual consensus and parties are **ad idem**, the Court will be loath to interfere, unless there are onerous terms or the effect is against public policy. Consequently, parties are at will to define what events will constitute default in their dealings with one another.

The Cape Town Convention allows a wide variety of remedies besides simple liquidation to satisfy the obligations under a security agreement. These include granting a lease of the object and collecting or receiving any income or profits arising from the management or use of the object (Art.8 (1)). Art.9 provides for vesting of the ownership of the object by the agreement of the chargee and other interested parties or by the court in to order satisfy the secured obligations by. Moreover, if the international interest is a title reserved by the conditional seller or a lessor's right, as opposed to an interest under a security agreement, there is no need for the creditor to pay the balance to the debtor even when the amount of the balance is larger than the amount of the secured obligation[13]

The remedies enumerated in the Convention system are consistent with the practice under South Africa affording relief to a creditor in the event of an occurrence of an event agreed to as constituting default, provided that the creditor may not sell or deal in the affected property without leave of the court, whether such property is in possession of the creditor or remained with the debtor in question.

9.3.3   Treatment of Security Interests Under the Insolvency Procedure

Under the Cape Town Convention, an international interest can be exercised even after an insolvency procedure is commenced with the debtor, without being stayed automatically or by an order of the insolvency administrator.[14] All three Protocols provide alternatives that differ in the extent of the power that the creditor can exercise in case of insolvency of the debtor. The rules differ depending on whether the State Party made a declaration choosing either of the alternatives in the relevant

---

[12] *Juglal NO and Another v Shoprite Checkers (Pty) Ltd 2004* (5) SA 248 (SCA), at para 12.

[13] Goode, Official Commentary, supra note 5, para. 4.101.

[14] Art.XI of the Aircraft Protocol; Art.IX of the Rail Protocol; and art.XXI of the Space Assets Protocol)

provision. However, even under an alternative less favourable to the creditor (Alternative B), the insolvency administrator or debtor in possession shall either cure all defaults and agree to perform all future obligations or give the creditor the opportunity to take possession of the secured object. Alternative C of Art IX of the Rail Protocol seems to be the only exception, which enables the insolvency administrator or the debtor to apply to the court for an order suspending its obligation.[15]

South Africa opted to apply Alternative A of Article XI for all types of insolvency proceedings and the waiting period will be thirty (30) days. Alternative A provides that

> **upon the occurrence of any insolvency-related event, the insolvency administrator or the debtor, as applicable, shall....give possession of the aircraft object to the creditor no later that the earlier of (a) the end of the waiting period; and (b) the date on which the creditor would be entitled to the possession of the aircraft if this Article did not apply**

Under the present Companies Act of 2011, a company in financial distress may be protected from adverse creditor action where there are reasonable prospects of rescuing that company.

During such a business rescue process, the rights of creditors are drastically curtailed and thus in direct conflict with the provisions of the Convention. A business rescue practitioner is appointed to supervise the affairs of a financially distressed company upon application by any affected person, the resolution of the Board of Directors of such a company, or court order.[16]

Section 133 provides that during business rescue proceedings, no legal proceeding concerning the property of the company, including enforcement action, *may be commenced with or proceeded with in any forum*, except with the written consent of the business recue proceeding or leave of court. In terms of section 134(1)(a) of the Companies Act, a company may, during business rescue proceedings, dispose or agree to dispose of property only in the ordinary course of business, or in *bona fide* transaction at arm's length for fair value if approved in advance and in writing by the practitioner. Similarly, the company's performance obligations under contracts entered into by the company prior to the commencement of business rescue proceedings are suspended or even cancelled.

Alternative A, which South Africa has elected to follow, specifically states that "*no remedies permitted by the Convention or this Protocol may be prevented or delayed after the date specified in paragraph 2*", Furthermore, "no obligations of the debtor under the agreement may be modified without the consent of the creditor". The effect of the relevant provisions in the Companies Act is that a general moratorium on performance obligations and suspension of legal proceedings is in place during the business rescue process in contradiction to the speedy relief provisions contained in the Convention system upon default of a debtor.

---

[15] Prof. Souichirou Kozuka, Chap. 2 of this volume.

[16] Section 129, Companies Act of 2009, www.gov.za/pub/Acts, accessed 20 July 2014.

9.4   General Considerations

The protection of debtor's interests is a primary considerations that led to support of the Aircraft Protocol and continues to be a motive force for the airline industry to urge the Government to consider amendments to the current implementation prescripts, reform the declarations to conform to constitutional requirements and ensure that the qualifying declarations as required for admission to the Cape Town List are legally adequate. Yet, the same underlying consideration for protecting debtor's interests prompted the South African delegation to the Diplomatic Conference for the Adoption of the Space Asset Protocol to introduce a resolution that clearly spelt out debtor's interests will be taken into consideration in the implementation of the Space Asset Protocol.

It is clear that, but for the Aircaft Sector Understanding, debtor's interests would have been a minimal consideration in the Convention system. This consideration is paramount to the local industry whose consensus as a precondition for legislative interventions.

The Airline industry, led by the Association of Airlines of South Africa, has embarked on an awareness raising crusade to appeal to the Government to effect the necessary amendments to the CIIME Act, the Insolvency Act and the Companies Act for domestic air law to be fully compliant with the requirements of the Cape Town Convention. This is so because the local airline is not deriving the economic benefits accruing to State jurisdiction who implement the Convention system in a satisfactory manner.

Adv. Phetole Sekhula   practices law in the High Court mainly in fields of commercial, contracts and local government laws. He holds a Juris Doctor degree from Georgetown University in Washington, DC, where he majored in Air and Space Law. He completed his undergraduate program at Morehouse College in Atlanta, Georgia where he trained on property development, construction and urban planning.

In his legal practice, Adv. Sekhula has advised municipalities on many aspects of local government law including township establishment regulations, Municipal Systems Act, the MFMA and implementing labour law legislation such as Basic Conditions of Employment and employment equity laws. He has assisted in drafting by-laws and contract management systems for local governments. He has chaired disciplinary hearings involving Municipal Managers and section 57 employees.

Adv. Sekhula serves as a Council member at the South African Council for Space Affairs (SACSA), a government agency responsible for regulating space activities in South Africa. As Chair of the Policy and Legal Committee, he is responsible for research and drafting policy papers on behalf of SACSA to guide the development of a coherent space regulatory framework. Presently, he is engaged in review of the current space legislation and drafting a new Space Act.

- Admitted to practice in 1993 and practised as member of Johannesburg Society of Advocates, Johannesburg Bar from 1993 to 1995 (2 years);
- Worked as Senior Manager: Legal Services for Department of Posts, Telecommunications and Broadcasting, 1995
- General Manager: Corporate Affairs, M-NET, 1996–1998 (2 years)
- Private Practice (Not at Bar) 2000–2005 (5 years)
- Johannesburg Bar, 2006–2008 (2 years)

- Private Practice, 2009–2014 (5 years)
- Pretoria Society of Advocates, September 2014—

Adv Sekhula is currently the Chairperson of the International Air Services Council (IASC) a statutory Government agency mandated to issues internal air services license to both local and foreign operators. The IASC advises the Department of Transport on all international air services regulations and relies on an economic regulatory model when assessing and adjudicating license application.

Chapter 10
The Cape Town Convention and Its Implementation in Spanish Law

Teresa Rodríguez de las Heras Ballell

10.1 Introductory Remarks: Convention Without Protocols

The analysis of national law on security interests on transport vehicles and the implications of Cape Town Convention (Convention and Protocols) is significantly conditioned by the fact whether the country is a Party jurisdiction or a non-Party jurisdiction. Whereas in the former case, reforms in domestic law aimed to implement uniform rules upon ratification can be identified and explained; in the latter one, only expected changes, both in material and registry issues, in preparation of the ratification in the future or possible conflicts of uniform rules with the domestic legal framework in case of ratification may be anticipated.

Spanish legal system represents at present a particular case in relation to the Cape Town Convention. On 28 June 2013, Spain deposited with UNIDROIT, together with several declarations, the instrument of accession to the Convention on International Interests in Mobile Equipment (hereinafter, the Convention).[1] Afterwards, the instrument of accession was published in the Official State Bulletin

---

Publication elaborated within the framework of the Research Project *La modernización del derecho español de garantías mobiliarias para facilitar el acceso al crédito y a la financiación en un contexto internacional* (DER2013-46070-P) funded by the Spanish program to promote excellent research.

[1] The Convention on International Interests in Mobile Equipment (hereinafter, Convention) was adopted in Diplomatic Conference that was held in Cape Town, South Africa, on the 16th of November of 2001 under the auspices UNIDROIT (International Institute for the Unification of Private Law *nnnn Institut International pour l'Unification du Droit Privé*) and ICAO (International Civil Aviation Organization). Pursuant to Article 49(1) CTC, the Convention entered into force on the 1st of March of 2006 together with the Protocol thereto on matters specific to aircraft equipment (hereinafter, Aircraft Protocol).

T. Rodríguez de las Heras Ballell (✉)
Faculty of Law and Social Sciences, University Carlos III of Madrid, Madrid, Spain
e-mail: tla@der-pr.uc3m.es

© Springer International Publishing AG 2017
S. Kozuka (ed.), *Implementing the Cape Town Convention and the Domestic Laws on Secured Transactions*, Ius Comparatum - Global Studies in Comparative Law 22, DOI 10.1007/978-3-319-46470-1_10

dated on 4 October 2013, along with the entire text of the Convention, the list of Contracting States and all declarations made to date.[2] Nevertheless, no Protocol was ratified either simultaneously or as a continuation of the accession until 27 November 2015 with the deposit of the instrument of accession with UNIDROIT to the Aircraft Protocol.[3] Consequently, Spain is a Contracting Party of the Convention since October 2013 but no instrument of ratification, approval, acceptance or accession to any of the Protocols was deposited until 2015. On 1 March 2016, the Convention as regards aircraft objects has entered into force for Spain and is now part of the Spanish legal system. Before the depositing of the instrument of accession to the Protocol, on May 22, 2015, new Regulations for the Aircraft Register (*Registro de Matriculación de Aeronaves Civiles*)[4] were adopted. The new legal text presumed the prompt accession to the Aircraft Protocol and the designation by Spain of a national entry point. Accordingly, in an additional provision (*Disposición Adicional 6°*), rules and procedures aimed to govern the relationship between the future national entry point (*Registro de Bienes Muebles,* hereinafter, RBM), the Aircraft Register and the International Registry are laid down. As per the instrument of accession, the designation of the RBM as the national entry point has been confirmed.

Due to the original and pragmatic multidivisional[5] structure under which the Cape Town system works, the staggered ratifying process followed by Spain resulted in an anomalous situation, as further explained below, to the extent that the expected ratification of any of the Protocols was deferred. Today, the transitional situation is totally concluded and the CTC is effective in Spain, but it might well be worth analysing the effects that derived from the staggered and prolonged process of ratification.

The functioning of the Cape Town system is based on a brilliant combination of general rules at the Convention level and equipment-specific rules provided for by each Protocol. Many practical advantages in the drafting process and in the application stage derive from that original structure. As a result, sector needs could be more properly met, negotiations and adoption processes might progress at different pace and the long-term benefits of formulating uniform general rules for all the categories

---

[2] Published in the Official Bulletin (*Boletín Oficial del Estado*) num. 238, of 4 October of 2013 (www.boe.es).

[3] During the second semester of 2015, the accession to the Aircraft Protocol was expected soon. In August 2015, Spanish Government requested the Parliament approval to proceed to deposit the instrument of accession to the Protocol. On August 25, 2015, the Committee on International Affairs of the Spanish Parliament issued its opinion favourable to the granting of the requested approval. As published in the Official Bulletin of Spanish Parliament (BOCG), Serie C: Tratados y Convenios Internacionales, Congreso de los Diputados, X Legislatura, 5 de agosto de 2015, Núm. 207–1, pág. 1, 110/000184 (available at http://www.congreso.es/public_oficiales/L10/CONG/BOCG/C/BOCG-10-C-207-1.PDF)

[4] Royal Decree 384/2015, published in the Official Bulletin, BOE num. 144, June 17th, 2015.

[5] Following my description of the system in Teresa Rodríguez de las Heras Ballell, *Las garantías mobiliarias sobre equipo aeronáutico en el comercio internacional. El Convenio de Ciudad del Cabo y su Protocolo,* Marcial Pons, Madrid, 2012, Chapter I.F (p. 42).

of equipment were not compromised by a multi-centred negotiation. Likewise, the Cape Town system, thanks to its modular structure, may grow to cover new categories of objects in other sectors other than the originally contemplated (aeronautic, space and rail industries).

The "multidivisional" Convention/Protocol design operates according to several criteria that confer upon the Protocol a significant controlling role. So, the Protocol does not merely elaborate on the Convention provisions but adapt them to each sector particularities, control the coming into force of the Convention in relation to the corresponding category of mobile equipment and specify the material scope of the latter in each case. Article 6(1) on interpretation rules, Article 6(2) confirming the prevalence of the Protocol over the Convention in case of discrepancy, and meaningfully Article 49(1) controlling the entering into force underpin the important role of the Protocol. As a matter of fact, the Convention entered into force on the 1st of March of 2006, along with the Aircraft Protocol (Article XXVIII). As a matter of law, the Convention cannot work independently.

Accordingly, along the whole transitional period until the last accession, Spanish position in relation to the Cape Town Convention displayed dysfunctional effects.[6] The Convention was considered to enter in force for Spain from 1st of October of 2013 and Spain is treated as a Contracting State for the purposes of the Convention; but in practical terms, the Convention could not be applied to any category of mobile equipment within its sphere of application and its provisions remained inactive as from the time of the entry into force of the Protocol for Spain (Aircraft Protocol, on March 2016) and then as regards of the corresponding category of equipment (aircraft objects). For the Convention provisions cannot have any effect unless linked to a specific category of equipment as covered by a Protocol. Although there are a few provisions that are not object-related (Arts. 47, 48, 51, 52, 59 and 61).

The accession to the Convention is a critical decision for Spanish strategic economic sectors that has to be applauded. Upon the deposit of the instrument of accession, Spain confirms a firm support for the Cape Town system as a stimulus of strategic industries and an enabler of a modernization process in domestic legislation. The deferred ratification of any of the Protocols, presumably, the Aircraft Protocol, already in force and widely ratified, in the first place (as it has finally been confirmed), was arguably justified by the need to carry out a prior reform of domestic legislation (both in material rules and in registry system) dealing with issues involved in and related to secured transactions over mobile equipment in order to be prepared for adopting the Protocols subsequently.

Certainly, the proposal for a modernisation of the existing system on secured transactions is timely and very convenient, but it has proved to require a longer time and entail a complex process. Notwithstanding this, from the outset an early adoption of the Protocols was highly desirable without making it dependant on the success of an all-embracing reform. Even more importantly, the CTC and the Protocol can reasonably work in Spain with a limited number of amendments to domestic rules.

---

[6] Further analysed in Teresa Rodríguez de las Heras Ballell, 'The accession by Spain to the Cape Town Convention: a first assessment', *Uniform Law Review,* 2014, pp. 1–23.

As a matter of fact, the CTC is already in force considering that the actions adopted so far aimed to implement the uniform system have been essentially focused on and led to enable the functioning of the designated national entry point. Although a profound and comprehensive reform of the secured transactions domestic framework has to be encouraged and is still an urgent undertaking that the Spanish legislator should not avoid, it proved not to be a *conditio sine qua non* for the Convention to take effect. Even if it is our understanding that a truly effective implementation of the Convention does still require further reform regarding certain issues. In particular, to align insolvency provisions with Alternative A of Article XI of the Protocol aiming to produce an equivalent result, to review domestic rules in the light or Article X, to ensure that procedural rules are suitable for the exercise of all remedies provided for by the Convention and the Protocol, and to amend the inadequate rules applicable to the national entry point.

For the purposes of the present study, Spain will have to be considered as a hybrid jurisdiction at an unusual midway position between a Party jurisdiction and a non-Party jurisdiction until the effective date of entering into force on 1 March 2016. Since then, Spain constitutes a proper Party jurisdiction in the terms of the initial and subsequent declarations made to the Convention and the declarations made to the Aircraft Protocol.

10.2 Economic Rationale and the Importance of Cape Town System for Spanish Economy

Despite the initially anomalous process of ratification and the partial accession to the Cape Town Convention for almost 2 years, the decision of Spain to deposit the instrument of accession to the Convention is a clear signal of acceptation of a positive expected economic impact of the uniform system on strategic industries for domestic economy.

Aeronautic sector, airspace industry and high-speed railway[7] manufacturing industry are strategic sectors in Spanish economy that have experienced a rapid and appreciable growth in last years. The accession to the CTC represents a visible impetus to their growth and financing. All these industries are highly innovative, capital intensive and with an intense supranational integration. Spain holds a representative fifth position in Europe airspace market in terms of turnover as well as employment. Likewise, high-speed railway manufacturing industry has been fostered and plays today a notable role in the international scene.

Considering that, it may be affirmed that the Cape Town system is interpreted as an enabler of credit in adequate conditions and a promoter of strategic industries. Economic impact assessments are not unknown in Spain so as to evaluate the need

---

[7]Data on Spanish railways in the European context in the report published by the Railway Observatory available at http://www.observatorioferrocarril.es/archivos/Ofe2011/Observatorio Ferrocarril_2011.pdf

of reforms, to design more effective legal solutions or to anticipate costs and risks likely to arise from an envisaged action. Notwithstanding that awareness, an economic analysis is not always conducted in the process of legal reform or, if undertaken, it is rarely the only deciding factor. In any case, it may be reasonably said that economic benefits of the Cape Town Convention may have been one of the factors considered in the decision to ratify. Nevertheless, no specific empirical analysis supporting that statement has been expressly mentioned or made public knowledge along the process. Other factors may have been relevant as well. The ratification of the Convention is a strategic decision. It is a sign of modernization and a visible first step forwards among European countries,[8] especially, those ones holding leading positions in the key sectors.

Along with such specific benefits on selected industries, secured transactions rules are commonly seen as enablers of the financing market as a whole. In that regard, it may be asserted that the idea that a strong security interest facilitates access to credit and globally benefits both creditors and debtors is widely shared in business-to-business transactions. When consumers and non-professional debtors are involved, however, social perception is probably the opposite. The distorting effects of last economic crisis aggravated by high levels of over-indebtedness[9] in certain social groups depict a very different image of secured transactions. Hence, in consumer financing transactions, security interests can be to some extent interpreted as instruments of abuse aimed to solely protect strong creditors, mainly financial entities, against weak parties. Such an economic situation could have debilitated the mainstream idea that security interests encourage credit flow.

Nevertheless, since the Cape Town Convention deals with high-value transactions between sophisticated parties in strategies industries, value perception is not, as previously stated, conditioned by such sociological factors or the economic situation, at least, not so intensively.

A total exploitation of economic benefits and strategic advantages requires completing the international commitment with the prompt ratification of any of the Protocols, predictably the Aircraft Protocol. Insofar as the reason to postpone the ratification of the Protocol seemed to be the need of a prior reform in the domestic legal framework and the registry system, seminars, workshops and professional meetings have been organized to discuss critical issues, contrast opinions and dis-

---

[8] On December 7, 2014, besides European Union as a regional economic integration organisation (Article 48 Convention), only Ireland, Luxembourg, Netherlands, Malta, Latvia and Spain have accessed to the Convention. And all of them, save for Spain, have also accessed to the Aircraft Protocol.

Namely, France, Germany, Italy and United Kingdom that rank among the first four economies in the European aerospace industry. Encouragingly, an announcement on UK's decision to proceed with ratification of both the Convention and Protocol as it relates to aircraft has been published in December 2013. Since further steps are required, ratification is expected in the near future.

[9] From the perspective of suretyships, some comments on that social perception in Teresa Rodriguez de las Heras Ballell, 'Protection from Unfair Suretyships in Spain', in Aurelia COLOMBI CIACCHI; Stephen WEATHERILL (Eds.), *Regulating Unfair Banking Practices in Europe: The Case of Personal Suretyships*, Oxford University Press, Oxford, 2010.

close concurring interests. On the occasion of those meetings, it has been repeatedly emphasized the importance of paying careful attention to implementation. Should Convention provisions be not properly implemented or should existing domestic rules or practices be likely to hamper the functioning of the International Registry, expected benefits might greatly vanish.

Special concerns were aroused in relation to the registry system and registration rules. Although Spain counts on a sound, modern, efficient and highly computerized registry system and some existing registry regulations are already in process of reform[10] to contemplate the operation of the International Registry, registry models and philosophies are visibly divergent, albeit not irreconcilable. Very simply, as a mere sign of that divergence, Spanish registration model is overall based on a document-filling registry (with some nuances) conducted by active Registrars. To the extent that Spain opts for, as it was highly expected and was indeed finally confirmed, designating a national entry point and principles governing national registry systems may differ from the registry model designed by the Cape Town Convention, it should be carefully considered the interrelation between registry systems in order to anticipate and minimize contradictions (eventual fees, required documentation, Registrar review). In that regard, I have expressed[11] my deep concerns about the rules and procedures laid down by the new Regulations for the Aircraft Register aimed to regulate the operation of the national entry point and its interaction with the International Registry. To my mind, such rules and procedures are not consistent with the spirit, the conceptual scheme and the rules of the Cape Town system. Contrarily, in its current version, a prior registration of international security interests in the national entry point seems to be required in clear contradiction with the autonomous, independent and *sui generis* character of international security interests that are not dependant on national requirements nor registration in local registries. A 'last-minute' resolution adopted on 29 February 2016 by the General Directorate of Registrars and Notaries approving the form to apply for the issuing of the Unique Authorization Code by the national (authorising) entry point and the IDERA form aims rightly to amend the previous inadequate rules. Nonetheless, some questioning comments on the said resolution can still be posited. Such subsequent actions have tried to amend the effects of those above-referred wrong

---

[10] The old Decree 419/1969, of 13 of March of 1969, regulating the Registry of Aircraft is in process of reform. The new text would include express provisions regulating interconnection between the Registry of Aircrafts and the Registry of Movable aimed to enable the application of the Cape Town Convention.

[11] Teresa Rodriguez de las Heras Ballell, 'El nuevo Reglamento de matriculación de aeronaves civiles, y el Convenio de Ciudad del Cabo y su Protocolo sobre garantías internacionales en elementos de equipo aeronáutico', 15 *Revista de Derecho de Transporte: Terrestre, Marítimo, Aéreo y Multimodal, 2015, pp.* 235–257; and Teresa Rodríguez de las Heras Ballell, 'La adhesión de España al Protocolo Aeronáutico del Convenio de Ciudad del Cabo y su implementación: una primera valoración del nuevo Reglamento de Matriculación de Aeronaves', 2 *Bitácora Millenium DIPr* 88, 2015 – Part I http://www.millenniumdipr.com/ba-29-la-adhesion-de-espana-al-protocolo-aeronautico-del-convenio-de-ciudad-del-cabo-parte-i, Part II: http://www.millenniumdipr.com/ba-30-la-adhesion-de-espana-al-protocolo-aeronautico-del-convenio-de-ciudad-del-cabo-parte-ii -.

provisions and ensure today a normal functioning of the national entry point on a regular basis.

In that point, the conviction that a proper implementation is crucial is conducting discussion in professional and institutional forums. A proper implementation casts on two dimensions. On the one hand, a carefully pondered list of declarations and an adequate wording of them. On the other hand, a reform of national system in those aspects likely to hamper, if not duly amended, the full exploitation of the uniform instrument's expected efficiencies.

10.3   Some Notes on Spanish Security Interests on Transport Vehicles

10.3.1   Categories of Objects

All objects covered by the Cape Town system in the three Protocols – aircraft equipment, railway rolling stock and space assets (Article 2) -, adopted so far, can be used as collateral in the different security devices provided for by the Spanish legal system on secured transactions. Some of them are expressly mentioned in specific legislation (as aircrafts or train cars) but most of them do easily fall into the general category of movable or personal property susceptible of being pledged or subjected to other forms of security interest under the domestic law even before becoming a State Party. Therefore, transport vehicles and other mobile equipment as described by the Cape Town Convention are subject to the same asset-based secured transactions rules as personal property in general.

Notwithstanding, it might be well worth pointing some considerations out.

Firstly, in certain cases, when assets are expressly mentioned in special legislation, parties are not free to choose the most appropriate security agreement. For instance, according to legislation regulating non-possessory pledges and mortgages on chattels (movable mortgage),[12] train cars and aircrafts can only be mortgaged (using movable mortgage) but not pledged under the same law (non-possessory pledge).

Secondly, as per the scope of application of the Aircraft Protocol, an aircraft in its entirety is not treated as an object in conformity with the Protocol. Aircraft equipment comprises airframe, helicopter, and engines. Contrarily, aircrafts are expressly contemplated in Spanish legislation on non-possessory pledges and mortgages on chattels (movable mortgage). Interestingly, aircraft equipment could be alternatively subject to different security forms other than movable mortgage (leasing, conditional sale with title reservation, non-possessory pledge). But, since aircrafts are described as a compound asset, the principle of accession by incorporation

---

[12] *Ley sobre Hipoteca Mobiliaria y prenda sin desplazamiento de posesión*, of 16 December 1954, published in the Official Bulletin, num 352, 18 of December of 1954.

entails that the interest is presumed to extend over all component parts. As a consequence, once the engine is installed, it would become part of the aircraft and lose autonomy. Despite that traditional principle, there is not an insurmountable obstacle to adopt Cape Town system's classification. Additionally, it has been admitted[13] the separate registration of engines and even of component parts provided that they do sufficiently meet identifiable criteria to access to the Registry of Movables.[14] As a matter of fact, contracting parties, who allowed to depart from legal provision and agree on a different extension of the interest, do frequently include in their security agreements provisions limiting the legal extension of a mortgage and separating engines, due to its high value and in accordance to industry practices.[15] Nonetheless, once the Convention and the Aircraft Protocol are in force in Spain, their provisions are part of Spanish legal system replacing, and hierarchically prevailing over domestic rules contradicting them.

Thirdly, as regards space assets, even if no specific references to this category of objects are found in existing secured transactions rules; there is no reason to question that these assets may be pledged or subjected to other forms of security agreements with the whole extent of effects (lease agreements, title reservation sales, non-possessory pledge, depending on the nature of each specific asset).

10.3.2 Security Interests and Title-Based Devices

As regards types of security agreements (security interests and title-based devices) as provided by the Convention, traditional pledges and mortgages, non-possessory security schemes, leasing agreements, and title reservation sales are known and, more widely or succinctly regulated, in Spanish legal system.

Rules governing such security agreements and title-based schemes are scattered in a selection of laws and regulations. An overview of most relevant rules may better illustrate the afore-mentioned fragmented image of the in force legal framework. Traditional possessory pledge and (real state) mortgage are essentially regulated in the Civil Code of 1889 along with the mortgage-related provisions of the Mortgage Act of 1946. The need to facilitate access to credit without dispossessing the debtor of most valuable assets devoted to his/her business activity led to the adoption of rules on non-possessory pledge and movable mortgage in 1954 (*Ley sobre Hipoteca Mobiliaria y prenda sin desplazamiento de posesión*, of 16 December 1954). Leasing agreements lacks however a systematic regulation with a succinct description in an additional provision of supervisory legislation of financial markets (*Ley 26/1988*, of 29 July 1988, *de Disciplina e Intervención de las Entidades de*

---

[13] Resolution of 29 of January of 2001, *Dirección General de Registros y del Notariado*.

[14] Article 6 of the Ordinance of 19 of July of 1999 regulating the Registry of Hire Purchase of Movables. – *Ordenanza para el Registro de Venta a Plazos de Bienes Muebles* -.

[15] See Rodríguez de las Heras, *Las garantías mobiliarias sobre equipo aeronáutico en el comercio internacional.* (n. 3) pp. 51–57.

Crédito).[16] Title reservation clauses are laterally referred in the legislation of hire purchase agreements of 1998 (Ley 28/1998 de Venta a Plazos de Bienes Muebles). More recently, and among others, Royal Decree-Law 5/2005, of March 11, on financial collateral arrangements, which implements in Spain Directive 2002/47/EC of the European Parliament and of the Council of June 6, 2002, has been adopted. Likewise, a set of rules on registration issues and defining the role of Registrars and Public Notaries in secured transactions, as set out in different texts, is part of the full regulatory image.

Needless to say, a systematizing effort to unify, provide coherency and modernize domestic rules on secured transactions is very much desirable, to my mind, on an urgent basis. Despite some legislative proposals for a general law on secured transactions, aimed to devise a unified legal framework based on registered pledge, have limitedly circulated, no specific legislative initiative seems to be at present in the legal horizon.

Surprisingly, even if Spanish legal system seems to be based on a formal more than a functional model, functional approach is not unfamiliar and is indeed adopted in certain issues. Even more, the distinction between traditionally pure security interests and title-based devices is not totally undisputed. So, although both leasing agreements and conditional sales would be traditionally deemed title-based devices, today, the legal nature of title reservation[17] or of the title held by the lessor in a leasing agreement[18] is disputed among scholars (and in case law) – ownership or security interest.

Likewise, an express reference to "functional equivalence" can be even found in Spanish legal rules for the purposes of registration. Thus, it is laid down that, along with pure hire purchase agreements on identifiable assets, any other agreement by virtue of which parties pursue same economic goals as a hire purchase agreement will be registered in the Registry of Movables. These examples reveal that even if Spanish model cannot be described as a functionalist one on secured transactions, it

---

[16] Published in Official Bulletin num 182 of 30 July 1988.

[17] Rodrigo Bercovitz Rodríguez-Cano, *La cláusula de reserva de dominio. Estudio sobre su naturaleza jurídica en la compraventa a plazos de bienes muebles,* Editorial Moneda y Crédito, Madrid, 1971; Ángel Carrasco Perera, and others, *Tratado de los Derecho de Garantía, Tomo II: Garantías Mobiliarias,* Aranzadi, Cizur Menor, 2008, pp. 416–417.

[18] Rodrigo Bercovitz Rodríguez-Cano, 'El pacto de reserva de dominio y la función de garantía del *leasing* financiero', in Ubaldo Nieto Carol, and others, *Tratado de Garantías en la Contratación Mercantil,* Tomo II, Vol. 1, Civitas, Madrid, 1996, pp. 377–416.

Antonio Cabanillas Sánchez, 'La configuración del arrendamiento financiero (leasing) por la Ley de 29 de julio de 1988, en la jurisprudencia y en el Convenio sobre Leasing Internacional', *III Anuario de Derecho Civil,* 1991, p. 961; Francisco González Castilla, *Leasing financiero mobiliario. Contenido del contrato y atribución del riesgo en la práctica contractual y la jurisprudencia,* Civitas, Madrid, 2002, pp. 156–178; María José Morillas Jarillo, 'Algunos aspectos del leasing de aeronaves en España', 208 *Revista de Derecho Mercantil,* 1993, p. 471; Rafael Illescas Ortiz, 'El *leasing:* aproximación a los problemas planteados por un nuevo contrato', 119 *Revista de Derecho Mercantil,* 1971, p. 74; Rafael Jiménez de Parga, and others, 'La operación de *leasing,* ¿es una operación de crédito?', 31 *Revista de Derecho Bancario y Bursátil,* 1988, p. 487.

can be asserted that a functional approach is not totally unknown and that the equivalence of economic effects in legal transactions is not certainly disregarded in Spanish jurisdiction.

10.4   Registration

As previously indicated, special legislation is not linked to the nature of the asset but the security form or the type of security agreement. Likewise, registration system – Registry of Movables or Registry of Movable Property or Registry of Personal Property (*Registro de Bienes Muebles*) – is common to all personal property including transport vehicles and other mobile equipment, albeit they might be registered in different sections of the Registry. In case of aircrafts, however, Spanish Registry system is dual: on the one hand, the Aircraft Registry for aircraft registration), recently modified as it has been previously noted, maintained by an authority of administrative nature (*Registro de Aeronaves* for public/administrative purposes); on the other hand, the Registry of Movables for the registration of interests over certain objects.

10.4.1   Types of Registries and Principles Governing the Registry System

For the purposes of studying the scope and effects of registration, it might be well worth pointing out first the distinction between "administrative registries" and "legal registries" under the Spanish legal system. Both of them can be involved in the registering of transport vehicles, as mentioned in the precedent section. As far as transport vehicles are concerned, whereas the Aircraft Registry, the Vehicle Registry[19] and the Ship Registry are "administrative registries", the Registry of Movables, that plays a central role in the implementation of the Cape Town system, is, as the Commercial Registry or the Property Registry, a pure "legal system" instead. Each kind of registry serves for specific and different aims. Not surprisingly, an efficient inter-connection between them is necessary and, in fact, carefully ensured.

Apart from differing in scope, aim and kind of information susceptible of being registered, most importantly, "administrative registries" and "legal registries" deploy different legal effects.

Very briefly, "administrative registries" serve Public Administration's interests and, accordingly, even if there are not totally hermetic, they provide a quite limited

---

[19] According to Article 2 of the Royal Decree 2822/1998, of 23 of December, the aim of the Registry of Vehicles is to identify the owner of the vehicle, its technical characteristics, road-worthiness, completed inspections, compulsory insurance and compliance with all legal obligations.

access to public. Contrarily, "legal registries" feature wide accessibility (at least to those holding a legitimate interest, that is presumed in certain cases[20]), *erga omnes* effectiveness and attribution of legal effects to registered information.

In order to gauge how different the registry model created by the Cape Town system is from the domestic model, comparison has to be made with "legal registries" and, in particular, with the Registry of Movables that has been designated as a national entry point.

Thus, "legal registries" run in accordance to the following principles:

Firstly, they are essentially public registries in the sense that registered data can be searched and/or requested by anybody claiming an interest in that information. Since registries are broadly operating as electronic systems, any communication to and from the Registry can be conducted by electronic means (e-mail or more frequently through the electronic platform) and on an interactive basis. Such an open access to registered data is not subject to the participation of any professional or intermediary, unless the interested party wishes so. Therefore, anybody can freely request information from the registry.

Nevertheless, the reply to the information request can be produced under two formats: simple notes for only informative purposes or certificates that, as literal transcriptions of registration, previously treated by the Registrar, reliably prove the legal situation of the searched object. Both simple notes and certificates can be requested and issued either paper-based or in digital format with a certified electronic signature of the Registrar when necessary.

Secondly, "legal registries" are intended not only to give notice but, above all, to confer legal value to registered information. Specifically, in relation to the titleholder, registration acknowledges and attributes the corresponding rights and legal effects to the holder. As far as third parties are concerned, registration deploys *erga omnes* effects to those circumstances susceptible of being registered.

As a consequence, it is clearly laid down, as regards the Registry of Movables, that "it is presumed that everybody knows any registered right, then ignorance cannot be invoked". Accordingly, in an opposite sense, any act or contract, susceptible of being registered, that, however, has not been properly registered, cannot be detrimental to any third party.

Hence, registration in a "legal registry" is the legal mechanism to prove, in or out of the court, the existence, extent, scope and limits of the registered situation and that the registered holder is the only person entitled to exercise it according to the law. Notwithstanding, registration is not able to validate null and void transactions. However, the principle of public faith entails that a good faith acquirer of an object from whom is registered as the owner will not lose his/her rights on the acquired object if afterwards the right of the original owner as registered is annulled or

---

[20] Contracting parties, lawyers, financial entities, detectives, accountants, public entities and any other professional or entity whose business or professional activity is related to the personal property traffic.

revoked. Good faith is presumed unless knowledge of the inaccuracy of the registration is proved.[21]

Thirdly, considering the strong legal effects deriving from registration, data to be registered are, not surprisingly, carefully reviewed to ensure accuracy and veracity. Hence, Registrar plays a central and active role in accrediting, certifying and supervising the information to be registered. To that end, Registrar certifies, on his/her own responsibility, the compliance of extrinsic formalities, capacity and right to dispose of parties, authority of courts, judges or authorizing professionals, and the material conformity with the law (any infringement of binding rule will be declared by the Registrar).

From this schematic outline of the Spanish model for "legal registries", some points likely to conflict with the Cape Town registry model can be easily perceived.

10.4.2 The Model of the Registry of Movables in the Context of the Cape Town System

The Registry of Movables (*Registro de Bienes Muebles*) has been designated as the national entry point for the purposes of the Cape Town Convention upon the accession to the Aircraft Protocol – more specifically, the *Registro Provincial de Bienes Muebles de Madrid* -.

As a "legal registry", the Registry of Movables is expected to share all the aforementioned general principles.[22] Even if that statement is quite certain today, a full coherency of registry principles among all registries has not been totally achieved. Indeed, scholars disagree on the complete applicability of strong registry principles as devised for real state property to the Registry of Movables. A significant heterogeneity of "registries" (sections) covered by the organizational umbrella of the Registry of Movables complicates the devising of a consistent framework of principles governing the registration of titles and security interests on movables. In accordance with the additional provision of the Royal Decree 1828/1999, of December 3,[23] the Registry of Movables comprises six sections whose scope and nature appreciably differ: ships and aircrafts; automobile and other motor vehicles; industrial machinery, commercial premises and equipment; other security interests; other registrable movable property; standards contract terms.

From its inception, the Registry is evolving to become a real registry of personal property with the registration of titles and security interests on identifiable movable

---

[21] As stated by Article 34 of the Mortgage Law for the purposes of the Real State Mortgage. Decree of 8 of February of 1946, published in the Official Bulletin num 58, dated on 27 of February of 1946.

[22] As clearly advocated by Francisco Javier Gómez Gálligo, 'Principios hipotecarios de los Registros Mobiliarios', *Revista Crítica de Derecho Inmobiliario*, num. 651, March-April 1999.

[23] As published in the Official Bulletin num. 306, date on December 23, 1999.

property (along with the registration of standard contract terms). However, scholars disagree on the complete transformation of the nature of the Registry. In fact, it is argued that the Registry is still far from operating as a real registry of personal property that is a *desideratum* more than a reality in the current state of evolution.[24] Important consequences derive from such an uncertain nature. In particular, effects on the transfer of titles and third parties' rights will be different in each case.

Among other reasons, the proper categorization of the Registry as a registry of titles is questioned insofar as the prior registration of ownership over the object as a condition to register further interests on it is not compulsory in all cases but merely facultative. Notwithstanding, within the field of our interest, in the case of ships and aircrafts the first registration has to be that of the ownership; otherwise, the Registrar will refute any further registration of interests on an aircraft or a ship lacking the registration of the ownership.

Thus, currently, the scope of the Registry of Movables is the registering of the following: agreements referred to personal property, such as sales, with or without deferred payment, ordinary leasing agreements and special leasing agreements (financial leasing, renting, lease back), movable mortgages and non-possessory pledges, naval mortgages, notices of seizure and notices of lawsuits and any other security interest, encumbrance or limitation on such assets with effects against third parties. Likewise, standard contract terms and court orders about them are registrable as well.

From an organizational viewpoint, it is organized as an asset-based model; accordingly, the registry system is based on registration against assets. Likewise, in general terms, it replicates a "full documentary model" in contrast to the notice-based formula of the International Registry. In that regard, a pair of considerations has to be made. Firstly, after a subsequent reform, the Registry is not a depositary of contracts but an extract of the agreement is transliterated for the purposes of the registering. Secondly, despite that the general rule is that only public deeds, administrative documents or court orders can access to the Registry, this formality has been attenuated in the case of hire purchase agreements, since private documents in an official form are admitted for the purposes of registration. The traditional limits to private documents were explained by their lack of a prior control ensuring veracity and accuracy by the corresponding competent organ.

Priority rules overall work on a time basis. Then priority is given to the secured creditor who filed first. In the same way, those registrable interests that however are not duly registered will exert no detrimental effect on third parties. Interestingly, on the occasion of the accession to the Convention, Spain did make no declarations under Articles 39 and 40, but as expected, upon the accession to the Aircraft Protocol, Spain has made several subsequent declarations under Articles 39(1)(a), 39(1)(b) and 40. Any further declaration will take effect under the conditions laid down by Article 57.

---

[24] Eduardo Vázquez de Castro, *La publicidad registral en el tráfico de bienes muebles,* Civitas – Thomson Reuters, Madrid, 2012, p. 87.

Unlike the Cape Town system, the actual knowledge of the existence, or more exactly, the lack of actual knowledge, may still have some relevance in the Spanish legal system on secured transactions, albeit with an uncertain extent. As a matter of law, the creation of a non-possessory pledge will not have any detrimental effect on previous third parties' rights on the object as perfected in a document with a previous authentic date (if these rights are not registrable). Likewise, it is stated that any acquirer of an object acquires its interest in it subject to any previous interest (ordinary) pledge insofar as he/she knew it or should have known it. It has to be remembered that ordinary (or possessory) pledge are not registered. Nevertheless, considering the doubtful nature of the Registry of Movables as a real registry of personal property, the applicability of the presumption of good faith to those third parties relying on the registered data seems to be questionable.

10.5   Enforcement

Spain's instrument of accession to the Convention was deposited with UNIDROIT together with declarations under Articles 52 and 54(2) of the Convention. Other than the classical declaration regarding Gibraltar status under Article 52, the declaration made under Article 54(2) is particular pertinent for enforcement purposes.

According to Article 54(2), "(a) Contracting State shall, at the time of ratification, acceptance, approval of, or accession to the Protocol, declare whether or not any remedy available to the creditor under any provision of this Convention which is not there expressed to require application to the court may be exercised only with leave of the court". Spain does accordingly declare that all remedies available to the creditor in the Convention may be exercised only with leave of the court. Since the declaration is made at the time of accession to the Convention without ratification of any Protocol, the scope of the declaration has to be further considered.

To solve that asynchronous situation up, all three Protocols[25] provide a rule stating that: "(d)eclarations made under the Convention, including those made under Articles 39, 40, 50, 53, 54, 55,57, 58 and 60 of the Convention, shall be deemed to have also been made under this Protocol unless stated otherwise". Therefore, the need of leave of the court for the exercise of remedies in case of defaults will be applicable to all further ratified Protocols unless otherwise declared by Spain at the time of ratification, acceptance, accession to, approval of any of the Protocols.

An immediate conclusion that can be reasonably inferred from the aforementioned declaration appears to be that Spain departs from any extra-judicial enforcement of security interests over assets. Even if the categorical statement of the declaration under Article 54(2) does unavoidably implies that, non-judicial enforcement is not nevertheless unfamiliar to Spanish legal system on secured transactions. Contrarily, extra-judicial enforcement proceedings before a Public Notary are contemplated in the legislation regulating non-possessory pledges and mortgages

---

[25] Article XXXI Aircraft Protocol; Article XXIX(1) Protocol on Matters specific to Railway Rolling stock, Article XLI Protocol on Matters specific to Space Assets.

on chattels[26] whose exercise requires no prior agreement between the parties, and, to a certain extent, acknowledged in hire-purchase agreements and leasing contracts too – as well as the effects of Law 5/2015, of July 2, on *Voluntary Jurisdiction.*[27]

The instrument of ratification of the Protocol has represented the opportunity to clarify the scope of the declaration as further explained below.

A schematic outline of the non-judicial enforcement model in the aforementioned cases may better illustrate its features and its scope. As an example, Article 16 of the Spanish law on Hire Purchase Agreements[28] will be split up in its component parts. Along with the logical affirmation that the creditor is entitled to enforce his/her interest in a declarative proceeding or an executive one before a court in conformity with domestic procedural rules, a special proceeding for hire purchase agreements is provided for. The special enforcement proceeding in case of default can be applied provided that the hire purchase agreement is duly registered in the Registry of Movables according to the official form. In case of default, the creditor is entitled to ask a Public Notary to claim the debtor the fulfilment of his/her obligations.

- Within the next three working days after being claimed, the debtor can pay the claimed amount or transfer the possession on the object to the creditor or the designated person for that purpose.
- If the debtor neither pays nor delivers the object, a court will order to foreclose the object in an executive proceeding. Should the debtor voluntarily convey the possession of the object, two procedural options are possible. Either the object is sold in public auction under the supervision of a Public Notary; or the creditor decide to satisfy the secured obligations by vesting the ownership of the object without public auction according to the tables values and scale of depreciation indexes included in the contract.
- If the value of the object is larger than the amount due by the debtor, the creditor will pay to the creditor the excess. Likewise, if the value of the object is not enough to satisfy the due amount, the creditor will conserve his/her rights against the debtor to claim the remaining debt.

10.5.1 The Scope of the Declaration Under Article 54(2)

Framing the declaration under Article 54(2) within the Spanish legal context, some unexpected results might arise. Should the scope of the declaration be literally meant that only pure judicial remedies can be applied in the enforcement of security interests, an undesirable consequence might result. Out-of-the-court enforcement as

---

[26] Articles 86–88 and 95–96, *Ley sobre Hipoteca Mobiliaria y prenda sin desplazamiento de posesión*, of 16 December 1954, published in the Official Bulletin, num 352, 18 of December of 1954.

[27] *Ley 5/2015 de la Jurisdicción Voluntaria*, published in BOE num. 158, 3 July 2015.

[28] *Ley 28/1998*, of 13 of July, *de venta a Plazos de Bienes Muebles,* published in Official Bulletin num 167, dated on 14 of July of 1998.

enshrined by domestic legislation would be deactivated in the international context. It make no sense, and it unlikely leads Spain's instrument of accession, an intentional decision to grant a worse treatment to international security interests than the one provided for by domestic rules. Considering that Notary-supervised proceedings are purportedly preferable in terms of agility and efficiency, it might be contented instead that, either under Article 13 as additional remedies permitted by the applicable law or under Article 14, creditors would benefit from exercising any remedy provided by the Convention, subject to Article 54(2), in conformity with the procedure prescribed by the law of the place where the remedy is to be exercised, and, consequently, following the procedural requirements of those enforcement procedures to be conducted before a Public Notary when applicable. It is my contention is that the latter interpretation should take priority.[29]

On the occasion of depositing an instrument of ratification, further declarations to the Convention can be made. Specifically, according to Article 53 a Contracting State may, at the time of ratification, acceptance, approval of, or accession to the Protocol, declare the relevant 'court' or 'courts' for the purposes of Article 1 and Chapter XII of the Convention. Hence, in the instrument of ratification Spain has rightly declare that *all of the competent courts of the Kingdom of Spain, as determined in accordance with the Spanish laws and regulations*, are the relevant courts for the purposes of Article 1 and Chapter XII of the Convention. The circular expression 'all the competent courts' is not particularly transparent but at least provides a helpful interpretative instrument to avoid the exclusion of notary-supervised proceedings by the declaration under Article 54(2) insofar as any organ, tribunal or authority empowered to enforce security interests in accordance with Spanish laws and regulations will be covered by the 'leave of the court' requirement. The aim of the declaration under Article 53 seems to be to defuse the undesirable rigidity of the previous declaration under Article 54(2); nevertheless, it is doubtful whether it is enough to satisfy Article X of the Protocol with a substantially similar domestic solution. It has to be pointed out here that, as a subsequent declaration, the declaration under Article 53 did not become effective until 1 June 2016.

That extension is particularly pertinent and absolutely coherent in light of the recently enacted Law on Voluntary Jurisdiction (15/2015, July 2) that modernizes and systematizes the Spanish system of protection mechanisms and allocates power and jurisdiction in certain civil and commercial issues among courts, judicial secretaries, notaries and registrars.

---

[29] Contrarily, however, Encarna Cordero considers that the wording of the declaration entails that CTC remedies could not be enforced before a Notary. Encarna Cordero, 'Garantías internacionales sobre elementos de equipo móvil', *Diario La Ley*, num 8189, 12 November 2013.

10.5.2   Remedies in Case of Default

In the Spanish jurisdiction, parties[30] are allowed to define the meaning of default that entitles the creditor to exercise remedies from the legal catalogue of available remedies in each case.

Interestingly, the Convention widens the remedies traditionally available to creditors in case of default under Spanish legal system – auction and more rarely enforcement agreements *(convenios de realización)*[31] -: take possession or control, sell or grant a lease, collect or receive any income or profits arising from the management or use of the object (Article 8 Convention). All said remedies should be exercised in a commercially reasonable manner. The standard of commercial reasonability is measured in conformity with the provisions of the security agreement provided that they are not manifestly unreasonable. According to Spanish legal provisions in force and judicial practice, foreclosure in auction, public tender or bidding process would be deemed commercially reasonable.[32] Other than those cases, any procedure implying a competitive bidding might be predictably declared reasonable as well.

As regards Article 10, remedies available to conditional sellers and lessors (terminate the agreement and take possession or control of the object) do not differ substantially from remedies provided for domestic legislation to date. Nevertheless, according to domestic legislation in force, conditional sellers and lessors cannot request a speedy relief from the court enabling the creditor to manage the object and collect income therefrom.[33] Such a remedy is only provided for in favour to chargees.[34] Regardless of that divergence between both legal regimes, Article 13 configures a uniform concept of interim reliefs distinct from those ones provided for by domestic rules. Therefore, interim reliefs will be exercised in accordance with Convention provisions and, if applicable, relevant Protocol ones, instead of being subject to domestic procedural rules. In the absence of any declaration under Article 55, such uniform interim reliefs are applicable under their own conditions along with those reliefs additionally provided for by domestic legislation. Spain has not made any declaration under Article 55 at the time of accession to the Convention,

---

[30] Some limits on parties' freedom to define "default" might be relevant in case of consumer transactions that are not however falling within the scope of application of the Cape Town system. For instance, the non-payment of two fees or the non-payment of the last fee is needed in consumer leasing agreements to declare "default" able to activate some remedies in favour to the creditor.

[31] According to Article 64 of Civil Procedure Act, *Ley 1/2000 de Enjuiciamiento Civil* as cited above.

[32] In compliance with rules on auctions as stated in Articles 643–654 Civil Procedure Act, *Ley 1/2000 de Enjuiciamiento Civil*.

[33] As remarked by Encarna Cordero, 'Garantías internacionales sobre elementos de equipo móvil', p. 5.

[34] Article 676 and following Civil Procedure Act, *Ley 1/2000 de Enjuiciamiento Civil*.

but the declaration made by the European Community pursuant to the said provision has to be taken into account.[35]

In the vesting of object in satisfaction as set out in Article 9, another historical controversy, likely to also explain the cautious move of Spain by making the Article 54(2) declaration when accessing to the Convention, is latent. As per Article 9(1) the chargee and all the interested persons may agree that ownership of (or any other interest of the chargor in) any object covered by the security interest shall vest in the chargee in or towards satisfaction of the secured obligations. If no leave of court is required, the possibility that the chargee may become the owner of any object covered by the security in satisfaction of the secured obligations has been always seen with suspicion. A wide range of reasons of moral, legal or procedural nature have been traditionally argued by scholars[36] to support and justify the strict classical prohibition of the so called "pacto comisorio"[37] in our legal systems. With the declaration made under Article 54(2), all concerns would be totally averted. The subsequent declaration under Article 53, as it has been interpreted, does not change that assertion.

However, it may be well worth taking the opportunity to carry out a more careful analysis of the provisions of the Convention regulating the remedies under debate and assess whether the apparent frontal contradiction with the national ban of "pacto comisorio" is indeed real. It is my contention[38] that the Convention contains rules framing the exercise of the controversial remedy that might, as a matter of fact, elude a direct collision with the said prohibitive rule. As per Article 9, the agreement for the vesting of object in or towards satisfaction of the secured obligations is to be adopted at any time after default according to Article 11. When the agreement is

---

[35] Declaration by the European Community pursuant to Article 55 of the Convention:

Pursuant to Article 55 of the Cape Town Convention, where the debtor is domiciled in the territory of a Member State of the Community, the Member States bound by Council Regulation (EC) No 44/2001 of 22 December 2000 on jurisdiction and the recognition and enforcement of judgments in civil and commercial matters will apply Articles 13 and 43 of the Cape Town Convention for interim relief only in accordance with Article 31 of Regulation No 44/2001 as interpreted by the Court of Justice of the European Communities in the context of Article 24 of the Brussels Convention of 27 September 1968 on jurisdiction and the enforcement of judgments in civil and commercial matters.

[36] Manuel Ignacio Feliu Rey, *La prohibición del pacto comisorio y la opción en garantía*, Civitas, Madrid 1995, pp. 74, 75; Federico de Castro y Bravo, 'La acción pauliana y la responsabilidad patrimonial. Estudio de los artículos 1911 y 1111 del Código Civil' *Revista de Derecho Privado*, 1932, p. 193; Francisco Capilla Roncero, *La responsabilidad patrimonial universal y el fortalecimiento de la protección del crédito*, Fundación Universitaria, Jerez, 1989, p. 206.

[37] The traditional prohibition of *pacto comisorio* is however limited by two exceptions: financial collateral arrangements and pledges of credit rights. In both cases, public auction is not required. Royal Decree-Law 5/2005, of March 11, which implements in Spain Directive 2002/47/EC of the European Parliament and of the Council of June 6, 2002, on financial collateral arrangements, regulates, among other matters, financial collateral arrangements.

[38] As reasoned as well in Rodríguez de las Heras Ballell, 'The accession by Spain to the Cape Town Convention: a first assessment' and previously in Rodríguez de las Heras Ballell, *Las garantías mobiliarias sobre equipo aeronáutico en el comercio internacional*.

adopted after default, many of the concerns underlying the banning do significantly temper insofar as the freedom to deal is not compromised and creditors' interests are not menaced by the fact that the prospective appropriation of the object is not actually conditioning any more the prior financing decision. As a consequence, the judgement about the validity of the agreement does essentially become a matter of time. Accordingly, the so called "pacto comisorio *ex intervallo*", agreed at any time after the conclusion of the main financing agreement involving a security device, has been traditionally deemed valid and enforceable or at least it has been argued that it should not be null and void *per se*.[39] More conclusive is the previous affirmation of validity if the vesting of the object is agreed when the secured obligation is already due. In such a case, parties are only agreeing on an alternative way to fulfil the obligation.[40]

In conclusion, an agreement for the vesting of object in or towards satisfaction of the secured obligations, provided that is adopted at any time after default, would manage to elude the confrontation with the rule banning the "pacto comisorio". Given that a declaration requiring leave of court has been made by Spain together with the instrument of accession to the Convention with the above-discussed implications of the subsequent declaration under Article 53, the collision has been in any case avoided at its roots.

10.6   Insolvency

The impact of insolvency provisions in European jurisdictions is determined by the declarations made by the European Union[41] under the Convention and the Aircraft Protocol.[42] The European Union deposited as a Regional Economic Integration Organization (Article XXVII Aircraft Protocol) the instrument of approval to the Aircraft Protocol on 28 April 2008 together with declarations.[43] Accordingly, as far as provisions on remedies on insolvency are concerned, it has been interpreted that

---

[39] Ángel Carrasco Perera, and others, *Tratado de los Derecho de Garantía, Tomo II: Garantías Mobiliarias,* p. 208.

[40] Reglero Campos, 'El pacto comisorio' I-XVI *Aranzadi Civil*, 2007, pp. 1907, 1921–1922.

[41] Berend Crans, 'The Implications of the EU Accession to the Cape Town Convention' 35 *Air and Space Law* 1, 2010, p. 7.

[42] On 18 December 2014 the European Union's instrument of approval to the Luxembourg Protocol to the Convention on International Interests in Mobile Equipment on Matters Specific to Railway Rolling Stock, adopted at Luxembourg on 23 February 2007, albeit not yet in force, was deposited with UNIDROIT. In this case, the European Union has made a declaration under Article XXII(2) of the Luxembourg Protocol.

[43] Interestingly, the European Union declared that "at the time of accession to the Aircraft Protocol, the Community will not make a declaration pursuant to Article XXX(1) concerning the application of Article VIII nor will it make any of the declarations permitted under Article XXX(2) and (3). The Member States keep their competence concerning the rules of substantive law as regards insolvency".

EU Member States are unable to make declarations under Article XI Aircraft Protocol (and the corresponding Article in other Protocols), although they would be able to amend their domestic laws so as to produce same substantive outcomes as if the declaration had been made. Hence, despite the advocating of pondering OECD "qualifying declarations", declarations concerning insolvency provisions are not expected in further instruments of ratification – see, however, declarations made by other EU Member States -.

In accordance to Spanish legislation on insolvency, currently in force[44] – noting that 2014[45] and 2015[46] reforms have entailed a notable impact on (asset-based) secured creditors' position -, after insolvency procedure is commenced with the debtor, enforcement of security interests and other title-devices agreements are stayed under the following circumstances. Those security interests on assets devoted to and necessary for the continuation of the debtor's business or professional activities, as held by the insolvency court, cannot be enforced (or will be suspended) until the first of the following milestone occurs: the approval of an agreement not affecting the exercise of the said security interest or the course of one year after insolvency was declared without being any liquidation initiated. Likewise, within the aforementioned period enforcement of the following agreements will be stayed as well: in particular, hire purchase agreements, title reservation agreements or leasing agreements provided that they are registered in the Registry of Movables.

It might be well worth reminding that those agreements whose obligations are still pending are not affected by the commencement of the insolvency procedure. Clauses entitling parties to avoid or terminate the contract on grounds of insolvency declaration are indeed null and void. Hence, agreements in force have to be expressly declared avoided upon the insolvency procedure. Otherwise, those obligations due by the debtor will be paid against the insolvency state (*masa*).

In the order of preference to pay claims in insolvency procedure, asset-based secured creditors are deemed to hold "privileged" claims, in particular, claims with

---

[44] Article 56 of Law 22/2003, of 9 of July, on Insolvency (*Ley Concursal*) as drafted by Law 17/2014, of 30 of September, adopting a number of urgent measures on refinancing and restructuring business debt (*Ley 17/2014, de 30 de septiembre, por la que se adoptan medidas urgentes en materia de refinanciación y reestructuración de deuda empresarial*), published in the Official Bulletin of 1st of October of 2014 and in force since 2nd of October of 2014.

[45] The enactment of the Law 17/2014 derives from the legislative processing as an ordinary law of the Royal Decree Law 4/2014, March 7, adopting urgent measures in refinancing arrangements and debt restructuration. BOE 1 October 2014.

[46] Royal Decree Law 1/2015, February 27, BOE 28 February 2015, introducing a 'fresh start' (or 'second chance') solution in insolvency laws and Law 9/2015, May 25, BOE 26 May 2015. 'Fresh start' solutions had been previously introduced, for certain debtors and under specific conditions, by Law 14/2013 providing support to entrepreneurs and promoting internationalization. The extent of the 'fresh start' is nonetheless limited. The debtor was required, among other requirements, to entirely pay off secured creditors (mortgage and pledges). Under the RDL 1/2015, the 'fresh start' model has been substantially amended. Interestingly, the total payment to privileged creditors is not always required for the cancelation of debts. Other formulas are laid down to allow the debtor being eligible for 'fresh start' benefits. Finally, Law 25/2015, July 28, on second chance, reduction of financial burder and other social measures, BOE 29 July 2015.

a "special" privilege (Article 90 Insolvency Act). Accordingly, in the liquidation phase, those claims will be first paid with the proceeds of the sale of those assets or rights.

In particular, now it should be considered the convenience to align insolvency provisions with Alternative A of Article XI of the Protocol aiming to produce an equivalent domestic result, since the option under that provision was not available for European Union Member States.

10.7   Concluding Remarks

Spanish Laws governing secured transactions have evolved in last decades and experienced several reforms mainly aimed to better meet new financing needs and facilitate access to credit, to counteract economic situations entailing financing constraints and to enable local businesses access to international financial markets in competitive conditions. Likewise, the registry system has carried out a significant modernizing process resulting in modern, professional and highly computerized registries. In particular, the establishment of the Personal Property Registry/Registry of Movables (*Registro de Bienes Muebles*) appreciably facilitated the evolution of the secured transactions system towards non-possessory security devices.

Despite the latest reforms, Spanish rules governing secured transactions are scattered, fragmentary and, in some cases, even antiquated. The modernizing impetus has not affected uniformly all areas of secured transactions laws. Whereas reforms in insolvency laws have been numerous and substantial, legal regime of traditional security interests has remained largely intact instead, except for the modern rules on financial collateral arrangements. Then, a comprehensive reform aimed to modernize, unify and provide consistency to the legal framework governing secured transactions is long awaited and still pending.

In 2005, the incorporation into Spanish jurisdiction of European rules on financial collateral arrangements entailed a profound reform in secured transactions system. Although the scope of that reform is limited, some basic principles underpinning the whole legal conception of secured transactions have been challenged and put under consideration. Consequently, a debate is open about the need to undertake a deep and all-embracing reform of existing legal system.

The accession by Spain to Convention in 2013 and the subsequent, albeit belated, ratification of the Aircraft Protocol, as above anticipated, have also significantly contributed to trigger such discussion and foster proposals to reform among practitioners, scholars and market players. Nevertheless, all economic benefits of Cape Town system are not automatically deriving from the mere accession. Particular care requires and special attention is to be paid to effectively implement the uniform system in domestic jurisdiction. Inadequate domestic actions lead to a dysfunctional implementation likely to undermine expected economic efficiencies from joining the uniform system. In sum, given the strategic value of a full incorporation into the Cape Town system, an effective implementation of its rules on material matters and in relation to the registry system, as discussed above, is crucial.

References

1. Bercovitz Rodríguez-Cano, Rodrigo. 1971. *La cláusula de reserva de dominio. Estudio sobre su naturaleza jurídica en la compraventa a plazos de bienes muebles*. Madrid: Editorial Moneda y Crédito.
2. Bercovitz Rodríguez-Cano, Rodrigo. 1996. El pacto de reserva de dominio y la función de garantía del *leasing* financiero. In *Tratado de Garantías en la Contratación Mercantil*, ed. Ubaldo Nieto Carol, Tomo II, Vol. 1. Madrid: Civitas.
3. Cabanillas Sánchez, Antonio. 1991. La configuración del arrendamiento financiero (leasing) por la Ley de 29 de julio de 1988, en la jurisprudencia y en el Convenio sobre Leasing Internacional. *III Anuario de Derecho Civil*, 961.
4. Capilla Roncero, Francisco. 1989. *La responsabilidad patrimonial universal y el fortalecimiento de la protección del crédito*. Jerez: Fundación Universitaria.
5. Carrasco Perera, Ángel, et al. 2008. *Tratado de los Derecho de Garantía, Tomo II: Garantías Mobiliarias*. Cizur Menor: Aranzadi.
6. Crans, Berend. 2010. The implications of the EU accession to the Cape Town convention, 35. *Air and Space Law* 1, 7.
7. De Castro y Bravo, Federico. 1932. La acción pauliana y la responsabilidad patrimonial. Estudio de los artículos 1911 y 1111 del Código Civil. *Revista de Derecho Privado*, 193.
8. Rey, Feliu, and Manuel Ignacio. 1995. *La prohibición del pacto comisorio y la opción en garantía*. Madrid: Civitas.
9. Gómez Gálligo, Francisco Javier. 1999, March–April. Principios hipotecarios de los Registros Mobiliarios. *Revista Crítica de Derecho Inmobiliario*, num. 651.
10. González Castilla, Francisco. 2002. *Leasing financiero mobiliario. Contenido del contrato y atribución del riesgo en la práctica contractual y la jurisprudencia*. Madrid: Civitas.
11. Illescas Ortiz, Rafael. 1971. El *leasing:* aproximación a los problemas planteados por un nuevo contrato, 119. *Revista de Derecho Mercantil*, 74.
12. Jiménez de Parga, Rafael et al. 1988. La operación de *leasing,* ¿es una operación de crédito? *Revista de Derecho Bancario y Bursátil* 31, 487.
13. Morillas Jarillo, María José. 1993. Algunos aspectos del leasing de aeronaves en España. *Revista de Derecho Mercantil*, 208, 471.
14. Reglero Campos, Luis Fernando. 2007. El pacto comisorio. *Aranzadi Civil*, I-XVI.
15. Rodríguez de las Heras Ballell, Teresa. 2010. Protection from unfair suretyships in Spain. In *Regulating unfair banking practices in Europe: The case of personal Suretyships*, ed. Aurelia Colombi Ciacchi and Stephen Weatherill. Oxford: Oxford University Press.
16. Rodríguez de las Heras Ballell, Teresa. 2012. *Las garantías mobiliarias sobre equipo aeronáutico en el comercio internacional. El Convenio de Ciudad del Cabo y su Protocolo*. Madrid: Marcial Pons.
17. Rodríguez de las Heras Ballell, Teresa. 2014. The accession by Spain to the Cape Town Convention: A first assessment. *Uniform Law Review*, 1–23.
18. Rodriguez de las Heras Ballell, Teresa. 2015. El nuevo Reglamento de matriculación de aeronaves civiles, y el Convenio de Ciudad del Cabo y su Protocolo sobre garantías internacionales en elementos de equipo aeronáutico. *Revista de Derecho de Transporte: Terrestre, Marítimo, Aéreo y Multimodal*, 15, 235–257.
19. Rodríguez de las Heras Ballell, Teresa. 2015. La adhesión de España al Protocolo Aeronáutico del Convenio de Ciudad del Cabo y su implementación: una primera valoración del nuevo Reglamento de Matriculación de Aeronaves. *Bitácora Millenium DIPr* 88, 88–112 – Part I http://www.millenniumdipr.com/ba-29-la-adhesion-de-espana-al-protocolo-aeronautico-del-convenio-de-ciudad-del-cabo-parte-i, Part II: http://www.millenniumdipr.com/ba-30-la-adhesion-de-espana-al-protocolo-aeronautico-del-convenio-de-ciudad-del-cabo-parte-ii.

20. Rodríguez de las Heras Ballell, Teresa. 2016. Key points for the effective implementation of the Cape Town Convention: The accession of Spain to the Aircraft Protocol. *Uniform Law Review*, 1–30.
21. Vázquez de Castro, Eduardo. 2012. *La publicidad registral en el tráfico de bienes muebles.* Madrid: Civitas – Thomson Reuters.

Teresa Rodríguez de las Heras Ballell is currently Associate Professor of Commercial Law at University Carlos III of Madrid where she teaches in all areas of Business Law since 1999. She is also Deputy Vice-Chancellor in International Relations at her university. She graduated in Law and in Business Administration in 1999 with honors (fist in her class) and got her PhD with Award of Special Distinction in 2005. She is an Arbitrator of the Court of Arbitration of Madrid and of the Spanish Court of Arbitration in commercial and financial disputes, Expert in arbitrating conflicts on domain names .es, and member of the Advertising Standards Tribunal (Autocontrol). She has an extensive experience as an international legal consultant in pre-legislative projects: member of the Expert Group on the elaboration of a Fourth Protocol for the Cape Town Convention on international security interests (UNIDROIT); Legal adviser to national and regional legislators in the drafting of new legislation on electronic commerce; member of the Common Core Project on "Immoral Contracts", European Union; and Short Term Expert in the EU Twinning Project Spain-Turkey on maritime law. She is also member of the Aviation Working Group (AWG)'s Spanish Contact Group for work relating to the Cape Town Convention and its Aircraft Protocol for the implementation in Spain. In 2011, she was designated Vice-President of the International Working Group on "New Technologies, Prevention and Insurance", Association Internationale de Droit des Assurances (AIDA). She has developed her research in prestigious universities and research centers: currently, Visiting Scholar at Columbia Law School; Fellow at Transatlantic Technology Law Forum, Stanford Law School; James J. Coleman, Sr. Distinguished Visiting Professor of Law, Tulane Law School; Visiting Fellow at Harris Manchester College, Oxford University; Marie Curie Fellow at the Centre of European Law and Politics (ZERP) of the University of Bremen (Germany); Researcher at UNIDROIT, Visiting Scholar at University of Washington; University of Arizona; Project Researcher at the University of Tokyo; University College of London; Fordham University. Besides, she regularly gives lectures abroad in several universities: University College of London, Columbia Law School, Shanghai University of Finance and Economics, Tulane University Law School, Kapodistrian University of Athens, Abo Akademi/Turku University, Reykjavík University, Paris II Pantheon Assass, Aarhus University, Örebro University (Sweden), Paris I Sorbonne, Universidad de la República del Uruguay, Universidad de Buenos Aires, Università di Bologna (Italy). Her research activity has been awarded with several prizes (among others, Excellence in Research Prize, W30 Santander/UCLA; First Prize Freshfields-Financial Times). Professor Rodríguez de las Heras is author of numerous publications both in English and in Spanish in a variety of topics.

Chapter 11
United States of America: Reconsidering the Transaction Document Filing Requirement for National Registry

Charles W. Mooney Jr.

11.1 Introduction

This National Report for the United States of America (USA) has benefited greatly from the General Report chapter by Professor Souichirou Kozuka. The report adopts the terminology mentioned in the About This Book section of this book and used in the General Report chapter.[1] The report first generally outlines secured transactions law in the USA. It then discusses the Cape Town Convention and, in particular, the Aircraft Protocol and their relationship to USA law. The United States ratified the Convention and Aircraft Protocol in 2004 and these instruments entered into force on March 1, 2006. The discussion of the Cape Town Convention generally follows the structure suggested by the national questionnaire for jurisdictions that are parties to the Convention.

11.2 Background: Secured Transactions Law in the USA

In the USA's federal system secured transactions law is primarily *state* law—primarily Article 9 of the Uniform Commercial Code ("UCC"). Each state has enacted a substantially uniform version of UCC Article 9.

Article 9 applies to any transaction that creates a security interest in personal property (*i.e.*, movables).[2] A "security interest" is a unitary concept that embraces transactions in any form (*e.g.*, possessory pledges or title-reservation agreements) in

---

[1] *See* General Report [3].

[2] UCC § 9-109(a)(1).

C.W. Mooney Jr. (✉)
University of Pennsylvania Law School, University of Pennsylvania, Philadelphia, PA, USA
e-mail: cmooney@law.upenn.edu

© Springer International Publishing AG 2017
S. Kozuka (ed.), *Implementing the Cape Town Convention and the Domestic Laws on Secured Transactions*, Ius Comparatum - Global Studies in Comparative Law 22, DOI 10.1007/978-3-319-46470-1_11

which personal property (the "collateral") secures an obligation.[3] It also applies to outright transfers (sales) of most receivables.[4] A security interest becomes enforceable ("attaches") when a debtor (a person with rights in the collateral or power to transfer rights) enters into a security agreement creating a security interest and value is given (*e.g.*, a loan made by the secured party to the debtor).[5] In general a security interest becomes effective against most third parties when it becomes "perfected."[6] Perfection occurs when a security interest has attached and one of several applicable perfection steps have been taken.[7] The most common and generally applicable perfection steps are the filing in a public office of a financing statement[8] and the secured party's taking possession of the collateral (as to collateral that is capable of being possessed, such as goods (tangible movables) or negotiable instruments).[9]

Financing statements are to be filed in a central filing office in each state, usually the office of the state's Secretary of State.[10] A financing statement must contain the name of the debtor, the name of the secured party, and a description of or indication of the collateral that it covers.[11] (Also, unless a financing statement contains certain additional information (*e.g.*, addresses of the parties) it may be rejected by the filing office.[12]) Financing statements are indexed against,[13] and searchable by,[14] the name of the debtor. Inasmuch as a financing statement reflects only limited and very basic information, the Article 9 filing system often is referred to as a "notice filing" system.[15]

The basic priority rule as between competing Article 9 security interests is the so-called "first-to-file-or-perfect" ("FTFOP") rule.[16] For example, suppose SP-1 files a financing statement against a debtor at Time 1 (T-1) covering certain collateral. Then, SP-2 files at T-2 and a security interest attaches in favor of SP-2 to the same collateral on that date. At T-2, SP-1 does not have any interest in the collateral so competing security interests do not exist. However, now suppose that at T-3 a security interest in the collateral attaches in favor of SP-1. Although SP-2's security interest was the first to be perfected, SP-1 was the first to file. SP-1 has priority under the FTFOP rule. SP-2 should have searched the filing office records, discovered SP-1's filing, and refused to proceed in the face of SP-1's earlier filed financing

---

[3] UCC § 1-202(b)(35) (defining "security interest").

[4] UCC § 9-109(a)(3).

[5] UCC § 9-203(a), (b).

[6] *See, e.g.*, UCC § 9–317.

[7] UCC § 9-308(a).

[8] UCC § 9-310(a).

[9] UCC §§ 9-310(b)(6); 9–313.

[10] *See* UCC § 9-501(a)(2).

[11] UCC § 9-502(a); 9–504.

[12] UCC § 9-516(b); UCC § 9-520(a).

[13] UCC § 9-519(c).

[14] UCC § 9-523(c).

[15] UCC § 9–502, official comment 2.

[16] UCC § 9-322(a)(1).

statement. The FTFOP rule applies irrespective of a secured party's knowledge of a competing interest.

Article 9 also provides several priority rules that are exceptions to the FTFOP rule. For example, qualifying purchase-money security interests are afforded priority even if a financing statement perfecting a competing security interest has been filed first.[17]

Perfected security interests generally have priority over later-in-time judicial lien creditors.[18] That priority also extends over a debtor's trustee in bankruptcy, which has the rights of a hypothetical judicial lien creditor at the time a bankruptcy case is opened.[19] Innocent buyers and lessees of collateral for value and which receive delivery of the collateral, as well as licensees of collateral, generally take free of unperfected security interests but subject to perfected security interests.[20] In addition, a buyer in ordinary course of business of goods takes free of a security interest even if it is perfected,[21] but a buyer does not qualify if, *e.g.*, it knows that the sale violates the rights of another person as to the goods.[22]

After a default (the definition of which is left to the parties[23]) a secured party is entitled to take possession of collateral that is capable of being possessed[24] and to dispose of the collateral (as by sale, lease, or other disposition) in a commercially reasonable manner after giving reasonable notice to the debtor and other interested persons.[25] A secured party may take possession of collateral without judicial process if it can do so without a breach of the peace.[26] After default a secured party also is entitled to collect and enforce receivables and other intangible collateral.[27]

UCC Article 9 contains its own internal set of choice-of-law rules. The general rule is that perfection and priority are governed by the local law of the jurisdiction in which a debtor is located.[28] However, for tangible collateral capable of being possessed, *perfection and priority* with respect to a possessory security interest are governed by the local law of the location of the collateral[29] and for non-possessory security interests *priority* is governed by the local law of the location of the collateral.[30]

---

[17] UCC § 9–324.

[18] UCC § 9-317(a)(2).

[19] 11 U.S.C. § 544(a)(1).

[20] UCC §§ 9-201(a); 9-317(b) – (d).

[21] UCC § 9-320(a).

[22] UCC § 1-201(b)(9) (defining "buyer in ordinary course of business").

[23] UCC § 9–601, official comment 3.

[24] UCC § 9-9-609(a).

[25] UCC §§ 9–610; 9-611-9-614.

[26] UCC § 9-609(b).

[27] UCC § 9–607.

[28] UCC § 9-301(1).

[29] UCC § 9-301(2).

[30] UCC § 9-301(3)(C).

11.3 The Cape Town Convention and Its Relationship to Past and Current National Laws in the USA

11.3.1 Registration Issues

The Cape Town Convention awards priority to the international interest that is registered first, whether or not the creditor had actual knowledge of the existence of a pre-existing but unregistered interest.[31] As discussed above in Part I, the FTFOP rule under UCC Article 9, both before and after the USA became a Contracting State, is similar in effect to the Convention's priority rule. However, in some situations under UCC Article 9 the rights of buyers and other non-secured party transferees would be affected by the existence or not of knowledge that the transfer violates the rights of a secured party.

Under USA federal law there exists a national registry, operated by the Federal Aviation Administration (FAA) in Oklahoma City, for the recordation of conveyances, leases, and instruments for security purposes affecting interests in airframes, aircraft engines, and helicopters.[32] This is an object-based registry—indexed and searchable based on the aircraft asset's description (not unlike, for this purpose, the international registry under Cape Town). The recordation applies to actual transaction documents that are filed for recordation—bills of sale, mortgages, conditional sale (i.e., title reservation) agreements, leases, and the like. Before the Cape Town Convention entered into force recordation in the FAA registry was necessary for the validity of interests as against most third parties and USA federal law continues to so provide.[33]

Under USA federal law one can access the international registry only through the FAA as an entry point (except with respect to aircraft engines).[34] Moreover, access to the international registry through the FAA as an entry point is conditioned upon the filing for recordation of the transaction documents in the FAA registry in exactly the same fashion as was required before the entry into force of Cape Town. Access is further conditioned on the FAA's authorization of an international registration.[35] Even though under Cape Town it is the international registration—not the filing for recordation of documents in the FAA registry—that controls issues of third-party effectiveness and priority, USA federal law requires compliance with *both regimes*. This structure was thought necessary to obtain the support and cooperation of the FAA and Oklahoma City-based interests (such as attorneys and title companies) in the process of obtaining USA ratification of Cape Town.

---

[31] Convention art. 29(1), (2).

[32] 49 U.S.C. § 44107.

[33] 49 U.S.C. § 44108(a), (b).

[34] Convention art. 18(5) (protocol may provide for Contracting States to designate entry points); Aircraft Protocol art. XIX(1) (Contracting State may designate entry points), (2) (designation may permit but may not compel use of entry points for aircraft engines).

[35] 49 U.S.C. § 44107(e)(3); 14 C.F.R. § 49.63).

This redundant registration structure is difficult to justify based on the costs and meager (if any) benefits of the system. It should be reconsidered. It is understandable that the FAA would want to ensure a reliable system for maintaining a registry of ownership of aircraft for purposes of *nationality* registration.[36] But maintaining a USA federal registry for all transaction documents seems unwarranted given the presence and role of the international registry.

Security interests in railroad cars, locomotives, and other railroad rolling stock generally are governed by UCC Article 9. Leases of such assets are governed by UCC Article 2A. However, such assets are subject to a special federal law requiring the filing for recordation of transaction documents (*e.g.*, mortgages, leases, conditional sale agreements, and the like) with the Surface Transportation Board registry as a condition for perfection.[37] Security interests in and leases of space assets are treated under USA law in general in the same manner as are rail equipment. However, space assets are not subject to any special registration system.

The International Registry under the Cape Town Convention is an object-based system based on registration (and searches) against an aircraft object (generally identified by manufacturer, model, and serial number) as opposed to another identifier such as a debtor's name.[38] Moreover, it is a "notice filing" system, containing only limited information that provides notice to third parties that there may be an international interest that warrants further investigation.[39] In that respect the International Registry is similar in approach to the UCC Article 9 name-based notice filing system. However, it was a novel approach for aircraft equipment, and would be for rail equipment, which have been (and remain) subject to transactional document recordation systems under USA federal law, as described above.

11.3.2   Treatment of Types of International Interests

Under the Cape Town Convention an "international interest" includes three types of interests: the interest granted by a chargor to a chargee under a security agreement (*i.e.*, a security interest securing an obligation), the interest of a conditional seller under a title reservation agreement, and the interest of a lessor under a leasing agreement.[40] The Convention leaves to the applicable law the determination of which category of international interest is created by an agreement.[41] Under USA law (*i.e.*, UCC Article 9), interests in aircraft assets, rail assets, and space assets that

---

[36] *See* Chicago Convention on International Civil Aviation (1944) art. 77(maintenance of national registry).

[37] 49 U.S.C. § 11301; 14 C.F.R. §§ 1177.1–1177.5.

[38] Convention art. 18(1); Aircraft Protocol art. XX(1); Registry Regulations Section 5.3(c).

[39] Roy Goode, *The Convention on International Interests in Mobile Equipment and Protocol thereto on Matters Specific to Aircraft Objects: Official Commentary* ¶ 2.122 (3d ed. 2013).

[40] Convention arts. 1(o); 2(2).

[41] Convention art. 2(4).

are created under a security agreement and under a title reservation agreement are treated identically—as security interests under Article 9's unitary system. Leasing agreements covering such assets, on the other hand, are governed by UCC Article 2A. Of course, the provisions of UCC Articles 9 and 2A must yield to the Cape Town Convention in the case of any inconsistencies.

11.3.3 Enforcement of International Interests—Outside of a Debtor's Insolvency Proceedings

Under the Cape Town Convention in the event of a default a chargee under a security agreement[42] is entitled to take possession of an object, sell or lease the object, and collect income or profits from the management of the object[43] and may apply for a court order in aid of these remedies.[44] The parties may by agreement determine which events constitute a default and give rise to the Convention's remedies provisions.[45] Convention remedies must be exercised in a commercially reasonable manner.[46] A chargee must give reasonable notice to interested persons of a proposed sale or lease of an object.[47] Sums received or collected from a chargee's exercise of its remedies must be applied towards the satisfaction of the secured obligation.[48] The chargee must distribute any surplus in excess of the secured obligation and reasonable expenses to junior interest holders in the order of their priorities.[49] The Convention also permits a chargee and all interested persons to agree, after default, that the chargor's interest vests in the chargee in (or towards) satisfaction of the secured obligation. These remedies and duties are remarkably similar to those applicable to the enforcement of security interests under UCC Article 9.[50]

---

[42] Because under UCC Article 9 a title reservation agreement is treated as a security agreement, Article would apply also to an agreement structured as a title reservation agreement.

[43] Convention art. 8(1).

[44] Convention art. 8(2).

[45] Convention art. 11(1).

[46] Convention art. 8(3). This requirement extends to remedies under art. 8(1) and 13 (relief pending final determination. Under the Aircraft Protocol, however, this requirement extends to all remedies. Aircraft Protocol art. IX(3). If a remedy is exercised in accordance with a provision of the parties' agreement such exercise is commercially reasonable "except where such a provision is manifestly unreasonable." Convention art. 8(3); Aircraft Protocol art. IX(3).

[47] Convention art. 8(4).

[48] Convention art. 8(5).

[49] Convention art. 8(6).

[50] See, e.g., UCC §§ 9–601, official comment 2 (circumstances giving rise to a default left to the agreement of the parties); 9–607 (collection and enforcement); 9–608 (application of proceeds of collection or enforcement); 9–609 (right to take possession following default); 9–610 (disposition of collateral after default); 9–611 – 9–614 (notification of disposition); 9–615 (application of proceeds of disposition); 9–620 (acceptance of collateral full or partial satisfaction of secured obligation).

The United States has made the following declaration in connection with Article 54 of the Convention:

Pursuant to Article 54 of the Convention, all remedies available to the creditor under the Convention or Protocol which are not expressed under the relevant provision thereof to require application to the court may be exercised, in accordance with United States law, without leave of the court.[51]

As mentioned above, UCC Article 9 permits a secured party to take possession of collateral following a default without judicial process if it does so without a breach of the peace. It also permits non-judicial collections on and dispositions of collateral.

Article 10 of the Convention provides that on default a conditional seller or lessor is entitled to take possession of an object and to terminate the agreement and to apply to a court in aid of these remedies. Otherwise it leaves the remedies to the applicable law. Under UCC Article 9 a conditional seller is treated as a chargee under a security agreement. The remedies of a lessor are governed by UCC Article 2A.[52]

11.3.4   Enforcement of International Interests—In a Debtor's Insolvency Proceedings

Article XI of the Aircraft Protocol outlines a creditor's remedies if its debtor becomes insolvent. A Contracting State that is a debtor's "primary insolvency jurisdiction"[53] may use a declaration to opt for either Alternative A or Alternative B of Article XI, or it may decide not to make a declaration at all.[54]

Alternative A closely resembles section 1110 of the United States Bankruptcy Code.[55] Alternative A is substantially more protective of a creditor's interests than Alternative B. Under Alternative A, the debtor's "insolvency administrator"[56] must give possession of the relevant aircraft object to the creditor holding an international

---

[51] Declarations lodged by the United States of America under the Cape Town Convention at the time of the deposit of its instrument of ratification, *available at* http://www.unidroit.org/status-2001capetown?id=496.

[52] *See* UCC §§ 2A-523 – 2A-532 (lessor's remedies on lessee's default).

[53] Aircraft Protocol art. I(2)(n) (defining "primary insolvency jurisdiction" as "the Contracting State in which the centre of the debtor's main interests is situated").

[54] Aircraft Protocol arts. XI(1) (Article XI applies only if a declaration is made under Article XXX(3)); XXX(3) (declarations concerning Article XI). There are similar provisions under the Rail Protocol and the Space Protocol. *See* Rail Protocol art. IX (Alternatives A, B, and C); Space Protocol art. XXI (Alternatives A and B).

[55] 11 U.S.C. § 1110.

[56] Convention art. 1(k) (defining "insolvency administrator" as "a person authorised to administer the reorganisation or liquidation, including one authorised on an interim basis, and includes a debtor in possession if permitted by the applicable insolvency law").

interest in the object before the expiration of the "waiting period."[57] Instead of specifying a period of time following the commencement of insolvency proceedings, such as the 60 day period provided by section 1110, Alternative A permits a Contracting State, in its declaration, to specify the applicable "waiting period" that will apply when the Contracting State is a debtor's primary insolvency jurisdiction.[58] However, as under section 1110, if the insolvency administrator or debtor "cures all defaults . . . and has agreed to perform all future obligations under the agreement," the insolvency administrator or debtor "may retain possession of the aircraft object."[59]

Because Section 1110 of Chapter 11 of the United States Bankruptcy code specifies a 60-day period and is substantially to the same effect as Alternative A of Art. XI, the United States has not made a declaration relating to Art. XI of the Aircraft Protocol.

11.3.5 *Additional and General Considerations*

This subpart of the report first offers some observations on the attitudes and perspectives of USA constituencies toward the Cape Town Convention. It then contrasts with those observations the motivating factors that led to the USA's actual ratification of the Convention and the Aircraft Protocol.

From the beginning the USA government and aircraft finance professionals were quite favorably disposed toward the Convention project. Early empirical and economic analyses of the prospective economic benefits of the Convention were highly influential.[60] More recently, emphasis has been placed on the importance of the implementation of and compliance with the Convention by Contracting States.[61] Suffice it to note that there is considerable support in the USA for the Cape Town Convention and the Aircraft Protocol to be widely adopted around the world.

---

[57] Aircraft Protocol art. XI(2) (*Alternative A*).

[58] *Id.* art. XI(3) (*Alternative A*).

[59] *Id.* art. XI(7) (*Alternative A*). However, "a default constituted by the opening of insolvency proceedings" need not be cured. *Id.*

[60] *See* Anthony Saunders et al., The Economic Implications of International Secured Transactions Law Reform: A Case Study, 20 *University of Pennsylvania Journal of International Economic Law* 309 (1999).

[61] *See* Jeffrey Wool, Treaty Design, Implementation, and Compliance Benchmarking Economic Benefit—a Framework as Applied to the Cape Town Convention, 17 *Uniform Law Review* 633, 640 (2012); Jeffrey Wool, Compliance with Transnational Commercial Law Treaties—A Framework as Applied to the Cape Town Convention, 3 *Cape Town Convention Journal* 5 (2015); Charles W. Mooney, Jr., The Cape Town Convention's Improbable-but-Possible Progeny Part Two: Bilateral Investment Treaty-Like Enforcement Mechanism, 55 *Virginia Journal of International Law* 451 (2015).

But this support likely had little to do with motivating the USA to ratify the Convention and Protocol. USA support for widespread adoption of the Convention and Protocol quite clearly is consistent with the interests of USA-based manufacturers and exporters of aircraft equipment—read: Boeing (aircraft), Pratt & Whitney/ United Technologies (aircraft engines), General Electric (aircraft engines). It is also consistent with the interests of USA-based providers of asset-based financing for foreign buyers and users aircraft equipment. But those benefits were not materially enhanced by the USA's ratification. The Convention and Protocol are unlikely to have reduced the costs of financing for USA buyers, borrowers, and lessees or increased sales and leases by USA manufacturers to USA-based entities. This is because Article 9 of the UCC, supplemented by the FAA aircraft registry, has provided a solid legal framework for aircraft financing for many years before the USA's adoption of these instruments.[62] If anything, the Cape Town Convention may have disadvantaged USA air carriers to the extent that it has lowered the costs of financing for those carriers' foreign competitors.

Why, then, was the USA motivated to ratify the Convention and Protocol? USA interests could actually realize the potential benefits of these instruments only if an operational International Registry were in place. Without the *volume* provided by USA debtor transactions, the registry would not be economically viable. Providing the volume and resulting revenues to the registry appears to be the principal—and completely rational—motivating factor behind USA ratification. But, of course, even with such a motivation the USA likely would not have ratified had the product—the Convention and Protocol—not been of a high quality that would support efficient asset-based financing.

References

1. Goode, Roy. 2013. *The convention on international interests in mobile equipment and protocol thereto on matters specific to aircraft objects: Official commentary*, 3rd ed. Rome: UNDROIT.
2. Mooney Jr., Charles W. 2015. The Cape Town Convention's improbable-but-possible progeny part two: Bilateral investment treaty-like enforcement mechanism. *Virginia Journal of International Law* 55: 451.
3. Saunders, Anthony, Anand Srinivasan, Ingo Walter, and Jeffrey Wool. 1999. The economic implications of international secured transactions law reform: A case study. *University of Pennsylvania Journal of International Economic Law* 20: 309.
4. Wool, Jeffrey. 2012. Treaty design, implementation, and compliance benchmarking economic benefit—A framework as applied to the Cape Town Convention. *Uniform Law Review* 17: 633.
5. Wool, Jeffrey. 2015. Compliance with transnational commercial law treaties—A framework as applied to the Cape Town Convention. *Cape Town Convention Journal* 3.

---

[62] In fairness, it is clear that in some situations being a Contracting State party to the Convention and Protocol may afford USA-based financers of aircraft equipment to greater cooperation from courts and administrators in other Contracting States.

Charles W. Mooney Jr. is Charles A. Heimbold, Jr. Professor of Law at the University of Pennsylvania Law School. Professor Mooney received his J.D. from Harvard Law School in 1972 and a B.A. from the University of Oklahoma in 1969. He practiced law with the Oklahoma firm of Crowe and Dunlevy and as a partner of the New York firm of Shearman & Sterling. Professor Mooney joined the Penn faculty in 1986, and during 1999 and 2000 he served as Interim Dean of the Law School. From 1998 to 2000 and from 2008 to 2009 he served as Associate Dean for Academic Affairs. He has been an active member of the American Law Institute and the American Bar Association. He served as a member of the Uniform Commercial Code Permanent Editorial Board Article 2 (Sales) Study Committee and also served as a reporter for that Board's Article 9 (Secured Transactions) Study Committee and as a reporter for the Revised Article 9 drafting committee. He served as a member of the U.S. Security and Exchange Commission's Advisory Committee on Market Transactions. Mooney was awarded the Distinguished Service Award, presented by the American College of Commercial Finance Lawyers. He is a Fellow and former Director of the American College of Bankruptcy and a Director of the International Insolvency Institute. He also served as U.S. Delegate and Position Coordinator (appointed by U.S. Department of State) at the Diplomatic Conference for the Cape Town Convention on International Interests in Mobile Equipment and the Protocol on Matters Specific to Aircraft Equipment, in Cape Town, South Africa. He also served as a U.S. Delegate for the UNIDROIT Geneva Securities Convention at the Diplomatic Conferences in Geneva. In recent years he has participated in the work of UNCITRAL's Working Group VI (secured transactions) as a member of the observer delegation of the International Insolvency Institute. Recently he served as member of the UNIDROIT Study Committee for a Fourth Protocol for the Cape Town Convention on mining, agriculture, and construction equipment. His current research centers on intermediated securities, security interests in bankruptcy, international harmonization of secured transactions law, restructuring of sovereign debt, and bankruptcy policy and theory. He has published widely in the fields of secured transactions and bankruptcy law.

Chapter 12
Finnish Mortgage System for Means of Transport: Outdated and Overly Complex?

Teemu Juutilainen

12.1 Overview

To date, Finland is not a party to the Cape Town Convention on International Interests in Mobile Equipment. This chapter focuses on Finnish domestic law on security over means of transport. It should be noted, though, that the Convention may significantly affect the future of domestic law (see Sect. 12.14).[1]

As a general rule, to use an individual tangible movable object as security for credit under Finnish law, one has to settle for a possessory pledge.[2] To make a possessory pledge effective against the pledgor's other creditors, the pledgor has to surrender possession of the object to the pledgee, or at least be unable to

---

[1] In this chapter, references to statutes are given with their respective numbers in the Statutes of Finland, for example, "the Vessel Mortgage Act (211/1927)". The latter part of the number indicates the year when the statute was published, which is usually also the year of enactment. Most of the statutes have been amended on several occasions, but the numbers do not reveal amendments. The statutes can be found in their original form as well as in their amended and consolidated form, indicating the dates of amendment, in the Finlex Data Bank: http://www.finlex.fi/en. While Finnish statutes are official only in the Finnish and Swedish languages, the data bank provides unofficial translations in other languages, mostly in English. These translations, when available, have been used in this chapter. In addition, the terminology of the chapter has been supplemented by translations used by The Finnish Transport Safety Agency (Trafi), which functions as the main register authority. The author wishes to thank Janne Kaisto, University of Helsinki, for comments on an early draft, and Christopher Goddard for language editing.

[2] With certain exceptions, the entire movable property of an enterprise can be used as a "floating" security for credit by an enterprise mortgage, under the Enterprise Mortgage Act (634/1984).

T. Juutilainen (✉)
Faculty of Law, University of Helsinki, Helsinki, Finland
e-mail: teemu.juutilainen@helsinki.fi

© Springer International Publishing AG 2017
S. Kozuka (ed.), *Implementing the Cape Town Convention and the Domestic Laws on Secured Transactions*, Ius Comparatum - Global Studies in Comparative Law 22, DOI 10.1007/978-3-319-46470-1_12

independently decide on its whereabouts.[3] This kind of security device is obviously unsuitable for situations where the security provider, usually the debtor, needs to use the encumbered object to conduct its own business.[4]

As an exception to this general rule, special legislation exists establishing a mortgage system for certain types of means of transport. The key pieces of this statutory framework are the Vessel Mortgage Act (211/1927), the Aircraft Mortgage Act (211/1928), and the Vehicle Mortgage Act (810/1972). The Vessel Mortgage Act is a general act in that it also applies to aircraft and vehicle mortgages, unless otherwise provided by the other two acts (Aircraft Mortgage Act, Section 2; Vehicle Mortgage Act, Section 22).

Preconditions for mortgaging a means of transport are that it falls within the scope of application of the relevant mortgage act and is registered in the relevant register. These registers are the Register of Vessels governed by the Register of Vessels Act (512/1993), the Aircraft Register governed by Chapter 2 of the Aviation Act (864/2014), and the Vehicle Traffic Register governed by the Act on Vehicle Traffic Register (541/2003). They all are maintained by The Finnish Transport Safety Agency (Trafi), with the exception that the Register of Vessels regarding vessels registered in the Region of Åland is maintained by the State Department of Åland.[5]

The purpose of this chapter is twofold: besides describing the main features of the current mortgage system for means of transport, it discusses the need for reform in this area of law.[6]

12.2 "System of Two Promissory Notes": Bearer Bond as Mortgage Instrument

According to the mortgage acts, a means of transport can be mortgaged to secure fulfillment of a monetary obligation (financial obligation). The promissory note or other document expressing this obligation must be appended when registration of a mortgage is applied for from the register authority. The original idea underlying the acts is that the document appended, with respect to which the mortgage is sought to be registered, expresses an actual debt owed to a creditor. Yet, financing practice has

---

[3] Jarno Tepora, Janne Kaisto, and Esa Hakkola, 2009, *Esinevakuudet* (Helsinki: CC Lakimiesliiton Kustannus), 39–40; Erkki Havansi, 1992, *Esinevakuusoikeudet*, 2nd ed. (Helsinki: Lakimiesliiton Kustannus), 141–145.

[4] See generally Ulrich Drobnig, 2011, Security rights in movables, in *Towards a European civil code*, 4th ed., ed. Arthur Hartkamp et al., 1025–1042 (The Hague: Kluwer Law International), 1026–1031.

[5] The Region of Åland is an autonomous part of the Republic of Finland. It is located on the Åland Islands, which are an archipelago in the Baltic Sea, at the entrance to the Gulf of Bothnia.

[6] Of course, the mortgage system is not the whole of Finnish law on security over means of transport. For example, see Hans Wassgren, 2004, Rights of financiers in aircraft: A Finnish perspective on the 2001 Cape Town instruments, *Uniform Law Review* 9: 557–572, 562–565. He also discusses retention of title and financial leasing in the context of aircraft finance.

long since abandoned this idea.[7] Instead, in pursuit of flexibility, a practice known as the "system of two promissory notes" has emerged.

In this practice, a mortgage can be registered even before the existence of any actual debt, repayment of which the mortgage could secure. The document appended to the application for registration of a mortgage is typically a bearer bond (negotiable promissory note), which does not, as such, represent any actual debt owed by the owner of the means of transport. Bearer bond forms for all types of mortgageable means of transport are linked to the Trafi website: http://www.trafi.fi.[8] Registration means that the register authority makes an entry concerning the mortgage in the relevant register and, importantly, on the bearer bond.

> This chapter is written under the assumption that the document expressing the monetary obligation with respect to which a mortgage is registered, or registration is applied for, is a bearer bond, created by filling in a bearer bond form provided by Trafi. This assumption simplifies and clarifies the discussion below, and is justified in that it corresponds to the normal course of action in current financing practice. Note, though, that the law does not require use of a form provided by Trafi, or a bearer bond or other negotiable document. If an ordinary, non-negotiable promissory note is used, the applicable legal norms are partly different.[9] It is also assumed in this chapter, for the sake of simplicity, that the debtor of a secured claim, or a claim to be secured, is the owner of the means of transport.

A mortgage over a means of transport is not, as such, a security right over that means of transport, but rather an element of a security right, needed in order to bring about third-party effects as well as to fix the secured amount and priority position.[10] Indeed, a mortgage can be registered before the owner of the means of transport provides a security right to a creditor. In that case, registration of mortgage can be seen as preparation for creating a security right in the future. When the owner wishes to provide a creditor with a security right over a means of transport, the owner makes a disposition (or enters into an agreement) concerning that right. This disposition is hereinafter called "charging", and the resulting security right a "charge".[11]

---

[7] KM 1992:44, *Kuljetusvälineiden velkakiinnitystoimikunnan mietintö* [Committee Report 1992:44], 4.

[8] Website accessed 6 Oct 2016.

[9] See Havansi 1992, 187–192, 278.

[10] In a comparative perspective, using the term "mortgage" like this may be misleading. "Mortgage" is by no means a perfect translation of the Finnish term *kiinnitys* and the Swedish term *inteckning*, both of which rather denote a technical act of register entry.

[11] "Charge" is not the only possible translation for the Finnish term *panttioikeus* and the Swedish term *panträtt*. For example, in the unofficial translation of the Real Estate Code (540/1995) available in the Finlex Data Bank, the term "lien" is used to denote a security right in the context of the mortgage system for real estate. Still, "lien" could be misleading in that it often denotes non-consensual security rights or entitlements to retain possession of the security object until the secured obligation has been discharged. See, for example, Gerard McCormack, 2004, *Secured credit under English and American law* (Cambridge: Cambridge University Press), 44–46. Another option would be "pledge", seeing that the above-mentioned Finnish and Swedish terms denote possessory and non-possessory security rights alike. Then again, "pledge" is generally understood as a possessory security right. Against these difficulties, "charge" seems to be the best option available. In comparative legal literature, it has been used "for all security rights in movables or in claims which

However, mere registration of a mortgage and charging do not create a charge in the sense of a security right that is effective against the security-provider debtor's other creditors. To that end, the creditor has in addition to receive possession of a bearer bond that contains the register authority's entry concerning the mortgage (hereinafter: "bearer bond with mortgage entry").[12] It is also possible that charging takes place first, and registration of a mortgage is applied for after that. If registration is applied for by the creditor whose claim is to be secured, which is possible with the owner's consent (see Sect. 12.4), a charge comes into existence upon registration of the mortgage.[13]

In short, the actual security right over a mortgaged means of transport is a charge. The mortgage acts prohibit possessory pledges over mortgageable means of transport (Vessel Mortgage Act, Section 23(3); Aircraft Mortgage Act, Section 1(2); Vehicle Mortgage Act, Section 2(2)).

The term "system of two promissory notes" refers, on the one hand, to a bearer bond, and, on the other, to a promissory note (or credit agreement) expressing the actual debt owed by the owner of a means of transport to a secured creditor. In legal literature, a bearer bond with mortgage entry is often referred to as a "charge promissory note". A promissory note (or credit agreement) expressing the owner's actual debt is often referred to as a "wrap promissory note". As a matter of fact, a charge promissory note is a promissory note only in a formal sense. Its function, besides that related to third-party effectiveness of a security right ("perfection" by possession of the bearer bond with mortgage entry), is to establish the amount of money that the secured creditor is entitled to from the value of the means of transport if the debtor defaults. Priority between two or more charges over the same means of transport is determined by the time of registration of mortgage – first in time, first in right. If the debtor repays the secured creditor, and the secured claim thus ceases to exist, the bearer bond is returned to the debtor. A feature of the system of two promissory notes is that the debtor is able to use the returned bearer bond to secure another claim, be it by the same or another creditor, with the same priority position that was fixed at the time of registration of the mortgage.[14]

---

are neither a security transfer of ownership nor a security assignment nor a possessory pledge". Eva-Maria Kieninger, ed., 2004, *Security rights in movable property in European private law* (Cambridge: Cambridge University Press), 154. In the same source, the Finnish vehicle mortgage is referred to as "vehicle charge" (p. 471).

[12] Ari Saarnilehto et al., 2012, *Varallisuusoikeus*, 2nd ed. (Helsinki: Sanoma Pro), 1206–1207; Tepora, Kaisto and Hakkola 2009, 126–127; Jarno Tepora, 2008, *Johdatus esineoikeuden perusteisiin* (Helsinki: Helsingin yliopiston oikeustieteellinen tiedekunta), 110–111; Havansi 1992, 278–279.

[13] Saarnilehto et al. 2012, 1207. In that case, the creditor receives the bearer bond with mortgage entry directly from the register authority.

[14] Havansi 1992, 279.

12.3   Mortgageable Means of Transport

According to Section 23 of the Vessel Mortgage Act, vessels "entered in the register" are mortgageable. This means vessels registered under the Register of Vessels Act. Section 1 of this act prescribes compulsory registration for Finnish vessels used for commercial seafaring and of at least 15 m in length. Section 2 provides for voluntary registration for smaller vessels used for commercial seafaring but of at least 10 m in length. In addition, Section 3 provides for voluntary registration of vessels under construction in Finland in the Vessel Building Register, if they will fulfill the requirements of Section 2 or 3 when completed.[15]

Section 1 of the Aircraft Mortgage Act provides that aircraft "registered in Finland or entered in the Annex of Aircraft Register" are mortgageable. Provisions on the Aircraft Register, including those on preconditions for registration, are in Chapter 2 of the Aviation Act.

According to Section 1 of the Vehicle Mortgage Act, the following vehicles are mortgageable: (1) truck (lorry), bus, coach; (2) truck trailer (trailer accepted as attached to a truck); (3) special car, tractor, motorised work machine, motorised device. Class definitions for vehicle types are provided in the Vehicles Act (1090/2002). Moreover, Section 38 of the Decree on Vehicle Registration (893/2007) provides that certain vehicles that cannot be registered for road traffic due to their measurements, mass or other features, can nevertheless be registered for the purpose of mortgaging.

Perhaps counter-intuitively, ordinary automobiles (cars) and vans are not mortgageable under the Vehicle Mortgage Act, or otherwise as individual objects. Automobiles and vans can be covered by an enterprise mortgage, or be subject to a possessory pledge, which however is unlikely to serve the security-provider debtor's needs – due to the very possession requirement, which prevents use by the security-provider debtor.

The lists of mortgageable means of transport in the above-mentioned legislation are exhaustive. No mortgage system or other special security rights legislation exists on railway rolling stock or space assets. These assets, too, can be covered by an enterprise mortgage, or be subject to a possessory pledge.

12.4   Registration of Mortgage

Registration of a mortgage should be applied for from the authority maintaining the relevant register, which in most cases is Trafi (see Sect. 12.1). Eligible to apply are the owner of the means of transport or, with the owner's consent, the creditor whose claim the mortgage is meant to secure (Vessel Mortgage Act, Section 24; Vehicle

---

[15] Section 23(5) of the Vessel Mortgage Act confirms that uncompleted vessels entered in the Vessel Building Register are also mortgageable.

Mortgage Act, Section 3). A mortgage expires 10 years after the date of registration, but can be renewed (Vessel Mortgage Act, Section 32; Vehicle Mortgage Act, Section 6).

A mortgage is registered against a means of transport, not against the debtor or other owner of the means of transport. Accordingly, a registered mortgage continues to encumber a means of transport even if its ownership is transferred to another person.

The mortgage system for means of transport resembles notice filing systems in that a registered mortgage only indicates that a security right (a charge) over the means of transport may exist, with a certain priority position. It is possible, for example, that the owner of a means of transport registers mortgages "just in case", but never creates security rights. However, a registered mortgage gives more information to a person searching the register than a filed notice does. In particular, it indicates the maximum amount of money that the secured creditor is entitled to from the value of the means of transport with priority over other creditors, assuming a charge has been created. A bearer bond or other document expressing a monetary obligation must be appended when registration of a mortgage is applied for from the register authority. This requirement brings the mortgage system closer to a deed registration system, even if the document does not express an actual debt owed by the owner, and even though it does not indicate creation of a security right.[16]

The amount of money for which registration of a mortgage is applied for is up to the applicant to decide (when creating the bearer bond). "Accuracy" in the sense that the amount should correspond to some particular secured claim is not relevant from the register authority's point of view. It is in the applicant's interest that the amount fits the purpose for which registration of mortgage is applied for. As noted in Sect. 12.2, the idea of the "system of two promissory notes" is that a bearer bond with mortgage entry can be reused to secure several successive claims.

At present, the State does not guarantee that registered information reflects the true state of titles,[17] but the mortgage acts are supposed to ensure that this is so, as follows: According to Section 25(1) of the Vessel Mortgage Act, the register authority will not register a mortgage if the person who consented to registration is not recorded in the register as the owner of the vessel.[18] Subsections (2) and (3) concern situations where ownership of a vessel, or of a part of a vessel, has been transferred to another person, and registration of a mortgage is applied for based on the earlier owner's consent. A mortgage can be registered if the application has been submitted before the register authority is requested to register the new owner's acquisition of ownership. If this request comes before the application for mortgage registration,

---

[16] On notice filing and deed registration systems, see Sjef van Erp, 2004, The Cape Town Convention: A model for a European system of security interests registration? *European Review of Private Law* 12: 91–110; 96–97, 103–108.

[17] See Committee Report 1992:44, 10.

[18] This provision should rule out the possibility of conflict between a charge and an earlier retention of title or financial lease. See Jarno Tepora, 1984, *Omistuksenpidätyksestä* (Vammala: Suomalainen Lakimiesyhdistys), 309.

the mortgage will not be registered. According to Section 26(1), an application for mortgage registration will be rejected if it concerns a vessel, or part of a vessel, which is subject to distraint by the enforcement authority, belongs to a bankruptcy estate, or is subject to an ownership dispute before a court of law. Subsection (2) prescribes that a mortgage is void if it has been registered while a vessel, or part of a vessel, was subject to distraint or part of a bankruptcy estate, but before the register authority was informed about these circumstances. All these provisions apply to aircraft mortgages by virtue of Section 2 of the Aircraft Mortgage Act. The Vehicle Mortgage Act has its own provisions, which however largely correspond to those of the Vessel Mortgage Act.[19]

12.5 Questions of Priority

If several mortgages have been registered with respect to the same means of transport, an earlier registered mortgage has priority over later registered mortgages, and mortgages registered on the same day have the same priority (Vessel Mortgage Act, Section 30). Of course, a later registered mortgage cannot obtain priority over an earlier registered mortgage on the basis that the creditor applying for registration of the later mortgage had no actual knowledge of the existence of the earlier registered mortgage.

Anyone is entitled to information on registered mortgages from the register authority. To check whether a means of transport has been mortgaged (whether one or more mortgages have been registered with respect to it) one can make a telephone inquiry.[20] For more detailed information, one can order (in writing, for example by fax or e-mail, and subject to a charge) an encumbrance certificate.

While priorities between several registered mortgages are clear, difficult situations may arise from conflicting dispositions made by the owner of a means of transport. As explained below, possession of a bearer bond with mortgage entry often plays a central role in resolving such priority conflicts.

Consider first a situation where owner A, who has one bearer bond with mortgage entry, charges a means of transport in favour of creditor B, and subsequently, before giving the bearer bond to B, charges the same means of transport in favour of creditor C. This priority conflict is resolved according to general principles on negotiable promissory notes, because a bearer bond is a negotiable promissory note.[21] The default norm is that priority belongs to B, the earlier chargee (first in time with respect to the conflicting dispositions). However, under certain conditions, C may achieve priority over B. Priority belongs to C if the bearer bond was in A's possession,

---

[19] See Section 4 of the Vehicle Mortgage Act. The difference is that the transfer of ownership situations covered by Section 25 Subsections (2) and (3) of the Vessel Mortgage Act are not mentioned.

[20] As for vehicle mortgages, inquiries by text message or via online service are also possible.

[21] A central source of these principles is Chapter 2 of the Promissory Notes Act (622/1947).

if A then transferred possession of the bearer bond to C, and if C was in "well-founded good faith" at the time of receiving possession. Well-founded good faith means that C did not know, and had no reason to know, about the earlier charge in favour of B. The creditor who loses the priority conflict may still not be left with nothing, but may get a secondary charge. This is a right to satisfaction of the claim to the extent that the amount of the mortgage (the amount of the bearer bond) exceeds what is needed to satisfy the claim secured by the primary charge.[22]

The principles are probably applied similarly if a bearer bond with mortgage entry did not yet exist when A charged the means of transport in favour of B. That is, priority belongs to B unless, after registration of the mortgage, C receives possession of the bearer bond in well-founded good faith.[23]

The scenario changes if A operates with more than one bearer bond. Consider the following situation: A charges a means of transport in favour of B, promising to register a mortgage with respect to bearer bond X, but subsequently charges the same means of transport in favour of C, and creates bearer bond Y. A registers a mortgage with respect to bearer bond Y before registering a mortgage with respect to bearer bond X, and transfers possession of bearer bond Y to C. Now, it is uncertain how this priority conflict is resolved. The prevailing opinion appears to be that in this case the default norm giving priority to the earlier chargee does not apply, and that B can achieve priority over C only on some special grounds. It has been argued that one such ground could be C's actual knowledge about the earlier charge in favour of B, at the time when charging in favour of C took place.[24]

This would be consistent with a solution that has been proposed for the situation where A, having charged a means of transport in favour of B, and before any bearer bond with mortgage entry exists, transfers ownership of the means of transport to C. Here, too, it has been argued that a default norm giving priority to the earlier disposition (charging in favour of B) would not apply. However, so the argument goes, B's charge could continue to exist despite the transfer of ownership either if C accepts it or, which is a more uncertain view, if C actually knew about the earlier charging in favour of B at the time of transfer of ownership.[25]

Section 30(3) of the Vessel Mortgage Act, Section 4(2) of the Aircraft Mortgage Act, and Section 5(2) of the Vehicle Mortgage Act concern claims that take priority over claims secured by a charge over a mortgaged means of transport. The Vehicle Mortgage Act and Aircraft Mortgage Act provisions mention claims secured by a

---

[22] Tepora, Kaisto and Hakkola 2009, 160–162. A secondary charge is made effective against third parties by notification addressed to the creditor with the primary charge. See Havansi 1992, 125.

[23] Tepora, Kaisto and Hakkola 2009, 164.

[24] Ibid., 165.

[25] Ibid., 158–159. See Mia Hoffrén, 2008, *Tieto ja sivullissuoja* (Helsinki: Suomalainen Lakimiesyhdistys), 33. She observes that willingness to give weight to actual knowledge in resolving priority conflicts has increased in more recent legal literature.

right of retention.[26] According to Chapter 3 of the Maritime Act (674/1994), maritime liens and rights of retention rank above a charge over a mortgaged vessel.

12.6 Limited Functionalism

The mortgage system for means of transport has little to do with the idea of functionalism as generally understood in the context of systems of security rights. A mortgage can be used for just one purpose, to create a security right of just one type, that is, a charge over a means of transport with respect to which a mortgage is registered. Besides, legislation provides exhaustive lists of mortgageable means of transport. A seller's right based on a retention of title clause or a lessor's right under a leasing agreement cannot be registered, and need not be registered for effectiveness against third parties.[27]

As a general proposition, though, Finnish law on security rights subscribes to functionalist thinking. This can be seen in the underlying aim, namely, to afford similar treatment to arrangements that pursue similar economic purposes. Two examples may serve as an illustration: First, the same third-party effects as by using a retention of title clause can be achieved by a clause on the right to recover the object of sale if the buyer fails to pay the purchase price. This is so because the clauses have a similar economic purpose.[28] Thus, the seller's protection against, say, the buyer's other creditors does not depend on resorting to concepts like "title" or "ownership".[29] Second, a (non-possessory) security transfer of ownership is not effective against the transferee's creditors because such a transfer has a similar economic purpose to a possessory pledge. Effectiveness would thus enable circumvention of the possession requirement concerning pledge, and the policy according to which this requirement is needed for publicity purposes.[30]

---

[26] The Aircraft Mortgage Act provision does not seem up to date. It also refers to certain claims related to a repealed Aviation Act (595/64).

[27] See Wassgren 2004, 564–565. He discusses the risk and unexpected consequences of a financial lease being recharacterised as hire purchase.

[28] See Tepora, Kaisto and Hakkola 2009, 370–373. They go a step further, suggesting that a retention of title clause and a recovery clause can be seen as indistinguishable not only as to economic purposes but even as to legal content.

[29] Bankruptcy Act (120/2004), Chapter 5 Section 7. See HE 26/2003, *Hallituksen esitys Eduskunnalle konkurssilainsäädännön uudistamiseksi* [Government Proposal 26/2003], 75. Cf. the outdated judgment of the Finnish Supreme Court 1983 II 132, where a recovery clause was regarded as "obligational by nature", and therefore effective only between the seller and the buyer. Furthermore, unlike in bankruptcy (collective liquidation proceedings), in enforcement (debt recovery proceedings), a seller with retention of title is not protected "as the owner" of the object of sale. That is, the object can be distrained against and realised, and the seller is protected "only" by way of a priority position in distribution of the realisation proceeds. See the Enforcement Code (705/2007), Chapter 4 Section 15.

[30] Tepora, Kaisto and Hakkola 2009, 414; Havansi 1992, 512–513. See Torgny Håstad, 2001, Nordiska önskemål vid en integration av säkerhetsrätten, in *Civilrättens integration ur nordisk*

12.7   Agreement on Private Enforcement

In the case of debtor default, a creditor holding a charge over a mortgaged means of transport does not have an independent power of realisation directly by operation of law. In contrast, this power exists, by virtue of Chapter 10 Section 2 of the Trade Code (3/1734), with respect to possessory pledges over ordinary tangible movable objects or negotiable documents.[31] The normal way to go about enforcement in the case of a charge over a mortgaged means of transport is through the district court. The chargee is supposed to bring a so-called "hypothec action" against the owner of the means of transport. In that action, the chargee requests the court to order the owner to pay a certain amount of money out of the value of the means of transport. If the court makes this order, the chargee still needs to turn to the enforcement authority, which will take care of selling the means of transport.[32]

A chargee of a mortgaged means of transport may wish to acquire an independent power of realisation by agreement with the owner of the means of transport. This could be arranged so that the owner authorises the chargee to sell the means of transport and satisfy the secured claim out of the proceeds of sale. However, this arrangement involves two kinds of uncertainty for the chargee: First, the law probably does not allow irrevocable authorisation. The owner might thus be able to revoke the independent realisation power at will. Second, authorisation would probably not survive transfer of ownership of the means of transport, or remain valid in the owner's bankruptcy (collective liquidation proceedings).[33]

12.8   Notion of Debtor Default

The parties to a security arrangement on a means of transport enjoy broad freedom to agree on the circumstances that entitle the secured creditor to exercise remedies. The starting point for the notion of default in the "system of two promissory notes" is, of course, the debtor not discharging their obligations under the promissory note (or credit agreement) that expresses the actual debt owed to the creditor ("wrap

---

synvinkel, ed. Salla Tuominen, 49–73 (Helsingfors: Juridiska fakulteten vid Helsingfors universitet), 55. Håstad sees the aim of functional solutions as a hallmark of Nordic property law. According to him, hollowing out the rules on pledge by having different rules for security transfer of ownership would be a "self-deception".

[31] HE 1/1988, *Hallituksen esitys Eduskunnalle laiksi kauppakaaren 10 luvun muuttamisesta, laiksi elinkeinonharjoittajan oikeudesta myydä noutamatta jätetty esine ja laiksi merilain 215 §:n muuttamisesta* [Government Proposal 1/1988], 9. The provision probably also applies, for example, to charges over book-entry securities and intellectual property rights. Saarnilehto et al. 2012, 1211; Havansi 1992, 389–399; Markku Tuominen, 2001, *Teollisoikeudet vakuutena* (Helsinki: WSLT), 220–221.

[32] Saarnilehto et al. 2012, 1214; Tepora, Kaisto and Hakkola 2009, 183–185; Tuula Linna and Tatu Leppänen, 2007, *Ulosmittaus ja myynti* (Helsinki: Talentum), 89.

[33] Tepora, Kaisto and Hakkola 2009, 178–179.

promissory note"). By contrast, a bearer bond with mortgage entry ("charge promissory note"), which is a promissory note only in a formal sense, is irrelevant for this purpose.

For example, if the parties agree that even one late periodical payment can make the entire debt fall due and immediately payable, then that delay entitles the secured creditor to seek satisfaction out of the value of the means of transport. Without such an agreement, a single late payment may not have the same effect if the sum of this payment is but a negligible part of the entire debt or the value of the means of transport. Common in financing practice are agreements that entitle a secured creditor to claim additional security or payments in advance, alternatively to make the entire debt fall due, if the security for the credit extended somehow deteriorates.[34] It should be noted, however, that the mortgage acts already provide solutions to some such situations.[35]

12.9   Remedies Besides Simple Liquidation

Other than on insolvency, the parties' freedom of agreement is also the main rule when it comes to remedies alternative to simple liquidation. For example, if a secured creditor and debtor consider it appropriate that upon default the secured creditor may take possession and start using the means of transport, or start collecting income generated by it, they can so agree.[36]

As regards remedies that involve vesting ownership of a means of transport in a secured creditor, Section 37 of the Contracts Act may cause complications. It provides as follows: "A term under which property pledged as security for an obligation is forfeited if the obligation is not discharged shall be void."

This so-called *lex commissoria* prohibition does not mean that a forfeiture term is never possible. In legal literature, Section 37 is often understood as meaning that a secured creditor is only entitled to receive the amount of their secured claim out of the value of the encumbered asset, whereas any surplus belongs to the owner of the asset. Accordingly, vesting ownership in a secured creditor by a forfeiture term is considered possible if that vesting is made conditional on the value surplus, if any, being returned to the owner.[37] It has even been suggested that Section 37 may not

---

[34] Havansi 1992, 383. He also notes that limits to the parties' freedom of agreement may result from Section 36 of the Contracts Act (228/1929). Subsection (1) provides as follows: "If a contract term is unfair or its application would lead to an unfair result, the term may be adjusted or set aside. In determining what is unfair, regard shall be had to the entire contents of the contract, the positions of the parties, the circumstances prevailing at and after the conclusion of the contract, and to other factors."

[35] Vessel Mortgage Act, Sections 38 and 39; Vehicle Mortgage Act, Section 11.

[36] Cf. Wassgren 2004, 566. He states that allowing a chargee to grant a lease over a mortgaged aircraft in a default situation is "currently unknown under Finnish law". However, he probably does not mean that this cannot be agreed on by the parties in a non-insolvency context.

[37] Tepora, Kaisto and Hakkola 2009, 305–306.

apply to situations in which forfeiture has been agreed on at some point after the security arrangement is initiated and credit extended. In such situations, *in casu*, so the argument goes, the creditor's bargaining power may have weakened to the extent that the security-provider debtor no longer needs the special protection that Section 37 is meant to provide.[38] Furthermore, because Section 37 only concerns conditional forfeitures, it does not prevent the debtor from transferring ownership to the creditor, say, in exchange so that the creditor releases the debtor from the payment obligation.[39]

12.10   Effect of Commencement of Insolvency Proceedings

The types of insolvency proceedings to be dealt with in this section and the next are (1) enforcement (debt recovery proceedings), (2) bankruptcy (collective liquidation proceedings), (3) restructuring of an enterprise, and (4) adjustment of the debts of a private individual. Security rights over a means of transport discussed in these sections are presumed to be "fully developed" as regards protection against the security-provider debtor's other creditors. Accordingly, in the context of the mortgage system for means of transport, it is presumed that in addition to registration of a mortgage and charging the mortgaged means of transport in favour of a creditor, possession of a bearer bond with mortgage entry has been transferred to that creditor.

Even if subject to a charge, a mortgaged means of transport can be subject to distraint as a part of enforcement proceedings initiated by another creditor. The distrained means of transport is realised in accordance with Chapter 5 of the Enforcement Code (705/2007), and the charge entitles the chargee to payment with a high ranking among the other claims involved. Enforcement Code provisions concerning real estate auctions largely apply to vessel and aircraft auctions, too (Chapter 4 Section 3, Chapter 5 Section 72).[40]

When bankruptcy proceedings begin, claims that have not yet fallen due are generally considered due between creditor and debtor (Bankruptcy Act (120/2004), Chapter 3 Section 9(1)). A creditor holding a charge or a right of pledge has a "separatist position" in relation to the bankruptcy estate (Bankruptcy Act, Chapter 17 Section 11). In the case of a charge over a mortgaged means of transport, this entails that a secured creditor can seek distraint against the means of transport after notifying the bankruptcy estate of the secured claim, as required by the Bankruptcy Act. Thus, the means of transport can be realised in accordance with Chapter 5 of the Enforcement Code. However, under Chapter 17 Section 12(1) of the Bankruptcy Act, the bankruptcy estate can prevent sale of an encumbered asset for two months (once) to scrutinise the secured creditor's (chargee's or pledgee's) rights or to

---

[38] Tepora 2008, 23–24. He presents this argument in discussion of security transfer of ownership (sale and lease-back with a security purpose).

[39] Tepora, Kaisto and Hakkola 2009, 306.

[40] See Linna and Leppänen 2007, 506, 611–618.

safeguard the interests of the estate. In certain situations specified in Chapter 17, the bankruptcy estate can sell assets that belong to the estate but are subject to a charge or right of pledge. Such sale requires either consent of the secured creditor or permission granted by the court. Court permission is possible (once) if a purchase offer has been made to the estate, the offer exceeds the likely auction price, and the secured creditor does not establish the probability of a better result of sale were the asset to be sold by other means. The bankruptcy estate can also resort to realisation under the Enforcement Code. This is possible at any time with the secured creditor's consent. Without such consent, it is possible as a final means of realisation if three years have passed since commencement of the proceedings.[41]

Commencement of restructuring of an enterprise or adjustment of the debts of a private individual, which are rehabilitation proceedings, cause a stay on realisation efforts. Realisation belongs to the scope of "interdiction of debt collection". This interdiction and the grounds on which the court can grant exceptions to it are found in Chapter 4 of the Restructuring of Enterprise Act (47/1993) and Chapter 4 of the Act on the Adjustment of the Debts of a Private Individual (57/1993).

12.11   Effectiveness Under Insolvency Proceedings

In short, a charge over a mortgaged means of transport remains effective in all insolvency proceedings discussed in the previous section. In enforcement and bankruptcy proceedings, this effectiveness means that a charge entitles a secured creditor to payment out of the realisation proceeds with a high priority position.[42] Under Section 1(2) of the Act on the Ranking of Claims (1578/1992), which applies in both types of proceedings, a claim secured by a charge over a mortgaged means of transport, or a higher ranking claim, will be satisfied out of the value of the means of transport ahead of other claims, as separately enacted. That is, these secured claims rank above other claims mentioned in the Act on the Ranking of Claims, including child maintenance claims, claims secured by enterprise mortgage, and unsecured claims. As noted in Sect. 12.5, certain claims referred to in the mortgage acts, and elsewhere in legislation, take priority over claims secured by a charge over a mortgaged means of transport. Other higher ranking claims include enforcement costs and the like (Enforcement Code, Chapter 5 Section 33; Bankruptcy Act, Chapter 17 Section 7).

In restructuring of an enterprise or adjustment of the debts of a private individual, claims secured by a charge over a mortgaged means of transport may count as a "secured debt", which has a special position. In these types of proceedings, the court is generally allowed to alter the content of debt relations. This is done in an instrument called a "payment plan". Generally, the payment schedule can be altered,

---

[41] Tepora, Kaisto and Hakkola 2009, 254–260.

[42] See also the remarks in Sect. 12.10 on a charge or pledge holder's "separatist position" in relation to the bankruptcy estate.

it can be decided that payments primarily amortise the principal amount and only after that credit costs, costs concerning the rest of the credit period can be lowered, and the outstanding principal amount can be lowered. By contrast, the special position of a secured debt means, in slightly simplified form, that the principal amount of that debt cannot be lowered (Restructuring of Enterprise Act, Section 45; Act on the Adjustment of the Debts of a Private Individual, Section 26).[43]

Section 3(1) of the Restructuring of Enterprise Act and Section 3(1) of the Act on the Adjustment of the Debts of a Private Individual define a secured debt as follows: a debt where the creditor holds a proprietary security right, which is effective against third parties, over property that belongs to or is in the possession of the debtor, insofar as the value of the security (the encumbered asset) at the commencement of the proceedings would have sufficed to cover the amount of the creditor's claim after deduction of liquidation costs and claims with a higher priority.

12.12   Economic Analysis in Designing the Law on Security Rights

The more general observations in this and the next section on the role of economic analysis and overall attitude on security rights may offer useful background information for understanding policy choices behind the Finnish law on security over means of transport. Additionally, they may help to assess its readiness for reform.

In *travaux préparatoires* for legislation on security rights, it is customary to discuss the anticipated economic effects in general terms. This discussion is, of course, based on general (however crude) economic analysis and assumptions of the functions of security rights. Availability of effective security rights, with a broad scope of assets eligible to be encumbered, is frequently noted to improve enterprises' financing possibilities. For example, Government Proposal 190/1983 for legislation on the enterprise mortgage states as follows:[44]

> Financing is a central factor in creating prerequisites for business activities. [...] Organising the debt financing needed is often hampered by the entrepreneur's lack of assets eligible as security for credit. [...] The proposal aims at improving enterprises' possibilities to use their own movable property as security for credit. This would diminish the need to resort to security rights provided by third parties. [...] The purpose of developing a mortgage system for movable property is to improve the conditions for conducting business in general, and particularly to facilitate financing arrangements of small and medium-sized enterprises.[45]

Another example is Government Proposal 133/2003 for the Act on Financial Collateral Arrangements, implementing the European Parliament and Council Directive 2002/47/EC on financial collateral arrangements:

---

[43] See Tepora, Kaisto and Hakkola 2009, 262–268.

[44] All translations in this section are free and selective.

[45] HE 190/1983, *Hallituksen esitys Eduskunnalle yrityskiinnityslainsäädännöksi* [Government Proposal 190/1983], 1–2.

Unification of legislation promotes functioning of the financial market within the European Union, and improves the stability of the financial system. This also contributes to enterprises' chances to acquire financing from other Member States on more beneficial terms. [...] Regulation concerning security rights significantly affects the availability of credit and its price. [...] New types of security rights may make the functioning of the financial market more efficient, and increase the amount and liquidity of securities eligible as security for credit.[46]

To the author's knowledge, no studies aiming to predict concrete (monetary or otherwise measurable) effects on the availability and price of credit have been presented or cited in *travaux préparatoires*. The Government Proposal for the Act on Financial Collateral Arrangements even states as follows:

At this point it is impossible to make monetary assessment of the proposal's effects on different parties' direct costs, the volume of credit extension, or enterprises' financing costs. Taxation essentially directs market practices. Also for this reason, it cannot be credibly assessed to what extent new types of security rights will become utilised. The price of credit is affected by so many other factors that the direct value of individual security clauses cannot be calculated.[47]

Expected distributional effects of security rights on insolvency have been analysed in *travaux préparatoires*. A notable example of this is Government Proposal 181/1992 for legislation on reform of the priorities system.[48]

Use of actual empirical analysis appears to be relatively uncommon and limited as to its purposes. One example, however, is the Committee Report 1981:56, by the Committee on Enterprise Mortgage. On the basis of various public and private statistics, the Committee studied use of the then existing mortgage types for movable property and their significance in financing practice, also separating different business sectors. Informed by the empirical evidence gathered, the Committee ended up proposing broadening the possibilities to use movable property as security for credit.[49]

12.13   Overall Attitude Towards Security Rights

The attitude of Finnish law towards security rights is in accordance with the growing international consensus that "secured credit is a general social and economic good".[50] Security rights are generally thought to increase the availability of credit and lower its cost, thus stimulating economic activity to the benefit of society at

---

[46] HE 133/2003, *Hallituksen esitys Eduskunnalle rahoitusvakuuslaiksi ja eräiksi siihen liittyviksi laeiksi* [Government Proposal 133/2003], 15, 23–24.

[47] Ibid., 24.

[48] HE 181/1992, *Hallituksen esitys Eduskunnalle etuoikeusjärjestelmän uudistamista koskevaksi lainsäädännöksi* [Government Proposal 181/1992].

[49] KM 1981:56, *Yrityskiinnitystoimikunnan mietintö* [Committee Report 1981:56], 33–59. This led to Government Proposal 190/1983, and finally to the Enterprise Mortgage Act (634/1984).

[50] On various manifestations of this consensus, see McCormack 2004, 15–22.

large. In *travaux préparatoires*, one regularly finds passages that emphasise the importance of security rights for enabling enterprise financing, especially small and medium-sized businesses.[51] The same holds true for legal literature.[52]

Yet, Finnish law does not always strive to offer "security rights of maximal strength", but rather to strike a balance between the interests of different types of creditor on insolvency.[53] Probably the best example here is the treatment of enterprise mortgages ("floating" security rights) in bankruptcy proceedings. According to Section 5 of the Act on the Ranking of Claims (1578/1992), claims secured by an enterprise mortgage are entitled to payment with priority over other claims, but in bankruptcy proceedings only with respect to 50 % of the value of the (enterprise) mortgaged property. Moreover, even then certain other claims rank higher, such as those secured by a charge, a right of pledge, or a right of retention. The 50 % rule was introduced in 1993, as part of a general reform of priority rules. The explicit aim of this rule was to promote equality between creditors, and to reserve assets to be distributed among unsecured creditors. In the same reform, certain statutory privileges, such as those for tax and wage claims, were abolished, and the role of the 50 % rule was to maintain the priority accorded to enterprise mortgages, the same as it was when statutory privileges existed.[54]

Another example concerns mortgages on land-based means of transport, and the fact that ordinary automobiles (cars) and vans are not mortgageable under the Vehicle Mortgage Act. Leaving these vehicles outside the scope of the act was mainly motivated by the desire to keep the workload of the register authority manageable,[55] at a time when information technology was not yet widely used. However, distributional concerns have also been raised in later legal literature. It has been suggested that to include automobiles in the scope of the act (or basically enabling any non-possessory security right over individual automobiles) could considerably weaken the position of unsecured creditors. At present, for example in

---

[51] See Government Proposal 133/2003 (for the Act on Financial Collateral), 15; Government Proposal 190/1983 (for legislation on enterprise mortgages), 1–2; Committee Report 1992:44 (on reform of the mortgage system for means of transport), 6.

[52] See Tepora, Kaisto and Hakkola 2009, 19–24; Tepora 2008, 104–106; Havansi 1992, 1–5.

[53] The question of justification for priority of secured over unsecured claims on insolvency has not sparked heated debate in Finnish legal literature, although the issues involved have been recognised. See Eva Tammi-Salminen, 2001, *Sopimus, kompetenssi ja kolmas* (Helsinki: Suomalainen Lakimiesyhdistys), 133–151; Teemu Juutilainen, 2007, Security rights and the lack of a priority debate: How to proceed with choice of law and harmonization?, in *Private law and the many cultures of Europe*, ed. Thomas Wilhelmsson, Elina Paunio, and Annika Pohjolainen (Alphen aan den Rijn: Kluwer Law International), 343–363.

[54] Government Proposal 181/1992, 12–19. See Clas Bergström, Theodore Eisenberg, and Stefan Sundgren, 2004, On the Design of Efficient Priority Rules for Secured Creditors: Empirical Evidence from A Change of Law, *European Journal of Law and Economics* 18: 273–297.

[55] HE 165/1976, *Hallituksen esitys Eduskunnalle laeiksi autokiinnityslain 1 ja 22 §:n sekä irtaimistokiinnityksestä annetun lain 3 §:n muuttamisesta* [Government Proposal 165/1976], 1–2.

enforcement (debt recovery proceedings), an automobile may form a significant part of the property that can be distrained against.[56]

12.14 Prospects for Reform

The Finnish mortgage system for means of transport is generally considered outdated and overly complex. In particular, dissatisfaction centres on the old-fashioned "system of two promissory notes". This practice begs the question why a mortgage should be registered with respect to a promissory note, be it a bearer bond or of another type, in the first place. Indeed, registration with respect to promissory notes was abandoned in the mortgage system for real estate, which was thoroughly reformed alongside other real estate legislation in 1995.[57] The flexibility added by the system of two promissory notes seems to have come at the cost of increased complexity.[58] Creation of security rights and achieving effectiveness against third parties could be simplified by rethinking the register system. One aim should be to abandon the requirement of "perfection" by document possession. Clear-cut rules would be needed to resolve priority issues arising from conflicting dispositions by the owner of the means of transport (see Sect. 12.5).

All in all, the legislation on the mortgage system for means of transport is deemed fragmentary and deficient.[59] The current mortgage acts, and other relevant legislation, make up an unnecessarily complicated whole. This is not only a problem with organisation of rules, impeding access to information on the law, but also makes one doubt the consistency of policy choices with respect to the content of the law. Examples include the asset scope of the mortgage acts. At least in the case of vehicle mortgage, this has been affected by considerations hardly relevant in today's perspective, namely, the register authority's workload at a time when information technology was uncommon.

An often-deplored detail of the mortgage system for means of transport is that priority is fixed according to the day of registration of mortgage, rather than the day when the register authority received the application for mortgage registration.[60] Examples of other, probably more serious shortcomings include the fact that rights in valuable parts of aircraft, such as engines, cannot be separately registered.[61] This is known to be problematic for the industry practice of pooling aircraft engines and

---

[56] Tepora, Kaisto and Hakkola 2009, 48, 415–416.

[57] See Real Estate Code, Part IV on Real Estate Liens. Instead of bearer bonds or other promissory notes with mortgage entry, standardised "mortgage instruments" are used.

[58] Symptomatic of this is that the system had to be described in Sect. 12.2 with the help of simplifying assumptions.

[59] Committee Report 1992:44, 10–11.

[60] Tepora, Kaisto and Hakkola 2009, 138; Havansi 1992, 279.

[61] Tepora, Kaisto and Hakkola 2009, 138.

spare parts.[62] A related matter is that the question of what belongs to a means of transport as component or accessory, and is thus within the scope of a mortgage, would need a legislative solution in the interest of legal certainty.[63]

Various reform needs have long been recognised. The latest reform proposal is the Committee Report 1992:44 (from 1992, that is). The Committee, commissioned by the Finnish Ministry of Justice, proposed a new system, unifying the rules on mortgages and charges with respect to different types of means of transport, and concentrating them in a single act. Both substantive and procedural norms were to be clarified. Instead of a bearer bond or other type of promissory note with mortgage entry, a standardised document called a "mortgage instrument" was to be used.[64] The proposed act includes provisions on, among other things, mortgage registration procedure, State liability for damages caused by mistakes in the register, and the content of a security right (still a charge) over a means of transport.

The Committee Report 1992:44 has not resulted in legislation. However, the Ministry of Justice lists "unification of mortgage systems for means of transport" as a pending legislative project.[65] The Ministry refers to the Committee Report 1992:44 as "background information", but notes that the schedule for continued preparation has not yet been decided. Interestingly, the Ministry links continued preparation to international developments: "In this matter, solutions in implementation of the Convention on International Interests in Mobile Equipment should be followed." It is difficult to say whether this means that Finland, according to the Ministry, should "do as others do", "keep an eye on what others do", or simply decide its position on the Convention before continued preparation.[66] Be that as it may, decisions taken by other European Union Member States can especially be expected to affect Finnish choices.

A more recent item on the Ministry's list of pending legislative projects is the "Convention on International Interests in Mobile Equipment". At this point, the aim of the project is to "examine the need to sign and ratify" the Convention and the Protocols on Aircraft and Railway Rolling Stock.[67] Should Finland decide to sign and ratify the Convention and the Protocols, the required reform will go much further than the ideas of the above Committee Report, and beyond the mere mortgage system.[68]

---

[62] Wassgren 2004, 563.

[63] Jarno Tepora, 2013, *Rahoitusmuodot ja vakuudet* (Helsinki: Lakimiesliiton Kustannus), 225–232.

[64] "Mortgage instrument" is the translation for the Finnish term *panttikirja* and the Swedish term *pantbrev* in the unofficial translation of the Real Estate Code available in the Finlex Data Bank. A more literal translation would be "charge deed" or "charge document".

[65] http://oikeusministerio.fi/fi/index/valmisteilla/lakihankkeet/esine-jaymparistooikeus.html. *Kuljetusvälineitä koskevien kiinnitysjärjestelmien yhtenäistäminen*. Webpage accessed 6 Oct 2016.

[66] The Finnish verb *seurata*, "to follow" is ambiguous in this sense.

[67] http://oikeusministerio.fi/fi/index/valmisteilla/lakihankkeet/esine-jaymparistooikeus.html. *Liikuteltaviin laitteisiin kohdistuvat kansainväliset oikeudet*. Webpage accessed 6 Oct 2016.

[68] See Wassgren 2004, 565–571.

References

1. Bergström, Clas, Theodore Eisenberg, and Stefan Sundgren. 2004. On the design of efficient priority rules for secured creditors: Empirical evidence from a change of law. *European Journal of Law and Economics* 18: 273–297.
2. Drobnig, Ulrich. 2011. Security rights in movables. In *Towards a European civil code*, 4th ed, ed. Arthur Hartkamp et al., 1025–1042. The Hague: Kluwer Law International.
3. van Erp, Sjef. 2004. The Cape Town Convention: A model for a European system of security interests registration? *European Review of Private Law* 12: 91–110.
4. Finnish Ministry of Justice. Pending legislative projects in property law and environmental law. http://oikeusministerio.fi/fi/index/valmisteilla/lakihankkeet/esine-jaymparistooikeus. html. Accessed 6 Oct 2016.
5. Finnish Transport Safety Agency (Trafi). http://www.trafi.fi. Accessed 6 Oct 2016.
6. Havansi, Erkki. 1992. *Esinevakuusoikeudet*, 2nd ed. Helsinki: Lakimiesliiton Kustannus.
7. HE 133/2003. *Hallituksen esitys Eduskunnalle rahoitusvakuuslaiksi ja eräiksi siihen liittyviksi laeiksi* [Government Proposal 133/2003].
8. HE 26/2003. *Hallituksen esitys Eduskunnalle konkurssilainsäädännön uudistamiseksi* [Government Proposal 26/2003].
9. HE 181/1992. *Hallituksen esitys Eduskunnalle etuoikeusjärjestelmän uudistamista koskevaksi lainsäädännöksi* [Government Proposal 181/1992].
10. HE 1/1988. *Hallituksen esitys Eduskunnalle laiksi kauppakaaren 10 luvun muuttamisesta, laiksi elinkeinonharjoittajan oikeudesta myydä noutamatta jätetty esine ja laiksi merilain 215 §:n muuttamisesta* [Government Proposal 1/1988].
11. HE 190/1983. *Hallituksen esitys Eduskunnalle yrityskiinnityslainsäädännöksi* [Government Proposal 190/1983].
12. HE 165/1976. *Hallituksen esitys Eduskunnalle laeiksi autokiinnityslain 1 ja 22 §:n sekä irtaimistokiinnityksestä annetun lain 3 §:n muuttamisesta* [Government Proposal 165/1976].
13. Hoffrén, Mia. 2008. *Tieto ja sivullissuoja*. Helsinki: Suomalainen Lakimiesyhdistys.
14. Håstad, Torgny. 2001. Nordiska önskemål vid en integration av säkerhetsrätten. In *Civilrättens integration ur nordisk synvinkel*, ed. Salla Tuominen, 49–73. Helsingfors: Juridiska fakulteten vid Helsingfors universitet.
15. Juutilainen, Teemu. 2007. Security rights and the lack of a priority debate: How to proceed with choice of law and harmonization? In *Private law and the many cultures of Europe*, ed. Thomas Wilhelmsson, Elina Paunio, and Annika Pohjolainen, 343–363. Alphen aan den Rijn: Kluwer Law International.
16. Kieninger, Eva-Maria (ed.). 2004. *Security rights in movable property in European private law*. Cambridge: Cambridge University Press.
17. KM 1992:44. *Kuljetusvälineiden velkakiinnitystoimikunnan mietintö* [Committee Report 1992:44].
18. KM 1981:56. *Yrityskiinnitystoimikunnan mietintö* [Committee Report 1981:56].
19. Linna, Tuula, and Tatu Leppänen. 2007. *Ulosmittaus ja myynti*. Helsinki: Talentum.
20. McCormack, Gerard. 2004. *Secured credit under English and American law*. Cambridge: Cambridge University Press.
21. Saarnilehto, Ari, et al. 2012. *Varallisuusoikeus*, 2nd ed. Helsinki: Sanoma Pro.
22. Tammi-Salminen, Eva. 2001. *Sopimus, kompetenssi ja kolmas*. Helsinki: Suomalainen Lakimiesyhdistys.
23. Tepora, Jarno. 2013. *Rahoitusmuodot ja vakuudet*. Helsinki: Lakimiesliiton Kustannus.
24. Tepora, Jarno. 2008. *Johdatus esineoikeuden perusteisiin*. Helsinki: Helsingin yliopiston oikeustieteellinen tiedekunta.
25. Tepora, Jarno. 1984. *Omistuksenpidätyksestä*. Vammala: Suomalainen Lakimiesyhdistys.
26. Tepora, Jarno, Janne Kaisto, and Esa Hakkola. 2009. *Esinevakuudet*. Helsinki: CC Lakimiesliiton Kustannus.

27. Tuominen, Markku. 2001. *Teollisoikeudet vakuutena*. Helsinki: WSLT.
28. Wassgren, Hans. 2004. Rights of financiers in aircraft: A Finnish perspective on the 2001 Cape Town instruments. *Uniform Law Review* 9: 557–572.

Teemu Juutilainen is a postdoctoral researcher at the University of Helsinki, Faculty of Law, Finland. He is a member of the project "European Bonds: The Moral Economy of Debt", funded by the Academy of Finland and the University of Helsinki. He teaches courses on secured transactions law, property law and private international law, and has published research in these areas.

Chapter 13
La Convention du Cap et sa reconnaissance en droit français

Philippe Delebecque

Abstract The Cape Convention knows a great success with about 60 ratifications from important States or organizations in international business, like Russia, India, United States, Brazil, China and European Union. The main idea governing the instrument is to give the most efficiency to securities or bonds which have an utmost economic importance.

Indeed the Convention provides for the constitution and effects of an international interest in certain categories of mobile equipment and associated rights.

The scope of application of the Convention is defined without any reference to the situation of the material or equipment given in guarantee. The Convention applies if, when at the conclusion of the agreement creating for the international interest, the debtor is located in a contracting State.

The basic framework of the Convention relies on the establishment for registration of an International Registry. A registered interest has priority over any other interest subsequently registered and over an unregistered interest.

The Convention includes also several provisions related to some issues concerning the constitution and the effects of an international interest.

This Convention is not in opposition with French law as recently modernized. Nevertheless, France has not ratified the Convention and ratification by EU remains limited to issues on which EU has jurisdiction. Therefore, difficulties remain because the *lex rei sitae* could prevail on the law of the registered international interest.

This paper after having presented the Convention and its principal provisions, discusses the differences between substantial French law and the law provided by the Convention. Finally, the paper concludes to the consistency between both systems.

P. Delebecque (✉)
Université Paris 1 Panthéon-Sorbonne, Paris, France
e-mail: ph.delebecque@wanadoo.fr

© Springer International Publishing AG 2017
S. Kozuka (ed.), *Implementing the Cape Town Convention and the Domestic Laws on Secured Transactions*, Ius Comparatum - Global Studies in Comparative Law 22, DOI 10.1007/978-3-319-46470-1_13

1. La Convention Unidroit relative aux garanties internationales portant sur des matériels d'équipements mobiles a été adoptée au Cap en 2001. Cette convention, ratifiée par l'Union européenne[1] et liant ainsi, dans les limites de la ratification, ses Etats membres, dont la France,[2] est doublement originale. Elle l'est d'abord par sa conception reposant sur des dispositions générales, de droit commun pourrait-on dire, complétée par des dispositions spéciales selon le type d'équipement en cause, aéronautique, ferroviaire et spatial. Plus concrètement, la Convention ne s'applique que dans la mesure où elle est accompagnée d'un Protocole visant telle catégorie de biens d'équipements mobiles (aéronautiques, ferroviaires et spatiaux). Le protocole aéronautique a été adopté en même temps que la convention elle-même : il est actuellement en vigueur dans 44 pays. Le protocole ferroviaire n'a été signé que par 4 pays et l'UE, mais n'est pas encore en vigueur. Le protocole spatial n'a pas encore été signé par l'UE. Les textes applicables ne concernent donc pour l'instant que les matériels aéronautiques.

La Convention Unidroit est ensuite originale par la matière qu'elle envisage, à savoir les garanties sur les biens d'équipements. Les instruments internationaux sur les garanties ne sont pas très nombreux : on ne peut guère que citer, pour ce qui est de textes liant la France, la Convention de 1926 sur les privilèges et hypothèques maritimes, ainsi que la Convention de 1948 (très proche de la précédente) relative à la reconnaissance internationale des droits sur aéronefs.[3] Les instruments sur les garanties portant sur des biens d'équipement sont encore moins nombreux : on ne connaît, à ce jour, que la Convention du Cap et son protocole sur les biens aéronautiques

2. La Convention du Cap et son protocole aéronautique forment un seul même instrument (art. 6, précisant qu'en cas d'incompatibilité entre les deux textes, le Protocole l'emporte). Ces textes ont été préparés en étroite collaboration avec les milieux professionnels et spécialement avec l'Association internationale du transport international (IATA). Ils sont cependant très largement méconnus et n'ont pas encore reçu d'applications pratiques. Cela s'explique par leur nouveauté, mais aussi par certaines de leurs dispositions dont on peut se demander si elles sont parfaitement conciliables avec le droit commun des sûretés, du moins au regard des exigences du droit civil français.

---

[1] L'UE a considéré que la matière régie par la convention tombait dans sa compétence. C'est donc l'UE et non les Etats membres qui l'ont ratifiée. L'adhésion européenne ne vaut toutefois que pour les aspects de la Convention relevant des compétences de l'UE (cf. règlement Rome I sur la loi applicable aux obligations contractuelles; règlement Bruxelles I sur la compétence des tribunaux; règlement relatif aux procédures d'insolvabilité). Les Etats membres ont conservé leur compétence sur de nombreuses questions, dont sur le droit matériel en matière d'insolvabilité. L'applicabilité de la Convention n'est donc que relative.

[2] La France est donc un Etat partie. Mais la France n'a pas, elle-même ratifié la Convention.

[3] Le Protocole précise (art. XXIII) qu'il l'emporte, en cas de besoin, sur la Convention de 1948. Il l'emporte également sur la Convention de 1933 relative à l'unification de certaines règles relatives à la saisie conservatoire des aéronefs ainsi que sur la Convention d'Unidroit de 1988 sur le crédit-bail international.

C'est ce à quoi il faut essayer de répondre. Aussi, après une présentation générale de la convention, nous pourrons insister sur les difficultés d'articulation entre la Convention du Cap et la législation française sur les sûretés.

13.1 Présentation générale de la Convention du Cap et du Protocole aéronautique

3. L'objectif de la Convention[4] est d'assurer l'efficacité du financement des matériels d'équipements mobiles grâce à un régime juridique international de garanties dûment unifié. En pratique, plusieurs techniques sont utilisées : le crédit-bail (*leasing*); la vente avec réserve de propriété et le prêt assorti d'une sûreté. Ces trois formules sont parfaitement connues en droit français et bien appréciées par les professionnels, étant précisé que le crédit-bail et la réserve de propriété ont la faveur des créanciers en raison de l'exclusivité conférée par le droit de propriété sur le matériel. L'idée est en tout cas de laisser aux parties la possibilité de recourir à ces différents mécanismes tout en les subordonnant à des règles communes tenant à la forme du contrat constitutif de sûreté, à son objet et à la localisation du débiteur. Cette pluralité de techniques permet d'assurer plus facilement la reconnaissance de la garantie dans tous les Etats contractants et offre au créancier un grand choix dans les mesures à prendre en cas de défaillance du débiteur.

Le régime de la sûreté est donc attrayant, mais cette efficacité suppose la réunion de plusieurs exigences préalables.

13.1.1 A. Exigences préalables

4. La première condition préalable tient aux règles de droit international privé : la *lex rei sitae* n'est pas ici adaptée, compte tenu de la mobilité des équipements. On pourrait se perdre dans la détermination de la loi applicable : loi d'origine, loi actuelle … D'où des règles uniformes et lorsque celles-ci ne trouvent pas à s'appliquer expressément, le recours aux « principes généraux » dont la Convention s'inspire ou, à défaut, à la loi applicable (art. 5.2). Ce renvoi aux « principes généraux » de la Convention est particulièrement intéressant, mais dans la mesure où aucune autorité n'est instituée pour les dégager, il est à craindre que leur détermination ne se fasse que sur des bases nationales.

Le Protocole aéronautique a toutefois le mérite de renvoyer à la loi choisie par les parties, puisqu'il est dit (cf. art. VIII) que les parties à un contrat de vente ou à un

---

[4]Le champ d'application est particulièrement ouvert, car la Convention est applicable lorsqu'au moment de la conclusion du contrat qui crée ou prévoit la garantie internationale le débiteur est situé dans un Etat contractant. Le fait que le créancier soit situé dans un Etat non contractant est sans effet sur l'applicabilité de la Convention (cf. art. 3).

contrat constitutif de garantie ou encore à un accord de subordination accessoire, peuvent convenir de la loi qui régira tout ou partie de leurs droits et de leurs obligations aux termes de la Convention. Ce renvoi à la loi d'autonomie est certainement approprié, compte tenu de la qualité de professionnel des parties.

5. La seconde condition préalable concerne les biens susceptibles d'être grevés par une garantie : ces biens sont énumérés par l'article 2.3 du texte principal, ce qui vise tout bien, ainsi que les droits accessoires portant sur ce bien, appartenant à l'une des catégories suivantes : cellules d'aéronefs, moteurs d'avions et hélicoptères. Le Protocole est dans le même sens et précise que par cellules d'aéronef, il faut entendre les cellules d'avion (à l'exception de celles qui sont utilisées par les services de l'armée, de la douane et de la police) qui, lorsqu'elles sont dotées de moteurs d'avion appropriés, sont de modèle certifié par l'autorité aéronautique comme pouvant transporter au moins 8 personnes ou des biens pesant plus de 2750 kg. Le même texte ajoute que les cellules d'aéronef comprennent aussi tous modules et autres accessoires, pièces et équipements qui y sont posés, intégrés ou fixés.

6. Il faut enfin observer que la Convention et son protocole admettent des dérogations dans les relations entre les parties elles-mêmes.[5] La Convention est à cet égard très libérale (v. art. 15). Le protocole l'est beaucoup moins, car ce dernier texte (cf. art. IV.3) n'admet que des dérogations écrites, très précises et portant sur les dispositions suivantes : paragraphes 2 à 4 de l'art. IX; elles peuvent également exclure par écrit les dispositions de l'article X.

13.1.2   B. Régime de la garantie

7. *1°. Constitution.* La garantie est constituée en tant que garantie internationale conformément à la convention si le contrat qui la crée ou la prévoit est conclu par écrit et porte sur un bien sur lequel le constituant, le vendeur conditionnel ou le bailleur a le pouvoir de conclure un tel contrat de garantie, c'est-à-dire a le pouvoir de disposer. La garantie est valablement constituée si ces conditions sont respectées, quelles que soient les dispositions du droit interne applicable. Peu importe que le droit interne connaisse ou non la sûreté constituée. Le contrat doit en outre indiquer clairement la volonté des parties de procéder à l'enregistrement de la garantie. Il doit également identifier le bien formant l'assiette de la garantie et préciser les obligations garanties.

8. *2°. Assiette.* Les biens formant l'objet de la garantie doivent faire l'objet d'une description et plus précisément, s'agissant des biens aéronautiques, comporter le numéro de série assigné par le constructeur, le nom dudit constructeur et la désignation du modèle (art. VII).

---

[5] Le principe de la liberté contractuelle est ainsi reconnu, ce qui est aujourd'hui assez habituel dans les conventions internationales. Il reste que cette liberté ne peut concerner que les parties elles-mêmes, puisqu'on ne peut, par contrat, disposer des droits des tiers.

En cas de perte ou de destruction physique du bien, la sûreté est reportée sur les indemnités d'assurance versées (art. 2.5), ce qui n'est qu'une application de la subrogation réelle bien connue du droit français.

9. *3°. Publicité.* La sûreté doit faire l'objet d'une publicité sur un Registre international doté de la personnalité juridique (Conv. art. 16s.; Protocole, art. XVI s.) et dont la responsabilité peut être engagée en cas de dommages causés par les pertes encourues à la suite d'une inscription ou d'un défaut d'inscription. La publicité est requise à des fins d'opposabilité aux tiers et doit permettre au créancier de prendre rang utile.

Ce système de publicité est l'innovation de la Convention et fait l'objet d'une réglementation très complète portant, notamment sur les consultations susceptibles d'être faites par les tiers. Les modalités d'inscription sont assez simples (Conv. art. 17s. et textes correspondants du Protocole), d'autant que le système est conçu pour être géré de manière électronique. Il suppose l'intervention d'un conservateur, ce qui lui confère la fiabilité requise. S'agissant des biens aéronautiques, l'OACI a été naturellement investie de la fonction d'autorité de surveillance (art. XVI).

10. *4°. Effets de la garantie.* La garantie une fois publiée, prime toute autre garantie inscrite postérieurement et toute garantie non inscrite. C'est là l'un des effets fondamentaux de la garantie : conférer un droit de préférence au créancier, droit qu'il pourra mettre en œuvre pratiquement comme il le souhaite (v. infra). La date d'inscription fait foi. Elle est opposable au syndic de la faillite du débiteur. Mais, la Convention ne porte aucune atteinte à la *lex concursus*, laquelle déterminera si la garantie est frauduleuse et susceptible d'être annulée (art. 30).

11. *5°. Prérogatives du créancier.* La Convention et le Protocole détaillent les mesures accordées au créancier en cas de défaillance du débiteur (art. 8s.; art. IX s.). Ces mesures sont diverses, variées et très favorables au créancier. Elles le sont d'une manière générale et d'une manière plus particulière en envisageant des situations d'urgence et l'hypothèse d'insolvabilité du débiteur.

12. D'une manière générale d'abord. En cas d'inexécution d'une obligation garantie,[6] le créancier peut mettre en œuvre les prérogatives que la Convention lui offre et plus précisément, pour autant que le constituant y ait consenti, ce consentement pouvant être donné à tout moment :

prendre possession du bien formant l'objet de la sûreté ou en prendre le contrôle;
vendre ou donner à bail le bien en cause;
percevoir tout revenu ou bénéfice produit par la gestion ou l'exploitation du bien[7];
Le créancier peut aussi demander au tribunal une décision autorisant ou ordonnant l'un des actes susvisés.
Le vendeur sous réserve de propriété ou le crédit-bailleur peut également mettre fin au contrat et prendre possession du bien formant l'objet du contrat (art. 10).

---

[6] Les parties peuvent définir ce qu'elles entendent par inexécution (art. 11); à défaut, l'inexécution se comprend d'une inexécution substantielle.

[7] Ces trois premières mesures doivent être mises en œuvre d'une manière commercialement raisonnable (art. IX.3).

De plus, à tout moment après l'inexécution d'une obligation garantie, le créancier et toutes les personnes intéressées peuvent convenir que la propriété de tout bien grevé sera transférée au créancier en règlement ou en vue du règlement de tout ou partie des dettes garanties (cf. art. 9). Le pacte commissoire est ainsi dûment admis. Le créancier peut par ailleurs, demander au tribunal compétent d'ordonner l'attribution du bien grevé en pleine propriété.

13. Mesures conservatoires. Le créancier, dans la mesure où il apporte la preuve de l'inexécution par le débiteur de ses obligations, c'est-à-dire s'il justifie en somme d'un principe de créance, peut solliciter du juge compétent des mesures conservatoires tendant à la conservation du bien ou de sa valeur, à la mise en possession du bien ou encore à en assurer le contrôle, la garde ou la gestion. Il peut également solliciter des mesures visant à se faire attribuer des produits ou des revenus du bien ou encore à immobiliser le bien. L'article X du Protocole complète ce dispositif, sans le remettre aucunement en cause.

14. Insolvabilité. La Convention indique (art. 30) qu'une garantie internationale est opposable au syndic de faillite du débiteur dans la mesure où la garantie a été régulièrement inscrite, *i.e.* conformément à la Convention, antérieurement à l'ouverture de la procédure. La disposition est importante : elle est de nature à préserver l'efficacité de la garantie dans les situations les plus compromises. Le Protocole (art. XI) contient des dispositions matérielles qui ne sont toutefois applicables que si l'Etat contractant fait, au moment de sa ratification, une déclaration en leur faveur. Deux variantes sont prévues. La première prévoit en substance que le débiteur doit restituer le bien formant l'objet de la garantie et que le créancier peut, en attendant, prendre toute mesure conservatoire. La seconde variante est plus équilibrée et dispose que le débiteur doit d'abord informer le créancier de l'ouverture de la procédure et de l'alternative qui s'offre à lui : payer ou restituer le bien. A défaut, le tribunal peut autoriser le créancier à prendre possession du bien, étant entendu que le créancier doit justifier sa créance.

En tout cas, même si le créancier a de fortes assurances et conserve ses droits en cas de procédure collective frappant le débiteur, il n'est pas possible d'ignorer ce qui se passe dans le pays où la faillite a été ouverte : une obligation de coopération entre les tribunaux de l'Etat où se trouve le bien et les tribunaux chargés d'administrer la procédure de faillite est instituée (art. XII).

15. 6°. *Cession et subrogation.* Toujours dans le même esprit de faveur pour le créancier, la Convention permet au créancier de transmettre ses droits (art. 31). La forme de la cession, les rapports entre le cédant et le cessionnaire ainsi que la question de la défaillance du cessionnaire donnent lieu à des dispositions assez précises.

16. 7°. *Compétence.* On notera, enfin, que la Convention s'est efforcée de définir des règles de compétence, ce qui est, en l'occurrence, particulièrement original, mais très heureux. En effet, la Convention admet les clauses attributives de compétence (exclusive) (art. 42) et détermine des règles de compétence en matière de mesures conservatoires.

13.2   L'articulation de la Convention du Cap et du Protocole aéronautique avec le droit français des sûretés

17. La garantie internationale instituée par la Convention du Cap et son Protocole aéronautique est construite sur un certain nombre de règles dont on peut se demander si elles s'articulent bien avec les dispositions du droit français des sûretés. C'est évidemment au regard du droit du gage, sûreté mobilière corporelle par excellence, que la question doit être envisagée. Avant la réforme française de 2006, il eût été permis d'hésiter, car le droit des sûretés était encore assez rigide.[8] Depuis la réforme de 2006, la situation est différente, dans la mesure où les dispositions du Code civil sur les sûretés réelles ont été sensiblement assouplies. Plus précisément, le droit du gage a été repensé. Le gage est devenu un contrat solennel – conclu nécessairement – par écrit (C. civ. art. 2336)[9] et ne suppose plus de dépossession, la dépossession étant, avec l'inscription sur un registre (cf. art. 2337, al. 1er), une simple mesure de publicité. Il peut porter sur un bien présent ou futur et garantir une créance présente ou future, si du moins cette créance future est déterminable. Ces conditions correspondent aux exigences de la Convention (cf. art. 7). De plus, les prérogatives du créancier ont été renforcées, puisque le pacte commissoire est considéré comme valable (art. 2348) et que l'attribution judiciaire du bien en pleine propriété est valorisée (art. 2347).

Il faut ajouter que le droit français maîtrise parfaitement la technique de la vente avec réserve de propriété (C. civ. art. 2367 s.) et que le crédit-bail est parfaitement reconnu (C. monétaire et fin. art. 313-7 s.).

Dans ces conditions, les deux régimes sont loin d'être incompatibles, ce qui ne signifie pas qu'il n'y ait aucune difficulté d'articulation entre ces deux régimes. Autrement dit, si, sur le plan des principes, l'articulation ne pose pas de véritable problème, il n'en va pas de même sur le plan des modalités.

13.2.1   A. La garantie internationale sur un bien aéronautique et les principes du droit interne français du gage

18. L'une des règles essentielles de la Convention du Cap est contenue dans l'article 29 où il est dit qu'une garantie internationale sur un bien aéronautique dûment inscrite prime toute autre garantie inscrite postérieurement et toute garantie non inscrite (art. 29). Précisons immédiatement que cette priorité joue quelle que soit la technique sous jacente : contrat constitutif de garantie, vente avec réserve de propriété ou crédit-bail.

---

[8] Réserve étant faite de l'hypothèque mobilière à laquelle ressemble la garantie étudiée.

[9] Il peut aussi être conclu par un mandataire ou même par un agent de sûreté (C. civ. art. 2328-1). L'art. VI du Protocole est dans le même sens. Les dispositions internes et internationales se rejoignent encore sur cette question importante de la représentation.

En cas de vente avec réserve de propriété, la sûreté repose sur la propriété conservée par le vendeur, ce qui le place dans une situation d'exclusivité. Le vendeur peut, en cas de défaillance de l'acheteur, obtenir la restitution du bien afin de recouvrer le droit d'en disposer, la valeur du bien repris étant imputée, à titre de paiement, sur le solde de la créance garantie.

La situation est à peu près la même en cas de crédit-bail.

Lorsqu'en droit interne, un gage est régulièrement constitué, puis publié, il prend rang et est opposable aux tiers. En outre et surtout, rien ne s'oppose à ce que plusieurs gages soient constitués sur le même bien. En ce cas, le rang des créanciers est réglé par l'ordre des inscriptions (art. 2340).

Par conséquent, la règle posée par l'article 29 de la Convention du Cap ne se singularise pas dans l'environnement juridique français. Elle est parfaitement compatible avec les principes retenus en droit interne. Elle ne heurte aucun principe du droit interne.

19. La compatibilité de la Convention du Cap avec les principes du droit interne français des sûretés se vérifie de la même manière lorsque l'on considère les prérogatives reconnues au créancier. Aucun problème ne se pose pour le vendeur avec réserve de propriété ou le crédit-bailleur : il leur appartient de reprendre le bien entre les mains de leur débiteur, étant précisé qu'en matière de crédit-bail, la valeur du bien n'est pas imputée sur la créance, contrairement à ce que l'on admet aujourd'hui en matière de réserve de propriété.[10]

En cas de gage, le créancier peut, en droit interne français, faire vendre le bien et se payer, par préférence, sur le prix dégagé par la vente. Il peut aussi demander que le bien lui soit attribué en pleine propriété ou encore mettre en œuvre le pacte commissoire convenu. Ces mesures rejoignent celles que la Convention du Cap a pris le soin d'organiser (supra, n° 12). Sans doute y-a-t-il quelques détails techniques qui divergent,[11] mais les dispositions du Code civil sur les prérogatives du créancier gagiste ne sont pas fondamentalement différentes de celles prévues par la Convention du Cap.

20. Enfin, en précisant qu'une garantie internationale valablement constituée avant l'ouverture de la procédure collective frappant le débiteur, est opposable à la faillite (art. 30), la Convention du Cap ne pose pas un principe qui heurte de front les règles du droit français de l'insolvabilité. En droit interne français, le créancier titulaire d'une sûreté valablement constituée ne perd pas ses droits dans une procédure collective, même s'il se trouve soumis à la discipline collective qu'implique la procédure. Le vendeur sous réserve de propriété et le crédit-bailleur sont dans une

---

[10] Dans le crédit-bail, contrairement à ce que l'on observe dans la réserve de propriété, la propriété garantit l'opération dans son ensemble et ne garantit pas précisément le ou les créances du crédit-bailleur sur l'utilisateur. La restitution du bien ne s'apparente pas à la réalisation d'une sûreté, en ce sens qu'elle ne fait pas perdre au crédit-bailleur la créance de loyers échus et impayés.

[11] La Convention permet en effet au créancier de prendre la possession ou le contrôle du bien, ce que ne prévoit pas le droit interne français. Quant à la perception des fruits, le droit interne français est plus ouvert que la Convention, l'art. 2345 C. civ. disposant que le créancier perçoit les fruits du bien et les impute sur les intérêts ou, à défaut, sur le capitale de la dette, alors que cette faculté n'est reconnue par la Convention qu'en cas de défaillance du débiteur (art. 8.1, c).

situation encore plus avantageuse, car ils n'ont pas à déclarer leurs créances. Il reste que le créancier gagiste ne peut réaliser son pacte commissoire dès l'instant que la procédure est ouverte (C. com. art. L. 622-7). Au demeurant, le Protocole renforce ici les droits des créanciers (art. XI), mais il faut rappeler que les dispositions prévues ne jouent qu'en cas *d'opting-in* de l'Etat contractant.[12] C'est déjà aborder notre dernier point.

13.2.2   *B. La garantie internationale sur un bien aéronautique et les modalités du droit interne français du gage*

21. Le système français de publicité des sûretés réelles est assez clair et ne soulève pas de difficulté particulière. En matière de gage, c'est aujourd'hui le décret du 23 décembre 2006 qui règle les différentes questions qui peuvent se poser : formalités d'inscription, formalités modificatives, effets de l'inscription, radiation, tenue du fichier, obligations des greffiers, recours.[13] En matière de crédit-bail, la publicité est organisée par les articles R. 313-4 à R 313-14 du code monétaire et financier, cette publicité rendant opposable le droit de propriété aux créanciers et ayants cause à titre particulier du crédit-preneur; le défaut d'accomplissement de la publicité n'empêche pas le crédit-bailleur d'établir son droit de propriété à l'égard des créanciers par tous moyens s'il peut prouver par tous moyens qu'ils avaient eu connaissance de l'existence de ce droit.[14] Quant à la réserve de propriété, aucune publicité n'est en principe prévue; du moins n'est-elle pas obligatoire.

Le système international est de son côté unitaire. Peu importe la technique sous jacente : gage, réserve de propriété ou crédit-bail. Il ne dépend pas du type de garantie en cause. En outre, la publicité est réelle et non personnelle, en ce sens que les textes fixent les critères d'identification du bien faisant l'objet de la sûreté, sans se préoccuper de l'identification de la personne du créancier et du débiteur (cf. art. 18; le Protocole n'envisage pas ces conditions).

22. Les différences entre les deux systèmes sont donc assez nettes, d'autant que les modalités techniques reposent sur des mécanismes qui ont chacun leur spécificité. Cela ne signifie pas pour autant qu'il n'y ait pas d'analogies. Ainsi en est-il relativement à la portée de l'inscription, du moins en matière de gage. Dans l'un et l'autre système, la bonne foi des tiers importe peu. Dès l'instant que la sûreté est inscrite, elle prime toute autre garantie (Conv. art. 29.1 et 2; C. civ. art. 2337).

---

[12] A notre connaissance, l'UE n'a pas fait une telle déclaration. L'art. XI du protocole n'est donc pas applicable.

[13] Par ailleurs, les ayants cause à titre particulier du constituant, resté en possession, ne peuvent pas invoquer cette possession pour revendiquer le bénéfice de l'art. 2276 C. civ. Autrement dit, ces tiers (acquéreur, créancier saisissant, deuxième gagiste, …) doivent nécessairement respecter les droits du gagiste dûment inscrit.

[14] Cass. com. 25 mars 1997, Bull. civ. IV, n° 81. A l'égard d'un acquéreur, le crédit-bailleur peut prouver sa mauvaise foi, afin d'écarter l'application de l'article 2276 C. civ.

23. Les différences entre les deux systèmes s'accusent si l'on s'arrête sur les dispositions concernant les procédures collectives. La loi interne française est, comme le sait, particulièrement complexe entre les procédures de conciliation, de sauvegarde, de redressement et de liquidation. Il est impossible d'entrer dans tous les détails qui ont tous leur justification. Ce qui est prévu par le Protocole (art. XI) est plus simple et plus direct, mais reste subordonné au bon vouloir de chaque Etat contractant. Ce n'est donc pas demain que les règles seront sur ce terrain des procédures collectives unifiées.

24. En définitive, la garantie internationale prévue et organisée par la Convention du Cap et son Protocole aéronautique ne manque pas d'attraits. La souplesse est l'une de ses premières caractéristiques, puisqu'une large place est faite à la liberté contractuelle. L'efficacité en est une autre, eu égard aux fortes prérogatives reconnues au créancier. Les droits des tiers sont également respectés grâce à un système de publicité moderne et centralisé. Il reste, même si l'on mesure parfaitement les difficultés de mettre au point un instrument international consensuel, que le texte n'a pas encore reçu une véritable adhésion de la communauté internationale et que les conflits de lois demeurent donc.[15] En outre, l'instrument aurait sans doute mérité d'être rédigé plus simplement et autour d'un plan plus cartésien. Quoiqu'il en soit, la balle est maintenant dans le camp de la pratique. On ne doute pas qu'elle saura tirer profit des réels intérêts de la nouvelle convention d'Unidroit.

Philippe Delebecque est le Professeur à l'Université de Paris-I (Panthéon-Sorbonne). Leur principales matières enseignées sont droit civil; droit maritime, droit aérien et des transports; droit du commerce international. Les principales publications incluent :

- *Cours de droit civil* (1. Le contrat – 2. La responsabilité – 3. Régime des obligations), Litec;
- *Droit civil, Les sûretés* (Précis Dalloz), en collaboration avec Ph. Simler;
- *Droit civil, Contrats civils et commerciaux* (précis Dalloz), en collaboration avec F. Collart;
- *Droit maritime*, Précis Dalloz, éd. 2014;
- *Droit du commerce international* (Précis Dalloz, 3ème éd. 2014), en collaboration avec JM Jacquet;
- *Droit commercial, Traité de Ripert et Roblot*, t. 2 (en collaboration avec M. Germain); (nouvelle édition en préparation avec A. Gaudemet).

Professeur Delebecque est le membre de l'Académie de Marine; Président de la Chambre Arbitrale Maritime de Paris; Président d'honneur de la Société Française de Droit Aérien et Spatial; Vice Président de l'Association Française du Droit Maritime; Membre du Comité Maritime International; Administrateur de l'Institut Méditerranéen des Transports Maritimes.

---

[15] Si une garantie est constituée sur des biens se trouvant dans un Etat non contractant, il n'est pas exclu que l'Etat en cause ne reconnaisse pas l'efficacité des droits inscrits sur le registre international ou ne leur accorde un traitement moins favorable que celui résultant de la Convention. Dans ces conditions, le titulaire de la garantie inscrite risque d'être primé par un autre créancier. Le problème tient encore une fois au jeu trop systématique de la *lex rei sitae*. Il reste que le droit français des sûretés est aujourd'hui très ouvert et qu'il y a peu de risque de voir un juge rejeter, au nom de l'ordre public international, une sûreté reconnue dans un Etat encore plus libéral que ne peut l'être la France et ayant ratifié la Convention du Cap.

Chapter 14
Security Interests in Mobile Equipment Under German Law – Some Notes on the Similarities and Differences in Relation to the Cape Town Regime

Benjamin von Bodungen

14.1 Introduction

So far, the Federal Republic of Germany has not ratified any of the instruments provided for under the Cape Town regime. Hence, Germany currently is a non-Party jurisdiction. However, Germany so far is the only state that has signed the Convention and all three related Protocols, i.e., the Aircraft Protocol, the Rail Protocol and the Space Assets Protocol. What is more, the German Government has played a very active role in the development of the Cape Town Convention. This is evidenced, *inter alia*, by the fact that the Diplomatic Conference to adopt the Space Assets Protocol took place in Berlin from 27 February to 9 March 2012.

The following analysis of the legal situation in Germany focuses on three key issues: First, the security interests available under German law with respect to mobile equipment such as aircraft, railway rolling stock and space assets are highlighted (*infra* no. 14.2). In this context, special attention is paid to the registration requirements in Germany. Thereafter, the enforcement of security interests in mobile equipment will be dealt with in greater detail and distinguished from the default remedies pursuant to the Cape Town Convention (*infra* no. 14.3). Finally, this report intends to shed some light on the question of how German law security interests are treated after insolvency procedures have been commenced in relation to the debtor (*infra* no. 14.4).

B. von Bodungen (✉)
Faculty of Law, German Graduate School of Management and Law, Heilbronn, Germany
e-mail: benjamin.vonbodungen@ggs.de

© Springer International Publishing AG 2017
S. Kozuka (ed.), *Implementing the Cape Town Convention and the Domestic Laws on Secured Transactions*, Ius Comparatum - Global Studies in Comparative Law 22, DOI 10.1007/978-3-319-46470-1_14

14.2   Security Interest in Mobile Equipment and Registration Requirements

For the creation of *in rem* collateral, strict requirements apply under German law. First, only certain types of security interests are available under German law (*numerus clausus* of property rights). Next, only specifically identified assets can be subject to a security interest (so-called principle of speciality). Finally, the content of most security interests is not at the parties' discretion but – to a large extent – defined by mandatory law. This is in stark contrast to the emphasis the Cape Town Convention places on party autonomy. On the other hand, no filing or registration requirements exist under German law for the creation or perfection of security interests in mobile equipment (subject to the exceptions for aircraft and ships specified below).

More specifically, German law provides for the creation of a possessory pledge in relation to moveable assets of – almost – any kind for the benefit of the pledgee.[1] Transfer of possession to the pledgee is required for the creation of this security interest. In the absence of a registry where notice of the pledge could be given to third parties, transfer of possession is the legally prescribed method of making the existence of the pledge public and thus satisfying the so-called principle of publicity. This, in turn, brings about that the pledgor is barred from exercising physical control over the collateral for the purpose of generating revenue that could be utilized towards discharge of the obligations secured by the pledge.

Against this background, the security transfer of ownership (*Sicherungsübereignung*) is the security interest that is usually granted in relation to moveable assets as it allows the security provider to retain possession of the collateral.[2] Full ownership of a moveable asset (but not its possession) is hereby transferred to the creditor who assumes the legal position of a fiduciary. The security agreement usually requires the debtor to turn over the collateral to the secured creditor for the purpose of its sale (only) in the event of a debtor default. Because the debtor retains possession of the collateral prior to the occurrence of a default, the security by outright transfer of ownership is not apparent to third parties. By way of an example, third parties will not be able to tell without further enquiry whether or not the operator of railway rolling stock has transferred ownership of such railway rolling stock to a financier for security purposes. The financier, in turn, will be under an obligation to re-transfer the ownership to the debtor once the secured debt has been satisfied.

In the case of aircraft (and also ships) registered in Germany, the legal situation is different. The adequate security interest in relation to these assets is a registered mortgage. Special rules, filing and registration requirements, which are similar to those for real estate mortgages, apply. Pursuant to the German Aircraft Mortgage Act (*Gesetz über Rechte an Luftfahrzeugen*), German law mortgages over aircraft

---

[1] Cf. Sections 1204–1259 of the Civil Code (*Bürgerliches Gesetzbuch*).
[2] Cf. Sections 929, 930 of the Civil Code (*Bürgerliches Gesetzbuch*).

must be registered in the Aircraft Mortgage Register (*Register für Pfandrechte an Luftfahrzeugen*) which is maintained by the local court (*Amtsgericht*) in the city of Brunswick.

The registration of a mortgage in the Aircraft Mortgage Register is a constitutive element of the creation of this security interest.[3] It will also accord the mortgage priority.[4] In the absence of knowledge to the contrary, a creditor can rely upon the content of the Aircraft Mortgage Register (provided that no opposition to its accuracy has been registered therein).[5] Aircraft mortgages created pursuant to the German Aircraft Mortgage Act extend to engines not permanently separated from the aircraft if ownership of the engine rests with the owner of the aircraft that is subject to the aircraft mortgage.[6] The creation and registration of separate security interests in aircraft engines is not provided for under German law at present. For this reason, ratification of the Cape Town Convention is expected to significantly ease aircraft financing in Germany.

Retention of title and leasing agreements are generally not treated as secured transactions under German law. What is more, it is not possible to file or register retention of title arrangements or lease agreements with a registry or authority in Germany in order to establish, protect or perfect the rights and interests of the seller or lessor. Hence, ownership of, or interests in, a leased asset that is in the possession of the lessee can be acquired from the lessee by a third party according to the principles of good faith acquisition. In order to reduce the risk of such good faith acquisition, lessors typically request the installation of a nameplate or other evidence of their ownership on the asset. Registration of the lessor position in the International Registry under the Cape Town Convention will require a paradigm change under German law and greatly improve the legal protection of lessors and conditional sellers.

14.3 Enforcement of Security Interests in Mobile Equipment

Enforcement of German law security interests depends upon the type of security granted under the security documents. A multitude of mandatory statutory provisions must be observed with respect to certain types of security while in other cases the enforcement is chiefly governed by the contractual arrangements between the parties.

As a general rule (and with a very limited number of exceptions only), no self-help remedies are available in Germany to expedite repossession if the defaulting debtor does not voluntarily deliver the asset to its creditor. Enforcement of a repossession claim therefore usually requires the assistance of official bodies (i.e., courts, bailiffs).

---

[3] Cf. Section 5 (1) of the Aircraft Mortgage Act (*Gesetz über Rechte an Luftfahrzeugen*).

[4] Cf. Section 25 (1) of the Aircraft Mortgage Act (*Gesetz über Rechte an Luftfahrzeugen*).

[5] Cf. Section 16 (1) of the Aircraft Mortgage Act (*Gesetz über Rechte an Luftfahrzeugen*).

[6] Cf. Section 31 of the Aircraft Mortgage Act (*Gesetz über Rechte an Luftfahrzeugen*).

In order to enforce an aircraft mortgage, the mortgagee must act in accordance with the provisions of German procedural law. Once the creditor has initiated the enforcement process, the competent court (i.e., the local court in Brunswick) will take all necessary steps to secure the aircraft and proceed with a public sale of the aircraft by way of an auction pursuant to the Act Governing Auctions and Sequestrations (*Gesetz über die Zwangsversteigerung und die Zwangsverwaltung*) which mainly deals with immoveables.[7] In principle, this is the only permissible way of realizing an aircraft mortgage in Germany. A private sale of the aircraft by the mortgagee is ruled out by law unless specifically agreed between the mortgagor and the mortgagee *after* the mortgage has become enforceable.[8] Similarly, prior to the mortgage becoming enforceable the parties cannot validly agree that ownership of the aircraft shall vest in the mortgagee, which is fully in line with Article 9 (1) of the Convention.

In contrast, the sale of collateral that is subject to a security transfer of ownership is far more flexible and can be sketched out in detail by the parties in their security agreement. For instance, financiers of railway rolling stock usually insist on being granted the right to sell the rolling stock by private sale or private auction on behalf of the debtor if the latter defaults under the financing agreements. The proceeds from such sale will be used towards the satisfaction of the secured debt. In addition, the parties may stipulate in their security agreement that the creditor's default remedies include the right to grant a lease over the collateral and collect the lease rentals in satisfaction of the secured debt. However, rolling stock of railways providing public transportation which is subject to a security transfer of ownership cannot be sold for the purposes of debt recovery without the consent of the relevant governmental supervisory authority.

In the context of leasing agreements, the lessor has the right to demand delivery of the lease object from the lessee if and when the lease has terminated. To the extent the lease is governed by German law, the lessor has a statutory right to termination of the lease without a notice period for compelling reasons (including payment defaults of a certain magnitude).[9] It is important to note that as long as the lease agreement is in place, the leased asset remains subject to the lessor's covenant of quiet enjoyment vis-à-vis the lessee. Consequently, any attempt by the lessor to recover the possession of the lease object would be unlawful prior to termination of the lease agreement.

Depending on the factual situation and the asset category, additional laws and procedures may become relevant. For instance, preliminary measures (*einstweilige Verfügungen*) which a secured creditor, lessor or conditional seller initiates with a view to grounding an aircraft are subject to restrictions under German law if the aircraft is used for postal services or public transportation on scheduled routes, or if the aircraft is about to take off for the commercial transportation of people or goods.

---

[7] Cf. Section 47 (1) of the Aircraft Mortgage Act (*Gesetz über Rechte an Luftfahrzeugen*).

[8] Cf. Section 49 of the Aircraft Mortgage Act (*Gesetz über Rechte an Luftfahrzeugen*).

[9] Cf. Section 543 of the Civil Code (*Bürgerliches Gesetzbuch*).

14.4   Security Interests in Insolvency Proceedings

It is important to note at the outset that all rights of enforcement and repossession, as set out above, may be suspended or precluded under German insolvency laws.

In the context of secured financings, creditors holding a security interest in a moveable asset forming part of the debtor's insolvency estate will in most cases not be able to obtain possession of the asset. Instead, they will have to rely on the insolvency administrator's sale of the asset and the preferential disbursement of the proceeds therefrom (*Absonderungsrecht*).[10] This also applies in case of a security transfer of ownership although – as outlined above – this is a full transfer *in rem*. Against this background it is evident that, at present, German insolvency law deviates from the remedies on insolvency pursuant to the Aircraft, Rail and Space Assets Protocols which rest upon the idea that secured creditors ultimately are given possession of the collateral.

As a general rule, the insolvency administrator will take possession of the debtor's assets and proceed to liquidate them for the benefit of all of the debtor's creditors. Although a secured creditor enjoys a priority claim over unsecured creditors in relation to the proceeds from those assets in which it was granted a security interest, this claim will be subordinated to the insolvency administrator's costs for ascertainment and utilization of the assets.[11] The costs for ascertainment of an asset are set by statute at 4 % of the utilization proceeds therefrom while the costs for the utilization of an asset will usually amount to 5 % of the utilization proceeds.[12] If the utilization entails the insolvency estate incurring VAT (currently at 19 %), this amount will also be added and in total 28 % of the utilization proceeds will be deducted prior to the remainder of the proceeds being disbursed to the secured creditor. Creditors holding mortgages in aircraft (which in many respects are treated as real estate for legal purposes in Germany) will be entitled to preferential disbursement (*Absonderungsrecht*) under the above-mentioned Act Governing Auctions and Sequestrations (*Gesetz über die Zwangsversteigerung und die Zwangsverwaltung*).

As far as leasing agreements are concerned, the insolvency administrator in most cases can choose whether or not to continue a lease.[13] The lessor may demand from the insolvency administrator to make a decision without undue delay as regards the continuation of the lease. In the past, courts have granted a consideration period of up to 3 months to the insolvency administrator. If the insolvency administrator decides to continue the lease, all of the insolvent lessee's obligations under the lease stay in full force and effect and – going forward – have to be borne by the insolvency estate with priority. In contrast, if the insolvency administrator decides not to continue the lease, the lessor is entitled to claim the separation (*Aussonderung*) and

---

[10] Cf. Sections 50, 51 of the Insolvency Code (*Insolvenzordnung*).

[11] Cf. Section 170 (1) of the Insolvency Code (*Insolvenzordnung*).

[12] Cf. Section 171 of the Insolvency Code (*Insolvenzordnung*).

[13] Cf. Section 103 of the Insolvency Code (*Insolvenzordnung*).

return of the lease object from the lessee's insolvency estate.[14] What is more, if the insolvency administrator does not live up to this obligation, the lessor could initiate proceedings against the insolvency administrator for the delivery of the possession of the lease object.

Finally, lease agreements concerning aircraft (which – as mentioned above – German law in many respects regards as real estate) remain in place in case of the lessee's insolvency but can be terminated by the insolvency administrator.[15] In case of such termination, the lessor will be entitled to request the return of the aircraft from the lessee's insolvency estate.

Benjamin von Bodungen (LLM Auckland 2002, PhD Manheim 2008) is Professor of Law at the German Graduate School of Management and Law in Heilbronn where he teaches German and international commercial and corporate law, finance and tax law. He also is an Of Counsel in the Banking & Finance practice group of Bird & Bird LLP, based in Frankfurt. Prior to joining the German Graduate School of Management and Law, he worked in the Frankfurt office of Freshfields Bruckhaus Deringer LLP, where he specialised in asset and structured finance.

---

[14] Cf. Section 47 of the Insolvency Code (*Insolvenzordnung*).

[15] Cf. Sections 108, 109 of the Insolvency Code (*Insolvenzordnung*).

Chapter 15
The Greek Law on Security Interests Burdening Transport Vehicles as Compared with the Cape Town Convention

Elina N. Moustaira

The initial idea, when the text of the Cape Town Convention was being prepared, was to create a uniform security interest, following the model of the "security interest" of the article 9 of the USA's Uniform Commercial Code, assimilating practically the conditional sale agreements and the leasing agreements with the security agreements.[1] This "functional" approach was partly abandoned afterwards, because it was thought that it might find hindrance in the non-common law States.[2]

Nevertheless, the "basic framework" of the Cape Town Convention is "that which applies to secured transactions in the UCC and other legal systems which have been influenced by the UCC".[3]

Finally, Cape Town Convention applies to all three mentioned agreements which create the so-called by the Cape Town Convention "interest". What is more, it is foreseen that the according to the rules of conflict of law applicable law will have the competence to determine if and in what category among the covered by this common name, will an international interest be included.[4]

Its rules are valid as a uniform law and they apply, not only to the international cases, but also to absolutely national [internal] transactions, except if a Member

---

[1] Stanford, M. (1996), Completion of a First Draft of Unidroit's Planned Future Convention on International Interests in Mobile Equipment, *Uniform Law Review*, 1(2), 275, 277 (274–283); Cumming, R.C.C. (1990), International Regulation of Aspects of Security interests in mobile equipment, *Uniform Law Review*, 62–206.

[2] Moustaira, E.N. (2001), Convention on International Interests on Mobile Assets as it is applied in aircraft equipment [*in Greek*], *Koinodikion* 367–390.

[3] Deschamps, M. (2013), The perfection and priority rules of the Cape Town Convention and the Aircraft Protocol. A comparative law analysis, *Cape Town Convention Journal*, 53 (51–64).

[4] Foex, B. (1999), La réserve de propriété dans l'avant-projet de Convention d'UNIDROIT : un point de vue suisse, *Uniform Law Review*, 4(2), 416 (409–424).

E.N. Moustaira (✉)
School of Law, National and Kapodistrian University of Athens, Athens, Greece
e-mail: emoustai@law.uoa.gr

© Springer International Publishing AG 2017
S. Kozuka (ed.), *Implementing the Cape Town Convention and the Domestic Laws on Secured Transactions*, Ius Comparatum - Global Studies in Comparative Law 22, DOI 10.1007/978-3-319-46470-1_15

State declares that, as far as it is concerned, the Cape Town Convention will not be applied to the internal transactions.[5]

Greece has ratified the Geneva 1948 Convention on the International Recognition of Rights in Aircraft (Law Decree 543/1970), but has neither signed nor, obviously, ratified the Cape Town Convention.

15.1 Registration System

As far as the recognition of foreign [security] interests is concerned, it is the law of the State of reception that decides whether a certain form of publicity – here, the registration – constitutes a part of the international public order.[6]

(a) No.
(b) The registration of aircraft, in Greece, is the responsibility of the Civil Aviation Authority (CAA). According to article 1 of the Law 1340/1983: "The Civil Aviation Authority constitutes a Public Service of the Ministry of Transport, Infrastructure and Networks and is administered by its Director and Assistant Director".

The following records, inter alia, are maintained with the CAA:

(a) Record of mortgages over aircraft and engines;
(b) Record of Arrests of aircraft and engines;
(c) Record of Ownership Claims over aircraft and engines;
(d) Record of Aircraft Leases.

There is no separate register maintained in respect of spare parts.

According to article 1339 of the Civil Code, which is applied to aircraft by analogy (art. 73 of the Code of Aviation Law), it is provided that the mortgage registers are public and anyone may consult them. The mortgage should also be noticed in the aircraft's Certificate of Registration (article 108 par. 3 of the Presidential Decree 7/1931).

A Presidential Decree should be issued concerning the manner of keeping the above records, but until now no such Decree has been issued. Consequently, the CAA currently does not keep a Register of Claims over aircraft and engines or a Register of Aircraft Leases. The relevant registrations are made in the general register.

---

[5] Bollweg, H.-G./Kreuzer, K. (2000), Entwürfe einer UNIDROIT/ICAO – Konvention über Internationale Sicherungsrechte an beweglicher Ausrüstung und eines Protokolls über Luftfahrtausrüstung, *ZIP*, 1361, 1364.

[6] Kreuzer, K. (1996) La propriété mobilière en droit international privé, 259 *Recueil des Cours de l'Académie de Droit International*, 254, 9–318; Moustaira, E.N. (1999), Security interests and private international law [*in Greek*], *Koinodikion*, 29, 31–32.

The mortgage covers the aircraft, its engines and – if there is no agreement to the contrary – its accessories (article 51 Code of Aviation Law).

A mortgage may also be recorded over an aircraft under construction, on the condition that the aircraft has been registered in the appropriate register (article 52 Code of Aviation Law). An engine not attached to an aircraft may be subject to a separate mortgage, provided that it has been recorded with the appropriate registry (article 53 par. 1 Code of Aviation Law).[7]

The mortgage may be of two types: a simple mortgage and a preferred mortgage. The simple mortgage is granted by unilateral declaration of the owner, written and registered in the Record of Mortgage (article 50 Code of Aviation Law). The preferred mortgage is granted by contract (article 58 Code of Aviation Law) and may be registered only over aircraft of a maximum take-off weight of over 5700 Kg (article 65 Code of Aviation Law).

The simple mortgage grants priority to the mortgagee over subsequent mortgagees, simple or preferred, and other simple creditors, but does not give a right to private sale or to the possession and management of the aircraft. The preferred mortgage gives the mortgage a right to the management of the aircraft as soon as his claim becomes due and payable or in any other case provided for by the terms of the preferred mortgage (article 57 Code of Aviation Law). Each and every detail must be noted in the Record of Mortgages.[8]

Registration of a mortgage secures priority for the mortgagee over all other mortgages which will be registered later in time. In case more mortgages are registered on the same day, they will be considered of equal value and will rank in the same order – *pari passu* (article 1272 Civil Code).[9]

A registered mortgage attaches the whole aircraft, its engines and any accessories – the latter, only if there is no agreement to the contrary (article 51 Code of Aviation Law).

Everything about an aircraft mortgage that is not regulated by the Code of Aviation Law, is governed by the provisions of the Civil Code, applied by analogy. According to article 973 of the Civil Code, the mortgage is a "real right".

A big percentage of the investments of many industrial and commercial enterprises refer to such assets of professional equipment, as the aircrafts. It is well known, that in international commerce the aircrafts financing is very often taking place by leasing agreements.[10]

---

[7] Kalantzis, A./Metaxotou-Bontza, C./Roufos-Kanakaris, L./Warren-Kalaidopoulos, H. (2012), GREECE, in: *Aircraft Finance. Registration, Security and Enforcement*, Volume 2, Sweet & Maxwell, 8–9 (1–61).

[8] Kalantzis, A./Metaxotou-Bontza, C./Roufos-Kanakaris, L./Warren-Kalaidopoulos, H. (2012), GREECE, in: *Aircraft Finance. Registration, Security and Enforcement*, Volume 2, Sweet & Maxwell, 15 (1–61).

[9] Kalantzis, A./Metaxotou-Bontza, C./Roufos-Kanakaris, L./Warren-Kalaidopoulos, H. (2012), GREECE, in: *Aircraft Finance. Registration, Security and Enforcement*, Volume 2, Sweet & Maxwell, 13 (1–61).

[10] Mauri, G. (2009), La Convenzione di Città del Capo e il protocollo aeronautico, *Contratto e Impresa/Europa*, 503, 506.

According to the Greek law, the aircraft may constitute object of leasing (article 1 par. 3 Law 1665/1986, as amended by article 11 par. 2 Law 2367/1995).

Article 1 par. 1 Law 1665/1986 allows that the entrepreneur, who is interested in acquiring the use of the aircraft for his/her business's equipment, is addressed to a leasing company, which buys in its name from the supplier or imports from abroad the aircraft in which the lessee is interested, pays the price and assigns its use to the entrepreneur – lessee.

The lessee pays a certain installment over the duration of the leasing contract and at the end of it, the lessee has the options either to extend unilaterally the leasing for a certain time period, at a certain rent, or to consider the leasing as terminated or to buy, on a unilateral declaration, the leased object, by paying the agreed amount.

According to article 1 par. 2 Law 1665/1986, the object of the leasing agreement may be a movable that the leasing company had previously bought from the lessee (lease-back). A lease-back agreement allows that a business owner of an asset, sells it to the leasing company, keeping it though in its possession and using it as a lessee, on paying its value.

The lessee obtains the possession of the aircraft in order to use and exploit it during the whole time of the leasing agreement. The lessee has the obligation to preserve the leased aircraft accordingly to the agreed use. He assumes the risk of the leased aircraft's accidental destruction or deterioration and has the obligation, according to the article 5 par. 2 Law 1665/1986, to insure the aircraft for the risk of its accidental destruction or deterioration.

From the above, it follows that the lessee assumes not only the use of the aircraft but also its commercial exploitation.

In order that the ownership right of the leasing company is secured – as a security interest –, the leasing agreement must be in writing and the relevant document must be registered with the specific Records kept by the First Instance Courts (article 4 paragraphs 1 & 2 Law 1665/1986).

The leasing agreement will be null, according to the article 159 par. 1 Civil Code, if it is not in writing and if it is not registered.[11]

Some commentators believe that the financing of mobile equipment suffers from the differences between the national laws and that adopting a uniform regulation would contribute to stop the increase of the cost of credit transactions for airline companies.[12]

Nevertheless, things are not so simple and the differences between the various legal systems cannot be deleted just by forcing upon them a new, internationally agreed, regime.

(c) The Cape Town Convention, following the opinion of its initial drafters, common law lawyers, adopted the "notice-filing" system. It had been considered as

---

[11] Chadjinikolaou-Angelidou, R. (2001) *The Aircraft as an Object of Transactions* [in Greek], 3rd edition, Sakkoulas Editions, Athens – Thessaloniki, 261–267.

[12] Sagaert, V. (2004), The UNIDROIT Convention on International Interests in Mobile Equipment: a Belgian Perspective, *European Review of Private Law* 89–90 (75–90).

the best possible one, since the "only aim" of the registration, according to the Cape Town Convention would be to assure the priority of an international interest on an object, over other international interests, of creditors who have acquired a preference (privilege) by judgment or by law and of insolvency administrators.[13]

The legal system of Greece, as far as the registration of security interests is concerned, falls under the category of the "document-filing" systems.[14] The advantages of this system are, among others, the following: the users of the national registries consider as very important the fact that they can have access to all documents gathered in one place. Furthermore, is also considered as very important the fact that whoever is interested to proceed in some transaction over an object, may be informed about previous transactions over the same object.

(d) As it was above mentioned, specific interests constituted by a security agreement, a title reservation agreement and a leasing agreement, "merge to form an autonomous international interest". Or, according to another, very accurate, description, the "international interest" under the Convention is a property interest which derives its force from the Convention and not from national law, "it is an artificial concept".[15]

Nevertheless, it is rightly pointed out that the characterization of these legal devices which will constitute the basis of an international interest is of the utmost importance.[16] In many civil law States, there is a clear distinction between proprietary and contractual rights, between real rights and personal rights. Under the national property laws of these States, the interests derived from a title reservation agreement and/or a leasing agreement are not treated the same as the interests derived by a security agreement. And that is the case for Greece, too.[17]

Title reservation agreement's definition by the Cape Town Convention is broader than the definition provided by Greek law, according to which[18] title retention (reservation) only secures the purchase price payable by the buyer.[19]

---

[13] Mooney, Jr, Ch. W (1999). Relationship between the prospective UNIDROIT International Registry, Revised Uniform Commercial Code Article 9 and national civil aviation registries, *Uniform Law Review* 4(2), 337–338 (335–345).

[14] Moustaira, E.N. (2001), Convention on International Interests on Mobile Assets as it is applied in aircraft equipment [*in Greek*], *Koinodikion*, 367–390.

[15] Kronke, H. (2011), Financial Leasing and its Unification by UNIDROIT – General Report, *Uniform Law Review* 16(1–2), 35 (23—44).

[16] Honnebier, B.P.(2004), The Dutch real rights of airlines can be the basis of international interests under the Convention of Cape Town, just like their equivalent American security interests, *European Review of Private Law* 9(1) 62 (46–66).

[17] Kalantzis, A. (2013), *Greece, in: Aircraft Liens & Detention Rights*, Sweet & Maxwell, 7 (1–22).

[18] The same is true, according to other laws too.

[19] Deschamps, M. (2013), The perfection and priority rules of the Cape Town Convention and the Aircraft Protocol. A comparative law analysis, *Cape Town Convention Journal*, 55 (51–64).

The term "security agreement" is very broad. It reflects the mentality of the USA's Uniform Commercial Code and, although some commentators say that this fact should not impede the other States from adopting the Cape Town Convention, it really creates many difficulties.

The absence of exceptions to the 'first in time to register' principle may provide greater certainty to a creditor who registers its interest in the International Registry, nevertheless a dual, parallel system could be somewhat created in the States in which there are differences between the various agreements which constitute the basis for international interests according to the Cape Town Convention.

15.2 Enforcement of a Security Interest

(a) No. For a security interest to be enforced, an enforceable title is needed. The documents which constitute such titles are final court judgments, notarial deeds and foreign titles declared enforceable in Greece (articles 904 & 905 Code of Civil Procedure).
(b) No.

A mortgagee who has a preferred mortgage on a Greek aircraft may take possession of the aircraft when his claim becomes due and payable, without any court process provided that the mortgagee is in the form of a notarial deed.[20]

Various issues cause concerns to the jurists of the non-common law countries. One of them is the "Relief pending final determination", of the article 13. As it is very well described by a commentator, it "does not seem to correspond to any relief traditionally found in national legal systems" and, among other problems, one can have strong doubts whether there could be a harmonized procedural remedy, when there is the international customary rule that procedure is governed by the *lex fori*.[21]

Furthermore, there are doubts about this article's qualities: Is it an interim relief or not? For example, the Aircraft and the Luxembourg Protocols allow contracting states to add to the remedies of Article 13 the sale of the object, an issue that had caused heated discussions during the Cape Town Diplomatic Conference, since the sale of the object had been initially included in the remedies. In common law systems, a sale may be a form of interim relief, while in other systems of law it is not the case. "Selling the object is not an interim measure", "it actually enforces the interest".[22]

---

[20] Kalantzis, A./Metaxotou-Bontza, C./Roufos-Kanakaris, L./Warren-Kalaidopoulos, H. (2012), GREECE, in: *Aircraft Finance. Registration, Security and Enforcement*, Volume 2, 24 (1–61).

[21] Cuniberti, G. (2012), Advance relief under the Cape Town Convention, *Cape Town Convention Journal* 80 (79–94).

[22] Cuniberti, G. (2012), Advance relief under the Cape Town Convention, *Cape Town Convention Journal*, 84 (79–94).

15.3 Treatment of Security Interests Under the Insolvency Procedure

The international interest, created by the Cape Town Convention, as a supranational substantive law instrument, supersedes any conflict of laws rule. Nevertheless, Cape Town Convention is not an all-inclusive codification of asset-based secured financing. Therefore, there is room for application for domestic substantive law rules, which will be determined either directly by uniform conflict of laws rules of the Cape Town Convention, or indirectly by domestic conflict of laws rules.[23]

In case of a company's insolvency the international insolvency law and the private international law of real rights, of proprietary rights, are on a crossroad.[24] So, when a creditor claims having a contractual security that confers to him a proprietary right, that is, a security interest, according to the Greek law he will be able to exercise it, without it being automatically or by order of the insolvency administrator stayed. Publicity of this security interest is absolutely required.

As far as the title reservation agreement is concerned, some decades ago, the predominant view in the case law (courts' decisions) was that this agreement had no effect whatever in case of the purchaser's insolvency. However, the view of part of theoreticians of law was that if the title reservation agreement had no effect in case of the purchaser's insolvency, in the name of the creditors' protection, then this agreement would practically have no validity in transactions between merchants and this would be a "*coup dur*" for the credit agreements, which are of vital importance for the national economy.

Actually, it is accepted by both theory and courts, that title reservation agreement is "saved" in case of the purchaser's insolvency and that the seller – proprietor of the asset may take possession of the asset, since the insolvent purchaser had never acquired the ownership of it and therefore it could not be included in the insolvency estate.[25]

15.4 General Considerations

(a) One could say that it has been customary, these last years, due to influences by the mentality of foreign laws, mainly those of the common law tradition.

---

[23] Kreuzer, K. (2013), Jurisdiction and choice of law under the Cape Town Convention and the Protocols thereto, *Cape Town Convention Journal*, 156–157 (149–164).

[24] Moustaira, E.N. (1998), La mise en œuvre des sûretés dans le cadre d'une faillite internationale, *Revue Hellénique de Droit International* 89, 96.

[25] Rokas, N. (1974), Title reservation agreement in case of bankruptcy of the purchaser [*in Greek*], *Nomiko Vima* 449, 456–460; Moustaira, E.N. (1998), La mise en œuvre des sûretés dans le cadre d'une faillite internationale, *Revue Hellénique de Droit International* 89, 97–98.

(b) Generally, yes. Still, the Cape Town Convention is considered by Greek jurists as very much complicated and difficult to be adopted by Greece, given the system that is already in existence.[26]

A very important issue is that of the Public Service and the way the Cape Town Convention deals with it. Things in Greece's economy and the structure of it, change fast, too fast most probably. The three Protocols took different approaches, or, to be more accurate: they took non-identical approaches, in relation to this issue. The least interested in dealing "directly with the on-going possibility of a public interest in protecting certain assets from creditor repossession" is the Aircraft Protocol. It might be because, as it is pointed out, "governments are persuaded that the political gain of facilitating cost-effective private sector finance for aircraft operators, and therefore a highly competitive aviation industry and cheap flights for the public, outweighs the political downside of withdrawal of service",[27] but it is not always so simple and, obviously, not all governments have the same attitude.

In Greece, by law 3710/2008, the National Council of Railways was constituted, which became the competent institution for the purchase of the railway services. By law 3891/2010, all necessary legislatives were taken for the restructuring of the rail sector, while, in parallel, the Regulative Authority of Railways was constituted, being mainly competent for the purchase of railway services.

The article 29 of the law 4111/2013 provides that the "Hellenic Company of Preservation of Rail Rolling Stock" will be competent, as the agent of the Hellenic State, for the management and the leasing to third parties of the rail rolling stock that either belongs to the Hellenic State or belongs to EUROFIMA and is leased by the Hellenic State.

The Luxembourg Protocol follows a "successful" Cape Town Protocol, as far as the success is counted on the number of ratifications. The problems persist though, and, for example, a much discussed issue of the Luxembourg Protocol is that of the prospective liability of the Registrar.[28]

As already mentioned, in Greece many things change and one of them is that many parts of the public sector are being privatized or, at least, using private financing.[29]

---

[26] However, there are also voices in favour of the adoption and ratification of the Cape Town Convention. For example, Voulgaris, I. (2010), La location-financière (leasing) en Grèce, *Revue Hellénique de Droit International* 223, 239, believes that is not possible that Greece adheres to the UNIDROIT Ottawa Convention 1988, which includes ships and other naval constructions, but, on the contrary, considers the idea of adoption and ratification by Greece of the Cape Town Convention and Protocols as rather positive.

[27] Rosen, H. (2013), Public Service and the Cape Town Convention, *Cape Town Convention Journal* 133 (131–147).

[28] Bollweg, H.-G./Schnell, K. (2007), Liability of the Registrar for the Registration of International Interests Pursuant to the Luxembourg Railway Protocol, *Uniform Law Review* 12(3) 571–572 (559–572).

[29] The same thing ascertain Bollweg, H.-G./Kreuzer, K. (2008), Das Luxemburger Eisenbahnprotokoll. Zum Protokoll zum Übereinkommen über international Sicerungsrechte an

This fact has stirred a lot of heated debates and one could express the opinion that the picture of the legal and economic system is not yet clear.

The Space Assets Protocol, for now, does not really concern Greek jurists. HellasSat, the only satellite that Greece had, has been purchased by foreign capitals, a few years ago.

It should once more be stated that the Cape Town Convention and Protocols, as legal texts are brilliantly structured, though very much complicated in practice and very difficult to be implemented in the various and very different between each other legal systems, especially since the whole texts' mentality is more or less evidently common law oriented.

References

1. Bollweg, H.-G., and K. Kreuzer. 2000. Entwürfe einer UNIDROIT/ICAO – Konvention über Internationale Sicherungsrechte an beweglicher Ausrüstung und eines Protokolls über Luftfahrtausrüstung, *ZIP*, 1361
2. Bollweg, H.-G., and K. Schnell. 2007. Liability of the registrar for the registration of international interests pursuant to the Luxembourg railway protocol. *Uniform Law Review* 12(3): 559–572.
3. Bollweg, H.-G., and K. Kreuzer. 2008. Das Luxemburger Eisenbahnprotokoll. Zum Protokoll zum Übereinkommen über international Sicerungsrechte an beweglicher Ausrüstung betreffend Besonderheiten des rollenden Eisenbahnmaterials vom 23.2.2007. *IPRax* 176.
4. Chadjinikolaou-Angelidou, R. 2001. *The aircraft as an object of transactions* [in Greek]. 3rd ed. Athens – Thessaloniki: Sakkoulas Editions.
5. Cumming, R.C.C. 1990. International regulation of aspects of security interests in mobile equipment. *Uniform Law Review* 1: 62–206.
6. Cuniberti, G. 2012. Advance relief under the Cape Town Convention. *Cape Town Convention Journal* 2012: 79–94.
7. Deschamps, M. 2013. The perfection and priority rules of the Cape Town Convention and the Aircraft Protocol. A comparative law analysis. *Cape Town Convention Journal* 2013: 51–64.
8. Foëx, B. 1999. La réserve de propriété dans l'avant-projet de Convention d'UNIDROIT: un point de vue suisse. *Uniform Law Review* 4(2): 409–424.
9. Honnebier, B.P. 2004. The Dutch real rights of airlines can be the basis of international interests under the Convention of Cape Town, just like their equivalent American security interests. *European Review of Private Law* 9(1): 46–66.
10. Kalantzis, A., C. Metaxotou-Bontza, L. Roufos-Kanakaris, and H. Warren-Kalaidopoulos. 2012. Greece. In *Aircraft finance. Registration, security and enforcement*, vol. 2, 1–61. London: Sweet & Maxwell.
11. Kalantzis, A. 2013. Greece. In *Aircraft liens & detention rights*, 1–22. London: Sweet & Maxwell.
12. Kreuzer, K. 1996. La propriété mobilière en droit international privé. *Recueil des Cours de l'Académie de Droit International* 259: 9–318.
13. Kreuzer, K. 2013. Jurisdiction and choice of law under the Cape Town Convention and the protocols thereto. *Cape Town Convention Journal* 2013: 149–164.

beweglicher Ausrüstung betreffend Besonderheiten des rollenden Eisenbahnmaterials vom 23.2.2007, *IPRax*, 176.

14. Kronke, H. 2011. Financial leasing and its unification by UNIDROIT – General report. *Uniform Law Review* 16(1–2): 23–44.
15. Mauri, G. 2009. La Convenzione di Cittá del Capo e il protocollo aeronautico. *Contratto e Impresa/Europa* 503.
16. Mooney Jr., C.W. 1999. Relationship between the prospective UNIDROIT International Registry, Revised Uniform Commercial Code Article 9 and national civil aviation registries. *Uniform Law Review* 4(2): 335–345.
17. Moustaira, E.N. 1998. La mise en œuvre des sûretés dans le cadre d'une faillite internationale. *Revue Hellénique de Droit Internationale* 51: 89.
18. Moustaira, E.N. 1999. Security interests and private international law [in Greek]. *Koinodikion* 29.
19. Moustaira, E.N. 2001. Convention on International interests on mobile assets as it is applied in aircraft equipment [in Greek]. *Koinodikion* 367–390.
20. Rokas, N. 1974. Title reservation agreement in case of bankruptcy of the purchaser [in Greek]. *Nomiko Vima* 449.
21. Rosen, H. 2013. Public service and the Cape Town Convention. *Cape Town Convention Journal* 2: 131–147.
22. Sagaert, V. 2004. The UNIDROIT convention on international interests in mobile equipment: A Belgian perspective. *European Review of Private Law* 89–90: 75–90.
23. Stanford, M. 1996. Completion of a first draft of Unidroit's planned future convention on International interests in mobile equipment. *Uniform Law Review* 1(2): 274–283.
24. Voulgaris, I. 2010. La location-financière (leasing) en Grèce. *Revue Hellénique de Droit International* 63: 223.

Elina N. Moustaira is Professor at the School of Law, National and Kapodistrian University of Athens, Greece. Prof. Moustaira was *Delegate of Greece*: at the UNIDROIT-ICAO Governmental Experts' Conference in Rome (2000), at the Diplomatic Conference for the adoption of the Cape Town Convention/Aircraft Protocol in Cape Town (2001), at the Diplomatic Conference for the adoption of the Rail Rolling Stock Protocol in Luxembourg (2007), at UNIDROIT Experts' Committees in Rome and Berlin (2008), at the UNCITRAL General Assembly in New York (June-July 2008), at UN Committees in Vienna (2009). Prof. Moustaira is *Member of the*: Hellenic Council of Nationality, Ministry of Interior (2000-2013), Società Italiana per la Ricerca nel Diritto Comparato, Wissenschaftiche Vereinigung für Internationales Verfahrensrecht, Hellenic section of the Commission Internationale de l'Etat Civil, International Law Association and of its Cultural Heritage Law Committee, International Academy of Comparative Law, World Society of Mixed Jurisdictions Jurists, Editorial Board of the International Journal of Cultural Property, Deutsche Vereinigung der Zivilprozessrechtslehrer, Juris Diversitas, Board of Directors of the Hellenic Society for Technology and Construction Law, and various other Foreign and Hellenic law associations. Legal advisor of the Minister of Justice (2009). She is author of 9 books and of about 100 articles, chapters in collective books, commentaries on courts' decisions, book reviews.

Chapter 16
The Cape Town Convention and Italian Law on Secured Transactions

Anna Veneziano

16.1 Introduction

The subject of this book concerns the (possible) impact on national law of a uniform law instrument developed by an inter-governmental organization, the International Institute for the Unification of Private Law (UNIDROIT). The International Academy of Comparative Law had already specifically addressed other UNIDROIT's instruments in past congresses.[1] The 2014 session from which this volume arose focused in particular on the Cape Town Convention on International Interests on Mobile Equipment[2] and the Protocols thereto (relating to aircraft,[3] railway-rolling stock[4] and space assets[5]).

---

[1] Regarding international contracts see the General Report by Michael Joachim Bonell in Bonell, MJ (ed), *A New Approach in International Commercial Contracts. The UNIDROIT Principles of International Commercial Contracts* (Kluwer Law Int, 1999); in the field of asset-based financing see the General Report by Herbert Kronke: Kronke, H, Financial Leasing and its Unification by UNIDROIT, (2011) *Unif L Rev* 23.

[2] 2001 Convention on International Interests in Mobile Equipment, available at http://www.unidroit.org/instruments/securityinterests/cape-town-convention. From now on "Cape Town Convention" or "Convention".

[3] 2001 Protocol to the Convention on International Interests in Mobile Equipment on Matters Specific to Aircraft Equipment, available at http://www.unidroit.org/instruments/securityinterests/aircraft-protocol. From now on "Aircraft Protocol".

[4] 2007 Luxembourg (Rail) Protocol to the Convention on International Interests in Mobile Equipment on Matters Specific to Railway Rolling Stock, available at http://www.unidroit.org/instruments/securityinterests/rail-protocol. From now on: "Rail Protocol".

[5] 2012 Protocol to the Convention on International Interests in Mobile Equipment on Matters Specific to Space Assets, at http://www.unidroit.org/instruments/securityinterests/space-protocol. From now on: "Space Protocol".

A. Veneziano (✉)
International Institute for the Unification of Private Law (UNIDROIT), Rome, Italy

Faculty of Law, University of Teramo, Teramo, Italy
e-mail: a.veneziano@unidroit.org

© Springer International Publishing AG 2017   253
S. Kozuka (ed.), *Implementing the Cape Town Convention and the Domestic Laws on Secured Transactions*, Ius Comparatum - Global Studies in Comparative Law 22, DOI 10.1007/978-3-319-46470-1_16

As is well known, the field of secured transactions has recently been at the centre of a number of harmonization initiatives, differing in their nature[6] and geographical sphere of application (being both global and regional[7]).

The Convention and the Aircraft Protocol can be counted amongst the most successful of such harmonization efforts, and indeed, more generally, of commercial law treaties so far, both in terms of ratifications[8] and volume of transactions.[9] On a more theoretical level, the Convention introduces a uniform and innovative regime in the field of secured transactions, which is notorious for its complexity and for the

---

[6] Ranging from instrument intending to become legally binding such as Cape Town Convention and its Protocols, to soft law products such as the 2010 Legislative Guide on Secured Transactions (and its 2012 Supplement on Electronic Registries) by the UN Commission on International Trade Law UNCITRAL (a legislative guide discussing policy issues and containing recommendations with the aim of paving the way to domestic law reforms), or the recently approved UNCITRAL Model Law. Other instruments at global level have specifically addressed security rights in the capital markets: 2006 Hague Convention on the Law Applicable to Certain Rights in Respect of Securities Held with an Intermediary; 2009 UNIDROIT (Geneva) Convention on Substantive Rules for Intermediated Securities. See Goode R, Kronke H, McKendrick E, *Transnational Commercial Law. Text, Cases and Materials* (2nd ed., OUP, 2015), 432; 453.

[7] One of the most interesting achievements at a regional level was the European Bank for Reconstruction and Development (EBRD) Model Law on Secured Transactions, originally published in 1994 and aimed at facilitating the transition to capital market economies and the introduction of efficient systems of security rights over movables in Central and Eastern European countries. Other regional bodies have recently developed model laws in this field: as an example see the 2002 Organization of American States (OAS) Model Inter-American Law on Secured Transactions. Finally, whilst the European Union has limited its legislative intervention to the financial markets with the 2002 Financial Collateral Directive (expanded in 2009), an entire book of the Draft Common Frame of Reference project was dedicated to 'Proprietary security in movable assets' (Book IX, in von Bar, Ch, Clive, E (eds.), *Principles, Definitions and Model Rules of European Private Law, Draft Common Frame of Reference (DCFR)*, Vol. 6 (Full ed., Sellier, 2009) 5389.

[8] In the relatively short time since the July 2014 IACL Congress, twelve additional States have ratified or otherwise accessed to the Convention, for a total of 72 States; the contracting States to the Aircraft Protocol are 65, the Aircraft Protocol being the only one that entered into force so far, triggering the effects of the Convention (data checked up to 3 October 2016). This is a staggering number in view of the recent adoption of the two instruments and is steadily increasing every year. The European Community/European Union has also approved the Convention and the Aircraft Protocol, and end of 2014 the Rail Protocol, in its capacity as a Regional Economic Integration Organisation (REIO. Most recently, the Rail Protocol (already ratified by Luxemburg and signed by four other States including Italy) has been signed by the United Kingdom with a view towards ratification.

[9] The International Registry, operated by Aviareto, a joint venture between the private company SITA SC and the Irish Government, appointed and supervised by the International Civil Aviation Organisation (ICAO), that adopted the Convention and the Aircraft Protocol jointly with UNIDROIT, has received more than 700,000 entries since the beginning of its activity in 2006.

difference in the approaches developed in domestic laws.[10] Work towards the adoption of the Convention system started from the assumption that though a wider use of cross-border asset-based financing would be beneficial, it was hampered by the interplay between the conflict-of-law regime generally applicable to proprietary rights and the existing divergences in the national legal systems. This was considered to be particularly the case for high value mobile equipment.[11]

Italy has signed the Convention as well as the Aircraft and Rail Protocols, but has not (yet) ratified them.[12] In the case of a non-Party jurisdiction, the questionnaire prepared by the General Reporter, Professor Kozuka (see Appendix in this volume), invited to compare domestic law with the Cape Town Convention (and its Protocols) and consider the implications of its possible future introduction in the national legal system.

Such analysis will be conducted against the backdrop of Italian general secured transactions law, the main features of which will be summarized at the outset, focusing on the regime of security devices that can be effectively created over the kind of equipment asset covered by the Convention.[13] Specific key aspects of the Cape Town Convention will be then compared with Italian law. For the purposes of this Chapter, again referring to the scope of application of the Cape Town Convention, the term 'security device' will encompass a traditional security agreement (pledge or mortgage), a title reservation agreement, as well as a leasing agreement (Art. 2 (2) Conv.).

By way of conclusion, two aspects will be briefly touched upon: the economic advantages for Italy of becoming part of the Cape Town Convention system; the compatibility of the main architecture of the Cape Town Convention with principles and rules underlying general Italian secured transactions law.

---

[10] See for all: Drobnig U, Security Rights in Movables, in Hartkamp, AS, Hesselink, MW et al. (eds.) *Towards a European Civil Code* (4th ed., Wolters Kluwer, 2010), Chapter 43, 1025; Kieninger, E-M (ed.) *Security Rights in Movable Property in European Private Law* (CUP, 2009); Beale H, Bridge M, Gullifer L, Lomnika E, *The Law of Security and Title-Based Financing*, (2nd ed., OUP, 2012).

[11] See Cuming, RCC, International Regulation of Aspects of Security Interests in Mobile Equipment, (1991) *Unif L Rev* 75; Goode, R, Transcending the Boundaries of Earth and Space: the Preliminary Draft UNIDROIT Convention on International Interests in Mobile Equipment, (1998) *Unif L Rev* 52.

[12] Italy is among the ten States that have adhered to the 1988 UNIDROIT *Convention on International Financial Leasing* (Ottawa Convention), which represented a – very limited – first step in the direction of cross-border recognition of leasing on equipment and as such, opened the path to the work on the future Cape Town Convention (see above, fn 1).

[13] Security rights over movables and immovables were the topic of an earlier Italian national report to the International Academy: see Bussani, M, Le présent et l'avenir des sûretés réelles, in *Rapports nationaux italien/Italian National Reports, XVI International Congress of Comparative Law, Brisbane 2002* (Milano, Giuffrè, 2002) 245.

16.2 Italian Secured Transactions Law as Applicable to the Financing of Mobile Equipment: A Brief Overview

From the outset, it should be made clear that the current Italian legal regime of secured transactions is generally considered to be far from satisfactory. The complexity and, at the same time, insufficiency of Italian secured transactions law to meet the needs of present-day economy have been repeatedly denounced by Italian scholars.[14] This critical approach was echoed in recent efforts to entrust the Government with the task of preparing an organic reform, based on the recognition that the present system discourages foreign investments and hampers growth.[15]

The insufficiency of the present legal regime is particularly evident with respect to traditional security devices on tangible goods. Using the value of tangible goods for financing purposes is difficult for enterprises due to the lack of efficient instruments allowing the collateralization of assets that cannot be handed over to the creditor. At the same time, this area of Italian law is confused, as a number of particularized exceptions to the principle of equal treatment of creditors[16] have been introduced overtime through specific legislation without a coherent rethinking of the whole system, and to such an extent that the generality of the principle itself can be questioned.[17]

The 1942 Italian Civil Code (*Codice civile*) only allows for possessory pledges where tangible assets are concerned (*pegno con spossessamento*).[18] Until the very

---

[14] See among others (in English and French): Tucci, G, Towards a Transnational Commercial Law for Secured Transactions: the Preliminary Draft UNIDROIT Convention and Italian Law, (1999) *Unif L Rev* 371; Ferrarini, G, Changes to personal property security law in Italy: a comparative and functional approach, in Cranston, R (ed.), *Making Commercial Law. Essays in Honour of R.M. Goode* (OUP, 1997) 477; Bussani, M, Rapport italien, in *Les garanties de financement, Travaux de l'Association Henri Capitant* (LGDJ, Paris, 1998) Vol. XLVII, 213.; Veneziano, A, Italy, in Sigman, HC and Kieninger, E-M (eds), *Cross-Border Security over Tangibles* (Sellier, 2007), 159; Italian Report by Graziadei, M and Candian, Alb, in Kieninger, E-M (ed.) (above, fn 10).

[15] A first attempt was made through one provision contained in a proposal to delegate to the Government the legislative power to introduce reforms towards, inter alia, the reoganisation of secured transactions law, presented to the Parliament on 12.2.2014 but never approved. This provision recently resurfaced in another legislative proposal aimed at reforming insolvency law and approved by the Council of Ministers on 12.2.2016 not yet approved by Parliament; Finally, a parallel legislative initiative was approved when this book was in its final stages of editing and will be only mentioned here: a new registered non-possessory pledge for enterprises was introduced by way of Governmental Decree (3 May 2016, No. 59). The new pledge is not yet operational since it awaits secondary legislation on the setting up of the centralised, fully electronic registry. It excludes, however, from its scope of application "registered mobile assets" such as aircraft.

[16] Art. 2740 (1) Italian Civil Code.

[17] See Tucci, G, *Garanzia*, in Digesto IV, Discipline privatistiche, sez.civ., Vol. VII (Torino, Utet, 1991) 579.

[18] On the pledge in Italian law and its recent developments see among others Gabrielli, E, *I diritti reali*, Vol. 5, *Il pegno*, in Trattato di diritto civile directed by R Sacco (Torino, UTET, 2005);

recent introduction of the new registered non-possessory pledge for enterprises (not yet operational, see fn 15), there was no general consensual non-possessory security right on specific assets (either held for use or to be resold). Except where a specific chattel mortgage exists (see below, para. 3), the kind of equipment covered by the Cape Town Convention could be collateralised by granting the special 'non- posses- sory lien' in favor of banks only, regulated in Art. 46 of the 1993 Banking Law (*privilegio ex Art. 46*, hereinafter 'Art. 46 Bank Charge') to secure medium- to long- term financing to enterprises.[19] Art. 46 Bank Charge replaced a veritable maze of different preexisting 'consensual liens' (*privilegi consensuali*), and is more accu- rately described as a 'charge', being the result of an agreement between the parties, connected to a loan, and needing publicity (though registration) to be opposable to third parties. The uncertainties regarding its priority against other security rights and in insolvency, however, as well as the limited effectiveness of the enforcing procedures rendered its use unattractive in practice.

Italian law recognises some title-based devices in the context of equipment acquisition finance, in particular retention of title and financial lease. They are usu- ally not classified as security rights but as ownership vested in the vendor/lessor. Two important consequences ensue: first of all, the requirements for effectiveness are different than those applicable to traditional security devices. Secondly, vendor and lessor do not usually have to compete with other creditors.

As far as retention of title under a sales contract is concerned, its statutory rules make it impractical to use on a large scale in commercial transactions.

Leasing is, on the other hand, widely used for equipment assets. The main rea- sons for its success, beside the fiscal ones, are the relatively rapid conclusion of the contract, the lack of formalities (as opposed to the granting of a traditional security right but also of a retention of title), the simple enforcement procedures and its high priority in insolvency, being the lessor considered as the 'true owner' of the goods.

Because of the limited possibilities offered by the legal system and the burden- some rules regarding both creation and enforcement of their rights, creditors that do not choose to remain unsecured (including sellers) do not usually rely on proprie- tary security but primarily on other devices such as personal security or bank guar- antees. Company and Insolvency law have introduced additional rules to protect financiers against competing creditors when a specific economic venture of a stock company is financed that cannot be classified as 'asset-based security'.[20]

Mastropaolo, F, De Vecchis, P and Mastropaolo, EM, in Mastropaolo, F (ed.), *I contratti di garan- zia*, 1, Trattato dei contratti directed by P Rescigno and E Gabrielli (Torino, UTET, 2006), 1192; Fiorentini, F, Il pegno, in Gambaro, A and Morello, U (eds), *Trattato dei diritti reali, Vol. V, Diritti reali di garanzia* (Milano, Giuffrè, 2014) 1 (with a comparative introduction).

[19] See Gabrielli, E, *Delle garanzie rotative* (Napoli, Jovene, 1998).

[20] See for example the provisions on 'dedicated assets' (*patrimoni destinati*) introduced in the Civil code, in conjunction with the Insolvency Law (Art. 2447 bis-decies Civil Code and Art. 72-ter Royal Decree 16 March 1942, No. 267 (Insolvency Law), as amended). This device does not, however, constitute an encumbrance over the equipment itself but on the "returns" of the economic venture.

16.3   General v. Specific Rules Applicable to Transport Vehicles and Other Mobile Equipment

The Maritime Code (*codice della navigazione*) and the Civil Code regulate specific chattel mortgages which are required to be filed in specialized (and separate) asset-based registries. A chattel mortgage can be created only on easily identifiable goods of relatively high unit value and for which a registry concerning title is set up: ships, aircrafts and motor-vehicles.[21]

As far as non-registered equipment is concerned (of the kind contemplated in the Rail and the Space Assets Protocol, but also in the case of aircraft engines) the general rules apply. Thus, pending entry into operation of the new registered non-possessory pledge for enterprises (see fn 15), a security right would only be effectively created if a specific consensual lien exists or under Art. 46 Banking Law. On the other hand, financial lease would be available for all types of equipment, while a sale with retention of title could also, at least in principle, be generally used, except for those movable assets that have to be registered in a public registry.

16.4   Comparison with Some Aspects of the Cape Town Convention System

16.4.1   Traditional Security v. Title-Based Devices

Cape Town Convention   The Cape Town Convention provides for an 'international interest' which is autonomous from any national counterpart. The term covers not only traditional (limited) rights *in rem* (an agreement granting – or transferring – a property right to secure a loan), but also acquisition finance devices based on retention of title, such as a conditional sale and a lease. The three categories are subjected to the 'same basic framework'[22]: in particular, the creation, registration and priorities rules apply generally. The characterization of an agreement as security, conditional sale or lease essentially only affects their enforcement. If the creditor is a chargee, it will be satisfied out of the value of the collateral up to the amount of the secured sum, with an obligation to account for the remaining proceeds, and the exercise of its remedies will be subject to notice requirements and some other

---

[21] Cf. Art. 565 Italian Maritime Code (mortgage over ships); Art. 1027 Italian Maritime Code (mortgage over aircrafts); r.d.l. 15.3.1927, No. 436, implemented by Law 19.2.1928, No. 510, and Art. 2810 Italian Civil Code (consensual lien (that is, a mortgage) over motor-vehicles). See Lefebvre D'Ovidio, A, Pescatore, G, Tullio, L, *Manuale di diritto della navigazione* (13th ed., Milano, Giuffrè, 2013) 723 et seq.; Chianale, A, L'ipoteca, Trattato di diritto civile diretto da R. Sacco, *I diritti reali*, Vol. 6 (2nd ed., Torino, UTET, 2010) 142, 189.

[22] See Deschamps, M, The perfection and priority rules of the Cape Town Convention and the Aircraft Protocol- A comparative law analysis, (2013) *Cape Town Convention Journal*, 51, at 53, available at http://www.ingentaconnect.com/content/hart/ctcj/2013/00002013/00000001/art00004.

restrictions depending on the contracting State's declarations in this respect.[23] The conditional seller and the lessor, being the "owners" of the equipment, are allowed to simply terminate the agreement and take possession.[24] The qualification of the agreement as a security or a title-retention device depends on the applicable domestic law. Thus, if under Italian law, as specified below, conditional sales and financial leases are not characterized as security rights, they will be treated accordingly. Where, on the other hand, the applicable domestic law, differently than Italian law, re-characterized such devices, the corresponding rules for security rights will come into play.[25]

Italian Law   Within the limits set forth above (paras 2 and 3), Italian law recognizes all three types of security devices covered by the Cape Town Convention. In practice, the most commonly used among them for high value equipment is finance lease (to allow both acquisition and manufacturing of the asset).

Retention of title and finance lease are not classified as (non-possessory) security rights and are usually treated in different parts of commentaries and general treatises. A tendency seems to be developing, however, especially among comparative law scholars, to consider them alongside the more traditional devices when addressing secured financing, whilst by no means always implying that the same legal regime should apply.[26] Their functional role is therefore increasingly taken into account, though their regulation – especially as regards creation, opposability in insolvency proceedings and enforcement – has not been affected so far.

16.4.2   Effectiveness as Against Third Parties and Role of Publicly Accessible Registries

Cape Town Convention   The Cape Town Convention provides for the setting up of an asset-based international registry, wholly electronic, for each type of collateral regulated in a Protocol, with the purpose of determining the priority of the creditor as against competing secured creditors and subsequent buyers, as well as against the debtor's insolvency administrator. Filing in the registry is therefore not necessary to create a valid international interest *inter-partes* nor to grant the creditor the right to enforce its security upon debtor's default. There is furthermore no need to register the agreement as such, but only a simplified document containing a limited number of required elements which will allow a subsequent interested party to search

---

[23] Arts 8 and 9 Conv.; Art. IX Aircraft Prot. See also below, para. 4.3.

[24] Art. 10 Conv. The Aircraft Protocol extends the obligation to exercise any remedy in a commercially reasonable manner to sellers and lessors. See below, para. 4.3.

[25] Goode, R, *Convention on International Interests in Mobile Equipment and Protocol Thereto on Matters Specific to Aircraft Equipment, Official Commentary* (3rd ed., Rome, UNIDROIT, 2013) 45.

[26] See above, fn. 14.

whether there are existing or prospective encumbrances on the equipment ("notice filing").[27] The Convention system allows for registration of a prospective interest, i.e. an interest which is still under negotiation between the parties, as long as the collateral is identified.[28]

As to the priority of the registered creditor, the Cape Town Convention adopts a strict first-to-file rule, with no exceptions for acquisition finance devices such as retention of title or lease, nor for subsequent buyers. This is justified both by the specialized character of the industry sectors involved and by the nature of the collateral, that is high value equipment as opposed to inventory or receivables.[29]

Italian Law In Italian law there is as yet, no single comprehensive filing system for security devices. Thus, a "first-to-file" rule for priority among all subsequent creditors cannot exist, not even when a filing system is in place for a specific type of device. Registration, however, has always been the traditional means to give "publicity" to charges in lieu of dispossession. There are different registries for various purposes (collateral-specific, such as the ones for aircraft and ship mortgages, or transaction-specific, such as the ones for retention of title). They differ widely as to their location, the necessary formalities for filing and the effectiveness of the filed interest vis-à-vis third parties. Some of them (such as the ones for aircrafts, ships and motor-vehicles) are not exclusively dedicated to security rights but serve as title registries as well. One common feature is that they are all "transaction filing" as opposed to 'notice filing', and the operative document establishing the transaction must be presented and evaluated by the registrar. The extent of computerization of the registries is also varied, but there is, for the moment, no completely electronic registry with remote access facilities similar to the one set up for the international interest under the Cape Town Convention.

As mentioned above, the role played by the registry is diversified.

For an aircraft chattel mortgage, title and other property rights on aircrafts are filed in a national registry. Registration of an aircraft mortgage is possible only if the transaction is contained in a notarized document[30] and is a necessary prerequisite for their *valid creation*, and not only for priority purposes. This is, in my view, an obsolete approach to registration of security rights on movables and should not be favored.

An interesting feature to be considered is the fact that the Maritime Code introduced an exception to the rule according to which a mortgage on a future asset is

---

[27] The term 'notice' filing as opposed to 'transaction' or 'transactional' filing, originally specific to the US UCC Article 9 model, is now widely used in scholarship and international instruments on secured transactions and was even adopted by Book IX of the *Draft Common Frame of Reference*.

[28] Goode, R, *Official Commentary* (above fn. 25), 44.

[29] Goode, R, *Official Commentary*, (above fn. 25) 67.

[30] This requirement was later simplified by allowing also a mere 'registration' of a written document by other competent authorities, cf. Law No. 248/2006.

validly registered only when the asset comes into existence (contained in Art. 2823 Civil Code) It is possible to create a mortgage on an aircraft which is still under construction or the construction of which is planned (Art. 1028 Maritime Code). It must be underlined, however, that the registry for aircrafts under construction is not the same as the general one.

As to the opposability of the creditor's rights to third parties, a registered chattel mortgage prevails over later-in-time registered rights and subsequent buyers and enjoys a high priority ranking vis-à-vis other competing interests (with the exception of a number of specific non-consensual liens, see below, para. 4.4).

For an Art. 46 Bank Charge, registration is needed to achieve effectiveness against third parties (including competing creditors) at the *Tribunale* (first or low instance court) of both the place where the grantor is located and the place where the bank has its seat (when different). Thus, registration is not a condition of the validity of the charge, though Art. 46 still requires a relatively high level of formality even as between grantor and bank.[31] As between Art. 46 creditors, a simple first-to-file rule would be applied. All other competing limited rights on the assets prevail over the Bank Charge if created with an 'ascertained date' (*data certa*), that antedates registration of the charge. In practice, it would be difficult for a lender to determine whether a prior in time interest prevails over its security since the ascertainment of the date is not done through a public filing but through notarization or authentication by a public official, and is mainly a way to prevent fraud.[32]

In the case of a retention of title in a sales contract, differently than in most other (especially European) jurisdictions, retention of title in certain items, i.e. 'machinery'[33] whose value exceeds what has now become a negligible sum is also subject to registration,[34] in the registry kept at the *Tribunale* of the place where the asset is located at the time of the stipulation. It is important to note, however, that the seller's rights are protected only as against *sub-buyers* (superseding the general *bona fide* acquisition provision in Art. 1153 Civil Code), and only if the asset remains within the jurisdiction of the same *Tribunale*. In relation to competing *creditors* (in particular judgment creditors) the retention of title does not have to be filed, but has to be previously agreed upon between the parties in writing, confirmed

---

[31] The charge must be create by a written document 'exactly describing' (1) the collateral; (2) names of lender and debtor or third party provider of security; (3) amount of the loan and its terms; (4) sum secured.

[32] Veneziano, A, Italy (above fn. 14), 172.

[33] With the exception of assets that are registered in public registries.

[34] Art. 1524 (2) Civil Code: € 15,49 – the amount has never been adjusted to the decrease in value of the nominal sum in Italian old *lire*. Furthermore, in the case of equipment exceeding the value of € 258,23 an additional requirement of a marking – a plate containing the seller's name and its property right in the machine as well as particulars concerning the machine – is provided for by special legislation, but again only to protect the title-retaining seller from sub-buyers.

in the sale invoices, with ascertained date prior to the date of attachment and duly registered in the buyer's accounts.[35]

Interestingly, the registry for the retention of title is the same which should be used also for Art. 46 bank charges. This did not result, however, in any coordination of the priority rules, not even as between the two registrable interests, and was apparently done solely to avoid the setting up of another registry.[36] The question is to be considered of little practical import due to the scant attention that Art. 46 Bank Charge has received until now in financing practice.

16.4.3 *Enforcement Measures*[37]

Cape Town Convention The default remedies under the Convention system are characterized by two essential elements. First of all, they leave wide room to parties' autonomy, and secondly, they provide for speedy enforcement measures. A set of opt-in and opt-out declarations by contracting States complemented the conventional design in order to ensure a wider adoption of the Convention and the Protocols. The only mandatory declaration under the Convention relevant to a contracting State concerns the possibility for the creditor to exercise out of court remedies (if the leave of the court is not required in the Convention itself).

Default remedies are different depending on whether the creditor is a chargee or the holder of a retention of title. A chargee may repossess the collateral, sell it, lease it unless declared otherwise by the contracting State where the asset is located at the time of enforcement, or may collect or receive any income or profit from the operation of the asset. The debtor's agreement is needed to exercise any self-help remedy. Surplus proceeds are to be accounted for and due notice should be given to all interested persons. The chargee may also appropriate the collateral by agreement with the debtor and other interested parties or by court order if the value of the outstanding obligations is commensurate with the value of the collateral. A conditional seller or a lessor, on the other hand, may either terminate the contract or exercise possession or control, without the need for debtor's agreement and with no accounting of

---

[35] This is the resulting regulation after the implementation of the 35/2000/EC Late Payment Directive (Legislative Decree No. 231/2002, Art. 11 (3)) and the decision of the European Court of Justice 26 Oct 2006, *Commission v. Italy*, C-302/05, according to which Italy did not fail to implement the Directive by providing for additional acts of the part of the seller in order for the title retention to be opposable to the buyer's creditors).

[36] For this comment and a review of what could be the abstractly possible solutions as to the relative priorities see Veneziano, A, Italy (above, fn. 14), 173.

[37] Arts 8–15 Conv. And IX–XIII Aircraft Prot. On the following see Goode, R, *Official Commentary* (above, fn. 25), 51; Wool, J, *Treaty Design, Implementation and Compliance Benchmarking Economic Benefit - a Framework as Applied to the Cape Town Convention*, (2012) *Unif L Rev* 633.

surplus proceeds.[38] All remedies (including the conditional seller's and lessor's) must be exercised in a commercially reasonable manner.[39]

The Cape Town Convention contains a further set of rules that are crucial to an efficient enforcement system, i.e. the provisions on relief pending final determination.[40] Under specific objective circumstances,[41] the holder of an international interest may obtain from the competent national court speedy relief pending final determination of the creditor's claim, in the form of one or more of the orders listed in Article 13(1) (a) to (d)[42] and as requested by the creditor.

Again, contracting States may modify the conventional regime by opting out of Art. 13, in whole or in part (a choice that was not, however, favored by contracting States) and/or by opting in the Protocols provisions on interim relief (which allow States to determine the number of days within which a remedy under Article 13 will be granted and parties to exclude the court's power to impose protecting terms in favor of the interested persons' for the contingency that the creditor breaches its obligations or fails to eventually establish its claim).[43]

Italian Law   One important obstacle to a more widespread use of non-possessory security rights in Italian law is represented by the cumbersome enforcement procedures. Possessory pledgees enjoy speedier remedies upon debtor's default and may choose between the normal execution rules of the Civil Procedural Code (*Codice di procedura civile*) and the self-help provisions contained in the Civil Code (the latter allowing the creditor to ask a court for appropriation of the collateral after appraisal of its value and with an accounting to the debtor of any excess, or to seize the asset and have them sold by an official agent – at auction or market price – or, if previously agreed upon with the debtor, to use a different method of sale). No such direct remedy is available to the creditor in the case of a non-possessory security right: the ordinary rules of the Procedural Code must be followed (Art. 502 et seq. Civil Procedural Code), which require a judicial decision and formal (and lengthy) enforcement proceedings, aiming at liquidation. This is especially true for consensual liens and for Art. 46 Bank Charge. Relatively more flexible enforcement provisions were introduced for the recently approved (and not yet operational, see fn 15) non-possessory pledge for enterprises.

---

[38] According to the Aircraft Protocol, furthermore, all creditors may ask for deregistration of the aircraft and export or physical transfer of an aircraft object (Art. IX Aircraft Prot.).

[39] A remedy is deemed to be exercised in a commercially reasonable manner if exercised in conformity with the provisions of the agreement, except where such provision is manifestly unreasonable (Art. IX (3) Aircraft Prot.).

[40] Art. 13 Conv.; Art. X Aircraft Prot.; see also Art. VIII Rail Prot.; Art. XX Space Prot.

[41] The creditor should adduce evidence of default; the debtor has to have agreed to the relief at any time: Art.13 (1) Conv.

[42] Art. 13 lists the following orders: (a) preservation of the object and its value; possession, control or custody of the object; (c) immobilisation of the object; (d) lease or, except when covered by (a) to (c), management of the object and the income therefrom. The Aircraft Protocol adds the possibility of asking the court to sell the collateral and apply its proceeds to the creditor's satisfaction.

[43] Art. X (2) and (5) Aircraft Prot.

Chattel mortgages on aircrafts are governed by specific enforcement rules that are no less cumbersome than the ordinary ones.[44] An interesting aspect, however, is the fact that the competent court may permit the continuing use of the equipment if adequate insurance is provided. The proceeds of such activity may be sufficient to cover the mortgagee's outstanding credit thereby avoiding the enforced sale and its inefficiencies.[45]

Italian procedural law allows for interim relief remedies under Arts. 669 *bis* et seq. of the Procedural Code (and in particular Arts. 700 et seq. for urgent measures – left to the court's discretion – if the creditor demonstrates a well-founded risk of imminent and irreparable prejudice). Such rules do not admit derogations by party autonomy (differently from what is provided in the Aircraft Protocol) nor do they set a mandatory time-limit for the giving of relief.[46]

Conditional sellers and lessors are, in contrast, considered to be the "owners" of the asset and, as such, can exercise all actions available to the holder of title. The title-retaining seller may terminate the contract and recover the asset. Special provisions protect the defaulting buyer from abuse in the case of an installment sale.[47] The financial lessor's rights upon default depend on the contract; the lessor is usually granted automatic termination and may repossess the asset, while the protective measures applicable for installment sales do not apply.

16.4.4 Effectiveness in Insolvency Proceedings

Cape Town Convention The provisions on the effectiveness of creditor's rights in debtor's insolvency are at the core of the Cape Town Convention system. A prior-in-time registered creditor enjoys a very strong position and may exercise all its default remedies as against the insolvency administrator of the debtor.

There are some provisions in the Convention that operate as a balance and take into account the possible existence of other interests that a State may wish to protect. Thus, the Convention does not affect the domestic law rules on avoidance of a transaction as a preference or a transfer in fraud of creditors (Art. 30(3) Conv.). Moreover, States are permitted to declare in advance which (already existing) domestic non-consensual rights will preempt the creditor's interest (Art. 39 Conv.), and which domestic preferential claims can be filed in the international registry to obtain priority over later-in-time international interests (Art. 40 Conv.). In the

---

[44] See Art. 1055 et seq. Maritime Code. Righetti, G, *Ipoteca navale ed aeronautica*, in Digesto IV, Discipline privatistiche, sez. comm., Vol. VII (Torino, UTET, 1992) 535, 557.

[45] Art. 1063 Maritime Code. D'Ovidio Lefevbre, A, Pescatore, G and Tullio, L (above, fn. 21), 764.

[46] See Tucci, G, *The preliminary draft UNIDROIT Convention* (above, fn. 14), at 390.

[47] Arts 1525 and 1526 Italian Civil Code.

absence of such declarations, all national rights or liens will be preempted by the international interest.

The Convention contains a further exception for rescue or similar proceedings, where the administrator has the power to limit or delay the enforcement rights of secured creditors.[48] The rationale of such an exception is not to interfere with the policies pursued by national legislators in this field. The Protocols, however, deviate from the Convention on this point, introducing a set of alternative provisions left to the choice of the contracting State of the primary insolvency jurisdiction. The first option[49] gives the creditor the greatest protection, reducing any powers of an insolvency administrator to stay or limit creditor's rights of enforcement on the collateral, be it during liquidation, rescue proceedings or even prior to insolvency, during a fixed period of time indicated in a State's declaration. The second option[50] substantially leaves it to courts to decide what is appropriate in each circumstance, unless the debtor gives notice that it will either cure all defaults or give the creditor the opportunity to take possession of the equipment in accordance with the applicable law.[51] If no declaration is made, the domestic insolvency law will apply.

It is important to note, from an economic perspective, that the aviation industry expressed a strong preference for Alternative A that was included in the list of so-called 'Qualified Declarations' under the *OECD Aircraft Sector Understanding on Export Credits for Civil Aircraft* (1 September 2011). According to this agreement, States that comply with the required declarations will be eligible for officially supported export credits for the sale or lease of aircraft and related materials at a discount rate.

Italian Law The rules on the effectiveness of financier's rights in insolvency proceedings vary, in Italian law, according to whether the financier is a chattel mortgagee, a chargee with a non-possessory security over the equipment (in particular, an Art. 46 chargee), a seller under a retention agreement or a lessee under a financial lease.

A chattel aircraft mortgagee is satisfied with priority on the proceeds from the sale of the collateral, but is preempted by a (limited) number of specific non-consensual liens pertaining to the aircraft and its operation (such as the ones in

---

[48] The Convention does not expressly refer to rescue or similar procedures, which are not autonomously defined in the Convention, but mentions "rules of procedure relating to the enforcement of rights to property which is under the control or supervision of the insolvency administrator". The *Official Commentary*, however, refers to an automatic stay on the enforcement of proprietary rights after commencement and illustrates it with a case concerning reorganization. See Goode, R, (2013) *Official Commentary*, cit. above, fn. 25, 344.

[49] Alternative A, see Art. XI Air Prot.; Art. IX Rail Prot.; Art. XXI Space Prot.

[50] Alternative B

[51] The Rail and Space Protocols introduced a third option (Alternative C), which is aimed at striking a balance between the other two alternatives, for more details see Goode, R, *Convention on International Interests in Mobile Equipment and Luxembourg Protocol Thereto on Matters Specific to Railway Rolling Stock. Official Commentary* (2nd edn., UNIDROIT, Rome, 2014), 421.

favour of recovery of the costs of the execution proceedings, unpaid taxes and duties, employees' wages and social security payments, salvage costs, etc.).[52]

The Art. 46 Bank Charge is expressly given the rank of a lien under Art. 2777 of the Civil Code. This means that the bank will be satisfied on the proceeds of the sale of the collateral but will be postponed to a number of preferred claims that enjoy a special priority. Moreover, recent Insolvency Law reforms added other categories of super-priority that take precedence even over the afore-mentioned preferred claims, including, among other, costs relating to the insolvency administration when provisional operation is authorized within a liquidation procedure and claims deriving from post-commencement financing.[53]

The above-mentioned regime is modified when an alternative procedure to the traditional liquidation is opened (such as in the case of the extraordinary receivership arrangement which can be used by (relatively) large firms)[54] or when other "rescue" procedures are initiated (voluntary arrangements entered into before or during insolvency).[55] A recent reform of the latter procedures (that seem to be the object of continuous adjustments by the legislator), reinforced the insolvency administrator's powers towards creditors secured by a lien, a mortgage or a pledge in the interest of reaching a viable rescue plan.[56]

In the case of buyer's insolvency, a seller with retention of title prevails if the conditions for opposability to conflicting creditors are satisfied (see above, para. 4.2). According to Art. 73(1) Insolvency Law, the insolvency administrator has the option of either keeping the contract (in which event the seller has the right to ask for the setting aside of a sum for future payment of the price unless the sum is immediately liquidated) or terminating it (in which event the seller may repossess the asset with no obligation to account for any excess of value).

The position of the lessor in the lessee's insolvency is expressly regulated in Art. 72-*quater* of the Insolvency Law. The insolvency administrator may decide whether to continue the contract or terminate it. In the event of termination the lessor has the right to retake the asset and must pay over to the insolvency administrator any monies exceeding the unpaid rent that derive from the sale or other use of the asset.

---

[52] Art. 1023 Italian Maritime Code.

[53] For example, Art. 111 (1) 1) and 111-*bis* Insolvency Law.

[54] Legislative Decree No. 270/1999 (*Amministrazione straordinaria delle grandi imprese in crisi*).

[55] *Concordato fallimentare* (Art. 124 et seq. Royal Decree No. 267/1942 on insolvency law); *concordato preventivo* (Art. 160 et seq. ins.law).

[56] See Guglielmucci, G, *Diritto fallimentare* (5th ed., Torino, Giappichelli, 2012) 272; 321.

16.5 The Cape Town Convention and Italian Law: A First Assessment in the Prospect of a Future Ratification by Italy[57]

16.5.1 The Economic Advantages of Ratification

First of all, the potential economic significance of the Cape Town Convention for Italy should be addressed.

As regards the aircraft industry, and similarly to what happened in other jurisdictions, present-day air transport regulations in Italy opened the market to competition and forced participants to operate on an entrepreneurial basis. The need to make recourse to private financing has considerably grown, also in view of the restrictions to State aids provided by the European legislation. Competition of services has, moreover, extended to foreign companies and in particular European ones. The Protocol would facilitate the obtaining of financing at lower rates and strengthen the competitiveness of Italian actors in the market.

Similar consideration appear to apply in regard to the Rail Protocol, though it is difficult at present to gauge their potential extent. The private market is still much more limited, the role of institutions is prevailing and the financing of construction and operation of rail rolling stock equipment follows alternative routes. The introduction of a measure of market competition and the need for investments in this sector, however, point to a growing relevance of private or mixed financing and to a possible important role to be played by the Rail Protocol in this respect. In order to provide economic benefits the Rail Protocol should be implemented on a wider European scale. The recent approval of the Rail Protocol by the European Union opened the way for European States to ratify (or access to) the Protocol.

Finally, concerning the Space Protocol, facilitating the influx of private capitals in this rapidly growing sector would certainly be of great benefit to the Italian industry, that is currently one of the major actors in Europe in this area.

---

[57] From a public international law perspective, Italy is a party to both the 1933 Rome Convention on the precautionary arrest of aircrafts and the 1948 Geneva Convention on the recognition of rights in aircrafts. According to Arts. XXIV (1) and XXIII of the Aircraft Protocol, the Cape Town Convention prevails over both instruments. A derogation to Art. XXIV (1) would be possible by declaration of the State ratifying the Protocol, but does not appear to be advisable in the light of the limited international recognition of the Rome Convention and its obsolete regulation as regards modern developments of air services and the present needs of aircraft financing.

16.5.2   Compatibility of the Cape Town Convention Regime with the General Principles Underlying Italian Secured Transactions Law

In assessing the compatibility of the Cape Town Convention system with Italian law two relevant points should be highlighted from the start.

Firstly, Italian law is clearly obsolete in many respects, especially in the case of security devices on tangible goods. Internationally accepted provisions that deviate from current domestic regulation may turn out to be a welcome innovation and even an interesting model for a future organic reform of Italian general secured transactions law. This is especially true for those areas where no fundamental incompatibility exists, or where recent developments have already paved the way to a more modern approach. I am referring, in particular, to the introduction of a publicity system through registration to solve priority issues and of speedier and more efficient enforcement proceedings.

Other aspects of the uniform provisions, such as the impact on insolvency law, deserve a more careful consideration, in view of the potentially disruptive effect vis-à-vis policy choices made by the national legislator. In this respect, however, it is important to consider the scope of application of the Cape Town Convention. The Cape Town 'international interest' does not purport to displace already existing domestic devices, but only to introduce an autonomous instrument, limited to enumerated high value, uniquely identifiable collateral, that would be effective against third parties and in insolvency wherever the equipment be at the time of enforcement (within the territorial scope of application of the Convention). Thus, the central aim of the uniform regime is to efficiently solve certain (cross-border) issues that are currently not addressed, in relation to a specific type of mobile equipment. This element, in my view, should play a fundamental role when analyzing the acceptability of deviations from current domestic law provisions and may well lead us to consider them proportionate to the economic benefits linked to the participation in the Cape Town Convention system.

Turning to the specific issues that were touched upon in para. 4, the introduction of a system of publicity through a public registry is perfectly compatible with Italian law. It is indeed a time-honored solution to the problem of admitting non-possessory security rights, and not only for uniquely identifiable, high value mobile collateral such as aircrafts or ships, for which a title registry exists. Consensual 'liens' or charges provided by special legislation were and are characterized by registration, and even sales with retention of title are supposed to be registered (though only for the purpose of superseding the good-faith acquisition rule). The main difference with the Cape Town Convention lies in two interconnected features: the choice of a 'notice-filing' approach, and the exclusive purpose of the registry (i.e. solving the priority conflicts between the holder of an international interest and other creditors with proprietary rights on the same asset, subsequent buyers and the debtor's insolvency administrator). Both features, coupled with the development of a sophisticated software for electronic filing, provide a more efficient solution to priority issues than the current haphazard and diversified systems. The recently introduced non-possessory pledge for enterprises (see fn 15) was designed to enjoy the benefit of a more modern, dedicated and fully electronic registry. The extent to which other elements will be also introduced (e.g. preference for a notice-filing approach; limited role of the registrar etc.) will depend on the content of the forthcoming implementing ministerial regulations.

It should be noted that the Cape Town Convention opted for asset-based registries (separate registries for each type of collateral). Whilst an asset-based registry would not be ideal for a general non-possessory security device, the Cape Town choice is justified by the specific nature of the collateral and the high specialization of the financing and industry sectors involved (particularly so for aircrafts and satellites).

Another key set of provisions of the Cape Town Convention is devoted to enforcement remedies upon the debtor's default. It is a sensitive area in respect to many domestic laws,[58] as demonstrated by the fact that the uniform regime allows derogation through a variety of opt-out and opt-in State declarations. Party autonomy certainly plays a much more important role in the Cape Town system than in Italian law. On the other hand, two critical points should be highlighted. Enforcement proceedings for charge creditors are excessively cumbersome in Italy when the suppler provisions of the possessory pledge are not applicable, so that the current discipline cannot be easily defended and a reform would be welcome, independently of the conventional rules. Furthermore, recent developments in other commercial sectors, such as financial markets, have already challenged the traditional limitations affecting the validity of the collateral agreement and/or the formalities of the enforcement mechanisms. In particular, the implementation of the EU Financial Collateral Directive has forced Italian courts and scholars to cope with the new concept of commercial 'reasonability' in enforcement as a substitute for the above-mentioned limitations.[59]

The insolvency provisions of the Cape Town Convention represent a further area where a contradiction with national law may be found. Enforceability against the debtor's insolvency administrator is an essential element in any efficient secured transactions regime. As seen above, however, under the Protocols the holder of an international interest may prevail over the administrator not only in liquidation, but also in reorganization or 'rescue' proceedings, if 'Alternative A' in the insolvency provisions is chosen by the contracting State. Furthermore, national consensual and non-consensual liens would be postponed to the duly registered international interest, except when a State declared their status as preferred priorities under Art. 39 Conv. or when they were registered at an earlier time under Art. 40 Conv. This solu-

---

[58] Tucci, G, *The preliminary draft convention* (above, fn. 14) 392: 'The remedies provisions (…) and the realisation of the international interest via the procedural law of each State is naturally the part of the future Convention which could potentially create the most significant problems in so far as they will need to be applied in conjunction with the domestic law rules of each State'.

[59] See in particular Murino, F, *L'autotutela nell'escussione della garanzia finanziaria pignoratizia*, (Milano, Giuffrè, 2010), 83.

tion appears to be justified in restricted and highly specialized economic sectors such as the ones within the scope of application of the Cape Town Convention. For the Aircraft Protocol, there is the additional incentive of the compliance with the so-called 'Qualifying Declarations' of the OECD Aircraft Sector Understanding (see above, para. 4.4). It would be more difficult to accept such unfettered creditor's rights as a model on a wider scale.

Finally, treatment of (financial) leases under the Cape Town Convention should be briefly addressed. It is true that leases are not classified as security devices nor subject to any kind of publicity under current Italian law. The filing procedure under Cape Town, however, is simple and relatively inexpensive, so that it does not appear to constitute an excessive burden, especially when compared to the benefits of a full cross-border recognition of the lessee's rights. Furthermore, as seen above (para. 4.1) the Convention simply extends to title reservation devices the basic regime applicable to traditional security rights, with some exceptions. In particular, leases (and sales with retention of title) are subject to different rules of enforcement. The resulting regime for lessors is perfectly compatible with Italian law.

References

1. von Bar, C., and E. Clive (eds.). 2009. *Principles, definitions and model rules of European private law, Draft Common Frame of Reference (DCFR).* (Full ed., Sellier). vol. 6, 5389.
2. Beale, H., M. Bridge, L. Gullifer, and E. Lomnika. 2012. *The law of security and title-based financing,* 2nd ed. Oxford: OUP.
3. Bonell, M.J. (ed.). 1999. *A new approach in international commercial contracts. The UNIDROIT principles of international commercial contracts.* The Hague: Kluwer Law Int.
4. Bussani, M. 1998. Rapport italien, in *Les garanties de financement, Travaux de l'Association Henri Capitant.* vol. XLVII. Paris: LGDJ, 213.
5. Bussani, M. 2002. Le présent et l'avenir des sûretés réelles, in *Rapports nationaux italien/ Italian National Reports, XVI international congress of comparative law, Brisbane 2002.* Milano : Giuffrè. 245.
6. Chianale, A. 2010. L'ipoteca, Trattato di diritto civile diretto da R. Sacco. In *I diritti reali,* vol. 6, 2nd ed, 142. Torino: UTET.
7. Cuming, R.C.C. 1991. International regulation of aspects of security interests in mobile equipment. *Unif L Rev,* 75.
8. Deschamps, M. 2013. The perfection and priority rules of the Cape Town Convention and the Aircraft Protocol- A comparative law analysis. *Cape Town Convention Journal* 2: 51.
9. Drobnig U. 2010. Security Rights in Movables. In *Towards a European Civil Code,* 4th ed. Hartkamp A.S., Hesselink M.W. et al. eds.. Wolters Kluwer, Chapter 43, 1025.
10. Ferrarini, G. 1997. Changes to personal property security law in Italy: A comparative and functional approach. In *Making commercial law. Essays in honour of R.M. Goode,* ed. R. Cranston, 477. Oxford: OUP.
11. Fiorentini, F. 2014. Il pegno. In *Trattato dei diritti reali, vol. V, Diritti reali di garanzia,* ed. A. Gambaro and U. Morello, 1. Milano: Giuffrè.
12. Gabrielli, E. 1998. *Delle garanzie rotative.* Napoli: Jovene.
13. Gabrielli, E. 2005. *I diritti reali,* vol. 5, *Il pegno.* In Trattato di diritto civile directed by R Sacco. Torino: UTET.

14. Goode, R. 1998. Transcending the boundaries of earth and space: The preliminary draft Unidroit Convention on international interests in mobile equipment. *Uniform Law Review* 3: 52.
15. Goode, R. 2014. *Convention on International interests in mobile equipment and Luxembourg Protocol thereto on matters specific to railway rolling stock. Official commentary*, 2nd ed. Rome: Unidroit.
16. Goode, R. 2013. *Convention on international interests in mobile equipment and protocol thereto on matters specific to aircraft equipment, official commentary*, 3rd ed. Rome: Unidroit.
17. Goode, R., H. Kronke, E. McKendrick, and J. Wool. 2012. *Transnational commercial law. International instruments and commentary*, 2nd ed. Oxford: OUP.
18. Graziadei, M., and Alb. Candian. 2009. Italian report. In *Security rights in movable property in European private law*, ed. Kieninger, E-M. Cambridge: CUP.
19. Guglielmucci, G. 2012. *Diritto fallimentare*, 5th ed. Torino: Giappichelli.
20. Kieninger, E.-M. (ed.). 2009. *Security rights in movable property in European private law*. Cambridge: CUP.
21. Kronke, H. 2001. Financial leasing and its unification by Unidroit. *Uniform Law Review*: 23.
22. Lefebvre D'Ovidio, A., G. Pescatore, and L. Tullio. 2013. *Manuale di diritto della navigazione*, 13th ed. Milano: Giuffrè.
23. Mastropaolo, F., P. De Vecchis, and E.M. Mastropaolo in Mastropaolo, F (ed.). 2006. *I contratti di garanzia*, 1, Trattato dei contratti directed by P Rescigno and E Gabrielli, 1192. Torino: UTET.
24. Murino, F. 2010. *L'autotutela nell'escussione della garanzia finanziaria pignoratizia*, 83. Milano: Giuffrè.
25. Righetti, G. 1992. *Ipoteca navale ed aeronautica*. In Digesto IV, Discipline privatistiche, sez. comm., vol. VII, 535. Torino: UTET.
26. Tucci, G. 1991. *Garanzia*. In Digesto IV, Discipline privatistiche, sez.civ., vol. VII, 579. Torino: Utet.
27. Tucci, G. 1999. Towards a transnational commercial law for secured transactions: The preliminary draft UNIDROIT Convention and Italian law. *Uniform Law Review* 4: 371.
28. Veneziano, A. 2007. Italy. In *Cross-border security over tangibles*, ed. H.C. Sigman and E.-M. Kieninger, 159. München: Sellier.
29. Wool, J. 2012. Treaty design, implementation, and compliance benchmarking economic benefit - A framework as applied to the Cape Town convention. *Uniform Law Review* 4, 633.

Anna Veneziano is Professor of Comparative Law at the University of Teramo, Italy. She is currently serving as Deputy Secretary-General of the Institute for the Unification of Private Law Unidroit. She is also affiliated to the University of Amsterdam (UvA), The Netherlands, as Professor of European Property Law.

A graduate with honours of the University of Rome I La Sapienza, she was awarded a Fulbright scholarship and received her LL.M. from the Yale Law School in 1993 and obtained a PhD degree in Comparative Law from the University of Florence (Italy) in 1996.

Among her policy making activities, before joining Unidroit she was a member of the Italian delegation with respect to the Cape Town Convention on International Interests on Mobile Equipment and the Protocol thereto relating to Aircraft (2001) as well as the Protocol thereto relating to Space Assets (2012). She was also a member of the Study Group on a European Civil Code and of the Compilation and Redaction Group on a Draft Common Frame of Reference on European Private Law (DCFR), as well as of the restricted Expert Group set up by the European Commission for the redaction of a common European law on sales (CESL).

Her main work, research and publication areas are on secured transactions and international insolvency as well as international, comparative and European contracts and sales law.

Chapter 17
The Security Interest in Transport Vehicles in Japan

Haruna Fujisawa

17.1 Introduction

As the General Report chapter of this book describes, the Cape Town Convention has been a great success. Unfortunately, Japan is not a party to this Convention. This Chapter aims to explain the Japanese law concerning security interests in transport vehicles.

This Chapter proceeds in four parts: first, the creation of a security interest will be discussed; second, registration will be analyzed; third, enforcement topics will be reviewed; and fourth, insolvency proceedings will be examined.

17.2 Creation of a Security Interest

17.2.1 Security Interests Provided by the Civil Code

In Japan, aircraft, railway rolling stock, and space assets are treated as movables.[1] Generally, security interests in movables are governed by the Japanese Civil Code (*Mimpô*). However, the Civil Code is flawed in that the security interests in movables are merely a pledge. In other words, it does not provide a method to create a security interest in a movable without depossession (a non-possessory security interest in a movable). Moreover, there is a principle of *numerus clausus* in the

---

[1] Article 86(2) of Civil Code (*Mimpô*) provides, "Any Thing which is not real estate is regarded as movable."

H. Fujisawa (✉)
College of Law and Politics, Rikkyo University, Tokyo, Japan
e-mail: fujisawa@rikkyo.ac.jp

© Springer International Publishing AG 2017   273
S. Kozuka (ed.), *Implementing the Cape Town Convention and the Domestic Laws on Secured Transactions*, Ius Comparatum - Global Studies in Comparative Law 22, DOI 10.1007/978-3-319-46470-1_17

Civil Code.[2] Therefore, security interests in movables without depossession do not exist in the Japanese law.

17.2.2 Title-Based Security

Because of the strong need to create security interests in movables without depossession, title-based securities are often used in business practices. As such, transfer of ownership, retention of title, or lease are mainly utilized.

The Supreme Court has recognized the rights of title-based security holders. It is important to note that these rights are not considered equivalent to ownership. As discussed below, the Supreme Court often treats them like secured creditors who holds a security interest.

17.2.3 Aircraft Mortgages

The Aircraft Mortgage Act (*Kôkûki Teitô Hô*) specially provides for mortgages of aircraft. According to this Act, a creditor can acquire a security interest in an aircraft without possession, similar to a real estate mortgage. It is possible to perfect the mortgage by registration in the registry established by the Aviation Act (*Kôkû Hô*).

However, a lease plays an important role in the practice of aircraft finance.

17.2.4 Railway Mortgages

The Railway Mortgage Act (*Tetsudô Teitô Hô*) makes it possible to create a mortgage covering railway rolling stocks. According to this Act, a mortgage can be created on a railway estate, which comprises real estate connected with railway (e.g., railway premises and station buildings), and movables used for railway (e.g., rolling stocks and machines for maintenance).

Historically, a car trust was used as a means of finance of rolling stock. Today, a lease and lease-back are utilized.

---

[2] Article 175 of Civil Code (*Mimpô*) provides, "No real rights can be established other than those prescribed by laws including this Code."

17.3   Registration

17.3.1   Perfection of Title-Based Security

A transfer of ownership takes effect solely by the manifestation of intent of the relevant parties.[3] To assert it against a third party, however, perfection is necessary. To perfect a transfer of ownership of a movable, the Civil Code requires delivery of the movable.[4]

In this context, "delivery" does not always mean that the location of the movable must change. The Civil Code permits constructive transfers.[5] Therefore, a transfer of ownership can be perfected without a change in the appearance.

Arguably, this provision benefits creditors. Nevertheless, the law must address immediate acquisition by a third party. Therefore, the Civil Code states that if a third party peacefully and openly commences the possession of the collateral, by a transactional act, the third party will acquire ownership immediately if the proceedings are commenced in good faith and the third party is faultless.[6]

17.3.2   Registration for Assignment of Movables

To avoid immediate acquisitions by third parties, creditors may utilize the provisions regarding registration for assignment of movables. The Act on Special Provisions, etc. of the Civil Code Concerning the Perfection Requirements for the Assignment of Movables and Claims (*Dôsan Saiken Jôto Tokurei Hô*), states that when a registration of assignment is made in a movables assignment registration file, the movables are deemed to have been delivered as set forth in Article 178 of the Civil Code.[7]

A registration of assignment of movables follows an application of the assignor and assignee once the following matters in a movables assignment registration file are recorded: (i) the name and address of the assignor (in the case of a juridical person, its trade name or other name and its main office or principal office); (ii) the name and address of the assignee (in the case of a juridical person, its trade name or

---

[3] Article 176 of Civil Code (*Mimpô*) provides, "The creation and transfer of real rights shall take effect solely by the manifestations of intention of the relevant parties."

[4] Article 178 of Civil Code (*Mimpô*) provides, "The transfers of real rights concerning movables may not be asserted against a third party, unless the movables are delivered."

[5] Article 183 of Civil Code (*Mimpô*) provides, "If an agent manifests an intention that the thing possessed by it shall thenceforward be possessed on behalf of its principal, the principal shall thereby acquire possessory rights." In this context, "agent" means transferor-debtor, and "principal" means transferee-creditor.

[6] Article 192 of Civil Code (*Mimpô*)

[7] Article 3(1) of Act on Special Provisions, etc. of the Civil Code Concerning the Perfection Requirements for the Assignment of Movables and Claims (*Dôsan Saiken Jôto Tokurei Hô*).

other name and its main office or principal office); (iii) if the main office or principal office of the assignor or the assignee is located in a foreign country, its business office or other office located in Japan; (iv) the cause of registration regarding the registration of assignment of movables and the date thereof; (v) any matters necessary for identifying the assigned movables, which are specified by Ordinance of the Ministry of Justice; (vi) the duration of the registration of assignment of movables; (vii) the registration number; and (viii) the date of registration.[8]

The registration does not certify the existence of the movables or the assignor's ownership; however, it does provide notice of the assignment of the movables.

In contrast to the International Registry System, this registration is searched by the name of assignor.

17.3.3 Retention of Title and Lease

In the case of retention of title or lease, because there is no transfer of ownership, sellers or lessors are not required to perfect their rights for asserting them against a third party. Furthermore, they cannot utilize the provisions regarding registration of assignment of movables because there is no assignment.

However, a third party may acquire the ownership by immediate acquisition. Therefore, sellers and lessors have been known to put nameplates on the collaterals to provide notice of their rights to a third party.

17.4 Enforcement

17.4.1 Enforcement of Title-Based Security

Title-based security holders can repossess collaterals if debtors default. Furthermore, according to the security agreements, they may sell or evaluate the collateral and apply it to their debt.

In contrast, the Civil Code states that security holders may not repossess the collateral; however, they may exercise their security interest only through the court proceedings provided by the Civil Execution Act (*Minji Sikkô Hô*).

---

[8] Article 7(2) of the Act on Special Provisions, etc. of the Civil Code Concerning the Perfection Requirements for the Assignment of Movables and Claims (*Dôsan Saiken Jôto Tokurei Hô*).

17.4.2   Liquidation Duty

In Japanese law, however, title-based security holders are at a disadvantage compared with the rights provided to secured creditors in the Cape Town Convention. The Supreme Court restricts the rights of title-based security holders in two ways.

First, a liquidation duty is imposed on a title-based security holder. If the value of collateral is larger than the amount of the balance due, then the security holder must pay the surplus to the debtor.[9]

In practice, there are two methods of liquidation. First, there is an "acquisition-of-ownership liquidation," where title-based security holders may acquire complete ownership and appraise the collateral. If the value of collateral is larger than the balance due, the security holder must pay the surplus to the debtor. If the price of collateral is smaller than the amount of the balance due, then the security holder must notify the debtor that there is no surplus.

Second, the "sale liquidation" method allows a title-based security holder to sell the collateral and acquire the proceeds. If the price of collateral is larger than the amount of the balance due, the security holder must pay the surplus to the debtor. If the price of collateral is smaller than the amount of the balance due, the security holder must notify the debtor that there is no surplus.

Title-based security holders may choose the more convenient method.

17.4.3   Debtor's Right to Recover the Collateral

Second, debtors have an opportunity to recover ownership of the collateral after a default.[10] The debtor may pay the balance due and acquire complete ownership of the collateral until either of the following events occurs: first, in the cases utilizing the acquisition-of-ownership liquidation method, until the title-based security holder pays the surplus or provides notice that there is no surplus; and, second, in the cases of sale liquidation, until the title-based security holder sells the collateral to a third party.[11]

Clauses that attempt to contractually grant a creditor the right to acquire the collateral immediately in the event of a default are considered to be invalid.

---

[9] Supreme Court, March 25, 1971, Minshu Vol.25, No.2, p.208.

[10] Supreme Court, January 22, 1982, Minshu Vol.36, No.1, p.92.

[11] Supreme Court, February 12, 1987, Minshu Vol.41, No.1, p.67.

17.5   Insolvency Proceedings

17.5.1   Three Types of Insolvency Proceedings

In Japan, there are three main types of insolvency proceedings: bankruptcy proceedings, civil rehabilitation proceedings, and corporate reorganization proceedings.

Bankruptcy proceedings are liquidation proceedings; however, civil rehabilitation and corporate reorganization proceedings are reorganization proceedings.

Civil rehabilitation proceedings are basically debtor-in-possession procedure, and are appropriate for reorganizations of relatively small companies and individuals. Characteristically, civil rehabilitation proceedings allow secured creditors to exercise their security interest outside of the proceedings. In contrast, corporate reorganization proceedings involve large companies.

17.5.2   Treatment of Security Interests in Insolvency Proceedings

In bankruptcy proceedings and civil rehabilitation proceedings, secured creditors are thought to have "the right of separate satisfaction."[12] The security interests are exercised outside of the proceedings. In contrast, in corporate reorganization proceedings, secured creditors are thought to have "secured reorganization claim."[13] The secured creditors are prohibited from exercising their security interests and are repaid through the proceedings.

Property possessed but not owned by the debtor is not affected by the commencement of insolvency proceedings. That property owner may segregate their property from the estate.[14]

Although title-based security holders nominally have ownership, they actually are secured creditors. Therefore, the Supreme Court has found that they have "the rights of separate satisfaction" or "secured reorganization claims" in insolvency proceedings.[15]

---

[12] Article 2 (9) of Bankruptcy Act (*Hasan Hô*) states, "The term "right of separate satisfaction" as used in this Act means a right that a person who holds a special statutory lien, pledge, or mortgage against property that belongs to the bankruptcy estate may exercise at the time of commencement of bankruptcy proceedings pursuant to the provision of Article 65(1) against the property that is the subject matter of these rights."

Article 65(1) of Bankruptcy Act (*Hasan Hô*) states, "The right of separate satisfaction may be exercised without going through bankruptcy proceedings."

[13] Article 2(10) of Corporate Reorganization Act (*Kaisha Kôsei Hô*).

[14] Article 62 of Bankruptcy Act (*Hasan Hô*), Article 52(1) of Civil Rehabilitation Act (*Minji Saisei Hô*), Article 64(1) of Corporate Reorganization Act (*Kaisha Kôsei Hô*).

[15] Supreme Court, April 28, 1966, Minshu Vol.20, No.4, p.900.

In stark contrast to the rules of Cape Town Convention, in the Japanese law, even title-based security holders are restricted in exercising their security interests through the insolvency proceedings.

17.5.3 Permission for Extinguishment of Security Interests

In insolvency proceedings, the most important restriction imposed on security interests is the permission for extinguishment.

In bankruptcy proceedings, if it is in the common interests of bankruptcy creditors to extinguish the security interests and sell the collateral, the bankruptcy trustee may file a petition with the court seeking permission for extinguishment of security interests. If successful, the security interests will be extinguished once a sum is received by the court.[16]

In civil rehabilitation proceedings, if the collateral is indispensable to the continuation of the rehabilitation debtor's business, the rehabilitation debtor or trustee may file a petition with the court seeking that the extinguishment of security interests be terminated by paying the amount of money equivalent to the value of the collateral.[17]

In corporate reorganization proceedings, upon the petition of a trustee, if the court finds that it is necessary for the reorganization, it may order that all security interests that exist on the collateral be extinguished by paying to the court the amount equivalent to the value.[18]

Title-based security holders as well as secured creditors are subject to extinguishments of their interests.

17.5.4 Stay of Exercise

In corporate reorganization proceedings, once an order of commencement of proceedings is made, commencements of exercise of security interests are not allowed; proceedings for exercise that have been initiated are stayed.[19]

In civil rehabilitation proceedings, secured creditors are generally allowed to exercise their security interest; however, if it conforms to the common interest of rehabilitation creditors and is not likely to cause undue damage to the secured creditor, the court may order the stay of exercise of the security interest.

These rules apply to title-based security holders as well as secured creditors.

---

[16] Article 186(1) of Bankruptcy Act (*Hasan Hô*).

[17] Article 148(1) of Civil Rehabilitation Act (*Minji Saisei Hô*).

[18] Article 104(1) of Corporate Reorganization Act (*Kaisha Kôsei Hô*).

[19] Article 50(1) of Corporate Reorganization Act (*Kaisha Kôsei Hô*).

Haruna Fujisawa (Ph.D in Law) is a Professor at the College of Law and Politics of Rikkyo University, Japan. She teaches courses on the Civil Code. Her main research subject is secured transactions law.

Chapter 18
The Cape Town Convention and Polish Law on Security Interests

Maria Dragun-Gertner, Zuzanna Pepłowska-Dąbrowska, and Jacek Krzemiński

18.1 Registration System

Polish civil law provides a creditor with different methods of securing his interest, which can be divided into two categories: personal and real security rights. The former entails full of surety for the debtor's obligations with all his assets, while the latter liability solely from certain asset, irrespective of its ownership. Among personal securities there are for example: suretyship, bank guarantee, blank bill of exchange, whereas among proprietary securities for example: a hypothecation, pledge (including the registered pledge), right of retention, transfer of ownership for security purposes.

From the abovementioned forms of securities the registered pledge is mostly similar to the system created under the Cape Town Convention. As all pledges, the registered pledge is a limited proprietary right having *erga omnes* character. It is an accessory right that follows the right which it secures. A creditor whose rights are secured by the registered pledge may be satisfied from a movable object irrespective of its ownership. The registered pledge allows the creditor (pledgee) to secure his interest in a movable object which remains in hands of a pledgor. Transfer of possession is not required, instead such pledge is evidenced in a special registry which is run by the district courts (commercial courts). In particular, a court in which circuit pledgor's domicile or his place of business is situated is competent to register the pledge. Registration has a constitutive effect what means that the registered pledge is created upon registration. The registry has an open character and everybody who wishes to do so may review the registry as well as require certified excerpts from it.

M. Dragun-Gertner (✉) • Z. Pepłowska-Dąbrowska • J. Krzemiński
Nicolaus Copernicus University in Toruń, Toruń, Poland
e-mail: mgertner@law.uni.torun.pl; zpeplow@law.umk.pl

© Springer International Publishing AG 2017   281
S. Kozuka (ed.), *Implementing the Cape Town Convention and the Domestic Laws on Secured Transactions*, Ius Comparatum - Global Studies in Comparative Law 22, DOI 10.1007/978-3-319-46470-1_18

18.1.1 Priority Among Creditors

In relation to the issue of priority generally Polish law relies on a Latin rule of *prior tempore, potior iure*. Accordingly, who files for the registration earlier entertains priority. Precisely, the day of filling an application for registration at the court decides upon the priority among the registered interests. When two applications are filled at a court at the same day it is assumed they were filed simultaneously (art. 16 of the Act on Registered Pledge and the Registry of Pledges,[1] hereinafter 'the Registered Pledge Act'). Moreover, the creditor secured by the registered pledge entertains priority before any creditors with personal security, with exception of those enumerated in special provisions (among them f. ex. the enforcement costs or maintenance charges). Knowledge of any previous secured creditors does not influence the creditor's priority. Thus, Polish law is not different from the Convention's solution in that respect. The same principle of priority concerns also continental hypothecation since its priority is defined by the day of filling application for registration (art. 12 and 29 of the Real-State Register and Hypothecation Act[2]). Additionally, all limited proprietary rights are governed by the above priority rule. Thus, a limited proprietary right which has been established earlier entertains priority (art. 249 of the Polish Civil Code[3]). An exception is made to a regular pledge (a proprietary security, which allows a creditor – pledgee to secure his interest in a movable object which possession is transferred to him), which has priority over any other limited proprietary right, even if the latter was established earlier, unless the pledgee has acted in bad faith (art. 310 of the Polish Civil Code).

18.1.2 Forms of Security Interests in Transport Vehicles

The Registered Pledge Act does not limit the objects of security interests, except ships entered in the register of ships and ships in construction which may be the object of mortgage or continental hypothecation. Thus, almost all movable objects may be subjected to the registered pledge, including the aircrafts, railway rolling stocks and space assets. In fact the Registered Pledge Act includes a specific provision relating to the aircrafts, according to which in cases of registering a pledge in the civil aircraft a court of registration files a copy of a decision on registration including its number to an authority responsible for civil aircrafts registration in order to reveal that pledge in the registry of civil aircrafts (in art 41a of the Registered Pledge Act). For a period of time there has been a controversy over the exact moment of creation of such registered pledge on an aircraft due to an inconsistency between

---

[1] J. of L. 2016, item 297.

[2] J. of L. 2013, item 707.

[3] J. of L. 2016, item 380.

the Registered Pledge Act and the Aviation Law Act.[4] That inconsistency was removed by the amendment of the latter act. It is now unquestionable that the registered pledge on an aircraft is effective from the time of its registration in the registry of pledges, which is followed by its disclosure in the civil aircraft register [1].

There is no registration system, nor special law concerning interests in the aircrafts, railway rolling stocks or space assets. They cannot be subjected to hypothecation, which is a limited proprietary right relating solely to an immovable object, with the exception of vessels entered in register of ships. According to art. 76 and 82 of the Maritime Code[5] vessels and vessels under construction can be subjected to the maritime hypothecation which is a lien governed by the provisions of civil law concerning hypothecation or according to the contract for instituting a maritime hypothecation may be a kind of mortgage (art. 84 to art. 88 of the Maritime Code).

18.1.3   Documentary Type System of Registration

The Polish system of pledges' registration is of a documentary type, not the notice filing system. It is a system of registration against an asset. Generally entry into the pledge registry is made upon an application by pledgor or pledgee. Such application must be accompanied with a document establishing validity of titles. Most commonly a contract on establishing pledge will be provided; however other types of documents are allowed as for example a contract of acquiring shares in a movable subjected to the registered pledge (art. 39 of the Registered Pledge Act). Only in rare occasions courts will proceed without an application. Such a possibility is envisaged in art. 18a of the Registered Pledge Act according to which a court may erase an entry after the lapse of 20 years from the moment of the entry, unless the parties have agreed to maintain registration for longer period (under the condition it is less than 10 years). To facilitate the availability of information there has been an electronic system established which gathers information from all the courts running the registry (art. 42 of the Registered Pledge Act).

The requirement of providing the document proving the validity of titles flows from the fact that the registration affects third persons. It is stated that from the day of registration nobody can plead ignorance of the data provided in the registry. Accordingly, a presumption of general knowledge of the registered data is introduced. Such a presumption may be overturned if a third party proves that regardless of due diligence he could not have known about it. Moreover, Polish law introduces a presumption of truthfulness of the registered information. Therefore, the pledgor or pledgee aiming at questioning the data revealed in the registry bears the onus of proof to the contrary (art. 38 of the Registered Pledge Act). With regard to a third party in good faith the pledgor or the pledgee may not assert that the data evidenced in the registry are false, unless the entry in the registry was not made in accordance

---

[4] J. of L. 2016 item 605.
[5] J. of L. 2016, item 66.

with the application and the pledgor or the pledgee immediately requested a motion to correct, complete, or erase the entry from the registry.

18.1.4   Interests Considered as Forms of Security

The registered pledge, as a limited proprietary right of an accessory character may secure an interest flowing from different contractual relationship. To the contrary, a leasing agreement and a title reservation agreement (conditional sale) may be regarded in Polish law as forms of securities in so far as they safeguard the performance in the contract of leasing or sale respectively. Furthermore, the pledge, including the registered pledge, is effective against third parties. Rights under the conditional sale contract, as well as leasing, have an relative character, i.e. they are effective solely between the parties to that contract. An exception is made for the conditional sale. According to art. 590 of the Polish Civil Code if the object is released to the buyer the reservation of ownership shall be confirmed in writing. It shall be effective with respect to the buyer's creditors if it has an authenticated (certified) date. Moreover, a general exception to the *inter partes* efficacy exists when conclusion of some contract makes impossible to fulfill partially or in whole a claim of a third party, that party may demand such contract being ineffective towards himself, provided that the parties knew of his claim or the contract was gratuitous (art. 59 of the Polish Civil Code). To conclude, one can argue that in an economic sense as far as it concerns movable objects all three institutions: pledge, conditional sale and leasing provide forms of security interest. Yet, such effect is served primarily by rights having the *erga omnes* effect as the pledge and the registered pledge. The agreements of leasing and conditional sale have the *inter partes* effect with possibility of extending it in cases of conditional sale if a reservation of title is carried out in a special form.

18.2   Enforcement of a Security Interest

Freedom of contract is the general rule governing contractual relations between the parties under Polish law (art 353[1] of the Polish Civil Code). Thus the parties are free to create terms of their agreement as long as they do not contravene statute or principles of community co-existence (art. 58 of the Polish Civil Code). However, by choosing to secure his interest in a form of a real right the creditor limits himself to the closed list of the real rights which includes the registered pledge. Furthermore, in cases of interests secured by the real rights generally no latitude is given for the parties as to the enforcement method. Yet in cases of the registered pledge parties have limited range of freedom as they may choose in a contract between defined remedies.

18.2.1   Meaning of Default

A question whether the parties are free to define the meaning of default triggering creditor's remedies has a twofold answer. A principle of parties' freedom applies in relation to the conditional sale agreement and the leasing agreement. In case of the leasing contract where parties did not contractually specify such default art. 709[11] of the Polish Civil Code allows a financing party to terminate the contract without notice if, despite financing party's written warning, the leasing party infringes his duties. To the contrary, in case of the registered pledge a contractual agreement does not influence the proprietary title in an object. According to art. 5 of the Registered Pledge Act only monetary claims may be secured by the registered pledge. Such pledge secures also the interest on a sum of money and incidental claims specified by the parties in the pledge agreement, as well as the cost of satisfying the creditor falling within the amount mentioned in the entry of the registered pledge. The security agreement which is the basis of the registered pledge should mention the secured claim and may determine only terms concerning relative (*inter partes*) relations between the parties.

18.2.2   Remedies Available

The creditor securing his interest in the form of the registered pledge has a limited set of remedies provided to him. Priority is given to the judicial enforcement proceedings (art. 21 of the Registered Pledge Act). However, the Act allows for other remedies in certain situations. First of them being transfer of ownership, which is possible in some situations. Particularly, if in a contract of the registered pledge a value of a movable has been strictly set the creditor may be remedied by vesting the ownership to him, under the condition that the contract provided for such remedy (art. 22 of the Registered Pledge Act). Moreover, a contract of registered pledge may call for sale by tender conducted by an official – a notary or bailiff. In both cases before commencement of the remedy proceedings the creditor is requested to inform about intended activity the pledgor who may choose to satisfy the pledgee or commence the court proceedings in order to establish that the secured interest does not exist or a claim is not mature (art. 25 of the Registered Pledge Act). There has been a debate whether lack of such information renders those remedies invalid or merely imposes a duty to compensate the debtor. Majority of scholars seem to favor the former solution [1]. Additionally, a contract of pledge may call for satisfaction from the profits of an enterprise in cases where pledge has been established on a group of things or rights constituting a single economic unit. Then an enterprise is taken under the administration of the creditor or other receiver. Alternatively, the creditor may ask for lease of such enterprise. Above options are available only when provided for in a contract of pledge. Moreover a contract of pledge may require pledgees consent for conclusion of a lease agreement (art. 27 of the Registered Pledge Act).

In relation to the balance payment generally all contracts (of leasing, conditional sale and registered pledge) allow for satisfaction up to the value of due interest. Nevertheless, parties are free to create their contractual relation as they wish, for example excluding the obligation of paying the balance by the creditor. Provisions on the registered pledge though are of a *ius cogens* character. According to art. 23 of the Registered Pledge Act, in cases of vesting an ownership to a pledgee when the value of a movable is higher than the amount of the secured obligation the creditor is obliged to pay the balance to the pledgor. He is not required to distribute the surplus among holders of subsequently ranking interests which have been registered. In the case of the leasing agreement when the financing party terminates the contract of leasing due to the circumstances for which the user is liable, the financing party may demand that the user forthwith pay him all the instalments stipulated in the contract and not having been paid yet, reduced by the benefits the financing party obtained as a result of the payment of the instalments before their due date and the dissolution of the contract of leasing (art. 709[15] of the Civil Code).

18.3   Treatment of a Security Interests Under the Insolvency Procedure

Polish insolvency procedure is mainly regulated by the Act on Bankruptcy from 2003,[6] which was substantially amended by a new restructuring law of 15 May 2015.[7] According to art. 10 of the Act on Bankruptcy if the debtor became insolvent, the court declares bankruptcy including liquidation of the debtor's assets. Earlier, that is before the aforementioned reform, the court could declare also bankruptcy of the debtor with an option of an arrangement with creditors if there was substantial evidence that the creditor's claims would be satisfied to a greater extent than would be in the case of liquidation of the debtor's assets. After the reform this type of insolvency procedure was replaced by four new procedures including: (1) arrangement approval proceedings, (2) accelerated arrangement proceedings, (3) arrangement proceedings and (4) sanation proceedings. Nevertheless, since majority of cases concerns the liquidation of the debtor's enterprise, all further considerations applies to this type of insolvency procedure.

---

[6] J. of L. 2015, item 233.

[7] J. of L. 2016, item 1574.

18.3.1 Effectiveness of the Security Interests in the Insolvency Proceedings

Polish insolvency law recognizes similar rule of effectiveness of the security interests as the Convention which means that the security interests are effective even after an insolvency procedure is commenced with the debtor. Noteworthy, this rule is not affected in any way by any provision of Council Regulation (EC) No 1346/2000 of 29 May 2000 on insolvency proceedings.[8] Although, there are several types of the security interests in Polish civil law, the widest range of remedies for the secured creditor provides the security in form of the registered pledge.

As of the day of the court's ruling declaring bankruptcy, the secured assets of the debtor are part of the bankrupt estate which is used to satisfy the claims of the bankrupt entity's creditors. The composition of the bankruptcy estate is determined by the bankruptcy trustee in the way of making a list of inventory and list of dues (art. 69 of the Act on Bankruptcy). It must be noted that the bankruptcy trustee is appointed by the court in its ruling declaring bankruptcy and his role is to manage the bankruptcy entity's assets as of the day of bankruptcy declaration the bankruptcy entity loses its right to use and maintain its assets (art. 75 of the Act on Bankruptcy). The bankruptcy trustee also values the bankruptcy estate and prepares a liquidation schedule.

While declaring bankruptcy, the court summons the bankrupt entity's creditors to notify, in specified period of time, no later than 30 days, their receivables in order to drawn up a list of receivables. It is the bankruptcy trustee duty to drawn up a list of receivables. In principle, the notification procedure is necessary for all of the creditors. However, the bankruptcy trustee is obliged to place secured receivables on the list of receivables ex officio. If the bankruptcy trustee fails to fulfill this obligation, the secured receivables shall be placed on the list of receivables by a judge that supervises insolvency procedure called the Judge – Commissioner. Notification should be done in writing in two identical copies.

As it was mentioned above, Polish insolvency law provides for similar remedies upon the declaration of bankruptcy of the debtor as the Cape Town Convention. It is especially true in relation to security interest in the form of the registered pledge. Accordingly, the creditor has the right to take over ownership of or sell the secured asset (art. 327 of the Act on Bankruptcy). However, the secured creditor (pledgee) can take over possession or sell the object only if the security agreement provides such remedies for the creditor. If the secured asset is in possession of the bankruptcy trustee and the secured creditor has the right to take over the ownership of an asset, the Judge – Commissioner marks the time in which the secured creditor can make use of his right, not shorter than 1 month. If the secured creditor does not use his remedy in fixed time, the asset will be sold by the bankruptcy trustee in accordance with the rules of the Act on Bankruptcy. If the security agreement provides only for

---

[8] O.J. L. 160/1, 30.06.2000.

the sale of the asset and the asset is in the possession of the bankruptcy trustee, the sale is conducted by the bankruptcy trustee. It must be underlined that if the value of the asset exceeds the value of the creditor's receivables, then the creditor is obliged to pay the bankruptcy trustee the surplus. In some circumstances the secured creditor's right to take over ownership is limited, even if the security agreement provides for such remedy. It is the case when the secured asset is part of the bankrupt entity's enterprise and it is more favorable to sell the bankrupt entity's enterprise with this asset than to sell it separately. The value of the secured asset is then separated from the general purchase price of the bankrupt entity's enterprise and is distributed to the secured creditor.

The rule governing the allocation of the sums obtained from the sale of the secured asset under the provisions of the Act on Bankruptcy is that those sums are distributed first of all to the secured creditors (art. 336 of the Act on Bankruptcy). The remaining sums are part of the bankruptcy estate and are paid to other creditors by the bankruptcy trustee. Therefore, the bankruptcy trustee is obliged to drawn up a separate schedule of distribution of the sums obtained from sale of the secured asset (art. 348 of the Act on Bankruptcy). There is a possibility to challenge this schedule by referring it to the Judge – Commissioner.

18.3.2 Effectiveness of the Security Agreement in the Insolvency Proceedings

It is the general rule of Polish insolvency law that all agreements to which the bankruptcy entity is a party are valid and effective even after the commencement of the insolvency procedure. Therefore no obligation of the debtor may be modified without the consent of the creditor. This principle is however limited by the regulation of art. 127 (1) of the Act on Bankruptcy which provides for ineffectiveness in regard to the bankruptcy estate of any legal acts that were undertaken by the bankruptcy entity 1 year before filling the bankruptcy request to the court, if those act were gratuitous or against payment, yet value of the obligation of the bankruptcy entity widely exceeds the value of benefits.

Polish insolvency law provides similar limitation as to the effectiveness of the security agreement. According to art. 127 (3) of the Act on Bankruptcy, the security agreement to which the bankruptcy entity is a party is ineffective in regard to the bankruptcy estate if it was signed 6 months before filling the bankruptcy request to the court. The creditor who holds the security interest may however demand the court to acknowledge the validity of the security agreement if he proves that on the day of signing the agreement, he was not aware of the grounds to declare bankruptcy.

Furthermore, the Judge – Commissioner may, on the request of the bankruptcy trustee, make the security interest on the assets of the bankruptcy entity ineffective, if the bankruptcy entity is not personally liable, the security interest was given

1 year before filling the bankruptcy request and the bankruptcy entity did not receive any benefits from it or it received grossly inadequate benefits (art. 130 (1) and art. 130 (2) of the Act on Bankruptcy). The Judge – Commissioner will make the security agreement ineffective irrespectively to the value of received benefit if those agreements secure the obligations of spouse, some categories of relatives or in-laws, partners or related companies.

18.4   General Considerations

18.4.1   Requirement of Economic Analysis

It might be argued that the general requirement of pursuing an economic analysis of every legal regulation can be derived from the Preamble of the Polish Republic Constitution according to which public institutions ought to proceed effectively and reliably. Specific requirements as to the assessment of the economic effects flow from the rules on the legislative technique. Accordingly, a research as to social, economic, organizational, legal and financial effects should be pursue before commencing works over any act, including the law of secured transactions, or generally private law (§1 of the annex to the Decree on Rules of Legislative Technique).[9] Moreover, the Statute of the Sejm (lower house of the Polish Parliament) requires that each proposal of an act has to be accompanied by a justification including foreseeable social, legal, financial as well as economic consequences (art. 34 of the Polish Republic Sejm Statute).[10] For the proposals coming from the Polish Government an in-depth study of the economic effects is necessary. According to the Statute on the Council of Ministers' Work an Impact Assessment of Legislation is an integral part of a justification preceding a proposal.[11] The Legislation Impact Assessment shall include primarily an analysis of the act's influence on: entities affected by the proposed act, the State's budget as well as the budgets of the local governments' units, labor market, competitiveness of the economy, including the functioning of enterprises (§ 28 of the Statute on Council of Ministers' Work). Indispensable elements of the impact assessment are results of consultations with the interested partners. Since majority of act proposals is of the governmental origin, they are accompanied by the Impact Assessment of an empirical nature. Formal requirement of the Legislative Impact Assessment does not concern, however, proposals coming outside of the government, from the Sejm deputies, the President of the Republic, the Senat or introduced by way of popular initiative.

---

[9] J. of L. 2006, item 283.

[10] M. P. 2012, item 32.

[11] M. P. 2013, item 979.

18.4.2   Advantages of Effective Security System

The idea which assumes that stronger security interest is beneficial for both, a creditor and a debtor is generally supported in the Polish jurisdiction. The more confident is the creditor, the more eager is he to give a loan/credit. Effective security system influences both, the availability and costs of borrowing. An example of provisions aiming at strengthening the position of a creditor are those providing the creditor secured by a registered pledge with the alternative remedies as taking ownership of an object or its sale by tender. Such a solution is also adopted in the case of the mortgage instituted on the registered vessels.

Reference

1. Gołaczyński, J., and M. Leśniak. 2009. *Zastaw rejestrowy i rejestr zastawów. Komentarz.* Warszawa: C.H. Beck.

Maria Dragun-Gertner is Professor of Law, Head of Department of Civil Law and International Commercial Law at the Faculty of Law and Administration Nicolaus Copernicus University in Torun, Poland. She is the Chair of the Polish Codification Committee for Maritime Law, as well as the President of the Polish Maritime Law Association and former Director of the Department of Maritime Administration in the Ministry of Transport and Maritime Economy (1991–1998).

Zuzanna Pepłowska-Dąbrowska PhD is an assistant professor at the Nicolaus Copernicus University in Toruń, Poland and a Fulbright scholarship holder at Tulane Law School in 2008–2009. She is a member of the Polish Codification Committee for Maritime Law and the Polish Maritime Law Association.

Jacek Krzemiński is a PhD candidate at the Nicolaus Copernicus University in Torun, Poland and attorney-at-law at local law firm "Minkiewicz Urzędowski Sobolewski Torba" also in Toruń. He specializes in international commercial arbitration and competition law.

Chapter 19
Security Interests in Transport Vehicles: The Cape Town Convention and Portuguese Law

Maria Helena Brito

19.1 Introduction

I. The main objective of the Convention on International Interests in Mobile Equipment, held at Cape Town on 16 November 2001, is the efficient financing of mobile equipment with high value.[1]

The Convention does not establish the specific rules to a particular kind of equipment and so it will be applied to each category of object referred to in Article 2 of the Convention through separate Protocols: airframes, aircraft engines and helicopters,[2] railway rolling stock[3] and space assets.[4]

The complete version of the Portuguese report presented for the XIXth International Congress of Comparative Law, on the subject "Security interests in transport vehicles – The Cape Town Convention and its implementation in national law", is available on the website of the Cape Town Academic Project (http://www.ctcap.org). This paper contains a reduced text and, for that reason, only includes references to Portuguese literature.

[1] M.H. Brito, "A Convenção da Cidade do Cabo relativa a garantias internacionais sobre equipamento móvel e o Protocolo Anexo sobre questões específicas relativas a equipamento aeronáutico", *Nos 20 anos do Código das Sociedades Comerciais*, Vol. III, Coimbra, 2007, p. 447 ff (p. 455); L.M. Leitão, "A Convenção do Cabo e o Protocolo sobre equipamento aeronáutico. Registo internacional de aeronaves", *Estudos de Direito Aéreo*, Coimbra, 2012, p. 617 ff (p. 618).

[2] Protocol to the Convention on International Interests in Mobile Equipment on Matters Specific to Aircraft Equipment (Cape Town, 16.11.2001).

[3] Protocol to the Convention on International Interests in Mobile Equipment on Matters Specific to Railway Rolling Stock (Luxembourg, 23.02.2007).

[4] Protocol to the Convention on International Interests in Mobile Equipment on Matters Specific to Space Assets (Berlin, 9.03.2012).

M.H. Brito (✉)
Faculty of Law, NOVA University of Lisbon, Lisboa, Portugal
e-mail: MariaHelenaBrito@fd.unl.pt

© Springer International Publishing AG 2017
S. Kozuka (ed.), *Implementing the Cape Town Convention and the Domestic Laws on Secured Transactions*, Ius Comparatum - Global Studies in Comparative Law 22, DOI 10.1007/978-3-319-46470-1_19

The Cape Town Convention intends to encourage and facilitate financing transactions regarding such mobile equipment, as well as to reduce the corresponding
costs by providing uniform rules of law applicable to international security interests
in certain categories of mobile equipment and associated rights.

The financing of aircraft equipment, railway rolling stock and space assets may
be the effect of different kinds of agreements: secured loan agreements, title reservation agreements or leasing agreements.

The efficiency and the success of these financing transactions depend on the
confidence of the creditor in the possibility of exercising his rights and remedies in
case of default of the debtor.

However, the criterion to determine the law applicable to the referred transactions is different from a system of conflict of laws to another. Furthermore, the
material law on security interests is one of the sectors where the disparity between
legal systems is more evident.

The traditional rule of conflict of laws means that international security interests
on mobile equipment should be governed by the law of the country where the mobile
equipment is located – the *lex rei sitae*.

But, in the case of aircraft equipment, railway rolling stock and space assets, the
equipment is permanently moving from one state to another, making the determination of the *lex rei sitae* difficult.[5] Additionally, there is the possibility of conflicting
regimes, through changes in time of the connecting factor ("*conflit mobile*").

Therefore, the conflict of laws method, based on the *lex rei sitae*, has been considered to be "manifestly inadequate" to determine the law applicable to financing
transactions concerning mobile equipment with high value.

Even if it were possible to attain an agreement about a uniform private international law – as, in a way, it was achieved by the Convention on the International
Recognition of Rights in Aircraft, signed at Geneva, on 19 June 1948[6] –, such a
solution, based on the application of a state law, would be questionable.

So the option for the uniformity fell upon the material law applicable to international security interests.

II. The fundamental aim of the Cape Town Convention is carried out through the
following features:

– the establishment of provisions about the creation and the effects of international
   security interests concerning mobile equipment with high value, in order to permit their recognition in all Contracting States;

---

[5] Some systems of Private International Law adopt a special connecting factor for certain categories of objects. This is the case of Portuguese law. Article 46(3) of the Civil Code (hereafter CC)
sets up that: "The creation and transfer of rights *in rem* pertaining to means of transport subject to
a matriculation are ruled by the law of the country where the matriculation has been effected". See
D. MOURA VICENTE, "O estatuto jurídico da aeronave", *Estudos de Direito Aéreo*, p. 571 ff (p. 583
f).

[6] The 1948 Geneva Convention on the International Recognition of Rights in Aircraft is in force in
Portugal since 12.03.1986.

- the creation of an electronic international registry system that ensures the publicity of international security interests concerning mobile equipment with high value as well as the priority of competing interests;
- the allocation of rights and remedies to the creditor in case of default of the debtor.

19.2   The International Interest

19.2.1   The International Interest Under the Cape Town Convention

I. The Convention rules the constitution and effects of an international interest in certain categories of mobile equipment and associated rights (Article 2(1)).

Paragraph 2 of Article 2 defines "international interest in mobile equipment", for the purposes of the Convention, as "an interest, constituted under Article 7, in a uniquely identifiable object of a category of such objects listed in paragraph 3 and designated in the Protocol:

(a) granted by the chargor under a security agreement;
(b) vested in a person who is the conditional seller under a title reservation agreement; or
(c) vested in a person who is the lessor under a leasing agreement".

Paragraph 4 of Article 2 clarifies that "the applicable law determines whether an interest to which paragraph 2 applies falls within sub-paragraph (a), (b) or (c) of that paragraph".

II. The Convention does not specify any condition to qualify an agreement or contract as a "security agreement", a "title reservation agreement" or a "leasing agreement". It is incumbent to the applicable law determined by the conflict of laws rules of the forum to answer the question if a "title reservation agreement"[7] or a "leasing agreement" must be considered an "international interest in mobile equipment", for the purposes of the Convention.

In principle, the Convention does not apply to security interests created by a unilateral act ("negócio jurídico unilateral"). However, through declaration of a Contracting State, the Convention may become applicable to certain categories of non-consensual rights or interests created in accordance to a national law (Articles 39 and 40 of the Convention).

In any case, these expressions – as also the expressions used in other provisions of the Convention – should be interpreted autonomously, beyond any national law. Regard is to be had to the purposes of the Convention as set forth in the preamble,

---

[7] About the law applicable to "title reservation agreement", L. LIMA PINHEIRO, *A venda com reserva da propriedade em direito internacional privado*, Lisboa, 1991, specially, p. 87 ff.

to its international character and to the need of promoting uniformity and predictability in its application.

The Convention does not include a contract of sale other than a title reservation agreement in its material scope; indeed, such an agreement does not create any special security that binds the debtor.

Nevertheless, Article 41 states that the Convention shall apply to the "sale" or "prospective sale" of an object as provided for in the Protocol with any modifications therein.[8]

19.2.2 Some Kinds of Interests Under Portuguese Law

I. The "international interest" may include the interest under a security agreement, the title reserved by the conditional seller under a title reservation agreement, the right of the lessor under a leasing agreement. Whether to treat all these interests as "security" or not is left to the applicable domestic law.

We will analyse some kinds of security interests according to Portuguese law:

- the most relevant "security agreements";
- the "title reservation agreement";
- the "financial leasing agreement";
- the "title transfer financial collateral arrangement" ("alienação fiduciária em garantia").

II. Among the security agreements ruled in Portuguese law, we must mention the mortgage ("hipoteca") and the pledge ("penhor").

In principle, mortgage concerns immovable property and pledge concerns movable property. However, mortgage also relates to some kinds of movable property subject to registration (Articles 686 to 689 CC). That is the case of motor vehicles,[9] aircrafts[10] and ships.[11]

Mortgage does not empower the creditor with the possession of the object and, as a rule, pledge is characterised by the transfer of the possession of the object to the creditor or to a third person (nevertheless there are many examples of pledge without the transfer of the possession of the object to the creditor or to a third person[12]).

---

[8] Article III of the Aircraft Equipment Protocol; Article IV of the Space Assets Protocol.

[9] Article 4 of Decreto-Lei 54/75, 12.02.1975.

[10] Articles 205 and 206 of Regulation on Air Navigation ("Regulamento de Navegação Aérea"), approved by Decreto 20.062, 25.10.1930.

[11] Articles 584 ff of Portuguese Commercial Code. About mortgage over ships, S. Aires, "Hipoteca sobre navios", *Estudos em Homenagem ao Prof. Doutor José Lebre de Freitas*, Vol. II, Coimbra, 2013, p. 447 ff.

[12] The most important is the pledge over tangible assets in favour of credit institutions (Decreto-Lei 29.833, 17.08.1939). For more examples and details, M.J. Almeida Costa, *Direito das Obrigações*,

Both mortgage and pledge give the creditor the right to be paid before any common creditor (Articles 686(1) and 666(1) CC). Mortgage must be registered by a public registry office ("Conservatória do Registo Predial", in what concerns immovable property). Besides, in Portuguese law, the registration of a mortgage has a constitutive nature: if the mortgage is not registered, it is not effective even between the parties.

III. A title reservation agreement (*pactum reservati dominii*) usually assumes the nature of a contractual clause, included in a sales contract or in another contract having as purpose the transfer of property over an object.

As an exception to immediate transfer of property by the contract, Article 409 CC states: (1) "in contracts having as purpose the transfer of property, the transferor may reserve the property over the object until the total or partial performance of the obligations of the other party or until the occurrence of another event"; (2) "if the contract concerns immovable property or movable property subject to registration, only the registered clause may have effect against third parties".

By means of title reservation agreement, the parties agree that the transfer of the property over the object is deferred to a moment subsequent to the conclusion of the contract. In general, the event that determines the transfer of the property is the full payment of the price by the purchaser: this is the typical modality of title reservation agreement. However, under the principle of party autonomy, the parties may establish that the transfer of the property depends upon any other event (for instance, a fixed future date).[13]

Publicity of title reservation agreement is only required in cases of immovable property or movable property subject to registration (Article 409(2) CC); in other cases publicity it not required and title reservation agreement may have effect against third parties.

The function of title reservation agreement does not consist in permitting the transferor to exercise the faculties as if he remains the owner of the object – because the object is delivered to the purchaser in order to empower the purchaser with those faculties (in short, with the use of the object). Differently, the function of this agreement consists in protecting the transferor from the consequences of non-performance of the contract by the purchaser, giving him a guarantee of payment.

Then, whatever may be the characterisation of the juridical position of the transferor and of the purchaser emerging from a title reservation agreement,[14] there is no

---

11th ed., Coimbra, 2008, p. 926.

[13] A. Cristas & M.F. Gouveia, "Transmissão da propriedade de coisas móveis e contrato de compra e venda. Estudo comparado dos Direitos Português, Espanhol e Inglês", *Transmissão da propriedade e contrato*, Coimbra, 2001, p. 15 ff (p. 56 ff).

[14] About that problem: G.F. Dias, "Reserva de propriedade", *Comemorações dos 35 Anos do Código Civil e dos 25 Anos da Reforma de 1977*, Vol. III, Coimbra, 2007, p. 417 ff (p. 425 ff); L. Carvalho Fernandes, "Notas breves sobre a cláusula de reserva da propriedade", *Estudos em Homenagem ao Professor Doutor Carlos Ferreira de Almeida*, Vol. II, Coimbra, 2011, p. 321 ff (p. 334 ff).

doubt that such an agreement may be considered as a security agreement in favour of the transferor.[15]

IV. The financial leasing agreement is a financial transaction under which one party (the lessor) grants the other party (the lessee), in return for the payment of rentals, the right to use a movable or immovable object. Such object must be acquired or constructed according to the specification of the lessee, who may purchase it, after the agreed period, for a price determined or determinable by application of the criteria set out therein.[16]

When the financial leasing agreement concerns immovable property or movable property subject to registration, it must be registered.[17]

Financial leasing is a complex transaction, involving several contracts: (i) a sales contract between the seller and the financial institution; (ii) a contract between the lessor and the lessee granting the lessee the use of the object in return for the payment of rentals; (iii) an option to a new sales contract between the lessor and the lessee.

The property right remains with the lessor and it will be transferred to the lessee only when the lessee exercises the option to buy the object, after payment of all the rentals and the agreed sum. Therefore, financial leasing agreement may be considered as a security agreement in favour of the lessor: (i) leasing is a financial transaction that expresses a loan; (ii) the creditor (the lessor) maintains the property right both in front of the debtor (the lessee) and in front of third parties, although the possession of the object remains with the lessee for the time of the financial transaction.[18]

This conclusion about the function of leasing agreement is more obvious in the case of "sale and lease-back", under which a party transfers the property right over an object (normally, an equipment or an immovable necessary to its activity) to the other party (a financial institution) and at the same time this party grants the first a sum of money and the use of the object, in return for the payment of rentals. It is essential in this kind of leasing agreement that the seller has the right to reacquire the object, in accordance with an option clause which establishes the transfer to the seller of the property right over the object when the agreed sum is totally paid.

---

[15] R.P. DUARTE, *Curso de direitos reais*, 3rd ed., Cascais, 2013, p. 305 ff; L.P. VASCONCELOS, *Direito das garantias*, Coimbra, 2010, p. 358 ff (p. 359, 363, 377 ff); L.L. PINHEIRO, *A cláusula de reserva de propriedade*, Coimbra, 1988, p. 109 ff; G.F. DIAS, "Reserva de propriedade", p. 436 ff. In the same sense, in recent decisions of Portuguese Courts: STJ, 07.07.2010; STJ, 09.10.2008; TRL, 28.02.2013; TRP, 29.04.2013; TRC, 19.12.2012; TRG, 21.05.2009; TRE, 07.10.2009.

[16] Article 1(1) of Decreto-Lei 149/95, 24.06.1995. See also Article 1 of the UNIDROIT Convention on International Financial Leasing.

[17] Article 3(5) of Decreto-Lei 149/95.

[18] R.P. DUARTE, "A locação financeira (Estudo jurídico do *leasing* financeiro)" (1981), *Escritos sobre leasing e factoring*, Estoril, 2001, p. 9 ff (p. 85 ff); ID., "Aspectos contratuais do aluguer, da locação financeira e de outros contratos afins à face da lei portuguesa" (1992), *Escritos...*, p. 161 ff (p. 164 ff); ID., *Curso de direitos reais*, p. 265. In the same sense, in recent decisions of Portuguese Courts: TRL, 10.04-2008; TRL, 20.01.2011; TRL, 09.06.2011; TRL, 03.11.2011.

Consequently "sale and lease-back" is a financial transaction (similar to a loan) where property right is transferred as a security.[19]

V. The "title transfer financial collateral arrangement" was introduced in Portugal by a statutory law of 2004. It is one of the modalities of financial collateral arrangements admitted by Decreto-Lei 105/2004, 8 May 2004, the legal act that implemented Directive 2002/47/EC of the European Parliament and of the Council of 6 June 2002 on financial collateral arrangements[20].[21]

Article 2(2) of Decreto-Lei 105/2004 states that the modalities of financial collateral arrangements are, *inter alia*: (i) the title transfer financial collateral arrangement (alienação fiduciária em garantia,[22] *pactum fiduciae cum creditore*); and (ii) the financial pledge. The distinguishing feature between the two modalities of financial collateral arrangements is the following: the first one (title transfer financial collateral arrangement) has the effect of transferring full ownership of financial collateral to a collateral taker for the purpose of securing or otherwise covering the performance of relevant financial obligations; the second one (financial pledge) has not that effect.

In general, by means of the title transfer financial collateral arrangement, the debtor, or a third party, transfers an object to the creditor, for the purpose of securing or otherwise covering the performance of relevant financial obligations; the creditor is bound to use that object only to obtain the performance of his credit; the object must be given back to the transferor when the obligation is performed.

The material scope of this legal act is narrow, because financial collateral arrangements may only concern cash (i.e., bank account balance), financial instruments and some credits (Article 5).

So, the title transfer financial collateral arrangement referred to in Decreto-Lei 105/2004 does not apply to the equipment covered by the Convention.

However, the opinion of Portuguese authors is not unanimous about this matter and some of them admit the validity of title transfer financial collateral arrangement with a general scope, covering any assets.[23]

---

[19] J.P. Remédio Marques, "Locação financeira restitutiva (*sale and lease back*) e a proibição dos pactos comissórios – negócio fiduciário, mútuo e acção executiva", *BFDUC*, 2001, p. 575 ff (p. 604); A.F. Morais Antunes, *O contrato de locação financeira restitutiva. Do diálogo difícil com a proibição legal do pacto comissório*, Lisboa, 2008, p. 23, 57. In the same sense, in recent decisions of Portuguese Courts: STJ, 28.10.1999; TRL, 24.01.2012.

[20] OJ L 168, 27.06.2002, p. 43–50.

[21] Decreto-Lei 105/2004 was modified by Decreto-Lei 85/2011, 29.06.2011. Its new version takes into account Directive 2009/44/EC of the European Parliament and of the Council amending, among others, Directive 2002/47/EC (OJ L 146, 10.6.2009, p. 37–43).

[22] The Portuguese version includes a word – "fiduciária", equivalent to "fiduciary" – without correspondence in the English text of the Directive.

[23] P. Pais Vasconcelos, *Contratos atípicos*, 2nd ed., Coimbra, 2009, p. 277 ff (p. 282 ff); L.C. Fernandes, "A admissibilidade do negócio fiduciário no direito português", *Estudos sobre simulação*, Lisboa, 2004, p. 243 ff (p. 269 ff); Id, *Teoria Geral do Direito Civil*, Vol. II, 5th ed., Lisboa, 2010, p. 347 ff (p. 354 f); V.P. Neves, *A cessão de créditos em garantia*, Lisboa, 2005, p. 157 ff; L.P. Vasconcelos, *A cessão de créditos em garantia e a insolvência*, Coimbra, 2007,

19.3 The Registration System

19.3.1 General Remarks

I. The establishment of an International Registry is one of the essential aspects of the Cape Town Convention (chapters IV to VII).

The objective of the system is to protect the creditor against third parties; in fact, registration is not necessary to protect the creditor against his own debtor.

The registration system intends, basically, to give public notice of international interests and so it enables the creditor to preserve its priority and the effectiveness of such international interests in insolvency proceedings against the debtor.

The registration shall not focus on the property of the equipment. Only in an indirect way the registration relates to property rights, since the rules on priority contained in the Convention determine that, in certain circumstances, the interest of the creditor is not effective against third parties if the registration was not made or was subsequent to that of a competing interest. In any case the registration may not base a presumption of property in favour of the creditor. The question of property is, in principle, ruled by the applicable national law.

On the other hand, the registration of "prospective international interests" and of "prospective assignments" of international interests (admitted in Article 16 of the Convention) is very important, as it is possible to fix a position of priority concerning the registered international interest. Indeed, pursuant to Articles 19(4) and 29, the relevant moment for the establishment of the priority is the date of the registration and not the date of the conclusion of the contract which creates the international interest. In addition, under Article 41 of the Convention, Article III of the Aircraft Equipment Protocol adopts the same solution concerning "contracts of sale" and "prospective sales" of aircraft equipment.[24]

After all, the International Registry under the Cape Town Convention is a system based on registration against an asset, not against a debtor (it is an asset-based registry, not a debtor-based registry[25]).

II. Different international registries may be established for different categories of object and associated rights (Article 16(2) of the Convention).

There shall be a Supervisory Authority as provided by the Protocol, and that Authority shall, in particular, establish or provide for the establishment of the International Registry, appoint and dismiss the Registrar and, after consultation with the Contracting States, make or approve and ensure the publication of

---

p. 83 ff. Against this view, C. Ferreira de Almeida, *Contratos III*, Coimbra, 2012, p. 176 ff (with other references).

[24] In the same sense, Article IV of the Space Assets Protocol in what concerns "contracts of sale" and "prospective sales" of space assets. In this aspect, the system of the Railway Rolling Stock Protocol seems to be different (Article XVII).

[25] Comparing to the system created by Article 9 of the *Uniform Commercial Code*, L.M. Leitão, "A Convenção do Cabo…", p. 622.

regulations pursuant to the Protocol dealing with the operation of the International Registry (Article 17).

The Protocol and the regulations shall specify the requirements, including the criteria for the identification of the object, in order to further the objectives defined in the Convention (Article 18(1)).

Articles 19 and 20 of the Convention define the conditions for the validity and time of registration.

Any person may, in the manner prescribed by the Protocol and the regulations, make or request a search of the International Registry by electronic means concerning interests or prospective international interests registered therein (Article 22).

Article 24 relates to the evidentiary value of certificates: a document in the form prescribed by the regulations which purports to be a certificate issued by the International Registry is prima facie proof: (a) that it has been so issued; and (b) of the facts recited in it, including the date and time of a registration.

The registration of an international interest remains effective until discharged or until expiry of the period specified in the registration (Article 21); Article 25 describes the situations for discharge of registration.

19.3.2 Effects of an International Registered Interest as Against Third Parties Under the Cape Town Convention. Priority of Competing Interests

I. Article 29 of the Convention lays down some rules governing the priority of a registered interest in relation to other registered interests and also to every kind of unregistered interests, whether or not registrable.

Paragraph 1 contains two fundamental priority rules:

– a registered interest has priority over any other interest subsequently registered;
– a registered interest has priority over an unregistered interest;

According to paragraph 2, the priority of the first-mentioned interest under the preceding paragraph applies: (a) even if the first-mentioned interest was acquired or registered with actual knowledge of the other interest; and (b) even as regards value given by the holder of the first-mentioned interest with such knowledge.

In the following paragraphs of Article 29 we find some consequences of these priority rules:

– the buyer of an object acquires its interest in it: (a) subject to an interest registered at the time of its acquisition of that interest; and (b) free from an unregistered interest even if it has actual knowledge of such an interest (paragraph 3)[26];

---

[26] This regime does not apply in its terms to "aircraft equipment", to "space assets" and to "railway rolling stock", because the relevant Protocols create special priority rules (Article XIV of the Aircraft Equipment Protocol; Article XXIII of the Space Assets Protocol; Article VIII of the Railway Rolling Stock Protocol).

– the conditional buyer or lessee acquires its interest in or right over that object: (a) subject to an interest registered prior to the registration of the international interest held by its conditional seller or lessor; and (b) free from an interest not so registered at that time even if it has actual knowledge of that interest (paragraph 4).

Under Article 29(6), any priority given by this Article to an interest in an object extends "to proceeds", as defined in the Convention.

On the other hand, Article 29 does not deal with the priority between competing unregistered interests: this question is left to the applicable law.

II. The priority of competing interests or rights under Article 29 may be varied by agreement between the holders of those interests, but an assignee of a subordinated interest is not bound by an agreement to subordinate that interest unless at the time of the assignment a subordination had been registered relating to that agreement (paragraph 5).

Article 29 also states that the Convention does not affect the rights of a person in an item (other than an "object", in the meaning of the Convention[27]), held prior to its installation on an object if under the applicable law those rights continue to exist after the installation; and does not prevent the creation of rights in an item (other than an "object", in the meaning of the Convention), which has previously been installed on an object where under the applicable law those rights are created (paragraph 7).

III. By declaration of a contracting State, it is possible:

– to give priority, without registration, to certain categories of "non-consensual right or interest" created under a national law (Article 39);
– to register in the international registration certain categories of "registrable non-consensual rights or interests", created under a national law, which by these means are treated as registered international interests (Article 40).

19.3.3 Effects of Registration Under Portuguese Law

I. In Portuguese law, both the mortgage and the pledge give the creditor the right to be paid before any other creditor (Articles 686(1) and 666(1) CC).

However, mortgage must be registered. In Portuguese law, the registration of a mortgage has a constitutive nature: if the mortgage is not registered, it is not effective even between the parties (Article 687 CC and Article 4(2) of the Registry Code on Immovable Property – Código do Registo Predial, hereafter CRPred).[28]

---

[27] That is, an item not included in the categories "aircraft object", "railway rolling stock" or "space asset", as defined in the relevant Protocol.

[28] About the constitutive nature of the registration of the mortgage in Portuguese law: L.C. Fernandes, *Lições de direitos reais*, 6th ed., Lisboa, 2009, p. 133 f; L.M. Leitão, *Direitos reais*, Coimbra, 2009, p. 467 f.

According to the general rule (Article 5(1) CRPred), the facts subject to registration only have effect against third parties[29] after the date of registration.

Article 6 of this Code sets up some basic priority rules:

- the right registered in the first place prevails over the subsequent for the same property, following the order of the date of registration and, within the same date, following the order of the corresponding application (paragraph 1);
- the definitive registration maintains the priority of the provisional registration (paragraph 3).

Article 7 CRPred deals with the presumption effect of the registration: the definitive registration creates the presumption that the right exists and that it belongs to the registered owner, in accordance with the terms defined in the registration.

Moreover, the judicial appeal contesting the registration act makes it possible to presume the application for discharge of the registration (Article 8(1) CRPred).

So, in Portuguese law, as between registered interests priority goes to the first to be registered and a registered interest has priority over an unregistered interest. A registered interest has priority over an earlier unregistered interest even if this was known to the holder of the registered interest at the date of registration.

Nevertheless, we must stress that, in Portuguese law, security interests over tangible goods are not subject to registration.

II. Under Portuguese law all kinds of vehicles covered by the three Protocols to the Cape Town Convention are able to be mortgaged or subject to other forms of security interests.

Indeed, as mentioned, the mortgage must pertain to immovable property and also to similar property, i.e., some kinds of movable property subject to registration – that is the case, for present purposes, of aircrafts. In turn, railway rolling stocks and space assets may be the object of pledge.

There is a special law and a special registration system concerning aircrafts. The registration system regarding aircrafts remains ruled in ancient and outdated Decreto 20.062 (25.10.1930); the competence for the registration belongs to the National Institute of Civil Aviation ("Instituto Nacional de Aviação Civil", in short, INAC).[30]

---

[29] Although the differences in the opinion of the Authors and in Court decisions about the notion of "third parties" for the purposes of registration rules, Portuguese Supreme Court, in a non-unanimous "uniformity ruling" (No. 3/99, 18.05.1999), adopted the traditional meaning: "«third parties» for the purposes of Article 5 CRPred are the acquirers, in good faith, from the same common transferor, of incompatible rights over the same asset". So, Article 5 CRPred was modified by Decreto-Lei 533/99, 11.12.1999, by means of the addition of paragraph 4, as follows: "«third parties», for the purposes of registration rules, are the acquirers, from the same common transferor, of incompatible rights among them". See an overview on this question in STJ, 30.06.2011.

[30] INAC was established by Decreto-Lei 133/98, 15.05.1998, and is now ruled in Decreto-Lei 145/2007, 27.04.2007. Its Regulation was approved by Portaria 543/2007, 30.04.2007.

That Aircraft Registration System ("Registo Aeronáutico Nacional") includes the license number of the aircraft, the name and domicile of the constructor and of the owner (what is consistent with Annex 7 of Chicago Convention on International Civil Aviation[31]), the transfer of property, and other acts related to the aircraft or to aircraft objects (such as assignment, leasing, mortgage).

19.4 Enforcement of Security Interests

19.4.1 Default Remedies Under the Cape Town Convention

19.4.1.1 Meaning of Default

I. The regime contained in Chapter III of the Convention ("Default remedies") is based on party autonomy, regarding the existence of the default as well as the organisation of the remedies that the creditor may exercise.

The remedies set out in Articles 8 and 9 (and also in Article 10) are extra-judicial remedies, if the parties have so agreed. The application to the court is, in this context, an option of the creditor.

However, in many jurisdictions, some of these remedies may be exercised only with leave of the court.[32]

II. Article 11 of the Convention deals with the meaning of default.

First, the debtor and the creditor may at any time agree in writing as to the events that constitute a default or otherwise give rise to the rights and remedies specified in this Chapter (Article 11(1)). Therefore the events of default may comprise the debtor's failure to perform and also some non-default events giving rise to the impossibility of performance such as the debtor's insolvency or an adverse change in taxation law applicable to the transaction.

Secondly, where the debtor and the creditor have not so agreed, "default" only means a failure which substantially deprives the creditor of what it is entitled to expect under the agreement (Article 11(2)).

The criterion used in this provision to define "default" reminds the notion of "fundamental breach of contract", contained in Article 25 of the United Nations Convention on Contracts for the International Sale of Goods.

---

[31] The Convention on International Civil Aviation, signed in Chicago on 7.12.1944, entered into force on 4.04.1947. Portugal is bound by this Convention from the beginning.

[32] This is the case in Portuguese law, in what concerns the execution of mortgage: L.C. FERNANDES, *Lições de direitos reais*, p. 159; R.P. DUARTE, *Curso de direitos reais*, p. 249 f; L.M. LEITÃO, *Direitos reais*, p. 480.

19.4.1.2 Remedies of Chargee

I. According to Article 8(1) of the Convention, in the event of default, the chargee may, to the extent that the chargor has at any time so agreed, exercise any one or more of the following remedies:

(a) "take possession or control of any object charged to it;
(b) sell or grant a lease of any such object;
(c) collect or receive any income or profits arising from the management or use of any such object."

The chargee may alternatively apply for a court order authorising or directing any of the acts referred to in preceding paragraph (Article 8(2)).

II. Article 8(3) and (4) state the *conditions* for the exercise of the remedies set out in Article 8(1)(a), (b) and (c):

– any remedy shall be exercised "in a commercially reasonable manner", i.e., in conformity with a provision of the security agreement except where such a provision is manifestly unreasonable (Article 8(3));
– a chargee proposing to sell or grant a lease of an object under paragraph 1 shall give reasonable prior notice in writing of the proposed sale or lease to the "interested persons" (Article 8(4), with reference to Article 1(m), in what concerns "interested persons").

Article 8(5) and (6) establish the *effects* of the collecting or receiving, by the chargee, of any sum, as a result of the exercise of any remedy set out in Article 8(1) or (2):

– such sums shall be applied towards discharge of the amount of the secured obligations (Article 8(5));
– where such sums exceed the amount secured by the security interest and any reasonable costs incurred in the exercise of any such remedy, then unless otherwise ordered by the court the chargee shall distribute the surplus among holders of subsequently ranking interests which have been registered or of which the chargee has been given notice, in order of priority, and pay any remaining balance to the chargor (Article 8(6)).

In principle, any remedy provided by Chapter III of the Convention shall be exercised in conformity with the procedure prescribed by the law of the place where the remedy is to be exercised (Article 14).

III. Article 54 admits the following declarations regarding remedies:

(1) "A Contracting State may [...] declare that while the charged object is situated within, or controlled from its territory the chargee shall not grant a lease of the object in that territory.

(2) A Contracting State shall [...] declare whether or not any remedy available to the creditor under any provision of this Convention which is not there expressed to require application to the court may be exercised only with leave of the court".

19.4.2 Enforcement Under Portuguese Law

19.4.2.1 Overview of Default Remedies

I. In brief, "default" in Portuguese law includes: (a) non-performance; (b) impossibility of performance; (c) delay in performance (*mora debitoris*, but not *mora creditoris*); (d) defective performance.[33]

If the contractual obligation is not performed by the debtor and the non-performance is not excused, the creditor has the right to damages for any loss caused by the debtor's non-performance (Article 798 CC). The fault of the debtor is presumed in cases of non-performance and of defective performance (Article 799 CC).

When the impossibility of performance is excused, the obligation extinguishes (Article 790(1) CC).

If performance becomes partially impossible the debtor will be discharged by performing the obligation to the fullest extent possible; the creditor's obligation will be proportionately reduced. However, if the creditor's interest in performance is justifiably lost, he may terminate the contract (Article 793 CC).

When the impossibility of performance is not excused, the debtor is liable as in case of non-performance (Article 801(1) CC). If the obligation results from a bilateral (synallagmatic) contract, the creditor, regardless of the right to damages, may terminate the contract and, if he has performed, he may claim for restitution (Article 801(2) CC). Therefore, in that case, the creditor may choose between the right to damages and the termination of the contract.

In the case of delay in performance, the debtor is liable for damages for any loss caused to the creditor (Article 804 CC).

In conclusion:

Non-performance of a contractual obligation will be excused if performance becomes impossible for reasons that do not result from the debtor's fault. An impediment to perform will discharge the debtor, unless it is temporary and the creditor's interest in performance is unaffected by the delay.

When non-performance of a contractual obligation is not excused, the creditor may resort to one or more of the remedies set out in the law. Different remedies may be accumulated, provided they are not incompatible.

---

[33] For developments on this matter: A. Menezes Cordeiro, *Tratado de Direito Civil Português*, Vol. II – *Direito das Obrigações*, Tomo IV – *Cumprimento e não cumprimento, transmissão, modificação e extinção, garantias*, Coimbra 2010, p. 103 ff; M. Lima Rego & C.F. Almeida, "Contract Law", *Portuguese Law. An Overview*, Coimbra, 2007, p. 187 ff (p. 191 ff).

II. According to Portuguese law, it is null and void the clause under which the creditor renounces in advance to any rights emerging from non-performance or delay in performance by the debtor (Article 809 CC).

However, the parties may, by agreement (named "penalty clause"), fix the amount of damages due by the debtor to the creditor (Articles 810 ff CC).[34]

19.4.2.2 Rules Concerning the Enforcement of Security Agreements

I. As a general rule, if the obligation is not voluntarily performed, the creditor has the right to demand judicial compliance and to execute the assets of the debtor, as stated in the Civil Code and in the rules of procedure (Article 817 CC).

The law gives the creditor the right to bring forth two actions in court: first, the creditor is entitled judicially to enforce his rights under the contract and demand performance; second, the creditor may execute the assets of the debtor. In certain circumstances the creditor may initiate an execution proceeding, without precedence of a declarative proceeding, based on an enforcement order, for instance, on a public deed.

The execution of the debtor's assets, in order to enforce the payment of a sum of money, includes the seizure of debtor's property ("penhora"), the judicial sale of seized property and the payment to the creditors. If the execution aims at the delivery of goods, those goods are also seized in order to be delivered to the execution creditor.

II. In particular, the enforcement of the mortgage must be exercised with leave of the court.

So, after the registration and upon verification of the event that triggers the guarantee (non-performance of the guaranteed obligation; seizure of the assets covered by the mortgage in an execution proceeding initiated by another creditor[35]; or insolvency of the holder[36]), the creditor is entitled judicially to enforce his priority right by appointing the guaranteed assets to seizure or by claiming for his credits in the context of insolvency.[37]

With the objective of preventing any abuse by the creditor, the Portuguese Civil Code forbids the *pactum commissorium* ("pacto comissório") in the context of a mortgage, i.e., the agreement under which there is an automatic appropriation

---

[34] About "penalty clause": A. PINTO MONTEIRO, *Cláusula penal e indemnização*, Coimbra, 1990; N. PINTO OLIVEIRA, *Cláusulas acessórias ao contrato: Cláusulas de exclusão e de limitação do dever de indemnizar e cláusulas penais*, 3rd ed., Coimbra, 2008, p. 71 ff.

[35] Even if the credit guaranteed by a mortgage is not yet due (Articles 788(7) and 791(3) of the Portuguese Civil Procedure Code, Código de Processo Civil, hereafter CPC).

[36] According to the Portuguese Insolvency and Recovery Code (Código da Insolvência e da Recuperação de Empresas, approved by Decreto-Lei 53/2004, 18.03.2004, as amended, hereafter CIRE), the declaration of insolvency determines the maturity of all the obligations of the debtor, which are not subject to a condition precedent (Article 91(1)).

[37] Articles 752(1) and 788(1) CPC and Article 128(1)(c) CIRE.

by the creditor of the mortgage object in case of default of the debtor (Article 694 CC).[38]

III. This rule applies, with the necessary adjustments (*mutatis mutandis*) to the pledge (Article 678 CC).

However nowadays it is permitted the agreement of the parties pertaining to the extra-judicial enforcement of the pledge (Article 675(1) CC). On the other hand, the interested parties may agree that the pledged object is awarded to the creditor for the value decided by the court (Article 675(2) CC).

The reasons for the prohibition of *pactum comissorium* are multiple and complex; first, it is necessary to protect the debtor from any extortion by the creditor; secondly, there is a general need of the juridical traffic not to fraud the principle of *par conditio creditorum*, through an unjustified privilege conferred to one of the creditors.[39]

IV. In recent times, the abovementioned Decreto-Lei 105/2004 (which transposed Directive 2002/47/EC on financial collateral arrangements) appears to admit the *pactum comissorium*, in the context of financial pledge, in certain circumstances (Article 11, in its original version); it is also stated that the contract of financial pledge may confer to the beneficiary of the financial collateral the right to dispose of the object (Article 9). But only a few years after that, the law was amended and discarded the wording *pactum commissorium* ("pacto comissório") (see Article 11, in its actual version[40]).

Nevertheless, Portuguese authors consider that the prohibition of *pactum comissorium* does not include the "pacto marciano", i.e., the agreement under which the beneficiary of the collateral – who may appropriate the object provided as collateral – is obliged to reimburse the guarantor of an amount corresponding to the difference between the value of the object of the collateral and the value of the guaranteed obligations. This is after all the meaning and the objective of the law (Decreto-Lei 105/2004, even in its first version).[41]

---

[38] The law also forbids the prohibition of selling the mortgaged objects – Article 695 CC.

[39] About *pactum comissorium*: J. Vieira Gomes, "Sobre o âmbito da proibição do pacto comissório, o pacto comissório autónomo e o pacto marciano – Acórdão do STJ de 30.1.2003, Rec. 3896/02", *Cadernos de direito privado*, No. 8, 2004, p. 57 ff; I. Andrade Matos, *O pacto comissório. Contributo para o estudo do âmbito da sua proibição*, Coimbra, 2006, in special, p. 107 ff.

[40] Article 11 of Decreto-Lei 105/2004, as amended by Decreto-Lei 85/2011, 29.06.2011, under the epigraph "Enforcement of contacts of financial pledge": "(1) In the context of financial pledge, the beneficiary of the collateral may enforce it, by appropriating the object provided as financial collateral, through sale or taking its possession, either setting-off its value or applying it to pay the guaranteed financial obligations: (a) if the parties have so agreed; (b) if the parties have agreed on the valuation of the financial instruments and of the credits over third parties provided as collateral. (2) The beneficiary of the collateral is obliged to reimburse the guarantor of an amount corresponding to the difference between the value of the object of the collateral and the value of the guaranteed financial obligations. (3) The provision of sub-paragraph (b) of paragraph (1) shall not affect any legal obligation under which the realisation or valuation of financial collateral and the calculation of the relevant financial obligations must be conducted in a commercially reasonable manner [...]."

[41] In this sense, STJ, 16.03.2011.

V. Regarding the aforesaid, we may ask if some of the remedies admitted in the Convention (Articles 8, 9 and 10) give rise to a conflict with the general rule that in Portuguese law prohibits the *pactum comissorium*.

The answer to this question must take into account the *conditions* laid down in the Convention to the use of such remedies: any remedy shall be exercised "in a commercially reasonable manner" (Article 8(3)) and shall be noticed in writing and in advance to the "interested persons" (Article 8(4)).

On the other hand, it is also necessary to consider the *effects* of the collecting or receiving of any sums by the chargee as a result of the exercise of such remedies: the sum collected or received by the chargee shall be applied towards discharge of the amount of the secured obligations (Article 8(5)) and where the sums collected or received by the chargee exceed the amount secured by the security interest and any reasonable costs incurred in the exercise of any such remedy, then in principle the chargee shall distribute the surplus among holders of subsequently ranking interests, in order of priority, and pay any remaining balance to the chargor (Article 8(6)).

Equivalent conditions are laid down in Articles 9 and 10 in what concerns the remedies available to a conditional seller or a lessor.

Moreover, the Convention qualifies some of these provisions as mandatory (Article 15).

And, definitely, Contracting States are allowed to declare under Article 54(2) of the Convention that any remedy available to the creditor may be exercised only with leave of the court.

It is therefore sure that in such cases the court controls the valuation of the objects, the allocation of those objects to the guaranteed obligation and the distribution of any surplus obtained by the creditor.[42]

19.5 Treatment of Security Interests Under the Insolvency Procedure

19.5.1 Effects of Insolvency Under the Cape Town Convention

I. The general rule is included in Article 30(1) of the Convention: in insolvency proceedings against the debtor an international interest is effective if that interest was registered in conformity with this Convention prior to the "commencement of the insolvency proceedings".

This provision about the effects of insolvency does not affect:

– the effectiveness of an international interest in the insolvency proceedings where that interest is effective under the applicable law (Article 30(2));

---

[42] V.P. NEVES, *A cessão de créditos em garantia*, p. 499.

– any rules of the law applicable in insolvency proceedings relating to the avoidance of a transaction as a preference or a transfer in fraud of creditors (Article 30(3)(a));
– any rules of procedure relating to the enforcement of rights to property which is under the control or supervision of the insolvency administrator (Article 30(3)(b)).

II. Article XI of the Aircraft Equipment Protocol makes some changes in Article 30(3) of the Convention, by establishing two categories of remedies (Alternatives A and B). The purpose is to strengthen the position of the creditor before the insolvency administrator or before the debtor, in cases of commencement of the insolvency proceedings against the debtor, as well as in cases of declared intention to suspend payments (or of actual suspension of payments) by the debtor. But this provision only applies where a Contracting State that is the primary insolvency jurisdiction has made a declaration pursuant to Article XXX(3).[43]

19.5.2   Effects of Insolvency Under Portuguese law

19.5.2.1   The Insolvency Proceeding

I. The modifications introduced in Portuguese insolvency legislation by the above-mentioned Insolvency and Recovery Code (CIRE) aimed to implement a more correct perspective of the purpose and the structure of insolvency proceedings.[44]

The principal purpose of insolvency proceedings is the satisfaction in a more efficient way of the creditors' rights. As the assets of the debtor represent the general security of the credits, it is incumbent to the creditors to decide about the effectiveness of that security. Using the wording of the normative act that approved the CIRE, this will be the better way to protect "public interest in good functioning of the market".

When the insolvency includes a business enterprise which did not create the necessary income to comply with its obligations, the better solution for creditors may either be the closure of the enterprise or the continuity of its exploration. But the option for the continuity of business must depend on the valuation of the creditors. That valuation will always represent the better way to protect the public interest in good functioning of the market, by maintaining viable enterprises and eliminating those which are not feasible.

In conclusion – and repeating the preamble of the CIRE –, insolvency law must regulate the elimination or the financial reorganisation of the enterprise, in

---

[43] See also: Article XXI of the Space Assets Protocol; Article IX of the Railway Rolling Stock Protocol.

[44] For developments about insolvency in Portuguese law: *Novo Direito da Insolvência, Themis,* special edition, 2005; C. Serra, *O Regime Português da Insolvência,* 5th ed., Coimbra, 2012; L.M. Leitão, *Direito da insolvência,* 5th ed., Coimbra, 2013.

accordance with a market approach, by assigning the central role to the creditors (converted, by virtue of the insolvency, in "economic owners of the enterprise").

II. The CIRE intended to unify the various proceedings in a unique proceeding of insolvency, based on the liquidation of the assets of the debtor, but granting the creditors the possibility of approving a special plan outside this regime, either providing for the liquidation in different terms, or providing for the reorganisation of the enterprise, whether or not in the ownership of the insolvent debtor.

Indeed, Article 1 CIRE in its original version stated: "The insolvency proceeding is an executive universal proceeding which has as purpose the liquidation of the assets of the insolvent debtor and the distribution among the creditors of the sum obtained, or the payment to the creditors according to an insolvency plan based, in particular, on the recovery of the business enterprise included in the insolvency".

In consistency with that approach, Article 192(1) CIRE fixed: "The payment of the credits over the insolvency, the liquidation of the assets of the insolvency and its distribution among the owners of those credits and the debtor, as well as the responsibility of the debtor after the conclusion of the insolvency proceeding, may be regulated within an insolvency plan, by derogation of the rules of the present Code".

The abolition in the CIRE of the dichotomy "recovery/bankruptcy" and the approach based on the insolvency as the only objective foundation of the procedure determined the change of terminology and the characterisation of the procedure as an "insolvency proceeding". In this context, "insolvency" is different from "bankruptcy": the impossibility of compliance with the obligations (the basis of "insolvency") does not imply inevitably the impossibility of the financial reorganisation of the enterprise (the basis of "bankruptcy").

III. As a general rule, upon the declaration of insolvency the debtor is immediately deprived of the administration and disposition powers concerning the assets belonging to him; those powers shall be exercised by the insolvency administrator (Article 81(1) CIRE).[45]

Nevertheless, in the decision declaring the insolvency of an enterprise, the judge may determine that the administration of the insolvency is assigned to the debtor, if: (a) the debtor has claimed for the administration of the insolvency; (b) the debtor has presented, or commits himself to present within a period of 30 days after the decision declaring the insolvency, a plan for the continuity of the exploration of the enterprise; (c) there is no reason to fear delays in the proceeding or other disadvantages to creditors; (d) the applicant for the insolvency, who is not the debtor, agrees on that solution (Article 224(1) and (2) CIRE).[46]

IV. The rationale of insolvency proceedings is the principle of *par conditio creditorum*: all the creditors of the same debtor must exercise their credit claims in the scope of the same proceeding and according to the same conditions. Each creditor

---

[45] R.P. DUARTE, "Efeitos da declaração de insolvência quanto à pessoa do devedor", *Themis*, special edition, 2005, p. 131 ff.

[46] The administration of the insolvency is also assigned to the debtor if the creditors so agree in the assembly where the report was examined, in the conditions laid down in Article 224(3) CIRE.

only has the privileges and the security interests recognised by insolvency law and within the limits recognised thereby.

As a result, Article 90 CIRE determines that creditors of the insolvency may only exercise their rights according to the provisions of the Code, during the insolvency proceedings. They have no recourse to the courts to initiate or to continue independent actions outside the insolvency proceedings.

Furthermore, the declaration of insolvency determines the maturity of all the obligations of the debtor, which are not subject to a condition precedent (Article 91(1) CIRE).

After the declaration of insolvency, set-off between credits and debts of the insolvency is not permitted except in very strict conditions (Article 99 CIRE).

Additionally, the decision declaring the insolvency determines that all limitation periods that operate to the advantage of the debtor don't run during the insolvency proceedings (Article 100 CIRE).

V. All the creditors of the insolvent at the time of the declaration of insolvency are considered insolvency creditors, whichever may be their nationality or domicile.

Some of the credits over the insolvency are "secured credits", since they benefit from security interests *in rem* (Article 47(a) CIRE).

However, the declaration of insolvency implies the extinction of certain security interests. Article 97 CIRE states the extinction, *inter alia*, of security interests *in rem* concerning immovable property or movable property subject to registration, which are already created, but at the time of the declaration of insolvency are neither registered nor object of an application for registration.

"Secured credits" are paid after deduction of the amounts necessary to satisfy the debts of the insolvency (Article 172(1) CIRE). The payment to the "secured creditors" is effected immediately after the corresponding liquidation – before any "common creditor" –, and following the correspondent priority (Article 174(1) CIRE).

VI. Regarding ongoing business, the law assigns to the insolvency administrator a right of option between the performance of the contract and the refusal to comply (see the "general principle" in Article 102 CIRE, with the conditions of its exercise, the "waiting period" and the exceptions to the "general principle").[47]

This right of option assigned to the insolvency administrator is the consequence of the basis of insolvency. Indeed, the insolvency-related event is the cessation of payments and if the insolvent were complied to the performance of ongoing contracts, such payments would represent an advantage to some creditors in detriment of the others. So, as the performance of some contracts may be useful for the insolvency, the insolvency administrator has the possibility to opt between the performance of the contract and the refusal to comply, as the case may be.

VII. In cases of title reservation agreement or of financial leasing agreement, Article 104(1) and (2) CIRE state that the insolvency of the conditional seller or of the lessor does not affect the possibility of the buyer or of the lessee to claim for the

---

[47] J. Oliveira Ascensão, "Insolvência: efeitos sobre os negócios em curso", *Themis*, special edition, 2005, p. 105 ff.

performance of the contract, if the asset has been delivered to him at the time of the declaration of insolvency.

This solution intends to protect the expectations of the buyer or of the lessee to acquire the property right over the asset and complies with Council Regulation (EC) 1346/2000 of 29 May 2000 on insolvency proceedings (see its Article 7(2)).

VIII. If the insolvent is the buyer or the lessee and if the asset remains in his possession, Article 104(3) CIRE determines the applicability of the right of option of the insolvency administrator, as laid down in Article 102, with a special provision concerning the "waiting period".

The title reservation agreement, in contracts of sale of a certain asset, when the insolvent is the buyer, is only opposable to the insolvency if it were agreed in writing before the delivery of the asset (Article 104(4) CIRE). This rule does not exist for leasing agreement.

IX. After the Court hearing – where the insolvency administrator and the commission of the creditors may provide their statements –, the judge takes the decision about the verification and graduation of the credits.

The graduation is universal regarding the assets of the insolvency and it is specific for the assets that are object of a security right (Article 140(1) and (2) CIRE).

X. The insolvency administrator must provide for conservation of insolvent's rights and for continuity of the exploration of the enterprise, preventing, when possible, the deterioration of its economic situation (Article 55(1)(b) CIRE).

When the decision declaring the insolvency is *res judicata*, the insolvency administrator must sell all the assets included in insolvency; however, he is required to provide for the anticipated sale of the assets which may not be preserved because they are subject to deterioration or depreciation. The insolvency administrator shall notify the debtor, the commission of the creditors and the judge about this situation (Article 158 CIRE).

19.5.2.2 The Revitalisation Proceeding

I. In 2012, the CIRE was modified[48] and the revitalisation proceeding was introduced in Portuguese insolvency law.

The revitalisation proceeding pursues the recovery of the debtor, by means of an agreement with the creditors. It may be used by companies or by individuals.

This special proceeding is ruled by the CIRE (by new Articles 17-A to 17-I and subsidiarily by the rules concerning the insolvency proceeding); when necessary Civil Procedure Code applies.

II. The revitalisation proceeding begins with the requirement of the debtor and the declaration of, at least, one of the creditors in order to initiate the negotiations looking for the plan of recovery (Article 17-C(1)); the court appoints a provisional judicial administrator (Article 17-C(3)(a)).

---

[48] By Lei 16/2012, 20.04.2012.

According to Article 17-E(1), the revitalisation proceeding hinders any claim to collect debts against the debtor and, during the negotiations with the creditors, suspends any existing claim against him with the same object. On the other hand, the debtor is not allowed to perform, without consent of the provisional judicial administrator, "acts of special relevance" to the insolvency proceedings (Article 17-E(2)), such as: the sale of the enterprise or of the place of business; the sale of the assets necessary to the continuity of the exploration of the enterprise; the sale of shares in other companies; the acquisition of immovable property; the conclusion of long term contracts; the assumption of obligations of third parties or the creation of security interests (Article 161(2)).

If the negotiations come to an end with the approval by the creditors of the plan of recovery and revitalisation of the debtor, that plan shall be submitted to the court for confirmation or refusal. The decision of the court is binding to the creditors, even if they have not taken part in the negotiations (Article 17-F).

If the debtor or the majority of the creditors conclude that it is not possible to attain an agreement on the recovery of the debtor, the negotiations terminate and the provisional judicial administrator reports the fact to the court (Article 17-G(1)). In cases where the debtor is not yet in an insolvency situation, the closure of the revitalisation proceeding results in the extinction of all its effects; in cases where the debtor is in an insolvency situation, the closure of the revitalisation proceeding results in the insolvency of the debtor, which will be declared by the court in a short time (Article 17-G(2) and (3)).

The closure of the revitalisation proceeding, as ruled in these special provisions of the CIRE, prevents the debtor from using the same proceeding for a period of 2 years (Article 17-G(6)).

19.6   Concluding Comments

I. The Cape Town Convention provides the regulation of a sector where there is a special need for the adoption of uniform material law. That objective is achieved through a set of rules detached from national legislations.

The area covered by the Cape Town Convention – *property law* – has been commonly away from the efforts towards uniform law. So, this is the first important merit of this Convention.

In order to reach its fundamental aim – to facilitate financing transactions regarding equipment with high value – the Cape Town Convention rules the creation and the effects of international security interests concerning mobile equipment with high value, so as to permit their recognition in all Contracting States. It also establishes an electronic international registry system that ensures the publicity of international security interests pertaining to that equipment and the priority of competing interests. Finally, it determines the rights and remedies to the creditor in case of default of the debtor.

The international security interest and the electronic international registry system correspond to original constructions of the Cape Town Convention.

The program is ambitious and appropriate to the intended purpose. Correctness and technical quality of the approved provisions are evident.

The option for regulation at the level of material law simplifies the complex problems of conflict of laws emerging from the recognition in different States of security agreements concerning mobile equipment.

The 1948 Geneva Convention on the International Recognition of Rights in Aircraft – in a restrict scope – intended to solve some problems regarding the international recognition of rights in aircraft. But it was a Convention based on conflict of laws rules, which refers, in many aspects, to the competent applicable law of a Contracting State.

On the other hand, under the Geneva Convention, rights in aircraft were registered in national records and consequently the creditors should consult the registration system of various Contracting States in order to know if certain aircraft was burdened with any security right. Instead, we have now a worldwide registration.

Therefore, the Cape Town Convention brings a very significant progress when compared to the 1948 Geneva Convention in what concerns predictability and transparency of financing civil aviation.

II. However, the Cape Town Convention contains some elements of complexity.

First, it is not easy to determine the rules governing the security interests concerning mobile equipment with high value, because, regarding each question, it is necessary to coordinate the dispositions of the Convention and those of the relevant Protocol. Such difficulty is the result of the option on the structure for this international treaty, based on two instruments (one Convention and, for each category of equipment, a separate Protocol). The Convention contains only the basic rules and it will be completed by different Protocols and regulations.

Afterwards, the approved regime, which is believed to be uniform, may eventually differ from a State to another, regarding the possibilities of *opting in* and *opting out* offered by the Convention and by the Protocols.

III. The decision of Portuguese authorities in view of the accession to the Cape Town Convention implies a detailed examination of the Convention and the Protocols and a careful valuation about the Declarations to be made by Portugal.

Essentially, there is no significant incompatibility between the Convention and Portuguese law. However, in my opinion, it is necessary that in a clear Declaration made at the time of ratification of the Cape Town Convention, under Article 54(2), Portugal states that the remedies available to the creditor may be exercised only with leave of the court, thus expressly excluding the *pactum commissorium*, incompatible with Portuguese public policy.

References

1. Aires, Sandra. 2013. "Hipoteca sobre navios", *Estudos em Homenagem ao Prof. Doutor José Lebre de Freitas*, vol. II, 447 ff. Coimbra.
2. Almeida, Carlos Ferreira de. 2012. *Contratos III*, Coimbra.
3. Antunes, Ana Filipa Morais. 2008. *O contrato de locação financeira restitutiva. Do diálogo difícil com a proibição legal do pacto comissório*, Lisboa.
4. Ascensão, José de Oliveira. 2005. "Insolvência: efeitos sobre os negócios em curso", *Themis*, special edition, 105 ff.
5. Brito, Maria Helena – "A Convenção da Cidade do Cabo relativa a garantias internacionais sobre equipamento móvel e o Protocolo Anexo sobre questões específicas relativas a equipamento aeronáutico", Nos 20 anos do Código das Sociedades Comerciais, vol III, 447 ff. Coimbra.
6. Cordeiro, António Menezes. 2010. *Tratado de Direito Civil Português*, Vol. II – *Direito das Obrigações*, Tomo IV – *Cumprimento e não cumprimento, transmissão, modificação e extinção, garantias*, Coimbra.
7. Costa, Mário Júlio de Almeida. 2008. *Direito das Obrigações*, 11th ed. Coimbra.
8. Cristas, Assunção, and Gouveia, Mariana França. 2011. – "Transmissão da propriedade de coisas móveis e contrato de compra e venda. Estudo comparado dos Direitos Português, Espanhol e Inglês", *Transmissão da propriedade e contrato*, 15 ff. Coimbra.
9. Dias, Gabriela Figueiredo. 2007. "Reserva de propriedade", *Comemorações dos 35 Anos do Código Civil e dos 25 Anos da Reforma de 1977*, vol III, 417 ff. Coimbra.
10. Duarte, Rui Pinto. 2001. "A locação financeira (Estudo jurídico do *leasing* financeiro)" (1981), *Escritos sobre leasing e factoring*, Estoril, 9 ff.
11. Duarte, Rui Pinto. 2001. "Aspectos contratuais do aluguer, da locação financeira e de outros contratos afins à face da lei portuguesa" (1992), *Escritos sobre leasing e factoring*, Estoril, 161 ff.
12. Duarte, Rui Pinto. 2005. "Efeitos da declaração de insolvência quanto à pessoa do devedor", *Themis*, special edition, 131 ff.
13. Duarte, Rui Pinto. 2013. *Curso de direitos reais*, 3rd ed, 305 ff.. Cascais.
14. Fernandes, Luís Carvalho. 2004. – "A admissibilidade do negócio fiduciário no direito português", *Estudos sobre simulação*, 243 ff, Lisboa.
15. Fernandes, Luís Carvalho. 2009. *Lições de direitos reais*, 6th ed. Lisboa.
16. Fernandes, Luís Carvalho. 2010. *Teoria Geral do Direito Civil*. vol II, 5th ed. Lisboa: Universidade Católica.
17. Fernandes, Luís Carvalho. 2011. "Notas breves sobre a cláusula de reserva da propriedade", *Estudos em Homenagem ao Professor Doutor Carlos Ferreira de Almeida*, vol II, 321 ff. Coimbra.
18. Freitas, José Lebre de (ed.). 2005. *Novo Direito da Insolvência, Themis*. Special edition.
19. Gomes, Júlio Vieira. 2004. Sobre o âmbito da proibição do pacto comissório, o pacto comissório autónomo e o pacto marciano – Acórdão do STJ de 30.1.2003, Rec. 3896/02. *Cadernos de direito privado*, 57 ff. No. 8.
20. Leitão, Luís Menezes. 2009. *Direitos reais*. Coimbra.
21. Leitão, Luís Menezes. 2012. A Convenção do Cabo e o Protocolo sobre equipamento aeronáutico. Registo internacional de aeronaves. *Estudos de Direito Aéreo*, 617 ff. Coimbra.
22. Leitão, Luís Menezes. 2013. *Direito da insolvência*. 5th ed. Coimbra.
23. Marques, João Paulo Remédio. 2001. Locação financeira restitutiva (*sale and lease back*) e a proibição dos pactos comissórios – negócio fiduciário, mútuo e acção executiva. *BFDUC*, 575ff.
24. Matos, Isabel Andrade. 2006. *O pacto comissório. Contributo para o estudo do âmbito da sua proibição*, Coimbra.
25. Monteiro, António Pinto. 1990. *Cláusula penal e indemnização*. Coimbra.
26. Neves, Vítor Pereira das. 2005. *A cessão de créditos em garantia*. Lisboa.

27. Oliveira, Nuno Manuel Pinto de. 2008. *Cláusulas acessórias ao contrato: Cláusulas de exclusão e de limitação do dever de indemnizar e cláusulas penais*, 3rd ed. Coimbra.
28. Pinheiro, Luís de Lima. 1988. – *A cláusula de reserva de propriedade*, Coimbra.
29. Pinheiro, Luís de Lima. 1991. *A venda com reserva da propriedade em direito internacional privado*. Lisboa: McGraw-Hill.
30. Rego, Margarida Lima, and Almeida, Carlos Ferreira de. 2007. Contract law. *Portuguese Law. An Overview*. Coimbra.
31. Serra, Catarina. 2012. *O Regime Português da Insolvência*, 5th ed. Coimbra: Almedina.
32. Vasconcelos, Luís Miguel Pestana de. 2007. *A cessão de créditos em garantia e a insolvência*. Coimbra: Coimbra Editora.
33. Vasconcelos, Luís Miguel Pestana de. 2010. *Direito das garantias*. Coimbra: Almedina.
34. Vasconcelos, Pedro Pais de. 2009. *Contratos atípicos*, 2nd ed. Coimbra: Almedina.
35. Vicente, Dário Moura. O estatuto jurídico da aeronave. *Estudos de Direito Aéreo*, 571 ff.

Maria Helena Brito (JD (University of Coimbra); LL.M; Ph.D (University of Lisbon)) is a Professor at NOVA University of Lisbon, Faculty of Law (Private International Law, International Trade Law, International Arbitration, Private Comparative Law, Legal Research, Civil and Commercial Contracts), Portugal. She is Former Judge of the Constitutional Court of Portugal (1998–2007). Her key publications include:

– *O contrato de concessão comercial. Descrição, qualificação e regime jurídico de um contrato socialmente típico*, Coimbra, Almedina, 1990
– *O factoring internacional e a Convenção do Unidroit*, Lisboa, Cosmos, 1998
– *A representação nos contratos internacionais. Um contributo para o estudo do princípio da coerência em direito internacional privado*, Coimbra, Almedina, 1999
– *Direito do Comércio Internacional*, Coimbra, Almedina, 2004
– "A Convenção da Cidade do Cabo relativa a garantias internacionais sobre equipamento móvel e o Protocolo Anexo sobre questões específicas relativas a equipamento aeronáutico", in *Nos 20 anos do Código das Sociedades Comerciais. Homenagem aos Profs. Doutores A. Ferrer Correia, Orlando de Carvalho e Vasco Lobo Xavier*, vol. III, Coimbra, Coimbra Editora, 2007, p. 447–501
– "Private International Law", in *Portuguese Law. An Overview* (ed. Carlos Ferreira de Almeida, Assunção Cristas, Nuno Piçarra), Coimbra, Almedina, 2007, p. 287–303 (with Eugénia Galvão Teles)
– "Portugal", in *Derecho de los contratos internacionales en Latinoamérica, Portugal y España* (dir. Carlos Esplugues Mota, Daniel Hargain, Guillermo Palao Moreno), Madrid, Edisofer, Montevideo-Buenos Aires, Editorial BdeF, 2008, p. 665–733 (with Eugénia Galvão Teles)
– "Portugal", in *Application of Foreign Law* (ed. Carlos Esplugues, José Luis Iglesias, Guillermo Palao), Munich, Sellier. european law publishers, 2011, p. 301–316 (with Dário Moura Vicente)

Chapter 20
Rapport suisse sur le thème « Les sûretés grevant les moyens de transport – La Convention du Cap et sa transposition en droit national »

Bénédict Foëx*

Abstract 20.1. Switzerland has signed the *Cape Town Convention on international interests in mobile equipment* as well as the *Aircraft Protocol* and the *Rail Protocol*. However, it has not ratified these instruments (yet) and has not signed the *Space Protocol* either.

20.2.1 There is a limited number of rights *in rem* under Swiss law. The main security rights which can be created in a movable are : pledges, transfers of ownership for security purpose and financial leases (all of which require that possession of the asset be transferred to secured creditor), as well as retentions of title (whose validity require a registration in a public registry); mortgages may encumber only certain categories of movables (aircraft, ships, cattle, etc.).

Switzerland keeps an *Aircraft Records Register* (not to be confounded with the *Swiss Aircraft Registry* maintained in accordance with Sect. 17 *et seq.* of the *Chicago Convention on international civil aviation*, of December 7, 1944) enabling the registering of rights *in rem* (and of certain personal rights) concerning aircrafts. If an aircraft is registered in this *Records Register* (which is not compulsory), it may be encumbered by way of filing the security rights in the register (mortgage, transfer of ownership for security purpose and financial lease [including lease-back]).

Aircrafts which are not registered in the *Aircraft Records Register*, railway rolling stock and space assets may be encumbered by possessory security rights (pledge, transfer of ownership for security purposes and financial lease) or be subject to a retention of title clause.

---

*Professeur à l'Université de Genève. Le présent texte a également été publié *in* Rapports suisses présentés au XIXe Congrès international de droit comparé. Collection de l'Institut suisse de droit comparé, vol. 73 (L. Heckendorn Urscheler, éd.), Zurich 2014, p. 269 ss.

B. Foëx (✉)
University of Geneva, Faculty of Law, Geneva, Switzerland

Schellenberg Wittmer, Geneva, Switzerland
e-mail: Benedict.Foex@unige.ch

© Springer International Publishing AG 2017
S. Kozuka (ed.), *Implementing the Cape Town Convention and the Domestic Laws on Secured Transactions*, Ius Comparatum - Global Studies in Comparative Law 22, DOI 10.1007/978-3-319-46470-1_20

20.2.2 Under Swiss law, ownership of a secured creditor (be it a lessor or an acquirer for security purpose) is a full ownership, whereas a mortgage is a limited right *in rem*. Ownership and mortgage follow different legal regimens and produce distinct effects.

20.2.3 The *Swiss Aircraft Records Register* is an asset-based registry. On the other hand, it is not a "notice-based" registry: rights (ownership, security rights, etc.) are filed by a registrar, upon production by the parties of the required documents (contracts, etc.); such filing is necessary to transfer ownership or to create a mortgage; in addition, a specific provision provides for the protection of the acquisition of ownership or of a mortgage relying in good faith in an entry in the *Aircraft Records Register*.

20.2.4 The rank of aircraft mortgages created by the parties (as opposed to those arising by operation of law) does not depend on the date of filing, but on the rank indicated by the parties upon registration. The parties may thus establish a mortgage in a second (or lower) rank, even though no other mortgage encumbers the aircraft yet, provided the amount taking precedence is specified in the entry; a mortgage may be established subsequently in the first rank and will have priority even though its date is posterior to that of the second-ranked mortgage; this system presents some similarities to that of the prospective international interests provided by Articles 16.1(a), 18.3 and 19.4 of the Cape Town Convention, although the parties are not the same (grantor and secured creditor to be subordinated under Swiss law; [prospective] chargor and [prospective] secured creditor under the Convention).

Likewise, if a mortgage is deleted from the registry, lower-ranked mortgages do not advance in rank and a mortgage may be registered in place of the one that has been deleted.

20.3.1 Under Swiss law, parties may agree "as to the events that constitute a default or otherwise give rise to the rights and remedies" (as provided by Article 11.1 of the *Cape Town Convention*).

20.3.2 The secured creditor may in principle realize the encumbered asset by private sale (as provided by Article 8.1(b) of the *Cape Town Convention*). The creditor who has acquired the ownership of the aircraft as security may sell the aircraft to a third party or keep it in payment; in either case, the creditor must account to the grantor and remit any excess proceeds resulting from the realization.

On the other hand, Swiss law is interpreted as not allowing the creditor to proceed by way of private sale if its security interest is an aircraft mortgage; in this case, the creditor must in principle resort to enforced sale proceedings (see also Article VII.1 of the *Geneva Convention on the international recognition of rights in aircraft*, of June 19, 1948).

20.3.3 Under Swiss law, the parties to a security agreement are at liberty to agree on other remedies in the case of an event of default, within the limit of compulsory law.

If the security at stake is a transfer of ownership for security purpose or a financial lease, the parties may in particular provide (in advance or upon the occurrence of an event of default) that the secured creditor is allowed to grant a lease of the aircraft received as security or to collect any income or profit arising from the management or use of such aircraft (cf. Article 8.1 (b) and (c) of the *Cape Town Convention*).

It is usually accepted that the parties may agree after default that the asset encumbered by a limited right *in rem* security interest shall vest to the secured creditor in satisfaction of the secured obligation (cf. Article 9.1 of the *Cape Town Convention*); likewise, the creditor who is entitled to realize the asset by way of private sale may acquire it itself, provided it accounts to the grantor and remits any excess proceeds resulting from such sale. It can be argued that the beneficiary of an aircraft mortgage may be contractually allowed to resort to these two remedies provided no enforcement proceedings have been initiated yet.

20.4.1 Security interests encumbering an aircraft, if validly created, are effective and enforceable towards third parties in enforcement proceedings (cf. Article 30 of the *Cape Town Convention*).

20.4.2 Aircraft mortgages are not immune to insolvency proceedings; the remedies under Alternative A or Alternative B of Article XI of the *Aircraft Protocol* are not fully compatible with the present state of Swiss law.

20.1   Introduction

Le présent rapport soumet les réponses de droit suisse au questionnaire préparé par le prof. Souichirou Kozuka, rapporteur général. Conformément aux instructions reçues, il reprend la structure générale proposée, en réaménageant toutefois dans la mesure du nécessaire l'ordre des réponses aux questions posées.

Il est par ailleurs rappelé que si la Suisse a signé la Convention du Cap[1] ainsi que ses protocoles aéronautique et ferroviaire, elle ne les a pas ratifiés; elle n'a en outre pas signé le protocole portant sur les questions spécifiques aux biens spatiaux.[2]

---

[1] Convention relative aux garanties internationales portant sur des matériels d'équipement mobiles, du 16 novembre 2001.

[2] Pour l'état des signatures et ratifications de ces instruments, cf. http://www.unidroit.org/french/implement/i-main.htm.

20.2   Sûretés mobilières moyennant inscription dans un registre

20.2.1   Types de sûretés

20.2.1.1   Généralités

En droit suisse, les droits réels (droits *in rem*) sont énumérés limitativement par la loi.[3] Ce *numerus clausus* vaut également pour les sûretés réelles : les parties ne peuvent pas créer d'autres types de sûretés réelles que ceux mis à leur disposition par le législateur.

Les principales sûretés réelles mobilières connues du droit suisse sont les suivantes :

- Le *droit de gage*, qui procure au créancier gagiste, s'il n'est pas désintéressé lorsque la créance garantie devient exigible, la faculté de (faire) procéder à la réalisation du bien grevé et de se payer par préférence sur le produit de cette réalisation (cf. notamment l'art. 891 al. 1 CC[4]).

  Corollaire du *numerus clausus*, l'art. 884 al. 1 CC prévoit qu'« en dehors des exceptions prévues par la loi, les choses mobilières ne peuvent être constituées en gage que sous forme de nantissement ».

  En d'autres termes, la mise en gage des choses mobilières s'effectue en principe moyennant transfert de possession de l'objet grevé au créancier gagiste (*nantissement*). Ce n'est qu'à titre exceptionnel que le droit suisse admet l'engagement d'une chose mobilière sans dépossession,[5] par l'inscription dans un registre; peuvent notamment être grevés d'une telle *hypothèque mobilière* : les choses mobilières immatriculées dans des registres *ad hoc* (ou « choses mobilières immobilisées » : aéronefs, navires, bateaux) et le bétail (art. 885 CC).

- Le *transfert de propriété aux fins de garantie* (ou propriété-sûreté; *fiducia cum creditore*), en vertu duquel la propriété d'une chose est transférée au créancier en garantie d'une créance (ou de plusieurs créances).[6] Le créancier acquiert la pleine propriété de l'objet ainsi transféré[7] (et non une propriété *sui generis*); en revanche, ce fiduciaire s'engage contractuellement envers le transférant

---

[3] Cf. STEINAUER, Les droits réels, Tome I, p. 69.

[4] CC : Code civil suisse, du 10 décembre 1907 (Recueil systématique du droit fédéral, 210; ce Recueil systématique du droit fédéral est accessible à l'adresse suivante : http://www.admin.ch/bundesrecht/00566/index.html?lang=fr).

[5] Cf. à cet égard l'art. 884 al. 3 CC : « le droit de gage n'existe pas, tant que le constituant garde exclusivement la maîtrise effective de la chose ».

[6] Voir par exemple : STEINAUER, Les droits réels, Tome III, p. 427 ss.

[7] Voir par exemple : Arrêt du Tribunal fédéral suisse 5A_189/2010, du 12 mai 2010, *in* Revue du notariat et du registre foncier 2012, p. 294 ss, p. 298 s.

(ou fiduciant) à n'exercer la propriété ainsi acquise que dans les limites du but de garantie de l'opération et à retransférer la propriété au fiduciant à l'extinction de la créance garantie.

Toutes les choses mobilières peuvent faire l'objet d'un transfert de propriété aux fins de garantie. A noter toutefois, s'agissant des choses mobilières « ordinaires » (à savoir, non immatriculées dans un registre), que le transfert de propriété n'est pas opposable aux tiers si la possession est transférée au fiduciaire par constitut possessoire (cas dans lequel le fiduciant reste en possession immédiate de la chose) (art. 717 al. 1 CC).

– La *réserve de propriété*, qui a pour effet de retarder le transfert de la propriété de la chose mobilière aliénée jusqu'à ce que la contreprestation due par l'acquéreur (soit, en général, le paiement du prix de vente) ait été exécutée.[8] Pour produire ses effets, la réserve de propriété doit être inscrite dans un registre spécial, intitulé registre des pactes de réserve de propriété (art. 715 al. 1 CC). La propriété réservée est une pleine propriété.

Seules les choses mobilières « ordinaires » peuvent faire l'objet d'une réserve de propriété; les choses mobilières immatriculées dans un registre et le bétail ne peuvent pas être aliénées sous réserve de propriété.[9]

– Le *leasing financier*, en vertu duquel le donneur de *leasing* acquiert auprès d'un tiers la propriété de la chose (mobilière[10]) désignée par le preneur de *leasing* pour en laisser l'usage et la jouissance au preneur pendant une durée déterminée en échange du versement d'une redevance périodique.[11] La propriété du donneur de *leasing* est également une pleine propriété.[12]

Toutes les choses mobilières peuvent faire l'objet d'un *leasing financier*.

A noter que le *lease-back* (dans lequel le preneur transfère la propriété de la chose au donneur, lequel laisse l'usage et la jouissance de celle-ci au preneur contre versement d'une redevance périodique[13]) procure en principe au donneur une propriété qui n'est pas opposable aux tiers (art. 717 al. 1 CC)[14] et n'est donc pas pratiqué en Suisse.

---

[8] Cf. par exemple: STEINAUER, Les droits réels, Tome II, p. 316 ss.

[9] Cf. par exemple : STEINAUER, Les droits réels, Tome II, p. 319. Voir en particulier l'art. 715 al. 2 CC s'agissant du bétail.

[10] Il s'agit en principe d'un bien d'investissement; cf. Arrêt du Tribunal fédéral du 30 avril 1992, publié au Recueil officiel des Arrêts du Tribunal fédéral 118 II 150/152 s. (traduit au Journal des Tribunaux 1994 II 98/102).

[11] Cf. par exemple : STEINAUER, Les droits réels, Tome III, p. 426.

[12] STEINAUER, Les droits réels, Tome III, p. 426.

[13] Cf. KUHN, Schweizerisches Kreditsicherungsrecht, p. 366.

[14] Arrêt du Tribunal fédéral du 25 mai 1993, publié au Recueil officiel des Arrêts du Tribunal fédéral 119 II 236/241; KUHN, Schweizerisches Kreditsicherungsrecht, p. 366 s.

20.2.1.2 Sûretés réelles portant sur un moyen de transport

1. *Aéronefs* (avions, hélicoptères, etc.[15]) : à l'instar de nombreux pays, la Suisse connaît l'hypothèque aérienne. Il s'agit d'un gage sans dépossession, qui naît moyennant inscription dans un registre (art. 15 al. 1 et 28 al. 1 LRA[16]) : le « registre des aéronefs ». Ce registre des aéronefs est un registre destiné à rendre publics certains rapports de droit privé (propriété, hypothèque, contrats de location et d'affrètement, etc.)[17] concernant les aéronefs.

L'immatriculation d'un aéronef au registre des aéronefs n'est pas obligatoire[18] et intervient à la demande du propriétaire de l'aéronef (art. 1 al. 2 LRA); un aéronef qui n'est pas immatriculé au registre des aéronefs ne peut pas être grevé d'une hypothèque aérienne : il suit le régime juridique applicable aux choses mobilières ordinaires (cf. art. 12 al. 1 LRA)[19] et sa mise en gage s'effectue moyennant transfert de la possession au créancier gagiste.[20] Une fraction seulement (environ 10%) des aéronefs suisses sont immatriculés au registre des aéronefs.[21]

Les aéronefs peuvent faire l'objet d'un transfert de propriété aux fins de garantie.[22] Si l'aéronef est immatriculé au registre des aéronefs, le transfert de la propriété au fiduciaire s'effectue moyennant inscription du fiduciaire comme propriétaire dans le registre (art. 14 et 23 al. 1 LRA); s'il s'agit d'un aéronef non immatriculé, le transfert de propriété implique le transfert de la possession (art. 714 al. 1 CC).[23]

L'aéronef immatriculé au registre des aéronefs ne peut pas faire l'objet d'une réserve de propriété.[24] En revanche, un aéronef non immatriculé dans ce registre

[15] L'art. 1 al. 2 de la Loi fédérale sur l'aviation du 21 décembre 1948 (« LA »; Recueil systématique du droit fédéral, 748.0) définit les aéronefs comme étant « les appareils volants qui peuvent se soutenir dans l'atmosphère grâce à des réactions de l'air autres que les réactions de l'air à la surface du sol (véhicules à coussin d'air) »; cf. également à cet égard l'annexe VII de la Convention internationale relative à l'aviation civile internationale, du 7 décembre 1944 (« Convention de Chicago », en vigueur pour la Suisse à compter du 4 avril 1947; Recueil systématique du droit fédéral, 0.748.0).

[16] LRA : Loi fédérale sur le registre des aéronefs, du 7 octobre 1959 (Recueil systématique du droit fédéral, 748.217.1).

[17] Cf. les art. 3 ss LRA.

[18] Ce registre est distinct du registre (appelé en Suisse « registre matricule »; art. 52 LA) destiné à recevoir les immatriculations d'aéronefs prévues par les art. 17 ss de la Convention de Chicago).

[19] Cf. McNally, Recht der Sicherung, p. 27.

[20] Cf. BK-Zobl and Thurnherr, Das Fahrnispfand, Systematischer Teil, N 385; Gross, L'hypothèque aérienne, p. 54.

[21] Pour des statistiques, voir notamment McNally, Recht der Sicherung, p. 28 (n. 102); Kuhn, Schweizerisches Kreditsicherungsrecht, p. 295.

[22] Cf. Kuhn, Schweizerisches Kreditsicherungsrecht, p. 294. *Contra* : McNally, Recht der Sicherung, p. 90.

[23] Cf. l'art. 717 al. 1 CC (*supra*, 20.2.1.1 [deuxième tiret]) si le transfert de possession a lieu par constitut possessoire.

[24] Cf. Steinauer, Les droits réels, Tome II, p. 319; Kuhn, Schweizerisches Kreditsicherungsrecht, p. 294; McNally, Recht der Sicherung, p. 90.

peut être transféré sous réserve de propriété[25]; l'art. 715 al. 1 CC[26] est alors applicable.

Les aéronefs peuvent faire l'objet d'un *leasing* financier.[27] Si l'aéronef est immatriculé au registre des aéronefs, le contrat de *leasing* peut être annoté dans le registre si sa durée est supérieure à six mois[28]; les droits du preneur deviennent ainsi opposables aux droits acquis postérieurement sur l'aéronef.[29]

De même, les aéronefs immatriculés au registre des aéronefs peuvent faire l'objet d'une opération de *sale and lease-back*[30] : l'art. 717 al. 1 CC[31] n'est pas applicable, le transfert de la propriété s'effectuant par inscription du donneur de *leasing* comme propriétaire dans le registre (et non moyennant transfert de la possession). La propriété du donneur de leasing dans un tel *lease-back* d'aéronef immatriculé au registre des aéronefs est une pleine propriété.

2. *Matériel roulant ferroviaire* : jusqu'à récemment, le droit Suisse permettait la mise en gage du matériel roulant ferroviaire avec inscription dans un registre. Il ne s'agissait toutefois pas d'un gage visant uniquement le matériel roulant ferroviaire, mais d'un gage général grevant toute une installation ferroviaire (voies, gares, hangars, ateliers, matériel d'exploitation, etc.) et englobant à ce titre le matériel roulant ferroviaire.[32]

Par une modification entrée en vigueur le 1er janvier 2010,[33] le législateur suisse a exclu le matériel roulant ferroviaire des objets susceptibles d'être grevés par ce gage ferroviaire.[34] Il s'agissait de permettre à l'avenir la mise en gage séparée du matériel roulant ferroviaire[35]; le législateur n'a cependant pas introduit à cette occasion un gage nouveau et s'est réservé de tenir compte ultérieurement des « efforts entrepris […] pour mettre en place un droit de gage international »[36] (à savoir, la garantie internationale prévue par la Convention du Cap et le Protocole de

---

[25] McNally, Recht der Sicherung, p. 90.

[26] Inscription de la réserve au registre des pactes de réserve de propriété; cf. *supra*, 20.2.1.1 (troisième tiret).

[27] McNally, Recht der Sicherung, p. 95 ss.

[28] Art. 5 lit. d LRA. Kuhn, Schweizerisches Kreditsicherungsrecht, p. 295; McNally, Recht der Sicherung, p. 97.

[29] Cf. art. 959 al. 1 CC (applicable en vertu de l'art. 7 LRA). Voir aussi : Kuhn, Schweizerisches Kreditsicherungsrecht, p. 295; McNally, Recht der Sicherung, p. 97.

[30] Frick, Finanzleasinggeschäfte, p. 249 s.

[31] *Supra*, 20.2.1.1 (deuxième tiret).

[32] Cf. par exemple : Kuhn, Schweizerisches Kreditsicherungsrecht, p. 306; Luciani, Les chemins de fer, p. 66.

[33] Recueil officiel du droit fédéral 2009 pp. 5622 et 5628.

[34] Voir l'art. 9 al. 2 de la Loi fédérale concernant la constitution de gages sur les entreprises de chemins de fer et de navigation et la liquidation forcée de ces entreprises, du 25 septembre 1917 (Recueil systématique du droit fédéral, 742.211).

[35] Cf. le Message du Conseil fédéral sur la réforme des chemins de fer 2, du 23 février 2005, *in* Feuille fédérale 2005 p. 2269 ss, p. 2323.

[36] Message du Conseil fédéral (n. 35), p. 2323.

Luxembourg[37]). Dans l'intervalle, le matériel roulant ferroviaire ne peut donc être grevé de gage que moyennant transfert de possession au créancier gagiste (nantissement).

Le matériel roulant ferroviaire peut faire l'objet d'un transfert de propriété aux fins de garantie (moyennant transfert de possession; art. 714 al. 1 CC), d'un contrat de *leasing* financier et d'une réserve de propriété (moyennant inscription au registre des pactes de réserve de propriété; art. 715 al. 1 CC).

3. *Biens spatiaux* : le droit suisse ne connaît pas de règles spécifiques concernant l'engagement de biens spatiaux.[38] Ce sont donc les règles ordinaires qui s'appliquent : la mise en gage des satellites et autres engins spatiaux nécessite le transfert de possession du bien grevé au créancier gagiste; l'on doit probablement admettre que si le bien spatial en cause se trouve dans l'espace, le créancier a une possession suffisante s'il a le contrôle[39] de celui-ci.

En théorie, rien ne s'oppose à ce que les biens spatiaux fassent l'objet d'un transfert de propriété aux fins de garantie (moyennant transfert de possession; art. 714 al. 1 CC) et d'une réserve de propriété (moyennant inscription au registre des pactes de réserve de propriété; art. 715 al. 1 CC). Leur financement par le biais d'un *leasing* financier de droit suisse est également possible.

4. Pour mémoire, l'on rappellera ici que le droit suisse connaît en outre la mise en gage par inscription dans un registre (hypothèque) de ces autres moyens de transport que sont les *navires et bateaux* enregistrés dans des registres *ad hoc*.[40] Un transfert de propriété aux fins de garantie, un *leasing* financier ainsi qu'un *lease-back* sont également envisageables. En revanche, les navires et bateaux immatriculés ne peuvent pas faire l'objet d'une réserve de propriété.[41]

Ces moyens de transport n'étant toutefois pas visés par le questionnaire, on les laissera de côté dans le présent rapport.

5. Il résulte de ce qui précède qu'en droit suisse, les aéronefs peuvent être grevés d'une hypothèque (s'ils sont immatriculés dans le registre des aéronefs) et que tel n'est le cas ni du matériel roulant ferroviaire, ni des biens spatiaux. La comparaison avec le régime juridique prévu par la Convention du Cap (et son Protocole aéronautique) s'avère donc plus fructueuse pour les aéronefs que pour les deux autres moyens de transport. Les développements qui suivent se limitent dès lors aux sûretés sur

---

[37] Cf. KUHN, Schweizerisches Kreditsicherungsrecht, p. 307.

[38] A noter que la Suisse est l'un des nombreux Etats ayant ratifié la Convention internationale sur l'immatriculation des objets lancés dans l'espace extra-atmosphérique, du 12 novembre 1974 (Recueil systématique du droit fédéral, 0.790.3).

[39] Cf. art. 8 al. 1 *lit*. a de la Convention du Cap et art. XIX du Protocole relatif aux biens spatiaux; voir aussi l'art. II al. 2 de la Convention mentionnée *supra*, n. 38.

[40] Voir à cet égard les art. 38 ss de la Loi fédérale sur le registre des bateaux (du 28 septembre 1923; Recueil systématique du droit fédéral, 747.11) et les art. 37 ss de la Loi fédérale sur la navigation maritime sous pavillon suisse (du 23 septembre 1953; Recueil systématique du droit fédéral, 747.30).

[41] STEINAUER, Les droits réels, Tome II, p. 319; KUHN, Schweizerisches Kreditsicherungsrecht, p. 323.

aéronef immatriculé au registre des aéronefs, en se concentrant avant tout sur l'hypothèque aérienne des art. 26 ss LRA.

20.2.2 Respect de l'autonomie privée

Conformément à sa tradition de pragmatisme et de respect de l'autonomie privée, le droit suisse ne soumet pas les différents types de sûretés à un régime juridique unique ou commun : la propriété du donneur de *leasing* ou de l'acquéreur aux fins de garantie est une pleine propriété (*plena in re potestas*), l'hypothèque (aérienne) est un droit réel limité (qui ne confère à son titulaire que certaines des facultés que l'on peut tirer du bien grevé); la propriété et l'hypothèque sont des droits réels distincts, dont les effets et les régimes juridiques ne sont pas les mêmes.

En outre, contrairement à la Convention du Cap (cf. art. 2 al. 2), le droit suisse ne range pas même les différentes formes de sûretés sous une appellation commune.[42]

20.2.3 Inscription d'une sûreté au registre des aéronefs

1. A l'instar du registre international prévu par la Convention du Cap, le registre suisse des aéronefs est un registre fondé sur le système réel (« asset-based ») : il est tenu en fonction des aéronefs (cf. notamment les art. 8 al. 1 LRA et 3 al. 1 RERA[43]), et non en fonction de la personne du propriétaire (ou du débiteur).

2. Il ne s'agit en revanche pas d'un registre fondé sur le simple avis d'enregistrement (« notice filing »). En particulier, la constitution d'une hypothèque aérienne suppose la réunion des conditions suivantes : un contrat revêtu de la forme écrite (art. 28 al. 2 LRA),[44] une demande écrite d'inscription émanant du propriétaire (art. 8 RERA) et l'inscription de l'hypothèque dans le registre (art. 28 al. 1 LRA). L'inscription produit un effet constitutif, en ce sens que l'hypothèque ne naît pas sans elle (cf. aussi l'art. 14 LRA). L'inscription est opérée par le préposé du registre, pour autant que les conditions (contrat et demande écrits) en soient réunies[45]; l'effet de l'inscription rétroagit au jour où la demande d'inscription a été

---

[42] On peut notamment citer comme exception les art. 31 et 32 de la Loi fédérale sur les titres intermédiés (du 3 octobre 2008; Recueil systématique du droit fédéral, 957.1) qui réunissent sous l'appellation unique « sûreté » toutes les catégories de sûretés pouvant porter sur un titre détenu auprès d'un intermédiaire. Cf. par exemple : KUHN, Schweizerisches Kreditsicherungsrecht, p. 475.

[43] RERA : Règlement d'exécution de la loi fédérale sur le registre des aéronefs, du 2 septembre 1960; Recueil systématique du droit fédéral, 748.217.11.

[44] Les droits réels suisses sont soumis au système de causalité, si bien que l'inscription doit reposer sur un contrat constitutif valable; cf. McNALLY, Recht der Sicherung, p. 40.

[45] Cf. par exemple: GROSS, L'hypothèque aérienne, p. 42.

reçue par le registre et consignée dans un registre chronologique appelé « journal » (art. 15 al. 2 LRA et art. 4 RERA).

3. Le transfert de propriété aux fins de garantie ainsi que l'acquisition de la propriété par le donneur de *leasing* financier (ou de *lease-back*) nécessitent l'inscription du bénéficiaire de la sûreté comme propriétaire au registre des aéronefs[46]; cette inscription produit également un effet constitutif (art. 14 et 23 al. 1 LRA). La propriété du fiduciaire ou du donneur de *leasing* étant une pleine propriété,[47] l'inscription ne révèle pas le but de garantie de l'opération : l'acquéreur aux fins de garantie et le donneur de *leasing* sont inscrits au registre en qualité de propriétaire. Le droit du preneur d'utiliser l'aéronef peut apparaître au registre sous la forme d'une annotation si le contrat a une durée supérieure à six mois.[48]

4. Les inscriptions ainsi opérées bénéficient d'une certaine foi publique; en particulier, l'art. 16 al. 1 LRA dispose que « celui qui a acquis la propriété ou un droit de gage en se fondant de bonne foi sur une inscription du registre des aéronefs est maintenu dans son acquisition »; en outre, l'art. 18 LRA prévoit que « la Confédération est responsable de tout dommage résultant de la tenue du registre des aéronefs ». Il s'agit là de différences importantes par rapport au système prévu par la Convention du Cap.[49]

20.2.4   Rang des sûretés inscrites au registre des aéronefs

1. Le rang des hypothèques aériennes (conventionnelles)[50] est fixé non pas en fonction de la date de leur constitution, mais selon la « case hypothécaire » occupée par le gage.[51] Les parties peuvent par exemple convenir que l'hypothèque qu'elles créent occupera une « case » de deuxième rang (ou un rang plus élevé encore), alors même que l'aéronef n'est encore grevé d'aucune hypothèque; il suffit pour cela qu'elles indiquent le montant par lequel le gage de deuxième rang sera primé.[52] La case ainsi réservée sera de premier rang; le constituant a alors la faculté de créer en tout temps une hypothèque (en respectant le montant maximum fixé à l'avance) et de convenir avec le nouveau créancier gagiste qu'elle occupera cette case : cette

---

[46] Cf., s'agissant du *leasing* : Kuhn, Schweizerisches Kreditsicherungsrecht, p. 295; Frick, Finanzleasinggeschäfte, p. 248 s. Voir en outre, s'agissant du transfert de propriété aux fins de garantie : Kuhn, Schweizerisches Kreditsicherungsrecht, p. 294.

[47] Cf. *supra*, 20.2.1.1 (deuxième et quatrième tirets).

[48] Cf. *supra*, 20.2.1.2.1 (appels de note 28 et 29). Aucune possibilité d'annotation n'est prévue s'agissant du transfert de propriété aux fins de garantie.

[49] Voir notamment les art. 28 al. 2 de la Convention du Cap. Voir pour le surplus McNally, Recht der Sicherung, p. 267.

[50] Les hypothèques naissant *ex lege* priment les hypothèques conventionnelles (art. 49 al. 1 LRA).

[51] Art. 26 al. 2 et 7 LRA, art. 813 al. 1 CC. Gross, L'hypothèque aérienne, p. 72; McNally, Recht der Sicherung, p. 40.

[52] Art. 7 LRA et art. 813 al. 2 CC. McNally, Recht der Sicherung, p. 41; Gross, L'hypothèque aérienne, p. 72.

hypothèque primera l'hypothèque créée antérieurement (et aura priorité sur elle), car elle occupe une case de rang préférable.

Ce système est appelé système des « cases fixes »[53] : si une case se libère suite à la radiation d'une hypothèque (par exemple, parce que le paiement de la créance garantie a entraîné l'extinction de l'hypothèque), les hypothèques de rang postérieur ne profitent pas de cette radiation pour avancer en rang.[54] Le propriétaire de l'aéronef a au contraire la faculté de constituer une nouvelle hypothèque en lieu et place de celle qui a été radiée[55] (dont la créance garantie ne doit pas dépasser le montant initialement attribué à la case en cause); cette hypothèque primera les hypothèques occupant une case de rang postérieur, alors même qu'elle a été constituée après celles-ci. Les parties peuvent déroger à ce système et convenir qu'une hypothèque profitera des cases qui se libèrent[56]; cette convention de nature purement contractuelle peut être annotée dans le registre (art. 5 *lit.* c LRA), aux fins d'être opposable aux droits acquis postérieurement sur l'aéronef.[57]

2. Ce système est en apparence assez éloigné de celui institué par l'art. 29 al. 1 de la Convention du Cap, selon lequel « une garantie prime toute autre garantie inscrite postérieurement ». Mais en réalité, les cases hypothécaires du droit suisse ont un rang, qui est déterminé par leur date de constitution : le principe de la priorité dans le temps s'applique aux cases hypothécaires.

Les parties bénéficient d'une liberté appréciable puisqu'elles peuvent librement décider si elles entendent d'emblée créer une case libre de rang préférable à la case qu'occupera l'hypothèque qu'elles sont en train de créer; elles peuvent en outre déterminer, lorsqu'une case se libère, si une hypothèque à créer occupera cette case ou non, et peuvent enfin déroger au système des cases fixes.

3. On observera par ailleurs que la « réserve de rang » est possible dans les deux systèmes : l'article 16 al. 1 *lit.* a de la Convention du Cap prévoit que des garanties internationales futures peuvent être inscrites dans le registre international; lorsque cette garantie future devient une garantie internationale (art. 18 al. 3 de la Convention du Cap), elle « est réputée avoir été inscrite lors de l'inscription de la garantie internationale future » (art. 19 al. 4 de la Convention du Cap) et acquiert ainsi le rang attaché à cette inscription. Il en va de même en droit suisse : une hypothèque aérienne inscrite dans la case initialement réservée bénéficiera du rang attribué à cette case.[58] Les principales différences résultent du fait que le montant maximal du gage à créer doit être précisé lors de la réserve de rang en droit suisse[59] (alors que tel n'est pas le cas selon la Convention du Cap[60]) et que les parties ne sont pas les mêmes :

---

[53] Cf. Art. 26 al. 2 LRA. McNally, Recht der Sicherung, p. 40; BK-Zobl and Thurnherr, Das Fahrnispfand, Systematischer Teil, N 385; Gross, L'hypothèque aérienne, p. 72.

[54] Art. 7 LRA et art. 814 al. 1 CC. McNally, Recht der Sicherung, p. 41.

[55] Art. 7 LRA et art. 814 al. 2 CC. McNally, Recht der Sicherung, p. 41.

[56] Gross, L'hypothèque aérienne, p. 72; McNally, Recht der Sicherung, p. 41.

[57] McNally, Recht der Sicherung, p. 41.

[58] Cf. *supra*, 20.2.4.1.

[59] Cf. *supra*, appel de note 52.

[60] Cf. art. 7 *lit.* d de la Convention du Cap.

en droit suisse, il s'agit du propriétaire et du créancier dont l'hypothèque sera primée par le gage à constituer,[61] alors que selon l'art. 20 al. 1 de la Convention, il s'agit du futur constituant et du futur créancier garanti.

4. On notera enfin qu'en droit suisse, l'hypothèque inscrite au registre des aéronefs l'emporte sans autre sur une hypothèque non encore inscrite. Cela tient au fait que l'inscription de l'hypothèque au registre des aéronefs produit un effet constitutif[62] : à la différence de ce que prévoit l'art. 7 de la Convention du Cap pour la garantie internationale, une hypothèque dont la constitution est convenue par contrat n'existe pas tant qu'elle n'est pas inscrite. Il n'existe dès lors pas à proprement parler de problème de rang entre une hypothèque aérienne inscrite et une hypothèque non encore inscrite; les droits du créancier titulaire de la première l'emportent sans autre sur les droits de nature purement contractuelle du second, même si le créancier gagiste a connaissance de la convention tendant à constituer la deuxième hypothèque (cf. art. 19 al. 1 et 2 de la Convention du Cap).

5. De même, les droits du propriétaire (auquel la propriété a été transférée aux fins de garantie ou qui est un donneur de *leasing*) l'emportent sur les droits de nature contractuelle qu'il n'a pas concédés; il en va différemment si le droit personnel en cause (dérivant d'un contrat de leasing, de location ou d'affrètement d'une durée supérieure à six mois) a été annoté au registre des aéronefs (art. 5 *lit.* d LRA) avant l'acquisition de la propriété (par le fiduciaire ou le donneur de leasing) : le droit annoté est en effet opposable à tout droit acquis postérieurement sur l'aéronef.[63]

20.3   Mesures en cas d'inexécution

20.3.1   *Définition contractuelle de l'inexécution*

En principe, la réalisation du bien grevé par la sûreté ne peut intervenir que si le débiteur ne s'exécute pas alors que la créance garantie est devenue exigible.[64] A cet égard, les parties sont libres de convenir en droit suisse des modalités d'exigibilité de la créance.[65] Elles peuvent également convenir que le créancier aura la faculté de procéder à la réalisation même si sa créance n'est pas encore exigible (par exemple, en cas de violation de telle obligation ou à la survenance de tel événement).[66]

Les parties peuvent donc convenir, à l'instar de ce que prévoit l'art. 11 al. 1 de la Convention du Cap, « des circonstances qui constituent une inexécution, ou de tout autre circonstance de nature à permettre l'exercice des droits » du créancier. Le droit

---

[61] Cf. *supra*, 20.2.4.1.

[62] Cf. *supra*, 20.2.3.2.

[63] Cf. *supra*, n. 29.

[64] Cf. par exemple Kuhn, Schweizerisches Kreditsicherungsrecht, p. 168 s.

[65] Cf. par exemple Kuhn, Schweizerisches Kreditsicherungsrecht, p. 169.

[66] Cf. par exemple Kuhn, Schweizerisches Kreditsicherungsrecht, p. 169.

suisse ne pose à cet égard aucune exigence de forme (cf. art. 11 al. 1 CO[67]), contrairement à la Convention du Cap, dont l'art. 11 al. 1 exige que de telles stipulations
relatives à l'inexécution soient convenues « par écrit ».[68]

20.3.2   Réalisation privée

1. A l'instar de l'art. 8 al. 1 *lit.* b de la Convention du Cap, le droit suisse reconnaît
en principe la validité des clauses contractuelles autorisant le créancier à procéder à
la réalisation privée de l'objet grevé par sa sûreté.[69]

2. S'agissant du transfert de propriété aux fins de garantie et du *leasing*, une
réalisation forcée ne serait d'ailleurs pas envisageable : le créancier étant propriétaire de l'aéronef servant de garantie, il ne peut en droit suisse demander à l'autorité
d'exécution forcée de procéder à sa réalisation forcée.[70] En cas d'inexécution de la
part du débiteur, le créancier qui a acquis la propriété aux fins de garantie peut
procéder à la réalisation privée ou conserver lui-même la propriété de l'aéronef;
dans les deux cas, il doit fournir un décompte au constituant et restituer à ce dernier
la différence éventuelle entre la valeur de réalisation et le montant de sa créance.[71]
Quant au donneur de *leasing*, il dispose sauf convention contraire des facultés que
réserve l'art. 107 al. 2 CO au créancier envers son débiteur en demeure dans les
contrats synallagmatiques : il peut à son choix exiger l'exécution du contrat ainsi
que le paiement de dommages-intérêts de retard, renoncer à l'exécution du contrat
et exiger des dommages-intérêts pour cause d'inexécution, ou encore se départir du
contrat et exiger la réparation du dommage résultant de la caducité du contrat[72]; il
n'est pas rare que les parties précisent dans leur contrat les droits du donneur en cas
d'inexécution.

3. Selon les auteurs, l'hypothèque aérienne fait exception au principe de
l'admissibilité de la réalisation privée.[73] L'art. 46 LRA prévoit en effet que « faute
par le débiteur de satisfaire à ses obligations, le créancier a le droit de se payer, par
voie d'exécution forcée, sur le prix de vente de l'aéronef »; la loi prescrit donc la
réalisation forcée et paraît exclure par là même la réalisation privée. Cette disposition

---

[67] CO : Loi fédérale complétant le Code civil suisse (Livre cinquième : Droit des obligations), du
30 mars 1911 (Code des obligations; Recueil systématique du droit fédéral, 220).

[68] Pour la définition du terme « écrit », voir l'art. 1er *lit.* nn de la Convention du Cap.

[69] Voir notamment : KUHN, Schweizerisches Kreditsicherungsrecht, p. 178 s.

[70] Cf. par exemple, s'agissant du transfert de propriété aux fins de garantie : BK-ZOBL AND
THURNHERR, Das Fahrnispfand, Systematischer Teil, N 1488.

[71] Cf. STEINAUER, Les droits réels, Tome III, p. 431. Voir aussi: BK-ZOBL AND THURNHERR, Das
Fahrnispfand, Systematischer Teil, N 1488 s.

[72] Cf. KUHN, Schweizerisches Kreditsicherungsrecht, p. 301.

[73] Cf. MCNALLY, Recht der Sicherung, pp. 56 et 217; EGLI, Die Luftfahrzeugverschreibung, p. 67.
Voir aussi: Message du Conseil fédéral à l'Assemblée fédérale à l'appui d'un projet de loi sur le
registre des aéronefs, du 13 mars 1959, *in* Feuille fédérale 1959 I 452 ss, p. 470.

a été édictée pour tenir compte de l'art. VII al. 1 de la Convention de Genève sur la reconnaissance internationale des droits sur aéronef,[74] qui est interprété comme autorisant uniquement la réalisation forcée.[75]

A vrai dire, le texte de cette dernière disposition se contente de désigner le droit applicable à la réalisation forcée,[76] sans se prononcer sur les éventuels autres moyens à disposition du créancier gagiste. La Convention de Genève contient d'autres dispositions dont on pourrait tirer (directement ou *a contrario*) que la réalisation privée d'un aéronef n'est en soi pas exclue.[77] On peut dès lors légitimement se demander si l'art. VII al. 1 de la Convention de Genève peut véritablement être compris comme interdisant aux parties de convenir d'une réalisation privée.

Il reste que l'art. 46 LRA n'est guère ambigu en tant qu'il prescrit de suivre la voie de l'exécution forcée. Compte tenu de ce qui précède, il y a cependant lieu d'interpréter restrictivement cette disposition. Il n'y a par exemple aucune raison d'interdire aux parties, si aucune procédure d'exécution forcée n'est pendante, de convenir de la vente de l'aéronef avec affectation du prix de vente au remboursement de la créance garantie par l'hypothèque. De même (et toujours sous réserve qu'une procédure d'exécution forcée ne soit entamée), le propriétaire doit pouvoir valablement autoriser le créancier gagiste à vendre l'aéronef (en qualité de représentant direct ou indirect) en se payant sur le produit de la vente[78] et en restituant un surplus éventuel au constituant de l'hypothèque. De tels engagements doivent pouvoir être valablement pris non seulement lorsque la créance garantie devient exigible, mais également à l'avance (par exemple, dans le contrat tendant à la constitution de l'hypothèque); leurs effets cessent si l'aéronef grevé fait l'objet d'une procédure d'exécution forcée ou si le propriétaire de celui-ci fait l'objet d'une procédure d'exécution collective.

20.3.3 Autres mesures

1. La liberté contractuelle étant la règle (art. 19 al. 1 CO), les parties peuvent en principe convenir librement des conséquences de l'inexécution de la créance garantie. Leurs stipulations doivent évidemment respecter les règles de droit impératif. En particulier, elles doivent avoir un contenu licite (art. 20 al. 1 CO) et ne pas

---

[74] Convention relative à la reconnaissance internationale des droits sur aéronef, du 19 juin 1948 (entrée en vigueur pour la Suisse le 1er janvier 1961; Recueil systématique du droit fédéral, 0.748.217.1).

[75] Cf. McNALLY, Recht der Sicherung, p. 56; EGLI, Die Luftfahrzeugverschreibung, p. 67. Voir aussi le Message du Conseil fédéral (*supra*, n. 73), p. 470.

[76] « Les procédures de vente forcée d'un aéronef sont celles prévues par la loi de l'Etat contractant où la vente est effectuée ».

[77] Voir par exemple les art. VII al. 3, VIII et IX de la Convention de Genève.

[78] De cet avis semble-t-il, si l'aéronef n'est grevé que par l'hypothèque du créancier gagiste : EGLI, Die Luftfahrzeugverschreibung, p. 67.

consister en une aliénation contraire aux mœurs de la liberté d'un des contractants (art. 27 al. 1 CC).

2. Cela étant, si la sûreté consiste en un transfert de propriété aux fins de garantie, rien ne s'oppose à ce que les parties conviennent que le créancier aura la faculté, en cas d'inexécution, de remettre l'aéronef à bail et d'en percevoir les loyers ou de percevoir les autres revenus ou profits produits par l'aéronef, ainsi que le permet l'art. 8 al. 1 *lit.* b et c de la Convention du Cap. Le titulaire d'une hypothèque aérienne peut également se faire concéder ces facultés contractuellement.[79] De telles mesures peuvent en théorie également être convenues entre les parties à un contrat de *leasing* ayant pour objet un aéronef.

3. Le transfert de propriété en règlement de la créance garantie (art. 9 al. 1 de la Convention du Cap) n'a de sens que dans le cas de l'hypothèque aérienne : dans le cas du *leasing* et du transfert de propriété aux fins de garantie, le créancier est déjà propriétaire de l'aéronef constituant la garantie.[80]

Le droit suisse frappe de nullité les clauses contractuelles autorisant le créancier à s'approprier l'objet grevé du gage faute de paiement. Cette prohibition du pacte commissoire est ancrée aux articles 816 al. 2 (gages immobiliers) et 894 CC (gages mobiliers); elle a une portée générale[81] et vaut en particulier pour l'hypothèque aérienne.[82]

Cela étant, il est admis que cette interdiction ne frappe pas les clauses conclues après l'exigibilité de la créance garantie (hypothèse également visée par l'art. 9 al. 1 de la Convention du Cap) : dès cette échéance, les parties peuvent valablement convenir de l'acquisition de la propriété du bien grevé par le créancier gagiste à titre de paiement (dation en paiement).[83]

Par ailleurs, il est également admis que l'interdiction du pacte commissoire n'empêche pas le créancier gagiste de se porter lui-même acquéreur de l'objet grevé vendu conformément à la clause contractuelle l'autorisant à procéder à la réalisation privée (« Selbsteintritt »)[84]; il ne s'agit en effet ici pas à proprement parler d'une appropriation, le créancier gagiste devant acquérir l'objet au prix du marché (objectivement déterminable), fournir un décompte et remettre au constituant le surplus éventuel (à savoir, la différence entre le montant de la créance garantie et le prix d'acquisition).[85]

---

[79] D'un avis contraire, semble-t-il : McNally, Recht der Sicherung, pp. 217 et 269; Kuhn, Schweizerisches Kreditsicherungsrecht, p. 301.

[80] Cf., s'agissant du *leasing* financier : Kuhn, Schweizerisches Kreditsicherungsrecht, p. 301.

[81] Kuhn, Schweizerisches Kreditsicherungsrecht, p. 179.

[82] McNally, Recht der Sicherung, p. 56. Voir aussi, s'agissant des hypothèques mobilières en général : Kuhn, Schweizerisches Kreditsicherungsrecht, p. 179; BK-Zobl, Das Fahrnispfand, N 22 *ad* art. 894.

[83] Cf. notamment : Kuhn, Schweizerisches Kreditsicherungsrecht, p. 180; BK-Zobl, Das Fahrnispfand, N 18 *ad* art. 894.

[84] Cf. Kuhn, Schweizerisches Kreditsicherungsrecht, p. 180.

[85] Cf. Kuhn, Schweizerisches Kreditsicherungsrecht, p. 180.

Les deux possibilités qui viennent d'être évoquées (dation en paiement convenue après l'exigibilité de la créance garantie; « Selbsteintritt ») sont également ouvertes au titulaire d'une hypothèque aérienne, aussi longtemps qu'aucune procédure d'exécution forcée n'est ouverte.[86]

4. A l'instar de ce que prévoit l'art. 10 de la Convention du Cap, le donneur de *leasing* peut, en cas d'inexécution de la part du preneur, mettre fin au contrat[87] et exiger d'être mis en possession immédiate de l'aéronef[88]; les parties peuvent convenir que le donneur ne devra aucune indemnité au preneur de ce fait.

20.4 Sort des sûretés en cas de mesures d'exécution forcée

1. Les sûretés réelles mobilières grevant un aéronef et valablement constituées sont opposables dans les procédures d'insolvabilité de droit suisse dirigées contre le constituant et le débiteur. En particulier, la propriété de l'acquéreur aux fins de garantie[89] et la propriété du donneur de *leasing*[90] sont reconnues dans les procédures d'exécution forcée dont le fiduciant ou le preneur de *leasing* peuvent faire l'objet. Quant à l'hypothèque aérienne, elle confère à son titulaire la faculté d'être payé par préférence sur le produit de la réalisation de l'aéronef grevé.[91] Le droit suisse est ainsi conforme à l'exigence posée à l'art. 30 al. 1 de la Convention du Cap.

2. Pour le surplus, l'aéronef grevé d'une hypothèque aérienne est affecté par les mesures d'exécution forcée. Ainsi et par exemple, si l'aéronef fait l'objet d'une saisie (à la demande d'un tiers créancier par exemple) ou d'une procédure en réalisation de gage (intentée par un créancier titulaire d'une hypothèque aérienne), l'office des poursuites (à savoir, l'autorité étatique en charge de la réalisation de l'aéronef) est chargée de l'administration de l'aéronef.[92] En cas de faillite du constituant, l'aéronef grevé tombe dans la masse en faillite (art. 198 LP) et est géré par l'entité en charge de la liquidation des biens, l'administration de la faillite. On le constate, le droit suisse ne prévoit pas de solution comparable à l'alinéa 2 *lit.* b de la Variante A de l'article XI du Protocole aéronautique; il paraît également difficilement

---

[86] Cf. *supra*, 20.3.2.3. D'un avis contraire, semble-t-il : McNally, Recht der Sicherung, pp. 217 et 269; Kuhn, Schweizerisches Kreditsicherungsrecht, p. 301.

[87] Cf. Kuhn, Schweizerisches Kreditsicherungsrecht, pp. 301 et 368. Voir aussi *supra*, appel de note 72.

[88] Sur la question de savoir dans quelle mesure le donneur peut à cet égard recourir à des actes de justice propre, voir notamment : Kuhn, Schweizerisches Kreditsicherungsrecht, p. 369 s.

[89] Voir par exemple: BK-Zobl and Thurnherr, Das Fahrnispfand, Systematischer Teil, N 1478 ss.

[90] Voir par exemple: Kuhn, Schweizerisches Kreditsicherungsrecht, p. 364.

[91] Art. 46 LRA. McNally, Recht der Sicherung, p. 56.

[92] Art. 56 al. 1 et 2 LRA. Cf. McNally, Recht der Sicherung, p. 67 s.; Gross, L'hypothèque aérienne, p. 121 s.

envisageable de satisfaire, en l'état du droit, l'exigence posée à l'alinéa 2 *lit.* b de la Variante B de l'article XI du Protocole aéronautique.[93]

20.5 Considérations générales

1. L'analyse économique du droit suscite un certain intérêt en Suisse, notamment dans les domaines du droit de la concurrence, du droit des sociétés et du droit de la responsabilité civile. L'influence de ces réflexions sur le processus législatif est difficile à apprécier, mais paraît de prime abord limitée; on peut toutefois relever qu'en vertu de l'art. 141 al. 2 *lit.* g LParl,[94] les « Messages » du gouvernement suisse (« Conseil fédéral ») au parlement (« Assemblée fédérale ») à l'appui de projets de loi doivent en principe notamment contenir des indications sur les conséquences économiques du projet de loi en cause[95] (fondées généralement sur une analyse d'impact de la législation proposée).

2. Le principe selon lequel un système performant de sûretés réelles (mobilières) favorise l'octroi de crédit et contribue au développement économique semble admis par de nombreux auteurs.[96]

Bibliographie

1. Egli, Arthur. 1958. *Die Luftfahrzeugverschreibung nach dem Entwurf eines Bundesgesetzes über das Luftfahrzeugbuch.* Winterthur: Université de Zurich (thèse).
2. Eigenmann, Antoine. 2004. *L'effectivité des sûretés mobilières.* Fribourg : Université de Fribourg (thèse).
3. Frick, Joachim. 2000. Finanzleasinggeschäfte am Beispiel von Aircraft Finance-Transaktionen – Strukturen, Vorteile und Risiken. *Revue suisse de droit des affaires et du marché financier:* 242–250.

---

[93] Cf. McNally, Recht der Sicherung, p. 236 (qui préconise qu'en cas de ratification de la Convention du Cap et du Protocole aéronautique, la Suisse s'abstienne de faire une déclaration au sens de l'art. XI al. 1 du Protocole aéronautique).

[94] LParl : Loi sur l'Assemblée fédérale, du 13 décembre 2002 (Recueil systématique du droit fédéral, 171.10).

[95] Voir par exemple : Message du Conseil fédéral relatif au code de procédure civile suisse (CPC), du 28 juin 2006, *in* Feuille fédérale 2006 p. 6841 ss, p. 7017; Message du Conseil fédéral concernant la révision du Code civil suisse (Cédule hypothécaire de registre et autres modifications des droits réels), du 27 juin 2007, *in* Feuille fédérale 2007 p. 5015 ss, p. 5077.

[96] Voir par exemple: Kuhn, Schweizerisches Kreditsicherungsrecht, p. 4; Eigenmann, L'effectivité, notamment p. 53 ss; Giovanoli, Tendances modernes, p. 69 (qui rappelle l'adage « sûretés traquées=crédit détraqué »); Graham-Siegenthaler, Das Bedürfnis nach Sicherheit, p. 450; Graham-Siegenthaler, Kreditsicherungsrechte, p. 724. Voir aussi, à titre d'illustration, le Message du Conseil fédéral concernant la révision du Code civil suisse (*supra*, n. 95), pp. 5027 et 5077; etc.

4. Giovanoli, Mario. 1997. Tendances modernes du droit des sûretés bancaires et contrôle prudentiel des banques. In *Sûretés et garanties bancaires,* éd. Nicolas Iynedjian, 23–69. Lausanne: Cedidac.
5. Graham-Siegenthaler, Barbara Elisabeth. 2006. Das Bedürfnis nach Sicherheit – Möglichkeiten und Schranken des Rechts. *Revue suisse de jurisprudence:* 449–457.
6. Graham-Siegenthaler, Barbara Elisabeth. 2005. *Kreditsicherungsrechte im internationalen Rechtsverkehr.* Berne: Université de Zurich (thèse d'habilitation).
7. Gross, Jean-Pierre. 1967. *L'hypothèque aérienne suisse.* Lausanne : Université de Lausanne (thèse).
8. Kuhn, Hans. 2011. *Schweizerisches Kreditsicherungsrecht.* Berne: Stämpfli.
9. Luciani, Pierre-Xavier. 1999. *Les chemins de fer et l'exécution forcée.* Lausanne: Université de Lausanne (thèse).
10. McNally, Maya. 2009. *Recht der Sicherung und der Finanzierung von Luftfahrzeugen.* Lucerne: Université de Zurich (thèse).
11. Steinauer, Paul-Henri. 2012. *Les droits réels,* Tome I, 5e éd. Berne: Stämpfli.
12. Steinauer, Paul-Henri. 2012. *Les droits réels,* Tome II, 4e éd. Berne: Stämpfli.
13. Steinauer, Paul-Henri. 2012. *Les droits réels,* Tome III, 4e éd. Berne: Stämpfli.
14. Zobl, Dieter, and Thurnherr, Christoph. 2010. Das Fahrnispfand. In *Berner Kommentar,* vol. IV.2.5.1, 3e éd. Berne: Stämpfli.
15. Zobl, Dieter. 1996. Das Fahrnispfand. In *Berner Kommentar,* vol. IV.2.5.2, 2e éd. Berne: Stämpfli.

Bénédict Foëx is a professor at the University of Geneva Faculty of law; he also practices law in a Swiss law firm. His teaching and research mainly focus on secured transactions, property law and contracts. He was a member of the Swiss delegation to the diplomatic conference that adopted the *Cape Town Convention on international interests in mobile equipment* and is a member of UNCITRAL's Working Group VI on Security Interests. He also has been the president of the Swiss Society of Jurists.

Part IV
Comments from the Practice

Chapter 21
Analysing the Effects of the Cape Town Convention on Four Selected Issues That Hinder the International Financing and Leasing of Aircraft and Engines

B. Patrick Honnebier

21.1 Introduction

Due to the worldwide economic problems, currently there exists a very strong competition in the air transport industry. A successful business strategy of the airlines in developed, emerging and undeveloped[1] countries alike is to advertise that they only fly with new aircraft. However, this kind of business promotion requires that they regularly update their fleets. Therefore, despite the existing recession there is an ever-growing[2] need of modern aircraft and aircraft engines (*aircraft objects*[3]). At present, the total demand for helicopters seems to have decreased. However, it is

---

[1] Not only in the Middle East, Asia, Western Europe and the U.S.A. the airlines operate modern aircraft. A prime example is Ethiopian Airlines which keeps ordering new aircraft, also in June, 2015. Ethiopia was the second state to adopt the Cape Town Convention in 2003. Since that time it has benefitted from the substantial advantages of the treaty. www.unidroit.org Moreover, in the global aviation industry it is a well-known fact that the financial effects of the treaty, particularly as a result of obtaining the 'Cape Town Convention Discount', have been very beneficial for Air Canada, Cargolux, several Eastern European carriers and other airlines which recently acquired new aircraft.

[2] For example, Airbus obtained orders and commitments for aircraft worth US $ 57 billion and Boeing for aircraft worth US $ 50.2 billion during the June, 2015 Paris Air Show in France. See Reuters, 18 June, 2015. See also Boeing's forecast, http://www.boeing.com/boeing/commercial/cmo/; Airbus Global Market Forecast 2015–2035, available at http://www.airbus.com/company/market/forecast/

[3] In this contribution the term 'aircraft objects' means aircraft (airframes), helicopters and aircraft engines. For a definition see article I(1)(c) Aircraft Equipment Protocol. For particular aircraft engines problems see Chapter 21.6, *infra*. However, the present contribution concentrates on aircraft (airframes) and engines.

B.P. Honnebier (✉)
Gomez and Bikker Law Offices, Amsterdam, The Netherlands
e-mail: b.honnebier@gobiklaw.com

© Springer International Publishing AG 2017
S. Kozuka (ed.), *Implementing the Cape Town Convention and the Domestic Laws on Secured Transactions*, Ius Comparatum - Global Studies in Comparative Law 22, DOI 10.1007/978-3-319-46470-1_21

assumed that this specialized market will recover before 2019.[4] The present publication focuses on the topics that relate to aircraft and engines. Nevertheless, it should be noted that to a large extent these issues also arise in regard to helicopter-specific finance and lease transactions. Historically, in most countries the aircraft and engines were acquired and owned by the local 'flag-carriers'. In turn, the 'national airlines' were financially controlled by the governments of the states in which they had their head-offices. The purchase of the aircraft and engines was realized by means of public funds. Today, most of the flag-carriers have been privatized[5] which implies that private funding is needed to acquire these aircraft objects. As the price of a large *aircraft* can exceed more than $ 200 million and of an engine to $ 20 million, the financing and leasing of these objects is extremely capital intensive. Besides, it is estimated that for every four aircraft engines, one *spare-engine*[6] is needed. Accordingly, it is necessary that a financier or lessor (owner) can adequately uphold its *proprietary interests*[7] in the certain aircraft (i.e. airframe) or engine in the event that the debtor is in default or becomes insolvent. Moreover, aviation financing and leasing transactions are often structured by means of Special Purpose Vehicles (SPV's). For valid legal, tax, accountancy, air safety supervision and other reasons, the SPV's will be established in different jurisdictions.[8] On the one hand, this useful scenario makes the related finance and lease agreements inherently international in kind. On the other hand, the transnational nature of aviation finance and lease arrangements imposes a burden on the financiers, lessors *and* operators.[9] For example, it has been submitted that this is because:

---

[4] See for example: Global helicopter market forecast and opportunities, 2019.

[5] For instance, the Portuguese state-owned airline TAP was intended to become totally privatized in June 2015. However, these plans did not materialize due to local political reasons. It is one of the few commercial carriers in the Member States of the European Union in which a national government still had a controlling stake.

[6] Unfortunately, the fundamental legal and practical differences between the financing and leasing of 'engines' on the one side and 'spare engines' on the other are not understood by all legal practitioners. See B.P. Honnebier, The merits and pitfalls of the Handbook 'Aviation Financing and Leasing 2014', Zeitschrift für Luft- und Weltraumrecht/German Journal of Air and Space Law (ZLW), 2014–4, p. 559, at p. 577.

[7] In this publication the term 'proprietary interest' or 'property right' includes all the interests and the right of ownership.

[8] For example, well-known 'Flag-States of Choice' where the needed SPV's are purposely established are Aruba, the Caribbean Netherlands, the Cayman Islands and Bermuda. See B.P. Honnebier and A.P. Berkhout, The Caribbean Netherlands is the Flag-State of Choice for cross-border aircraft lease transactions, Tax Planning International Review (TPIR), 2014–10, p. 30; The new legal and fiscal regimes that facilitate the financing and leasing of aircraft in the Netherlands and Dutch Caribbean, TPIR, 2012–6, p. 18; The new legal and fiscal aviation finance and lease opportunities in the Kingdom of the Netherlands, Journaal LuchtRecht/Netherlands Journal of Air Law (JLR), 2012–2, p. 38; B.P. Honnebier, Comparing the property laws of the aircraft registries of choice the (Caribbean) Netherlands, Bermuda, Ireland and Malta, JLR, 2014–3, p 55.

[9] This publication submits in Chapter 21.3 that not only the rights of the owners and financiers of aircraft must be secured. It is argued that also the *proprietary interests* of the commercial and private *operator-lessees* of aircraft must be guaranteed in the event that the *lessor* is in default or becomes insolvent. The author personally presented this view at the annual meeting of the

"[T]he widely *differing approaches of legal systems* to security and title reservation rights [engender] uncertainty among intending financiers as to the efficacy of their rights. The result is to inhibit the extension of finance [...] and to increase borrowing costs" (*emphasis added*).[10]

More specifically, at the global level exist excessive discrepancies between the applicable national *substantive property laws* that govern the financing and leasing of aircraft and engines.[11] Additionally, not many countries have *properly* established *aviation-specific* finance and lease laws (*lex specialis*). For example, the European Netherlands has created aviation finance laws. These special regulations provide a substantive property regime for *recorded* aircraft and a new conflict of laws rule. Unfortunately, as far as the finance and lease of aircraft engines is concerned these rules are not adequate. See further Sect. 21.5 and Sect. 21.6 of this contribution. Besides, it is noted that the majority of the Member States of the European Union have neither adopted aviation-specific legislation nor general laws covering *financial* and *operational* lease agreements. Consequently, the legal systems governing the creation, validity, effects and enforcement of proprietary rights in financed and leased aircraft objects vary between all the countries in which they are operated.[12] In addition, globally the *conflict of laws rules* of the states that cover international aviation finance and lease contracts differ fundamentally. Accordingly, it is not guaranteed that the proprietary interests of the financiers, lessors and operators in aircraft which have been validly created in a certain jurisdiction, can be upheld abroad. It is concluded that due to the lack of uniformity of local aviation-specific substantive laws and conflict of laws rules, the financing and leasing of aircraft objects is severely frustrated.[13] The devastating outcome of the English case *Blue Sky v. Mahan Air* (2010)[14] confirmed that the above-described problems do not just concern an academic discussion.[15] To the contrary, it demonstrates that these matters are of ample practical significance for the aviation industry at large. This is

---

American Bar Association (ABA), Aircraft Finance Subcommittee, August 2004 in Atlanta. See B.P. Honnebier, New Protocols and the financing of aircraft engines, published in the ABA Forum on Air and Space Law's journal The Air &Space Lawyer (TASL), 2006–1, p. 15.

[10] R.M. Goode, The Cape Town Convention on International Interests in Mobile Equipment, ULR, 2002–1, p. 4.

[11] Similar issues occur in relation to the finance and lease of trains and space assets. However, this article concentrates on aircraft and engines.

[12] B.P. Honnebier, JLR, 2014–3, p 55.

[13] B.P. Honnebier and J.M. Milo, The Convention of Cape Town: the creation of international interests in mobile equipment, European Review of Private Law (ERPL), 2004–1, p. 3.

[14] *See for example the English cases in which the transfer of title to the aircraft was disputed: Blue Sky One Limited & O'rs v Mahan Air* [2009] EWHC 3314 (Comm); *Blue Sky One Limited & O'rs v Mahan Air & Ano'r [2010] EWHC 631 (Comm); Air Foyle Ltd* v *Center Capital Ltd* [2002] EWHC 2535 (Comm), 2 Lloyds Rep 753. The rights of the *mortgagee* could not be enforced in the latter case.

[15] B.P. Honnebier, The devastating 'Blue Sky' judgment compels the member states of the European Union to adopt the Cape Town convention, The Aviation & Space Journal, 2012–2, p. 10; The English Blue Sky case shows that the aircraft finance practice needs uniform international substantive mortgage laws as the existing conflict rules fail, Tijdschrift Vervoer en Recht (TVR), 2011–2,

because the English mortgage that was established in the certain English aircraft could not be enforced. Consequently, the financier was damaged for $ 43.1 million. The fact that the property interests of the financiers, lessors and operators may not be enforceable in other jurisdictions is a considerable *economic risk*. This prospect negatively influences the position of the stakeholders of the international aviation finance and lease practice. In turn, the existing economic challenges lead to unnecessary high finance and lease costs. These expenses undesirably increase the prices of airline tickets and cargo-transport. Consequently, an *international uniform substantive property law treaty* is needed to solve the existing global problems.[16]

21.2   The Goal and Structure of This Contribution

The *goal* of the present article is to investigate *four* noteworthy legal and practical issues that have played a major role in the worldwide aviation finance and lease practice. More specifically, it briefly[17] addresses the related provisions of the 'Convention on International Interests in Mobile Equipment' (Convention) and the 'Protocol on Matters specific to Aircraft Equipment' (Protocol) which were realised in Cape Town, South Africa in 2001. In practice, jointly the Convention and Protocol are called the Cape Town Convention. This contribution only discusses the following significant matters which each have a major impact on the international aviation finance and lease industry. It addresses the *secured interests of the operator-lessees*, the effect of *non-consensual interests*, the impact of *choice of law clauses* in agreements and the alleged application of the *doctrine of accession* to engines. These subjects are all covered by the Cape Town Convention. The present article only considers these four topics as space restraints make it impossible to review the entire regime of this treaty.[18] The general intent of the Cape Town Convention is to

---

70; The Rectified contribution to Contemporary Issues and Future Challenges in Air and Space Law, November 2011; ZLW, 2011–1, p. 47.

[16] B.P. Honnebier, The need for clear rules to facilitate the international financing of the acquisition and use of aircraft, Notarius International, 2000–4, p. 146; The European air transport sector requires an international solid regime facilitating aircraft financing: the Cape Town Convention, TVR, 2007–5, p. 151.

[17] Due to the scope of this book, in this contribution the five topics can only be discussed summarily. For more extensive publications concerning the intent, need and effects of the Cape Town Convention, see the Introduction and country-specific chapters of this book, as well as the related earlier publications. See for example B.P. Honnebier, The Convention on International Interests in Mobile Equipment and the Aircraft Equipment Protocol Encourage European Property Law Reform, Edinburgh Law Review (ELR), 2004–1, p. 115; The fully-Computerized International Registry for Security Interests in aircraft and Aircraft Protocol that will be effective toward the beginning of 2006, Journal of Air Law and Commerce (JALC), 2006–1, p. 63. See also the Special Issue concerning the Cape Town Convention and the three different Protocols thereto, ERPL, 2004–1.

[18] The significance of the instruments is evident as currently, and in a very short time, 66 states have adopted the Convention and 58 of them the Protocol. These countries are representative of eco-

facilitate the international financing and leasing of aircraft, aircraft engines and heli-copters.[19] For this purpose, jointly the Convention and Protocol provide for a solid legal regime protecting the substantial interest of the financiers, lessors and opera-tors of aircraft. It makes the purchase and use of aircraft objects more available and affordable.[20] It is emphasised that *only* the Cape Town Convention provides for the long-needed aviation-specific *international uniform regime covering substantive property law*. Nevertheless, some lawyers[21] have proposed that also the 'Convention on the international recognition of rights in aircraft' (Geneva Convention, 1948) has established an international substantive property law regime. Their view is errone-ous as this instrument is merely a conflict of laws (*private international law*) treaty which requires that its Contracting States *recognize* certain rights in aircraft. This matter is further discussed in Sect. 21.6, *below*.

This contribution is *structured* as follows. In Sect. 21.3, the existing national *secured interests* of the *lessees* (operator-lessees) of aircraft are discussed. For example, in the United States, the Kingdom of the Netherlands and other countries the local airlines can obtain these greatly valued secured rights. This publication argues that also at the global level an operator-lessee needs adequate protection of its financial interests in the event that the *lessor* defaults or becomes insolvent. In addition, it explains that the national secured interests of operator-lessees fall under the sphere of application of the Cape Town Convention. Sect. 21.4 addresses the major problem of the *non-consensual* rights that can be established in aircraft. Where certain requirements are met, under the regime of the Cape Town Convention the holders of *national liens* may be protected. For example, in the United States, United Kingdom, India, Ireland and Malta these third-party rights have priority over the *registered international interests* of the financiers, lessors and operator-lessees. Anecdotal evidence shows that not all the (large) stakeholders of the aviation finance and lease industry are aware of this important fact which may have a negative impact on their own interests. The popularity and legal effects of *choosing the applicable law* in aviation finance and lease agreements are reviewed in Sect. 21.5. For exam-ple, repeatedly it is contended that New York law and English law offer the most predominant and valuable form of security in aircraft finance transactions. The pres-ent publication submits, however, that worldwide many lawyers (purposefully)

---

nomically developed and developing regions. In addition, they represent aircraft objects manufac-turing as well as purchasing countries.

[19] R.M. Goode, The Official Commentary on the Convention on International interests in Mobile Equipment and Protocol Thereto on Matters Specific to Aircraft Equipment, 2013; B.P. Honnebier, Review of the Official Commentary, International and Comparative Law Quarterly, 2005–1, p. 268; ASL, 2003–6, p. 334. For the text of the Convention and Protocol in several languages see www.unidroit.org

[20] For the tremendous financial impact of the Cape Town Convention see for example V. Linetsky, Economic benefits of the Cape Town Treaty, 18 October 2009; A. Saunders and I. Walter, The proposed Convention: an economic impact assessment, 1988.

[21] See for erroneous interpretations of the regime of the Geneva Convention B.J.H. Crans, How Many Engines on a Boeing 737, Air & Space Law (ASL), 2013–3, p. 229; M.L. Jakobsen and L.B. Gabelgaard, The Aircraft Engine Dispute in Denmark, ASL 2014–3, p. 214.

ignore the fundamental legal concept that any choice of law clause in a contract has a very limited effect. This view is endorsed by the Cape Town Convention. In Sect. 21.6 the grave consequences of the alleged application of the *doctrine of accession* to aircraft engines finance and lease transactions are investigated. This theory implies that the owner of the airframe becomes the owner of the engine as soon as the latter object is attached to the former. The Cape Town Convention dictates that engines are financed and leased separately from the airframe. Finally, Sect. 21.7 provides some *concluding remarks*.

21.3 The Matter of the Secured Interests of the Operator-Lessees

For a very long time in the international legal aviation practice there is consensus that the rights of the lessors (owners) and financiers of aircraft and engines must be properly secured. However, also the *proprietary interests* of the commercial and private *operator-lessees* of aircraft need adequate protection in the event that the *lessor* is in default or becomes insolvent.[22] Therefore, for instance under the national aviation finance law of all the territorial units of the Kingdom of the Netherlands (Kingdom) and the property law of the United States under a (true[23]) lease agreement the lessor of the aircraft may grant the operator-lessee a *secured interest* (security interest in the United States) to 'acquire' or 'possess' the aircraft. Under the *special* aviation finance law of the Kingdom such a secured interest (*zakelijk recht*) can be created, provided that the aircraft is *recorded* in the national *Aircraft Title Registry*. The latter party is the 'holder' (*houder*) of the aircraft. The secured right to *possess* the aircraft finds its origin in an 'operational lease agreement' which must include a term of at least 6 months (art. 8:1309 Civil Code). The secured right of the operator-lessee to *acquire and possess* (to purchase) the aircraft can be included in a 'financial lease agreement' (art. 8:1308 Civil Code).[24] In practice, this interest is

---

[22] B.P. Honnebier, The Cape Town Convention and the Aircraft Equipment Protocol: Protecting the registered secured interests of airline lessees, Air and Space Law (ASL), 2005-1, p. 27; The new international regimen proposed by UNIDROIT as a means of safeguarding rights in rem of the holder of an aircraft under Netherlands law, Uniform Law Review (ULR), 2001-1, p. 5.

[23] See article 2A Uniform Commercial Code (UCC) of the United States for the definition of a 'true lease agreement'.

[24] It is noted that the legal systems of all the territorial units of the Kingdom of the Netherlands do not provide for special operational or financial lease law (*lex specialis*). B.P. Honnebier, De (internationale) leasing transactie als financieringsmethode van roerende kapitaalgoederen, in: Dossier, 2007, p. 59; Een internationale uniforme materiële regeling voor het eigendomsvoorbehoud is tot stand gekomen. De conventie van Kaapstad, in: Nederlands Tijdschrift Burgerlijk Recht (NTBR), 2002-6, 233; De internationale financieringspraktijk heeft wederom behoefte aan de uitbreiding van het bestaande pakket van Nederlandse zakelijke rechten, Weekblad voor Privaatrecht, Notariaat Registratie (WPNR), 2000, 914.

called an 'option to purchase' the aircraft.[25] In the European Netherlands, the large commercial airlines will *generally* insist on obtaining these interests. In the Kingdom,[26] the secured interests of the operator-lessee originate in the Convention on the International Recognition of Rights in Aircraft which requires their *recognition* in the other member States.[27] In turn, the Geneva Convention-covered rights are based on the property laws which existed in the United States before article 9 Uniform Commercial Code (UCC) was established. These former property laws existed in New York and Pennsylvania and they protected the conditional buyer and lessee respectively. Currently, they fall under the application of Article 9 UCC[28] which is implemented in all the Constituent States of the United States. Similar laws exist in other jurisdictions.[29] In the Kingdom, United States and other countries the security interest of the operator-lessee is a full *right in rem*, as opposed to a *right in personam*. Accordingly, this *real right* has third-party effect (*erga omnes*) as long as it is recorded in an aircraft title registry in the Kingdom or perfected in the United States. It is emphasised that this type of interest is legally *not* characterised as a lessee's right of *quiet possession*. This is a *personal right* of the lessee which is frequently included in financial documents. Therefore, it only has effect against the contracting party (lessor). However, globally the problem arises that the local property laws of many jurisdictions are *hostile* to the secured rights of the operator-lessees. For example, the security interest of an airline that is validly established in

---

[25] B.P. Honnebier, The Cape Town Convention and the Aircraft Equipment Protocol: Protecting the registered secured interests of airline lessees, in: ASL, 2005–1, 27; The Dutch real rights of airlines can be the basis of international interests under the Convention of Cape Town, just like their equivalent American security interest, ERPL, 2004–1, 46; The new international regimen proposed by UNIDROIT as a means of safeguarding rights in rem of the holder of an aircraft under Netherlands law, in: ULR, 2001–1, 5.

[26] See articles 8:1308 and 8:1309 Civil Code of all the territorial units of the Kingdom of the Netherlands and article 9 Uniform Commercial Code (UCC) of the United States. See B.P. Honnebier, ERPL, 2004–1, p. 46.

[27] "The Contracting States undertake to recognise …: (b) rights to acquire aircraft by purchase coupled with possession of the aircraft; (c) rights of possession of aircraft under leases of six months or more". (article I (1)(b-c) Geneva Convention).

[28] For the situation in the United States see G. Gilmore, Security Interests in Personal Property (2 volumes), 1965; G. Gilmore, Security law, formalism and Art. 9, 47 Nebraska Law Review, 1987, p. 21; Repossession of Collateral and Foreclosure of Security Interests in Leveraged Lease Aircraft Finance Transactions, ASL-10, 1995, p. 9; O. Shrank, Commercial Concerns in Prepaid Rent Deals, Leader's Equipment Leasing Newsletter, June 1996, p. 6; J. Honnold, The Law of Sales and Sales Financing, 4th edition 1976, p. 30; R.E. Speidel, Advance Payments in Contracts for Sale of Manufactured Goods: a Look at the Uniform Commercial Code, 52 California Law Review, 1964, p. 281; F.R. Kennedy, The Trustee in Bankruptcy under the Uniform Commercial Code: Some Problems Suggested by Art. 2 and 9, 37 Rutgers Law Review, 1960, p. 518; W.E. Hogan, The Marriage of Sales to Chattel Security in the UCC, Massachusetts Variety, Boston University Law Review, 1958, p. 571.

[29] For example, most of the Canadian Provinces and Territories, Australia, New Zealand, Serbia and Surinam have similar laws. See for Canada's applicable law M. Deschamps, Les regles de propriété de la Convention du Cap, ULR, 2002–1, pp. 22–24.

New York, cannot be enforced in a number of foreign countries. Only an international aviation finance and lease law related treaty can dictate the opposite.

While the regime of the Cape Town Convention is not explicit, extensive legal research has established that the secured interests of the operator-lessees can fall under the sphere of application of this treaty. However, provided that these interests are covered by the definition of an *international interest*. Article 2(2) of the Convention provides the following broad definition: '…an international interest in mobile equipment (aircraft) is an (national) interest…: (a) *granted by the chargor under a security agreement*; (b) vested in a person who is the conditional seller under a title reservation agreement; (c) vested in a person who is the lessor under a leasing agreement'. The above-addressed Kingdom, United States or other secured interests of the operator-lessees do not belong to categories (b) and (c). This is because they are not interests which are offered to the conditional seller or lessor. Nonetheless, they do fall within category (a). A specific Kingdom, United States or other secured interest of the operator-lessee must be *characterized* by the applicable *national* special aviation finance law or general substantive property law. The secured interests of the operator-lessees to acquire or possess an aircraft can be enforced as follows. The regime of the Cape Town Convention provides for extensive *remedies* which can be upheld against third-parties, provided that they have been recorded in the *International Registry*. The operator-lessee's registered international interest has *priority* over any other interest subsequently registered and over an unregistered interest in the event that the lessor defaults. Furthermore, it is enforceable against a new and undesirable lessor in the event that the title to the leased aircraft is transferred. It can also be upheld against (non-secured) third-party creditors in the bankruptcy procedure of the lessor. Provided that it was registered in the International Registry before the beginning of the insolvency proceeding. It is emphasized that also under the Cape Town Convention the interest is *not* classified as a 'right of quiet possession' of the operator-lessee. This is just a *personal right* which *cannot* be registered as a separate international interest.[30] The operator-lessee has to rely on the lessor to register the latter's international interest in the International Registry. Accordingly, the personal right to quiet enjoyment is not offering the operator-lessee the equivalent protection as is provided to the holder of an international interest. Consequently, it is important for a Kingdom, United States airline or other operator which has been granted a secured interest by the lessor under the applicable national law, to obtain a registered international interest under the Cape Town Convention. Otherwise its substantial financial interests will not be adequately protected internationally.

Obviously, whether in practice a lessor will indeed provide a secured interest to an operator-lessee depends, inter alia, upon the economic and financial leverage of the parties to a certain lease and financial transaction. In addition, cultural differ-

---

[30] R.M. Goode. The Official Commentary, 2013. See articles 29(1)(4)(5), 30 Convention and XVI(1) Protocol. www.unidroit.org

ences that exist between one state and another play a significant role. For example, when an established airline is located in the European Netherlands, generally the United States and other lessors are willing to offer the operator-lessee a secured interest. On the other hand, this may not yet be so in a scenario which concerns a lessor and airline which are both situated in the United States. In such a case the lessor is often reluctant to provide a security interest to the operator-lessee. A reason for this concern could be that most United States trained aviation finance and lease lawyers have never heard of the possibility to create security interests of operator-lessees under article 9 UCC. Let alone that they have any idea that such a right can form the basis of a registrable international interest under the Cape Town Convention (article 2(2)(a) Convention). Due to their ignorance they do not feel at ease with advising their clients about these interests. This is true, despite the fact that historically the national secured rights of the lessees find their origin in United States (New York and Pennsylvania) substantive property laws. Furthermore, anecdotal evidence shows that some lawyers in the United States fear that offering the security interests to the operator-lessees will jeopardise the registered international interests of their clients which are financiers and lessors. However, in practice there is no threat. To create the desired *priority ranking* among the competing proprietary interests, the international interest of the financier will be registered at the International Registry first in time, the interest of the lessor afterwards and the one of the operator-lessee last. This procedure achieves that the international interests of the financier and lessor are properly protected. It is noted that under the Cape Town Convention by an agreement between the holders of these interests the priority may be varied.

It is concluded that the availability of national secured rights for the operator-lessees, which can form the basis of international interests under the Cape Town Convention, are critically important to any airline or other operator. Wherever the operator-lessee is situated, it may influence its decision to enter into an aircraft lease agreement. This policy has certainly been adopted by the leading local airlines in the European Netherlands. This is because these days also the lessor may default or become bankrupt and the lessee seeks to mitigate its damages. The Convention and Protocol supplement, or offer new remedies to, the rights that are locally available to the operator-lessees. However, first it is required that a Contracting State has already implemented the concept of secured rights of the operator-lessees in its national legal system. Otherwise, the airlines cannot obtain registrable international interests under the treaty. Therefore, in order to have the operator-lessees appreciate the needed predictability and consistency provided by the Cape Town Convention, the states are well-advised to create the local special substantive property laws. This is also true in a non-Cape Town Convention scenario as in every country the airlines require adequate protection.

21.4 The Issue of the Non-consensual Rights That Frustrate the Finance and Lease of Aircraft and Engines

The legal systems of most countries make a distinction between the *consensual interests* and *non-consensual interests* which can be established in aircraft objects. The former type of interests is *voluntarily* created by the parties of the contract, while the latter group is constituted *by operation of law*. For example, national security interests, charges, mortgages, pledges and hypotheques are based on agreements which have been entered into by the parties. Some non-contractually created rights which are applicable in many countries are airport fees, repairmen liens, taxes, other governmental fees and crew salaries. In India[31] and other countries such involuntarily established rights have led to undesirable expensive and time-consuming Court cases.[32] In India the aviation authorities demanded on several occasions that financiers and lessors would pay for the outstanding tax-related and other debts of the defaulting operators of commercial and private aircraft. These actions are unconscionable as legally the financiers and lessors (owners) were not the debtors of the substantial duties at hand. Even in the event that such demands arguably have a basis in Indian national law, the real reason for impeding the valid rights of the financiers and lessors may be based on ulterior motives. For instance, the government intends to protect the local airlines or favour other interested parties. These actions impose significant hardship on the financiers as due to undesirable and lengthy litigation the aircraft may be grounded for more than 6 years. Such practices may result in cannibalism of the aircraft and a substantial loss of its value. In addition, it means that the lessor is damaged as no lease rentals will be paid when the aircraft is grounded for a very long time.

An extraordinary and controversial non-consensual right concerns the navigation charges of the European Organisation for the Safety of Air Navigation

---

[31] Particularly India is notorious for the amount of unnecessary Court cases which have recently occurred. See for example the SpiceJet cases, Court Asks DGCA Not to De-register SpiceJet Planes till April 6 (March 26, 2015), http://profit.ndtv.com/news/industries/article-court-asks-dgca-not-to-de-register-spicejet-planes-till-april-6-7495452015; *Corporate Aircraft Funding v. Union of India & ORS*, W.P. (C) 792/2012, March 14, 2013; *Directorate of Revenue Intelligence v. Corporate Air Craft Funding Co.*, LPA 226/2013 ¶ 22 (May 10, 2013) (Del.) [India] which concerned a private aircraft which was grounded for four years; *Kingfisher Airlines cases DVB Aviation Finance Asia PTE Ltd v. Directorate General of Civil Aviation, et al.*, WP (C) 7661/2012 and CM No. 4208/2013 (8 April 2013)., 2013. All these cases, and more, which involved governmental agencies of India.

[32] N. Downs, Taking Flight from Cape Town: Increasing Access to Aircraft Financing, University of Pennsylvania Journal of International Law, 2014–4, p 863; D.N. Gerber and D.R. Walton, De-registration and Export Remedies under the Cape Town Convention, Cape Town Convention Journal, November 2014, p. 49.

(EUROCONTROL).[33] In Western Europe, only the United Kingdom[34] (UK) and Ireland[35] have offered EUROCONTROL extensive non-contractual rights in aircraft. In the UK, the Civil Aviation Authority (CAA) has the power to arrest an aircraft on behalf of EUROCONTROL until all the overdue air navigation charges have been fully satisfied. In addition, EUROCONTROL/CAA may at any time detain the aircraft in respect of which the debt was incurred, or any other aircraft which is operated by the same debtor. In practice, this right is called a 'fleet lien' as it covers all the aircraft of the local or foreign commercial or private operator. The attachment can only be circumvented if the lessor (owner) terminates the lease agreement when the lessee is defaulting. However, the termination must take place before the aircraft enters the United Kingdom and it is arrested. In addition, the debt may be incurred by flying to and from countries outside the United Kingdom where EUROCONTROL does not have similar non-consensual rights. Besides, the EUROCONTROL liens have priority over the consensual interests of the financiers, owners and lessors of national and foreign aircraft.[36] The leading financiers, lessors and manufacturers of aircraft objects are members of the Aviation Working Group (AWG)[37] which organisation intends to safeguard their interests. In respect to a certain Court case the AWG stated: "… putting it generally, … the exercise of the power in the U.K. 'leaves a financier or lessor of an aircraft with a significant risk which is difficult (if not impossible) to manage effectively'. The UK has ratified the Cape Town Convention on 27 July, 2015. To more or less extent, the Convention and Protocol also apply in the Crown-dependencies Gibraltar, the Cayman Islands and Guernsey. The generally phrased formal Declaration regarding article 39 Convention implies that in the UK the excessive EUROCONTROL liens still apply.[38] The Western Continental European states have not provided EUROCONTROL with extraordinary non-consensual rights in aircraft. As this organisation does not have privileges which are similar to the ones existing in the United Kingdom and Ireland, it cannot easily collect the outstanding air navigation charges in these jurisdictions.

---

[33] B.P. Honnebier, Collecting EUROCONTROL air navigation charges by precautionary arresting the aviation fuel of aircraft in the European Netherlands, JLR, 2013, no. 2–3, p. 33.

[34] Reg. 4 Civil Aviation (Chargeable Air Services Detention and Sale of Aircraft for EUROCONTROL) Regulations 2001.

[35] See the Irish Air Navigation and Transport (Amendment) Act 1998.

[36] See for example the unreported English case Irish Aerospace (Belgium) N.V. v. EUROCONTROL and CAA, Queens Bench Division, Commercial Court, 10 June 1991. For a more detailed review of EUROCONTROL liens and this case see T. Christopher and J.H. Bax, Air Law, 1992–1, p. 2.

[37] The primary goal of the AWG is to facilitate aviation financing and leasing and to address issues which hinder this intent. www.aero.com

[38] See www.unidroit.org/status-2001capetown?id=1887

The fundamental difference between the consensually and non-consensually established interests is incorporated in the regime of the Cape Town Convention.[39] The latter category finds protection under the treaty, provided that a Contracting state has made a special Declaration which addresses this matter. More precisely, article 39 of this instrument permits the creation of 'non-registrable' liens and 'retention' or 'detention' rights. In addition, article 40 allows non-consensual interests which must be 'registered' at the International Registry. The problem exists that several Contracting States have made the Declaration that many types of local liens *have priority* over registered international interests. Consequently, the rights of the financiers, lessors and operators are not guaranteed in these countries. For example, when the United States adopted the Convention and Protocol in 2006 it made a brief and broadly phrased Declaration regarding article 39 Convention.[40] However, in essence it has declared that a large amount of differing (forthcoming) non-consensual interests and detention rights have *priority* over the registered international interests of the financiers, lessors and operators. For instance, it was presented at a meeting of the American Bar Association, Aircraft Financing Subcommittee[41] that also *aircraft fuel liens* may have priority over the consensually created rights. While Ireland no longer offers EUROCONTROL the same extensive rights as the UK, it still provides this organisation special non-consensual rights. Irish law states that an aircraft can easily be sold when the operator does not pay the incurred Irish 'airport charges'. After these fees have been deducted from the sale proceeds of the forced execution, the total amount of the outstanding EUROCONTROL charges are paid as they have priority over the other debts of the operator. The non-contractual rights which the UK and Ireland have given to EUROCONTROL are of major concern to the financiers and lessors of aircraft. This is because they permit EUROCONTROL to hold them accountable for unpaid air navigation fees, while these debts are incurred by the operators of the aircraft. These debts may have run up to millions of US $. The Irish EUROCONTROL charges fall under the regime of the Cape Town Convention.[42] As is mentioned in Sect. 21.2 of this article, anecdotal evidence shows the following. It affirms that not all the stakeholders of the global aviation finance and lease practice know that the due to the controversial Declarations made by some Contracting States under the articles 39 and 40 Cape Town Convention the local non-consensual liens have priority over their international interests.

---

[39] J.F. Pritchard and D.L. Lloyd, Analysis of Non-Consensual Rights and Interests under Article 39 of the Cape Town Convention, 2013; M. Scott, Liens in aircraft: priorities, JALC, 1958, Volume XXV, p. 193; B.P. Honnebier, JLR, 2014–3, p. 29.

[40] For the United States Declaration under article 39 Convention see the UNIDROIT website www.unidroit.org.

[41] ABA, Annual Meeting, Aircraft Financing Subcommittee, FATCA, Ex-Im Bank Reauthorization and Fuel Liens, presented by Chubbuck and Draz, Chicago,12 September 2014.

[42] See www.unidroit.org/status-2001capetown?id = 1584

21.5 The Validity and Effect of Choice of Law Clauses in Aviation Finance and Lease Agreements

As is explained *supra*, a consensual right which is validly established in a certain jurisdiction, may not be enforceable in the countries where the aircraft is operated. A group of lawyers[43] propose that a 'choice of laws clause', which is included in an international aviation finance or lease agreement, may solve this major issue. They suggest that the parties must choose a state which has created modern aviation finance and lease laws. In their opinion, the selected legal system could be enforced in the national Courts of this country and abroad. Besides, they contend that the selected regime would have third-party effect (*erga omnes*). Therefore, allegedly also the *other* (foreign) creditors of the debtor would be bound by their choice of law clause. In particular, currently it seems customary that in aircraft financing and leasing contracts the parties choose the law of England or the state New York. In practice, it is often proposed that these jurisdictions have adequate aviation finance and lease laws. Furthermore, some lawyers contend that when the parties opt for the law of New York-state, the Cape Town Convention would be applicable. They suggest that because the United States has ratified this instrument, it will also apply to the agreement which includes a choice of law clause referring to New York law. This view is erroneous. The present contribution argues that a clause selecting the law of England or New York merely has a *limited* effect. In addition, it does not solve the aforementioned global issues. This is because the choice only has effect between the parties (*inter se*). A choice of law clause is solely enforceable as far as the *contractual* aspects of the agreement are concerned. In almost all countries the chosen law does *not* affect the proprietary interests of third-parties.

In regard to the possibility to select the applicable law in agreements the following general statement has been made:

> "That principle is that human beings have the right to agree upon what they will, due regard being had to the rights of others".[44]

This comment reflects the international common leading opinion which must always be observed. Therefore, the choice of English or New York[45] law does not bridge the elementary differences which exist in the substantive property laws of

---

[43] F. Sanders, Loophole in aircraft mortgages poses threat to lawyers and financiers, 8 November, 2011; G. Hill, Financing and Investing in Engines, 31 March 2011, p. 7; E. Lawless, Enforcement of security over an aircraft, February 2010, p. 4; C.A. Gee, Choice of law after England's Blue Sky One Case, June 2011; M. Hamilton, Aviation law areas of practice, 2011.

[44] See the treatise on chattel mortgages by G. Gilmore, Security interests in personal property, Vol. I–II, 1965, p. 422. This author has been described as the 'intellectual father' of the Uniform Commercial Code (UCC) which is implemented (differently) in the legal systems of all the states of the United States.

[45] Th.A. Zimmer and D. Pearson, Aircraft mortgages-English law or New York law?, see Aviation financing and leasing 2014, p. 6 The authors point out that a selection of New York or English law *merely* covers 'the contractual relations' between the parties to a mortgage agreement! See also Cheshire and North, Private International Law, 1999, p. 941.

the states. This is because the choice cannot be upheld against (foreign) third-parties when the debtor is in default or insolvent. It is submitted that the lawyers who suggest the opposite are making a fundamental legal mistake.

Significant English Court cases confirm that the applicable English conflict of laws rule forbids choosing English or another national substantive property law. For instance, this view has been affirmed in the English ruling *Blue Sky v. Mahan Air* (Blue Sky case, 2010).[46] In the Blue Sky case the English Court analysed the scope of the *lex contractus* conflict of laws rule which is also called the rule of the 'proper law of the contract'. See further *below*. In respect to the disputed validity of the English mortgage that was created in an aircraft which had the English nationality, the judge *refused* to apply English property law. He explicitly disregarded the circumstance that English law had been selected by the parties to apply to the English mortgage in the English aircraft.[47] In England and worldwide it is the *common leading opinion* of the doctrine that the raised issues concerning the creation, validity, effects and enforcement of property rights are *not* covered by the law that has been chosen by the parties to the contract. The Blue Sky case confirms that the custom to select English law has no effect on the proprietary aspects of international aviation finance and lease agreements. In other publications it is argued extensively that the devastating global impact of this ruling could have been avoided.[48] As far as the situation in the United Kingdom is concerned, since this jurisdiction has ratified the Cape Town Convention the problem of applying the lex situs conflict of laws rule to international aviation financing and leasing transactions is solved in regard to agreements that are entered into after the treaty has entered into force on 1 November 2015. This is because the treaty provides for a uniform *substantive property law regime* which governs the creation, validity, effects and enforcement of registrable international interests in aircraft objects.

Just recently, a handful of lawyers are promoting the conflict of laws rule called the proper law of the contract.[49] They are not successful as it is not endorsed by the local and international community. In regard to the disputed creation, validity, effects and enforcement of proprietary interests in a 'thing', historically the international doctrine[50] has argued that the *lex rei sitae* (*lex situs*) conflict of laws rule must

---

[46] *Blue Sky One Limited & O'rs v Mahan Air & Ano'r [2010] EWHC 631 (Comm).*

[47] Blue Sky under paragraph 156. See also *Glencore International AG v Metrotrading International Inc* [2001] 1 Lloyds Rep 284.

[48] B.P. Honnebier, The devastating 'Blue Sky' judgment compels the member states of the European Union to adopt the Cape Town convention, The Aviation & Space Journal, 2012–2, p. 10; The English Blue Sky case shows that the aircraft finance practice needs uniform international substantive mortgage laws as the existing conflict rules fail, TVR, 2011–2, 70; Rectified contribution to Contemporary Issues and Future Challenges in Air and Space Law, November 2011; ZLW, 2011–1, p. 47.

[49] G.M. McBain, Anglo-American conflict of law rules relating to the conveyance of aircraft, 1991, p. 3.

[50] A. Schlüter, Der Eigentumsvorbehalt im europäischen und internationalen Recht, Internationales Handelsrecht, 2001–4, p. 142; J.A. van der Weide, Mobiliteit van goederen in het IPR, pp. 181–184; B.P. Honnebier, ZLW, 2011–1, p. 61.

be applied. It is the *opinio iuris communis* that this rule governs all property rights in (registered) movable and immovable objects, regardless whether these rights have been consensually or non-consensually created.[51] Only in regard to very few matters another conflict rule is accepted. For example, only regarding the *consensual* rights in aircraft the special *lex registri(i)* conflict rule is proper. However, the *lex situs* rule is still appropriate to cover disputed *non-consensual* interests[52] in aircraft. This is because in these situations the *closest connection* of the disputed issue at hand is with the legal system of the situs (*connecting factor*) in which the aircraft object is located.

The fundamental legal principle that a choice of law clause is merely enforceable between the parties to a certain agreement is explicitly endorsed in article VIII(2) Protocol. This provision states that the parties to an agreement may agree on the law which is to govern their contractual rights and obligations.[53] Provided, however, that the relevant Contracting State has made a Declaration to this effect (articles VIII(2) and XXX(1) Protocol). Therefore, the Cape Town Convention endorses the *opinio iuris communis* that solely in relations between themselves the parties may select the applicable law. This international common legal opinion is also expressed in the Official Commentary to the Cape Town Convention. It clarifies that the possibility of a choice of law clause that would affect third-parties is *outside* its scope.[54]

In any event, the current publication submits that when the parties to finance and lease contracts *carefully* 'choose the flag' of the aircraft, to a large extent the existing problems may be solved. For this purpose, they can establish a Special Purpose Vehicle in this *jurisdiction of choice*. This scenario certainly resolves the existing issues where the Cape Town Convention applies as the aircraft is *registered as to nationality* in a Contracting State. Provided, that this country has made the relevant

---

[51] B.P. Honnebier, Collecting EUROCONTROL air navigation charges by precautionary arresting the aviation fuel of aircraft in the European Netherlands, JLR, 2013-2/3, p. 33, at p. 40.

[52] As per 1 January 2012, article 10:127, sub 4 of the Civil Code of the European Netherlands prohibits that the parties to an agreement choose the applicable law as far as property rights in aircraft are concerned. It dictates that the *lex registrii* conflict of laws rule applies to both *voluntarily* and *non-voluntarily* established interests in aircraft. The substantive property law of the state where the aircraft is *registered as to nationality* or is *recorded* (*teboekgesteld*) decides the existing issues. This rule is appropriate to cover *consensual* rights in aircraft. However, the new law makes an *elementary legal mistake* by applying it to *non-consensual* rights in aircraft. See B.P. Honnebier, JLR, 2013-2/3, p. 33, at p. 40; JLR, 2011–2, p. 34.

[53] See the comments to the draft CITEJA Conventions which refer to borrowed aircraft engines. It is stated that the legal accession of an engine is: ... un acte illicite et même susceptible de repression pénale", "... un vol...". Compte Rendu, Doc. 162, 1931, p. 40.

[54] R.M. Goode, The Official Commentary, 2013; The international interest as an autonomous property interest, 12 European Review of Private Law, 1/2004; International interests in mobile equipment and the Cape Town Convention and Aircraft Protocol: adding a new dimension to international law-making; The Cape Town Convention and Protocols and the Conflict of Laws, A commitment to private international law, 2013, p. 221; B.P. Honnebier, Bookreview, ICLQ, 2005, p. 268. See also www.unidroit.org/status-2001capetown-aircraft under Select Bibliography.

Declaration and it has implemented the treaty appropriately. This implies that the purposely chosen flag-state offers modern and adequate law which is attractive to the financiers, lessors *and* operators of aircraft.

21.6   The Grave Problem of the Alleged Accession of Aircraft Engines to Aircraft

At present, the most serious issue arising in the international aviation finance and lease practice is caused by the allegation that the 'doctrine of accession' applies to aircraft engines. In essence, the 'accretion theory' means that an engine which is installed in or on an aircraft (airframe) legally becomes a 'component part'. As from the 1990s, at the international level it is continuously debated whether *by operation of law* (*ex lege*) and under *all* circumstances the title to a financed or leased engine is transferred to the owner of the airframe as soon as the former object is mechanically attached to the latter. Therefore, if the strict accession theory applies it is not guaranteed that the interests of the financier or lessor (owner) of the high-value engine can be upheld. Considering the disastrous financial impact of the accession doctrine, the aviation industry has submitted since the 1930s that its application would be *improper*. More precisely, at that time it was already argued that this theory would 'legalize' *engine-stealing*.[55] Consequently, in most jurisdictions the title-shift theory is *not* applicable to aircraft engines.[56] Besides, *any* interpretation of a local or international *special* law (*lex specialis*) which frustrates aviation financing and leasing transactions is wrong *per se*. This is because the primary intent of a purposefully created lex specialis is to facilitate the availability of these arrangements as the applicable *general* property law (*lex generalis*) is not adequate. Therefore, interpreting the special legal regime[57] in such a manner that it would (even more than the lex generalis) hinder the finance and lease of aircraft and engines is by definition unjustified as such a view clearly contravenes its main goal.

---

[55] See the comments to the draft CITEJA Conventions which refer to borrowed aircraft engines. It is stated that the legal accession of an engine is: "… un acte illicite et même susceptible de repression pénale". "… un vol…". Compte Rendu, Doc. 162, 31 October, 1931, pp. 40–41. e

[56] See for example G. Elbing, Sind Triebwerke wesentliche Bestandteile von Flugzeugen?, ZLW, 1995, p. 387, V. Sagaert,De UNIDROIT Conventiebetreffende international zakelijke rechten op roerend uitrustingsmaterieel, 2002–1; De UNIDROIT Conventie, Een laatste strohalm voor de Belgische luchtvaartindustrie, Rechtskundig Weekblad, 2002, 1367.H. Schlegel, Eigentumserwerb, 1938, pp. 60–64. See also the Court ruling Urteil des Hanseatischen Oberlandesgericht, Hamburg, 8 October 1931, Zivilsenat Bf. II 299/31.

[57] See for example the special legal regime covering the possibility of *accession* of the *parts* to the *certain* aircraft, which is provided by Article 8:3a(2) of the Civil Code of *all* the territorial units of the Kingdom of the Netherlands. This provision dictates that *no* accession of *engines* takes place and that they are *not component parts* of *the* (particular) aircraft. Nevertheless, a few practitioners in the European Netherlands keep insisting the opposite while their view clearly hinders the finance and lease of aircraft engines. See further below.

Nevertheless, practice shows that the legal and practical implications of cross border engines-related *operational* or *financial* lease transactions are not always understood. More precisely, some lawyers do not comprehend the fundamental legal differences between the regimes of the 'Convention on the international recognition of rights in aircraft' (Geneva Convention, 1948) and the Cape Town Convention. When a finance or lease transaction is considered, the financier, lessor and operator must analyse the legal and economic risks that are involved. At that time, determining the type of regime of the applicable aviation treaty plays a pivotal role. The fundamental discrepancies between the two existing conventions are addressed subsequently.

It must be kept in mind at all times that the *Geneva Convention* is *not* a substantive property law treaty. In this respect, the following has been submitted:

> "It must be remembered that in the Geneva Convention there is *no intention or attempt* to achieve the international *unification* of air law which is inherent to the other Conventions. Since the subject dealt with was too complex, it was enough to establish certain principles concerning the *recognition* of rights in aircraft, and to refer frequently to the variety of national laws to resolve the numerous problems concerning details which might arise in this respect. Thus, the Convention was confined to binding member states only with regard to certain rules which constituted an urgent response. Since complete codification of financing on an international basis would, at that time, have been premature".[58]

In other words, the Geneva Convention does *not* envision to establish a *uniform international substantive property regime*. Therefore, it does *not* cover the creation, validity, effects and enforcement of *consensually* or *non-consensually* created rights in aircraft. Consequently, *no* proprietary rights can be derived from its regime. As its name indicates, it merely requires that its Contracting States *recognise* four[59] broadly defined categories of *contractually* created rights in the *specific* aircraft.[60] For this purpose the term aircraft extends to its airframe, engines and all other things, provided that they are *intended for use* in *the* (specific) aircraft. As it was not an aviation-related uniform substantive law treaty, from the day that the Geneva Convention was realised, it was considered to be a provisional regime. Its draftsmen and national lawmakers agreed that as soon as possible such a convention had to be realised. However, it took until 2001 when the Cape Town Convention was realised. Besides, the Geneva Convention does *not* apply to non-contractually constituted

---

[58] N. Matteesco-Matte, Treatise on Air-Aeronautical law, 1981, p. 566 (*emphasis added*).

[59] "The Contracting States undertake to recognise: (a) *rights of property in aircraft*; (b) rights to acquire aircraft by purchase coupled with possession of the aircraft; (c) rights of possession of aircraft under leases of six months or more; (d) mortgages, hypotheques and similar rights in aircraft which are contractually created as security for payment of an indebtness" (article I (1) (a-d) Geneva Convention).

[60] Article XVI of the Geneva Convention *describes* the aircraft as follows: "For the purpose of this Convention the term 'aircraft' shall include the airframe, engines, propellers, radio apparatus, and all other articles *intended for use* in *the* aircraft *whether installed therein* or temporarily separated there from". It is noted that this is not a legal definition.

rights in aircraft.[61] This fact is significant, as an installed engine becomes, or does not become, a component part of a specific aircraft *by operation of law*. Consequently, the Geneva Convention does *not* cover the matter of the accession of aircraft engines *per se*. Besides, the primary goal of the Geneva Convention is, as a conflict of laws treaty and in its limited way, to enhance the international financing of aircraft. Evidently, the suggested interpretation of article XVI would frustrate its scope. This fact is corroborated by the Minutes and Documents of the ICAO Legal Committee.[62] Accordingly, the view that the Geneva Convention covers the question whether the engines are component parts of the certain aircraft is inconsistent with its scope and intent.

Nonetheless, several legal practitioners, particularly in Denmark and the European Netherlands, persist that article XVI of the Geneva Convention would endorse the accession doctrine. Anecdotal evidence indicates that this has convinced the international aviation finance and lease practice that leasing engines is a major economic risk. For instance, one of the largest engines and aircraft lease companies[63] expresses its concern in an important financial document. This paper explicitly refers to European Netherlands, Finland, Greece and Jamaica. Consequently, the accession doctrine had a devastating impact on the global aviation practice. See particularly the unjustifiable consequences of the Danish Court case Cimber Sterling (2013).[64] To a large extent, the ruling was based on the *wrongful interpretation* of article XVI of the Geneva Convention. This is because the litigating parties had pleaded that the treaty would, somehow, dictate the accession doctrine to aircraft engines. The Danish case has seriously impacted the worldwide aviation finance and lease market. Also in the United States the application of the Geneva Convention in respect to the engines issue has led to confusion in the Federal Bankruptcy Courts.[65]

---

[61] B.P. Honnebier and A.P. Berkhout, TPIR, 2014–10, p. 30; 2012–6, 15; JLR, 2012–2, 38. Honnebier, Clarifying the alleged issues concerning the financing of aircraft engines, ZLW, 2007–3, 383; A. van de Velde, TVR, 2005, 44.

[62] See minutes and documents of the ICAO Legal Committee regarding the realisation of the Geneva Convention, ICAO Doc, 4635, March 1948, pp. 35–37 119–120.

[63] See Blade engine securitization, Private placement memorandum, p. 30, December 2006.It is noted that this document also refers to some other jurisdictions. However, these countries have adopted the Cape Town Convention which means that the aircraft engines dispute no longer exists there. See also Irish Stock Exchange, 2006.

[64] The Cimber Sterling ruling by the Bankruptcy Court of Sønderborg in Denmark, cases BS SKSk-1292/2012, 1301/2012, 1302/2012, 1303/2012, 1304/2012 and 1306/2012. The Danish Court wrongfully applied article XVI Geneva Convention. Its ruling had a devastating impact on the global aviation community. See B.P. Honnebier, JLR, 2014–3, p. 61. It is noted that Denmark has adopted the Cape Town Convention in 2015. See the UNIDROIT website. However, this instrument does not govern the mortgage, lease and other agreements which were entered into before it entered intio force in this country.

[65] See for example *First National Bank of South Georgia v. Ayers Aviation Holdings, Inc. v. GATX, General Electric (GE) Company*, United States Bankruptcy Court, Middle District of Georgia, Albany Division, Case 00–11881, 25 July, 2002. The ruling regarded, inter alia, the (wrongful)

The present publication reiterates that the Geneva Convention does *not* provide a uniform substantive aviation property law regime in general and that it does not cover the accession of engines problem in particular.

The *Cape Town Convention* endorses the international *opinio iuris communis* that engines are distinct aircraft objects. The international aviation industry regards aircraft engines as objects which can be financed and leased separately from the aircraft (airframe). Regardless whether these objects are attached to the aircraft. The prevailing legal opinion of the international aviation community is based on the views of the international organisations which supported the realisation of the Cape Town Convention. These institutions are the International Civil Aviation Organization (ICAO representing states), International Institute for the Unification of Private Law (UNIDROIT representing states) and International Air Transport Association (IATA representing airlines). In addition, as is stated in Sect. 21.4, *supra*, the Aviation Working Group represents the interests of the international aviation finance and lease sector. This group played an important role in the realisation of the treaty. The international prevailing legal opinion submits that the possibility that under *all* circumstances the ownership of an engine may be involuntarily transferred to another party is a major economic risk. This is because these objects are very expensive. Furthermore, engines are extremely mobile units, which are often financed and leased apart from the airframe. Besides, they are very often *interchanged* within an airline's fleet of aircraft. In addition, at present groups of airlines have concluded *engine pooling agreements* which have direct contacts with the problem-states where the accession doctrine is allegedly applicable.

Therefore, the Protocol clarifies:

"Ownership or another right or interest in an aircraft engine shall not be effected by its installation on or removal from an aircraft" (article XIV(3) Protocol-Modification of Priority Provisions)."

It is concluded that the engine mechanism envisioned by the Cape Town Convention considers airframes and engines to be distinct *aircraft objects* which can be financed and leased separately. Accordingly, distinct international interests can be created in the engines. Moreover, these international interests can be registered at the International Registry. After registration, the international interest in an engine can be enforced (by the offered remedies including repossession) against third-parties in the insolvency of the debtor. The Cape Town Convention supersedes the Geneva Convention where the latter treaty relates to aircraft as defined in the Protocol, and to aircraft objects. However, with respect to rights or interests not covered or affected by the former instrument, the latter is not superseded (article XXIII Protocol).

---

interpretation, validity and priority of the liens in the aircraft and engines. After much debate and other decisions, it finally ruled that based on the Geneva Convention the local law of the Czech Republic was the controlling law.

In the European Netherlands the doctrine of accession is *not* applicable to engines.[66] Nonetheless, some local lawyers seem to argue conversely.[67] Just for the sake of argumentation, it is assumed that the accession theory would apply in this jurisdiction. The issue arises here that the Cape Town Convention is only not applicable in the European Netherlands. On the other hand, it does apply in *all* the other territorial units of the Kingdom of the Netherlands since 1 September, 2010.[68] To circumvent the alleged engine-related problems the certain aircraft can be *registered as to nationality* in the Caribbean Netherlands (particularly the jurisdiction Bonaire) where the Cape Town Convention applies.[69] Since 10 October, 2010, jointly the Caribbean Netherlands and the European Netherlands form the jurisdiction 'the Netherlands'. This means that the aircraft obtains the flag (ICAO Prefix 'PH') of the Netherlands. Besides, under the laws of the European Union[70] this aircraft can be operated permanently in all the other Member States of the European Union. In this scenario, the doctrine of accession would definitely not create engine finance and lease problems in the European Netherlands.

---

[66] In the Kingdom of the Netherlands there should be no issue concerning the question whether aircraft engines are component parts of the certain aircraft. All the Courts, special aviation finance laws and prevailing legal opinion as formulated by the Legal Department of KLM conclude that there is *no* accession of aircraft engines. See the Supreme Court of the Netherlands (*Hoge Raad*), 26 March, 1936, Nederlandse Jurisprudentie (NJ), 1936, 757; Supreme Court of the Netherlands, NDS Provider, C06/082, 2008, 177; AAR Aircraft & Engine Group/Aerowings, Court of Appeals Den Bosch 2003–56; Volvo Aero Leasing/AVIA Air, Court of First Instance of Aruba, 25 June, 2003, no. 121. www.rechtspraak.nl The view of the combined Courts of First Instance of the European Netherlands is stated in their 'Handbook for precautionary arrests' (Beslagsyllabus), January 2016: no accession of engines occurs! This book is written by and for the judges and their view creates uniformity in cases concerning the dispute whether engines can be precautionary attached. See also B.P. Honnebier, TVR, ZLW, 2007–3, pp. 383–390; J.W. Wichers, 2002, pp. 13, 36, 37, 38, 48, 78, 102, 103, 104; C.H. Sieburgh, Toerekening van een onrechtmatige daad, 2000, pp. 202, 208; R.J.C. Flach, Scheepsvoorrechten, 2001, p. 206; B.G.P. Rogmans, Verkeersopvattingen, 2007, pp. 22, 28, 46; F.A. van Zoest, TVR 2002–6, pp. 183 and188; een fout van de wetgever?, TVR 2002–6, pp. 183 and188; E.B. Rank-Berenschot, Het luchtvaartuig als object van het vermogensrecht, WPNR, no. 6198, 1995, pp. 691, 695.

[67] M.H. ten Wolde and H.B. Reehuis, Zekerheid in de wolken?, Liber Amicorum Wim Reehuis, 2014, p. 489.

[68] For a more detailed analysis of the former and present different territorial units of the Kingdom of the Netherlands and the application therein of the Cape Town Convention, see the contribution to this book by S. van Erp. See also the documents which were lodged by the Kingdom of the Netherlands and deposited at the Secretariat of UNIDROIT. www.unidroit.org/nationalinfo-2001capetown

[69] B.P. Honnebier and A.P. Berkhout, TPIR, 2012–6, p. 15; JLR, 2012–2, p. 38.

[70] J. Balfour and R. Ricketts, Aircraft use, registration and leasing in the EC, ASL, 1993–1, p. 25.

21.7 Some Concluding Remarks

The serious problem exists that the proprietary consensual interests in aircraft and engines which have legally been properly established in a certain jurisdiction, may not be enforceable in this state or other countries. For example, in the event that the Cape Town Convention (2001) does not apply to a certain dispute, the devastating English Blue Sky v. Mahan Air case (2010) has proved that a valid English mortgage in an English aircraft may not be enforceable in a local English Court. Therefore, the financier, lessor *and* operator of the aircraft may not be appropriately protected in England or abroad. Accordingly, it is crucial that the country of the flag of the aircraft has created a modern legal aviation finance and lease regime. It is even more significant that it has adopted the Cape Town Convention as to a large extent this treaty adequately protects the financial interests of all the stakeholders. More specifically, the treaty also adequately safeguards the *secured interests of the operator-lessees*, it affirms the international prevailing legal opinion that *choice of law clauses* merely have an effect between the parties to an agreement and it *resolves* the grave problem of the alleged application of the *accession doctrine* to engines. Nevertheless, for example India, the United States, the United Kingdom, Ireland and other several other Contracting States of the Convention and Protocol have made stakeholder-unfriendly Declarations permitting various *non-consensual interests* in aircraft. Because of these Declarations many liens have priority over the registered international interests. This means that the aviation property regimes in these countries do not adequately protect the rights of the financiers, lessors and operators. Therefore, the stakeholders are well-advised to structure their financial and lease transactions by means of Special Purpose Vehicles (SPV's) in the Contracting States which did not make these negative Declarations. Keeping all this in mind, it is concluded that the Cape Town Convention provides for a modern and solid international substantive aviation finance and lease regime. The jurisdictions which have not yet adopted the instrument are encouraged to (re)consider their views very soon.

References

1. ABA, Annual Meeting, Aircraft Financing Subcommittee, FATCA, Ex-Im Bank Reauthorization and Fuel Liens, presented by Chubbuck and Draz, Chicago,12 September 2014.
2. Airbus Global Market Forecast 2015–2035. Available at http://www.airbus.com/company/market/forecast/
3. Balfour, J., and R. Ricketts. 1993. Aircraft use, registration and leasing in the EC. *Air & Space Law* 18(1):25.
4. Boeing's forecast. http://www.boeing.com/boeing/commercial/cmo/.
5. Cheshire and North. 1999. *Private international law*.
6. Christopher, T., and Bax, J.H. *Air law 2*.
7. Crans, B.J.H. 2013. How many engines on a Boeing 737. *Air & Space Law* 38(3): 229.

8. Deschamps, M. 2002. Les regles de propriété de la Convention du Cap. *Uniform Law Review* 1: 22–24.
9. Downs, N. 2014. Taking flight from Cape Town: Increasing access to aircraft financing. *University of Pennsylvania Journal of International Law* 35(4): 863.
10. Elbing, G. 1995. Sind Triebwerke wesentliche Bestandteile von Flugzeugen? *Zeitschrift für Luft- und Weltraumrecht* 387.
11. Flach, R.J.C. 2001. *Scheepsvoorrechten.*
12. Gee, C.A. 2011. Choice of law after England's Blue Sky One Case. http://www.vedderprice. com/Choice-of-Law-After-Englands-Blue-Sky-One-Case-06-30-2011/. June.
13. Gerber, D.N., and D.R. Walton. 2014. De-registration and export remedies under the Cape Town convention. *Cape Town Convention Journal* 3:49, November.
14. Gilmore, G. 1965. *Security interests in personal property,* vol. I–II. Boston: Little, Brown.
15. Gilmore, G. 1987. Security law, formalism and Art. 9. *Nebraska Law Review* 47:21.
16. Goode, R.M., The Cape Town Convention on international interests in mobile equipment, *Uniform Law Review,* 2002–1, 4.
17. Goode, R.M. 2004. The international interest as an autonomous property interest. *European Review of Private Law* 12(1): 18.
18. Goode, R.M. 2013. *The official commentary on the convention on international interests in mobile equipment and protocol thereto on matters specific to aircraft equipment,* 3rd ed.
19. Goode, R.M. 2013. The Cape Town convention and protocols and the conflict of laws. In *A commitment to private international law,* 221.
20. Goode, R.M. 2015. International interests in mobile equipment and the Cape Town convention and aircraft protocol: Adding a new dimension to international law-making. In *Transnational commercial law: Texts, cases and materials,* 2nd ed, ed. R. Goode et al., 393.
21. Hamilton, M. 2011. Aviation law areas of practice.
22. Hill, G. 2011, March 31. Financing and investing in engines. http://www.airfinancejournal. com/docs/London2011/Airfinance_Journal_CFM_Financing_and_Investing_in_Engines-_ Legal_Issues_-_31_March_2011.pdf.
23. Hogan, W.E. 1958. The marriage of sales to Chattel security in the UCC, Massachusetts Variety. *Boston University Law Review* 571.
24. Honnebier, B.P. 2000. De internationale financieringspraktijk heeft wederom behoefte aan de uitbreiding van het bestaande pakket van Nederlandse zakelijke rechten. *Weekblad voor Privaatrecht, Notariaat Registratie* 914.
25. Honnebier, B.P. 2000. The need for clear rules to facilitate the international financing of the acquisition and use of aircraft. *Notarius International* 5(4): 146.
26. Honnebier, B.P. 2001. The new international regimen proposed by UNIDROIT as a means of safeguarding rights in rem of the holder of an aircraft under Netherlands law. *Uniform Law Review* 6(1): 5.
27. Honnebier, B.P., Een internationale uniforme materiële regeling voor het eigendomsvoorbe-houd is tot stand gekomen. De conventie van Kaapstad, in: *Nederlands Tijdschrift Burgerlijk Recht,* 2002–6: 233.
28. Honnebier, B.P., The Dutch real rights of airlines can be the basis of international interests under the Convention of Cape Town, just like their equivalent American security interest, *European Review of Private Law,* 2004–1: 46.
29. Honnebier, B.P., The Convention on International Interests in Mobile Equipment and the Aircraft Equipment Protocol Encourage European Property Law Reform, *Edinburgh Law Review,* 2004–1: 115.
30. Honnebier, B.P. 2005. The Cape Town convention and the aircraft equipment protocol: Protecting the registered secured interests of airline lessees. *Air and Space Law* 30(1): 27.
31. Honnebier, B.P., Review of the Official Commentary, *International and Comparative Law Quarterly,* 2005–1: 268.
32. Honnebier, B.P., New Protocols and the financing of aircraft engines, published in the ABA Forum on Air and Space Law's journal *The Air &Space Lawyer,* 2006–1: 15.

33. Honnebier, B.P. 2006. The fully-computerized international registry for security interests in aircraft and aircraft protocol that will be effective toward the beginning of 2006. *Journal of Air Law and Commerce* 70(1): 63.
34. Honnebier, B.P. 2007. De (internationale) leasing transactie als financieringsmethode van roerende kapitaalgoederen. In *Dossier*, 59.
35. Honnebier, B.P. 2007. Clarifying the alleged issues concerning the financing of aircraft engines. *Zeitschrift für Luft- und Weltraumrecht* 56(3): 383.
36. Honnebier, B.P., The European air transport sector requires an international solid regime facilitating aircraft financing: the Cape Town Convention, *Tijdschrift Vervoer en Recht*, 2007–5: 151.
37. Honnebier, B.P., The Rectified contribution to Contemporary Issues and Future Challenges in Air and Space Law, *Zeitschrift für Luft- und Weltraumrecht*, 2011–1: 47.
38. Honnebier, B.P., The English Blue Sky case shows that the aircraft finance practice needs uniform international substantive mortgage laws as the existing conflict rules fail, *Tijdschrift Vervoer en Recht*, 2011–2: 70.
39. Honnebier, B.P., The devastating 'Blue Sky' judgment compels the member states of the European Union to adopt the Cape Town convention, *The Aviation & Space Journal*, 2012–2: 10.
40. Honnebier, B.P. 2013. Collecting EUROCONTROL air navigation charges by precautionary arresting the aviation fuel of aircraft in the European Netherlands. *Journaal LuchtRecht/ Netherlands Journal of Air Law* 12(2–3): 33.
41. Honnebier, B.P. 2014. Comparing the property laws of the aircraft registries of choice the (Caribbean) Netherlands, Bermuda, Ireland and Malta. *Journaal LuchtRecht/Netherlands Journal of Air Law* 13(3): 55.
42. Honnebier, B.P., The merits and pitfalls of the Handbook 'Aviation Financing and Leasing 2014', *Zeitschrift für Luft- und Weltraumrecht*, 2014–4: 559.
43. Honnebier, B.P., and A.P. Berkhout. 2012. The new legal and fiscal aviation finance and lease opportunities in the Kingdom of the Netherlands. *Journaal LuchtRecht/Netherlands Journal of Air Law* 11(2): 38.
44. Honnebier, B.P., and A.P. Berkhout, The new legal and fiscal regimes that facilitate the financing and leasing of aircraft in the Netherlands and Dutch Caribbean, *Tax Planning International Review*, 2012–6: 18.
45. Honnebier, B.P., and A.P. Berkhout. 2014. The Caribbean Netherlands is the flag-state of choice for cross-border aircraft lease transactions. *Tax Planning International Review* 41(10): 30.
46. Honnebier, B.P., and J.M. Milo. 2004. The convention of Cape Town: The creation of international interests in mobile equipment. *European Review of Private Law* 12(1): 3.
47. Honnold, J. 1976. *The law of sales and sales financing*, 4th ed.
48. Jakobsen, M.L., and L.B. Gabelgaard, The Aircraft Engine Dispute in Denmark, *Air and Space Law* 2014–3: 214.
49. Karesh, J.I. 1995. Repossession of collateral and foreclosure of security interests in leveraged lease aircraft finance transactions. *Air and Space Lawyer* 10: 9.
50. Kennedy, F.R. 1963. The trustee in bankruptcy under the uniform commercial code: Some problems suggested by Art. 2 and 9. *Rutgers Law Review* 37:518.
51. Lawless, E. 2010, February. Enforcement of security over an aircraft. http://www.dilloneustace.ie/download/1/Enforcement%20of%20Security%20over%20an%20Aircraft.pdf.
52. Linetsky, V. 2009, October 18. Economic benefits of the Cape Town Treaty. http://www.awg. aero/assets/docs/economicbenefitsofCapeTown.pdf.
53. Matteesco-Matte, N. 1981. *Treatise on air-aeronautical law*. Montreal: ICASL-McGill University.
54. McBain, G.M. 1991. *Anglo-american conflict of law rules relating to the conveyance of aircraft*.

55. Pritchard, J.F., and D.L. Lloyd. 2013. Analysis of non-consensual rights and interests under Article 39 of the Cape Town convention. *Cape Town Convention Journal* 3: 3.
56. Rank-Berenschot, E.B. 1995. Het luchtvaartuig als object van het vermogensrecht. *Weekblad voor Privaatrecht, Notariaat Registratie* (6198):691.
57. Rogmans, B.G.P. 2007. *Verkeersopvattingen.*
58. Reuters, 18 June, 2015.
59. Sagaert, V., De UNIDROIT Conventie betreffende international zakelijke rechten op roerend uitrustingsmaterieel: Een laatste strohalm voor de Belgische luchtvaartindustrie, *Rechtskundig Weekblad*, 2002, 1367.
60. Sanders, F. 2011, November 8. Loophole in aircraft mortgages poses threat to lawyers and financiers. http://www.ascendworldwide.com/2011/11/loophole-in-aircraft-mortgages-poses--threat-to-lawyers-and-financiers.html.
61. Saunders, A., and I. Walter. 1998. The proposed convention: An economic impact assessment. http://www.awg.aero/assets/docs/EIA.pdf
62. Schlegel, H. 1938. *Eigentumserwerb.*
63. Schlüter, A., Der Eigentumsvorbehalt im europäischen und internationalen Recht, *Internationales Handelsrecht*, 2001–4: 142
64. Scott, M. 1958. Liens in aircraft: Priorities. *Journal of Air Law and Commerce* XXV: 193.
65. Shrank, O. 1996, June. Commercial concerns in prepaid rent deals. *Leader's Equipment Leasing Newsletter* 6.
66. Sieburgh, C.H. 2000. *Toerekening van een onrechtmatige daad.*
67. Speidel, R.E. 1964. Advance payments in contracts for sale of manufactured goods: A look at the uniform commercial code. *California Law Review* 52: 281.
68. ten Wolde, M.H., and H.B. Reehuis. 2014. Zekerheid in de wolken? *Liber Amicorum Wim Reehuis* 489.
69. van der Weide, J.A. 2006. *Mobiliteit van goederen in het IPR.*
70. van Zoest F.A., Retentierecht op luchtvaartuigen in Boek 8 BW: een fout van de wetgever?, *Tijdschrift Vervoer en Recht* 2002–6: 183.
71. Wichers, J.W. 2002. Natrekking, vermenging en zaaksvorming. Opmerkingen bij de algemene regeling voor roerende zaken in het Burgerlijk Wetboek.
72. Zimmer, Th.A., and D. Pearson. 2014. Aircraft mortgages-English law or New York law? *Aviation Financing and Leasing* 6.

Cases

73. *Air Foyle Ltd v Center Capital Ltd* [2002] EWHC 2535 (Comm), 2 Lloyds Rep 753.
74. *Blue Sky One Limited & O'rs v Mahan Air* [2009] EWHC 3314 (Comm).
75. *Blue Sky One Limited & O'rs v Mahan Air & Ano'r [2010] EWHC 631 (Comm).*
76. *The Cimber Sterling ruling by the Bankruptcy Court of Sønderborg in Denmark,* cases BS SKSk-1292/2012, 1301/2012, 1302/2012, 1303/2012, 1304/2012 and 1306/2012.
77. *Corporate Aircraft Funding v. Union of India & ORS,* W.P. (C) 792/2012, March 14, 2013. *Directorate of Revenue Intelligence v. Corporate Air Craft Funding Co.,* LPA 226/2013 ¶ 22 (May 10, 2013) (Del.) [India].
78. *First National Bank of South Georgia v. Ayers Aviation Holdings, Inc. v. GATX, General Electric (GE) Company,* United States Bankruptcy Court, Middle District of Georgia, Albany Division, Case 00–11881, 25 July, 2002.
79. *Glencore International AG v Metrotrading International Inc* [2001] 1 Lloyds Rep 284.
80. *Irish Aerospace (Belgium) N.V. v. EUROCONTROL and CAA,* Queens Bench Division, Commercial Court, 10 June 1991.

81. *Kingfisher Airlines cases DVB Aviation Finance Asia PTE Ltd v. Directorate General of Civil Aviation, et al*, WP (C) 7661/2012 and CM No. 4208/2013 (8 April 2013)., 2013.
82. The Supreme Court of the Netherlands (*Hoge Raad*), 26 March, 1936, *Nederlandse Jurisprudentie* (NJ), 1936, 757.
83. The Supreme Court of the Netherlands, NDS Provider, C06/082, 2008, 177.
84. *AAR Aircraft & Engine Group/Aerowings*, Court of Appeals Den Bosch 2003–56.
85. Urteil des Hanseatischen Oberlandesgericht, Hamburg, 8 October 1931, Zivilsenat Bf. II 299/31.
86. *Volvo Aero Leasing/AVIA Air*, Court of First Instance of Aruba, 25 June, 2003, no. 121.

B. Patrick Honnebier Prof., LL.M., LL.M. (advanced), is Of Counsel at Gomez and Bikker Law Offices, Amsterdam, the Netherlands and particularly representing major aircraft and aircraft engines financiers and lessors; Adjunct Professor at the University of Mississippi (Ole Miss), School of Law, Master of Laws (LL.M.) in Air and Space Law program, Professor responsible for the full Spring Semester course of International Aviation Financing and Leasing law; Expert on International Aviation Financing and Leasing Law, Institute of Air and Space Law AEROHELP, St. Petersburg, Russia, since January 2016; Guest lecturer in the Netherlands at Utrecht University since 2007 and Groningen University since 2014. He committed himself to give guest lectures at the New York University in Shanghai and at the National University of Singapore in 2016. Professor Honnebier was responsible for the course International Aircraft Financing Law at the International Institute of Air and Space Law, Leiden University in the Netherlands from 2002-2013; Associate Professor at Utrecht University, Faculty of Law, Department of Commercial and Corporate Law from 1992-2007; Lecturer of commercial and corporate law at the University of Aruba from 1996-1999. Professor Honnebier was Observer at the Diplomatic Conference for the realisation of the Cape Town Convention, November 2001. He was the legal advisor of the Governments of Aruba, the former Netherlands Antilles and the Ministry of Foreign Affairs of the Netherlands concerning the adoption by the Kingdom of the Netherlands of the Cape Town Convention on September 1, 2010. Currently, he is the legal advisor of the Ministry of Infrastructure and Environment (Department of Civil Aviation) of the Netherlands in regard to the drafting of new national legislation covering problematic foreign aircraft deregistration and repossession cases. He is a frequent and worldwide speaker at aviation finance and lease law conferences. For example, he presented at the Law Section of the Royal Aeronautical Society in London on 29 January, 2016. He is the author of more than 60 publications in various law reviews and all the leading aviation law journals.

Chapter 22
The Luxembourg Rail Protocol to the Cape Town Convention: Some Practical Differences from the Aviation Protocol

Howard Rosen

It was an inspired decision of the drafters of the Cape Town Convention to allocate protocols to each industry sector. Clearly there are some commonalities between the different industries, but not only do circumstances differ in relation to the legal implementation following on from the status of domestic and private international law applying to the different industries as well as the requirements of the asset itself, but in terms of private finance, the rail and the aviation sectors are at different stages of development which means that some basic assumptions may exist for the aviation sector but do not necessarily apply in the same way for the rail sector.

What this note seeks to do is to look selectively at each of these aspects in turn as they are considered by the Luxembourg Rail Protocol (hereafter the Rail Protocol), by reference to the positions taken and assumptions made in relation to the Aircraft Protocol to the Base Convention.[1]

22.1 Legal Considerations

By the time the delegates from 42 different countries assembled in Luxembourg to review the draft Protocol for railway rolling stock, the Base Convention and the Aircraft Protocol had already been in place for over 5 years. Compromises made at the Diplomatic Conference in Cape Town could be re-evaluated and, whilst the general principle followed by delegates was not to make changes to the core

---

[1] For a more detailed comparison, see *Rosen/Fleetwood/von Bodungen*, The Rail Protocol – Extending Cape Town Benefits to the Rail Industry, 17 Unif. L. Rev. (2012), 609

H. Rosen (✉)
Rail Working Group,c/o Howard Rosen Solicitors,
Baarerstrasse 98, 7262, CH-6302 Zug, Switzerland
e-mail: howard.rosen@railworkinggroup.org

© Springer International Publishing AG 2017   363
S. Kozuka (ed.), *Implementing the Cape Town Convention and the Domestic Laws on Secured Transactions*, Ius Comparatum - Global Studies in Comparative Law 22, DOI 10.1007/978-3-319-46470-1_22

concepts contained both in the Base Convention and the Aircraft Protocol, there were areas where there were necessary divergences.

One obvious difference has been the treatment of the creditor rights on the insolvency of the debtor. Article IX of the Rail Protocol broadly follows the approach of Article XI of the Aircraft Protocol, but with one significant exception. Whilst there was a consensus that Alternative B would create some significant difficulties for creditors, the "self-help" provisions in Alternative A troubled lawyers from the civil law jurisdictions. And then there was a lingering concern that the absence of recourse to the courts for the debtor could even be considered unconstitutional in certain jurisdictions. Accordingly, Article IX of the Rail Protocol also contains an Alternative C, which is designed to provide essentially the same remedies to the creditors as Alternative A save that it preserves, in certain circumstances, the rights of a debtor or the insolvency administrator to apply to the court to suspend repossession as long as the creditor is essentially placed in the same position as what it had originally expected to be in at the inception of the transaction.[2]

In the European Union there is a further legal gloss in that the Cape Town Convention is seen as a split competence instrument where some competences are with the EU, as a Regional Economic Integration Organisation,[3] and some with the Member States. Under a compromise agreed between the EU and EU Member States, the EU claims "competence" on this matter[4] but declines from making any declaration and the Member States accept that they cannot make declarations under Article IX but can introduce parallel rules under domestic law.

In each case the move to a régime designed to be supportive of the creditor in the case of insolvency will often result in substantial changes to domestic insolvency law. Aside from the legal policy issue, there can be practical implications where certain states will wish to adopt the changes as part of general reform of domestic insolvency law – and this can in turn involve a lengthy consultation process. Accordingly bearing in mind the other benefits delivered by the Rail Protocol[5] the rail industry, by contrast to the aviation industry, is, in such a case, encouraging states to ratify without a declaration under Article IX (or corresponding domestic law implementation) and then revisits the issue later.[6]

A conceptually similar approach was taken in relation to the public service aspects of the rail industry. The railways can be lifelines for communities and it was understood that a creditor's repossession of financed rolling stock could cause

---

[2] And indeed there is scope for the court to make additional remedial orders prior to authorising suspension of the creditor repossession rights – see *Goode*, Official Commentary on the Convention on International Interests in Mobile Equipment and the Luxembourg Protocol thereto on Matters specific to Railway Rolling Stock, 2nd edition (2014), Comment [5.41]

[3] See Article 48 of the Base Convention

[4] Pursuant to Council Regulation (EC) No. 1346/2000 of 29 May 2000 on insolvency proceedings

[5] In particular the provision for the first time of a registry recording security interests in railway rolling stock – see below

[6] The so-called "half a loaf" approach – see *Rosen/Fleetwood/von Bodungen*, The Rail Protocol – Extending Cape Town Benefits to the Rail Industry, 17 Unif. L. Rev. (2012), 609 at 619 *et seq.*

disproportionate damage to the community as a whole (for example, commuters no longer being able to travel into a city on a working morning) compared to the loss being incurred by the creditor when not exercising its repossession rights. Some countries currently constrain repossession in these circumstances. So the public service exemption contained in Article XXV sets out to create a mechanism whereby, in certain circumstances, the drastic action of a creditor repossessing "Public Service Railway Rolling Stock"[7] could be restrained against, usually, the creditor continuing to receive the benefit of its original bargain.[8] But this could only apply to continue current restraints, not to invent new ones.[9] Moreover, any person (including a governmental or other public authority), other than the creditor, exercising a local law right to take possession of the public service railway rolling stock is placed under a duty to preserve and maintain the rolling stock until it is handed over to the creditor.[10]

A third policy change manifested itself in Article XXVI of the Rail Protocol, in turn modifying Article 60(3) of the Base Convention for the purposes of the Luxembourg Protocol. This deals with the difficult issue of pre-existing interests.[11] Railway rolling stock can operate for many decades and certain items have been known to operate for more than 60 years. Accordingly, financings or leases can easily last 15 years. So consideration has to be given to dealing with claims of creditors arising in relation to railway rolling stock under agreements in place prior to the date the Rail Protocol has come into force in the jurisdiction where the debtor has its principal domicile?[12]

Financiers need to know where they stand with some certainty and Article XXVI was designed to facilitate a clear cut-off point from which date the registry would accurately reflect both the security interests and their respective priorities in relation to a specific item of railway rolling stock. On balance, it was decided that it was best to create a definite fixed period, to be decided by the contracting state but to be no shorter than 3 years, and no longer than 10 years, after ratification, during which period the pre-existing security interests retained their priority rights.[13]

---

[7] Defined as "railway rolling stock habitually used for the purpose of providing a service of public importance" Art. XXV (1)

[8] For a more detailed discussion on this, see *Public Service and the Cape Town Convention*, Rosen, 2 Cape Town Convention Journal 2013, 131

[9] Art. XXV (1)

[10] Art. XXV (2)

[11] Defined as "a right or interest of any kind in or over an object created or arising before the effective date of this Convention as defined by Article 60(2)(a)" (Article 1 (v) of the Base Convention)

[12] See *Goode*, Official Commentary *ibid*, Comment 4.350.

[13] But of course these pre-existing interests do not constitute "international interests", with the corresponding creditor rights, for the purposes of the Rail Protocol

22.2 Practical Issues

The first question is how to define and then identify railway rolling stock.

The definition of railway rolling stock is wide, encompassing not just conventional railway equipment but also, because the Protocol applies to all vehicles running on rails or above, on or under permanent guideways, such diverse equipment categories as monorail carriages, trams, mountain railway carriages, cable cars and even cranes and gantries at ports.[14] But what constitutes an *item* of railway rolling stock? This can be an interesting issue in the context of articulated vehicles. The regulations being prepared for the International Registry and guidance notes will follow industry practice where ever possible but essentially, if a carriage is not permanently connected to another carriage or locomotive, it will be considered to be an item of railway rolling stock in its own right.

Once it is established what constitutes an item of railway rolling stock, the next problem is how to identify it. Since the objective of the Cape Town Convention is to facilitate true asset backed financing, it is essential that a creditor is able to identify precisely and unequivocally the equipment in which any security interest.[15] has been created.[16] But there is no uniform system globally for identifying railway rolling stock in a unique and commonly accepted way. This has had some significant practical implications. Initially it was thought that, like in the aviation sector, a manufacturer's identifier would be sufficient. This still remains as a possibility[17] but it was quickly apparent that, especially in the light of the broad spread of assets covered by the Protocol, not only did not all manufacturers have identification systems but they were potentially incompatible with each other and in certain cases identifiers could be duplicated or recycled, so were not unique as an identifier as required by Article XIV. Similarly immatriculation or running numbers can change so could not be used since the identifier has to be unique and permanent. There has been no alternative therefore other than to invent a new global unique numbering system where an URVIS[18] number will be allocated directly by the international registry as a unique and permanent identifier for one specific item of equipment.

This all represent a complete break with the identification system in the Aircraft Protocol but it has also raised important questions as to how the number is to be

---

[14] See Art. I.2(e), *Goode*, Official Commentary *ibid*, Comment 4.350 and RWG briefing paper R0556 *What Equipment is covered by the Luxembourg Protocol? More than you might think...* at www.railworkinggroup.org.

[15] "International Interest" under the Base Convention

[16] "For the purposes of Article 18(1)(a) of the Convention, the regulations shall prescribe a system for the allocation of identification numbers by the Registrar which enable the unique identification of items of railway rolling stock" – Article XIV.1

[17] Article XIV.1(b)

[18] Unique Rail Vehicle Identification System being a non-repeatable 20-digit number (including 1 or more check digits) allocated permanently to one specific item of railway rolling stock. See also RWG briefing paper R0480 *Identifying railway rolling stock it's time for a world-wide system* at www.railworkinggroup.org.

created, how it can be allocated as well as how it can be shown on the rolling stock concerned. So it is no longer a question, in the Rail Protocol "eco-system", of a creditor simply taking existing manufacturer identifiers and registering the international interest against that asset, but in the rail sector the creditor will first have to ensure that the rolling stock is carrying an URVIS number prior to effecting the registration. On the positive side, the creation of a new universal identification system will open up new opportunities for the rail sector, including lifetime records for assets and the potential to track the location of individual assets in real time worldwide. Moreover with millions of potential items of railway rolling stock to be registered at the International Registry, it will be a clear requirement from the outset that there is a system of registration of and search against specific groups of assets.

Lastly unlike the aviation sector, generally there are no national registries registering either title or security interests in relation to railway rolling stock. The absence of existing national registries has meant that there is no existing domestic legislation which can be adapted through the operation of the Rail Protocol and there is no publicly searchable system for identifying either ownership or secured party status in relation to an item of railway rolling stock. But the advantage is that the international registry then will play a significant role for domestic rail financing transactions, even where it is clear that the financed equipment will not cross jurisdictional boundaries. In addition, the fact of the registration of a notice of sale or security interest of itself (and the ability to search against an asset) will be a major step forward for industry as lawyers and transaction parties will be able to check, conclusively and in advance of closing a transaction, rival claims on assets to be financed, leased or purchased, as well as potentially to create additional rights for creditors in many jurisdictions, as a matter of domestic law, regardless of the terms and applicability of the Rail Protocol.

In conclusion, since the registry regulations will only be published shortly before it comes into force and practical issues will undoubtedly be revisited once it is in force, it is not entirely clear how the Rail Protocol will operate in practice. What is certain is that in most jurisdictions it will not only be providing an upgraded system for recording, prioritising and enforcing security interests but it will actually create those systems. The Protocol raises some legal policy challenges, but most importantly, provides significant new practical solutions for industry specific issues. When in force it will transform the rail industry. While many of the basic parameters of the Cape Town Convention still apply for the rail sector, there are specific industry considerations which have at times necessitated practical digressions. But that was what the drafters of the Cape Town Convention expected from the outset.

Howard Rosen CBE M.A. (Oxon.), Solicitor of the Senior Courts of England and Wales; Principal, Howard Rosen Solicitors, Zug, Switzerland, studied law at Oxford University and qualified as an English solicitor in 1980. He worked as an in house counsel for international leasing companies between 1980 and 1988 and since 1989 has led a boutique law firm, Howard Rosen Solicitors in Zug, Switzerland, specialising in international commercial and finance law, with a particular emphasis on aviation and rail finance. He is a member of the Law Society of England and Wales, the International Bar Association and the Society of Trust and Estate Practitioners. He is a

Correspondent of Unidroit, is Immediate Past President of the Council of British Chambers of Commerce in Europe and remains the chairman of its Public Affairs Committee. Since 1996 Mr Rosen has been chairman of the Rail Working Group (www.railworkinggroup.org), a world-wide not for profit industry association, constituted by UNIDROIT, which is dedicated to the implementation of the Luxembourg Rail Protocol to the Cape Town Convention on International Interests in Mobile Equipment. He is a regular writer, as well as a speaker and moderator at internationalrail conferences.

Chapter 23
Entering into Force: Promoting Unidroit's Space Protocol Among Emerging Space Actors

Daniel A. Porras

The Protocol to the Convention on International Interests in Mobile Equipment on Matters specific to Space Assets (hereinafter referred to as the *Space Protocol*) is, at heart, an instrument intended to facilitate the growth of space activities. With the ever-growing importance of space capabilities to modern society, it is not surprising that a new framework has emerged that proposes an additional method for the financing of very expensive space assets. As such, the Space Protocol sets out the rules by which public and private actors will be able to secure financing for tools such as satellites through asset-based financing, a practice not unlike getting a loan for a car and using the car as collateral. This type of financing is, of course, not new but the nature of space assets (i.e. the fact that they are bound for orbit) creates numerous technical complexities that requires a wholly new regimen to govern such loans. The International Institute for the Unification of Private Law (Unidroit), the institution under whose auspices the Space Protocol was developed and adopted, came across many of these complications during the development process. One such issue that demonstrates the nuanced difficulties of this project was simply finding a way for a creditor to "take possession" of an asset that is already in orbit.[1]

Given such challenges, some doubted whether establishing asset-based financing for space assets was feasible at all, or even desirable. The Space Protocol came under heavy criticism, particularly from certain established space powers and some major actors in the commercial sector who felt that this instrument would create more problems than it would solve.[2] However, the Space Protocol generated significant interest from one very important part of the space community that over-

---

[1] These challenges and their respective solutions are discussed at length in other parts of this publication and will not, therefore, be recounted herein.

[2] Unidroit 2011 – DCME-SP – Doc. 6, pp. 5–8.

D.A. Porras (✉)
LMI Advisors, Washington, DC, USA
e-mail: dporras@lmiadvisors.com

© Springer International Publishing AG 2017

S. Kozuka (ed.), *Implementing the Cape Town Convention and the Domestic Laws on Secured Transactions*, Ius Comparatum - Global Studies in Comparative Law 22, DOI 10.1007/978-3-319-46470-1_23

came lingering doubts: States with emerging economies.[3] These countries, many from the Latin American, African and South Asian regions, are currently the fastest growing States in terms of space capabilities, searching for the means to obtain critical technology that many in established countries take for granted. They are, therefore, the actors that have the most to gain from the establishment of an instrument such as the Space Protocol. Bolstered by that interest, the Space Protocol was finalised by bringing together members from all across the space community, including over 60 governments (including established space powers) and numerous private actors. The Space Protocol was adopted and opened for signature in Berlin on 9 March 2012.

For Unidroit and the States that actively supported the Space Protocol, this Instrument represents a tremendous achievement. However, there is still a long way to go. Under its own provisions, the Protocol will not come into force until ten States have ratified it and a Supervisory Authority has confirmed that an International Registry is fully functional.[4] Both of these tasks are considerable, particularly the former. In comparison to other international instruments of its like, ten ratifications is a high number, agreed to as a compromise in order to ensure that there will be enough transactions taking place under the Space Protocol for the effective operation of the International Registry.[5] However high this might seem, it has already been demonstrated that there is significant international will to see this regimen come into fruition, notably from emerging economies. States in rapidly developing regions of the world could once again prove to be a tremendous source of support for the Space Protocol, producing not only more than enough ratifications needed for its entry into force but also for the successful implementation of the Cape Town Convention in outer space, even if the Space Protocol is not adopted by wealthier States with established space capabilities.

The framework of the Cape Town Convention makes this possible by its very own provisions. Under Article 3(1), the Cape Town Convention applies "when, at the time of the conclusion of the agreement creating or providing for the international interest, the debtor is situated in a Contracting State". Article 3(2) goes on to specify that the location of the creditor does not affect the applicability of the Convention. Under these terms, a creditor located, for example, in Canada would be able to enforce the Space Protocol against a debtor located in Burkina Faso so long as Burkina Faso is a Contracting State. In this case, Canada would not need to be a Contracting State in order for the creditor to be able to enforce its interest. Financial

---

[3] Unidroit 2012 – DCME-SP – Report, pars. 18–22.

[4] Article XXXVIII(1) of the Space Protocol. The International Registry is a database where, under the Cape Town Convention system, all interests are recorded and are available for viewing 24 h a day, seven days a week.

[5] The other two Protocols to the Convention on International Interests in Mobile Equipment (hereinafter referred to as the *Cape Town Convention*), the Aircraft Protocol and the Railway Protocol, require eight and four ratifications respectively. It should be further noted that the number ten was a compromise between a proposal for twenty ratifications being required and another proposal that only five should be required.

institutions, such as banks, wishing to extend loans for such assets could be based anywhere in the world and have clients in numerous countries, all falling under distinct jurisdictions. So long as the debtors are located in Contracting States, the financial institution would only have to deal with a single set of regulations, namely the Space Protocol. This arrangement provides significantly more predictability and transparency than having to deal with a myriad of laws from jurisdictions that the creditor may or may not be familiar with. The list of Contracting States for the Space Protocol could, therefore, be made up entirely of States whose sole interest is to take on the role of debtor.

For additional protection, the drafters of the Space Protocol have included provisions that further ensure that a creditor will be able to enforce their interest in the event of default. One of the major concerns raised during the development of the Space Protocol was how a creditor would take control of a satellite that was already in orbit, not least of all since physical repossession of the satellite would be all but impractical. Under Article XIX of the Space Protocol, the parties to an agreement may place command codes and related data with a third party, thereby giving the creditor further assurance that they will be able to take control of the space asset and enforce their interest, even if it is already in orbit. The third party would also not need to be located within a Contracting State for the Space Protocol to apply.

In this context, one can see that for any given transaction conducted under the Space Protocol, there will likely be three parties: the creditor, the debtor and a third party who holds the command codes. Of these three, only the debtor must be located within a Contracting State. It is not, therefore, imperative for States with lingering doubts about the Space Protocol to ratify. Rather, it will be critical for the States wishing to avail themselves of the Cape Town regimen as debtors to ratify. This matches the entire *raison d'être* of the Space Protocol, which is to provide a new means of financing for those who need additional options for the acquisition of space assets.

Already, one can see that there is a greater willingness from States with developing economies to adopt this new financial regimen. At present, only four countries have signed the Space Protocol, with no ratifications: Burkina Faso, Germany, Saudi Arabia and Zimbabwe. Of these four, only Germany is an established space power. The list of countries that regularly expressed their support for the Space Protocol from Africa, Latin America and South Asia is extensive, with many of them also holding the titles of emerging space actors. This list includes Brazil, Colombia, Ghana, Indonesia, Iran, Mexico, Nigeria, Pakistan, Senegal, Turkey and Yemen. These are all countries who are looking to purchase space technology that is widely available all over the world. The Space Protocol will offer them a new financial option to do that very thing. By harnessing the willingness of these States to open up a new avenue for access to space assets, Unidroit will not only be able to achieve the necessary ratifications to bring the Space Protocol into force but, because these countries are also presently those that are looking to purchase the most space technology, it will create the critical mass necessary to ensure the successful operation of the International Registry.

This is not to say that established space powers should not be courted. Indeed, many wealthy countries will be the base of the financial institutions that will one day be asked for loans under the Space Protocol and should, therefore, be brought into the sphere of the Cape Town regimen. However, a concerted effort should be made to seek out the support of those countries who stand to gain the most from this important new achievement, namely those countries with emerging economies who are seeking to take a bold new step with outer space technology. By bringing these countries together, Unidroit will be achieving the aim of the Space Protocol: continued growth for human space activities.

Daniel A. Porras Mr Porras served as an Associate Officer for the Unidroit Secretariat during the development and adoption of the Space Protocol. Since then he has gone on to work further in the international space law and policy field at the UN Institute for Disarmament Research (Geneva) and the Observer Research Foundation (New Delhi). He is currently working as a consultant for LMI Advisors (Washington, DC), providing legal guidance on international telecommunication regulations. Mr Porras has just received his LL.M. from the Georgetown University Law Centre in International Business and Economics Law.

Appendix: Questionnaire to National Reporters

Preliminary Note

The subject of our session, "security interests burdening transport vehicles – The Cape Town Convention and its implementation in national law," is allotted to the session of "air and maritime law" but requires insights into the basic principles of the law on secured transactions. It is a pleasure of this humble general reporter to work with such knowledgeable national reporters, which he believes should ensure the success of the session.

As all of you must be aware, the Cape Town Convention[1] and its Aircraft Protocol[2] has marked a remarkable success in terms of the number of States Parties and the volume of transactions. Only few other uniform law instruments have paralleled their achievements. Not only have they had a significant impact on the practice of aircraft financing, but also their intellectual influence on the designing of secured transactions law deserves careful analysis. On the other hand, we note many important jurisdictions, in particular those belonging to the Civil Law family, have not become a Party to them. Further, the second and third Protocols to the Convention, on security interests in the railway rolling stocks[3] and space assets,[4] respectively, have not met as much enthusiasm as the Aircraft Protocol yet, though Unidroit and

---

[1] Convention on International Interests in Mobile Equipment, 2001. The text, States Parties, list of declarations and other information are accessible on the website of Unidroit http://www.unidroit.org/english/conventions/mobile-equipment/main.htm and of Aviation Working Group http://www.awg.aero/projects/capetownconvention/.

[2] Protocol to the Convention on International Interests in Mobile Equipment on Matters Specific to Aircraft Equipment, 2001.

[3] Luxembourg Protocol to the Convention on International Interests in Mobile Equipment on Matters Specific to Railway Rolling Stock, 2007.

[4] Protocol to the Convention on International Interests in Mobile Equipment on Matters Specific to Space Assets, 2012.

© Springer International Publishing AG 2017

S. Kozuka (ed.), *Implementing the Cape Town Convention and the Domestic Laws on Secured Transactions*, Ius Comparatum - Global Studies in Comparative Law 22, DOI 10.1007/978-3-319-46470-1

some collaborators are making efforts to bring them into operation. To give a fair evaluation of the Cape Town Convention and its Protocols, we need to place them in the context of global or regional developments of secured transactions law, such as the UNCITRAL Legislative Guide on Secured Transactions, Principles of European Law (PEL) project or Model Inter-American Law on Secured Transactions (OAS Model Law). The national reporters, when they find it appropriate, may feel free to refer to these developments relevant to their jurisdictions.

The subject may have different implications, depending on whether the national reporter is in a jurisdiction that has already become a Party to the Cape Town Convention and its Aircraft Protocol ("Party jurisdiction") or in a jurisdiction that has yet to become a Party to them ("non-Party jurisdiction"). In a Party jurisdiction, the national reporter is invited to report on the changes made to their domestic law when ratifying and implementing the Convention. In a non-Party jurisdiction, the national reporter is invited to compare the current domestic law with the Cape Town Convention and analyse the implications of the Cape Town Convention in their jurisdictions.

Further, as already hinted, even a Party jurisdiction may have issues to be considered differently with regards to the Rail Protocol and Space Assets Protocol. The national reporter is invited to examine what makes the difference, if any, and whether the difference lies in the legal system or rather in the economic situation surrounding the transactions of each type of equipment.

Basic Theme

The Cape Town Convention aims at establishing a legal framework that will facilitate financing and leasing mobile equipment with high value.[5] The drafter of the Convention and Aircraft Protocol argued in the process of the drafting that three principles were needed to establish such a framework. They are: (1) transparency in the priority among secured interests ("international interests" under the Cape Town Convention) through the registration system, (2) the prompt enforcement of secured interests in case of default by the debtor, including the admissibility of private enforcement, and (3) the enforcement of the secured interests without being qualified or modified under the insolvency procedure.[6] As indicated in the specific questions below, these principles have largely been adopted by the Convention and its Protocols.

The national reporter in a Party jurisdiction is invited to analyse whether, and to what extent, these principles were consistent with the national law before becoming

---

[5] Sir Roy Goode, *Convention on International Interests in Mobile Equipment and Protocol Thereto on Matters Specific to Aircraft Equipment: Official Commentary*, Third Edition, para. 2.1 (Unidroit, 2013).

[6] Anthony Saunders, Anand Srinivasan, Ingo Walter & Jeffrey Wool, The Economic Implications of Secured Transactions Law Reform: A Case Study, *University of Pennsylvania Journal of International Economic Law*, Vol. 20, p.309, at 324

a Party to the Cape Town Convention. The national reporter in a non-Party jurisdiction is invited to analyse in what respects the Cape Town Convention and the Aircraft Protocol differs from the existent national law. Further, the national reporters in both jurisdictions are asked to consider whether changing the national law and accepting the policy of the Cape Town Convention and implementing it was, or can be, justified by the policy consideration, such as the benefits to be brought to the aviation industry in their jurisdictions.

Specific Questions

The questions below may require technical analysis of the debtor-creditor law. While precise and in-depth reports are welcome, the national reporters are invited to examine the basic principles or policies underlying the law of each jurisdiction, not simply describing practical information.

The national reporter is invited to give answers to the questionnaire in an essay, referring to the questions below and adding other points that they find important. It is appreciated to avoid the style of "one answer to one question".

Questions for a National Reporter in a Party Jurisdiction

Registration System

(a) The Cape Town Convention gives priority to the secured creditor who filed first, whether or not the creditor had actual knowledge of the existence of another creditor having acquired a security interest in advance (art.29 of the Convention). Was this principle different from that of domestic legislation in your jurisdiction before becoming a State Party to the Convention?

(b) The three Protocols to the Cape Town Convention govern transactions involving aircrafts, railway rolling stocks and space assets (such as satellites). Were these vehicles able to be mortgaged or subjected to other forms of security interest under the domestic law of your jurisdiction before becoming a State Party? Was there any special law or registration system for the security interests in these vehicles, as opposed to personal property in general?

(c) The International Registry under the Cape Town Convention is a system based on registration against an asset, not against a debtor (see art.18 (1) of the Convention). Further, it is a "notice filing" system, which only gives a notice to third parties that there may be an interest that deserves further enquiries.[7] The Registrar assumes the accuracy of the provided information without any exami-

---

[7] Goode, *Official Commentary*, supra note エラー！ ブックマークが定義されていません。, para.4.132.

nation of it (see art.28 (2) of the Convention) and there is no guarantee that the registered information reflects the true state of titles. Was this a novel idea as compared with the filing or registration system for security interests in your jurisdiction when becoming a State Party?

(d) The Cape Town Convention defines the "international interest" to be registered in the International Registry as including the interest under a security agreement (similar to charge or mortgage in some jurisdictions), the title reserved by the conditional seller under a title reservation agreement, as well as the right of the lessor under a leasing agreement (art.2 (2) of the Convention). Whether to treat all these interests as "security" (functional approach) or not is left to the applicable domestic law (art.2 (4) of the Convention), while the rules governing the three kinds of international interest are almost the same. Were these ideas different from the rules of secured transactions law in your jurisdiction before becoming a State Party?

Enforcement of a Security Interest

(a) The Cape Town Convention affirms the validity of an agreement on privately enforcing an international interest as long as the method employed is commercially reasonable (art.8 of the Convention), unless the State makes a declaration otherwise upon becoming a State Party (art.54 (2) of the Convention). Did the national law (including the case law) of your jurisdiction affirm the validity of such an agreement in the absence of the Cape Town Convention? What declaration has your state made under Article 54 (2) of the Convention?

(b) The Cape Town Convention also allows the parties to define the meaning of default that entitles the creditor to exercise remedies (art.11 (1) of the Convention). Would such a clause in the agreement be held valid in your jurisdiction in the absence of the Cape Town Convention?

(c) The Cape Town Convention allows a wide variety of remedies besides simple liquidation, such as granting a lease of the object and collecting or receiving any income or profits arising from the management or use of the object (art.8 (1) of the Convention). It is also possible to satisfy the secured obligations by vesting the ownership of the object by the agreement of the chargee and other interested parties or by the court order (art.9 of the Convention). Further, if the international interest is a title reserved by the conditional seller or a lessor's right, as opposed to an interest under a security agreement, there is no need for the creditor to pay the balance to the debtor even when the amount of the balance is larger than the amount of the secured obligation[8] (compare art.10 with art.8 (6) of the Convention). Were these results the same under the domestic law of your jurisdiction before becoming a Party to the Convention?

---

[8]Goode, *Official Commentary*, supra note エラー！ ブックマークが定義されていません。, para. 4.101.

Treatment of Security Interests Under the Insolvency Procedure

(a) An international interest under the Cape Town Convention can be exercised even after an insolvency procedure is commenced with the debtor, without being stayed automatically or by an order of the insolvency administrator (art. XI of the Aircraft Protocol; art.IX of the Rail Protocol; art.XXI of the Space Assets Protocol).[9] The rules differ depending on whether the State Party made a declaration choosing either of the alternatives in the relevant provision. Has your State made any declaration regarding this provision? If it does, were the rules provided by the chosen alternative different from the treatment of a security interest under the domestic insolvency law of your jurisdiction in the absence of the Convention? If no alternative is chosen, what was the reason for doing so?

(b) The Cape Town Convention requires that the registered international interest remain effective under the insolvency procedure (art.30 (1) of the Convention). Further, if the State Party in its declaration choses an alternative more favourable to the creditor, no obligation of the debtor may be modified without the consent of the creditor (alternaive A of art.XI of the Aircraft Protocol; alternatives A and C of art.IX of the Rail Protocol; alternative A of art.XXI of the Space Assets Protocol). Did the insolvency law of your jurisdiction provide for the same rule on a security interest in the absence of the Convention? Which alternative has your state chosen?

(The answers under this section might vary, depending on the type of insolvency procedure, such as whether liquidation or reorganisation. In such a case, the national reporter is asked to respond with respect to major types of procedure in the relevant jurisdiction.)

General Considerations

(a) In the course of drafting the Cape Town Convention and the Aircraft Protocol, economic analysis was conducted to assess the benefits that the Convention would bring to the relevant industry and the society as a whole.[10] Is it customary in your jurisdiction to conduct such economic analysis, in particular, an empirical one, when designing the law of secured transactions (or private law in gen-

---

[9] All three Protocols provide alternatives that differ in the extent of the power that the creditor can exercise in case of insolvency of the debtor. However, even under an alternative less favourable to the creditor (Alternative B), the insolvency administrator or debtor in possession shall either cure all defaults and agree to perform all future obligations or give the creditor the opportunity to take possession of the secured object. Alternative C of art.IX of the Rail Protocol seems to be the only exception, which enables the insolvency administrator or the debtor to apply to the court for an order suspending its obligation.

[10] Saunders et al. supra note エラー! ブックマークが定義されていません。.

eral)? Was this empirical analysis useful in pushing your state to become a Party to the Convention?

(b) The basic idea of the Cape Town Convention, as mentioned above under **Basic theme**, seems to imply that a stronger security interest will enable the debtor to enjoy better conditions of finance and, as a result, bring larger benefit to both the creditor and debtor. Is such an idea commonly supported in your jurisdiction?

(c) The promoter of the Cape Town Convention recently emphasises the importance of the implementation of its rules by the States Parties and argues that the intended economic benefits will not be achieved if the implementation by the domestic law does not fully comply with the terms of the Cape Town Convention.[11] Is this idea supported in your state?

Questions for a National Reporter in a Non-Party Jurisdiction

Registration System

(a) The Cape Town Convention gives priority to the secured creditor who filed first, whether or not the creditor had actual knowledge of the existence of another creditor having acquired a security interest in advance (art.29 of the Convention). Was this principle different from that of domestic legislation in your jurisdiction?

(b) The three Protocols to the Cape Town Convention govern transactions involving aircrafts, railway rolling stocks and space assets (such as satellites). Are these vehicles able to be mortgaged or subjected to other forms of security interest under the domestic law of your jurisdiction? Is there any special law or registration system for the security interests in these vehicles, as opposed to personal property in general?

(c) The International Registry under the Cape Town Convention is a system based on registration against an asset, not against a debtor (see art.18 (1) of the Convention). Further, it is a "notice filing" system, which only gives a notice to third parties that there may be an interest that deserves further enquiries.[12] The Registrar assumes the accuracy of the provided information without any examination of it (see art.28 (2) of the Convention) and there is no guarantee that the registered information reflects the true state of titles. Is this system different from the filing or registration system for security interests in your jurisdiction?

---

[11] Jeffrey Wool, Treaty Design, Implementation, and Compliance Benchmarking Economic Benefit – a framework as applied to the Cape Town Convention, [2012] *Uniform Law Review* p.633.

[12] Goode, Official Commentary, supra note エラー! ブックマークが定義されていません。, para. 4.132.

(d) The Cape Town Convention defines the "international interest" to be registered in the International Registry as including the interest under a security agreement (similar to charge or mortgage in some jurisdictions), the title reserved by the conditional seller under a title reservation agreement, as well as the right of the lessor under a leasing agreement (art.2 (2) of the Convention). Whether to treat all these interests as "security" (functional approach) or not is left to the applicable domestic law (art.2 (4) of the Convention), while the rules governing the three kinds of international interest are almost the same. Are these ideas different from the rules of secured transactions law in your jurisdiction?

Enforcement of a Security Interest

(a) The Cape Town Convention affirms the validity of an agreement on privately enforcing an international interest as long as the method employed is commercially reasonable (art.8 of the Convention), unless the State makes a declaration otherwise upon becoming a State Party (art.54 (2) of the Convention). Does the national law (including the case law) of your jurisdiction affirm the validity of such an agreement?

(b) The Cape Town Convention also allows the parties to define the meaning of default that entitles the creditor to exercise remedies (art.11 (1) of the Convention). Will such a clause in the agreement be held valid in your jurisdiction?

(c) The Cape Town Convention allows a wide variety of remedies besides simple liquidation, such as granting a lease of the object and collecting or receiving any income or profits arising from the management or use of the object (art.8 (1) of the Convention). It is also possible to satisfy the secured obligations by vesting the ownership of the object by the agreement of the chargee and other interested parties or by the court order (art.9 of the Convention). Further, if the international interest is a title reserved by the conditional seller or a lessor's right, as opposed to an interest under a security agreement, there is no need for the creditor to pay the balance to the debtor even when the amount of the balance is larger than the amount of the secured obligation[13] (compare art.10 with art.8 (6) of the Convention). Are these results the same under the domestic law of your jurisdiction?

---

[13] Goode, Official Commentary, supra note エラー！ ブックマークが定義されていません。, para.4.101.

Treatment of Security Interests Under the Insolvency Procedure

(a) An international interest under the Cape Town Convention can be exercised even after an insolvency procedure is commenced with the debtor, without being stayed automatically or by an order of the insolvency administrator (art. XI of the Aircraft Protocol; art.IX of the Rail Protocol; art.XXI of the Space Assets Protocol).[14] The rules differ depending on whether the State Party made a declaration choosing either of the alternatives in the relevant provision. Are the rules provided by these provisions, in particular the alternative most favourable to the creditor, different from the treatment of a security interest under the domestic insolvency law of your jurisdiction?

(b) The Cape Town Convention requires that the registered international interest remain effective under the insolvency procedure (art.30 (1) of the Convention). Further, if the State Party in its declaration choses an alternative more favourable to the creditor, no obligation of the debtor may be modified without the consent of the creditor (alternaive A of art.XI of the Aircraft Protocol; alternatives A and C of art.IX of the Rail Protocol; alternative A of art.XXI of the Space Assets Protocol). Does the insolvency law of your jurisdiction provide for the same rule on a security interest?

(The answers under this section might vary, depending on the type of insolvency procedure, such as whether liquidation or reorganisation. In such a case, the national reporter is asked to respond with respect to major types of procedure in the relevant jurisdiction.)

General Considerations

(a) In the course of drafting the Cape Town Convention and the Aircraft Protocol, economic analysis was conducted to assess the benefits that the Convention would bring to the relevant industry and the society as a whole.[15] Is it customary in your jurisdiction to conduct such economic analysis, in particular, an empirical one, when designing the law of secured transactions (or private law in general)?

(b) The basic idea of the Cape Town Convention, as mentioned above under **Basic theme**, seems to imply that a stronger security interest will enable the debtor to enjoy better conditions of finance and, as a result, bring larger benefit to both the creditor and debtor. Is such an idea commonly supported in your jurisdiction?

---

[14] All three Protocols provide alternatives that differ in the extent of the power that the creditor can exercise in case of insolvency of the debtor. However, even under an alternative less favourable to the creditor (Alternative B), the insolvency administrator or debtor in possession shall either cure all defaults and agree to perform all future obligations or give the creditor the opportunity to take possession of the secured object. Alternative C of art.IX of the Rail Protocol seems to be the only exception, which enables the insolvency administrator or the debtor to apply to the court for an order suspending its obligation.

[15] Saunders et al. supra note エラー! ブックマークが定義されていません。

Printed in Great Britain
by Amazon

82399436R00224